D1030228

Toward Another Shore

Russian Literature and Thought
Gary Saul Morson, Series Editor

Toward Another Shore

Russian Thinkers Between Necessity and Chance

AILEEN M. KELLY

Yale University Press   New Haven and London

Designed by Sonia L. Scanlon.

Set in Minion type by Rainsford Type, Danbury, Connecticut.

Printed in the United States of America by Vail-Ballou Press, Binghamton, New York.

Library of Congress Cataloging-in-Publication Data

Kelly, Aileen.

Toward another shore : Russian thinkers between necessity and
chance / Aileen M. Kelly.

p.   cm.—(Russian literature and thought)

ISBN 0–300–07024–1 (alk. paper)

1. Intellectuals—Russia.   2. Russia—Intellectual
life—1801–1917.   3. Intellectuals—Soviet Union.   4. Soviet Union—
Intellectual life.   I. Title.   II. Series.

DK189.2.K45   1998   97–47188

947—dc21   CIP

A catalogue record for this book is available from the British Library.

The paper in this book meets the guidelines for permanence and durability of
the Committee on Production Guidelines for Book Longevity of the Council on
Library Resources.

10 9 8 7 6 5 4 3 2 1

О сколько нам открытий чудных
Готовят просвещенья дух
И Опыт, сын ошибок трудных,
И Гений, парадоксов друг
И Случай, бог изобретатель

O, how many and marvelous are the discoveries
prepared for us by the spirit of enlightenment,
by Experiment, the child of painful error,
by Genius, the friend of paradox,
and by the divine inventor, Chance

—Alexander Pushkin

To J. A. C. (O. B.), for services rendered

Contents

Acknowledgments ix

Introduction 1

1: Methods and Approaches

1 A Complex Vision 15

2 Leonard Schapiro's Russia 25

2: Insights and Ambivalences

3 Carnival of the Intellectuals 37

4 Dostoevsky and the Divided Conscience 55

5 Tolstoy in Doubt 80

6 The Nihilism of Ivan Turgenev 91

7 Liberal Dilemmas and Populist Solutions 119

8 The Intelligentsia and Self-Censorship 134

9 Which Signposts? 155

10 The Chaotic City 201

3: Delusions and Evasions

11 The Rational Reality of Boris Chicherin 221

12 Bakunin and the Charm of the Millennium 245

13 A Bolshevik Philosophy? 257

14 Brave New Worlds 285

4: Another Shore

15 Irony and Utopia in Herzen and Dostoevsky 307

16 Herzen versus Schopenhauer 326

17 The Divine Inventor, Chance 345

Notes 353

Permissions 399

Acknowledgments

I am indebted to the British Academy for the award of a Research Readership from 1992 to 1994 which enabled me to pursue my work on the theme of chance in Russian thought—the first results of which are the essays on Turgenev, Herzen's response to Schopenhauer, the *Signposts* movement, and "The Divine Inventor, Chance," in this volume.

This book owes its existence to the patience and learning of Professor John Campbell, an inexhaustible source of inspiration, propulsion, and *mots justes*.

I am deeply grateful to Robert Silvers of the *New York Review of Books* for encouraging me to write on subjects outside my immediate academic preoccupations. Through his enthusiasm for Russian literature, art, and ideas, he has done much to extend my horizons.

There is no adequate way to express my debt to Sir Isaiah Berlin, who inspired my interest in Russian thinkers and whose moral vision has been the constant standard by which I have measured their failings and their strengths.

Introduction

"Here, we may say, we are at home, and like the mariner after a long voyage in a tempestuous sea, we may now hail the sight of land": thus Hegel described the commencement (with Descartes) of the modern age in philosophy, when human thought began to seek to derive all its knowledge and values autonomously through reason. Quoting these lines in 1843, Aleksandr Herzen, then the leading radical Hegelian in Russia, offered a variation on Hegel's metaphor. Hegel believed that his philosophy was "the shore to which thought is sailing as to its peaceful harbour. . . . We, on the contrary, see [it] as the shore on which we stand, ready to quit it at the first favorable wind."[1]

Herzen would argue in his political journalism that even the most progressive European thinkers, inhibited by filial devotion to hallowed traditions and habits of thought, had been as reluctant as Hegel himself to explore the liberating implications of his philosophy and to subject all arbitrary authorities to the scrutiny of self-determining reason. In contrast, Russian intellectuals had no rich past or cherished traditions to command their allegiance and only contempt for the primitive despotism that oppressed them. In their struggle for freedom they would accept no half measures, questioning all those transcendent authorities—religious, political, or moral—that were habitually invoked to justify the coercion of living human beings. With the help of this iconoclasm, Herzen hoped that the Russian intelligentsia would build a new kind of freedom.[2]

Instead, it created a new kind of tyranny, and since then for many Western commentators Russian thought, particularly in its radical and revolutionary varieties, has been synonymous with intolerance, ideological intransigence, and a utopian mentality that is (as Martin Malia wrote of the form in which Herzen expressed his ideals) "alien and even disturbing to the empirical, pragmatic Anglo-Saxon mind."[3] When Soviet scholars were producing their hagiographical accounts of the Russian radical intelligentsia as heroic spokesmen for the masses, with the advent of the Cold War an influential school of Western liberal historians—primarily in the United States and Great Britain—began to contend that the intelligentsia's maximalist psychology and indifference as to means was principally responsible for the regime that had led to the horrors of Stalinism. One of the most distinguished proponents of this view, Leonard Schapiro, saw a fundamental division in Russian political thought between a small minority who sought to instill in their compatriots a respect for liberal institutions and the rule of law, and the majority, whose millenarian impatience and contempt for compromise paved the way for totalitarian despotism. Historians such as Malia, Richard Pipes, Robert Conquest, Adam Ulam, Robert Daniels, and Tibor Szamuely drew similar lessons from the Russian experience. Some portrayed the radical intelligentsia as misguided idealists, others represented them as psychotic personalities; all saw them as misfits divorced from the real world, obsessed by ideal abstractions, and fanatically convinced of their own moral rectitude and theoretical correctness. By the beginning of the 1960s, influenced by new approaches and quantitative methods being applied by social historians in other fields, a new generation of researchers had begun to question many of the presuppositions of the liberal school, in particular their view of the intelligentsia as an ideologically and psychologically monolithic group. However, as Edward Acton has observed (in a book published in 1990), although the Western consensus based on the traditional liberal interpretation has now broken down, "many of the most distinguished scholars in the field remain firmly committed to it and it continues to inform conventional wisdom among non-specialists in the West."[4]

Yet one powerful liberal voice has consistently dissented from that wisdom. The slow process of demythologizing the intelligentsia began in the 1950s with Isaiah Berlin's first essays on Russian topics. These were original above all in drawing no sharp dividing line between the radical intelligentsia and the great Russian writers whose humanism had long been admired in the West: Berlin pointed out that writers such as Turgenev (and even Dostoevsky on occasion) had expressed admiration for the moral commitment of the Left.

Berlin's interest in Russian thought, like that of the liberal school, is bound up with his faith in libertarian values. But while they believe these values to be inseparable from the legal and political structures of constitutional democracy, Berlin maintains that a truly liberal pluralism is irreconcilable with the view that there is one universal solution to the problems of social existence. John Stuart Mill regarded the desirability of representative democracy as "a question of time, place, and circumstance"; Berlin has suggested that the anarchistic socialism of the Russian populists should not be dismissed quite as easily as it has been, both by communist and liberal historians. He has pointed out that Russian radical thinkers laid the foundations not only of the dogmatic utilitarianism that has been so much highlighted by their critics but also of a strong tradition of libertarian humanism, which was defeated only in October 1917. Both strands cut across conventional political categories and can be traced to the dominant influence of Hegel in the Russia of the late 1830s and the 1840s. On one hand, radicals and conservatives alike were seduced by Hegel's positive doctrines, his historical theodicy of the march of history to the goals of truth and justice. But there were also, as Berlin has stressed, a minority of thinkers who were deeply affected by the negative aspect of Hegelianism, its undermining of the Enlightenment's optimistic belief that human beings and things could be classified and their behavior predicted according to precise scientific laws. Reality "for ever escapes all artificial ideological nets, all rigid, dogmatic assumptions, defies all attempts at codification, upsets all symmetrical moral or sociological systems": this was the version of Hegel's dialectic that shaped the outlook of (among others) Herzen and Turgenev.[5] Berlin has argued that the classification of Herzen's views as just one more variety of early socialism has done him a grave injustice by leaving out his most arresting ideas: above all, his prescient indictment of the destructive power of ideological abstractions over human beings. Other thinkers, like Tolstoy, longed for an ideal that would resist their corrosive critique; in their deep ambivalence Berlin found a precious source of illumination on the perennial and competing attractions of monist and pluralist visions of the world.

Berlin's formulation of the "accursed questions" besetting Russian thinkers was one of the motivating impulses of the research that led to the essays collected here. Written over a period of twenty years, they have one common theme: the struggle between ideological faith and nihilistic doubt expressed with varying degrees of lucidity and self-awareness during more than a century by some of Russia's most outstanding writers and intellectuals. My belief that this approach offers a better understanding of the fundamental conflicts of prerevolutionary Russian thought than the more usual political classifications is set out in Chapters 1 and 2, which contrast the approaches of Berlin and Leonard Schapiro.

While the Soviet Union was still a threat, to argue (as I do in this book) that we might be morally enlightened by the insights of Russian radical humanists was to swim against the ideological stream in the West. Liberal societies had never been more secure in their goals and values, and historians who identified with those values were not disposed to concede merit or insight to those whom they saw as having prepared the ground for the evils of Bolshevism. It has been noted that in dealing with the socialist tradition, such historians operate with a form of retrospective historicism that has peculiar affinities with the predictive historicism of Karl Marx: their verdicts on the ideals and motives of early socialists are delivered with the hindsight of those who know that socialism was destined for catastrophic failure.[6]

This approach is now much less common: a fact that has less to do with the demise of the "Evil Empire" than with a deeper and more pervasive revolution, whose form Herzen dimly discerned in his vision of another shore. The "post-modern condition" has been variously defined, but there is a consensus that its basic component is an acceptance that we can no longer credibly anchor our values in any universal ground, whether God, Reason, or History. The spectacular failure of twentieth-century attempts at the rational ordering of peoples and human affairs, combined with developments in science, philosophy, psychology, and social theory, has eroded our faith in all "grand narratives" of progress: those teleological accounts of the historical process whereby individuals and peoples have traditionally sought to situate themselves meaningfully in the flow of existence. The view that reality is inherently fragmentary, history a directionless flux, is the common ground of new theoretical developments across the range of intellectual disciplines.

One consequence of this is an increasing emphasis on a contextual approach to intellectual history—in particular, the early socialism of the nineteenth century, where thinkers previously classified by their place in retrospectively constituted traditions are being reappraised in the light of how they themselves viewed their goals and achievements. (As one commentator has put it, as it was this generation that coined the term *socialism,* it will simply not do to lecture them on the meaning of the term.)[7] Such historians are establishing a new kind of equality between the present and a past viewed as another present of inexhaustible richness, which we may continually consult for new insights into what remain open problems.

Ironically, the current popularity of a dialogical engagement with the past owes much to the influence of a Russian thinker. The "discovery" of Mikhail Bakhtin (who had been beavering away for nearly half a century in Russian provincial obscurity) led to a cult that spread in the early 1980s from Paris to the United States. More recently, Bakhtin's suspicion of all systems that ignore the "unfinished" quality of everyday existence has inspired new work on the Russian "countertradition" of anti-ideological thought, pioneered in the United States by Caryl Emerson and Gary Saul Morson.[8] Focusing mainly on literary examples (Lev Tolstoy's and Fyodor Dostoevsky's representation of how moral choice is exercised in the flux of daily events), they have defined this style of thinking as "prosaics" after Bakhtin's emphasis on the "prosaic wisdom" of the novel form. These two scholars have argued strongly that the critique of utopian thought by such writers has much relevance for our own time.

The essays collected in this book were written in the same belief. In particular, in recent years I have been struck by parallels between debates among the prerevolutionary Russian intelligentsia and current attempts to redescribe the nature of the self and experienced reality, in ways that avoid the teleological assumptions behind our inherited forms of knowledge and representation. The most unsettling of the new approaches to philosophy, science, and culture are based on the historicist thesis that there is no transcendental point outside empirical reality from which to judge human practices: that the categories and values of any human group are a function of their time, the localized product of contingent circumstances. One of the most influential and provocative of the new pragmatists, Richard Rorty, has developed the critique of foundationalism initiated by Friedrich Nietzsche: in his democratized version of the Nietzschean ideal of self-creation, future communities will break free of the past by generating radically new self-descriptions, experimenting with different philosophical and moral vocabularies in a spirit of Nietzschean gaiety. But some of Rorty's critics have probed the darker implications of the view that truth is "created" by those whose private visions "catch on" in their communities. In such a "postphilosophical" culture, they argue, the sole arbiter of truth and meaning will be the will to power.[9] The critic Christopher Norris expresses a common view that the radicalism of much poststructuralist and postmodern theory

> has now passed over into a species of disguised apologetics for the sociopolitical status quo, a persuasion that "reality" is constituted through and through by the meanings, values or discourses that presently compose it, so that nothing could count as effective counterargument, much less a critique of existing institutions on valid theoretical grounds.
>
> In short, we have reached a point where theory has effectively turned against itself, generating a form of extreme epistemological scepticism which reduces everything—philosophy, politics, criticism, and "theory" alike—to a dead level of suasive or rhetorical effect where consensus-values are the last (indeed the only) court of appeal.[10]

Such criticism reflects a common uneasiness about the fact that so much of the debate over postmodernist theories is curiously abstracted from the social contexts of everyday life, where the erosion of traditional faiths has led to widespread pessimism and a cynical nihilism. A similar mood, inflamed by half-digested Nietzschean ideas about "self-becoming" and personal authenticity, once produced legions of eager participants in mass murder. The power of ideas to inspire actions, good or bad, is a reality from which Anglo-Saxon intellectuals have hitherto been largely shielded: I believe that the Russian experience contains lessons that we would do well to note before it is too late.

We live in a time of "casual families" in which parents and children are not bound together by shared beliefs of the kind that used to constitute the moral order of society: "Nowadays . . . there is no such order because there is nothing general and binding, nothing in which all fathers believe. Instead there are: first, wholesale, sweeping renunciation of the past (renunciation and nothing positive); second, attempts to say something positive, yet neither general nor binding, but everyone in his own way,—attempts parcelled into units and individuals, devoid of experience, practice, even without full faith in them on the part of their inventors."[11]

No, not Western cities of the 1990s but the Russia of the 1870s, as observed by Dostoevsky in his *Writer's Diary*. As shown in two of the chapters in this book, by the beginning of the twentieth century Russian inventiveness had turned to considering the implications of the proposition that truth is not discovered but created and that the sole reality is the will to power. These notions were first seriously explored not in academic debate but by members of the Bolshevik elite and the terrorist wing of the Socialist Revolutionary Party; and in the wider discussions that ensued, the focus was firmly on the effect of such ideas on the moral makeup of those who preached them and on their attitudes to the rights of others.

Both critics and admirers of Russian thinkers have remarked on their tendency to develop Western ideas to their logical (and often absurd) extremes. In free societies new ideas are absorbed into an ongoing discussion, and their more abrasive edges softened or disguised by layers of interpretation. In the century before the Russian Revolution, the most extreme implications of the theories of Arthur Schopenhauer, Charles Darwin, Nietzsche, and other trailblazing thinkers, now recognized as progenitors of postmodern thought, were seized on by intellectuals eager to compensate for the impossibility of action by feats of intellectual daring. Their debates took place against a background of accelerating social change, as the Russian autocracy sought to transform itself into something resembling a modern state. As now in post-Soviet Russia, numerous intellectuals, horrified by what they saw as a process of social and moral disintegration, sought refuge in the reassertion of eschatological faiths. Some, like Dostoevsky, hesitated between faith and doubt, while a minority for whom, as for Nietzsche, philosophy was a matter of living "voluntarily in ice and on high mountains,"[12] relentlessly pursued the intellectual consequences of the critique of metaphysical thought launched by German radical Hegelians in the late 1830s. None of these people were scholars or full-time theorists. Some were revolutionaries, living in exile, like Herzen, or in constant danger of arrest; others were writers or journalists. Their knowledge of their Western sources was fragmentary, their attitude to them eclectic: complex arguments were sometimes built on a line or two from an authority often quoted out of context. But it would be a mistake to think that their criticism of ideological thought is merely of historical interest—a first timid step into a territory that now holds no terrors for us. The evasive strategies and varieties of self-delusion and cant in which some Russian thinkers indulged are alive and well within current criticism, and I believe that they are less often exposed now than they were in the debates chronicled below. Russian thinkers had sensitive antennae for detecting moral weaknesses in their opponent's case (if not always in their own); we may learn from them how better to discriminate among visions of freedom in our postideological age.

In their attitudes to the ideological ferment of their time, Russian intellectuals may be divided into three groups. One was torn between utopia and irony: between the search for a transcendent meaning in the conflicts of existence and a sense that process and conflict are all that there is. A second group, having dipped their toes in the Hegelian sea, retreated to a metaphysical shore, whence they interpreted the contemporary intellectual confusion and social disintegration as a transitional stage on the path to a new and more perfect order, variously defined in religious or rationalist terms. Third, a very few sought to carry the revolt against metaphysics through to its conclusion, by questioning the claims of all universal systems and ideals to enclose, predict, and regulate the flux of contingent existence.

These three categories are the subject of Parts II to IV of this book. Chapter 3, "Carnival of the Intellectuals," examines the unprecedented questioning by writers and intellectuals of received beliefs and absolutes that accompanied the beginning of the so-called Age of Great Reforms in mid-nineteenth-century Russia. We can see in this period the setting up of the battle lines between those who believed that such denial was the first step toward the definition of the one right way to live and libertarian humanists, who protested against the desire of radical critics to regiment human creativity by enlisting art in the service of politics. Most Russian writers and thinkers achieved no resolution of the conflict between their need for certainties and their revolt against dogmatic thought. I explore this conflict in the life and writing of Dostoevsky, who saw himself as the chronicler of discord and disintegration; of Turgenev, whose challenge to the Left's dogmatic optimism was ultimately grounded in a scarcely less dogmatic Schopenhauerian pessimism; and of Tolstoy, whose struggle to resolve the contradictions in his view of art and morality is one of the great tragic dramas in the history of ideas.

The Russian populist movement strove to reconcile its commitment to radical social change with a rejection of authoritarian methods and systems. But it could not resolve the conflict between its libertarian ethos and its demand for wholehearted dedication from its members. At the beginning of the twentieth century this erupted in painful discussions on the corrupting effects of violence employed in the pursuit of revolutionary goals, and led to calls both from outside and within the revolutionary movement for a "revaluation of values" that would replace the traditional ideal of the narrowly committed revolutionary hero with a more complex model, open to a wide variety of experience, recognizing the self-sufficient value of goals and ideals other than his own, and not equating doubt with betrayal of the cause. In debates over this issue the mystique of revolution was deconstructed by radicals as well as by their opponents (in particular, the famous *Signposts* group of writers.) Confusions and inconsistencies on both sides bore witness to the tenacity of messianic hopes that the right formula (whether revolutionary or, as in the view of some *Signposts* authors, religious) would lead to a final state of harmony; but when, in an early example of political correctness, the Bolshevik writer Maksim Gorky demanded the removal from a Moscow stage of Dostoevsky's *Possessed* on the ground of its negative portrayal of revolutionaries, he was opposed by the vast majority of the Russian Left, who claimed that open discussion of the shortcomings of the radical movement could do nothing but good. This little known but highly significant debate about censorship shows that on the eve of the Revolution many Russian radicals had gone a long way toward achieving freedom from "the great interior censor"—that voluntary submission to universal norms and moral absolutes which, as Bakhtin pointed out, are always the last of the authorities to fall in any political upheaval.

Both before and after the Revolution, the intelligentsia's sense of the chaotic conflicts in its moral world was expressed in literature and art through images of the capital, Petersburg-Leningrad. The fantastic, rootless city of Dostoevsky's novels, a natural seedbed for the doctrine "all is permitted," it was for the Symbolists a surreal world whose contradictions were about to explode into apocalypse. In productions staged on its streets and squares in the aftermath of 1917 members of the artistic avant-garde engaged in carnivalistic celebrations of the destruction of outdated values and the coming of the revolutionary state that would once and for all resolve the problem of how human beings should live together. It was not long before the poetry of Anna Akhmatova and Osip Mandelstam, through unforgettable images of a city in the grip of terror, began to probe the true nature of utopia in power.

A source of some confusion in the interpretation of Russian thought has been the fact that those thinkers most submissive to the dictates of the great interior censor have tended also to be among the most vigorous proponents of freedom—whether defending liberal freedom against socialist collectivism, anarchist freedom against all political constraints, Nietzschean freedom against Marxist determinism, or artistic freedom against philistine norms. Such theorists, who include the "conservative liberal" Boris Chicherin, the anarchist Mikhail Bakunin, the "Nietzschean Marxists" of the decade before the Revolution, and many of the artistic avant-garde of the 1920s, are the subject of Part III.

Chicherin is often cited as an archetypal political moderate, a defender of gradualism against the excesses of the Left. But his opposition to radical change was motivated not by liberal pragmatism but by a conservative variety of Hegelian theory, the source of his conviction that the Russian autocracy represented a necessary stage on the way to the "rational state" to which all historical development was tending. Bakunin has attracted an admiring following among some radicals in the West as the archetypal free spirit, the embodiment of anarchist spontaneity in revolt against all system-builders; but his goal of "absolute liberty" was a construct of German Idealism, inspired by its dream of the resolution of all conflicts in a final wholeness. In recent reappraisals of Russian Marxism the "Nietzschean Marxists," whose heresy was stamped out by Lenin before the Revolution, have been interpreted as representing a grassroots challenge to Bolshevik authoritarianism. True, they preached that human beings create truths, rather than discover them, in the process of adapting to new environments. But they also argued that human individuality was a temporary adaptation and that in the final state to which history was moving there would be neither conflict nor distinction between individual and collective purposes.

The same kind of utopia inspired those leaders of the artistic avant-garde who formed an uneasy alliance with Bolshevism in the 1920s. It has been suggested that they represent a vibrant strand of creative idealism, prematurely stifled by Stalin, to which Russians can turn for inspiration in the post-Soviet world. Yet their ideal of a new kind of human being, founded on the myth of a collective consciousness and the cult of the machine, would prove a welcome source of inspiration to Stalin's hacks.

All these individuals and movements professed the belief in the ultimate harmony of all purposes that is central to the rationalist utopia, and in each case this belief led to collusion with despotism. In his eagerness to ensure that Russia would not be forced by revolution off the appointed path of progress, Chicherin shocked his contemporaries by defending the rationality of autocratic diktats and of the bureaucrats and policemen who carried them out. Bakunin planned to enforce his principles through dictatorship and formed an alliance with the violent and criminal Sergei Nechaev. The Nietzschean Marxists, having proclaimed themselves collectivists, had no choice but to submit when their chosen collective ordered them to recant. The proponents of a rationalist idyll among the postrevolutionary avant-garde proved more intolerant of ideological deviation than many of the Bolshevik leaders of the time and, in their urge to harness art to political purposes, freely colluded in the mass manipulation that set the stage for Stalin's advent and their own destruction.

The new interest in the defeated rivals of the Marxist utopia is often explicitly motivated by a desire to fill the spiritual vacuum caused by the collapse of ideological certainties in East and West. Faced with the prospect of a nihilistic culture, it is tempting to settle for the devil one knows: to cast around for new and untried forms of the old faiths that used to legitimate our ideals and values. In Part IV, I discuss a third option: an alternative both to nihilistic pessimism and to ideological faith, as preached by Aleksandr Herzen, who believed that humane values are better grounded in an acceptance of our contingency than in the urge to escape it.

Herzen was among the first European thinkers to grasp the significance of the erosion of faith in all-embracing, teleological explanations of the world that Nietzsche would describe as the death of God. An early interest in the empirical methods of the natural sciences made him suspicious of theories of linear development in history and nature; a decade before the appearance of *The Origin of Species,* he published the essays collectively entitled *From the Other Shore* (the shore that Hegel had failed to reach), in which he interprets religious and rational doctrines of progress as the result of a cultural conditioning that has taught us to evaluate the observable world in the light of fictitious ends and purposes and to see chance as a purely destructive force. His critique of belief in the inherent rationality of the historical process was echoed by Dostoevsky in *Notes from Underground,* but Dostoevsky could not reconcile his religious faith with the absence of a providential order in the world, and he accused Herzen of a destructive pessimism, a view echoed by many later Russian thinkers, including the distinguished historian of Russian philosophy V. V. Zenkovsky, who construes Herzen's denial of an a priori order in the world as an expression of despair.

But Herzen vigorously rejected philosophical pessimism as a peevish overreaction to the loss of cherished illusions about our centrality in the universe and a refusal to face the consequences of our status as beings subject to time and chance. A significant, though small, minority of Russian thinkers followed him in maintaining that not only are freedom and morality possible in an unprogrammed world; they are inconceivable in any other. As I show in "Which Signposts?" the thinker Pyotr Struve drew on Herzen's ideas in his own humanistic crusade against the intelligentsia's eschatological faiths in the years leading up to the 1917 Revolution; and from a historical perspective one can see close parallels between Herzen and two other writers—Chekhov and Bakhtin—who have helped to shape our understanding of the relations between time and freedom.[13]

As a view of how history, society, morality, and the self will look if approached as a product of time and chance, *From the Other Shore* has lost none of its relevance. Stephen Jay Gould has observed that we have yet to come fully to terms with the ways in which the Darwinian revolution has transformed our understanding of the natural and historical world. Our everyday concepts and our stereotypes of science reveal a continued allegiance to the comforting but deeply misleading iconography of the ladder of progress: we are only beginning, fearfully, to explore the consequences of recognizing our dependence on chance. It has been argued that the demythologizing tendencies at work today are unlikely to stop us from seeking to trace universal patterns in history, that grand narratives are ways of formulating fundamental human needs: "Their 'grandness' is a measure of the urgency and intensity of the need."[14] But equally, these are going through a profound transformation; accounts of progress are giving ground to narratives of contingency, which tend to fall into two distinct categories: I shall call them here the Nietzschean and the Darwinian. Nietzschean narratives stress the endless relativity of meaning, precluding common standards or access to final truths. They replace rationalist accounts of morality and progress with visions of individuals and communities trying out new vocabularies in a spirit of ironic play. Darwinian philosophers, while agreeing on the need to revise our vocabulary, argue that what we now know about the role of chance in the historical and physical world does not support the claim that there is no reality independent of our shifting representations of it: in scientific enquiry and other rational activities (such as analytical moral philosophy) imaginative freedom is bound by constraints imposed by physical laws and the requirements of rational consistency. In Darwinian narratives (as in Darwin's account of evolutionary processes), contingency is not equated with directionless play; chance is seen to operate within a framework of laws, allowing for the plotting of continuities, the calculation of probabilities, and a prospect of progress, although not in a linear march toward a final goal. Typical Darwinians—hermeneutic philosophers such as Charles Taylor or Alasdair MacIntyre—while taking account of the self's historicity, argue that our sense of the past as the source of present situations that in turn shape the future allows us to make moral generalizations—and even moral progress.

In spite of their dubious history, free-floating Nietzschean fantasies tend to have a more seductive appeal (at least to theorists in the humanities) than do sober Darwinian narratives. This is why it is timely to draw attention to the ideas of a man who, though trained as a natural scientist and professing a Baconian empiricism, was acclaimed by Dostoevsky as a poet (and by Nietzsche as a man of "every outstanding quality"). Herzen did not live to cross swords with Nietzsche; but his negative response to the pessimism of Schopenhauer, whom Nietzsche acknowledged as his teacher, gives us an idea of how he would have reacted to the Nietzschean vision of an intrinsically meaningless world which has so much influenced our own age. Of all the thinkers discussed in this book, he was the most successful in avoiding in equal measure the traps of pessimism and of utopian faith. The Russian intelligentsia has for good or ill been associated with utopianism, but Herzen once predicted that its irony would be the source of its salvation. He may yet prove to be right.

PART I

Methods and Approaches

A Complex Vision

CHAPTER ONE

Do not look for solutions in this book—there are none;
in general modern man has no solutions.
—Aleksandr Herzen, *From the Other Shore*

In an attempt to explain Russian Bolshevism to Lady Ottoline Morrell, Bertrand Russell once remarked that, appalling though it was, it seemed the right sort of government for Russia: "If you ask yourself how Dostoevsky's characters should be governed, you will understand."[1]

In the eyes of many Western liberals, the Soviet tyranny was the inescapable outcome of the ideas and actions of Dostoevsky's "possessed": the Russian radical intelligentsia. In the degree of their alienation from their society and of their impact on it, the Russian intelligentsia of the nineteenth century were a phenomenon almost *sui generis*. Their ideological leaders were a small group with the cohesiveness and sense of mission of a religious sect. In their fervent moral opposition to the existing order, their single-minded preoccupation with ideas, and their faith in reason and science, they paved the way for the Russian Revolution and thereby achieved major historical significance. But they are too often treated by English and American historians with a mixture of condescension and moral revulsion—because the theories to which they were so fervently attached were not their own but borrowed from the West and often misunderstood and misapplied, and because in their fanatical passion for extreme ideologies they are held to have rushed, like Dostoevsky's devils, to blind self-destruction, dragging their country, and then much of the rest of the world, after them. The Russian Revolution and its aftermath have strengthened the belief, deeply entrenched in the Anglo-Saxon outlook, that a passionate interest in ideas is a symptom of mental and moral disorder.

One powerful liberal voice has never failed to dissent from this view of the Russian intelligentsia. Isaiah Berlin is one of the most widely admired political thinkers of the second half of the twentieth century, the proponent of what John Gray describes as a "stoical and tragic liberalism" of unavoidable conflict between competing values, which has injected new life into the liberal intellectual tradition.[2] His writings are penetrated with the conviction that liberal values are best defended by those who best understand the power of ideas, in particular the intellectual and moral attractions of what he has called the great despotic visions of the Right and Left. One of his distinctive contributions to English intellectual life has been as a counterforce to its parochial indifference to intellectual movements in Europe. In a succession of dazzling studies he has carried the personalities and ideas of some of the most original thinkers of the post-Renaissance world to a wide audience, and in essays brought together in the collection *Russian Thinkers* (1978), he has achieved the same for the phenomenon of the Russian intelligentsia.

Berlin's approach to Russian thought has been directed by his interest in how ideas are "lived through" as solutions to moral problems. Avoiding the common tendency to pronounce on Russian solutions with the wisdom of historical hindsight, he has focused instead on the dilemmas they were conceived to resolve. Though his essays on Russian subjects stand by themselves, with no need of philosophical annotation or cross-reference, they are also a substantial contribution to the central theme of all his writings on intellectual history, and their originality can best be appreciated if they are approached within this wider framework.

Berlin's writings have been centrally concerned with what he sees as one of the most fundamental of the open issues on which moral conduct depends: are all absolute values ultimately compatible with one another, or is there no single final solution to the problem of how to live, no one objective and universal human ideal? In the essays on liberty that encapsulate his thinking on this issue, he has explored the historical and psychological roots and consequences of monist and pluralist visions of the world. He argues that the great totalitarian structures built on Hegelian and Marxist foundations are not a terrible aberration but rather a logical development of the central assumption shared by the main currents of Western political thought: that a fundamental unity, deriving from a single universal purpose, underlies all phenomena. This can be discovered, according to some, through scientific inquiry or, according to others, through religious revelation or metaphysical speculation. When discovered, it will provide a definitive answer to the question of how one should live.

Although the most extreme forms of this faith, with their dehumanizing visions of individuals as instruments of abstract historical forces, have led to criminal perversions of political practice, Berlin emphasizes that the faith itself cannot be dismissed as the product of sick minds. It is the basis of all traditional morality and is rooted in a deep and incurable metaphysical need that arises from humanity's sense of an inner split and its yearning for a mythical lost wholeness. This craving for absolutes is often the expression of an urge to shed the burden of responsibility for one's fate by transferring it to a vast impersonal and monolithic whole—"nature, or history, or class, or race, or the 'harsh realities of our time,' or the irresistible evolution of the social structure, that will absorb and integrate us into its limitless, indifferent, neutral texture, which it is senseless to evaluate or criticize, and against which we fight to our certain doom."[3]

Berlin believes that precisely because monistic visions of reality answer fundamental human needs, truly consistent pluralism is rarely found in history. In the sense in which he uses the word, *pluralism* is not to be confused with that which is commonly defined as a liberal outlook—according to which all extreme positions are distortions of true values and the key to social harmony and a moral life lies in moderation and the golden mean. True pluralism, as Berlin understands it, is much more tough-minded and intellectually bold: it rejects the view that all conflicts of values can be finally resolved by synthesis and that all desirable goals may be reconciled. It recognizes that human nature generates values which, though equally sacred, equally ultimate, exclude one another, without there being any possibility of establishing an objective hierarchical relation among them. Moral conduct may therefore involve making agonizing choices, without the help of universal criteria, between incompatible but equally desirable values.

This permanent possibility of moral uncertainty is, in Berlin's view, the price that must be paid for recognition of the true nature of one's freedom: the individual's right to self-direction, as opposed to direction by state or church or party, is plainly of supreme importance if one holds that the diversity of human goals and aspirations cannot be evaluated by any universal criterion or subordinated to some transcendent purpose. But he maintains that although this belief is implicit in some humanist and liberal attitudes, the consequences of consistent pluralism are so painful and disturbing, and so radically undermine some of the central and uncritically accepted assumptions of the Western intellectual tradition, that they are seldom fully articulated. In seminal essays on Giambattista Vico, Niccolò Machiavelli, and Johann Gottfried von Herder, and in "Historical Inevitability" (1954) Berlin has shown that those few thinkers who spelled out the consequences of pluralism have been consistently misunderstood and their originality undervalued.

In *Four Essays on Liberty* he suggests that pluralist visions of the world are often the product of historical claustrophobia, during periods of intellectual and social stagnation, when a sense of the intolerable cramping of human faculties by the demand for conformity generates a demand for "more light," an extension of the areas of individual responsibility and spontaneous action. But as the dominance of monistic doctrines throughout history shows, people are much more prone to agoraphobia: at moments of historical crisis, when the need for choice generates fears and neuroses, they eagerly trade the doubts and agonies of moral responsibility for determinist visions, conservative or radical, that give them "the peace of imprisonment, a contented security, a sense of having at last found one's proper place in the cosmos." Berlin points out that the craving for certainties has never been stronger than in the twentieth century; and his essays on liberty are a powerful warning of the need to discern, through a deepening of moral perceptions—a "complex vision" of the world— the cardinal fallacies on which such certainties rest.[4]

Like many other liberals, Berlin believes that such a deepening of perceptions can be gained through a study of the intellectual background to the Russian Revolution. But his conclusions are very different from theirs. With the subtle moral sense that led him to radically new insights into European thinkers, he refutes the common view that the Russian intelligentsia were, to a man, fanatical monists: their historical predicament strongly predisposed them to both types of vision of the world, the monist and the pluralist—the fascination of the intelligentsia derives from the fact that the most sensitive among them suffered simultaneously, and equally acutely, from historical claustrophobia and agoraphobia, so that they were at once strongly attracted to messianic ideologies and morally repelled by them. The result, as he reveals, was a remarkably concentrated self-searching that in many cases produced prophetic insights into the great problems of our time.

The causes of that extreme Russian agoraphobia which generated a succession of millenarian political doctrines are well known: in the political reaction following the failure of the Decembrist rising of 1825 the Westernized intellectual elite became deeply alienated from their backward society. With no practical outlet for their energies, they channeled their social idealism into a religiously dedicated search for truth. In the historiosophical systems of German idealist philosophy, then at the height of its influence in Europe, they sought a unitary vision that would make sense of the moral and social chaos around them and anchor them in reality.

This yearning for absolutes was one source of that notorious consistency which, as Berlin observes, was the most striking characteristic of Russian thinkers—their habit of taking ideas and concepts to their most extreme, even absurd, conclusions: to stop before the ultimate consequences of one's reasoning was seen as moral cowardice, insufficient commitment to the truth. But there was a second, conflicting motivation behind this consistency. Among the Westernized minority, imbued through their education and reading with both Enlightenment and Romantic ideals of liberty and human dignity, the primitive and crushing despotism of Nicholas I produced a claustrophobia that had no parallel in the more advanced countries of Europe, and which was expressed in a radical questioning of traditionally accepted authorities and dogmas—religious, political, and social. As Berlin shows in his essay "Russia and 1848," the failure of the European revolutions in 1848 accelerated this process by increasing the intelligentsia's distrust of Western liberal and radical ideologues and their social nostrums.[5] The tensions and the insights generated by an iconoclasm that was driven by the thirst for faith are the central theme of Berlin's essays on Russian thinkers.

In a series of vivid portraits in *Russian Thinkers,* he presents the most outstanding members of the intelligentsia as continually torn between their suspicion of absolutes and their longing to discover some monolithic truth that would once and for all resolve the problems of moral conduct. Some succumbed to the latter urge: Mikhail Bakunin began his political career with a famous denunciation of the tyranny of dogmas over individuals and ended it by demanding total adherence to his dogma of the wisdom of the simple peasant; and many of the young "nihilist" iconoclasts of the 1860s accepted without question the tenets of a crude materialism. In other thinkers the battle was more serious and sustained. The literary critic Vissarion Belinsky is often cited as the arch example of the intelligentsia's fanatical attachment to the principle of logical consistency: from Hegelian principles he deduced that the despotism of Nicholas I was to be accepted as a necessary stage in the march of History. But as Berlin shows in a moving study of Belinsky, after a tormenting inner struggle he surrendered to the promptings of his conscience, fervently denouncing Hegel's doctrine of progress as a Moloch to whom living human beings were sacrificed. In their search for an ideal that would withstand their destructive critique, many other Russian intellectuals were led to question the great metaphysical systems that ruled over nineteenth-century European thought as well as some of the most cherished assumptions of progressive ideologies. In an essay on the populist tradition that dominated Russian radical thought in the nineteenth century, Berlin observes that this movement was far ahead of its time in pointing to the dehumanizing implications of contemporary liberal and radical theories of progress, which placed such faith in quantification, centralization, and the rationalization of productive processes.

Most Russian thinkers regarded their destructive criticism as a mere preliminary, the clearing of the ground for some great ideological construction; Berlin sees it as highly relevant to our time, when only a consistent pluralism can protect human freedom from the depredations of the systematizers. Such a pluralism, he has pointed out, was fully articulated in the ideas of a thinker whose originality had hitherto been largely overlooked: Aleksandr Herzen.

The founder of Russian populism, Herzen was known in the West mainly as a Russian radical with a utopian faith in an archaic form of socialism. In two essays on Herzen, and in introductions to his greatest works, *From the Other Shore* and *My Past and Thoughts,* Berlin established him firmly as "one of Russia's three moral preachers of genius," the author of profound reflections on liberty.[6]

Herzen had begun his intellectual career with a search for an ideal; he found it in an advanced form of socialism that he believed existed in embryo in the Russian peasant commune. But he argued that neither his nor any other ideal could be a universal solution to the problems of social existence: the search for such a solution was incompatible with respect for human liberty. He accused the revolutionaries of his time of being conservatives in their reluctance to confront the common source of all forms of political oppression: the tyranny of abstractions over individuals. Herzen's attacks on all deterministic philosophies of progress, Berlin argues, showed a prescient understanding that "one of the greatest of sins that any human being can perpetrate is to seek to transfer moral responsibility from his own shoulders to . . . an unpredictable future order," to sanctify monstrous crimes by faith in some remote utopia.[7]

Berlin depicts Herzen's predicament as a very modern one. Herzen was torn between the conflicting values of equality and excellence; he recognized the injustice of elites but valued the intellectual and moral freedom and the aesthetic distinction of true aristocracy. But while refusing, unlike other leading ideologists of the Russian Left, to sacrifice excellence to equality, he understood, with John Stuart Mill, something that has become much clearer in our day: that the common mean between these values, represented by "mass societies," is not the best of both worlds but more frequently, in Mill's words, an aesthetically and ethically repellent "collective mediocrity," the submergence of the individual in the mass. In a language as vivid as Herzen's own, Berlin has conveyed to the English-speaking reader the originality of Herzen's belief that there are no general solutions to individual and specific problems, only temporary expedients that must be based on an acute sense of the uniqueness of each historical situation and on a responsiveness to the needs and demands of diverse individuals and peoples.

Berlin's exploration of the self-searching of Russian thinkers includes studies of two writers—Tolstoy and Turgenev—that remove the widespread misconception that in prerevolutionary Russia literature and radical thought formed two distinct and mutually hostile traditions. Tolstoy's and Dostoevsky's well-known aversion to the intelligentsia has been frequently quoted to emphasize the gulf between Russia's great writers, who were concerned with exploring human spiritual depths, and its radical thinkers, perceived as obsessed with the external forms of social existence. Berlin maintains that the art of Tolstoy and Turgenev can be understood only as a product of the same moral conflict as that experienced by the radical intelligentsia. In his study of Tolstoy's view of history, "The Hedgehog and the Fox," and in his essay on Tolstoy and the Enlightenment, he interprets the relation between Tolstoy's artistic vision and his moral preaching as a titanic struggle between monist and pluralist visions of reality. Tolstoy's lethal nihilism demolished the pretensions of all theories, dogmas, and systems to explain, order, or predict the complex and contradictory phenomena of history and social existence, but the driving force of this attack was a passionate longing to discover a single unitary truth, encompassing all existence and impregnable to attack. He was thus constantly in contradiction with himself, perceiving reality in its multiplicity but believing only in "one vast, unitary whole."[8] In his art he expressed an unsurpassed feeling for the irreducible variety of phenomena, but in his moral preaching he advocated simplification, reduction to one single level, that of the Russian peasant or the simple Christian ethic. In some of the most psychologically delicate and revealing passages ever written on Tolstoy, Berlin suggests that his tragedy was that his sense of reality was too strong to be compatible with any of the narrow ideals he set up; the conclusions articulated in Herzen's writings were demonstrated in Tolstoy's inability, despite the most desperate attempts, to harmonize opposing but equally valid goals and attitudes. Yet his failure to resolve his inner contradictions gives Tolstoy a moral stature apparent even to those most mystified or repelled by the content of his preaching.

Few writers would seem to have less in common than Tolstoy, the fanatical seeker after truth, and Turgenev, a master of lyrical prose, the author of "nostalgic idylls of country life."[9] But in his essay on Turgenev, Berlin shows that although by temperament he was a liberal, repelled by dogmatic narrowness and opposed to extreme solutions, he had been deeply influenced in his youth by the moral commitment of his radical contemporaries and their opposition to the brutality of the Russian autocracy. He fully accepted his friend Belinsky's belief that the artist cannot remain a neutral observer in the battle between justice and injustice but must dedicate himself, like all decent people, to the search to establish and proclaim the truth. The effect of this was to turn Turgenev's liberalism into something quite distinct from the European liberalism of that time, much less confident and optimistic, but more modern. In his novels, which chronicled the development of the intelligentsia, he examined the controversies of the middle years of the nineteenth century between Russian radicals and conservatives, moderates and extremists, exploring with great scrupulousness and moral perception the strengths and weaknesses of individuals and groups and of the doctrines by which they lived. Berlin stresses that the originality of Turgenev's liberalism lay in the conviction he shared with Herzen (even though he thought that Herzen's populism was his last illusion), as against Tolstoy and the revolutionaries (even though he admired their single-mindedness), that no final solution to the central problems of society was possible. In an age when liberals and radicals alike were complacent in their faith in the inevitability of progress, when political choices seemed mapped out in advance by inexorable historical forces—the laws governing economic markets or the conflict of social classes—which could be made to assume responsibility for their results, Turgenev perceived the hollowness of the certainties invoked by liberals to justify the injustices of the existing order or by radicals to justify its merciless destruction. He thus anticipated the predicament of the radical humanist in the twentieth century, which one of the most morally sensitive political thinkers of our time, Leszek Kolakowski, has described as a continual agony of choice between the demands of *Sollen* and *Sein,* value and fact:

> The same question recurs repeatedly in different versions: how
> can we prevent the alternatives of *Sollen-Sein* from becoming
> polarizations of utopianism-opportunism, romanticism-
> conservatism, purposeless madness versus collaboration with
> crime masquerading as sobriety? How can we avoid the fatal
> choice between the Scylla of duty, crying its arbitrary slogans,
> and the Charybdis of compliance with the existing world, which
> transforms itself into voluntary approval of its most dreadful
> products? How to avoid this choice, given the postulate—which
> we consider essential—that we are never able to measure truly
> and accurately the limits of what we call 'historical necessity'?
> And that we are, consequently, never able to decide with cer-
> tainty which concrete fact of social life is a component of his-
> torical destiny and what potentials are concealed in existing
> reality.[10]

Kolakowski's formulation of this dilemma that has faced the twentieth century is surely valid. Yet Turgenev, a thinker of a very different type, faced it more than a century ago. Before proponents of one-sided visions, conservative or utopian, possessed the technological equipment for experiments on limitless human material, it was less difficult to defend the view that one or other extreme vision, or even a middle course, was the whole answer. Isaiah Berlin has demonstrated that, at a time when both liberals and the ideologists of the Left were still confident of the sufficiency of their systems, Turgenev had attained a more complex vision and had embodied it in his art.

Among the three central figures in these essays, there is no doubt where Berlin's greatest sympathies lie. As he shows us, for all Tolstoy's moral grandeur, his blindness at those moments when he relinquishes the humane vision of his art for a domineering dogmatism is repellent. And Turgenev, for all the clarity of his vision, his intelligence, and his sense of reality, lacked the courage and moral commitment he so admired in the radical intelligentsia: his vacillation between alternatives was too often a state of agreeable melancholy, ultimately dispassionate and detached.

It is Herzen who emerges as the hero of *Russian Thinkers.* Although Berlin concedes that there was substance in Turgenev's assertion that Herzen never succeeded in ridding himself of one illusion—his faith in the "peasant sheepskin coat"—for him this does not detract from a view of liberty that was both both profound and prophetic in its perception that "one of the deepest of modern disasters is to be caught up in abstractions instead of realities."[11] Berlin concluded his inaugural lecture as professor of social and political theory at Oxford with a quotation from an author whom he did not identify: "To realise the relative validity of one's convictions, and yet stand for them unflinchingly, is what distinguishes a civilised man from a barbarian."[12] Herzen, who had the subtle vision of a Turgenev along with a self-sacrificing commitment to the truth that was the equal of Tolstoy's, was in this sense both brave and civilized. He possessed to a great degree that consistent pluralism of outlook which for Berlin is the essence of political wisdom.

It is often said of the Russians that their national peculiarity consists in expressing in an extreme fashion certain universal characteristics of the human condition; and for many the historical significance of the Russian intelligentsia consists in the fact that they embodied the human thirst for absolutes in a pathologically exaggerated form. Berlin's essays present us with a very different and much more complex interpretation of the intelligentsia's "universality," showing that for a variety of historical reasons they embodied not one but at least two fundamental, and opposed, human urges. The urge to assert the autonomy of the self through revolt against necessity continually clashed with their demand for certainties, leading them to acute insights into moral, social, and aesthetic problems that in this century have come to be regarded as of central importance. That this aspect of their thought has aroused so little attention in the West is due in some measure to the glaring intellectual defects of the thought of most leaders of the intelligentsia. The repetitiousness, the incoherence, the proliferation of half-digested ideas from foreign sources in the writings of men like Belinsky, together with the political disasters for which they are held responsible, have led many Western scholars to echo the Russian thinker Pyotr Chaadaev's famous pronouncement that Russia exists only to teach the world some great lesson—apparently, that its example should be avoided at all costs. But with an acute instinct for quality, and with no trace of the condescension that is the frequent concomitant of historical hindsight, Berlin has discerned behind the formal shortcomings of the intelligentsia's writings a moral passion worthy of attention and respect, a vindication of the belief he has preached to his English audience over many years: enthusiasm for ideas is not a failing or a vice; on the contrary, the ability to think through political and social ideals in order to predict their ultimate consequences is the best safeguard we have against the tyranny of ideological systems.

As he points out in *Four Essays on Liberty,* no philosopher has ever succeeded in proving or refuting the determinist proposition that subjective attitudes do not influence historical events. But his studies of how Russian thinkers "lived" their beliefs, testing them in daily moral struggle, argue more powerfully than any logical demonstration in support of the message that penetrates all Isaiah Berlin's writings: that human beings are morally free and are (more often, at least, than the determinists would concede) able to influence events for good or ill through their freely held convictions and ideals.

Leonard Schapiro's Russia

CHAPTER   TWO

In the introduction to his book *The Soviet Political Mind,* Robert Tucker remarks that the history of twentieth-century politics can be seen as a process of realizing the dreams of the nineteenth. Few scholars of Soviet history were so passionately committed to demonstrating the truth of this view as Leonard Schapiro, and few were more qualified to do so. After the Second World War the study of Russian history and Soviet politics separated into two distinct specializations whose practitioners spoke no common language. Schapiro never respected this artificial boundary. For many years the doyen of Russian studies at the London School of Economics, and one of the most influential liberal historians of Russia, he is best known for his books *The Origins of the Communist Autocracy* and *The Communist Party of the Soviet Union,* but he also published a provocative study of nineteenth-century Russian political thought,[1] and one of his last books was a biography of Ivan Turgenev. Both the breadth of his interests and the central vision that inspired and ordered them are strongly evident in *Russian Studies,* a posthumous collection of articles, reviews, and talks that are the fruit of more than forty years of study of Russian history and thought.[2] From the Slavophiles to Solzhenitsyn, few Russian writers and thinkers of significance over the past two centuries do not appear somewhere in this volume—and all are measured by one dominant criterion: whether they embodied or opposed the dreams that led to the hideous reality of the Soviet era.

Schapiro was a leader of what from the 1940s to the 1960s was the dominant orthodoxy in Soviet studies in the West, based on the premise that Stalinism was the logical successor to Leninism and that the dynamics of Soviet history since 1917 can be explained by one determining factor: the ruling party's commitment to total power. As he emphasized in the first essay in *Russian Studies,* Schapiro considered this the only valid approach to the study of Soviet government. During the last twenty years of his life he expressed increasing alarm at new trends in Sovietology, which dismissed "totalitarianism" as a Cold War term, saw power struggles within the party as one among many conflicts of interest groups in the USSR, and even favored such approaches as "grass-roots sociology," under what Schapiro called the dangerous illusion "that at bottom the Soviet Union is reasonable and basically motivated by the same aims as the Western nations."[3]

By the end of the 1960s the new "fashions," as Schapiro dismissively labeled them, had destroyed the orthodox consensus in Sovietology, splitting the field into what the historian Stephen Cohen has called "totalitarianism" and "revisionist" schools.[4] Among the leaders of the totalitarianists (along with Schapiro) were Richard Pipes, Adam Ulam, and Zbigniew Brzezinski; the revisionists included Cohen himself, Jerry Hough, Moshe Lewin, and a number of younger Sovietologists. The advent of perestroika increased the distance between the two schools of interpretation, as each attempted to influence Western reactions to Gorbachev's reforms. Proponents of the totalitarian model of Soviet government (supported by many, but by no means all, Soviet dissidents who had been forced to emigrate during the Brezhnev period)[5] interpreted the reforms as cosmetic changes, tactical maneuvers designed to shore up the existing system and win credits in the West. Revisionists argued that the reforms showed that the party was not the frozen monolith it had been popularly assumed to be; that they reflected a genuine competition among factions and interest groups within the elite and a degree of responsiveness to the demands of society. They suggested that the Soviet Union was not, as the old orthodoxy claimed, a sui generis phenomenon: that what was then taking place could be understood as a conflict between reformism and conservatism. The totalitarianists warned that to respond to these new developments by relaxing hostility would be to play the Russians' game. The revisionists replied that a negative response to Mikhail Gorbachev on the part of the West would have the effect of creating an unholy alliance between their hardliners and ours and would, as has happened in the past, contribute to the defeat of the reformers.[6]

Although this debate was generally conducted in ahistorical terms, it was based on two irreconcilable views of the historical roots of the Soviet state. The revisionists believed that, like all other governmental systems, this was a complex product of many strands, including the nationalism and anti-Westernism of the tsarist bureaucracy and the Russian Right. The totalitarianists tended to ascribe the sole paternity of the Soviet system and all its evils to the Russian revolutionary tradition. As one of the most respected proponents of this view, Schapiro had a dominant influence in shaping Western attitudes to the Soviet Union. The historical grounds for his convictions are presented in the essays collected in *Russian Studies*.

Schapiro was concerned to refute what he saw as a "legend" fostered by Marxist historians: "that there was never any choice in Russia between dark reaction and red revolution, and that liberal order was an alien plant which could never have taken root.["7] He argued that the main impediment to the establishment of a liberal democracy in Russia was not the intransigence of the autocracy but the radical intelligentsia's opposition to the principle of legal order.

Schapiro described how he came to this belief: his study of law (he became an academic after sixteen years as a practicing lawyer) left him with the lifelong conviction that the rule of law was a necessary condition of human dignity, that "a society can only progress by evolution, and not by convulsions, by growth and not by surgery dictated by belief in some system . . . [and that] the only condition for ensuring organic growth, is a well-rooted legal system and a strong and independent judiciary to safeguard it."[8]

Approaching Russian history with this criterion in mind, he was deeply influenced by two books. The first, Karl Wittfogel's *Oriental Despotism,* revealed to him the gulf between the societies of the West, founded on legal order, and the historical nature of the Russian governmental system; while the conservative liberal Victor Leontovitsch's *Geschichte des Liberalismus in Russland* showed him why the government's reforming and Westernizing policies in the nineteenth century met with so little support and cooperation on the part of Russian society. The Russian intelligentsia, whatever their political differences, were united in seeing advocacy of law and order as "cold, calculating, immoral, selfish, un-Russian, or unpatriotic."[9] The Slavophile movement saw the absence of a legal order as evidence of a superior moral principle underlying the Russian state. In its idealized vision of the autocracy, the relations between governor and governed rested on patriarchal bonds of trust and love—the coercive force of legal guarantees was superfluous. The radical intelligentsia dismissed Western constitutional structures as empty forms and feared that liberal reforms would seduce Russia away from its "separate path" of development based on the allegedly socialistic principles inherent in the peasant commune.

The consolidation of capitalism in Russia and the foundation of a Constitutional Democratic (Kadet) Party at the beginning of the twentieth century did not, according to Schapiro, transform the intelligentsia's attitude to legal order. Quoting the Kadet leader P. N. Miliukov, who designated the revolutionary parties as "our allies on the Left," Schapiro argued that by their hostility to the government the liberals contributed to their own defeat. The intelligentsia "all dreamed of some short cut to freedom which would avoid the laborious construction of solidly based independent institutions such as had been slowly built up over the centuries in Western Europe."[10] As a result, their only positive achievement—the assassination of Alexander II—was futile and retrograde: it halted reform, polarized Russian society, and led eventually to the triumph of Bolshevism.

Few Western historians would dissent from the view that the intelligentsia's negative attitude to law contributed to the failure of liberal democracy to take root in Russia. But a number of scholars have questioned whether liberal doctrines were feasible at all as a basis for political behavior in a country that had neither a substantial middle class nor representative government and where those whose demands would have been regarded as mildly reformist in the West were treated as dangerous subversives by a government determined not to relinquish its claim to absolute power.[11] Hence the view, far from unique to radical historians, that would-be liberals had little choice but to align themselves with the Left against the autocracy.

Schapiro answered this by arguing the existence of a "tenuous, but more truly liberal Russian tradition," which maintained that once a major change has been accomplished, "the most important ally of liberalism is conservation, and not revolution."[12] He traced this "conservative liberalism" back to Pyotr Chaadaev, whose "Philosophical Letter," published in 1836, first advanced for public debate the problem of Russia's future as a country that was cut adrift by historical catastrophe (the Mongol invasion) from Western Europe and that had failed to develop the ideas of "duty, justice, law and order," which were the moral essence of European culture.

As Schapiro pointed out, such "Western" principles were basic to the outlook of Aleksandr Pushkin, among other writers, but he contended that they were elaborated systematically only by a few thinkers who were isolated and misunderstood in their time and subsequently consigned to the oblivion of history's losers. Among these Schapiro gives special attention to the legal philosopher Boris Chicherin, who maintained after the Emancipation Act of 1861 that once the government had embarked on the road of reform, the chief obstacle to the ultimate attainment of civil rights and political freedoms was the mentality and beliefs of the Left. Schapiro stressed Chicherin's significance in his book on nineteenth-century Russian thought and devoted one of his best-known essays (republished in *Russian Studies*) to those whom he regarded as the principal representatives of the same tendency in the early twentieth century: the authors of the symposium *Signposts,* several of whom (including the philosopher Nikolai Berdiaev) had been leading Marxists before moving to philosophical Idealism and religious belief. Published in 1909, *Signposts* attacked the Russian Left's tradition of opposing power and its maximalist demands and called for a moral rebirth of the intelligentsia through a reaffirmation of traditional cultural and religious values. Like Chicherin, the *Signposts* authors called for gradual evolution, based on a respect for law and the national cultural heritage. These calls, Schapiro observed, fell on deaf ears: the intelligentsia could not be weaned from its fanatical conviction that there is one complete answer to all questions, past and future, if only it can be found.

Schapiro's view of the importance of Chicherin and the *Signposts* authors is confirmed by the considerable body of work that has appeared on both since he brought them to the notice of historians. But subsequent scholarship has interpreted their significance rather differently. Few scholars now approach Russian liberalism from the narrow perspective of Leontovitsch, whose book so greatly influenced Schapiro and whose criterion of true liberalism was the Hegelian *Rechtsstaat* model. Some historians have emphasized the contrast between the pragmatic approach of classical, Anglo-Saxon liberalism and the doctrinaire nature of the Hegelian variety preached by a group of historians and jurists, Chicherin among them, who together founded the Russian "etatist" school of historiography,[13] based on Hegel's vision of the modern, centralized state as the incarnation of human rational consciousness and the crown of historical progress.

In the work of these thinkers, the interests of the people tended to be identified with the interests of the state and the interests of the state with those of the ruler. Their attempt to fit Russian history into a rigidly Hegelian frame led them to glorify autocrats like Ivan the Terrible (Ivan IV) and Peter the Great, who forced their centralizing designs on Russia at terrible human cost, and to idealize the contemporary autocracy as a progressive and rationalizing force. Some historians have argued that the major factor in the estrangement of this group from other sections of Russian progressive society was not their gradualism but their veneration of the state—their bizarre determination to present a primitive, corrupt, and floundering system of arbitrary rule as the historical instrument of rational reform. In this they were the forerunners of those Soviet historians whom Stalin pressed into service when he needed to invest his dictatorship with the authority of national tradition, and who obediently presented the bloodthirsty monster Ivan IV as a national hero and his reign of terror as the "historically inevitable" and "objectively necessary" means of controlling and unifying the Russian state.[14]

Similarly, the *Signposts* authors included (along with some liberals) proponents of a messianic nationalism that had some very illiberal implications. In prerevolutionary Russia, calls to uphold traditional values meant very different things to different groups; but a sense of historical context was a luxury the totalitarianism school frequently discarded: their politicizing of historical study precluded them from scrutinizing the liberal credentials of the prerevolutionary critics of the Russian Left.

Schapiro's brand of liberalism was wholly in the English empirical tradition. It is defined by Harry Willetts in his introduction to *Russian Studies* as being even more concerned with legal safeguards against the encroachment of the state on the rights of the citizen than with society's need to set limits to the disruptive activities of individuals. In other words, Schapiro was drawn to the classical liberalism of Locke, Bentham, and Mill, based on the concept of "negative liberty"—that human beings are free only inasmuch as they are granted a sphere of activity in which they can do as they like without interference from others and have freedom to consent to or dissent from particular forms of government.

Liberals of this sort have frequently pointed to the despotic implications in the concept of "positive liberty" outlined in Hegel's *Philosophy of Right*, which is the cornerstone of Rechtsstaat liberalism: the belief that the individual achieves liberty only through the state as the incarnation of his or her rational consciousness. Once the state is identified with the rational nature of humans, people can be seen to be free when they are most coerced, resistance on their part being interpreted as the expression of irrational urges. Schapiro, of course, was well aware that Russian liberal conservatism was rooted in Hegel and not in Mill; but the antilibertarian implications of this tradition are only lightly touched on in his book of essays, and then only in a non-Russian context: in a lecture on the general relation of law to the study of history and politics. Schapiro pointed to the weakness of the concept of the Rechtsstaat, as interpreted by the German positivist tradition of jurisprudence, which established the state as the source of the validity of law; it followed for those who embraced this concept that such travesties of law as Hitler's destruction of the Weimar Republic were valid and enforceable.

Schapiro did not pursue this line of thought—had he done so, he could scarcely have avoided discussing the affinities between the Russian ideologists of the Rechtsstaat and other offshoots, via Marx, of the Hegelian tradition. In their attachment to vast historical abstractions and universal principles Russian Hegelian liberals bear a remarkable resemblance to the "terribles simplificateurs" of the far Left. Those whose pragmatic and gradualist approach to change was genuinely motivated by a concern for individual liberty as the supreme value represented a far more "tenuous tradition" than that which Schapiro believed he had discovered, and it was one that did not respect party barriers. One of its representatives was the socialist Aleksandr Herzen. Another, and the only one who received detailed consideration in his essays on Russian thinkers, was Ivan Turgenev.

Isaiah Berlin has pointed out that Turgenev both created as a literary type and himself embodied a figure that has since become universal: "the well-meaning, troubled, self-questioning liberal, witness to the complex truth."[15] At a time of acute polarization of opinion in Russia, Turgenev possessed the rare ability to see many sides of a case; repelled by the fanaticism and simple solutions of many of the Left, he was unable to identify his cause with that of the generals and bureaucrats who persecuted radicals. His uncertainty was expressed in a political inconsistency that infuriated both Left and Right. He professed himself an old-fashioned liberal, in the English sense, who opposed revolution on principle. Yet he was friendly with leading revolutionaries and gave money to subversive publications. There was no Russian figure with whom Schapiro identified more closely than with this "English" liberal. His attachment to Turgenev is movingly expressed in an essay on the "triumph of humanity" in Turgenev's work—its acceptance of love and goodness as ends in themselves, and not for what they achieve in practice: "The important matter in life for Turgenev is neither system, nor abstract formula or theory, but human beings in their interrelation with one another."[16]

But Schapiro was curiously reticent and ambiguous about the political attitudes that flowed from Turgenev's humanism. On one occasion he included him in a list of Russia's only "true" (that is, conservative) liberals; on another he remarked, without elaboration, that Turgenev "almost" belonged to this tradition.[17] In his three essays on Turgenev in *Russian Studies* he discussed only the least contentious aspect of Turgenev's political vision: his consistent opposition to the idea that Russia should embark on a path of development separate from that of the West. Schapiro was clearly uncomfortable with the ambivalence that was an essential quality of Turgenev's liberalism but that could in no way be made to serve his own polemical ends. In his book on Turgenev he much underplayed this ambivalence, attributing his actions in the late 1870s (when he gave moral and financial support to the revolutionary cause) to a "romantic mood."[18] In this period, Schapiro noted disapprovingly, Turgenev let his heart rule his head.

Schapiro's mistake as a historian was perhaps to have let his head rule his heart. Those who knew him were struck by qualities that he shared with Turgenev—generosity, tolerance, commitment to liberal and humane values; the same qualities drew him with missionary zeal into the battle against the system that he believed to be the greatest threat to these values, and to the uncompromising position of the totalitarianism school, which represented the Soviet regime as wholly evil in its essence and intentions. It was the desire to show that the dream as well as the reality of that system had no moral legitimacy that attracted Schapiro to the Russian nineteenth century, and here the remorseless logic of the totalitarianism model dictated the simple scheme of oppositions one finds in much of his work. To have recognized the hesitations of Turgenev and others like him as the expression of a genuine liberal dilemma would have been to concede by implication some degree of legitimacy to the aims and motives of the Left. Hence the conclusion dictated by the wisdom of hindsight, that Turgenev was a liberal only when he was not a fellow traveler.

The perspective of the "totalitarianism" school justified its narrowness by the allegedly sui generis nature of the Soviet system, but Schapiro's essays show that when applied to prerevolutionary Russia, its analyses are alarmingly shallow and distorted, producing a history cleansed of complexity and gray areas, whose polarized schemas of oppositions resemble nothing so much as the Marxist patterns of thinking that Schapiro so greatly detested.

Fortunately, Schapiro was incapable of consistently following this approach. The same ambivalence that drew him equally to such opposing human types as Chicherin and Turgenev frequently resulted in judgments incompatible with the totalitarianism school's position. The leading revisionist historian Stephen Cohen pointed out that although Schapiro set out in *The Origins of the Communist Autocracy* to demonstrate that the Soviet government was a monolithic regime, "his work actually shows that this was not the case."[19] The same inconsistency is evident throughout his writing on Russian thought, in which his sympathetic and penetrating insights into character and motivation frequently refute his generalizations. Schapiro's essays on Lenin and Georgy Plekhanov are two such examples. But the most remarkable instance is his review of Cohen's book on Nikolai Bukharin, whose publication in 1974 was a major contribution to the revisionist approach, arguing that the New Economic Policy (NEP) (whose main architect was Bukharin) was not a tactical deviation from a predetermined path but a long-term strategy aimed at countering the effects of a premature seizure of power and bringing the peasantry to socialism through incentives and persuasion; that the brutal termination of the NEP by Stalin was neither necessary nor inevitable; and that (as shown by events in Czechoslovakia in 1968 and by demands for the "rehabilitation" of Bukharin by members of European Communist parties) the "Bukharinist" tradition continued to offer an alternative to Stalinism within European communism.

Schapiro welcomed Cohen's "magnificent" book, above all as a rebuttal of those "communisant" intellectuals (he had E. H. Carr principally in his sights) who argued that Stalin's policy was realistic and necessary.[20] He himself, from a very different standpoint, had frequently insisted on the necessity of Stalinism as the logical outcome of Leninism—and he would continue to do so; but here he agreed that Lenin in his last years developed a vision of socialism that was more ethical, conciliatory, and evolutionary, and he observed that Stalin's victory came from a number of contingent factors: his personal ruthlessness and mastery of the party apparatus, and his appeal to the most degenerate and corrupt aspect of the party—its self-seeking urge for power. In contrast, Schapiro pointed out, Bukharin, the principal theorist of Bolshevism in the early 1920s, although no democrat, expressed fears that a party enjoying a monopoly of power might become dangerously corrupt. Bukharin believed that socialism should be built on harmony and reconciliation, Schapiro wrote, and he should command our "respect and admiration" for his innumerable humanitarian acts and for the part he played in creating a relatively free and varied Marxist culture that survived until the 1930s.[21]

In his survey of the controversy between the two dominant approaches to Soviet history, Cohen blamed the Cold War origins of Sovietology for the fact that many Sovietologists, far from being enamored of their chosen discipline, "seemed to dislike or hate it."[22] Schapiro's essay on Cohen's book shows how far in spirit he was from the tendency with which he chose to identify himself. One of his most attractive qualities was his ability to respond with generosity and warmth to people with whose ideas he deeply disagreed. This capacity to distinguish between views he detested and the people who held them injected a note of hopefulness into his attitude to the Soviet scene, which was at sharp variance with his more deterministic prognostications. Schapiro's response to Bukharin's humanity and decency led him to a heretical conclusion in his re-view of Cohen's book. Agreeing with the author that Bukharin offered the only alternative to Stalinism and various forms of violent revolution—"a form of post-revolutionary revisionism"—he concluded: "The rehabilitation of Buk-harin may come—who can tell? If it ever does it will be a sure sign that real and substantial changes have taken place in the essential nature of the Soviet system of rule."[23]

It came. The changes that followed have made the weaknesses and limita-tions in Schapiro's historical thinking more evident, but they have also justified its essential—if thoroughly inconsistent—hopefulness.

PART II

Insights and Ambivalences

Carnival of the Intellectuals: 1855

CHAPTER THREE

The dominant vice of people in our time is *to seem, but not to be*. Everywhere and in everything are lies . . . in our hats, which don't protect our heads from the cold, in our skimpy, absurd frock coats, which cover the rear and leave the front unprotected; in our amiable smiles, in our minds which deceive and are deceived; in our tongues which are used, as Talleyrand put it, to conceal our thoughts. Our education—external, superficial, without depth, strength, or honesty—is a lie. Lies, lies, lies, an endless chain of lies. And the most remarkable thing about this state of affairs is the fact that it is at one and the same time falsehood and order.
—Aleksandr Nikitenko, 28 March 1855

Carnival is a lofty attitude toward the world which belonged *to the entire folk* in past centuries. It is an attitude toward the world that liberates from fear, brings the world maximally close to man and man close to his fellow-men . . . and with its joy at change and jolly relativity, stands opposed to the gloomy, one-sided official seriousness which is born of fear, is dogmatic and hostile to evolution and change, and seeks to absolutize the given conditions of existence and the social order.
—Mikhail Bakhtin, *Problems of Dostoevsky's Poetics*

One of the "men of the 1860s," Nikolai Shelgunov describes that decade on which Russia embarked with the end of the Crimean War as

a period of unusual spiritual intensity, of remarkable concentration of mental effort and remarkable sharpening of our critical faculties. . . . There was not a single field of knowledge that the critical faculty did not penetrate, not a single social phenomenon untouched by it. Earth and heaven, paradise and hell, problems of personal and public happiness, the peasant's hut and the nobleman's mansion—all these were scrutinized and subjected to critical appraisal. . . . The intellectual revolution we experienced in the sixties was not less in scope than the one France experienced after the middle of the eighteenth century.[1]

The political events of 1855 were not solely responsible for this revolution. Shelgunov points out that, unlike earlier crises that had stirred the Russian people to action, neither the death of Nicholas I nor the Crimean defeat threatened the nation's existence. A successor had ascended the throne, an honorable peace was in prospect: "everything could have gone on again in the old, traditional way, with a few small repairs and reforms." There was, nevertheless, a common sense that there was no way back: that history had arrived at one of those mysterious turning points at which a nation is roused from its slumber.[2]

Russia's intellectual ferment of 1855 can be described, in Mikhail Bakhtin's term, as a "carnivalization" of thought and literature. As Dominick La Capra has observed, this concept defines a kind of critical consciousness that (although Bakhtin exaggerated its links with popular culture) has an important contestatory function in modern societies, challenging existing conditions in the name of an ideal of free and unconstrained human relations.[3] I believe that Bakhtin's model helps us understand the mood of Russian intellectuals in that year of liberation from "official seriousness born of fear."

Bakhtin explores how the devices of folk carnival (ripping off masks, mocking the sacred, inverting hierarchies, juxtaposing opposites) have been used by artists and thinkers to question the established order of things and to force a re-thinking of accepted categories. At "frontier" periods in the development of cultures (Bakhtin gave the example of the early Renaissance), the "carnival-esque" extends to all areas of social existence. Overtaken by new events and discoveries, the official ideology loses authority and is replaced by a plurality of perspectives. In the social and ideological flux of such periods (as in the pageants and rituals of folk carnival), values and ideas break out of their closed systems and meet in challenging contact. Nothing is stable, all meanings are ambivalent, the familiar is made strange; rules are suspended and in topsy-turvy situations, new possibilities open up for the creative imagination.

At such periods, according to Bakhtin, humanist values may come to the fore. There is a shift in the sense of time; the present is seen not as a fragment of some transcendent, preprogrammed order but as fluid, inconclusive, responsive to the play of the creative imagination. Reverence for authority gives way to celebration of change (an attitude symbolized in the central rite of carnival: the crowning, followed by the uncrowning and subsequent beating, of the carnival king). While not eliminating oppression and censorship, carnival laughter has helped to liberate people from "the great *interior censor,* from the fear rooted in the human spirit for thousands of years; fear of the sacred, of official prohibition, of the past, of power."[4]

A carnivalesque attitude that fearlessly delivers the objects of its investigations into the hands of "free experimental fantasy" is, Bakhtin has argued, a precondition of progress in science, the arts, and society.[5] His model or ideal type of the carnivalesque can help us interpret that frontier year when experimental fantasy took possession of all areas of Russian life.

At the first rumors of the death of Nicholas I on 2 March 1855, Ivan Turgenev rushed to the Winter Palace and questioned a terrified sentry, who refused to comment on the report on the ground that if it proved false, he would be hanged on the spot.[6] Nicholas had devoted his life to suppressing independent thought: his death united his servants and victims in a common sense of release. The censor Aleksandr Nikitenko recorded in his diary the end of "a long, and, one must admit, cheerless page in the history of the Russian tsardom," while in his London exile the radical thinker Aleksandr Herzen declared: "The death of this nightmare has made me young."[7]

The news took nearly a month to reach the Siberian town of Semipalatinsk, where Dostoevsky, sentenced for his part in the Petrashevsky conspiracy, was living a dreary existence as a common soldier. With other political exiles he attended a funeral service at the Russian church. Release was much on all their minds: it was customary to start a new reign with an amnesty.

In the general euphoria, exaggeratedly high expectations of the successor were formed. The young officer Lev Tolstoy, stationed with his artillery battery above Sevastopol, took his oath to the new emperor, noting in his diary that the momentous epoch now beginning will demand "courage and effort" from all.[8] The young journalist Nikolai Chernyshevsky wrote piously to his parents in Saratov that all in St. Petersburg had great faith in the new tsar's magnanimity.

Soon the government signaled its intentions to embark on reform of the system (in particular, the situation of the serfs) and to sound out opinion on how to proceed. To understand how momentous this modest proposal of perestroika seemed at the time, one should bear in mind that in the eyes of its subjects the tsarist autocracy appeared scarcely less monolithic than its communist successor would seem. To Shelgunov, who as a forestry official had traveled widely in the Russian countryside in the early 1850s, the institution of serfdom seemed to exude both logical and juridical stability. Everyone, he wrote, knew his or her place; serf Russia operated like an enormous but simple machine, built like a beehive, in each cell of which there sat a small autocrat. To remove even a few stones from such a structure would be to risk destroying the whole, with consequences no one could foresee.

Utopian hope combined with the prospect of practical activity to create a wave of civic enthusiasm among the intelligentsia, who under Nicholas had been forced to channel its energies into metaphysical speculation. The extraordinary flowering of political journalism that characterized the 1860s began when Chernyshevsky joined the editorial staff of Nikolai Nekrasov's *The Contemporary* in May 1855, putting his radical stamp on a journal that had lacked direction since the death of its founder, Vissarion Belinsky, in 1848. Nikitenko was delighted to be given the task of drawing up a plan for reform of the censorship laws: "The time has come to put an end to . . . the arbitrariness of ignoramuses who have turned the censorship into a tribunal and treat ideas like thieves and drunkards." But soon he was ambivalent about the virtues of free speech. "Censorship," he noted in his diary, "is the most sensitive and painful nerve in our social existence: we must treat it with caution": it should not be abolished until Russians acquired the public morality and respect for law that are part of the concept of citizenship. He discovered, too, that the interests of glasnost did not necessarily coincide with those of firm government, complaining that the new tsar's openness to general advice meant that he took longer to make decisions than his father, who had relied on briefings from his ministers. In that sense, "Our work is managed less efficiently than . . . under the deceased tsar."[9]

The new force of public opinion revealed itself when news came of the fall of Sevastopol. The Russian public had come to identify with the fortunes of Nicholas's army through Tolstoy's *Sevastopol Tales,* which appeared in *The Contemporary* when the siege was still on. (Turgenev, who much admired them, begged Tolstoy to give up his military career: "I love Russian literature too much not to wish to know that you are safe from all stupid and indiscriminate bullets.")[10] In April, Tolstoy noted in his diary that his comrades' morale was sinking daily. By the summer the news was so bad that Turgenev confided to his friend the literary historian and critic Pavel Annenkov that he had stopped reading the foreign press. The city fell on 27 August. Tolstoy wrote to his aunt that he wept when, after a "great and glorious" battle, he saw it in flames, with French flags on its bastions.[11] In St. Petersburg, Turgenev exclaimed to Sergei Aksakov: "If only we can put this terrible lesson to good use, as the Prussians did with their defeat at Jena!"[12]

The defeat of the empire's military colossus shattered Russians' picture of the world. As Shelgunov put it, his country was like a ninety-year-old peasant woman who had never left her village. The average Russian's understanding of history and politics was highly limited and reposed on the belief "that Russia was the biggest, richest and strongest of all countries, and . . . [could], if absolutely obliged to do so, subjugate all peoples." Now it was up to individuals to fill the vacuum left by such beliefs through their own efforts, whether by discovering new truths or retrieving others from the past. "In a word, we had to start all over again from scratch."[13]

Some did so in secret. A group of students in Kharkov, motivated (as they later claimed) by shame and anger at Russia's defeat, formed a society devoted to fighting absolutism. Short-lived, it was a seed of the revolutionary groups of the 1860s.[14]

The image of heroic Russian soldiers betrayed by a corrupt and incompetent government radicalized many young people, among them the government official (and future revolutionary) Nikolai Serno-Solovevich. In a poem composed in prison some years later, he wrote that when Sevastopol began to groan, "this groan outraged everyone": from that day he resolved to work for his country's liberty.[15]

The hollowness behind the facade shocked even the governing elite. On news of the defeat, Nikitenko reflected: "My God, so many victims! . . . All at the behest of a mad will, drunk with absolute power and arrogance. . . . We have been waging war not for two years, but for thirty, maintaining an army of a million men and constantly threatening Europe. What was the point of it all? What profit, what glory has Russia reaped from this?" Only a few years earlier, he noted, the nationalists in Moscow were preaching that Europe was in decay and only the Slavs were flourishing: "And now Europe has proved to us in our ignorance and apathy, our arrogant contempt for her civilization, just how decayed she really is! Oh, what wretches we are!"[16]

The Crimean defeat gave fresh impetus to the rethinking of old categories. Shelgunov noted that everything began to be discussed—not only the present but the fate of future generations and the possibility of a total transformation of Russia and Europe. "Yes, Europe! We even speculated about renewal of the West through Russian principles—and not only Slavophiles, but also Westernizers, dreamt of such things."[17]

Here was the creative ferment of a "frontier" period: the official lie was discredited, new ideas had not yet hardened into dogma—no option seemed foreclosed. In A Writer's Diary, Dostoevsky described the "restless, unpacifiable" type, who makes his appearance at such turning points when, amid general disillusionment with traditional values, "each one seeks to invent something of his own, something new and unheard-of."[18] This type irrupted into the Petersburg salons of 1855 in the person of Lev Tolstoy.

Tolstoy had already established a brilliant literary reputation with the first two volumes of a trilogy, Childhood and Boyhood, and his Sevastopol Tales. At the end of 1855, Turgenev, with a prescient insight into Tolstoy's character, commented that "if he doesn't cripple his talent himself, he will go far, out of sight of us all."[19] The poet Afanasy Fet and Pavel Annenkov, who both met Tolstoy in Turgenev's apartment that winter, have left similar impressions of him. Fet was struck by his "automatic opposition to all generally accepted opinions" and his egregious rudeness. Annenkov described him as a very original mind, with whom one had to deal cautiously. He sought to resolve all questions by his own efforts, ignoring all existing traditions of thought on the ground that "these are invented on purpose by people in order to delude themselves or others." His judgments (such as his dismissal of Shakespeare) often seemed shockingly perverse, and he showed extreme intolerance of the social affectations to which Turgenev was prone: already then Tolstoy was searching for a truth characterized both by "simplicity and *commonsense*."[20]

This last observation is confirmed by the diaries Tolstoy kept during the long siege of Sevastopol, which are much concerned with meditations on his destiny—a question made more urgent by the ever-present threat of death and the army's lack of interest in his talents. He was irritated by "the fact that it does not enter anyone's head that I am good for anything except cannon-fodder, and the most useless kind of fodder at that." He sought, with military precision, to achieve self-perfection through "the most logical method": by first (through the exercise of reason) defining the supreme virtues and then formulating appropriate rules for his conduct. He succeeded in reconciling ambition with virtue by setting himself the twin goals of wealth and fame (in both the literary and military arenas), to be achieved through service to others and to his country. But he saw these as only "relative aims": his restless search for "rules" by which to live would lead him in a more original direction, already prefigured in a passage in his diary of March 1855, which sets down "an enormous idea, to whose realization I feel myself capable of consecrating my life. This idea is the founding of a new religion . . . , Christian, but stripped of faith and mystery, a practical religion, not promising future bliss, but giving bliss on earth."[21]

The dream of a kingdom of God on earth—a new just order and a new type of individual, intellectually, socially, and morally free—was the motivation behind much of the unmasking of falsehood that began in 1855. This mixture of ruthless iconoclasm and utopian faith would be characteristic of the Russian intelligentsia until 1917, and it owed much to the influence of Aleksandr Herzen in the first year of the new reign.

One of the most brilliant figures of the Russian 1840s, Herzen emigrated in 1847 to devote himself to political journalism in the service of the cause of freedom in his country. A friend of Pierre-Joseph Proudhon, Jules Michelet, Giuseppe Mazzini, and Giuseppe Garibaldi, he was a publicist of genius, and his memoirs, which he began to write in the 1850s, have been described by Isaiah Berlin as a literary masterpiece to be placed alongside the novels of Tolstoy, Turgenev, and Dostoevsky (all of whom admired his writing).[22] In Herzen we see the type of thinker whom Bakhtin described in his book on Rabelais: a leader of a humanist avant-garde who seeks to speed up the demise of outworn and oppressive belief systems by adopting the position of an ironic outsider in relation to the official discourse of his time. Subverting it through "carnival laughter," he strips authorities of their sacred aura, revealing the absurdity of the accepted order of things.

Herzen was influenced by the anthropocentrism of Ludwig Feuerbach, which claimed to rehabilitate "real" man, whom religion and philosophy treated as only a means for the realization of transcendent purposes. But he went further than most radical thinkers of his time in his suspicion of all ideological abstractions and systems in whose name individual liberty was suppressed. He described contemporary socialist doctrines of progress as mere secular versions of religious eschatology: to define a specific ideal as the goal of history was to deny the freedom of individuals to move in new and unpredictable directions. All social ideals should be flexible enough to reconcile the principle of the common good with the changing needs and aspirations of real people at specific periods; such an ideal, he suggested, already existed in embryonic form in the self-governing structure of the Russian peasant commune.

In 1853 in London, Herzen established the Free Russian Press, whose pamphlets, outlining the history of serfdom and the socialist potential of the commune, were clandestinely transported to Russia. On Nicholas's death he founded a new periodical, the *Polar Star,* and begged his compatriots to end thirty years of silence by sending him manuscripts that could not be printed in Russia. An anonymous source contributed Belinsky's correspondence with Nikolai Gogol to the first issue (in August 1855), which also contained an open letter from Herzen to the new tsar, urging him to take heed of the voice of his press, which, like an electric meter, would register the tension and activity of the repressed forces of the Russian people.

Herzen's humanism helped shape Russian socialism in its pre-Marxist, populist form. His articles were copied, distributed, and discussed by the Kharkov group and many other circles. But it was consistent with his convictions that he used the enormous influence of his press primarily to encourage the development of independent thought by acting as a forum for discussion. His own views on history, he claimed, were not a doctrine but, rather, "a fermenting agent, . . . [which] angers people and makes them think." Appropriately, he chose 1855 to publish the first Russian translation of *From the Other Shore,* the essays that sum up his iconoclastic vision, with a new foreword introducing them as "the protest of an independent individual against . . . absurd idols which belong to another age and which linger on meaninglessly amongst us, a nuisance to some, a terror to others."[23]

No work, it would seem, could have been more suited to the spirit of the times. "We do not build, we destroy . . . , we eliminate the old lie": Herzen argued that in the 1848 revolutions the European Left had shown itself no less dogmatic and authoritarian than the Right, revealing how deeply the reverence for transcendent powers and absolutes was rooted in European culture. In this regard, he believed, Russia had an enormous advantage over the West. In a speech made in London early in 1855 before an audience of European radicals (and subsequently published by his Free Russian Press), he argued that in Russia the question of revolution was "simplified" by the fact that the state, a foreign import introduced by force, had no roots in native traditions, and only a tiny minority had a vested interest in its existence.[24]

In Herzen's carnivalistic reversal of accepted wisdom, the mighty Russian state was stripped of substance, and the newly crowned tsar peremptorily uncrowned. Russia's future would be built on a survival from its remote past—the commune—with the help of a tiny and powerless minority—the dissident intelligentsia. The phenomenon that became known as Russian nihilism owed much to the self-image that Herzen helped this group to form at the outset of the new era. The philosopher Pyotr Chaadayev had taught the "men of the 1840s" to see their distance from Europe's cultural traditions as a historical tragedy. Herzen presents the same marginality as a unique advantage. The intelligentsia is "free, because we possess nothing. There is almost nothing that we can love."[25] Peter the Great's revolution had forced the educated classes to renounce their old beliefs, but the European values he had inculcated by means of the knout had never become part of the fabric of their being. Unrestrained by reverence for a past that was not theirs, they were, Herzen believed, better equipped than their European contemporaries to formulate a new vision of reality free from all metaphysical dualism.

The utopianism of Herzen's hopes was evident as soon as the details of the Emancipation of the serfs began to be discussed, revealing problems that not even the Left believed could be overcome by intellectual denial. Later Russian populists would be less optimistic about the advantages of backwardness and less critical of the achievements of the West. But that such questions should have been discussed at all in Russia in the mid-1850s was itself remarkable. Alternative models of progress would be a matter for debate in the West only much later, when the disadvantages of large-scale industrialized economies (capitalist and socialist alike) became evident. That Russian socialism anticipated some of these insights by almost a century was due largely to Herzen's ability to exploit his vantage point as an outsider on the Western cultural scene.

Ironically, Herzen's criticism of the West owed much to the stimulus of contemporary European thought; and those Russians who sought new values at the beginning of the 1860s were strongly influenced by the fact that European intellectuals were then also engaged in revising their picture of the world. German Idealism, which viewed history and culture as a march to some mysterious transcendent goal, had lost its preeminence with the growth of interest in social problems and new advances in science and technology. It was widely hoped that science, perceived as the source of ultimate truth about the individual and society, would complete the work of eighteenth-century rationalism in demolishing the outdated beliefs of Christian and monarchic Europe.

The young radicals of 1855 eagerly adopted the West's new faith, but their fathers were more ambivalent. Idealism had been a means of escape from reality under Nicholas, but it had also provided a moral basis for dissent. Agreed on the necessity of a new humanism, the intelligentsia would become bitterly divided on the question of what its epistemological basis should be. Their debate would have enormous repercussions on Russian literature, thought, and history; we are still living with its results today.

It all started with the publication of a rather dull dissertation: Nikolai Chernyshevsky's *The Aesthetic Relations Between Art and Reality.* Chernyshevsky defended his dissertation in May. The formal discussion, he told his parents, was disappointingly short and trivial, proving how little the ideas that he advanced were as yet understood in Russia.[26] Though philosophically unsubtle and confused, the work was revolutionary, signaling the young generation's adoption of the "new Enlightenment"—a materialist rationalism bolstered, as in the West, by the achievements of mid-nineteenth-century science. The authorities scented subversion. The censor Nikitenko (who, as a professor of literature, was Chernyshevsky's supervisor), thought it philosophically unsound, and it was not approved until three years later. But Chernyshevsky succeeded in publishing the dissertation some months after his unsuccessful defense. Reactions ranged from violent antipathy to reverent admiration. Shelgunov, one of Chernyshevsky's most ardent admirers, described it as a "humanistic sermon" that gave initial shape to the ideals of the 1860s.[27]

The work's hidden agenda was a socialist ideal supported by the anthropocentrism of Feuerbach and the new materialism. Chernyshevsky rejected the concept of an ideal beauty, a reflection of the infinite. Words like "infinite," he argued, are meaningless concepts that only produce confusion. He offered a definition free from transcendentalism: humanity is the supreme reality; therefore the most beautiful thing is life. The ideal of beauty is human beings in the plenitude and harmony of their powers, not some fantastic vision of the Absolute.

If art was (as Chernyshevsky implied) merely an inferior copy of reality, it could scarcely engage in criticism of that reality; but this was what he demanded of it. To defenders of the autonomy of art he replied that all art served ideological aims. Idealist aesthetics offered an escape from unpleasant social realities; the true role of art, as the "science of the beautiful," was to cooperate with the natural sciences in interpreting the world as a preliminary to mastering it.

The literary establishment greeted these theses with outrage. In letters to the writer Dmitry Grigorovich and the critics Ivan Panayev and Aleksandr Druzhinin, Turgenev expressed disgust with *The Contemporary* for giving serious attention to "this vile carrion, the offspring of spiteful blindness and stupidity."[28] All those involved knew that much more than art was at stake. Chernyshevsky's dissertation represented a break with the past no less significant than the death of Nicholas. The thinkers and writers who had matured under that regime saw themselves as a dissident brotherhood, with common values inspired by the humanism of Friedrich Schiller and the romantics. By dismissing their aesthetic idealism as no more than fine words, Chernyshevsky seemed to be accusing this generation of capitulating before despotism. His dissertation on aesthetics drove a wedge into Russia's intellectual elite: soon it would separate into two mutually hostile camps. This son of a priest represented a new force that would shape the new epoch: the *raznochintsy,* children of peasants, workers, minor clergy and petty officials, more impressed by science than by poetry and art, and uncompromising in their demands for radical change. In his private correspondence, Turgenev habitually referred to Chernyshevsky as "the one who smells of bugs": in Russia's crude "new people" the fastidious men of the 1840s sensed enemies rather than allies in a common cause.

The publication of the first critical edition of Pushkin's works (edited by Annenkov) was the occasion for a statement of position by both sides. Chernyshevsky used the pretext of a review to publish four long articles depicting Pushkin as a master of poetic form who belonged to a bygone age. He developed this theme in his *Essays on the Gogol Period of Russian Literature* (the first of which appeared at the end of 1855). Here he presented himself as the heir of the great critic Belinsky, with whose views, suppressed under Nicholas, he sought to reacquaint the Russian public: restating Belinsky's interpretation of Gogol's works as social satire, he asserted that Gogol, though no less a talent than Pushkin, was more sensitive to the needs of his time.

Infuriated by this view (and by Chernyshevsky's appropriation of Belinsky, whose criticism was rooted in Idealist categories), prominent critics rushed to defend traditional aesthetics. In a series of essays reviewing the Pushkin edition, Druzhinin proclaimed the self-sufficient value of art, praising Pushkin for standing above the battle of partisan schools and condemning the excessive concentration of the literary tendency known as the natural school on the negative aspects of Russian life. Druzhinin's essays met with a chorus of approval from Annenkov, Vasily Botkin, and other influential critics. Thus began the battle between the proponents of the "Pushkin" and "Gogol" tendencies in Russian literature. This unedifying polemic, in which both sides distorted the achievements of two great writers to suit their ideological purposes, was not a promising start to the new era.

Only Turgenev kept a distance from both camps. While praising Druzhinin's defense of Pushkin, he dissented from his condemnation of Gogol. It was true that the critical tendencies in Russian literature were currently overvalued; but in life as well as in literature, Russia needed its Gogols as much as its Pushkins. There are periods, he wrote Botkin, "when literature can't *only* be art, and there are interests higher than poetic interests"; such a period occurs when a nation reaches the stage of critical self-awareness.[29]

Turgenev believed that Russia had arrived at this momentous point. In October he remarked to the writer Sergei Aksakov: "The epoch through which we are living is of a kind that all too rarely repeats itself": at such a time all thinking people who loved their country should draw together and communicate on matters of the spirit.[30] Since the end of the 1840s, Turgenev had been preparing the ground for dialogues of this sort by chronicling his generation's disillusionment with romanticism and German metaphysics as guides to action. In his story "The Hamlet of Shchigrov District" a provincial landowner who has proved equally incompetent at managing his estate and his personal life ironically recalls his youthful infatuation with Hegel's philosophy: "Judge for yourself, what use, yes, what use, if you please, could I have made of Hegel's Encyclopaedia? What would you say there is in common between that Encyclopaedia and Russian life?"[31] It was Turgenev (in a story of 1850) who coined the term *superfluous person*, which the generation of the sixties would use against their fathers. In 1855 he published four stories (*Two Friends, A Correspondence, Yakov Pasynkov,* and *Faust*), depicting characters whose search to make sense of their existence through metaphysical speculation leads to debilitating self-analysis and paralysis of the will.

Bakhtin has drawn attention to how writers have used the cultural dissonances of transitional periods as a means of distancing themselves from their own values, which they explore and test in the light of competing beliefs.[32] This distancing, already evident in Turgenev's stories, is a striking feature of the work that occupied most of his time in the second half of 1855—*Rudin.* Turgenev's anxieties about the novel are a constant theme of his correspondence at this time. He told Nekrasov (who would publish it in *The Contemporary* at the beginning of 1856) that he had given long thought to the work, the first for which he had made a detailed plan in advance. He continually reshaped it over the summer and autumn, declaring that he had never labored over anything so much. Uneasy about the result, he confided to Druzhinin: "I somehow feel that my literary career is over. This story will decide that question."[33] In October he read it to a group of critics, including Nekrasov, who praised it; but he was still recasting it in December.

The action of the novel spans the 1840s. As Sergei Aksakov remarked, had it been written then, its eponymous main character would have been a hero.[34] Now, however, his values were under assault. Bakhtin, who believed that of all art forms the novel (through its capacity to represent a multiplicity of social universes and points of view in challenging contact with each other) was best capable of expressing the carnivalistic perception of the world, rated Turgenev's novels highly in this respect. He saw them (like Dostoevsky's works) as examples of the "novel of testing," in which the main character's beliefs are put to the proof in an unresolved battle of ideas, which express the multiple potentials of a period of social flux.[35]

In "polyphonic" novels of this kind the author's values are contested in open-ended debate. We have seen that Turgenev wanted 1855 to be a time of dialogue: his anxieties over *Rudin* sprang from the complex task he had set himself—to approach the values of his generation from the critical perspective of an outsider. Dmitry Rudin, we know, was modeled on Mikhail Bakunin, who had instructed Turgenev in Hegelian philosophy at the beginning of the 1840s before embarking on his career as a revolutionary in Europe. Like Bakunin, he possesses extraordinary eloquence: arriving unexpectedly as a guest at a country estate, he discourses inspiringly on the subject of "what gives eternal meaning to man's transient life" and the need to translate ideals into action. His meaning is obscure, "but that very lack of clarity lent a special charm to his words."[36] In his youth, we are told, he had used this charm to convince himself and the young men in his circle that they were a spiritual elect, destined to accomplish some great and mysterious mission. In this flashback to the 1840s, Turgenev captures all the seductive appeal of Idealism to a generation adrift in a hostile and alien environment. In return for the sense of rootedness and direction it offered, critical judgment was easily suspended: the orator who had so entranced his young comrades, we are told, had been a sponger, poseur, and manipulator, a sower of discord in the little circle. Now, when his hostess's daughter, inspired by his calls to resolute action, falls in love with him and proposes that they elope, he refuses out of a mixture of apathy and moral cowardice.

Distancing himself from a past to which he was still deeply attached, Turgenev treated the shortcomings of Idealism with far more devastating irony than Chernyshevsky ever did. But another point of view, seemingly contradictory, emerges in the course of the characters' debates. The most luminous personality in the novel (described in Lezhnev's account of the past) is based on the Schellingian idealist Nikolai Stankevich, whose memory Turgenev revered. Rudin himself emerges with credit from an encounter with the cynical Pigasov, who derides all metaphysical speculation and (as Chernyshevsky professed to do) respects only "facts." (This fearless critic of Idealism, we learn, was once a venal official.) In conversation with this character Lezhnev presents a different view of his former friend, in which Turgenev implicitly addressed the new generation: in pouring scorn on the absurdities of metaphysical philosophy, one risks condemning the genuine search for truth that inspired it. For all his defects, Rudin has a quality with which he can infect those who, unlike him, have the capacity to act: enthusiasm. "And believe me, a phlegmatic man myself, that is the most precious of qualities at our time. We have all become unbearably calculating, indifferent, inert. . . . We should be grateful to anyone who, even for an instant, rouses us and stirs us up!"[37] Chernyshevsky's crude materialism could never, in Turgenev's view, provide a satisfactory philosophical explanation for the nobler instincts of human beings. Lezhnev argues that the philosophy of his circle, for all its defects, had had an ennobling effect on them all: a view developed in the novel's epilogue, written after the publication of Chernyshevsky's dissertation, and responding directly to its attack on the values of the men of the forties.

Rudin and Lezhnev meet after a lapse of some years. The affected gloom of the young philosopher has now become a genuine melancholy after a life of failed projects, all undertaken with the desire to do practical good. Rudin talks of the difficulty of building anything when one has no foundations of one's own, no firm ground beneath one's feet. Without absolving him of moral responsibility for his failures, Turgenev reminds his readers of the predicament of those few who rebelled against the official ideology of Nicholas's regime and who, long before this became a popular preoccupation, were forced to construct an alternative vision of the world "from scratch." He reminds them, too, of the penalties involved: Rudin was dismissed from his post as a teacher because of his reforming enthusiasm. Now, when he confesses that his idealism has consisted of words but not deeds, his former critic springs to his defense: "good" words can be as valuable as deeds. But the novel remains ambivalent toward the values of Rudin's generation; he admits that he has often been repelled by his own rhetoric, not least in the mouths of his followers.

Rudin was generally perceived as a wreath laid on the grave of a type that had breathed its last along with Nicholas.[38] Chernyshevsky would give the work his patronizing approval, as a tribute to a past generation that had opened up the road along which the new men were confidently marching. But in his obsession with the need to act at all costs, Rudin was also a type of the future, like his real-life model who was then incarcerated in a dungeon in Petersburg (having been handed over to the Russian government by the Austrians, who had imprisoned him for his part in the 1849 insurrection in Dresden). Those who remembered Bakunin as an idealist philosopher would have been reminded of his subsequent revolutionary career by the new ending that Turgenev added to the third edition of his novel in 1860, in which Rudin dies on the barricades in

Paris, in the workers' rising of July 1848. This scene depicts a type only beginning to emerge among the intelligentsia in the greater freedom of the new reign: the Hamlet who seeks to resolve his inner divisions by assuming the role of a revolutionary Don Quixote. It anticipates the metamorphosis of superfluous men, who sought self-realization by communing with the Absolute, into revolutionaries drawn to the no-less-utopian dream of identifying with an idealized *narod*. (It is ironic that the rhetoric of the elderly Bakunin, after his escape to the West, would have a powerful influence on some émigré groups of populists.)

Turgenev was deeply ambivalent toward this emerging type. Lezhnev, his mouthpiece in the novel, admires, envies, and pities the Rudin of the epilogue. In their cult of action, such persons pay no heed to the obstacles in their path; hence their activity bears little fruit. Rudin knows nothing of the Russia he wishes to transform; in the revised ending of the novel he arrives on the barricades with a bent and rusty sword after the battle has been lost, and those who observe his final act of futile heroism take him for a Pole. But the enthusiasm that enables him to inspire others (even if only to similar mad feats) makes Lezhnev ashamed of his skepticism and sober common sense. The self-parodying ambivalence of Turgenev's treatment of Rudin poses the question which would dominate the 1860s: Hamlet or Don Quixote—a cautious gradualism that can be read as a capitulation to evil, or a leap of blind faith into the unknown?[39]

According to Bakhtin, the prose art presumes a "sense of the historical and social concreteness and the relativity of living discourse, a sense of its participation in historical becoming and social struggle; it deals in discourse still warm from that as yet unresolved struggle."[40] Turgenev summed up his aims as a novelist in similar terms: "I have striven to the limits of my strength and ability, consciously and dispassionately to portray and embody in appropriate types what Shakespeare calls 'the body and pressure of time.' "[41] Time's pressure is palpable in *Rudin*: the polemics that were shaping the new epoch were reflected in its writing as they took place. In order to convey the contending voices without the distorting intervention of his own prejudices and sympathies Turgenev continually submitted his manuscript to friends of different ideological standpoints, amending his portraits of social types in accordance with their reactions. He tells Annenkov that he found both the conservative Botkin and the radical Nekrasov useful sources of comment. Nekrasov's subsequent complaint that Rudin was a "contradictory" figure may be taken as a measure of Turgenev's success in showing his complex hero from a number of perspectives, not all of which could be reconciled.[42]

Turgenev played an active role in orchestrating the polyphony of 1855, seeking constantly to mediate between conflicting points of view and to explore their possibilities. His friends were angered by Tolstoy's rudeness to him, but he responded by christening him "the Troglodyte,"[43] confiding to Annenkov that he felt a fatherly affection for the irascible young man. He took pride in the fact that his St. Petersburg apartment was a "terrain neutre" on which people with the most diverse opinions could meet.[44] Botkin could be found there in amicable discussion with Nekrasov and the socialist thinker and poet Nikolai Ogarev, who would soon emigrate to become Herzen's co-editor in London. In this company, Turgenev tells Annenkov, even Vladimir Sollogub (an aristocratic literary dilettante) "tries to be a good fellow."[45] In December, Turgenev invited Aleksandr Nikitenko to his apartment for a gathering at which Ogarev was to read his poetry. This carnivalistic coming together of censor and socialist symbolized the utopian spirit of that year, in which old divisions and enmities appeared to be fast vanishing.

But new rifts were taking their place, and one event in 1855 seemed to demonstrate the fragility of Turgenev's hopes. In October, the funeral took place in Moscow of the historian Timofei Granovsky, one of the best-loved intellectual leaders of the 1840s, a liberal humanist who had played a reconciling role between Slavophiles and Westernizers. The crowd was very large, and the occasion unusually solemn. Turgenev noted the many young faces present: Granovsky had been an inspiring teacher. "Nothing for a long time," he wrote his friend Sergei Aksakov, "has affected me like this. To lose this man at such a moment is too bitter a blow."[46]

Yet no mediator could have bridged the divisions that were beginning to form. Turgenev managed for some years to maintain cordial relations with Chernyshevsky but could not bring himself to compromise with Chernyshevsky's views on art. He wrote to Nekrasov of the immense harmfulness of "this poorly concealed hatred of art. . . . Take *that* enthusiasm away from us, and we might as well do away with ourselves."[47] In his last meeting with Rudin, Lezhnev told him that for all their differences, they spoke a common language: "now . . . as new generations pass us by on their way to goals that are not ours, we should hold on tightly to each other."[48] At the outset of the new era, Turgenev perceived that Russia's "fathers" and "children" differed not merely on means but on ends; that the new men's utilitarian rationalism implied a vision of society in which creativity would be circumscribed in the service of narrowly prescribed goals. He told Botkin and Nekrasov that his main objection to Chernyshevsky's treatise was that it presented art as only a surrogate of reality and "essentially fit only for immature personalities. However much he may try to wriggle out of it, this idea is at the root of everything he writes." Although Hamlets have always existed among us, it took a Shakespeare to uncover the nature of Hamlet. If Chernyshevsky believed that his philosophy could get to the heart of reality in the same way, he was "taking rather a lot on himself."[49]

The debate over aesthetics that began in 1855 is commonly interpreted as a sign of the polarization between liberal and radical opinion that tends to begin after a system embarks on reform. Already, even before reforms began to be drawn up and discussed, battle lines were forming between those who hoped for peaceful evolution toward a constitutional monarchy and those whose aim was some variety of socialism, achieved if necessary by force. But there was another equally important distinction in approaches to the new realities that did not always coincide with political divisions.

Some, like Turgenev and Herzen, encouraged the variety and iconoclasm of the thought that emerged in the new epoch as the basis on which to build a pluralistic and unregimented society, tolerating a wide diversity of aims, beliefs, and creative fantasies. Others saw the destruction of a false picture of the world as the clearing of the ground for a monistically conceived truth, to which all would freely subscribe. Tolstoy was already dreaming of a new religion, while Chernyshevsky embraced the religion of science as the sole source of truth about humans and society. Bakhtin points to the very different attitudes of the Enlightenment and the Romantic movement to parody and satire. The Enlightenment employed satire against unreason, but never against its own sanctities. It had its Voltaire but not its Rabelais. Its abstract rationalism—excluding ambivalence, permitting neither question nor parody—represented an impoverishment of the creative consciousness. The Romantic movement that succeeded it, although it tended to confuse subjective fantasy with reality, did not impose an artificial rational unity on the historical process, whose conflicts and ambivalences it expressed through irony and self-parody.[50] The most reflective of Russia's Romantic rebels, on becoming "fathers" in the 1860s, shed the inward-looking subjectivism of their youth but retained their sense of the indeterminateness of historical existence, open to questioning and transformation by creative and rebellious individuals. Through their ability to parody their own discourse and see their values in a relativizing perspective they demonstrated the infinity of possible points of view on a world unprogrammed by transcendent powers. In comparison with Herzen's and Turgenev's vision, the "New Enlightenment" of the "children" seems impoverished to the point of blindness. Enlisting Gogol in the service of his doctrine of rational progress, Chernyshevsky failed to perceive the subversion of rationality and the despairing disbelief in human perfectibility that lay at the heart of Gogol's work. The men of the sixties would embrace Turgenev's label of "nihilists" to denote their freedom from the past; but Herzen would argue that on the contrary, in their dogmatism and harsh intolerance, some of them were mirror images of Nicholas's officials. The true nihilists, he claimed, were those of his generation who had rejected the absolutes of Idealism without replacing them with new ones.[51]

The carnival mood of 1855 respected none of the taboos of the past, challenging the censor in ever more ingenious ways; but only a small minority proved to be free from what Bakhtin called the "great interior censor." Most were uncomfortable, like Tolstoy, without "rules" laying down the path to preset goals. The revolutionaries of the mid-1860s would take their lead not from Herzen (who in *From the Other Shore* predicted that socialism itself would eventually fail to meet the changing needs of human beings and would be swept away by some new revolution) but from Chernyshevsky, whose propaganda novel *What Is to Be Done?* would set down an obligatory code of behavior for all "new people."

The dialogue on which Turgenev had placed such hopes in 1855 became, in his novel of 1861, *Fathers and Children*, a dialogue of the deaf. But it had always had an air of unreality: one participant was missing from the start.

The Hamlet of Shchigrov District would be happy to take lessons from Russian life, "but see here, my good fellow, it will not speak."[52]

In 1855 the Russian intelligentsia had hardly begun to interpret the mentality of those whom it saw as its natural allies in the fight against autocracy. From London, Herzen preached the virtues of the peasant commune, but (in an article published by the Free Russian Press in 1853) had warned against the error of ascribing one's own aims and ideals to "the people": "In our democratic century there is no word that is so little understood and so misused. . . . Some raise the people to the skies, turning it into a sort of seer . . . ; others trample it in the mud, calling it the vulgar multitude."[53] Meanwhile, the object of these fantasies leads its own mysterious life, remaining calm when its defenders throw down the gauntlet on its behalf, and rising in rebellion when least of all expected.

The unpredictability of the Russian people was a major factor in the tensions of 1855. The ever-present threat of peasant revolt had become more immediate during the mass mobilization of the previous year, when a rumor spread among the peasants that those who took up arms would gain their freedom, that an edict to this effect had already been signed but was being concealed from the people by local authorities and the clergy. A spontaneous movement began in Ryazan and soon engulfed neighboring provinces. Peasants left landowners' estates en masse, sending delegates to the tsar to plead for justice. Troops were sent to quell the movement, which spread to nine provinces in the heart of Russia. Its size helped convince the new tsar of the need to give the peasants their freedom. Meanwhile Herzen's pamphlets, sent from London, invoked the terrible memory of the Pugachev revolt a century before in order to persuade the nobility that its interests lay in averting bloodshed by working for a peaceful social revolution.

In April 1855 an event took place that, unlike Nicholas's death, the end of the war, or Chernyshevsky's dissertation, is not normally quoted as a turning point but was perhaps more significant than any of these. A former student of Kiev University, one Yosif-Anton Rozental, appeared in a village in the Kiev district and read to the peasants a manifesto purporting to be a letter to the Russian people from the French emperor and the queen of England, offering the sympathy of free peoples to those suffering the "yoke of Moscow" and promising them "equality and freedom." The peasants reacted by attempting to arrest the student and taking the message to the authorities. Rozental was imprisoned, condemned to death, and his sentence commuted to deportation for life to Siberia.[54] This is one of the first recorded cases in which a member of the intelligentsia is known to have attempted to make political contact with the peasants. But when these broke their silence, they spoke a language very different from that of the radical iconoclasts of 1855. Rozental's fate, anticipating the tragedies of so many intellectuals who went to the villages in the "movement to the people" of the 1870s, symbolizes the gulf between the revolts in which the peasants ritually acted out their beliefs and hopes and the carnival of the intellectuals in Petersburg and Moscow.

Dostoevsky and the Divided Conscience

CHAPTER FOUR

In the decade between the Russian Revolutions of 1905 and 1917, many of the Russian radical intelligentsia believed that Dostoevsky had anticipated their moral dilemmas.[1] Writers sympathetic to the Left like Dmitry Merezhkovsky argued that the experience of that turbulent period confirmed Dostoevsky's discovery about the nature of moral choice: namely, there existed no single system of beliefs, no coherent ethical code, that could resolve all problems of ends and means and that this was so because, on some of the most fundamental issues of moral choice, the promptings of reason and feeling could not be reconciled. To be internally consistent, all ethical systems (and the religious and political creeds that embodied them) must therefore ignore or deny some of the moral imperatives rooted in human nature. No system of belief, however compelling, could thus confer immunity from guilt, doubt, or self-contempt.

The émigré intelligentsia who pioneered Dostoevsky studies in the West saw no such pessimism in his work. Konstantin Mochulsky and many lesser critics pronounced the novels a triumphant vindication of the Christian ethic, accomplished through an annihilating critique of its chief rival, atheistic humanism. The "metaphysical school," as it has been called, shaped the popular view of Dostoevsky in the West, citing his nightmare visions in support of the reassuring belief that the enemy of compassion and humane values was outside the walls, on the other side of the great ideological divide.[2] In specialist studies, too, despite the pervasive influence of Bakhtin's "polyphonic" interpretation of the novels, the image of Dostoevsky as prophet has had a significant effect. Some of the representatives of the metaphysical school, such as Nikolai Berdiaev, may no longer be taken very seriously, but their role in setting the direction of Dostoevsky studies in the West should not be underestimated. It has been a source of confusion both about the moral "message" of the novels and Dostoevsky's personal views on the nature of moral choice. On both these issues, critics have often shown less insight than those Russian radicals who, at the beginning of the twentieth century, identified with Dostoevsky's portrayal of the divided conscience.

To argue, as one critic has done, that a polyphonic interpretation of the novels "is evident, more or less explicitly, in the great majority of modern studies of Dostoevskii" is to overstate the case.[3] "Monological" interpretations of his work are still advanced, although perhaps no longer as confidently as in René Wellek's introduction to the volume on Dostoevsky in the Twentieth-Century Views series, where Bakhtin's contention that there is "no final word" in the novels was dismissed as "patently false."[4] In an original interpretation Elizabeth Dalton presents Dostoevsky's work (exemplified by *The Idiot*) as the projection of an oedipal conflict in the author, submission to the social and religious order being construed as the alternative to the destruction of "the perilous internal equilibrium of repression, threatening the control and even the existence of the ego."[5] In a more familiar approach, Ellis Sandoz echoes Berdiaev in declaring the Legend of the Grand Inquisitor "a vindication of the Christian faith as powerful as any in literature," prophetic in its exposure of the spiritual and intellectual bankruptcy of socialist humanism. From a rather different standpoint, Sven Linnér argues that "there is no bakhtinian polyphony" in *The Brothers Karamazov*: Father Zosima's answers to Ivan's formulation of the problems of poverty, oppression, and criminality are intended to be a definitive denial that science and reason can be made to serve the good—a position that, in Linnér's view, must "to reformists no less than to revolutionaries—appear immoral, because it tends to make us forget the necessity of treating social questions rationally." There are signs both in Russia and in contemporary Western scholarship of a new emphasis on the image of Dostoevsky as a prophet offering an answer to the loss of the faith in secular doctrines of progress that was the guiding idea of modernity. Bruce Ward sees him as "primarily concerned with bringing to light the underlying meaning of modern civilization" and argues that he identified with the religious doctrine of progress expounded by Father Zosima, while in Russia Bakhtin's theories have been ingeniously linked with the discredited official Soviet ideology.[6]

Declared anti-Bakhtinians may be in a minority in contemporary Dostoevsky criticism, but their tradition flourishes under other guises. As Malcolm Jones has pointed out, many scholars, while paying lip service to Dostoevsky's pluralism, write about him as though all his works related to a single universal organizing principle.[7] To quote one eminent example: Robert Jackson, who has stressed the absence of doctrinaire answers in Dostoevsky's art (which he defines as a "permanent restiveness" shaped by a sense of contradiction between man's condition and his higher aspirations), nevertheless claims that the novels do provide "the formulas for being and nothingness, the principles governing life and spiritual death. The imperative remains for the reader—as for the heroes of the novels—to choose."[8] Faced with this formulation of the options, the reader's choice might well be free, but it would certainly be predictable.

Although many critics maintain that the novels present no objective criteria for verifying or refuting the arguments of faith or reason, few would follow Jones to the Bakhtinian conclusion that "it is therefore open to the reader to acknowledge the reality of religious experience, even to acknowledge its psychological value, but to deny its objective truth value . . . . the structure of the fiction invites such a reading, for . . . the fundamental motivating forces are psychological."[9] It is often argued that the religious viewpoint in the novels can be attained only through a "leap" from reason to faith, the implication being always that the leap is a flight to a higher ground. As Jean Drouilly puts it, Zosima's vision cannot be authenticated by reason, but neither can reason, with its "superficial" understanding of the universe, refute it. In this interpretation, Dostoevsky's outlook is no more pluralistic than that of any mystic who concedes that the ineffable character of his spiritual experience transcends the world of appearance.[10]

In the West, the arguments for and against Dostoevsky's pluralism have focused almost exclusively on his fiction. A notable exception is Gary Saul Morson's thoroughly Bakhtinian study of Dostoevsky's attitude to his own utopian ideal in *A Writer's Diary*. He argues that Dostoevsky consciously draws on the tradition of earlier "meta-utopian" works, alternately asserting his belief in the full realization of the Kingdom of God on earth and undermining it through satire and irony.[11] Morson's concern, however, is with a literary genre, and he does not analyze Dostoevsky's attitude in the *Diary* to the rival socialist utopia, leaving unchallenged what, as we shall see, is the dominant view among Western scholars: that Dostoevsky's nonfictional writings from the 1860s onward display a consistent and unchanging opposition to the humanist ethic of the Russian socialists. This view is not seen as incompatible with a Bakhtinian interpretation of his novels. Jan Meijer explains that the dialogical character of the novels was the product of artistic necessity rather than personal conflict: "Once the writer launched his characters on dialogue, when every idea called forth its opposite, it drove them . . . far beyond the opinions Dostoevskii the man held."[12]

To sum up: critics are increasingly focusing on what Ronald Fernandez has described as Dostoevsky's cognitive dissonance as the product of a society ideologically and structurally in the process of a transition from traditional to modern; but this perception tends to be combined with the more familiar claim that "a unifying view . . . permeates all of [Dostoevsky's] work." Fernandez himself concludes that Dostoevsky resolved his conflict by a fervent reaffirmation of the traditional in the form of Russian religious messianism. In his works "the cards are stacked against the new man": he cannot eliminate his dissonance unless he uses God."[13]

As Jones has noted, the Bakhtinian revolution is not as profound as it has seemed. Few of those who support it would not assent equally to Linnér's claim that "Dostoevskii belongs to the great idealistic tradition of the century. He stands at a line of defence that extended across the whole of Europe. Like innumerable other writers and thinkers, he met the assault of positivism and materialism with the contention that beyond the reality we perceive with our senses there also exists a spiritual reality, and that a part of man is not subject to the laws of Nature but belongs to the world of the spirit."[14] For all their differences in approach and attitude to their material, monological interpretations of Dostoevsky's work (of which the above is a small sample) all echo the version of Dostoevsky's "message" first preached to the West by embattled Russian émigrés. This message, despite its terrible warnings, is fundamentally complacent: the path to spiritual salvation and a peaceful conscience is assured to those who reject the blandishments of atheistic humanism in favor of the Christian ethic as preached by the monk Zosima. Consistently monological interpretations of the conflicts in the novels are now rare; but, as we have seen, a Bakhtinian approach to these conflicts is perfectly compatible with the view that, whether or not Dostoevsky wrote polyphonic novels for artistic reasons, he was doctrinaire in his own moral beliefs.

On the contrary: the ideological conflicts in the novels directly reflected unresolvable dilemmas in Dostoevsky's moral life. For him the enemy was never outside the walls. The great dialogues of the novels were not structured philosophical debates; rather, as the following pages will show, they expressed the chaotic experience of a practical moralist, observing the workings in Russian society and in his own conscience of two kinds of compassion, the Christian and the humanist, and forced by events constantly to reassess his position in relation to each.

The "metaphysical" critics have represented Dostoevsky's religious conversion as a sudden turn away from the world of empirical experience to the eternal verities, but the biographical evidence indicates otherwise. As Joseph Frank has pointed out, Dostoevsky had always been a Christian of sorts.[15] The goal of his early utopian socialism had been the implementation in society of the ideals of the New Testament, whereas his disenchantment with socialism was the result, above all, of close observation of human character in prison, where he discovered that the view of the common people that had inspired his Westernizing socialism was a naive Rousseauian fiction. At the same time, the occasional Christian reflexes and the yearning for psychic autonomy that he observed in the cruel and degenerate beings around him led to a number of conclusions that were later embodied in his messianic Christian nationalism.

Empirical observation thus played a significant role in Dostoevsky's move from utopian socialism to Orthodox Christianity, but his faith and his powers of observation were from the first uneasy allies. His case studies, made in prison, of destructive and irrational urges later served as ammunition for his attacks on the "scientific" utopias of the left; but they could (and would) equally serve as grounds for the fear that a society founded on Christian principles was an unattainable dream. Nor did he shrink from accepting scientific opinion on his epileptic seizures and the auras that preceded them; the description put into the mouth of Prince Myshkin is clearly autobiographical.[16] The onset of a seizure was accompanied by an overwhelming sense of harmony and beauty, an "ecstatic devotional merging with the highest synthesis of life."[17] But, given the diseased origin of this experience and the possibility that the convulsions that followed would end in idiocy, what was he to make of it? Myshkin's bewilderment before the paradoxical nature of his mystical insights was, clearly, also Dostoevsky's: he never used them to support his religious beliefs. His records of his seizures read like medical notes (he had a close interest in experimental medicine and advances in epileptology); they are devoid of metaphysical speculation.[18]

Dostoevsky's conversion was not the triumph of faith over reason and science: it was rather the beginning of a struggle whose outcome was never assured, as predicted in the famous letter written from exile in 1854, in which he describes himself as "a child of the century, a child of unbelief and doubt," destined to be tormented to the grave by "this thirst for faith, which is all the stronger in my soul the more arguments I can find against it." His only moments of calm come from the belief that "nothing is more beautiful, profound, sympathetic, reasonable, courageous, and perfect than Christ . . . if someone proved to me that Christ is outside the truth and that in reality the truth is outside Christ, then I should prefer to remain with Christ rather than with the truth."[19]

This confession is usually seen as representing (albeit in an uncommonly acute form) the clash between faith and reason characteristic of the Christian tradition, a conflict whose resolution is never seriously in doubt. As Frank explains, Dostoevsky had seen in the camp evidence of the power of the irrational and of faith as forces in human life and the limitations of reason when confronted with the crises of existence, and this evidence allowed him to make a "final and unambiguous" choice of faith over reason.[20]

I believe that neither the passage in question nor any subsequent self-revelations on this subject can be interpreted as showing that Dostoevsky ever established a hierarchy of this kind between the arguments of reason and faith or that he saw his conflict as a recurring Christian dilemma. The last sentence of the passage quoted above seems to convey fairly unambiguously the sensation of being torn between two mutually exclusive visions of ultimate truth, a predicament that Dostoevsky saw not as a constant in Christian experience but as specific to his century. This point is stressed even more in a reflection by Myshkin, into whom Dostoevsky put so much of himself: "The men of . . . the eighteenth century were absolutely not the same sort of people as we are now: not the same race as now, in our age. Really, it's as if they were a different species. In those days they were men of one idea, but now we are more nervous, more developed, more sensitive, men of two or three ideas at once. . . . Modern men have a broader outlook—and I swear this prevents them from being so all-of-a-piece as they were in those days."[21] For Dostoevsky and his heroes the struggle between reason and faith had been given a new tragic dimension through the challenge offered to Christian morality by atheistic humanism. Those of Dostoevsky's characters who believe with Myshkin that "compassion is the main, if not the only law of human existence" are faced with the necessity of choice between two irreconcilable perceptions of the causes of evil and suffering and the remedies for them.[22] The force with which Dostoevsky puts the humanist case in his novels owes much to the fact that his generation received its education in compassion not from the church but from the militant humanism of Vissarion Belinsky, exemplified in the *Letter to Gogol,* in which he castigated the Russian church for its passive acquiescence in the crimes of despotism and declared that the socialists, apostles of reason and material progress, were truer to the Christian vision of the dignity of humanity than was the church with its emphasis on the virtues of humility and asceticism. Dostoevsky would be arraigned for reading the *Letter* to a meeting of the circle of utopian socialists headed by M. V. Petrashevsky: its case against contemporary Christianity would be echoed much later in his private notebooks.

As we shall see, Dostoevsky's view of Belinsky would be revised more than once in his later life; but even when denouncing Belinsky's militant atheism (which he had never shared), Dostoevsky would acknowledge the profound effect on him of the great critic's humanism and his belief that it was the writer's duty to participate in the battle for social justice.[23] Dostoevsky's principal goal as a member of Petrashevsky's circle had been the abolition of serfdom, and his religious conversion did not diminish his concern with what Belinsky had defined as Russia's most vital social problems. Serfdom was abolished by Alexander II shortly after Dostoevsky's release from prison, and that fact became the cornerstone of his defense, in his political journalism, of the principle of reform from above against those who believed it could only be brought about from below. He believed (together with many liberals in the 1860s) that the government, terrified by the prospect of revolution, needed every encouragement to continue on the path of reform.[24] Although he refrained from public criticism of autocracy, his notebooks and the diaries of the last two decades of his life leave no doubt as to his loathing of the arbitrary exercise of power and of the contempt for human dignity expressed by the practice of corporal punishment, which he had been forced to witness as a prisoner and which he described in harrowing terms in *The House of the Dead,* declaring: "A society which looks indifferently on such a phenomenon is already infected in its very foundations."[25] In the early 1860s he tried to convince the young radicals grouped around the journal *The Contemporary* that, for the immediate present, the gulf between his and their views on human nature and on Russia's national destiny was less important than their common dedication to the cause of social justice. In his notebook he commented on the polemics between *The Contemporary* and his own journal, *Time:* "Why have we been quarreling when there's work to be done?" From this common ground he defended the leaders of the Left against conservative attempts to discredit them, pronouncing Nikolai Dobrolyubov to be "a great fighter for the truth."[26] Over the next decade evidence of the suffering and despair of the common people, gleaned from newspaper and court reports, would serve him not only as material for his novels but also as the basis for increasingly pessimistic reflections on Russia's potential for progress.

There are, therefore, no grounds for the view that Dostoevsky's conversion signified a switch from a Belinskian social engagement to the social quietism of Gogolian piety or (to put it in the more admiring terms of Berdiaev) that Dostoevsky turned away from the empirical world in order to immerse himself in "the profound realities of the spiritual universe."[27] Unlike most Russian conservatives, he never argued that the radicals' demands for social justice were a revolt against a God-given hierarchy, a trivialization of the spiritual essence of human beings, or a distraction from the central task of spiritual self-perfection. Had he done so, his own inner debate with the compassion of unbelief would have been resolved. Instead, he chose a far riskier enterprise: not questioning the goal of socialism (at least, in the form preached by the early utopian socialists—a Kingdom of God on earth, governed by the principles of brotherhood and love) but arguing that this would be achieved not through reason, science, and the revolutionary transformation of social and political institutions but through the means prescribed by Christian faith—humility, love, and a forgiving response to violence. Unable to accept that Christ was "outside" the truth of reason, he set out to prove the contrary, by confronting the rationalists of the Russian Left on their own ground, the observable reality of human nature.

He did so to devastating effect in *Notes from Underground* (1864), while in *Crime and Punishment,* published two years later, he undertook to show that the utilitarian ethic of the Russian radicals of the 1860s violated a religious sense of the absolute value of the individual that was fundamental to human nature. Outlining the plan of the work to his editor Mikhail Katkov, Dostoevsky claimed that Raskolnikov's sense of guilt was a simultaneous vindication of "God's truth and earthly law."[28]

But the problem of "two truths" could not be so easily resolved. Dostoevsky was aware that his claims for the Christian ethic had to be supported by a practical demonstration of its effects on social relations. He wrote to S. A. Ivanova that the aim of his next novel (*The Idiot*) was to create a "positively beautiful man" but admitted, "There is nothing on earth more difficult than that, especially now. . . . The beautiful is an ideal, and the ideal—ours and that of civilized Europe—is still far from assuming its final shape."[29]

These apprehensions (in marked contrast with the messianic nationalism of his political journalism) proved justified. Myshkin has all the Christian virtues that Dostoevsky believed to be the fundamental "law" of human nature—love, humility, forgiveness; and the author's didactic aim would seem to require that his hero's example should infect those around him. Tolstoy was to embody such a message in his novels: Those who "live by the heart" have a beneficial influence on people and social processes, an influence denied to those whose actions are regulated by reason. But Myshkin's compassion is at best ineffectual: at worst, it has a spectacularly disastrous effect on his milieu, arousing bitter resentment and precipitating murder in the denouement. Dostoevsky's didactic intentions seem to have been subverted by the same insight into unregenerate human character that he had used to such effect against the optimistic doctrines of the Left. The men and women who surround Myshkin are irritated rather than inspired by his charity and goodness; their irrational wills and misdirected energies destroy him along with themselves. Robin Feuer Miller has forcefully argued that Myshkin's increasing oddity and isolation toward the end of the novel are part of a complex narrative strategy by which the author invites the reader to reject the narrator's point of view and make his or her own positive judgment as to the truth Myshkin is seeking to convey.[30] If this is the case, the strategy did not pay off. Dostoevsky was dissatisfied with his novel: "It did not express even a tenth of what I wanted to express."[31] In one sense, it revealed much more than he had intended. His Christian hero was not the whole and harmonious personality that his faith required him to construct but a divided creature, drawn from experience. Impotent in the face of overwhelming forces of violence and aggression, he is tormented by the sense that "his soul is in darkness."[32] Two years after the publication of *The Idiot*, Dostoevsky wrote to A. N. Maikov that the subject of his next novel (to be called *The Life of a Great Sinner*) would be "the same question that has tormented me consciously or unconsciously throughout my entire life—the existence of

God." The novel, a triumphant defense of the Christian faith, would contain "a majestic, *positive,* holy figure." Elsewhere he describes the plot of the work in which at last "I will say all that I have to say": The hero would lose his faith and, after a long search, recover it through "the Russian soil, the Russian Christ, the Russian God."[33]

Dostoevsky's renewed confidence in his ability to embody his idea in a credible human psychology came after three years of self-imposed exile in Europe, where he had been driven by ill health and the importunities of creditors. From this distance he acquired a starkly simple view of the ideological conflicts between liberals, conservatives, and socialists about the future of Russia. He saw the ideals of European liberalism and its Russian counterpart as a cover for the selfish interests of a greedy and materialistic bourgeoisie, while his impressions of contemporary Russian socialism were formed largely by his reading of lurid newspaper accounts of the trial of Sergei Nechaev's group for the murder of one of their number and of the "Catechism" attributed to Nechaev, which proclaimed that the revolutionary end justified the use of any means.

Out of touch with the Russian Left, Dostoevsky saw the activities of the psychotic Nechaev and his tiny band of intimates as expressing the essence of Russian socialism, which he now conceived as a purely destructive force. His letters of this period contain his bitterest attacks on his former mentor Belinsky, as the progenitor of the "little liberals and progressivists . . . whose main pleasure and satisfaction is derived from cursing Russia," and it was in order to expose this "trash," as he called them, that he began a political novel, inspired by the Nechaev affair.[34] In 1872, after returning to Russia, he aligned himself firmly with the extreme Right by accepting the editorship of the ultraconservative paper *The Citizen.* Over the next decade, however, he was to discover that the configuration of moral forces in Russia was very different from what it had appeared to be from abroad. He came to see the conflict between contemporary conservatives and radicals not as the defense of "Russian Christianity" against the materialist poison from the West but rather as a confrontation between an institutional conservatism that used religion to sanction the existing social order and a radical humanism closely resembling that of Belinsky and the socialism of Dostoevsky's youth. In this reenactment of the polemic between Gogol and Belinsky, Dostoevsky could identify with neither side. Nor could he see signs of a third force, those "positive" Christian figures on which he believed Russia's future depended. His *Life of a Great Sinner,* with its triumphant affirmation of Christian faith, was never written. Instead, all his great idealists were to be men in the grip of "two or three ideas at once."

Dostoevsky's notebooks and diaries reveal that his last novels were written at a time of intense inner struggle, as he sought unsuccessfully to reconcile his religious conservatism with the data of experience. His *Writer's Diary* (which first appeared in *The Citizen* in 1873 and was resumed as an independent publication in 1876–77) was conceived as a means of illustrating and justifying his social theories and ideals by reference to current events. Instead, the impression given by the *Diary* (and confirmed by much more explicit notes and drafts) is one of increasing doubt as to the practical feasibility of his socioreligious ideal and growing disillusionment with the conservative forces with which he had aligned himself.[35]

On his return in 1871, Dostoevsky found Russia in the process of rapidly accelerating industrialization and was alarmed to discover over the next decade that neither the government nor its supporters on the Right displayed the intention or the ability to resist the embourgeoisement of Russian society, the pauperization of the peasantry, and the concomitant destruction of what he believed to be Russia's most precious national values and traditions. The *Diary* and his notebooks refer with increasing frequency over the years to the chaos in the countryside and the misery of the peasantry, whom he saw as the bedrock of society. The money needed desperately for the reform of agriculture after the Emancipation had been diverted to the building of railways; crushed by taxes, unprotected by the law, the peasantry expressed their despair in drunkenness and crime.[36] In the cities Dostoevsky noted a sharp increase in court records of crimes committed for gain, while an equally marked rise in cases of suicide and child abuse testified in his view to the breakup of the family unit and, with it, of the traditional fabric of Russian society.[37] The defenders of tradition with whom he had allied himself were far more concerned with the policing of society than with protecting what Dostoevsky saw as its moral core: a fact that soured his relations with the archreactionary Prince Meshchersky, the proprietor of *The Citizen*. In 1874 he gave up the editorship of the paper and immediately afterward agreed to the serialization of his new novel *The Adolescent* in the progressive journal *Notes of the Fatherland*. His notebooks reflect his disillusionment with the Russian Right, which he now labeled as intellectually bankrupt. "The conservative part of our society is as rotten as any other: so many swine have joined its ranks."[38]

Dostoevsky put much of the blame for the economic and spiritual plight of the peasantry on the venality, laziness, and petty despotism of Russian officialdom and on the "inexhaustible" cynicism of the tsar's advisers. He deplored the fact that nothing had been done to halt the economic decline of the gentry, who in Dostoevsky's scheme of things were the "living link" between tsar and people. He noted that the church seemed to be in a state of paralysis, and his study of court reports led him to conclude that the legal reforms of the 1860s had done far more to entrench the rights of property and privilege than to protect the weak. Throughout the 1870s he lamented the absence in the educated strata of society of moral leaders (*luchshie liudi*), who could help to ensure that Russia did not repeat the mistakes of the West.[39]

Unlike most of the Russian Right, Dostoevsky believed that the autocracy's role was not to preserve the status quo but to lead society in a radically new direction—toward the implementation of Christ's teachings in social relations. While denouncing the secular gospel of progress as preached in the West, he was equally critical of Russian conservatives—"men from the past"—for their indifference to the people's material welfare. A note of 1876 declares, "Life is good, and one must ensure that everyone on earth can confirm this,"[40] and his last notebook contains a contemptuous assessment of the morality of Konstantin Leontiev's ascetic Byzantinism: " 'It is not worth wishing the world well because it has been said that it will perish': this idea has something reckless and dishonest about it. It is, moreover, an extremely convenient basis for everyday conduct. If all are doomed, then why . . . love or do good? Let's live for our bellies' sake!"[41]

The issue that most clearly exposed the gulf between Dostoevsky and the leaders of the Right was that of popular education, which, as industrialization gained impetus in the 1870s, began to be hotly debated in the Russian press. In his contribution to the discussion the Pan-Slav propagandist, General Rostislav Fadeev, argued that in the interests of social stability higher education should be restricted to the gentry. This view was shared by Dostoevsky's friend, the highly influential conservative Konstantin Pobedonostsev (future director general of the Synod of the Orthodox Church). Nevertheless, Dostoevsky protested energetically in his *Writer's Diary* of 1876: "I have never been able to understand the idea that only one-tenth of the people should be given higher education, while the remaining nine-tenths should serve merely as material and means to that end, while themselves remaining in darkness. I do not wish to think, or to live, otherwise than with the faith that all the ninety millions of us Russians (or whatever number may eventually be born) will some day be educated, humanized, and happy. I . . . firmly believe that universal education can harm none of us."[42] In the published *Diary*, Dostoevsky softens his criticism by reassuring his readers that no one concerned with these matters in Russia "would argue that it was essential to bestialize one part of the people for the well-being of another part, representing civilization, as is done all over Europe." In his private notes for the *Diary*, however, his criticism of his powerful opponents is much more savage. The idea that "light and the supreme benefits of life should be willed to one-tenth of the population" is described as "horrible and totally anti-Christian," "vile (calculated and predatory)." On such conditions "I don't even want civilization. I believe in the full Kingdom of Christ: how it will come about it's hard to predict, but . . . it will come."[43]

This protest recalls an often-quoted passage in one of Belinsky's letters:

"Why should I care that a genius should live a heavenly existence on earth, when the mass wallows in the mud? Why should I care that the world of ideas in art, religion, and history should be open to me, when I cannot share this with all those who should be my brothers as men, my neighbors in Christ, but who are strangers to me, and whose ignorance makes them my enemies? Why should I care that there is bliss for the chosen, when the majority doesn't even suspect the possibility of bliss? I will have nothing of bliss, if it is to be given to me alone among thousands!"

In another well-known passage Belinsky denounced the Hegelian philosophy of progress for justifying the suffering of history's victims as a necessary part of the struggle to reach an ideal form of existence, and challenged Hegel: "I declare that if I succeeded in climbing to the highest step of the ladder of progress I would ask you there to give me an account of all the victims of . . . chance, superstition, the Inquisition, Philip II, etc., otherwise I would throw myself down head first from the highest step. I don't want happiness, even gratis, if I'm not at rest about each of my blood brothers, who are bone of my bone and flesh of my flesh."[44]

The letter containing the second of these passages was published in 1875 in the journal *The European Messenger,* and there seems little doubt that it was known to Dostoevsky and was the source for Ivan Karamazov's offer to "return his ticket" to divine harmony.[45] The irony cannot have escaped Dostoevsky, for only a few years previously he had condemned Belinsky for sowing the seeds of rebellion in Russian society. Now, in terms reminiscent of the *Letter to Gogol,* he, too, was challenging the belief in a God-given social hierarchy and accusing its proponents of betraying the Christian principles they professed.

As the government, supported by a vociferous Right, entered on a new era of repression, Dostoevsky began to reconsider the social ethic that he had once shared with Belinsky and the radical idealism that he had so decisively rejected in the late 1860s. In *A Writer's Diary* he presents a new evaluation of Belinsky, claiming that for all his respect for reason and science, the great critic "understood more profoundly than anyone else that reason, science, and realism alone can create only an ant-heap, not social 'harmony.' . . . He knew that the basis of everything was moral principles." Dostoevsky carefully distinguished Belinsky's moral feeling from the atheism in which he attempted to ground it (a "fatal error" in Dostoevsky's view), and his notebooks of the 1870s contained a number of sympathetic references to Belinsky's compassion and instinctive understanding of Russia, which compensated, Dostoevsky claimed, for the poverty of his practical knowledge. He contrasted this quality with the "aristocratic" condescension to the people that he saw as characteristic of contemporary political journalism and declared: "Belinsky is right, even when he is wrong."[46]

Through the paradox of Belinsky, Dostoevsky was forced to confront the paradox of Russian socialism, which he could no longer dismiss as a vile infection from the West. To recognize the genuineness of the moral impulses behind the compassion of unbelief was to question a fundamental belief of his own: that only the Christian ethic could express and satisfy the moral nature of human beings. Dostoevsky was aware of his inconsistency: the last years of his life were dominated by his struggle to resolve it.

A number of reflections in Dostoevsky's journalism and notebooks of the 1870s show that his changed view of Belinsky was part of a wider reconsideration of the relation between the socialist and Christian ethics, representing a moral reassessment of the Left that was simultaneously a confrontation with the legacy that his own radical past had left within him.

The new direction of Dostoevsky's thought was reflected in his article on *The Possessed* in *A Writer's Diary* of 1873,[47] in which he deplored the fact that his novel, along with the Nechaev affair, had been used by the right-wing press to support the argument that radicalism in Russia was an artificial implant on the healthy body of Russian society and attracted only the criminal and the mentally diseased. He reminded his readers: "I myself am a former Nechaevist." Given different historical circumstances, few of the members of Petrashevsky's circle would have hesitated to commit a politically motivated murder if it had been represented to them as a necessary act, not because they were scoundrels but because they believed that all means were justified in the pursuit of an aim "which seemed to us holy and moral in the highest degree": rebuilding the world on Christian principles. The message of his novel was not that scoundrels commit foul acts but that, in such unstable times as their own, "one can commit the most foul and loathsome act without, in some cases, being a scoundrel at all."

It is interesting to compare this defense of his youthful idealism with a passage in his private notebooks protesting the contemptuous dismissal of the utopian socialism of Charles Fourier (which had been one of the principal influences on the Petrashevsky circle) in a pamphlet by the Pan-Slavist General Fadeev:

> No, I'm for Fourier, . . . even though it was partly because of
> Fourier that I was punished, . . . and I rejected him long ago,
> but I'll defend him just the same. I'm sorry that the philosopher-
> General treats the poor socialist so condescendingly—i.e., all
> those scholars and youths who had such faith in Fourier were
> such fools that they had only to go to Fadeev to be immediately
> enlightened. Truly, there must be something else in this—either

> Fourier and his followers were not such fools as all that or the
> philosopher-General is exceptionally clever. I suspect the former
> is the case.[48]

Dostoevsky's suspicion that there was "something else" in humanistic socialism that made it less easy to refute than the conservatives believed was intensified by the rise of a new generation of Russian radicals whose moral idealism, reflected in the "movement to the people," had close affinities with that of the utopian socialists of his own generation. In his notebooks Dostoevsky frequently expressed admiration for the moral nobility of this "pure and generous youth" and, in a public letter addressed to a group of Moscow students, declared that "there has never been a period in our Russian life when the youth . . . were more honest and purehearted, thirsted more for truth and justice, were more prepared to sacrifice everything, even their lives, for the truth, than they are now." Although he now laid the blame for what he saw as their estrangement from God and the Russian people on historical circumstances rather than on their own moral makeup, he frequently insisted that their strivings lacked sense and coherence and denied that atheistic socialism was destined to implement the gospel of love.[49] At the same period, however, there are indications that Dostoevsky was increasingly less sure of this position. Much more positive assessments of the socialist ethic begin to appear in his notebooks and journalism. Soviet scholars gave these close attention,[50] but Western studies of his nonfictional writings of this period have chosen to focus on other issues,[51] reflecting what appears to be a general consensus: that in the 1870s there was no significant change in Dostoevsky's attitude to socialism.[52] Even his new sympathy with the personalities of the young Left tends to be seen, in Mochulsky's words, as merely a shift from hostility to a "disdainful condescension."[53]

The notebooks, in particular the comparisons Dostoevsky made between the young socialists and their opponents on the Right, show this judgment to be wide of the mark. In the mid-1870s he noted, "We should bow our heads in shame before the socialists!" On one side of the scales was the established order, which seemed "either paralysed or accursed"; on the other, the "reality and truth" of socialism's demands, the clear resemblance of its goals, if not its means, to the ideal of the gospels.[54] That this paradox tormented Dostoevsky may be inferred from the fury with which he lashes out in his private notebooks at those conservatives who exhibit moral condescension of the sort that critics have attributed to him. Given the chaotic instability of Russian society and its insoluble problems, he argues, the smug self-satisfaction of such figures as Fadeev is one of the most alarming of contemporary phenomena.[55]

Dostoevsky had castigated the conservatives for their smugness as far back as the early 1860s, when he defended the leaders of the Left against attacks by the *Russian Messenger*, edited by Mikhail Katkov, and a passage from his polemics with Katkov at that time is worth quoting here inasmuch as it encapsulates the dilemma that was to haunt him throughout the 1870s. Katkov had asserted that those who believed humans to be no more than a combination of chemical elements thereby precluded themselves from defending human rights or formulating a social ideal. Dostoevsky replied:

> I assure you that I, the writer of these lines, in no way think or believe that I am wholly the product of a test tube. . . . But, if I did believe precisely that, why could I not then talk about the rights of man, about his well-being and the improvement of his existence? . . . Surely, merely for a mechanically conceived benefit, merely in order to exist, people must agree among themselves, must come to a consensus, and, consequently mutually bind themselves with bonds of duty. There already, we have duty and consequently an aim in life. Without that, society is unthinkable. Whatever their convictions, after all, people would remain people, they could not destroy their nature? At the very least, this is a difficult question, and to resolve it as suddenly as you do is impossible. . . . Somehow you resolve it too calmly, too triumphantly, and that alone is suspicious.[56]

Katkov's proposition was essentially no different from what Dostoevsky had preached in his journalism and his art since his conversion and would continue to defend throughout his life: that the Christian belief in the immortality of the soul was fundamental to human nature, the source of love for others, and, therefore, the only basis for true morality. It was not this belief that he questioned but the smug certainty that it was unassailable. Hence his startling suggestion that reason, logic, and historical evidence supported the hypothesis of the Left that the instinct for solidarity was biological, not religious, in origin. This passage, with its contempt for those whose faith was impervious to the assaults of their reason, gives an insight into the nature of the "terrible torments" that Dostoevsky had anticipated in his confessional letter from exile.

The question Dostoevsky had put to Katkov recurs in many forms in his notebooks of the 1870s, where the debate between his reason and his faith was conducted in the form of reflections on contemporary events. The outcome was in the balance to the end: at times the scrupulously dispassionate observation of people, events, and social processes that had destroyed the young Dostoevsky's socialist faith came close to shattering his belief in the power of the Christian ethic to transform social relations without the need for compulsion.

Dostoevsky the believer asserts repeatedly in the notebooks that true morality and brotherhood are possible only on the basis of Christian faith. Socialist humanism, based solely on the conclusions of reason and science, made no allowance for the individual's irrational urge for freedom. It had "invented the milieu with its inevitable laws in order to destroy the personality." The socialists' emphasis on social solidarity and self-sacrifice sprang not from moral feeling but from vanity and a herd instinct, while their materialist cult of rational self-interest would give carte blanche to the most predatory elements of society in a future world of cannibalistic "darkness and horror."[57]

These generalized indictments contrast oddly with his observations (based on press reports and other contemporary sources) on the moral outlook of the young Russian radicals of the 1870s. He marvels at the "honesty and sincerity" of their faith, their dedication to the common good, and their lack of concern with material things: "They put their ideal above everything. . . . Earthly blessings come only after that." This characteristic of the revolutionary youth, he notes, "is the point of contact between our society and the people." He recalls that Belinsky's priorities were similar, alluding to Ivan Turgenev's description of the time hunger had made him seek to terminate a long debate with Belinsky on the question of the existence of God: Belinsky had expostulated indignantly, "First we'll decide the existence of God, then we'll have dinner."[58]

It was the resemblance between the Christian ethic and the humanist ideal of brotherhood (as preached both by his own and the new generation of socialists) that posed the greatest threat to the exclusive claims that Dostoevsky made for Christian morality.[59] He notes that the ideal of George Sand (who had been closely connected with the founders of utopian socialism) had been not a human "ant-heap" but the moral renewal of humanity and concludes, "She was a Christian, although she did not know it."[60]

Dostoevsky could not have been unaware of the speciousness of this argument, particularly if extended to the young socialists of the 1870s, whose spirituality and moral stature presented such a striking contrast with the qualities of some of Russian Orthodoxy's most zealous defenders. He was bitterly conscious of this irony, to the extent of expressing in print his rage at the incapacity of the establishment that he constantly defended to give him any sound justification for supporting it. In *A Writer's Diary,* commenting on the fact that the legal reforms of the 1860s seemed to have done little to promote the moral health of Russian society, he protested: "I simply desire that we should all become a little better: This is a very modest wish, but, alas, a most idealistic one: I'm an incorrigible idealist. I search for sanctities, I love them, my heart thirsts after them, for I'm so constructed that I cannot live without them: But all the same, I would prefer ideals that are just a little holier than those we have—otherwise is it worth worshiping them?"[61]

Dostoevsky's despair at the state of Russian society was expressed in the draft of a preface to *The Adolescent*, written in 1875, in which he claimed to be the first writer to have exposed the "deformed and tragic side" of the majority of his compatriots:

> Only I have portrayed the tragedy of the underground, which consists in suffering, self-laceration, the awareness of a better existence and of the impossibility of attaining it; and, above all, in the intense conviction of these unfortunates that all are the same and therefore that it's not worth trying to be better. What is there to support those who try to improve themselves? A re- ward? Faith? No one is offering a reward, and there is no one to believe in. Just one step from this, and we have extreme de- pravity, crime. . . . A mystery.[62]

The main support of Dostoevsky's faith in Russia's future remained his be- lief in the innate Christian virtues of the common people, the "diamonds" shining through the alluvial filth;[63] but even here his optimism had been damp- ened by his observation of the effects of contemporary social developments: he believed that the people's Christianity was threatened by the "worship of Mammon," which had permeated to the lowest reaches of society and could be cured only by drastic methods. Salvation might be at hand: writing on the eve of the Russo-Turkish conflict, Dostoevsky expressed high hopes of the benefi- cial effects of a just war on the moral fiber of the nation.[64]

The struggle of Dostoevsky's faith against the observable evidence may be summed up by a passage in his notebooks, written the year before his death:

> In our time, questions have arisen: is the good good? For in- stance, is Christ's patience and humility good? How should hu- man equality be brought about—through universal love, utopia, or through the law of inevitability, self-preservation, and scien- tific experiment? But the Gospel has foretold that . . . people are calmed not by the progress of intellect and the laws of inev- itability, but by a moral recognition of a higher beauty, serving as a universal ideal. . . . How can one make our literature yield up a positive ideal? . . . Belinsky was saved by dreams of the fu- ture: science and new foundations. I have said that one must seek ideals from the people, from Orthodoxy . . . . But these are merely attempts, hints. It is more possible to depict real figures of bewildered sufferers. Alas, I've been doing that all my life.

An even more eloquent testimony to Dostoevsky's inner divisions can be found in a note of 1876: "I declare—*as yet without proof*—that love for mankind is incomprehensible and quite impossible unless it is combined with faith in the immortality of the human soul."[65] The struggle between "Christ and the truth" revealed in that stressed parenthetical statement was worked through artistically in the great "sufferers" of his last three novels.

The first of these—*The Possessed*—was the political novel inspired by the Nechayev affair. Dostoevsky's initial satirical intention took shape in the sinister clown Pyotr Verkhovensky and the radical rabble whose vanity and inner emptiness made them his willing dupes. He expected to polish off the novel quickly before starting work on the religious quest of his "Great Sinner," but it proved much more difficult to complete than any of his earlier works. In an agonizing process of revision, Verkhovensky was edged out of its center by a new hero, Stavrogin, "also somber, also criminal but . . . tragic."[66] It is this tragic character who is the spiritual father of Nechaevism in the novel. The outlines of the "Great Sinner" are already present in Stavrogin, but the drama of faith and unbelief that Dostoevsky had sketched out for his future hero has been played out in Stavrogin's past, which does not appear in the final version of the novel. It is recalled only through his mysterious influence on the other main characters, who owe their various ideologies to him. He himself is a spent force. His search to test the limits of his will has led to the boredom of indifference to good and evil from which the only relief is self-destruction.

Stavrogin, however, is much more than just an unregenerated Raskolnikov: the author's attitude to the two characters is entirely different. Raskolnikov was his creature, directed to his fate and judged by him, but Stavrogin manipulates Dostoevsky. From his letters to Katkov we learn that Dostoevsky initially viewed his subject "aloofly" but that as he continually recast the novel he felt a strange sense of helplessness as he was taken over by his new hero: "He has captivated me." Dostoevsky was apprehensive that readers might find the character banal: "I have taken him from my heart." The one "positive" character in the novel, Shatov, the mouthpiece for Dostoevsky's Christian nationalism, expresses a similar feeling toward his former mentor Stavrogin. Bitterly attacking Stavrogin's atheism, he nevertheless admits that he still worships him: "I cannot tear you out of my heart."[67] It has often been pointed out that Stavrogin has some of the traits of Nikolai Speshnev, one of the most gifted members of the Petrashevsky circle, a powerful and mysterious personality who made a profound impression on the young Dostoevsky, but the reason for the author's identification with his hero lies deeper than this. It is to be found in the passage in which Shatov reminds Stavrogin of his former faith: "Did you not tell me that if it were mathematically proved to you that the truth is outside Christ, you would rather remain with Christ than with the truth?"[68]

This deliberate echo of Dostoevsky's own confession reveals how far he had strayed from his original intention of annihilating the enemy. The theme of the novel, together with contemporary developments in Russia, had forced him to reflect on the motives and personalities of his own radical past and to confront the implications of the discovery, made after his conversion, that the arguments of faith did not silence those of reason. The tormented sense of perpetual division already present in Prince Myshkin is dominant in all the main characters of *The Possessed*. It is not clear, we are told, whether Stavrogin is a believer or an atheist. What is important is that he believes in neither his belief nor his unbelief. With the exception of Verkhovensky, who is a moral nullity, all those influenced by Stavrogin experience an agonizing conflict between faith and reason. When, after a passionate defense of the views that Dostoevsky held most dear, Shatov is asked by Stavrogin whether he believes in God, he stammers out that he *will* believe. The half-demented Kirillov plans to kill himself as a supreme act of self-will to prove that God is dead and to open the way for the transformation of mortals into gods, but he confesses, in an echo of Dostoevsky's admission to Maikov, "God has tormented me all my life." God is necessary and must therefore exist: "But I know that he does not and cannot exist. . . . Surely you understand that a person with two such thoughts cannot go on living?"[69]

The Orthodox Christianity of the Russian people as the "final word," the supreme truth that will bring harmony into human relations—or godless self-will, leading inexorably to murder or self-destruction: this was the choice that Dostoevsky had intended to present in his political novel. In the execution of the work, however, the propagandist clashed with the artist, obedient to a different experience of moral choice. The two approaches are never reconciled, to the artistic detriment of the novel. Its plot remains true to the original didactic intention. Two visions of Russia's future are contrasted: the path to be taken by a Christian nationalism is outlined with obscure but passionate eloquence by Shatov, while the ultimate consequences of the proposition "everything that promotes the revolution is moral" are spelled out in the dream of the Nechaevist "philosopher" Shigalev: to control the violence it has spawned, the revolution will establish a system in which humanity will be divided into two parts. One-tenth will have unrestricted powers over the other nine-tenths, an obedient herd.

Between these two alternatives Dostoevsky clearly intended there to be no problem of choice. Yet the novel is permeated with the shadowy theme of agonizing moral choice, its content unexplained but located in the personality of Stavrogin, who we are told represents the "tortured, dichotomous nature of the people of our time."[70]

Dostoevsky's last two novels are an anatomy of this divided nature.

The Adolescent (published in 1875) reflected Dostoevsky's anxiety about the moral health of Russian society. In an early sketch of the work he wrote: "the main idea is disintegration." The theme would be the spiritual development of a youth who "seeks a guideline for his behavior, a means of distinguishing good from evil, which does not exist in our society."[71] The youth's search brings him into contact with a revolutionary organization modeled on the Dolgushin group, whose trial in 1874 Dostoevsky had followed closely. They occupy a very minor role in the final version of the novel, but their moral idealism, similar to that of the Petrashevsky group, is contrasted favorably with the preoccupations of the predatory society around them. Although the adolescent is not converted to their philosophy, their case—that contemporary society is so irredeemably corrupt that one cannot "do good" in it without first cleansing it by force—is never refuted in the novel.

The final version of the work is dominated by the portrait of the adolescent's father, Versilov, Dostoevsky's first attempt at a full-scale study of the new species that Myshkin had defined: he confesses that he "can, in the most convenient way, feel two opposite feelings at the same time," a faculty that lends a corresponding ambiguity to his actions.[72] An atheist who can demonstrate that all ideals are illusions, he defends Christianity and yearns for a Kingdom of God on earth, seeking to re-create his lost faith by an effort of reason and will.

Half-predator, half-idealist, devoured by doubts, Versilov remains a mysterious character, hardly less shadowy than Stavrogin. The species was still in embryo; five years later it would emerge fully formed in *The Brothers Karamazov.*

In the years in which Dostoevsky was working on his last novel, the Russian revolutionary movement took a new and violent direction with the formation of a terrorist group whose aim was to force the government to grant the civil liberties that would permit the people to express its will. Dostoevsky's attitude to these revolutionaries, who repudiated Nechaev's amoralism and his cult of force, was ambiguous—as attested by the strange conversation of 1880 recorded by his publisher, A. S. Suvorin. Some scholars, reluctant to admit any evidence of radical sympathies on Dostoevsky's part, have shed doubt on the reliability of this well-known passage; but Suvorin, a conservative, had no reason to paint Dostoevsky redder than he was, and the passage is so revealing that it is worth quoting at length. Referring to a recent attempt on the life of the tsar, Dostoevsky "commented on the odd attitude of the public to these crimes. Society seemed to sympathize with them, or, it might be truer to say, was not too clear how to look on them." He asked Suvorin whether, if he heard of a plot to blow up the Winter Palace, he would inform the police. Suvorin said he would not. Dostoevsky replied:

> Neither would I. Why not? After all, it is horrible, it is a crime. Perhaps we could have forestalled it. I was thinking about this before you came in. . . . I went through all the reasons that might have made me do this. They are basic, solid reasons. Then I considered all the reasons that would have stopped me from doing it. They are absolutely insignificant. Simply fear of being thought an informer. . . . The liberals would never forgive me. They would torment me, drive me to despair. Is this normal? Everything is abnormal in our society: That is why all these things happen, and nobody knows how to act—not only in the most difficult situations, but even in the simplest. I would have written about this . . . but one can't do so. In our society one is not allowed to speak about the most important things.[73]

Instead, Dostoevsky wrote a novel about parricide. But *The Brothers Karamazov* is saturated with the terrible dilemmas of moral choice in Russia at that time. The two "ideas" of Christianity and anti-Christian humanism confront each other on equal terms. The principle of rational self-interest, consistently pursued, bears fruit in the killing of Fyodor Karamazov and in the despotism of the Grand Inquisitor; but to maintain, as many critics have done, that the Legend of the Grand Inquisitor was intended to be a final refutation of the humanist "idea" is to ignore the extraordinary force with which Dostoevsky allows Ivan Karamazov to argue the case against the Christian ethic as a rule for social existence. In the central philosophical confrontation between Ivan and his brother Alesha, Dostoevsky gives the humanist case a depth and plausibility that he had hitherto denied it.

The Christian ethic, according to Alesha and his spiritual mentor Zosima, depends on a "precious, mysterious sense of our living bond with another world," the source of our impulses to love, humility, and forgiveness. Ivan protests that his "earthly Euclidian mind" is not equipped to deal with things "not of this world"; it can judge only on the evidence of things seen.[74] Affronted by the absurdity of the suffering of innocent human beings, he cannot accept that this will be redeemed by some future divine harmony and condemns as obscene and criminal an ethic that demands that the torturers of children be forgiven. Love of humanity demands the forcible remodeling of the world by any expedient means in accordance with the dictates of reason, to the end of securing the happiness of the greatest number.

Ivan is not a naive rationalist in the mold of Chernyshevsky. He does not deny that the Christian ethic expresses genuine human needs and aspirations.

As he makes clear in his legendary account of the Grand Inquisitor's meeting with Christ, he is merely arguing that this ethic is senseless when used as a basis for ordering social relations. The Inquisitor accepts that it has its validation in human striving to an ideal freedom but maintains that with very few exceptions people are too slavish, too weak, too vicious, and too self-deceiving to live by it. He draws on history, logic, and the observable evidence of the power of ungovernable instincts (evidence that Dostoevsky had once used to refute the rationalists in *The House of the Dead*) to prove that the Christian ethic is based on a model of humans as they ought to be, not as they are: irrational beings whose desire for freedom is predominantly expressed in barbaric rebellion and the destruction of their own kind, thereby frustrating another equally basic human need—for a tolerable existence in this world, attained by the satisfaction of material wants and personal security from violence. Proof of the depth of this need is the constant readiness of individuals to surrender their freedom in return for its satisfaction: this is the only ultimate good realizable for the vast majority. A social ethic based, unlike Christ's, on true compassion for people as they are, will justify the use of all means, including force, that will secure a stable social existence for the greatest number and protect them against those self-destructive impulses that are the expression of their urge for freedom. The only realizable social ideal is the contentment of an obedient flock, purged of disruptive impulses and subject to a small elite of rulers who will satisfy its every need except the need for freedom.

Many commentaries on the legend still conclude that its message is unambiguous: a "powerful vindication" (in Berdiaev's words) of the Christian ethic, achieved by exposing the false compassion of atheistic humanism.[75] But as Edward Wasiolek, among others, has pointed out, from the fact that the Christian view of humanity and the Christian ideal of liberty are shown to be more attractive than that of the Grand Inquisitor, it does not follow that they are more valid.[76] Indeed, Dostoevsky has put all the weight of factual evidence on the Inquisitor's side. The system he proposes follows with impeccable logic from the evidence of historical experience and of observable human behavior, which together suggest that fear of punishment and retributive justice are much more effective than all-forgiving love in deterring the authors of such outrages as the torture of children. On this evidence, the Inquisitor's ethic is incontestably more compassionate than Christ's (a point Dostoevsky stresses more in his notes than he dares in the final version). As Wasiolek puts it, the two ethics represent two discontinuous ways of understanding human nature, neither of which can refute the other because there are no basic assumptions common to both. That this is how Dostoevsky intended the Legend to be interpreted is suggested by his comment in a letter to N. A. Liubimov: "My hero [Ivan] has chosen a proposition which *in my opinion* is irrefutable: the senselessness of the suffering of children."[77]

This is not the dispassionate fairness of an opponent secure in his own position: there was too much of Ivan in Dostoevsky. The suffering that Ivan describes with a Belinskian passion was based on real cases that Dostoevsky had set down and brooded over in his notebooks. The Grand Inquisitor's view of observable human nature was a view that Dostoevsky had used to challenge the optimistic rationalism of the Russian Left and to frustrate Myshkin's compassion. In the legend he finally detaches the essence of the enemy from its contingent forms, and this essence turns out to be much more formidable than the narrow fanaticism of Nechaev, the naive materialism of the radicals of the 1860s, or even the utopian socialism of the 1840s and 1870s. In *The Brothers Karamazov* he goes beyond these transient manifestations to their permanent source in an inalienable part of the moral nature of human beings: the desire that justice should be done and be seen to be done, that evil should not flourish, and that the innocent should be vindicated on this earth. In a central scene of the novel, Ivan confronts the saintly Christian Alesha with a story of a general who has a peasant child torn to death by hunting dogs: Would "moral feeling" not demand that the general be put to death? Alesha is forced to admit that it would.[78]

When Dostoevsky asserted that Ivan's arguments were unanswerable he must have shocked his Orthodox friends, but he was only restating what he had foreseen at the time of his conversion: there could be no final resolution of the conflict between the moral data of empirical experience and an ethic rooted in the invisible world of faith because they shared no common ground. If one took one's stand with Christ against logic, it must be without the comforting belief that one had thereby scored a victory over logic. Hence the struggle that he had predicted for himself in 1854 and that he embodied in all his Christian heroes. The last and most radiant of these, the monk Alesha Karamazov, is no more secure in his faith than Shatov: see his confession to Lisa when, overcome with grief at the death of the child Iliusha and his father's murder, he asks: " 'Am I really a monk? . . . but it may be that I don't even believe in God.' . . . In those words, blurted out too suddenly, there was something too mysterious, too subjective, something perhaps unclear even to him, but already undoubtedly a source of torment to him."[79] Suvorin records in his diary that Dostoevsky told him that he intended to write a sequel to the novel in which Alesha would renounce his faith in his search for the truth, would "naturally" become a revolutionary, and would be hanged for a terrorist act.[80]

Those of Dostoevsky's heroes who choose logic over Christ are equally divided, conscious of betraying part of their natures. The Grand Inquisitor describes the despotic benefactors of humanity as "sufferers," cursed by the clarity of their insight into human weakness. Dostoevsky's moral vision challenged the mystique, promoted by the radical critics, that saw the revolutionary hero as serene and untroubled by doubt, a model of the integrated human being of the future. Only after the violence and slaughter of 1905 did moral doubts and self-questioning become common in some revolutionary circles, but Dostoevsky sensed the beginnings of these doubts. His notebooks show that his sympathy with the young radicals of the 1870s owed much to the affinities he discerned between his and their perception of the "accursed questions" of their confused time.[81] One of the most revealing passages in all his writings on his view of the nature of moral choice was prompted by the trial in 1878 of Vera Zasulich, the would-be assassin of General Fyodor Trepov, the governor of St. Petersburg. At her trial (which ended in an unexpected acquittal and a colossal moral defeat for the government) Zasulich declared that the attempt had been a response to Trepov's action in having a student detainee flogged for failing to remove his cap in his presence. She had resolved to prove, if necessary at the cost of her life, that no one who violated another person in such a way could be sure of doing so with impunity. "It is a frightful thing to raise one's hand against another human being, but I found that I had to do it."[82] Dostoevsky, who had followed the trial closely, copied the first part of this sentence into his notebook. It expressed perfectly the conflict between two kinds of compassion that had absorbed him and dominated his art since his conversion. Commenting that Zasulich's vacillation had been more moral than her resolution of it, he wrote: "What is moral cannot be completely reduced to the concept of consistency with one's convictions—sometimes it is more moral not to follow one's convictions . . . while retaining one's convictions, one stops short because of some feeling and does not complete the act. One curses oneself and feels self-contempt in one's mind, but one's feeling, that is, one's conscience, stops one from completing it."[83]

This fragment of self-revelation confirms the accuracy of Dostoevsky's prediction that his struggle would torment him to the grave. The choice that he made in 1854 to follow the promptings of feeling against reason was permanent, but so also (despite the strident dogmatism of some of his political journalism) was the sense of inner division that it caused. His greatest characters embody his personal discovery that not only conflict but also self-contempt and a sense of self-betrayal are inalienable characteristics of the truly moral life. This view is not calculated to have popular appeal, and the effort persists to make his works yield a more positive message, in support of certain moral and ideological absolutes. It is the more remarkable, then, that one of the greatest of all moral absolutists, Tolstoy, was among the first to detect (and detest) the true nature of Dostoevsky's perception of ethical choice. In a letter to the critic Nikolai Strakhov, written shortly after Dostoevsky's death, he expressed indignation and alarm at the fact that Dostoevsky was already being hailed as a prophet and a saint: "One simply cannot set up on a pedestal for the edification of posterity a man who was all struggle."[84]

Tolstoy in Doubt

CHAPTER FIVE

"**Y**ou think that I am one thing and my writing is another. But my writing is the whole of me." Thus Tolstoy wrote in 1885, in one of the long and bitter letters to his wife in which he sought to explain the appalling suffering that they had caused each other since his spiritual crisis of the 1870s. Their misery was all due, he believed, to one fatal mistake: she had succumbed to "the general opinion that a literary artist . . . should write works of art, and not think about his life or improve it, and that all that is a kind of folly or mental illness."[1]

Tolstoy's onslaughts on the principle of moral neutrality in art began in earnest only after the religious conversion he described in his *Confession*, which he began writing in 1879. But it was a principle that had always been alien to him. When as a young man in the 1850s he had turned for a brief period from writing to teaching and work on his estate, this was because he had temporarily ceased to find in art and beauty a sufficient answer to the central preoccupation of his life—the search for the truths by which humanity should live. When, having returned to writing in the early 1860s, he was working on *War and Peace*, he was apprehensive, as he wrote to the historian Mikhail Pogodin, that people would praise "the sentimental scene with the young lady . . . and other such rubbish" and might not notice "the chief thing"—his ideas on the limits of freedom and dependence and his views on history, which were part of an outlook "formed in me God alone knows by what toil and suffering."[2]

His fears were well founded: as Isaiah Berlin pointed out in *The Hedgehog and the Fox*, the "philosophical" passages in *War and Peace* have traditionally been seen as irrelevant digressions alien to the artistic structure of the work, early evidence of the tragic folly that would lead him to renounce his artistic calling for a role in which his talents were undistinguished: that of moralist and preacher.[3]

The common perception of Tolstoy in English-speaking countries continues to separate the artist from the thinker—a fact that can be partly accounted for by the decades in which there was a significant gap in the relevant material available in translation. Tolstoy's belief in the unity of his art and his life led him in his last years to give as much careful thought to the posthumous editing and publication of his letters and diaries as he had done with regard to his literary works. Throughout his life those letters that dealt with the questions that most preoccupied him were meticulously copied and preserved. He gave enormous importance to his diaries (which span a period of sixty-three years), rereading them and stressing their significance for understanding him and his art. Thirty-two volumes of the monumental ninety-volume Soviet edition of his works are devoted exclusively to his letters, and thirteen to his diaries and notebooks; but very little of this material was available in English translation until 1978, when R. F. Christian published a two-volume translation of selected letters, followed in 1985 by two volumes of extracts from the diaries. These judiciously chosen selections provide a taste of the material that is still inaccessible to English-speaking readers and will do much to eliminate what Christian (in his introduction to the letters) describes as the persistent fallacy that Tolstoy's "conversion" was a "sudden *volte-face,* the sour grapes of a man growing too old to enjoy the pagan, sensual and materialistic pleasures of life."[4]

The standard picture of Tolstoy the thinker, especially in his later life, tends to be static and singularly unattractive: a self-appointed and self-righteous sage with absurdly simplistic and utopian views on the organization of society; a moral despot and domestic tyrant whose narrow and unshakable dogmatism wrecked his marriage and drove his wife to the verge of madness. This picture is not consistent with the spiritual journey recorded in the letters and diaries. Their dominant note to the very end is not dogmatism but doubt, so intense as to bring Tolstoy close to suicide at one period. To read them in sequence is an overwhelming experience: Tolstoy's life, like his novels, does not encourage neat judgments about character and the nature of human error; but even *Anna Karenina,* with its sense of catastrophe issuing from inescapable contradictions, does not have the tragic power of Tolstoy's personal account of a lifetime of passionate and unremitting search. For the reader is soon aware of what Tolstoy would never accept—that his fleeting periods of intense happiness were deceptive tokens of hope, temporary distractions from the inexorable development of contradictions that his great gifts of mind and heart were impotent to resolve and that culminated in the horror of his last years of family life, his despairing flight, and his death at the railway station of Astapovo.

As Berlin showed in *The Hedgehog and the Fox,* in his search for fundamental laws of existence Tolstoy was torn between two opposing visions of reality. His artist's love of the variety and irreducible complexity of life led him to reject all intellectual constructions claiming to provide final explanations, whether religious, scientific, or philosophical, of the meaning of history and of individual destinies. Those characters in his novels whom he portrays as possessing true wisdom rely in their moral lives not on their reason but on an instinctive sense of the flow and direction of life. Yet Tolstoy's "nihilism," his contempt for those who sought to fix this instinct in doctrines and systems, was at odds with his longing for moral certainty, attainable only through some unitary vision of the world from which clear rules for conduct could be derived: hence his attempts to erect a set of absolutes based on the Gospels or the beliefs of simple peasants.

Berlin has shown how this conflict permeates Tolstoy's view of history. His letters and diaries reveal its effects on his daily moral life, which was a constant struggle between two opposing conceptions of self-perfection. His aesthetic intuition led him to see his goal as self-fulfillment, the harmonious development of all his capacities, guided only by an instinctive sense of the life force that united him with all living beings. But his intellect presented the process of self-perfection to him as one of self-mastery and self-denial, the control or elimination of instinctive drives in the name of norms and prescriptions advanced by reason and the conscious moral will as answers to the question of how human beings should live.

An account of the worldview that Tolstoy developed in the years before his religious crisis is found in his correspondence with his relative Aleksandra Tolstaia, to whom he confided throughout his life the most intimate details of his spiritual experience. A devout Orthodox Christian, she expressed frequent concern about Tolstoy's lack of Christian faith, and in reply he attempted to outline his beliefs. At the age of fourteen he had replaced the naive religion of his childhood with a "clear and logical" view of life in which religion had no place. Ten years later, in 1852 (after a restless succession of occupations—an unfinished university career, the running of his estate, followed by his first serious attempts at writing interspersed with dissolute interludes in Moscow society), he joined the army as a cadet and was posted to the Caucasus. In the tedium of garrison life he began to feel that life lacked not only mystery but meaning. There followed two years of intense intellectual searching, resulting in the discovery of an "old and simple" truth: "that there is immortality, that there is love, and that one must live for others in order to be happy for all eternity."[5]

The "religion" Tolstoy had adopted by the end of the 1850s was a form of pantheism, derived from his passionate love of nature combined with the influence of Rousseau, whose belief in the superiority of primitive, spontaneous virtue over the values of the civilized intellect found a deep response in Tolstoy during his life in the Caucasus. To Tolstaia, who disapproved of this "pagan" love of nature, he replied: "For me nature is religion's guide." It was among simple peasants, not the devout Christians of his own milieu, that he found the quality he saw as essential above all others: a serene sense of the natural order of things, instinctive harmony with universal processes and with the infinite principle that was the common ground of all being. Tolstoy experiences the joy of this sense himself, expressing it in his letters in marvelous passages that describe spring in the country. In one of these, "wild," as he says, with the intoxication of spring, he writes: "There may be moments of happiness stronger than these, but there is nothing to equal the fullness and harmony of such happiness."[6]

Tolstoy's Rousseauism was deepened by a visit in 1857 to Europe, where he witnessed a public execution—an event that profoundly affected his life. In a letter to his friend Vasily Botkin he expressed horror at the arrogance of the civilized intellect that assumed the right to ordain the killing of a healthy human being by reference to concepts of justice and truth on whose definition no two lawyers can agree. The political and moral norms accepted by civilized society were "terrible lies";[7] the conclusion to the short story "Lucerne," which Tolstoy published in the same year, contains a powerful expression of this view, which would lead him by logical steps to an uncompromising opposition to the modern state in all its manifestations.

Over the centuries, he writes, our dissecting, categorizing intellect has deceived us into believing that we can regulate our lives by fixed rules and eternal norms. We state categorically that civilization and freedom are good, barbarism and despotism evil, but these abstractions cannot help us make our daily moral choices in a world where every fact and every situation can be viewed from an infinity of competing perspectives, and where good is often inextricably bound up with evil. The false pretensions of our reason have stifled the instinctive moral sense that prompts us to act in harmony with the flow of all life. "We have one, and only one infallible teacher—the world spirit implanted in each and every one of us, instilling into each a striving for what ought to be—the same spirit which makes the tree grow toward the sun, makes the flower disperse its seeds by autumn, and makes us instinctively huddle close to one another."[8]

"Lucerne" touches on a theme that is prominent in Tolstoy's two great novels: that of the futility and sterility of virtue whose source is the head and not the heart. In 1859 he wrote Aleksandra Tolstaia: "To do good *deliberately* is shameful. The more so since I've experienced the happiness (however rarely) of doing it unconsciously, quite by accident, and straight from the heart."[9] Those of his characters who devote themselves to deliberate and reasoned altruism, whether in their personal relations or in social action, are shown as both impotent in their efforts to define the bounds of good and evil and sterile in their inner lives, lacking the vital force that animates such characters as Natasha Rostova and Kitty Shcherbatskaia. These women apparently live for themselves and their families, not for others, pursuing their personal happiness; yet as Tolstoy's alter ego, Levin, comes to believe, actions bear fruit not when they are consciously directed to "doing good to everyone, to humanity, Russia and the whole countryside," but when they spring from the unconscious urge for self-fulfillment inherent in all living beings.[10]

In spite of preaching this doctrine to Aleksandra, Tolstoy confesses to a conflict between the feeling of "love and tranquillity" that it has given him and certain "highly developed" Christian feelings of which he is conscious.[11] The nature of this conflict emerges clearly from his diaries of the 1850s. Although his aesthetic sense prompts him to strive for inner harmony, his intellect tells him he is the permanently divided being of Christian doctrine, for whom virtue consists in the victory of his higher, spiritual nature over his animal urges. He feels himself drawn simultaneously in opposing directions by two competing wills—and it is the principle of conscious self-mastery, not instinctive self-realization, that dominates his personal moral development. In 1856 he recorded in his diary a sudden insight that happiness lies not in submission to laws and sanctions but in "spinning out from oneself, like a spider, a sticky web of love in all directions, catching in it anything that comes by."[12] Such passages are rare, however. On the contrary, his daily struggle against what he considers to be his main vices—lust, laziness, gambling, vanity—is governed by a succession of naively devised rules and systems, according to which he sternly charts his progress in subduing his baser inclinations.

Tolstoy's vacillations between opposing paths to self-perfection reached their most acute phase between 1856, when he resigned from the army, and 1862, the year of his marriage, as he searched for an occupation to which he could devote his life. The central problem of those years was his relationship to the society whose goals and values he increasingly despised. At first his feeling for nature enabled him to follow the path he had prescribed in "Lucerne," retreating into his private world and seeking his personal fulfillment in art, in the certainty that he was thereby conforming to the natural order of things. He wrote to Aleksandra that after two months in "Sodom" (his time in Paris), a stay in the Swiss countryside had rid his soul of an "accumulation of filth," revealing to him "how good [things] are." Back in Russia in 1857, however, he was soon overcome by "a feeling of disgust for my country": against a background of patriarchal barbarism, a handful of intellectuals were engaged in political arguments that did not seem to him to reveal any understanding of the deep causes of injustice and corruption.[13]

At first he again found his salvation in the tranquillity of his inner vision and its embodiment in art; but in a letter written at the end of 1857 he noted the destruction of this refuge: "I tried and I still try to tell myself that I am a poet and that another reality exists for me . . . [but] I was horrified to see that all this painful, foolish and dishonest reality was not an accident, . . . but a necessary law of life." He tells Aleksandra that he has renounced his belief in the possibility of creating his own "happy and honest little world" in which he would do good peacefully and unhurriedly: "To live an honest life you have to . . . struggle endlessly, and suffer loss. As for tranquillity—it's spiritual baseness. That's why the bad side of our soul desires tranquillity, not being aware that its attainment entails the loss of everything in us that is beautiful, not of this world, but *of the world beyond.*"[14]

Tolstoy's views on art in the late 1850s reflect his hesitations between a view of the virtuous life as consisting in conscious struggle and a sense that it lies in tranquil conformity to elemental processes. He was on friendly terms with the proponents of the principle of art for art's sake in debates between liberal and radical critics at the period, and even planned in 1858 (together with Ivan Turgenev and the poet Afanasy Fet) to establish a journal that would defend the independence of art against the radical movement, which sought to turn it into a political weapon. But his conscience revolted against the apparent absence all around him of harmony and instinctive goodness, and in a letter of 1860 he repudiates the vocation of the pure artist as a justification of the "monstrous and foul" act of living by the exploitation of the labor of others. The death of his brother Nikolai in the same year provoked an agonized self-questioning on the meaning of human existence, to which neither his love of nature nor his art could provide answers. "Art is a lie, and I can no longer love a beautiful lie."[15] He embarked on a policy of conscious altruism of the kind that, not long before, he had stigmatized as futile, choosing to stifle his need to write in order to dedicate himself to the improvement of his peasants' lives by setting up a school on his estate and formulating theories of education designed to protect and develop the precious primitive instincts of human beings.

Tolstoy's struggle between two visions of the moral life was at its sharpest in the ideal of the family that he developed in the late 1850s. At that time a tranquil country life, lived in benevolent harmony with his peasants and combining his writing with the production and education of children, seemed to him the form of existence most closely attuned to the fundamental processes of nature. But he approaches this ideal of the heart with all the dogmatic rigor of his moralizing head. He selects the daughter of a neighbor, Valeria Arseneva, as a candidate for the role of wife, candidly announcing to her in a letter that he feels a "passionate longing" to fall in love with her for the purpose, but warning her that he will not indulge in the nonsense of "tender and exalted" feelings. He looks on married happiness much too sternly for that. "I'm staking everything on this one card. If I don't find complete happiness, I shall ruin everything, my talent, my heart; I'll become a drunkard and a gambler; I'll steal, if I haven't the courage to cut my throat."[16]

His correspondence with Arseneva reveals Tolstoy the moral dogmatist at his most naive and unattractively despotic. The path to the tranquil idyll of rural and domestic virtue that he paints for her is by way of the most unremitting self-mastery, the ruthless eradication of all her defects, which Tolstoy discusses at length, attributing them to a weakness for the pleasures of society that must be overcome. He warns her that he requires nothing less than perfection from her. Not the slightest moral backsliding can be tolerated: one false step and their happiness will be forever ruined. Their relationship—which, needless to say, was brief—was enshrined by Tolstoy in the moralizing story "Family Happiness," but by the time it was published in 1859 he had come to see its priggishness as loathsome. Three years later when he fell in love with Sonia Behrs, this was an affair of the heart, not the head. They were married after a brief courtship, and Tolstoy's letters to Aleksandra throughout the 1860s show that, in spite of intermittent upheavals, he felt himself close to his ideal of a "tranquil and moral" happiness. After a year of marriage he wrote: "I don't analyze my situation (I've given up *grübeln*) or my feelings—I only *feel* my family circumstances. . . . This condition gives me an awful lot of intellectual scope. I've never felt my intellectual powers, and even all my moral powers, so free and so capable of work."[17]

He gave up his teaching to devote himself to writing *War and Peace*, which was published in 1869. Throughout this period, the concept of self-perfection as identical with self-fulfillment is a constant theme of his letters and diaries. Thus, in a diary entry of March 1863, he writes: "Everything that people do is done because their whole nature requires it. The intellect just fabricates its own imaginary reasons for each act, which are called convictions, or faith in the case of the individual, and ideas when applied to nations in history. . . . The chess game of the intellect goes on independently of life. . . . What we call self-sacrifice and virtue, are only the satisfaction of one particular morbidly over-developed tendency. The ideal is harmony. Only art senses this."[18]

The artist is now reinstated in his eyes as the channel for the expression of the unconscious harmony of all being. In a letter of 1865 he asserts: "The aims of art are incommensurate . . . with social aims. The aim of an artist is not to solve a problem irrefutably, but to make people love life in all its countless inexhaustible manifestations."[19]

But Tolstoy was preaching, above all, to convince himself. If his new happiness made the ideal to which he aspired clearer to him than ever before, he was still, in his constant introspection, the divided man of the past. He writes in his diary: "There are no guilty beings in the world. To be happy is to be justified!";[20]

but a few days later he is tormented by the conviction that he does not deserve his happiness and sets out to earn it by a program of self-improvement. Reason, whose powers he had so much denigrated, continues obstinately to present him with a dualistic vision of the personality, according to which virtue consists in the triumph of duty over natural inclination. Tolstoy embodied his conflict in his short novel *The Cossacks.* Begun in 1852 but published only in the year after his marriage, it is the balance sheet of a decade of introspection. His hero, Olenin, shares Tolstoy's pantheistic love of nature and his idealization of primitive people who, he declares, live for themselves alone and for that reason are harmonious and beautiful. But Olenin's conscience, like the author's, urges him to seek "another kind of happiness," that of living for others through self-sacrifice.[21] Tolstoy could find no way to reconcile the aims of serving beauty and the good: self-denial, grounded in a vision of human beings as eternally at war with themselves, was hardly the path to the aesthetic goal of an undivided nature.

Marriage and his concentration on the writing of *War and Peace* distracted Tolstoy from this dilemma until the end of the 1860s, when his search for meaning in life entered a new, more desperate phase. He became too much oppressed by the injustice and corruption of the world around him for his reason to be satisfied with the pantheistic faith in the essential goodness of all things that had carried him through earlier crises. Yet, as is shown by his increasingly savage attacks on conventional moral and political beliefs, his instinct was never more suspicious of the attempts of intellectuals to produce a coherent explanation of the fundamental mysteries of life. It was on religious faith that Tolstoy placed his last hopes of a synthesis between the two ideals he longed to serve equally—the moral and the aesthetic.

In a letter of 1873 to Strakhov he outlined an approach to religion that would permit him at last to reconcile the artist with the moralist in him. What is wrong with existing religions, he writes, is that beauty—which is the fundamental principle of all great religions—has been usurped in them by reason. The good is best understood as beauty: "To turn the other cheek when you are struck on one is not clever or good, but senseless and beautiful." Dogmatic theology had confused people by introducing logic into religion, with the result that "there is no longer beauty nor a guide through the chaos of good and evil." Toward the end of the decade Tolstoy wrote to Strakhov that he had achieved "the most precious thing of all"—inner harmony—by an unquestioning and unreasoning acceptance of the traditions and observances through which simple Christians had for centuries expressed their answers to the "questions of the heart." "I swim just like a fish in water, in actions which make no sense, and only refuse to submit when tradition tells me to perform actions . . . which do not correspond to the fundamental irrationality of that vague consciousness which exists in my heart."[22]

Religion seemed to offer in permanence what nature had given him only in transitory experiences—a sense of unity with simple, uncorrupted people and elemental processes. But it could not last. Tolstoy's reason would not permit him to accept "actions which make no sense," and it soon ruthlessly demolished, along with faith in miracles and the divinity of Christ, all the other traditions and dogmas whose adherents included his beloved peasants. Tolstoy's version of Christ's teaching, purged of all that he saw as superstitious or superfluous, was reduced to a "law of love" based on the precepts of the Sermon on the Mount, which he took to their logical extreme in the two doctrines that were to be the essence of "Tolstoyism": total chastity and nonresistance to evil. In a letter to a Tolstoyan, he defended the intransigence of his interpretation of Christianity as follows: "Christianity, like any truth, has this peculiarity that if it is not accepted in its entirety, it may as well not be accepted at all."[23]

He had argued eloquently in "Lucerne" that every ideal is both true—in representing one side of human nature—and false, in that very one-sidedness. He had also poured scorn on those who claimed what he himself would later insist (in a letter of 1887): that it was "impossible . . . for a person to write without drawing a definite line for himself between good and evil." Few thinkers had argued more convincingly than Tolstoy that the need for certainties and moral absolutes, by falsifying our understanding of the complex truth, disorients us morally, setting us hopelessly at odds with ourselves and the world. But the need for faith was ultimately stronger in him than the instinct for harmony, even leading him to denounce the latter as a dangerous delusion. In a letter to Aylmer Maude in 1901 he criticizes John Ruskin's "hazy ecclesiastical-Christian understanding of the demands of life which enabled him to combine ethical ideals with aesthetic."[24] The last years of Tolstoy's life were governed by a rigidly dualistic view of reality: the conflict between beauty and good, matter and spirit, the aspirations of the spirit and the power of the flesh, is a constant theme of his correspondence and his diaries.

Tolstoy's relentless battle with himself is described with horrifying frankness in his diaries. Even his letters, which are much more reticent about the upheavals in his family life, make painful reading: they reflect all too well his fits of shame and self-loathing when his sexual drive, his hot temper and intolerance, and above all his artistic gifts, led him to betray his narrow principles. He had proclaimed that art, in order to serve the goal of universal brotherhood, must be didactic in content and accessible in form to the simplest peasants, and he contemptuously dismissed the novel form as "obsolete": "If I have anything to say, I won't describe a drawing-room or a sunset etc." In 1896 he wrote to Strakhov: "What a crude, immoral, vulgar and senseless work *Hamlet* is." Yet he never ceased to be ashamed of the "dreadful power" exercised over him by music that was incomprehensible to the masses, and he was unable to prevent himself from occasionally reverting to being the spontaneous artist of earlier years. After one such lapse—resulting in his comedy *The Fruits of Enlightenment*—he writes of his sense of shame: "What a soul-degrading occupation art is. A man may die at any time, and all of a sudden he jots down anxiously a phrase which is appropriate to a particular person and is funny; and he's glad to have found it."[25]

But it was not the difficulty of the tasks he had set himself that caused Tolstoy the greatest torment. He believed that "there is only one negative quality needed for everything in life, particularly in art—not to lie";[26] but he suffered perpetually from a sense of a fundamental falseness in his attempts to draw the dividing line between good and evil, some terrible flaw in the logic on which he based his gospel of love. He insisted repeatedly in his writings and in letters to the tsar and to public figures that all attempts to do good that made compromises, however temporarily, with violence and the institutions founded on it were sterile and self-defeating: "It's impossible to begin to do good without ceasing to do evil which is the direct opposite of that good; impossible for a landowner to help the starving people; impossible for a judge, tsar, ruler, or military man to oppose murders and violence."[27]

But this precept demanded that when famine struck in Russia in 1891 he should refuse to participate in the government-backed relief schemes, and this he could not bring himself to do. His well-publicized support of them attracted large sums of aid from outside Russia, but according to the logic of his principles his active charity was a betrayal of the law of love. When, on the other hand, he produced a story in which he preached his ideal of chastity in all its rigor, he was subsequently filled with self-disgust: "There was something nasty about "The Kreutzer Sonata," . . . something bad about the motives which guided me in writing it."[28]

The contradiction that finally defeated him lay in his relationship with his family. When his desire that they should renounce their possessions and thus cease to exploit the labor of others was met with incomprehension from his children and active hostility from his wife, he saw three choices open to him, all contrary to the law of love. To leave them would be to pursue the task of perfecting himself at the cost of his duty toward them; to use his authority to change their way of life would be to break the precept of nonresistance to evil; to remain with them (as he did) and to try to fight against evil "lovingly" was to continue living in a way opposed to his beliefs. As a result, "I don't achieve lovingness and gentleness, and I suffer twice over from life and from remorse." The sea of good and evil had not parted at the point where he had drawn his line; on the contrary, he observes with horror that his philosophy of love seems to foment division and hatred: "My friends, even my family, turn away from me. Some people—liberals and aesthetes—think me mad or feeble-minded like Gogol; others—revolutionaries and radicals—think me a mystic or a gasbag; government people think me a pernicious revolutionary, Orthodox people think me the devil. . . . What hurts is that the thing which constitutes the main aim and happiness of my life—loving relations with people—is destroyed."[29]

This sense of moral failure was the more intense because Tolstoy never surrendered his vision of the moral ideal as the harmonious fulfillment of demands implanted in human nature. Through physical work and on walks in the countryside he was still able to experience "the purest joy of all . . . the joy of nature," which gave him a feeling of the essential goodness of all things.[30] His reading of Chinese philosophy led to reflections on the nature of true wisdom that recall his former outbursts against "conscious" virtue. In 1884 he wrote in his diary: "Lao-Tzu says one should be like water. When there are no obstacles it flows; when there's a dam it stops. The dam breaks—and it begins to flow again; a square vessel and it's square, a round vessel and it's round. That's why it is more important and stronger than anything."[31]

A comparison he makes between Dostoevsky and Turgenev gives a rare insight into his awareness of the gulf between his ideal of wholeness and the path of struggle that he had chosen. He had often expressed deep admiration for Dostoevsky's moral passion and had frequently dismissed Turgenev's delicate, detached depiction of Russian society as shallow, lacking in warmth and moral commitment. But in a letter to Strakhov in 1883 we find a striking change of view. Tolstoy protests against the growing adulation of Dostoevsky as a religious thinker. He had died in the midst of a desperate struggle between good and evil, in which all his great brain and heart had not helped him. He was like a magnificent racehorse made almost valueless by a single flaw, whereas Turgenev was the sort of "sturdy little steed without a flaw," on which one always reached one's destination; for this quality (although not for his artistry), Turgenev would be remembered when Dostoevsky was forgotten.[32]

Tolstoy's more eccentric pronouncements on art were almost invariably the products of his efforts to attain consistency in his moral vision. This judgment, however, reflects a rare acceptance that his inner contradictions were not to be resolved, that his extraordinary intellectual powers were an insuperable barrier to the wholeness that his artist's sense told him was the moral ideal and that he believed was attainable by those simpler and less gifted than he. "The longer I live," he told Strakhov, "the more I value horses without a flaw."[33]

The Nihilism of Ivan Turgenev

CHAPTER SIX

T he "elegiac poet of the last enchantments of decaying country houses and of their ineffective but irresistibly attractive inhabitants"—this (as Isaiah Berlin has suggested) is the conventional picture of Ivan Turgenev.[1] The reality was a man intellectually and artistically ahead of his time, one of that avant-garde who, in the first half of the last century, already sensed in the iconoclasm of Feuerbach and the pessimism of Schopenhauer the beginnings of a rethinking of the nature of the self that would shake European thought to its ontological foundations. Nietzsche would announce that he was the first "to know myself in opposition to the mendaciousness of millennia,"[2] but writers like Turgenev had already prepared the ground for this new project of self-knowledge through their exploration of the devices by which the psyche seeks to escape the reality of its own contingency. In his fiction and his debates with his friend Aleksandr Herzen, one of the most original thinkers of the age, Turgenev wrestled with the question with which we are familiar in postfoundationalist debates about the nature of history, freedom, and the self: to what extent one may apply criteria of rationality, direction, progress, and freedom to historical and social processes. Herzen believed that these concepts become meaningful when stripped of their dualistic connotations, whereas Turgenev maintained that there was a tragic discontinuity between all human values and ideals and the objective processes of nature and history. As philosophical authority he would cite Schopenhauer, a pioneer of orientation in a godless world and one of the few thinkers whom Nietzsche would acknowledge as a worthy predecessor.

This chapter tracks Turgenev's efforts to reconcile Schopenhauerian pessimism with liberal values and a humanistic ethic, an enterprise which led, in Herzen's words, to "the most utter nihilism of *exhaustion and despair*."[3] I believe that Turgenev's struggle and his failure are closely relevant to discussions within postmodern theory on the problem of validating moral norms and ideals without recourse to foundationalist assumptions. Schopenhauer's ethic of compassion has been cited as a solution;[4] Turgenev's attempt to "live" this ethic, and to depict its consequences through the characters in his novels, suggests that it is not. In particular, his experience sheds light on a question central to current debates on cultural theory: whether, with the erosion of belief in the rationality of the self and the historical process, the realm of the aesthetic should be perceived as a source of occasional remission from the pain of existence in a meaningless world, or, alternatively, as an aid to moral orientation in that world and a means of healing its divisions. The first of these two views was a central plank of Schopenhauer's pessimism, and Turgenev (along with Wagner) was among the first of many major artists to find his vision compelling. The classic exposition of the second alternative is Schiller's treatise *On the Aesthetic Education of Man*, a text greatly admired by Turgenev's most formidable opponent, Herzen. In the concluding section of this chapter I interpret the well-known polemic between Turgenev and Herzen as a conflict between a Schopenhauerian and a Schillerian approach to an unprogrammed world. It has been argued that Schopenhauerian pessimism can provide a basis for a liberal humanism in such a world. Turgenev's experience, however, does not support that view. His attempt to apply his philosophy to specific problems of moral choice under a despotic regime adds a dimension lacking in current theoretical attempts to define criteria of meaning and morality that are not dependent on universalist assumptions. We shall see that his conception of the world as a moral void leads him in a very illiberal direction: to an envious admiration of those who by the intensity of their commitment to an inner demand or ideal, whatever its nature, have achieved a Nietzschean authenticity.

Turgenev was born in 1818 into the gentry milieu that he would lovingly depict in his novels. One of three sons of cultivated parents, he would later recall the indelible impression made on him by his mother's brutal treatment of her serfs. A voracious reader from early childhood, he was accepted at the age of fifteen as a student in the Faculty of Literature at Moscow University. His first literary effort, an undistinguished dramatic poem written when he was sixteen, reflects the preoccupations of his introspective generation: its hero (modeled on Byron's Manfred) struggles with the enigma of his destiny in an uncomprehending universe. In 1838 he left Russia for four years of travel and study in Europe, most of which he spent in Berlin, the philosophical mecca of his generation. There he attended lectures on Hegel with Mikhail Bakunin, who had taken it on himself to initiate all his Russian friends into the mystery of their place within the general Hegelian scheme. In Rome, Turgenev became intimate with the dying Nikolai Stankevich, whose Moscow circle had pioneered the study of German Idealism among the intelligentsia and who was revered as a model of spiritual harmony: Turgenev would later portray him in the novel *Rudin*, in the figure of the serene Pokorsky. As Andrzej Walicki has pointed out, Turgenev was always preoccupied not with the ideal of a perfect society "but rather with that of the perfect man, a man who combined inner harmony with the highest level of self-consciousness."[5] His early education in Idealism led him to hope (like Herzen at the same age) that the "reflection" which tormented his generation was a necessary transitional phase, the dialectical premise of a future harmony between the goals of enlightened individuals and the objective course of history.

This optimism was shaken by his return to St. Petersburg in 1841, where, after a brief spell in the civil service, he devoted himself to writing. His early short stories, in which youthful idealism is destroyed by the banality of everyday existence, reflect his frustrations under the suffocating despotism of Nicholas I. But hope returned through his friendship with Vissarion Belinsky, who admired his first published story, "Parasha," and in whose circle he met Herzen and other luminaries on their visits from Moscow. Like Belinsky, Herzen, and Nikolai Ogarev, he seized on the revolutionary implications of Feuerbach's invitation to mankind to reappropriate those qualities it had projected onto imagined entities;[6] on a visit abroad in 1847, he declared Feuerbach to be the only writer with individuality and talent among all the philosophical "scribblers" in Germany at that time. Reading the seventeenth-century Spanish Catholic dramatist Pedro Calderón in the light of Feuerbach's *The Essence of Christianity*, he acknowledges a horrified fascination with mankind's propensity to proclaim its own worthlessness before a divinity that it has itself created: "However, I prefer Prometheus, I prefer Satan, the embodiment of revolt and individuality. Atom though I am, I am my own master: I want truth, not salvation, and I expect it from my intelligence and not through grace."[7]

Inspired by the radical humanism of the Left Hegelians, Turgenev was ready to believe with them on the eve of 1848 that mankind was about to attain a state of rational autonomy. The failure of the revolution (which, like Herzen, he witnessed in Paris) would convince him that such a state was permanently beyond human reach.

Turgenev could identify with none of the protagonists in the French conflict. Although he had feared that the June uprising in Paris would end in the destruction of civilized values by a vengeful proletariat, he was sickened by the brutality with which it was suppressed and the cynicism of the victors. His experiences left him a committed gradualist, opposed in principle to revolution— "an old-style liberal in the English . . . sense," as he once put it—but without the faith in rational and inevitable progress that was to characterize liberalism in the Russian sense.[8] Like Herzen, he saw the events of 1848 as overwhelming proof that history was not an ascent to freedom. Writing to his friend the singer Pauline Viardot after the Hungarian revolt had been suppressed by the

Austrians and Russians (with the complicity of the French), he concedes that he is not a politically minded person; but any civilized man would be at a loss to know where to lead a tolerable existence at this historical juncture: "The young nations are still barbarians, like my dear compatriots, or, if they have got to their feet and wish to walk, they are crushed like the Hungarians; and the old nations are expiring, stinking with corruption in their cankered, rotting state. But anyway, who has said that man is destined to be free? History proves the opposite." Goethe's aphorism "Der Mensch ist nicht geboren frei zu sein" (Man is not born to be free) was a statement of fact, "no more, no less, a truth that he spelled out as a precise observer of Nature."[9]

Herzen would use the same quotation as the epigraph to one of the essays in *From the Other Shore,* his philosophical summing-up of 1848. But whereas Herzen argued there that mankind had deluded itself about the extent and nature of its freedom, Turgenev would conclude that history had demonstrated that the notion of freedom itself was an illusion.

Turgenev's pessimism owed much to a melancholy temperament (from early middle age he was haunted by the fear of illness, old age, and death) and to personal misfortunes. In April 1852 he was arrested for some incautious phrasing in an obituary of Gogol he had published. Exiled to his country estate until the end of the following year, he was not allowed to travel to Europe again until 1856. His unhappy infatuation with Pauline Viardot cast a gloom over his life, condemning him to a humiliating existence in her wake. When she moved with her husband to Baden-Baden in 1863, and thence to Paris in 1871, he followed them, despite his fear of the effect this self-imposed exile would have on his writing and his reputation among the younger generation in Russia, from whom he became bitterly estranged in the early 1860s. But although these events intensified it, Turgenev's pessimism was not a mood but a distinctive vision of the world, which his discovery of Schopenhauer's philosophy helped to shape and integrate.

Schopenhauer's pessimism served as a catalyst for impressions formed by reflection and experience, which had combined to destroy Turgenev's faith in religious and idealist theodicies.[10] He came to Schopenhauer already persuaded that human cruelty and destructiveness were part of the natural and immutable order of things, a reality from which we are distracted by the surface beauty of the world: "The nightingale can sing to us of enchanting raptures, while a miserable insect, half-crushed, is painfully expiring in its gizzard," he wrote in June 1849.[11] Henceforth one despairing note begins to resound insistently in his writings: the "small squeak"[12] of the human consciousness, impotently protesting against the blind, elemental forces that make nonsense of its aspirations to progress, perfection, and permanence. The contemplation of nature forced Turgenev to acknowledge the irrelevance of human ideals to a process in which human beings make so marginal and ephemeral an appearance. Before the indifferent glance of the goddess Isis, the individual "senses his isolation, his weakness, his contingency, and hastily, with a secret fear, he turns to the petty concerns and labours of his life: he is more comfortable in this world of his own creation. Here he is at home, here he still dares to believe in his significance and his strength."[13]

The extent of Schopenhauer's influence on Turgenev has been much debated. It is agreed that it was most marked in the first half of the 1860s (the period of his most intense polemical contacts with Herzen) but that throughout his literary career he used Schopenhauerian themes eclectically as a framework for his own views. Two themes in particular—conscious existence as suffering, alleviated only through forms of self-renunciation, and the individual's helplessness before the irrational forces of history and nature—are so prominent in his fiction from the mid-1850s that one commentator suggests that his acquaintance with Schopenhauer dates back to 1854.[14] The first work to point strongly to such an influence is the short story "Faust," published in 1856. Its hero, his hopes of happiness destroyed by the blind force of erotic love (Schopenhauer's "malevolent demon, striving to pervert, to confuse, and to overthrow everything"),[15] concludes that the secret meaning of life, "the answer to its riddle," lies in renunciation. In youth, we may entertain the belief that life's goal is freedom, or the fulfillment of cherished ideals: "But it is shameful to comfort oneself with illusions, when finally the stern face of truth comes to look you in the eye."[16]

The main characters of the two novels that Turgenev published at the end of the 1850s reach the same conclusion. Yelena, in *On the Eve,* takes the Schopenhauerian view that we are all guilty by virtue of our existence; she accepts that her egoistic striving for happiness deserved to be frustrated, inasmuch as it set her in contradiction with the unchangeable nature of the world. Her self-abnegation, like that of Lavretsky in *A Nest of Gentlefolk,*[17] is based on the same strange combination of fatalism and moral strenuousness that characterizes Schopenhauer's ethic—an ethic that Turgenev seems to share, declaring in a letter of 1860: "There's no point in complaining and whining. . . . It's now time to get used to *real* self-sacrifice, not the kind of which we talk so much in our youth and which we associate with love (which is, after all, pleasure),—but that kind . . . *which gives nothing to the individual,* except a sense of duty done." And to the poet Nikolai Nekrasov: "One must stand firm, not in order to attain certain goals, but just in order not to break."[18] In some of his stories the characters' sense of fate is intensified by dreams and visions that bring them face to face with the mysterious "unknown" (*nevedomoe*—Schopenhauer's *das verborgene Macht*). The Schopenhauerian view that one's given character, shaped by such forces, cannot be changed recurs in Turgenev's fiction, consoling one of his heroes and driving another to despair.[19]

The "stern face of truth" is the subject of the story "Enough" (subtitled "Fragments from the Memoirs of a Deceased Artist"), on which Turgenev began work as the Emancipation drew near and Russia looked forward to a new era. The message in this work is grim: the brevity of human life and the triviality of its concerns exclude all hope of moral or political progress. Nothing has changed since Shakespeare created Hamlet and Lear: all around us we see "the same credulity and the same cruelty, the same thirst for blood, gold, and mud, the same trivial pleasures, the same meaningless sufferings in the name of . . . well, let's say in the name of the same nonsense that Aristophanes mocked two thousand years ago, the same crude bait that so easily lures that thousand-headed beast, the human crowd; the same imperious behaviour, the same servile habits, the same natural duplicity—in a word, the same anxious and busy squirrel's leaps in the same old cage that no-one has even taken the trouble to repair."[20]

History is a "market-place of phantoms" where buyers and sellers, all equally deceiving and deceived, mask the pointlessness of their activity with a cacophony of noise.[21] The most terrible thing about human life is that there is nothing terrible about it at all; beneath its trivial surface there are no hidden depths. Words such as *justice, freedom,* and *mankind* lose their inspirational power once we have the courage to face the fleeting nature of our life: a repetition of other lives, equally brief, devoted to the pursuit of absurd or unattainable goals. But what about art and beauty? "The Venus of Milo, one must say, is less open to question than Roman law or the principles of 1789." Yet even art is impotent before the blind force of nature, whose destructive work is so enthusiastically helped along by the human race: "How can one withstand the crushing, crude, endless and ceaseless onslaught of those waves; how, in the last resort, can one believe in the meaning and dignity of those transient forms which we fashion in the darkness, on the edge of an abyss, out of ashes and for an instant of existence?" Like all human creative drives, the capacity to create beauty is a trap, encouraging us to believe that we are the conscious instruments of some purposive force. The greatest minds in history were also the most aware of the contradiction between our finite condition and our infinite aspirations, although the word "great" is scarcely apposite in this context. Other than self-annihilation or self-contempt, there is only one option for the person with a developed consciousness: "calmly to turn his back on it all, to say 'Enough!' and, folding his useless arms on his empty breast, to preserve the last and only dignity available to him: the dignity of knowing his own nothingness."[22]

That this dismal vision was Turgenev's own is evident from the following passage in a letter written shortly after the publication of "Enough," referring to a state of mind that he frequently experienced, when "this sphinx which appears at all times and to all people, has looked at me with its wide, motionless, empty eyes, all the more terrible in that they do not seek to terrify. It is cruel not to know the key to the puzzle; perhaps even more cruel to say to oneself that there is no key, because there is no longer any puzzle. Flies, beating incessantly against a pane of glass—that, I believe, is the most perfect symbol for what we are."[23]

"Enough" reads like a summary of Schopenhauer's reflections on the monotonous sameness of history and the vanity of all existence, but without his metaphysical resolution of the conundrum.[24] Nevedomoe—mysterious, seemingly supernatural forces that reason can neither explain nor control—appear in many of Turgenev's short stories (to the disgust of Herzen, who commented that a fascination with such phenomena was alien to people "with bones and sinews" like himself).[25] But Turgenev always vigorously denied that he had any tendency toward mysticism, assuring one of his critics: "I am interested exclusively in one thing: the physiognomy of life and its authentic representation."[26] This level of investigation offered no explanation or resolution of life's tragic dissonances. For Schopenhauer, a work of art fulfilled its function by revealing the universal forms of phenomena; for Turgenev, this revelation could not compensate for the finitude of the artwork and its creator. Nor, unlike the artist in his story, could he resign himself to loss of faith in progress. He chose instead to run the risk of self-contempt by defending values and goals that could not be reconciled with his view of the historical process.

The resulting tensions and ambivalences are expressed in his painfully personal essay of 1860, "Hamlet and Don Quixote," which presents the disease of "reflection" not (as he had held it to be in his optimistic youth) as a transitional stage in humanity's ascent to a harmonious existence but as a permanent characteristic of all developed individuals. He argues that among Russia's intellectual elite the urge to expose falsehood and serve the good has led to a tragic polarization between ironists and enthusiasts. The ironists' search for truth has locked them into an endlessly regressive process of denial, which destroys all meaning with its dissecting doubt. In the opposing type (which he sees as dominant among the new generation of radicals), reflection has been stifled by the need for faith. Their vision is shallow and narrow: but the mad and noble folly with which they pursue shadows without substance has a capacity to inspire others that is denied to the manysided and reflective Hamlets. By infecting others with their passion, the Don Quixotes supply the ferment that leads to change, but they are powerless to determine the results of the upheavals they produce: these lie "in the hands of fate"—not that Hegelian rational necessity from which some of Turgenev's fellow liberals expected such rich fruits but the blind irrational forces that thwart human designs.[27] Are not all ideals of progress thus illusions, the cause of futile sacrifices? The question hangs unanswered over this essay, which was read as a lecture to a St. Petersburg audience.

"Involuntarily, the questions arise: surely one does not have to be mad to believe in truth? and surely a mind that has gained control over itself does not thereby lose all its power?"[28] Turgenev saw no escape from the tragic paradox to which his generation's quest for self-knowledge had led them. Their iconoclasm had been motivated by the search for a faith that would withstand their destructive critique, but that critique had led them to an awareness of insoluble contradictions between their aspirations and their human condition. They had emerged from their reflections as "superfluous people," incapable of wholehearted commitment to any goal. The unattractive features of this self-absorbed type (on which Turgenev concentrates with masochistic eloquence) are redeemed in his eyes by the suffering that results from their self-knowledge.

Turgenev's novels and stories present a gallery of such people who had sought to decode the mystery of their existence with the help of German philosophy.[29] The most clear-sighted arrive at a resigned acceptance of their defeat, such as "The Hamlet of Shchigrov District." In his youth, this incompetent, impoverished, and embittered landowner in the remote Russian steppe goes to Berlin with other seekers after philosophical truth. But his studies sap his spontaneity and initiative, leaving him only with the habit of sterile meditation on a question to which no answer was forthcoming: what is the relevance of Hegel's *Encyclopedia* to Russian life? German philosophy having failed to provide guidance to the conduct of life on the Russian steppe, he reflects that he would have done better to have stayed at home and studied his environment firsthand: its demands, and his own calling, might then have become clear. But here, too, is an insuperable problem: "I would be happy to take lessons from Russian life, but see here, my good fellow, it will not speak."[30]

With no clear focus for his energies, the Shchigrov Hamlet sinks into lethargy and self-contempt. Nonetheless he is portrayed as a person of greater integrity than those who wrest a meaning from the Russian silence that satisfies their need for certainties. Turgenev's former mentor Bakunin was a model for the antihero of his novel *Rudin*, who persuades the young members of his circle that history has prepared for them some marvelous destiny, yet to be revealed. To his enchanted listeners, "Nothing remained senseless or accidental; everything evinced rational necessity and beauty . . . and we ourselves, with a kind of worshipful awe, with a sweet quivering of our hearts, felt as though we were living vessels of eternal truth, its instruments, called to accomplish something great."[31]

Rudin grows in stature at the end of the novel when, his grandiose aspirations having been defeated by the prose of Russian reality, he comes to recognize, like Turgenev himself, that "there is no firm ground beneath one's feet": his certainties have been stripped away until he realizes that he does not even possess a coherent sense of self. How can one build anything, he asks, "when one has yet to construct one's own foundations?"[32]

For a brief period, Turgenev had found an answer to this question in the great project of the Emancipation, officially announced in December 1857. He followed its progress with intense interest from abroad and composed a memorandum on the setting up of a new journal to discuss questions connected with the reform. But his proposal was deemed "premature" by the authorities and had to be abandoned. During three long visits to Russia between 1858 and 1861, he began preparations to transform the peasants on his estate into free workers. He soon discovered that his peasants interpreted the coming freedom as a license to plunder a master they need no longer fear. Although the frustrations of that period made him sharply critical of all those whom he suspected of idealizing the muzhik, he continued to place high hopes on the reform. Together with the critic Pavel Annenkov, he drew up a project for the dissemination of literacy in the countryside; this, too, was blocked by a government opposed to all initiatives but its own. When the Emancipation took place and it began to seem clear that the immediate disadvantages to the peasants outweighed the benefits, Turgenev's disenchantment was swift: he showed little interest in the reforms that followed, such as the introduction of a framework for local government and the reform of the legal system. The populists' faith in the socialist potential of the peasant commune, Slavophile and Pan-Slavist theories of the special historical calling of the Russian nation, and the liberals' insistence that its destiny was merely to follow the path of the West all seemed to him deluded efforts to read a sense into the Russian silence. In a letter to Annenkov in the spring of 1862 he comments on the feverish atmosphere in St. Petersburg, where the Slavophiles preached Russia's spiritual mission in their periodical *Day,* the radical leader Nikolai Chernyshevsky was hissed by liberal writers, and the prominent professor of law and self-styled "liberal conservative" Boris Chicherin was reviled by the progressives for urging the authorities to crush dissent in the universities: "They all whirl before one's eyes like faces in a *danse macabre,* while there below them, like a dark background to the picture, is the people-sphinx."[33]

There was no place for Turgenev in this dance. His distrust of all salvationary formulas and systems made it impossible for him to identify with any group or party in the immediate post-Emancipation period. He was repelled by the doctrinairism of the Hegelian school of etatist liberals represented by Chicherin and the historian Konstantin Kavelin. Unlike them, he foresaw only a "modest" civilizing role for the educated classes.[34] On the question of the significance of the peasant commune, he thought their views of less value than those of the Slavophiles. Kavelin's theory that the commune represented a primitive stage in a historically determined progression towards Hegel's ideal of the rational state was, he wrote to the Slavophile Konstantin Aksakov, an "artificial" construction "somehow reminiscent of our long-past gymnastic exercises in the philosophical arena." Like Herzen, Turgenev believed that the Slavophiles had helped bring the Russian intelligentsia down from the sterile heights of metaphysical speculation to an acquaintance with the humble realities of their national life. But, although the Slavophiles' study of Russian history had revealed much that was "interesting and new," he could not agree with their conclusions: "You paint a true picture, and then . . . exclaim—'How beautiful all this is!' "[35] To see poetic meaning in the brutalized state of the Russian people was as absurd as to believe that the latter were on the point of a dialectical emergence into the light of the rational state—or on the eve of a revolutionary apotheosis. His novel *Fathers and Children* (1861) depicted the liberal fathers as ineffectual and the radical sons as narrow and doctrinaire. Both sides took deep offence. Equally evenhanded, his next novel, *Smoke*, portrayed a selection of Russian courtiers, bureaucrats, and revolutionaries—all of whom were stupid, hypocritical, and self-seeking. As a result, he notes, he was attacked with an unprecedented unanimity: "Stones are flying at me from all sides."[36] Before the publication in 1876 of his last novel, he wrote to a friend: "If for *Fathers and Children* I was beaten with sticks, for *Virgin Soil* I will be beaten with staves—and in just the same way, by both sides."[37] The reactionary nationalism which grew apace in Russia after the defeat of the Polish rising of 1863 was also a target for Turgenev's satire, together with all the elements of what he called the "Moscow swamp": "Orthodoxy, nobility, Slavophilism, gossip, the Arbat, Katkov, Antonina Bludova,[38] ignorance, self-opinionatedness, haughty manners, the arrogance of officers, hostility to everything foreign, sour cabbage soup, the absence of soap—in a word, chaos!"[39]

In 1867, when the Slavic Ethnographic Exhibition in Moscow was the subject of passionate excitement in nationalist circles, Turgenev published a carefully timed defense of Western values.[40] It is put into the mouth of the ardent Westernizer Potugin in *Smoke*, who declares his devotion to Europe and the word *civilization*: "Everyone understands it, it is pure and sacred, while all the others, the national idea [*narodnost*] for example, the idea of glory, smell of blood."[41] But despite Potugin's inordinate long-windedness, it is not easy to understand precisely what he or Turgenev mean by civilization. The concept excludes all native Russian traditions, collectively dismissed as barbarous, and encompasses the science, art, and social institutions of the West, which Potugin deems to embody and promote the values of disciplined work, independence, and personal dignity. He insists that Russia's only hope of salvation is imitation of the West, but no program of action is specified, and the virtues he extols are conspicuously absent from the society of Baden-Baden, where much of the action takes place and which provides a congenial environment for members of the Russian gentry who describe themselves as liberals and have their peasants whipped back at home. Potugin's speeches have the false ring of propaganda aimed at rallying troops to a flagging cause. The author's authentic voice is to be found elsewhere in the novel, in the passage which unlocks the title's meaning. His hero, Litvinov, on his way back to Russia to embark on the kind of patient work that Potugin recommends, watches the cloud of smoke rising from the funnel of his train: "Suddenly it all seemed smoke to him, everything human and, above all, everything Russian. . . . Everything seemed to be constantly changing, new phenomena kept flashing past, but in essence everything was always the same, always in a hurry, racing to get somewhere, and always disappearing without trace, with nothing achieved. Another puff of wind, and everything rushes off in the opposite direction, again to commence the same ceaseless, agitated,—and unnecessary game."[42]

Schopenhauer (who uses the same metaphor for phenomenal existence) was in Turgenev's thoughts when he was composing this novel; his name appears in an early draft.[43] The influence of his ideas may be detected behind Turgenev's comments on the erotic passion that destroys his hero's hopes of personal happiness: "Down-to-earth people like Litvinov should not be carried away by passion—it destroys the very meaning of their lives. . . . But nature does not come to terms with logic, with our, human, logic. She has her own, which we neither understand nor recognize, until it crushes us under its wheel."[44]

Once, when asked to summarize his outlook, Turgenev described himself as a realist who sought to convey the "living truth" of human nature, believed neither in absolutes nor systems, and loved freedom above all else.[45] But only the most platonic love of freedom was compatible with the kind of realism represented by the dominant metaphor of Smoke. In 1849, like Herzen, Turgenev had seen on all sides only cankered senility or barbarous infancy; but unlike Herzen, he had desperately wished to believe in the capacity of the former to civilize the latter. Closer acquaintance with Russia's would-be civilizers, however, only confirmed the despairing view of the human condition that he expressed in "Enough" and Smoke. That novel was conceived during the most intense phase of his debates with Herzen over Russia's future. As his country whirled through the danse macabre of the 1860s, he sought to persuade Herzen that he avoided a similar despair only through the impermissible stratagem of utopian hope.

❋

The relationship between Turgenev and Herzen dates from the months Turgenev spent in Paris in 1848–49, when he became a friend of the Herzen family. The two corresponded intermittently in the 1850s and met twice in London (where Herzen had set up his Free Russian Press in 1853 in order to provide his compatriots with a forum for political discussion); their last such encounter was in 1862. Each admired the other's humanism; Herzen welcomed Turgenev's *Sketches from a Sportsman's Notebook* (published in collected form in 1852) as a powerful attack on serfdom. Both were intensely interested in their generation's habit of introspection (described by Turgenev as "our strength and our weakness, our downfall and our salvation");[46] they valued each other's insights into the tensions between the Russian radicals' iconoclasm and their need for faith. Herzen sent Turgenev chapters of his memoirs for comment, while Turgenev sent him drafts of his works. Their affinity was based above all on their common suspicion of doctrines, systems, and utopian faiths, which led both to distance themselves from all the political groups and ideologies that began to take shape in the first years of the new reign. But their natural sympathies lay with opposing camps, and the polarization of liberal and radical forces in Russia of the early 1860s would lead to a break between them.

After Turgenev's first visit to him in London in 1856, Herzen published an essay in the form of a letter to an unnamed friend, responding to Turgenev's criticism of the socialist propaganda of his immensely influential periodical *The Bell*. He had been accused, he wrote, of pointing to the defects of Western constitutional liberalism and thus undermining the faith in enlightened values so necessary to Russia at that juncture; his critics also claimed that by stressing the potential of the Russian peasant commune, he was echoing the romantic utopianism of the Slavophiles. In response, Herzen pointed to the deepening antagonisms in European societies and their failure to heal the wounds of 1848. He recapitulated the grounds for his belief in the possibility of a separate path for Russia: first, the absence of an entrenched economic and legal order supported by a strong middle class; and second, the survival of the commune with its democratic institutions, whose development with the help of Western technology might allow Russia to pass to an advanced form of socialism without the large-scale industrialization whose human cost had proved so terrible in the West.[47]

Five years later, in *The Bell*, Herzen published an extended reply to Turgenev, a cycle of essays entitled "Ends and Beginnings." Addressed once again to an unnamed friend, they were prompted by a second series of discussions which took place during Turgenev's visit to London in the latter half of May

1862. Their content can be deduced from Turgenev's letter to a mutual acquaintance noting that his main objection to the platform of Herzen and his co-editor, Nikolai Ogarev, was that "while despising the educated class in Russia, almost trampling it in the mud, they assume the existence of revolutionary or reforming principles in the people; in fact, quite the opposite is the case."[48] The capacity and motivation for genuine reform, he believed, existed only in a minority of the educated elite, by whom Turgenev meant those Westernizers who, like himself, were committed to civilized and liberal values.

"Ends and Beginnings" takes issue with Turgenev's view of contemporary Europe as a model for emulation. Herzen argues that those aspects of Europe's art and culture dearest to them both were products of its past. He cites John Stuart Mill's critique of the drive to standardization and rationalization in modern bourgeois democracies with the concomitant growth of a moral conformism hostile to originality, diversity, and creative experimentation (the "aesthetic element" of social existence), all of which seemed to be inexorably leading to domination by a "collective mediocrity" enforced by the tyranny of the crowd.[49] Herzen suggests that with the advent of the bourgeois state, European civilization has reached a settled equilibrium, a safe haven to which all Western nations aspired after the upheavals of the past. He contends that this was its attraction for Turgenev: he was no more enamored than Herzen of the hypocrisies, inequities, and limited horizons of the political culture he defended, but like the French liberal intellectuals of 1848, he valued its power to repress the discordant forces that threatened an ordered life. Pronouncing this view prudent but fainthearted, Herzen declares his own intention to pursue the dream he has glimpsed in the Russian fog: the possibility of a wholly new kind of society, an advanced form of socialism to be achieved by developing the potential of the peasant commune.

Turgenev had intended to publish a response to "Ends and Beginnings" in *The Bell*, but, preempted by an official warning not to contribute to a publication banned in Russia, he was constrained to conduct his side of the polemic in private responses to the essays as they appeared.

In one such letter, he protests that Herzen has misrepresented his position. His allegiance to Western political and civic principles is motivated by neither hedonism nor weariness but by the conviction that it is the duty of the educated class to acquaint the people with Western culture; it will then be up to the people itself to decide what parts of that culture it should accept.[50] He concentrated his attack on Herzen in one main volley: a letter of 8 November 1862, in which he congratulates his friend on his analysis of contemporary mankind:

But why does this have to be *western* mankind and not "bi-
pedes" in general? You are like a doctor who having analysed all
the symptoms of a chronic illness, announces that the cause of
all the trouble is that the patient is a Frenchman. An enemy of
mysticism and absolutes, you mystically abase yourself before
the Russian sheepskin coat and see in it a great paradise, the
new and original social forms of the future—*das Absolute,* in a
word; that same *Absolute* that you make such fun of in philosophy. All your idols have been shattered, but one cannot live
without an idol, so let's raise an altar to this new, unknown god
. . . and once again one can pray, and believe, and wait. . . .
History, philology, statistics—all count for nothing with you:
facts count for nothing—not even, for instance, that indubitable fact that we Russians belong linguistically and racially to
the European family, "genus Europaeum," and consequently, by
the invariant laws of physiology, must proceed along the same
path. I have yet to hear of a *duck* which, belonging to the genus *duck,* breathed through gills like a fish.[51]

Although penetrating in its sense of the tension between Herzen's skepticism and his faith, Turgenev's attack on his friend's "idols" has a gloomy dogmatism of its own. He contends that the Russian people's aims and ideals are
as yet unknowable, yet he is confident they do not include those positive tendencies that Herzen has discerned. It is notable that he finds fault not with
Herzen's diagnosis of the moral and aesthetic decline of modern culture but
with his view that this process may not be universal or irreversible. As an antidote to Herzen's hopes about Russia's future, he suggests: "Schopenhauer,
my friend, you should read Schopenhauer more attentively."[52]

Turgenev's reference to the "invariant laws of physiology" prompted Herzen
in his concluding essay to accuse him of the doctrinaire determinism which he,
Turgenev, was so quick to criticize in others. In physiology, Herzen points out,
the general plan of development permits endless unforeseen deviations, such
as the trunk of the elephant and the hump of the camel. The "genus Europaeum" contained peoples who had grown old without fully developing a
bourgeoisie; there were others "whom the *bourgeois* system suits as water suits
gills. So why should there not be a nation for whom the *bourgeois* system will
be a transitory and unsatisfactory condition, like gills for a duck?" Why should
it be "a wicked heresy, a defection from my own principles, and from the immutable laws of creation and the rules and doctrines, human and divine" not
to regard the bourgeois state as the final and predestined form of Russian so-

ciety? A historical accident, a change of environment, could combine in un-expected ways with old traditions and habits to set a people off on a new trajectory of development. In the United States, a new breed of the "European variety" had been formed before our eyes, Herzen noted. If fresh soil sufficed to make a new nation out of established peoples, why should a nation that had developed under conditions completely different from those of Western European states repeat Europe's past—"and that, too, when it knows perfectly well what that past leads to?" It was to be expected that the government sought to impose its autocratic straitjacket on the aspirations of the Russian people; but now we had the liberal intelligentsia "preaching to us that such is the im-mutable law of physiology, that we all belong to the *genus europaeum* and must therefore cut all the old capers to a new tune."[53] On the contrary, the fact that Russia evolved late and separately from the rest of Europe made it likely that it would develop structures of its own, "under the influence of the past and of borrowings, of its neighbours' examples and of its own angle of reflection."[54]

Both men claimed that their respective views on Russia's native potential were based on empirical evidence, but Turgenev's November letter had rather weakened his case in this regard. He had recommended the study of Schopen-hauer; replying in a private letter, Herzen suggests that he has thereby revealed the authority behind his tirade against the "Russian Messiah": "a nihilistic ide-alist, buddhist and philosopher of death." Had Turgenev noticed that under that blighting influence he, too, was becoming a nihilist? Turgenev had been accused of insulting the young generation by his use of that term in *Fathers and Children* to denote their rejection of established values; Herzen remarks on the contrast between their "nihilism of *energy and anger*" and "the most utter ni-hilism of *exhaustion and despair*" expressed in Turgenev's letter.[55] Some years later, reflecting on the social significance of Turgenev's novel, he elaborated on this distinction:

> Nihilism . . . is logic without structure, it is science without dogma, it is unconditional submission to experience and re-signed acceptance of all consequences, whatever they may be, if they follow from observation or are required by reason. Nihilism does not transform something into nothing, but shows that a nothing that has been taken for a something is an optical illu-sion, and that every truth, however much it contradicts our fan-tastic imaginings, is more wholesome than they are, and is in any case what we are in duty bound to accept. . . .
>
>   Of course, if by Nihilism we are to understand . . . the turn-ing of facts and thoughts into nothing, into barren scepticism, into haughty folding of the arms, into the despair which leads

> to inaction, then . . . one of the greatest Nihilists will be Turge-
> nev, . . . and another will be perhaps his favourite philosopher,
> Schopenhauer.[56]

A "haughty folding of the arms" was the stance recommended by the narrator of "Enough," on which Turgenev had begun working while "Ends and
Beginnings" was being published; the narrator's tirade against history's
monotonous repetitiveness can be read as an oblique response to Herzen's
hopes of new beginnings (the first manuscript of the story is headed "Some Letters without Beginning or End"). Toward the end of his life, Turgenev confided
to his publisher, M. M. Stasiulevich, that he regretted the publication of that
work, which "expressed memories and impressions that were so *personal* that
there was no need to share them with a public."[57] He expressed no such misgiv-
ings about *Smoke,* but the pessimism of that novel (which seems to have been
conceived in part as a response to the propaganda of *The Bell*) is relieved by its
ambivalences.[58] There is no note of hope in "Enough": hence Turgenev's admission to Stasiulevich that he would be "horrified" if the story were to resur-
face; fortunately, he observes, it had aroused no general attention at the time.[59]

Indeed, only Herzen had shown a discomforting interest in exploring the
contradictions between Turgenev's private philosophy and his public defense
of liberal values. But on this question Turgenev refused to be drawn. He rejects
Herzen's charge that he regards his country with nihilistic despair: "I see a
tragic side to the fate of *all* the *European* family (including, of course, Russia)."
Even so, this still does not make him a nihilist: "I'm nevertheless a European—
and I love the banner, I believe in the banner under which I came to stand in
my youth."[60]

This was Turgenev's parting shot in a debate which has been commonly interpreted as a robust and straightforward defense of the principles of freedom
embodied in Western democracies against a misty vision of a messiah in a
sheepskin coat.[61] Few commentators have echoed Herzen's awkward questions
as to what precisely political freedom and progress meant to a man who saw
the most perfect symbol of human existence in the image of flies beating themselves against a pane of glass. When the final letter of "Ends and Beginnings"
mocked the stultifying determinism of Turgenev's concept of the "invariant
laws of physiology," he did not protest. He could hardly have done so. "Old
Goethe was right: der Mensch (der *europäische* Mensch) ist nicht geboren frei
zu sein," he would remind Herzen when they resumed their correspondence in
1867, after a gap. He was prepared to concede that the European Peter was at

death's door, but it did not follow that the Russian Ivan was in any better shape.[62] This was the tragedy referred to in his deeply ambivalent confession of faith in the European banner: the pettiness and futility of the mass of human aspirations and achievements (not least those of the contemporary Western bourgeoisie) were part of an immutable cosmic order that stood in profound opposition to the values of the creative few. Not even the greatest achievements of reason and science had the power to release humanity from its suffocating sack and move history in new and unpredictable directions. As Herzen had suggested at the outset of their debate, Turgenev's commitment to the culture and institutions of Western Europe was principally motivated not by hope but by fear of something worse: he believed that however corrupt and unjust it might be, the order at which Western European states had arrived represented the best form of protection yet devised against the blind, deterministic forces that shape human lives. But he would have agreed with Schopenhauer on the pathetic inadequacy of any such protection: that human happiness is a "hollow, deceptive, frail, and wretched thing, out of which neither constitutions, legal systems, steam-engines, nor telegraphs can ever make anything that is essentially better."[63]

Turgenev had been irritated by Herzen's reference to his idealism: he had done no more than "*mention*" Schopenhauer yet was accused of bowing to his authority.[64] Rightly, he felt vulnerable on this point. It may seem odd that Herzen did not probe more deeply, and more publicly, into the intellectual premises of an opponent who had recommended that he cure his tendency to idealize reality by an immersion in German metaphysics, but to discuss Turgenev's personal philosophy in print would have been to identify his opponent. It is possible, however, to reconstruct the debate on first principles that was forestalled by the Russian police and by Turgenev's evasions: in one sense, it had already taken place. As expressed in his published works, and (more frankly) in his private correspondence, Turgenev's vision of the sameness and absurdity of the historical process is identical in all significant respects with that of Herzen's opponent in two dialogues of *From the Other Shore:* an idealist who, driven to despair by the catastrophes of 1848, concludes that if history is not the progressive realization of human ideals, "then our whole civilisation is a lie . . . our labours are absurd, our efforts ludicrous." The life of peoples becomes "mere idle play. . . . It was not for nothing that Shakespeare said that history was a tale told by an idiot, signifying nothing."[65]

Turgenev would cite the same line from *Macbeth* in the course of a similar tirade against what he described as history's "unnecessary game."[66] The same bleak view is behind the advice with which he concluded his November letter to Herzen: "Have the courage to look the devil *in both eyes,*" seeking no exemptions for any nation from the common fate of humanity. But in Herzen's two dialogues of 1849, the charge of cowardice was thrown back at his opponent: there was nothing admirable in retreating from a world that would not dance to one's tune. Instead of bewailing the chance forces that frustrate our heart's desires, we should cease to yearn to be what we are not, accept the contingent nature of all life, and adapt our purposes to it. Elsewhere in the same work Herzen notes that the search for an absolute meaning and a final goal in finite existence leads logically to utter nihilism: "If one looks for the final aim, then the purpose of everything living is—death."[67]

This was precisely the conclusion that Turgenev had reached with the help of the "philosopher of death" for whom the march of history was a funeral procession. Schopenhauer views physical existence as "only a constantly prevented dying, an ever-deferred death. . . . Every breath we draw wards off the death that constantly impinges on us. . . . Ultimately death must triumph, for by birth it has already become our lot, and it plays with its prey only for a while before swallowing it up."[68]

"Death is like a fisherman who has taken a fish in his net and leaves it in the water for a while. The fish continues to swim, but the net is on it and the fisherman will take it when he wants."[69] So wrote Turgenev in *On the Eve.* The "sentence of condemnation" which, as Schopenhauer observes, nature imposes on every will to live, was for Turgenev the most immediate of realities.[70] From the mid-1850s he poured out his despair in letters to intimate friends. Life cannot be other than a tragedy: after all, "we are all condemned to death— you could hardly have anything more tragic than that!"[71] Life is a fortress, constantly besieged by death; the inevitability of the outcome deprives the battle of its interest.[72] Life, according to Schopenhauer, "swings like a pendulum to and fro between pain and boredom";[73] Turgenev's most intimate letters, written over three decades, do much the same. *Taedium vitae,* the intrinsic worthlessness of an existence imminently to be annulled by death, is their dominant theme. To Countess Lambert, one of his closest confidantes, he confesses that his life is dominated by "the presence of one constant thought: the vanity of all earthly things and the nearness of something that I cannot name." When the pious countess accuses him of an excessive attachment to material existence, he regrets that she is mistaken: "If I have still not been able to make mental contact with things not of this earth, then *everything* that is of this earth has *long* since deserted me, and I find myself in some sort of void, misty and oppressive. . . . [Life] slithers away from me like a snake—there's no way I can catch hold of it—small hope, when I can't even get a glimpse of its shape, arrive at some idea of what it means! Meanwhile the days race by swiftly and sluggishly: these epithets are not often found side by side—but that's the way it is, nevertheless."[74]

In a grim travesty of Romantic yearning, empirical existence comes to have less substance and reality for him than its mysterious end. In January 1861, when all Russia was in a ferment of anticipation, he describes a mood of dull lethargy that frequently comes upon him: "Three months have gone by like smoke from a chimney, floating past in grayish puffs, all seemingly different, yet all monotonously the same."[75] At such times the battles between parties, opinions, and ideas appear to him, in a phrase from the poet Tiutchev which he was fond of quoting, as "a shadow cast by smoke."[76] He now focuses his utopian yearnings on remembered time. To Countess Lambert he writes: "All my life is in the past, and the present is dear to me only as a reflection of that past. . . . But what, in fact, was so particularly good about that past? Hope, the possibility of hoping, that is, the future. This sounds like a play on words; but that is just the way it is. Human life goes by just like that, *entre ces deux chaises*."[77]

By devaluing the present, Turgenev's philosophy saps creativity and purpose. At the age of forty, he told Lev Tolstoy of his sense that "my life has passed and yet at the same time, I have the feeling that it has not yet begun,— that I have still to face the indeterminateness of youth, along with all the sterile emptiness of old age." Only one thing attaches him to the present: his "living love of Good and Beauty."[78] But even these values are suspect. Like Schopenhauer, he sees consciousness as an illness, a pathological deviation from the universal order of things; hence all those aspects of culture in which humanity has enshrined its highest goods—philosophy, science, morality, art, poetry— are nothing other than sedatives, "*des palliatifs,*" against the pain of unfiltered reality and the horror of final extinction.[79] He regrets that the most "precious" of such remedies—religious faith—is not available to all. While counting it as his "personal misfortune" not to be a believer, he nonetheless insists that his philosophy is not a matter of individual temperament but rather the conclusion to which any developed and reflecting individual is inescapably led, once he renounces beliefs unsupported by empirical evidence.[80]

In the last years of his life, Turgenev's pessimism came increasingly to dominate his fiction. The first pages of his novella *Spring Torrents* read like a distillation of Schopenhauer's views on the vanity of life in the face of all-destroying death.[81] The most Schopenhauerian of all his works are the prose poems, written between 1877 and 1882, only some of which were published in his lifetime. Here the dominant tone is resignation, a search for remission from the suffering of existence through recourse to three "palliatifs": artistic creation and contemplation, self-forgetful compassion with all that lives and suffers, and annihilation of the "burdensome and odious ego" through ascetic denial of the will.[82] In 1877 he wrote to Gustave Flaubert: "Après quarante ans, il n'y a qu'un seul mot qui compose le fond de la vie: renoncer" (After forty years, I find only one word to constitute the essence of life: renunciation).[83]

Here, then, is the "nihilism of weariness and despair" that Herzen discerned behind Turgenev's profession of faith in Western values. Only to his most trusted correspondents does he give frank expression to his lack of hope in the improvement of the human condition. Garibaldi's campaign for Italian independence inspires this comment to Countess Lambert: "So there is still enthusiasm on this earth? People can still sacrifice themselves, rejoice, behave like madmen, be filled with hope? I'd like at least to take a look and see how it is done." But, he reflects, it would be too late: what passion he still had now flowed into his writing.[84] It was passion of a very masochistic sort: "Hamlet and Don Quixote" (on which he was working when he made this comment) presents humanity with a choice between deluded hope and clear-sighted awareness of the pathological deformity of human nature.

As Herzen makes clear in his definition of their respective forms of nihilism, he sees Turgenev's dilemma as self-imposed. The despair he represents as the lot of all self-awareness is merely the result of the haughty rejection of a world which contradicts our "fantastic imaginings." Like the disappointed idealist in *From the Other Shore,* he has chosen to play a stock role which was once tragic but is fast becoming ridiculous.

Herzen's insights into the psychology behind Turgenev's anguished self-questioning help to explain why that anguish so curiously fails to move. Turgenev's public image of pragmatic moderation concealed another persona, considerably more querulous and less mature, one bent on punishing a world that had deceived his immoderate expectations by denying it all value and meaning. He was right to have been nervous about having exposed that side of himself in "Enough": Dostoevsky would lampoon that work in *The Possessed,* in his cruel satire of Turgenev as the fashionable and self-important author Karmazinov, who struts before his audience, declaiming his farewell to the world: "Merci! Merci! Merci!"[85]

Herzen was right, too, in suggesting that cosmic pessimism played a much greater role than pragmatic considerations in Turgenev's opposition to the notion of a separate path of development for Russia. We have seen him vague in his affirmation of Western civilization, but dogmatic in his insistence that Russia had no indigenous political or cultural potential. When the government (together with most liberal opinion) moved decisively to the Right in the 1870s, Turgenev became increasingly sympathetic to the personalities of the young radicals, though not to their cause, which, he declared, "is so false that it cannot fail to lead to a total fiasco."[86] Pyotr Lavrov, one of the leaders of the radical émigré community to which Turgenev gave generous financial and moral support in the last years of his life, later summed up Turgenev's attitude toward Russian politics: "scepticism as to the possibility of anything really useful for

Russia emerging from the activities of anyone at all—government, liberals or revolutionaries." The welcome he gave to promising developments was nothing in comparison with the force of his attacks on whatever deceived his "fleeting hopes."[87] Nevertheless, the young radicals were grateful for his sympathy and gave him a touching welcome when he visited Moscow in 1879. But what they mistook for support was a mixture of pity, aesthetic admiration, and envy of those who were secure in a simple faith. He confides to Annenkov that his feelings for the radical youth can be expressed in one word—"compassion."[88] By that word he meant, like Schopenhauer, an identification with all that is condemned to the futility of finite existence. In one of the *Prose Poems* composed at that period he writes:

> I pity myself, others, . . . everything that lives. . . .
> I pity the murderer and his victim, ugliness and beauty, the oppressor and the oppressed. . . .
> O boredom, boredom, melting into pity! Man can sink no lower.[89]

The year before Turgenev died, he made this comment to a friend concerning his *Prose Poems:* "The public and the critics will greet them with indifference, or contempt; but that won't cause me any grief."[90] During his last years he became increasingly immune to criticism of the ideological content of his work. In a memoir on the controversy aroused by his novel *Fathers and Children,* he belatedly admits to the charge he had denied so indignantly in his correspondence with Herzen a few years before. He recalls that one woman had remarked to him that the book's title should have been *Neither Fathers nor Children:* "and you're a nihilist yourself!" Perhaps she was right, he reflects: "Everyone who is in the business of writing (I'm judging by myself), writes not what he wants to write, but what he has in him to express."[91]

Turgenev viewed his position vis-à-vis Herzen as that of an artist who expressed the truth as he saw it in defiance of ideological correctness. Herzen, he believed, had betrayed his artistic vision by suppressing those of his insights into the human condition that did not coincide with the theories of Russian socialism. But, as Herzen points out in "Ends and Beginnings," the question of the importance of art and the creative imagination ("our only indubitable good") was never an issue between them. Both rejected the notion of a predetermined pattern or purpose in history or human life and consequently gave a central role to aesthetic sensibility in interpreting the flow of experience: hence Herzen's celebrated comment in *From the Other Shore* that the truly free person "*creates* his own morality," guided by an aesthetic sense of relationships.[92]

His view of the relations between the aesthetic and moral realms is close to that of Schiller's treatise on aesthetic education, which he had hailed in the 1840s as a "prophetic" work.[93] Like Schiller, he called for the cultivation of a sense of harmony and proportion, based on an approach to phenomena as "living form," in the belief that an aesthetic delight in the "play" of contingent existence was a necessary corrective to the universalizing and systematizing drives of reason.[94] Here was the root of his differences with Turgenev: he saw the dominant role of chance in history not as a cause for cosmic pessimism but rather as an invigorating challenge to our capacity for creative improvization.

Turgenev's polemic with Herzen was conducted on a terrain that is now familiar to us. Thinking on culture and society has become increasingly skeptical of all attempts to comprehend history in rational and purposive terms and has fallen back on aesthetic models and analogues to describe a world and a self perceived as fluid and fragmentary, reinterpreting traditional notions of truth, knowledge, rationality, and progress as metaphors used to justify pragmatic practices. But at its most sophisticated and innovative, such criticism has tended to become an infinitely regressive process of deconstruction, an end in itself detached from practical moral concerns and the search for wisdom that was once philosophy's raison d'être. As Bernard Williams has observed, self-consciousness and reflective self-awareness, "when made into *the* distinctive attitude of a sophisticated philosophy, make it revolve ever faster; the owl of Minerva, robbed by later scepticism of Hegel's flight plan to the transcendental standpoint, notoriously finds itself flying in ever-decreasing circles."[95]

By the standards of the late twentieth century, Turgenev's debate with Herzen on the nature of history lacks sophistication, but it compensates for this in the depth and sharpness of its moral focus. Both participants had precise reasons for rejecting Hegel's flight plan: first in Russia and then in Europe, they had witnessed and recorded the ways providentialist visions of the world justified suffering, oppression, and violence and, by encouraging escapist fantasies and unreal hopes, provoked catastrophes such as that of 1848. Each, casting around for new ways of formulating the problem of moral and political freedom, had found inspiration in a thinker whose philosophy had sprung from similar practical moral concerns: Schopenhauer's view of the self was a challenge to the "wickedness" of optimistic theodicies, whereas Schiller's had been developed in opposition to the rigid rationalism that he held responsible for some of the worst excesses of the French Terror. Both innovatory in their stress on the importance of irrational drives in determining human purposes, these two thinkers diverged radically in their view of the relation between those drives and the moral consciousness—as did Turgenev and Herzen. The distinctive qualities of Turgenev's aesthetic nihilism emerge with particular clarity if one approaches his debate with Herzen as a head-on collision between a Schopenhauerian and a Schillerian view of the relation of the self to the world.

Schiller and Schopenhauer both gave central importance to aesthetic awareness as a means of transcending the limitations of our ordinary modes of perception. In Schopenhauer's famous phrase, when consciousness, detached from its everyday interests and goals, is given up to aesthetic contemplation, "we celebrate the Sabbath of the penal servitude of willing."[96]

Schopenhauer's concept of will-less contemplation echoes Schiller's description of the "play-drive" activated by the contemplation of beauty, which releases us from the dominion of those drives under whose compulsion we engage in goal-directed activity. But there the resemblance ends. Schiller maintains that, by uniting our intellectual faculties with the "blind" life of feeling, aesthetic awareness reveals to us the compatibility of these aspects of our nature and thereby "the practicability of the infinite being realised in the finite," the possibility of attaining a state of freedom in the world of everyday experience.[97] Beauty can transform the world by restoring us to it as integrated human beings, masters, to an equal degree, of all our powers. This state of equilibrium is momentary but provides us with a model for our relations with our human and physical environments, teaching us to balance principles with the demands of sense, releasing us from subservience to universal prescriptions, and enriching our responses to the contingent and the particular as the material for the creation of a unique moral self. The goal of an aesthetic education is to deepen and secure our sense of moral autonomy by teaching us to see that virtuous behavior consists not in strict conformity to universal laws and norms but in appropriate and sensitive responses to the needs of specific individuals and situations.

Schopenhauer, on the other hand, held that by penetrating to the inner, unchanging nature of being, aesthetic contemplation inculcates a horror of the contingent. Our pleasure in the sublime weakens our ties with phenomenal existence: "We feel ourselves urged . . . to give up willing and loving life." The highest degree of this feeling is achieved through tragic catastrophe: by presenting to us "the terrible side of life . . . the wailing and lamentation of mankind, the dominion of chance and error," tragedy brings with it the dawning of the knowledge that the world and life "can afford us no true satisfaction, and are therefore not worth our attachment to them."[98] For the same reason Schopenhauer sees the summit of pictorial art in the masterpieces of Raphael or Correggio, whose countenances of saints reflect the "perfect resignation" that follows on the surrender of the will. An appreciation of art prepares us for that awakening from the "long, heavy, confused dream" of existence in the world of phenomena[99] by giving us a knowledge of the changelessness of the inmost nature of the world and the self, it cures us of the restless and futile striving to become other than what we are and teaches us how to carry out the role dictated by our given characters "artistically and methodically, with firmness and grace."[100]

The aesthetic education that Schiller envisaged was intended to overcome the separation between aesthetic discourse and political and historical processes through the development of insights that could heal the divisions in modern societies. Schopenhauer sees the poet's and the historian's concerns as irreconcilable. The poet apprehends "the Idea, the inner being of mankind outside all relation and all time." The historian "must look at everything according to its relation, its concatenation, its influence on what follows, and especially on its own times." His material is found in "the transient complexities of a human world moving like clouds in the wind, which are often entirely transformed by the most trifling accident," scarcely worthy of the serious attention of the mind, which "should select for its consideration that which is destined never to pass away." Schiller's aesthetic education is designed to teach us to value "content"—the transient, unrepeatable forms of life in their multiplicity and diversity—as much as "form"; to Schopenhauer, it is self-evident that "the individual thing, in its individuality and contingency," is valueless: "this thing exists once, and then exists no more for ever." As manifestations of the phenomenal will, plurality and multiplicity are irredeemably malign: "Diversity of all beings, individuality, egoism, hatred, wickedness, all spring from *one* root." Schiller asks that we learn to exploit our contingency creatively. Schopenhauer reviles chance as a blind and malevolent force whose "constant interference" muddies our perception of the universal patterns of existence; "always bent on some mischievous trick," it mocks us by ensuring that, tragic though our existence is, "we cannot even assert the dignity of tragic characters, but, in the broad detail of life, are inevitably the foolish characters of a comedy."[101]

With his sweeping antitheses and schematic systems of dichotomies, Schopenhauer's "poet" is Schiller's "barbarian," in dire need of an aesthetic education that will moderate his "form-drive" and integrate it with the sensual sides of his nature. For all its insights into the workings of the will, Schopenhauer's system was far more bound by the past than Schiller's. His aesthetic ideal is built on traditional dualistic categories that he himself held to be suspect; Schiller dissolves them in the name of a radically new vision of moral autonomy.

Turgenev's and Herzen's respective visions of the self present a similar pattern of opposites. Turgenev conforms to the Schopenhauerian model of the artist, for whom creativity is a temporary escape from taedium vitae. He may have set out to be a "historian," depicting (as he once put it) "what Shakespeare calls 'the body and pressure of time,'" but he ended up as a "poet."[102] The characters in his novels all tend to conform to one of two eternal human types—Hamlet or Don Quixote, whose tragic conflicts bear witness to the tedious sameness of the historical process, that "market-place of phantoms" from which so many of his heroes and heroines retreat into quietistic resignation. Schopenhauer's ideas grafted smoothly onto the outlook of an artist schooled by the Russian idealist circles of the 1830s and 1840s to believe (like his alter ego in "Enough") that true values must lie beyond the corrupting reach of time. Herzen, on the other hand, had been centrally concerned from his earliest writings with the problem of the self-fulfillment of individuals in the here and now. Like Schiller, he had identified the main impediment to moral and political freedom as the belief that contingent phenomena and individual human beings derive their significance from timeless and universal principles and norms. The self-styled liberators of his time had mistaken the principal enemy, which was not just religion, monarchy, or the Right, but something much closer to home: the dualism that imbued all their values, judgments, and attitudes. Taking as his example Kant's view of virtue as successful self-coercion, Schiller had predicted that "philosophy . . . [will] lend her name to an oppression formerly authorised by the Church."[103] In *From the Other Shore* Herzen points to the moral confusion that has resulted from failure to scrutinize the concepts and categories with which we have made our transition to a desacralized world. Having discarded religion, "we have retained all the habits of religion," remaining faithful to that "perverted but completely consistent dialectic" that recognizes the infinite worth of the individual only for the purpose of destroying him the more solemnly in the name of some universal principle.[104]

Turgenev's inner struggles express precisely the kind of confusion that Herzen had in mind. It has been argued that Schopenhauerianism is not incompatible with liberalism: Schopenhauer ridiculed Hegelian notions of a supraindividual collective consciousness and regarded himself as a moderate liberal, defending the rule of law as a guarantee of individual rights.[105] But there are close analogies between Hegel's vision of the march of Spirit through history and Schopenhauer's doctrine of a noumenal will that determines all phenomenal existence. If one takes John Stuart Mill's defense of individual autonomy as a touchstone of true liberalism (admittedly a contentious view), then Turgenev's favorite philosopher will be seen to have drawn him in a very illiberal direction. He would (as he observed in a letter to Herzen) remain "an individualist until the end," irreconcilably opposed to the collectivist fantasies of socialists like Bakunin; yet he also yearned to be released from the burden of "the hated 'I.' "[106] Believing that a reflective consciousness must necessarily admit the impossibility of freedom and meaning in an irrational, purposeless world, he was consumed by an envious and undiscriminating fascination with forms of nonreflective spontaneity that shielded others from this horrible truth. Contingent existence is all "dust and ashes—and blessed is he who has not dropped anchor in those bottomless waves!" Those who lack faith "possess nothing"; among them he counts himself.[107] His attitude to the young Russian radicals whose trials he followed closely in the 1870s, and whose qualities he embodied in a series of literary figures, was complex: a liberal's revulsion against doctrinaire narrowness struggled in him with envy of those who had succeeded in "destroying" their ego through self-forgetful service to an ideal.[108] He confesses that his feelings about the radical hero of *Fathers and Children* "were confused (God knows whether I loved or hated him!)."[109] Critics of his novel had not understood his involuntary attraction to that character: they "do not suspect that pleasure of which Gogol speaks, and which consists in punishing oneself and one's own defects . . . through the imaginary types that one portrays."[110] His self-flagellation was intense: his fiction abounds in characters who, through wholehearted commitment to some passion or ideal, had achieved a harmony denied to him. Some (like Yelena in *On the Eve* and Natalia in *Rudin*) embody self-sacrificing love; others (Lavretsky and Liza in *A Nest of Gentlefolk,* Insarov in *On the Eve,* the woman terrorist in the prose poem "On the Threshold") serve a social ideal. Yet others (such as Maria Nikolaevna in *Spring Torrents*) are possessed by an elemental, predatory passion. As the Russian critic Mikhail Gershenzon has pointed out, no coherent moral message can be gleaned from Turgenev's fascination with all these varieties of inner harmony.[111] Whether displayed in the performance of austere duty or in the pursuit of selfish passion, unreflecting strength of purpose is presented as deeply desirable from the standpoint of those introspective personalities who occupy the foreground of his fiction. It is desired most intensely by Rudin, who preaches inspiringly on the sterility of skepticism and argues that life is worth living only when it is directed by a sense of destiny; but in his more introspective moments he admits that the unreflecting faith he so much admires is beyond his reach. "My fate is strange, almost comic—I am ready to surrender myself wholly and entirely, I thirst to do so—but I cannot. I will end by sacrificing myself for some rubbish in which I won't even believe." Turgenev once confessed that he had modeled Rudin partly on himself.[112] Herzen was unequivocal on this point, dismissing the common view that the principal model for Rudin had been Bakunin. "Turgenev," he wrote in his memoirs, "created Rudin in his own image and likeness."[113] Turgenev can be said to have recreated Herzen in the same image, projecting on to him the yearnings of a skeptic who had "grown sick of skepticism."

There is a curious passage in Turgenev's very ambivalent essay "Hamlet and

Don Quixote," where, having castigated the "mad," thoughtless enthusiasm of the latter type, he takes their side against the reflective Hamlets: "Who will take it on himself to say that always and in every case he will distinguish and has distinguished a barber's copper bowl from a magic golden helmet? Hence it seems to us that the most important thing is the sincerity and force of the conviction itself,—the result is in the hands of fate. The fates alone can tell us whether we have been fighting phantoms or real enemies, and with what armour we covered our heads. Our business is to take up arms and fight."[114]

Here Turgenev seems to be asserting (as Nietzsche and his existentialist followers would do) that with the demise of a religiously sanctioned morality, personal "authenticity"—the intensity of commitment to some inner imperative or ideal, whatever its nature—must be the supreme moral value and the criterion of good and evil. Herzen could not have written such a passage. In the absence of suprahistorical criteria of right and wrong he appealed not to the fates or the individual's given nature but to the autonomous moral consciousness, shaped by historical memory and by the "anthropological reality" of our sense of freedom.[115] Herzen shared Turgenev's fascination with the quixotic type. He devotes several pages of his memoirs to the more fanatical of the Italian revolutionaries, some of whom he knew intimately and who, he wrote, "overwhelm one with the grandeur of their sombre poetry." But he seems to have been better able than Turgenev to separate his admiration for their commitment from a moral evaluation of their acts, complex though he found that task to be. Such personalities as Orsini (the would-be assassin of Napoleon III) "amaze us by their goodness, they amaze us by their wickedness; they impress us by the strength of their passion and the strength of their will. . . . [They are] ready for any privation, any sacrifice, from a sort of thirst for enjoyment. Self-denial and devotion in them go hand in hand with vengefulness and intolerance. . . . They set no value on their own lives nor on the life of their neighbour, either." He contemplated such people with a "nervous pleasure, mingled with tremors," but without Turgenev's self-prostration. Their cruel energies, he observes, were no substitute for an understanding of the processes that they sought to turn to their advantage; Italy's freedom was currently being shaped by the diplomacy of self-interested powers, not by these bloodthirsty martyrs. "They are children, but wicked children."[116] Frozen at a primitive stage of moral awareness, they had reneged on the obligation of development that one owes to oneself.

Wickedness is not a category much used in Turgenev's judgments of those who are driven by an all-consuming passion. Like Schopenhauer, he is sometimes ambiguous on the question of whether moral criteria are applicable at all to a world determined by irrational forces—a "killing-field," as he once despairingly observes, in which all living creatures are intent on devouring their fellows: "Destroy or be destroyed—there is no middle way! Let us then be the destroyers!"[117] Bakunin gleefully used similar reasoning to justify his glorification of the elemental force of popular revolt.[118] Turgenev hated violence and Bakunin's revolutionary cant but, unlike Herzen, could offer no coherent moral opposition to either. In his fearful fascination with unreflective spontaneity, his self-castigating Hamlet seems to anticipate those twentieth-century liberals who have been overeager to admit to a moral inferiority before the "authenticity" of the Left.

Liberal Dilemmas and Populist Solutions

CHAPTER   SEVEN

To the Russian Marxists, the populist movement that dominated the Russian radical tradition for nearly half a century before them was all heart and no head, the creation of high-minded but ineffectual idealists, which formed a sentimental prologue to the real business of revolution. But many Western liberal historians have seen far greater significance in it, arguing that the roots of Soviet despotism are traceable ultimately to revolutionary populism, from which the Bolsheviks took the method of enforcing a socialist ideology through the violent action of a professional revolutionary elite.

As Edward Acton has observed, the traditional liberal interpretation of the revolutionary intelligentsia regards their ideas as the product of their own psychological needs, frequently explaining their protest in terms of some kind of personal deficiency.[1] A representative example of this approach as applied to Russian populism is Adam Ulam's study *In the Name of the People,* which focuses on the phenomenon of terrorism as the key to the populist psychology. Ulam's argument is as follows: the populist ideal of socialism based on the peasant commune had no roots in the outlook of the peasants themselves; rather, it was the construction of alienated intellectuals whose thirst for faith found satisfaction in worship of the democratic virtues of the primitive masses. Unable to arouse mass support for their religion, they channeled their desire for the speedy realization of utopia into a cult of violence, religious in its intensity and manifested at its most extreme in the notorious Sergei Nechaev's murderous cell of revolutionaries, which preached and practiced the dictum that all means were sanctified by the revolutionary end. The fanatical type who dominated in the first underground groups of the 1860s "hated and feared more than anything else . . . the prospect of Russia's peaceful evolution into a constitutional society—in which all his preparations for revolution, all his self-denial, would be in vain."[2]

In the mid-1870s it became clear that the radical intelligentsia's god had failed it when a mass pilgrimage to the countryside to preach socialism to the peasants revealed them to be politically apathetic and even hostile to their worshipers. Those who remained in the movement were able to salvage their illusions by returning to their obsession with political terror, forming a party whose immediate goal was the assassination of the tsar. They continued to deceive themselves that they were speaking for the people, when in reality they were merely satisfying, through childish and criminal means, their own hankering for heroics. Terror, deprived of its alleged justification of service to the people, became an end in itself, a form of existentialism. This tragic situation contained some of the seeds of twentieth-century totalitarianism: dispensing with the idealism of the populists, the Bolsheviks took over their party mystique and techniques and developed them to their logical conclusion by establishing the dictatorship of an elite over the masses.

This is strongly didactic history, leading us in logical steps from the initial delusion to the inevitably tragic denouement. But the neatness of the picture is achieved through a method of selection and emphasis that severely distorts the historical data. Starting with a paradigm that reduces conflicts of ideas to a schematic simplicity, Ulam develops a psychological approach to his subjects of the kind that, as one modern historian put it, surrounds a hard core of interpretation with a thin layer of facts. The attraction of this type of psychohistory is that it offers a clear and dramatic explanation of the origins of some of the great evils of our time; but it does so at the cost of overlaying truth so thickly with myth that it defeats its own didactic purpose. There are lessons to be learned from the history of Russian populism, but not when it is used to confirm a set of prior assumptions.

Ulam's book represents a common approach to Russian political thought of the last century which seeks to explain the ideological conflicts that led up to the 1917 Revolution as a battle between two opposing mentalities—the totalitarian, which dreamed of the total refashioning of human societies to conform to a single ideal model, and the liberal, which held individual liberty to be the supreme value and believed it best served by a gradual and pragmatic modification of existing institutions. The domination of the former, in its populist and Marxist forms, is perceived as having checked Russia's development toward democracy on the basis of the reforms of 1861. Ulam even pinpoints the moment at which the totalitarian tendency triumphed over the liberal—April 4, 1866, when, he argues, the momentum of liberalization was arrested by the attempt of the "deranged former student" Dmitry Karakozov to kill the tsar.[3]

But this distinction between liberal and totalitarian democrats (arising from the experience of Western constitutional democracies after the French Revolution) has limited explanatory power in the context of the Russian autocracy, where calls for restraint in political demands could be construed as support for despotism and where even many liberals came to believe that the total transformation of the existing order, by revolution if necessary, was a precondition for the realization of their minimum demands. (The last tsar began his reign by

declaring constitutional liberties to be "senseless dreams," and even the concessions forced by the 1905 revolution did not properly amount to the rule of
law.) The distinction between liberal sheep and extremist goats obscures much
more than it reveals about the spectrum of political ideas and options in the
special conditions of Russian absolutism. Above all, it obscures the originality
of Russian revolutionary populism as a libertarian and humanist protest
against those conditions, in which would-be liberals were constantly forced
into actions that contradicted their own values.

The predicament of those who sought to preach liberal moderation in
nineteenth-century Russia is richly documented in memoirs, letters, and diaries. Among the most important of these sources are the diaries of Aleksandr
Nikitenko, one of the most prominent public figures of his time.[4] Spanning a
period of fifty years and covering the reigns of Nicholas I and Alexander II,
they remind us of the specific context and the complex problems to which revolutionary populism was a response, a dimension often lacking in historians'
accounts of it.

Nikitenko was born a serf in 1804 and through his intellectual gifts secured
the patronage necessary to gain him his freedom. After graduating from St. Petersburg University, he embarked on a career in government service, reaching
high office in the censorship department and the ministry of education and
playing an active part on many government committees and commissions,
while simultaneously pursuing a distinguished career in literature. He was at
various times a professor of literature, a member of the Academy of Sciences,
the editor of newspapers and journals, and the author of articles on literary history and criticism. At the center of the political and cultural life of his age, he
was an extraordinarily acute observer of the oscillations, over half a century, in
the political climate of Russia.

Nikitenko was a very conservative liberal: he abhorred what he called the
"fantastic" utopias of the Left and even under the despotism of Nicholas I was
opposed to revolutionary solutions. He strongly welcomed the intention of Alexander II to emancipate the serfs and hailed the promised administrative and
judicial reforms (which included the relaxation of censorship, the reform of
the legal system, and the establishment of a network of local government institutions—zemstva) as the beginnings of the rule of law in Russia. Yet while
condemning the Left's demands for more radical change, he began to suspect
that the government's vacillations between reform and reaction were due less
to the fear of radical extremism than to a contradiction in its own attitude toward reform. Observing the operation of the new censorship laws, he concluded that they were "created only for show"—the preliminary censorship of
literature had been abolished only to deliver it more securely into the hands of

the Minister of Internal Affairs, who had the absolute authority to suppress all published material that he regarded as subversive and to order the arrest of editors and authors. This Nikitenko describes as "tyranny in its purest form," aimed at accomplishing what censorship under Nicholas I had failed to do—to turn literature into a loyal instrument of government. Similarly, his observation of the working of the administrative reforms in the early 1860s led him increasingly to doubt the sincerity of the government's intention to limit autocracy by law: he notes that the autonomy granted to the courts was constantly undermined by the intervention of ministers and the secret police in matters of censorship and political offenses, while the St. Petersburg zemstvo, when it attempted to use the freedoms granted to it on paper, was dissolved "like some secret nihilist society."[5]

By the end of the decade it was clear to Nikitenko that there was a contradiction at the heart of the reforms. If carried out with good faith, they must necessarily limit the tsar's power. But the authorities saw them as minor modifications which would modernize the country without undermining absolutism. "They expected that the most orderly existence, in harmony with their wishes, would logically follow [the reforms]; that our ways would immediately change for the better, that industry and agriculture would flourish; that wealth would flow through the entire country like a river. The press, they felt, would be given over to praising those who held the reins of government, and so on and so forth. All these golden dreams did not come true."[6]

Instead, the reforms awakened the desire of educated society to participate in political life, and Nikitenko predicted that if the government did not have the wisdom to dismantle autocracy from the top, others would begin from the bottom. In 1865 he asserted that such is the scorn for law and order generated by the government's arbitrariness and brutality that "one feels the inevitability of revolution in the air. . . . We stand at the brink of anarchy."[7]

This prediction was made the year before Karakozov's attempt on the tsar's life. Although he belonged to a small revolutionary group, the act seems to have been his personal initiative. An intense and solitary personality, he left a proclamation stating that as the tsar was ultimately responsible for the people's suffering, only his removal could open the way to true freedom. After the attempt, the government retreated from all its reforms, until by 1870, Nikitenko notes, all Russian society was under the rule of fear; but the history of reform in the early 1860s, recorded with scrupulous impartiality in his diary, leaves little doubt that the effect of Karakozov's act was not to turn the government back from a liberalizing course but rather to accelerate a process immanent in its attempt to "find the philosopher's stone," as Nikitenko puts it—to synthesize progress with autocracy.[8]

In seeking to maintain a liberal position in a society without the rule of law,

Nikitenko was forced into continual contradiction with himself. He urged the intelligentsia to campaign only for the elimination of abuses within the existing system and called on the government to enlist the support of the mature elements of society against the "absurd" demands of the Left. But at the same time he was forced to recognize that an autocrat finds the most moderate demands subversive: he notes that the government denounced as "revolution" even the results of its own reforms, appearing to believe, in its undiscriminating hostility to all independent thought, that Russia was inhabited only by nihilists, while in reality its policies were creating nihilists out of reasonable people. Nikitenko may have had himself in mind here: in 1872 he declared that "for society to wait for the administration graciously to yield to its desires, is knowingly to make a fool of itself"; it must fight for them, regardless of the government's prohibitions. Thus he implicitly concedes that in Russia liberal values cannot be defended by liberal methods. Indeed, there may be only one way out of the impasse: "Perhaps we shall have to be cleansed in fire and revolution."[9]

Underlying the problem of tactics were even more serious conflicts of principle. Believing that the only path to freedom was gradual evolution on the basis of existing institutions, Nikitenko was unable to discern the seeds of a free society in any of Russia's contemporary institutions. The spirit of society had been crushed under "a bureaucratic administration allied with sovereign despotism," while the masses remained steeped in ignorance, without the slightest understanding of social and political issues.[10] The church and the administration, motivated solely by the desire for self-preservation, had no interest in the task of guiding hearts and minds. When a group of revolutionaries connected with Nechaev was put on trial in 1871, Nikitenko reflected gloomily that the young radicals' contempt for their society was justified. He acknowledged that many of them had noble motives, but he loathed their violent methods and atheistic socialist morality.

The result was an insoluble dilemma. Nikitenko detested political extremism, but in mid-nineteenth-century Russia to protest against despotism was to be an extremist: he hated socialist morality, but the system he defended had no alternative morality to offer. At the beginning of the 1870s he expressed his bitter disillusionment with the moral idealism that had led him, a decade earlier, to seek to help the government to realize noble aims: "Autocracy is clinging to its divine power with both hands; government officials cling to autocracy and support it because they, like insects who appear and disappear with the sunshine, are wholly dependent on it for their existence; the people, not yet aroused from a thousand-year sleep, stir and toss from side to side without knowing whether and whither they should bestir themselves."[11]

What is left, he asks, "for a thinking, honest man, standing completely alone, to do?" The absence of an answer to this question led him to substitute a stoical determinism for the liberal's faith in human freedom: "It seems that no human effort can save us from our fate. We are in the hands of history, which is drawing us irresistibly towards a fatal, inevitable crisis."[12]

Nikitenko's dilemma is one which has become familiar in the twentieth century: that of an isolated intellectual elite seeking to defend enlightened values in an economically backward country where illiterate masses are held down by brute force. Ivan Turgenev captured it perfectly in his story "The Hamlet of Shchigrov District," whose hero, a member of the gentry, is defeated by the irrelevance of his Western education to his environment. Hegel's philosophy, with its vista of necessary progress, reduces him to despair: How is he supposed to apply Hegel to Russian life, he asks—and not just Hegel, "but German science in general, in fact I'll go further—science itself?" Liberals in nineteenth-century Russia were "superfluous people," often, like Nikitenko, reduced to a pessimistic determinism by their inability to reconcile their values with their primitive and brutal environment. Turgenev, who immortalized this type in his novels, was himself one of its most striking representatives. In a well-known letter to Aleksandr Herzen in the late 1860s he mocks the populists' faith in the Russian peasant but offers in its place not liberal optimism, but an aphorism of Goethe: Man is not born to be free.[13] Turgenev found his personal solution in the pessimism of Schopenhauer, achieving, like Nikitenko, a kind of resignation through a stoically deterministic view of the world.

The dilemma of liberals in Russia was not resolved by the formation of a liberal party after the revolution of 1905. They continued to be unable either to elicit a response from the masses or, in the continuing absence of a Western-style constitutional order, to define a platform that could distinguish them clearly from the parties of the Left.

The alternative proposed by the populists—that Russia should not attempt to copy Western models of the state but rather exploit the potential of a native institution, the peasant commune—has been seen by many liberal historians as not worthy of serious discussion ("silly," "puerile," "inept," are just a few of the adjectives Ulam uses to describe their ideas). But in the context of nineteenth-century Russia the populists' option can be seen as no more utopian than the hopes of liberal constitutionalists.

Populism was the collective term for a wide spectrum of radical theories and movements. It reached the height of its influence in the 1860s and 1870s, culminating in the assassination of Alexander II in 1881; its subsequent swift decline was due to both the efficiency of the police and the destruction of the commune through industrialization. The populists believed the liberals were mistaken in seeking Western remedies for Russian ailments. Following Herzen (whose ideas dominated the rise of the movement in the 1850s), they argued that constitutional freedoms had benefited only the middle classes in the West, which was now threatened with revolution by a desperate proletariat. They held that by developing the cooperative principles of the peasant commune and the artisan artels Russia could avoid the horrors of large-scale industrialization and the concomitant pauperization of the mass population: with the aid of Western technology and expertise, the communes could be transformed into federated associations of agricultural and industrial workers.

"Russian socialism" was presented as an empirical approach to the problem of social justice, which the West had signally failed to solve. But in addition there was a widespread expectation among populists that the destruction of evil and oppressive institutions would suffice to bring about a just and harmonious society. Like most revolutionary groups before and since, the populists dreamed the ancient millenarian dream of a world where all divisions would be overcome. Much has been written about the Russian intelligentsia's utopian hopes, which compensated for their extreme isolation in a peasant society ruled by a brutal despotism and encouraged them to fantasize about a future order in which they would live in harmony with an idealized peasantry. But less attention has been given to an equally striking consequence of the intelligentsia's alienation: its iconoclasm. As Herzen once observed, by giving them nothing to command their affection or allegiance, the government had encouraged them to apply all the ruthless logic of which they were capable to a critique of the existing order. Motivated by an individualistic humanism that had been shaped by their reading of the early French socialists, the intelligentsia set about the demolition of all dogmas, norms, authorities, and idols that fettered the human aspiration to self-direction. Their critique was aimed at the Left as well as the Right: the authoritarian collectivism of Marx's utopia was as abhorrent to them as the sham of existing liberal democracies in the West.

The iconoclast struggled with the utopian in the souls of individual populists and in conflicts within the movement over questions of ends and means. Until the early 1860s some radicals hoped for a peaceful social transformation, after which the tsar would preside over a federated system of communes; but the government pursued all socialists as subversives, and the question of the timing of the revolution, together with the connected problem of the intelligentsia's relation to the people, began to cause deep divisions within the movement. The great majority believed that the masses should be converted to the ideal of peasant socialism through persuasion and rational argument: to make the revolution for the people would be to go against the antiauthoritarian ethos of populism and to perpetuate the rule of coercive elites. However, one minority group, the "insurrectionists," believed that the intelligentsia should take a lead in inciting the masses to immediate revolt, whereas a small number of

Jacobins argued that a coup d'état by a tightly organized conspiratorial elite was the only way to ensure a transition to socialism before capitalism became entrenched in Russia. The latter two tendencies helped shape the outlook of the most notorious member of the movement, Sergei Nechaev. Nechaev's belief that the revolutionary end justified the use of any means whatsoever was the most extreme expression of the element of apocalyptic impatience in the populist movement. His closest rival in this respect was Mikhail Bakunin, whose philosophy, based on the dictum "the urge to destroy is a creative urge," led him to collaborate with Nechaev on violent propaganda intended to incite the peasants to revolt. But the millenarian tendency to devalue the present in the yearning for an ideal future was more commonly expressed in the intense asceticism of individuals and groups who sought to model themselves on the ideal of the "positive hero" as formulated by Nikolai Chernyshevsky and his generation in the 1860s: a revolutionary who suppresses all personal emotions and aspirations that might distract him from the fight to realize his vision of the future. In some cases this cult led to a morbid fascination with self-sacrifice and even death for the cause. But when Nechaev coupled the demand for self-renunciation with justification of the sacrifice of all others in the name of the revolution, he met with almost universal condemnation. The "Nechaev affair" caused a moral crisis throughout the movement, resulting in a general reaffirmation of its iconoclastic humanism as a corrective to its utopian hopes.

This humanism found its fullest expression in the writings of Herzen, who observed after the revolution of 1848 in France that most revolutionaries in the West were conservatives, seeking to free people from subjection to one set of absolutes in order to enslave them to another: *salus populi* had replaced the divine right of kings as the idol to which the needs and aspirations of living individuals were to be sacrificed. Herzen's attack on the idolatry of all collective abstractions, including the concept of progress itself, was echoed by later populist leaders, most notably Nikolai Mikhailovsky, who urged that collective social goals be brought into balance with the right of individuals to the maximum possible self-fulfillment. He denounced the kind of political theorizing that attributed to society an existence independent of the people who composed it, making idols of the "aims of history" or the "honor of the state." These idols demand sacrifices: "They feed on the human body, they gorge on human blood." Not even the commune should be viewed as a self-sufficient value: "All social unions, whatever high-flown names they may bear . . . have only a relative value. They should be dear to us only inasmuch as they promote the development of the individual personality, protect it from suffering, and extend the sphere of its enjoyment. . . . Words such as 'the common cause,' . . . 'the common good,' must not confuse you, because too often contraband is carried under this flag."[14] The extreme personalism of this passage is belied by

Mikhailovsky's unremitting toil for the populist cause: the movement never managed to resolve the contradictions between its individualism and its emphasis on the intelligentsia's duty to the people, as epitomized in Pyotr Lavrov's *Historical Letters*, which forthrightly condemns those who put their self-development before service to the people's needs. The clumsy attempts of Chernyshevsky's generation to reconcile egoism with altruism by appealing to biological determinism and their efforts to harness art to politics are notorious, as is their ideal of the totally dedicated revolutionary hero. But this model was increasingly challenged by later populists such as Mikhailovsky as the expression of a narrow utilitarianism that was alien to the goals of the movement. When in the first decade of the next century, the outlook of the radical intelligentsia as a whole came under fire from critics outside its ranks, the intellectuals of the Socialist Revolutionary Party (the populists' successors) had already begun to conduct their own self-examination; as will be seen in the next chapter, they took a lead in discussing the despotic implications of the cult of revolutionary heroism and the damage it had inflicted on the psyche of individuals in their movement.

For all its internal contradictions, Russian populism stands out among other socialist movements of the nineteenth century in the frequency with which its ideologists voiced the concern that the ends should not be corrupted by the means. When the more impatient suggested that the masses might have to be liberated against their will by those who understood their needs better than they did themselves, they were met with strongly argued opposition from within the movement, a noteworthy example being Herzen's polemics in the 1860s with Bakunin and the Jacobins. The depth and genuineness of this libertarian ethos was most clearly demonstrated by the overwhelming reaction of shame and revulsion among populists at the beginning of the next decade when, after the murder of one of his small group by the others, the principles of Nechaev's philosophy of violence became generally known.

The need for moral purification in the wake of these revelations was a primary motivation behind the "movement to the people" of 1873–74, during which thousands of young men and women turned their backs on conspiratorial methods and moved into the countryside to live and work among the peasantry as teachers, doctors, midwives, and artisans. This extraordinary exodus was not (as Ulam contends) conceived in a haze of mystical exaltation but was shaped by the writings of Herzen, Chernyshevsky, Mikhailovsky and Lavrov, whose dislike of misty abstractions and predilection for the experimental methods of the natural sciences was shared by these young populists. Thirsting for facts and statistics, they had begun to prepare themselves for their contact with the people at the beginning of the 1870s by forming circles in the major cities to educate themselves in economics and political culture. They collected money to buy and distribute in the provinces Marx's *Capital*, Louis Blanc's history of the French Revolution, and the works of Ferdinand Lassalle, persuaded sympathetic publishers to issue studies on economic and political theory which the censor would pass, and organized the transport of forbidden books to Russia. Some extended their educational activities to the workers in the Petersburg factories and created small ateliers of their own in which intellectuals could learn trades to prepare themselves for life in the villages. In their communal existence and mutual relationships the members of these circles strove to embody the principles of the cooperative socialism that was their ideal. The ensuing movement into the countryside was moral rather than political in inspiration, motivated not by a specific program but by a sense of guilt before the people and a desire to share their misery and understand their lives, so that the society of the future would be based on their needs and aspirations and not on the theories of an intellectual elite.

The suspicion with which the peasants greeted them, and the conservatism and apathy that they encountered, convinced the majority that it would require long and patient work to persuade the peasants to accept socialism freely. Faced with this task, some began to set up long-term colonies in the villages. But the authorities had harassed the enterprise from the start. Two to three thousand populists were arrested, and many were imprisoned after mass trials. Open propaganda of socialism was precluded, while at the same time the commune was disintegrating under the pressures of industrialization; if Russia was to avoid the horrors of mass pauperization, time was very short. It was these considerations that led to the formation of a conspiratorial party of full-time revolutionaries, known as Land and Freedom, in order to build a revolutionary force through covert agitation. It acquired a terrorist wing, the People's Will, which held that only the assassination of the tsar would force the government to grant the political liberties that would allow them to campaign openly for socialism. These groups have the dubious distinction of being labeled the prototypes for Lenin's professional revolutionary elite; but their ethos was far removed from Bolshevism. The majority of their members seem to have seen terrorist violence as an unavoidable and temporary distraction from the work of peaceful propaganda in the countryside, a weapon of last resort. Their periodical condemned the assassination of President James Garfield of the United States on the grounds that "in a country where personal freedom makes honourable ideological struggle possible . . . political murder as a means of struggle is an example of the very same spirit of despotism that we are seeking to destroy in Russia."[15]

This was no shrewd public relations move of the kind perfected by terrorists in the next century; the People's Will was made up of young propagandists of the movement to the people whose moral idealism had been admired by such experienced observers of human character as Turgenev and whose motives Ni-kitenko and Dostoevsky (also no supporter of the Left) compared favorably with the self-interestedness of the defenders of autocracy. Turgenev was not alone in discerning signs of saintliness in such women terrorists as Sofia Per-ovskaia, the daughter of a general and one-time governor of Petersburg who had worked as a midwife in the countryside before joining the terrorist group and who was hanged for her part in the assassination of Alexander II.

It is no coincidence that one of the most morally impressive of the leading socialists in nineteenth-century Europe, the anarchist Pyotr Kropotkin, was for two years a member of the circle headed by N. V. Chaikovsky, the most im-portant of the populist self-education groups of the early 1870s, before his im-prisonment and subsequent escape to the West. Those who knew him there were impressed by what Henri Barbusse called his "impeccable" moral har-mony, which made him consistently put the fate of individuals above the pu-rity of dogma and defend all victims of intolerance and cruelty, whether or not their causes were fashionable. In his memoirs the anarchist Rudolf Rocker de-scribes Kropotkin speaking at a demonstration held in London in 1903 to pro-test the recent pogrom against Jews in Kishinev: "His face pale with emotion, his grey beard caught by the wind. His first words were hesitant, as though choked by his deep feeling. Then they came rushing out fiercely, each word like the blow of a hammer. There was a quiver in his voice when he spoke of the suffering of the victims. He looked like some ancient prophet. All the thousands who listened to him were moved to their depths."[16]

There was the same incontestable moral authority in Kropotkin's indict-ment, in a letter to Lenin written shortly before his death, of the Bolsheviks' de-cision to take hostages in order to protect themselves against possible violence from their opponents: "How can you, Vladimir Ilich, you who want to be the apostle of new truths and the builder of a new State, give your consent to the use of such . . . unacceptable methods? Such a measure is tantamount to de-claring publicly that you adhere to the ideas of yesterday. . . . What future lies in store for Communism when one of its most important defenders tramples in this way on every honest feeling?[17]

In a speech made in 1893, Kropotkin argued that only one group (anarchists of his persuasion) "respects human life and loudly insists upon the abolition of capital punishment, prison torture and punishment of man by man altogether. All the other parties teach every day their utter disrespect of human life. Killing the foe, torturing him in prison, is their principle."[18]

This passage encapsulates the dual nature of Russian populism as a move-ment that radically subverted the tradition from which it sprang. From the more visionary French socialists it had inherited the millenarian faith in a fu-ture, perfected world where there would be neither sin nor punishment. But the iconoclastic humanism with which populists preached their message proved to be a double-edged weapon, used against those both outside and within the movement who sought to justify the victimization of unregenerated human beings in the present as a means of hastening the arrival of the future ideal mankind.

It is surely less significant that Russian populism generated a Nechaev than that it spawned only one and that his violent vision attracted so few followers. This is the more astonishing in that the vast majority of revolutionary populists were men and women in their early twenties; the older and wiser soon ended up either in prison or emigration. The collective image of these young people as dreamers who had constructed a fantasy of the peasant has little basis in fact. Bakunin's idealization of the instincts of the masses (with whom he had had no contact since emigrating in 1840) was highly untypical. Few populists had illusions about the stunted life of the communes. Chernyshevsky, whose journalism was a dominant influence on the movement, was a competent economist who had made a close study of the vast documentation on the commune and rural life produced by official committees and unofficial research in preparation for the Emancipation. Even before the movement to the people, the city intelligentsia were remarkably well informed about current realities in the countryside. One of the books most discussed in the city circles had been an impressive study of class differentiation in the villages and the breakup of the commune, based on the personal observations of a former official in the Ministry of Justice, V. V. Bervi-Florovsky, during a decade of exile in Siberia and southern Russia—his punishment for populist sympathies.

Such details can be found in abundance in Franco Venturi's monumental work *Roots of Revolution,* an early example of the detailed research done since the end of the 1950s which has disposed of the myth that the Russian revolutionary movement was created and kept going by groups of intellectuals isolated from the masses. After their early mistakes, the populists (like the Marxists after them) learned to adapt their programs to harmonize with the aspirations of those whom they claimed to represent. The number of revolutionary activists and sympathizers ready to help them rose steadily from the 1860s until, by the revolution of 1905, the two main revolutionary parties each had many thousands of members, of which intellectuals were a minority. Only a dwindling number of scholars continue to portray the Russian revolution as a duel between the tsarist regime and a handful of fanatical intellectuals, but this view is still frequently encountered in works written for a nonspecialized readership. The standard image of populism, in particular, continues to be shaped by studies like Ulam's that focus on the movement's most violent and least characteristic strand.[19] Out of two notorious acts—Nechaev's murder of a fellow revolutionary and the assassination of a tsar—a myth has been woven of a movement given up to a cult of violence, the forerunner of Bolshevik despotism. The bias of this approach can be measured by comparing Ulam's descriptions of the small Jacobin groups that sprung up in the 1860s with the biographical data supplied in Venturi's book. In Ulam's version the societies consisted of a mixture of psychopaths and sick minds out of touch with all reality, as evidenced by their violent manifestos. Venturi, on the other hand, documents the fact that the authors of the notorious revolutionary proclamations calling on the peasants to "lift up the axe" against their oppressors had gone into the countryside immediately after the Emancipation to study conditions there and that even the Jacobin groups devoted a major part of their energies to spreading education and creating cooperative societies among the urban workers.

The forcible termination of the movement to the people and the debates in the mid-1870s (again extensively covered by Venturi) on the moral and practical justification of terrorism suffice to refute Ulam's contention that terrorism was an easy option taken by intellectuals unprepared to cope through patient propaganda with the human failings of their deity, the people, and attracted instead to a religion of violence; but if his book is short on facts, it is long on interpretation. Populists do not just resort to terror, they succumb to its lure; when they take advantage of the chance to return to propaganda among the peasants, they are "fleeing from the overwhelming urge to go on killing."[20] The historian's interpretation of his subjects' motives always takes precedence over their own: compare the terrorists' version (from the memoirs of Vera Figner), "Reason told us that we must follow the course chosen by . . . the political terrorists. . . . But our hearts drew us to the world of the dispossessed,"[21] with Ulam's assertion that in the mid-1870s "intellectually [Land and Freedom] remained committed to education and agitation among the peasants and the growing industrial proletariat. . . . Emotionally most of its members became obsessed with terror." When historical evidence to prove a point is lacking, psychohistory produces its trump card. The revolutionaries of the 1860s, we are told, "viewed with dread, even if unconscious," the prospect of peaceful change in Russia. The most stubborn of the facts which contradict Ulam's thesis (Land and Freedom's opposition to the Jacobin idea of revolutionary dictatorship) is dealt with in the same way. The party, he claims, "never lived up to what we might describe as its subconscious ideal of a militant authoritarian party imposing its will on the masses."[22]

I shall not speculate on any unconscious motivation of Ulam's approach to Russian history. But it is clear that the view that a direct line of ideological descent can be traced from revolutionary populism through Leninism to Stalinism encouraged an interpretative bias among some Western historians comparable to that of their Soviet counterparts, who approached populism as the first stage in an ascent to the enlightenment of Russian Marxism. Both schools of interpretation served then to obscure (and to some extent still do) the most prescient aspect of the populist tradition: its rejection of theories that transferred responsibility for events from individuals onto such abstractions as progress and historical inevitability. As Herzen wrote to Bakunin (the only leading populist who was an exception to this rule), "To become the blind instrument of fate, . . . God's executioner, one must possess a simple faith, a naive ignorance, a primitive fanaticism and a kind of unsullied intellectual innocence."[23]

The populists were among the first of the European Left to perceive the hollowness of the god that subsequently failed; but their critique of the idolatry of progress is also pertinent to liberal cultures which retain some form of belief in a single ladder of ascent from "backward" through more "advanced" forms of social organization, to the final goal of liberal democracy, perceived as the system most capable of harmonizing the legitimate purposes of rational human beings. Debating on this subject with Turgenev, Herzen denied that it was "a defection from . . . the immutable laws of creation" not to regard the European bourgeois state as the goal of historical development.[24] He pointed out that we perceive history as a linear advance only because we forget the experiments that were aborted, the developments that were rechanneled by the influence of chance or local factors: history, like nature, is not acting out a script but perpetually improvising from the possibilities that lie to hand.

In the mid-nineteenth century this was a new kind of political discourse that radically subverted the assumptions of rationalist universalism. It was equally opposed to the romantic idealization of primitive cultures, as expressed in the Slavophiles' belief that the past achievements of the West were valueless in comparison with the spiritual insights embodied in the Russian peasant's way of life. Against rationalist and romantic versions of the one correct historical path, the majority of populists proposed an eclectic approach, seizing on a chance configuration of events—the survival of the commune into an age when it could be developed with the help of the West—to map out a new form of social organization that would combine the advantages of cooperative existence with the individual liberties whose importance had been so convincingly demonstrated by philosophers and social theorists in the West. Their thinking on this question was remarkably creative and flexible: they viewed the process of industrialization with none of the doctrinaire hostility that many Russian liberals displayed toward the commune. In the last quarter of the nineteenth century, a number of populist economists, such as V. P. Vorontsov, began to explore models of industrialization that would take account of the specific features of the Russian economy and the interests of the peasant, while allowing Russia to coexist with more developed capitalist countries.

This approach to the problem of progress removed the emphasis from the goal to the process itself, from the universal to the particular, from conformity to a preset future agenda to the exploitation of the unique potential of the present. This creative openness, which respected no ideological boundaries, allowed populist thought to be fertilized by some of the most innovative thinkers of the contemporary West. Herzen, for instance, invoked the new radical liberalism of John Stuart Mill against the doctrinairism of Russian liberals, citing *On Liberty's* crusade against rationalistic norms and universal systems that sought to eliminate human diversity and to crush spontaneity.

The view that (as Mill contended) human societies progress through a "plurality of paths" is now generally accepted by *bien pensant* intellectuals;[25] but the belief in a single ladder of progress is still deeply rooted in our culture and continues to inspire many of our prejudices and fears. We can learn from the struggle of the Russian populists against the inhumanity of doctrinairism both within and outside their movement. Could the aversion of some liberal historians toward the populists be based on an unconscious prejudice against the notion that we could be taught anything by a group of radicals in a country so far below us on the ladder? But I have said that I would not speculate on such questions.

The Intelligentsia and Self-Censorship
C H A P T E R E I G H T

How long ago was it that, terrified from childhood, we ceased to kill in ourselves the most innocent desires? How long ago did we cease to shudder when
finding in our souls passionate impulses unrecorded in the tariff of romanticism?
—Aleksandr Herzen, *From the Other Shore*

In a letter to his friends in Russia in 1850, Aleksandr Herzen complained
of the "democratic orthodoxy" that prevailed among the exiled revolutionaries of 1848:

> They have set up their own radical inquisition, their poll tax on
> ideas: ideas and thoughts that meet their requirements are
> granted rights of citizenship. . . . Those that do not are . . . the
> proletariat of the moral world: they have to be silent or win
> their place by a head-on attack. Subversive ideas have become
> subject to a democratic censorship that is incomparably more
> fearsome than any other variety, because it is not backed by
> police, or packed juries . . . or prisons, or fines. When the reac-
> tionary censorship takes a book from your hands, the book re-
> ceives universal respect: the author is hounded, the printing
> house closed, the machinery smashed, and the victimized words
> acquire the status of belief. Democratic censorship achieves the
> moral destruction of its object: its indictments are promulgated
> not . . . from a procurator's mouth, but from the distance of ex-
> ile, the darkness of prisons. A verdict written by a hand which
> bears the marks of chains leaves a deep impression on the heart;
> but that does not mean that it is not unjust.
>   [The revolutionaries of 1848] have formed a binding tradi-
> tion. . . . They preserve it in exile, in the face of persecution.
> . . . That is splendid, but hardly conducive to growth. . . . A per-
> secuted tradition, with its crown of thorns on its head, con-
> stricts the intellect, the heart and the will.[1]

A decade after this passage was written, democratic censorship in Russia was as much a force to be reckoned with as the official variety. According to S. Glagolev, the Orthodox Church's leading polemicist against Darwinism, during the 1860s "no-one in Russia was permitted to open his mouth to object to the 'eternal truths' enunciated by Darwin."[2]

Those interested in Russian thought are familiar with the features that radical censorship shared with the official version. Listing some of the measures taken by radical journalists of the 1860s to ensure that the authors of antinihilist novels were not published in the leading journals or allowed a hearing in public debate, Charles Moser concluded that it was "a very real question" which of the two censorships was the worse.[3] But the coercive aspect of radical censorship tends to be emphasized at the expense of an equally significant feature: the voluntary element stressed by Herzen. Radical censorship before the revolution was first and foremost self-censorship, operating against thoughts and feelings as much as against words and actions: a self-imposed fettering of the "intellect, heart and will" in accordance with the programmatic demands of freely accepted political goals. The literary censorship operated by the Russian radicals was ancillary to this task, its primary aim being to promote the self-constraint and self-mastery demanded by the revolutionary program by presenting persons who had achieved it as models for emulation. Much has been written about the radical intelligentsia's cult of the positive hero and criticism of it by the great Russian writers, but the opposition to this cult from within the radical camp itself tends to have escaped attention.[4] I shall argue that from the 1890s onward, increasing numbers of radicals showed an acute awareness of the damage inflicted on themselves and their movement by the practice of self-censorship and that this led, in the years between the 1905 revolution and the First World War, to a determined (if unsuccessful) attempt by a significant number on the Russian Left to dispense with the myth of the positive hero and with the principle of radical censorship as a whole.

Self-censorship was a product of the moral ethos of nineteenth-century Russian populism, which demanded that the radical vanguard, as the bearers of a new social ethic, embody it in their personal behavior and serve as models for the mass of society. From Vissarion Belinsky onward, radical critics declared the primary task of literature to be the discernment and encouragement of progressive forces in Russian society through the presentation of exemplary human types. When writers failed to fulfill their requirements, the critics showed them how: the single-minded dedication (or, in the eyes of nonradical writers, crippling narrowness) of Rakhmetov, hero of Chernyshevsky's *What Is to Be Done?* became the model for a generation of radicals. Their leaders expected them to become flawless monoliths, ruthlessly suppressing all private emotions, interests, and aspirations that stood in the way of the total and unhesitating subordination of their reason and will to a doctrine of revolutionary change. Not only art, literature, and personal relations but all intellectual enquiry, when not directly relevant to the cause, were prohibited as futile pastimes of superfluous people, as Pyotr Lavrov reminded his contemporaries in the late 1860s in his immensely influential *Historical Letters:* "The person who lets some personal considerations force him to stop halfway, who because of the beautiful head of a Bacchante, or some interesting observations on infusions, or an engrossing quarrel with a literary rival, has forgotten all the enormous quantity of evil and ignorance against which one must fight,—such a person can be anything you like—a fine artist, a marvelous scholar, a brilliant publicist—but he has withdrawn himself from the ranks of the conscious workers for historical progress."[5]

The same point was put more succinctly in the *Catechism of a Revolutionary,* composed in the following year by Sergei Nechaev: "The revolutionary . . . has no interests of his own, no cause of his own, no feelings, no belongings; he does not even have a name. Everything in him is absorbed by a single exclusive interest, a single passion—the revolution."[6]

There is no doubt as to the inspirational power of the monolithic model: Lenin, among others, has testified to the formative influence on him of Chernyshevsky's novel.[7] There are many examples in the revolutionary movement of a self-renunciation that came close to the ideal: Chernyshevsky himself, the Chaikovsky group, the women of the People's Will. But we know that the vast majority of revolutionaries did not come close at all. A few—for example, Nechaev or the members of Ishutin's terrorist cell in the 1860s—used the revolutionary ethic as an outlet for their pathological tendencies; some, like the unappetizing young bullies described by Herzen in his memoirs, believed that their dedication to the cause gave them the right to instant fulfillment of all their demands. In others, inability to conform to the model of unhesitating strength led to despair and sometimes suicide. Our picture of this gloomy reality, however, comes almost exclusively from sources outside the intelligentsia itself, which observed a strict taboo on public discussion of the stresses and setbacks involved in the fight to transform their personalities. The superfluous people of the 1840s had left no one in doubt as to the debilitating torment of their struggle to attain an inner unity; the next generation assured the world that the goal had been attained and patronized their introspective predecessors from an assumed position of personal harmony and unhesitating strength. Only occasionally, for example, in private correspondence, do cracks appear in the monolithic front, as in Chernyshevsky's moving confession in a letter to the poet Nikolai Nekrasov:

> I myself know by experience that convictions do not constitute
> everything in life: the demands of the heart exist. . . . I know
> that the poetry of the heart has the same rights as the poetry
> of the intellect; for me personally, the first is more attractive
> than the second. I have permitted myself this frankness not
> only to tell you that my approach to poetry is by no means ex-
> clusively political. On the contrary, it is only by force that poli-
> tics has entrenched itself in my heart. But my heart does not
> live by politics, or at least it has no wish so to live.[8]

There were no such tensions in the propaganda image of the "men of the sixties." The world was given to believe that they had carried out the amputation of their private selves with effortless ease. Hence Chernyshevsky's memorable declaration in a review of Turgenev's story "Asia": "Farewell, erotic questions! A reader of our times, preoccupied with questions of administrative and judicial improvements, of financial reforms, of the emancipation of the serfs, cannot be bothered with them."[9]

As Rufus Mathewson observed in his book on the positive hero, the image of the "new man" was as false as the recruiting placards in the post office and fulfilled essentially the same function: to boost enlistments to the cause.[10] This image, however, was not a deliberate invention for the benefit of credulous recruits. Its potency as myth depended on its propagandists' belief in it as existing reality. The radical critics all insisted that there be no falsification in the portrayal of heroes: the writer must be guided by the criteria of "truth" and "typicality." The meaning of these terms, however, was conditioned by a Hegelian determinism that interpreted history as an ascent toward the total emancipation of humanity through a dialectical conflict between progressive and retrogressive forces. The writer was expected to distinguish the "necessary" and "significant" aspects of this process from the extraneous and inessential: in other words, to detect and emphasize the incipient trends that contained the seeds of future development and thereby to accelerate history's upward movement. As Mathewson has pointed out, truth, as defined by the radical critics, contained a large element of prediction: the writer was expected to be a kind of prophet, his optimistic expectations dictating a "realism" that was highly selective.[11] Thus, in the eyes of radical ideologists, the mythical Rakhmetov, as a representative of the incoming phase of history, was more "real" (and hence more worthy of depiction) than the living multitudes of superfluous people.

In one sense, the prediction was self-fulfilling: radical individuals were under enormous psychological pressure to believe that they conformed to the monolithic model. To admit to the existence of inner struggles or indulge forbidden emotions and desires was, as they were constantly reminded, to withdraw themselves definitively "from the ranks of the workers for progress." Self-censorship did not remove the Russian radical's inner conflicts; on the contrary (as the great novelists perceived), it intensified them by denying expression to fundamental needs and depriving the intelligentsia of the possibility of analyzing and reconciling their conflicting drives. The Nechaev affair, with all its pathological undertones, provoked no significant move to self-examination on the part of Nechaev's contemporaries. It was left to the intelligentsia's critics to point to the alienation and psychological deformities caused by their self-mutilation. But a careful reading of the revolutionary memoirs and fiction of the last quarter of the century yields evidence of one of the more tragic aspects of the self-delusion created by the drive to self-censorship. Among the terrorists of the People's Will, egoism, deprived of healthier outlets, sometimes takes the form of a morbid obsession with personal sacrifice and death—to the detriment of the revolutionary's practical use to the cause. The modern reader of *Andrei Kozhukhov*, a propagandistic novel by the revolutionary Sergei Stepniak-Kravchinsky, is less likely to be impressed by the perfections of the selflessly dedicated terrorist hero than by one small psychological detail: consecrating the night before his assassination attempt to reflections on the sacrifice he is to make, he neglects to clean his revolver, which at the crucial moment on the next day misfires.[12]

After several failed attempts, the People's Will succeeded in killing Alexander II. However, the resulting reprisals destroyed the revolutionary organization. Marxist theories of the inevitable triumph of socialism restored the intelligentsia's historical optimism, but at a price: in the famous remark of Pyotr Struve, one of the founders of Russian Marxism, the individual personality was "a sociologically negligible quantity."[13] Historical materialism removed the objective justification for the only personal emotion sanctioned by the intelligentsia's model of revolutionary virtue: the moral satisfaction of the sacrificial feat. The crude rationalism that had helped intellectuals in the 1860s to escape the torments of philosophical introspection had led by a series of logical steps to the conclusion that the intelligentsia and its heroic aspirations were superfluous both to Russia and to history. For some Marxist ideologists, this was an acceptable price to pay for a correct understanding of the historical process; but others, including Struve himself, began to argue that historical materialism could not explain the role of moral ideals in history. Two revisionist movements arose at the end of the century to inject a voluntarist ingredient into Russian Marxism. Although philosophically very different—one was based principally on neo-Kantian Idealism, the other (sometimes called the "Nietz-schean Marxists") on the empiriocriticism of Richard Avenarius and Ernst Mach—both were responses to a crisis of identity among the intelligentsia that they defined in very similar terms.[14]

The revisionists saw the irrationalist currents in philosophy, psychology, art, and literature then percolating from Europe into Russia as the expression of aspects of human creativity that the revolutionary movement had ignored for too long. They pointed out that the ideal of the founders of socialism had been the realization of all human potential. In demanding that fighters for this ideal suppress their personal aspirations in the name of collective utilitarian goals (defined in narrow economic terms), Russian socialism had been moving in a different direction: toward a general leveling in the name of the "philis-tine" goal of material contentment.[15] Both revisionist groups were strongly in-fluenced by Nietzsche's aesthetic immoralism; they argued that self-denial for the common good was at best a regrettable necessity: it should never be pre-sented as a virtue. The revolutionary should see his activity as a means of self-fulfillment, the harnessing of all his creative energies to the battle for progress. The more multifaceted the personality of the individual revolutionary, the bet-ter able he would be to promote the many-sided development of all human be-ings. "We wish to liberate the life of the feelings," proclaimed Nikolai Berdiaev for the neo-Kantian revisionists, while the Nietzschean Marxist Anatoly Lu-nacharsky described the more orthodox members of the Marxist-inspired Rus-sian Social Democratic Workers' Party, led by Georgy Plekhanov, as spiritual descendants of Bazarov, the blinkered rationalist of Turgenev's *Fathers and Children*. The "new man" of the future, he declared, would be a harmonious personality whose every action would be dictated by his thirst for "fullness of life."[16]

Neither movement produced a satisfactory explanation of precisely how the new man would reconcile his search for personal self-fulfillment with the de-mands of collective action. Most of the neo-Kantian group subsequently with-drew from the political struggle in order to address themselves to religious and philosophical issues, while the Nietzschean Marxists, who had always stressed their allegiance to Marxist collectivism, ultimately recanted in obedience to the Bolshevik party line. Both movements were the precursors of a more general crisis of identity among the intelligentsia that became manifest after 1905.

In that year the role for which generations of the Russian Left had prepared themselves did not materialize. The masses made their own revolution with lit-tle help from positive heroes. In the violence and confusion, the distinction between idealists and thugs became blurred as ambiguous figures drifted into the revolutionary ranks, finding a field for their talents as terrorists, agents provocateurs, or members of Bolshevik expropriation brigades. Unedifying power struggles and squabbles over tactics within the radical parties contributed to the disillusionment and defection of significant numbers. In their mutual recriminations the hard core of the faithful accused one another of betraying the movement's ideals, but in 1909 the debate was moved to a different plane when *Signposts,* a volume of essays criticizing the radical intelligentsia, offered for public discussion the proposition that the ideals themselves, in particular the model of the positive hero, were to blame for the current moral confusion.

The seven authors (who included Struve, Berdiaev, and two other former neo-Kantian revisionists) launched a concerted attack on the theory and practice of self-censorship among the Left. They argued that the model it had set up for emulation was a crippled, neurotic personality, pathologically suspicious of all forms of creativity that did not promote the revolutionary cause, conceiving of both individual development and social progress as processes of extirpation and destruction rather than of creation and growth. This monster had been created by a despotic public opinion among the Left that scorned and ridiculed all who fell short of an ideal of self-censorship based on one supreme principle: "To think about one's own personality is unseemly egoism."[17] If a few remarkable personalities had achieved this ideal, for the rest, *Signposts* claimed, the cult of narrowness had been a pretext for avoiding the difficult task of personal development. As the literary historian Mikhail Gershenzon put it: "A bunch of revolutionaries went from house to house, knocking on all the doors: 'all out onto the streets—it's shameful to stay at home!'—and all the consciousnesses, lame, blind, one-armed, poured out onto the square. At home there was dirt, poverty, disorder, but the master of the house didn't care. He was out saving the people."

Speaking for the intelligentsia as a whole, Gershenzon also declared: "We are crippled, because we are divided personalities; we have lost the capacity for natural development, where the consciousness grows along with the will, because our consciousness, like an engine which has broken loose from its train, has whirled away into the distance and is tearing along empty, leaving the life of our emotions and will far behind."[18]

The other authors put their case less subjectively, pointing to the despotic implications in the cult of a revolutionary savior who rejected all values not directly relevant to the goal and recognized only one moral absolute: his duty to the people. They urged the intelligentsia to turn inward on itself and cultivate its spiritual resources, on the premise (which was the common platform of all seven authors) that the inner life of the individual was the only creative force in human existence, and the only solid basis on which a society could be built.[19]

There were few nuances in *Signposts'* critique of the Left. They pressed their point home with sweeping generalizations and a hefty dose of imaginative exaggeration. In intellectual circles the symposium was the sensation of the year, arousing a passionate debate in which, from the liberals to the parties of the extreme Left, the intelligentsia responded as a united front. In a stream of lectures, debates, articles, and symposiums they denied the existence of the crisis diagnosed by *Signposts,* pronouncing it a slanderous attack on the progressive elements in Russian society, designed, whether consciously or not, to serve the purposes of the Russian Right. Richard Pipes expressed what is still a common view among Western liberal scholars in accepting *Signposts'* critique as the unadorned truth about the radical movement and interpreting the unanimity of the opposition to the symposium as proof that the hard core of the intelligentsia had remained unchanged since the 1860s. Wholly unaffected by developments in psychology, literature, and art, it had preserved intact its crudely rationalist vision and its heroic self-image, together with its traditional methods of censorship: "The Russian intelligentsia, socialist and liberal alike, indignantly rejected all . . . criticism and pitilessly cast out of its midst those who had dared to question either its moral excellence or its historic mission."[20]

However, this image of the radical intelligentsia of the early twentieth century as superannuated Bazarovs does not correspond to the facts. The cultural developments to which Pipes refers contributed to the defection of many intellectuals from the revolutionary movement, but they also profoundly affected the movement itself, creating tensions that were exacerbated by the events of 1905.

Lunacharsky's contemptuous reference in 1908 to the Bazarovism of Plekhanov's faction was symptomatic of a widespread belief among the Left that rationalist self-censorship had produced personalities ill-equipped to deal with complex moral and social problems. The intelligentsia's collective response to *Signposts* was not the expression of smug certainty but a desperate propaganda exercise designed to cover up its considerable moral disarray. Unfortunately for its historical reputation, the exercise was a resounding success. The vehemence of the public outcry over *Signposts* has ensured the "Signposts debate" a place in the history of Russian thought out of all proportion to its real significance. In fact, the official party responses to the symposium were no more than a smokescreen behind which, in party organs and intelligentsia journals and newspapers, a genuine attempt was being made to address questions very similar to those raised by the *Signposts* authors, in particular, the effects of half a century of self-censorship on the psychological and moral profile of the Russian revolutionary. These discussions focused principally on two issues: a crisis within the Socialist Revolutionary (SR) Party over revolutionary ethics and an attempt by Maksim Gorky to prevent the staging of a dramatized version of

Dostoevsky's *The Possessed*. It is hard to find any mention of these two debates in later studies of the period, yet they were turning points in the history of the radical intelligentsia.

The SR Party's self-examination was precipitated by the discovery in 1908 that Yevno Azev, the leader of the party's elite Battle Organization (its terrorist wing), had been operating as a police agent since before the 1905 revolution.[21] Both the *Signposts* authors and the few Russian writers who defended their views in print had cited the Azev affair to support their argument that self-censorship had blunted the moral antennae of the Left to such a degree that it could not detect human motives without proof of a mathematical order. Vasily Rozanov, for instance, claimed that there was a direct line from Chernyshevsky's attack on aesthetics to the domination of an Azev in a party that claimed to have inherited the moral idealism of the nineteenth-century populists.[22]

The SR leadership naturally made no mention of the Azev affair in their official reply to *Signposts*, but their memoirs reveal that they took a remarkably similar view of its implications. According to the party leader Viktor Chernov, they felt they had been struck by a moral catastrophe.[23] They took the situation so seriously as to found in 1912 a journal, *Precepts*, devoted primarily to the discussion of revolutionary ethics. Chernov established the framework of the debate with three essays in which he asserted that large numbers had left the revolutionary movement through disgust at the tactics used in 1905. The "morally impure" elements that had then appeared in the ranks of the Left had been encouraged by the tendency (most pronounced among the Marxists) to replace moral criteria with considerations of political utility. Those who used blackmail, robbery, and indiscriminate murder to achieve their goals must be persuaded not merely that "they have miscalculated in their political arithmetic, [but] . . . that they have morally degraded themselves." On the grounds that "a movement which ignores the spiritual and moral physiognomy of its members . . . reveals itself to be bankrupt," Chernov set out to revitalize socialist morality, seeking inspiration, as the Marxist revisionists had done, from currents of thought to which Russian socialism had traditionally been hostile.[24] His method was well-meaning but crude: approaching the question of the relation of ends to means (epitomized by the problem of political terrorism) in the light of the opposing teachings on violence of Nietzsche and Tolstoy, he attempted to construct a middle way between the two. His reflections on this theme (which were philosophically of a very low order) ran concurrently in the journal with installments of an altogether more gripping work that was to play the central role in the ensuing debate—a semiautobiographical novel by Boris Savinkov, one of Azev's former fellow terrorists.[25]

In 1909 Savinkov had published a short novel entitled *The Pale Horse* in the liberal journal *Russian Thought*. As a minor work of fiction by an unknown decadent writer (both works were written under a pseudonym), it aroused limited critical interest, but by the time his much longer novel, *What Never Happened,* was serialized in *Precepts,* the author's real identity was known and *The Pale Horse* was republished.[26] Both novels, interpreted as a graphic illustration of the crisis afflicting SR intellectuals, were extensively analyzed in a general discussion on the moral profile of the revolutionary hero, in which the Left's taboo on public self-criticism was largely set aside.

The Pale Horse was a savage demystification of the monolithic hero. The central character, a terrorist, is portrayed as a personality crippled by his narrow rationalism. Equally indifferent to the fate of his victims and his fellow terrorists, he falls into an isolation relieved only by his cult of violence as an assertion of personal power. Bored, like Dostoevsky's Stavrogin, by a freedom without content and tormented by an obscure sense of guilt, he eventually commits suicide. Suicide (thinly disguised as reparation for his crime) is also the solution of a second terrorist, a committed Christian, whose religious and moral instincts are at war with the rationalism inculcated in him since childhood, which he believes to have destroyed the integrity of his personality.

Savinkov's second novel, set against the background of a party demoralized by loss of faith in its own incorruptibility, uses the problem of the right to kill as the basis for a wider exploration of the mystique of the revolutionary hero and its narrowing effects on the personality. The main character, one of the party elite, can no longer accept the party's claim to be the final arbiter on questions of revolutionary morality, but in the attempt to define an independent standpoint on the problem of ends and means, he discovers that it is he who has been defined by his ideology. His voluntary renunciation of relationships and experiences outside the circle of the party has deprived him of criteria with which to criticize the ideological clichés he now suspects. His search for moral autonomy involves a recognition that self-censorship was also self-deception: when a colleague comes to him for a party ruling on the justification of terrorism, he advises him to look for one in his own conscience and feels that for the first time in many years "he had dared to speak the truth." He blames the silence of a previous generation for the moral confusion of his own: "Why did the People's Will conceal from us that terrorism is not only sacrifice, but also blood, deceit and shame?"[27]

Stripped of his mystique, the model revolutionary is gradually revealed by the probings of Savinkov's hero as an inadequate human being, ripe for exploitation by an Azev: a moral automaton, unquestioningly accepting the party's goals and concentrating exclusively on means. The novel also charts the emergence of a new type in whom moral certainty has become moral indifference—the highly specialized technician of revolution. The confusion of Savinkov's hero turns into despair, making a point simultaneously illustrated by Chernov's laborious theoretical efforts in the same journal: that the destruction of the revolutionary mystique raised questions to which there were no easy answers.

The ironic title that Savinkov gave to his second novel did nothing to diminish the indignation in some quarters of the Russian Left at the SR Party's gross infringement of the rules of self-censorship. Gorky was so offended at the inclusion of the work in an issue of *Precepts* containing one of his own stories that he broke off all relations with the journal, referring to Savinkov in a speech many years later as a social degenerate in the style of Dostoevsky's Underground Man.[28] The "22 friends and supporters of the SR party" who signed a letter of protest to the editors argued that the novel presented a "completely false picture of the revolutionary movement . . . treated tendentiously, from a viewpoint totally alien to our beliefs."[29]

The editors replied that Savinkov might be mistaken but that he was sincere; it was better to argue with him than to silence him or force him to publish in journals hostile to the movement. Attempts then being made to have him expelled from the party were, they asserted, contrary to its tradition of freedom of thought and criticism. The journal's critics on the Left, however, had a different view of their traditions: as Lenin put it with characteristic directness, Chernov's defense of freedom of thought was "cowardly, evasive apostasy."[30]

But the majority of responses to the publication of Savinkov's novels indicate that, with the exception of the Bolsheviks, by 1912 apostates were in the ascendant on the Russian Left. The self-criticism of the SR leadership resulted from pressures within the party that they could not afford to ignore. Their memoirs reveal that Savinkov's conscience-stricken characters, far from being melodramatic inventions as some critics claimed, were closely modeled on prominent party members.[31] The terrorist intellectuals of the time, several of whom had studied at German universities at the height of the revival of idealism, were closely in touch with the new movements in philosophy and one of them, V. V. Zenzinov, records that they had devoted much earnest discussion to the question of the right to kill in the light of neo-Kantian moral theory.[32] Such people welcomed public discussion of their dilemmas. When the rumor circulated that Savinkov was to be expelled from the party, Yegor Sazonov, the assassin of the interior minister V. K. Pleve, wrote from prison demanding that if this happened, he too should be expelled.[33]

With few exceptions, the published responses to Savinkov's novels reflected a belief that the time had come to abandon the fiction of the monolithic hero and to explore the moral tensions generated by revolutionary activity. Plekhanov described the appearance of the works as "a major literary event."[34] They were the subject of lectures and debates throughout the country, and by 1914 more than forty articles had been published on them, most by critics sympathetic to the Left. Leading radicals contributed to the discussion. On a spectrum from liberal to far Left, most critics interpreted the works as reflecting the intelligentsia's disillusionment with a vision of reality that had proved too simplistic to cope with contemporary events. The exceptions were the Bolsheviks and other Marxists headed by Plekhanov who, while expressing sympathy with Savinkov's heroes, claimed that their dilemmas could have been instantly solved by a correct understanding of the historical process.[35] Some liberal critics welcomed what they saw as evidence that the Left was awakening from decades of self-hypnosis induced by the dream of martyrdom, seeking contact with a world outside party circles, and reaching out to currents of thought that had previously been forbidden territory to help them solve questions whose existence they had hitherto denied.[36] The marked influence of Dostoevsky on Savinkov's works was stressed; as the decadent critic Dmitry Merezhkovsky pointed out, the characters of *The Pale Horse* formulated their sense of inner division in the language of Ivan and Alesha Karamazov.[37]

There was a general view among both liberal and radical critics that the Russian Left's new sensitivity to conflicts between their reason and their moral instincts was not (as *Signposts* had hoped) the prelude to a mass desertion from the cause but rather the expression of a healthy need to regain a perspective on reality extending beyond the party and its immediate goals: a development seen as essential to the moral health of the individual revolutionary and of the movement itself. Critics within the SR Party interpreted this phenomenon as a sign of a new radical humanism that was a much needed counterbalance to contemporary trends among the Social Democrats.[38] One of the more perceptive of the liberal critics, S. A. Adrianov, writing in *Russian Thought*, summarized the significance of *The Pale Horse* as a portrayal of the self-mutilation that occurs when an individual turns himself into an instrument for the realization of an ideal:

> Violence is done to the most valuable part of the personality: that very thing in the name of which the sword was raised is destroyed. Fighting against tyranny in life, the individual creates tyranny in his own soul, crushing one part of his ego with another. Within the human personality there occurs the same horror that takes place in a society morally crushed by tyranny: both oppressor and oppressed are isolated and corrupted. When, sooner or later, there comes a decisive test, a question of life or death for the entire organism, its shattered and maimed components, incapable of united and efficient action, enter into cha-

otic, suicidal conflicts, and the organism vanishes from the
world of the living, in excruciating torments of . . . impotence
and despair.[39]

One has only to read the memoirs of terrorists of the SR Battle Organization
to recognize that this passage is no flight of poetic fantasy; it corresponds to
many haunting descriptions of tormented men and women who looked forward to their deaths not as martyrdom but as necessary reparation for guilt incurred and a welcome escape from insoluble dilemmas.

Much of the discussion of Savinkov's novels linked them with other works
by contemporary writers, in particular Leonid Andreev and Viktor Veresaev,
which dealt with the revolt by progressive intellectuals against the rationalist
self-censorship of the past and their attempt to resolve conflicts between the
promptings of feeling and the demands of reason.

Although the style and content of Andreev's works was strongly influenced
by the decadent movement, he managed, somewhat surprisingly, to retain the
friendship of Gorky (who nevertheless urged him to distance himself from decadent mysticism). Radical critics, while disapproving of his pessimism, recognized both his significance as a spokesman for the moods of the progressive
intelligentsia and the importance of the issues raised in his works. The populist
intellectual historian R. V. Ivanov-Razumnik even compared his significance
to that of Anton Chekhov and Gorky at the turn of the century, on the ground
that he had led the way in revealing the contemporary relevance of Dostoevsky's works, with their "eternal Karamazov questions."[40]

Many of Andreev's stories and plays are direct or allegorical treatments of
the moral confusion on the Left after 1905.[41] Their heroes are personalities in a
process of moral disintegration under the intolerable strain of the problem of
reconciling ends and means. Never slow in jumping onto intellectual band-
wagons, Andreev followed the appearance of The Pale Horse with a terrorist
novel of his own, whose eponymous hero, Sashka Zhegulyov, resolves his dilemmas of conscience in a manner then current among real-life terrorists: by
conceiving of his own future death (in the course of a terrorist act) as a form
of reparation for the crime of murder.[42]

The works of the Marxist Veresaev (a practicing doctor and member of the
Social Democrats) received a less ambiguous welcome from critics on the Left,
who seem without exception to have seen him as an honest and objective
chronicler of the moods of the radical intelligentsia.[43] In the mid-1890s he had
published the first of a series of novels in which radical intellectuals, forced by
the defeat of revolutionary populism to reexamine their motives and ideals, experienced a growing awareness of the limited role played by reason in human
motivation.[44] With the help of contemporary developments in philosophy and

psychology they begin to explore the hitherto forbidden area of the irrational and subconscious. For the hero of his first novel (published in 1895) the trauma of confronting these censored areas of the personality proves fatal: terrified by the chaotic impulses revealed to him, he kills himself. The more intrepid heroes of the two subsequent works (published in 1901 and 1908), who are familiar with the ideas of Eduard von Hartmann, Henri Bergson, and other thinkers of whom Bazarov would not have approved, explore the role of the irrational in human motivation in a search to integrate their personalities and to arrive at a social ethic that took account of the complexity of human needs and aspirations—an enterprise that, although optimistic, remains open-ended: the author's main concern is to demolish the claims of dogma to provide absolute answers to important questions.[45]

In the years immediately following the 1905 revolution, a number of other stories and novels depicting doubt-ridden revolutionaries appeared, mainly in liberal, but sometimes in radical, periodicals.[46] Taken by themselves, these works (none of which was as scandalously topical as Savinkov's) might not have aroused the interest they did, but together with Savinkov's novels, they added up, as several critics pointed out, to an impressive documentation of a general awareness among the Russian intelligentsia of the damage inflicted on their personalities by the tyranny of dogma. No longer willing that the content of their personalities should be determined by their ideological beliefs, many sought, as one critic put it, to keep something back for themselves, to legitimize impulses previously denied expression, and to explore hitherto closed areas of experience in an attempt to create a coherent moral identity from the fragmented elements of the self.[47]

Thus, on the eve of the First World War, it seemed that the moral concerns that had established the intelligentsia's tradition of self-censorship and the literary censorship designed to promote it were beginning to give way before greater pressures. But, as the protests addressed to the SRs' journal indicate, self-censorship still had committed defenders, the most vigorous of all being Maksim Gorky. The two sides came into direct confrontation in 1913 in a debate over Gorky's attempt to have Dostoevsky's *The Possessed* removed from the repertoire of the Moscow Art Theater.

The most prominent writer to identify himself with a party of the far Left (the Bolshevik faction of the Social Democrats), Gorky believed that the intelligentsia's crisis of identity could be resolved only by a return to the emulation of its traditional model. Between the revolutions of 1905 and 1917 he put much of his energies into an attempt to revive the tradition of the social criticism of literature (which had steadily lost ground since its heyday in the 1860s) and proclaimed once again the urgent need for monolithic positive heroes as role models to replace the complex and introspective personalities of superfluous people. Addressing himself, as Belinsky and his followers had, to the question of why Russian literature was failing to produce these exemplary types, Gorky argued that it reflected the twin diseases of Russian life—"Karamazovism" and "Karataevism." The sadism of Fyodor Karamazov and the masochistic fatalism of Tolstoy's Platon Karataev together epitomized the "Eastern principles" whose dominance in the Russian psyche had determined the country's barbaric history. In emphasizing these characteristics and exalting suffering and acceptance, Russia's two greatest writers had done immense damage to their country. The mysticism and pessimism of contemporary writers was in the same tradition: "All our literature is . . . an apologia for passivity."[48]

Gorky accuses Russian writers of having failed to fulfill their social function, which he defines as promoting an "education in democracy" and the "development of mankind's spiritual energies" in the service of socialism, through the depiction of exemplary types.[49] Russian literature was deficient in typicality and universality—terms to which Gorky gives the same highly conditional meaning as Belinsky and his pupils had.[50] He affirms that it is the duty of the artist (equipped with an understanding of the present as a stage in history's inevitable progression to a glorious future) to isolate and emphasize the tendencies in contemporary life that point to that future. Gorky saw this as no easy task. In his polemical journalism he supports his case for the urgent need of positive heroes with a survey of existing Russian types that is far more pessimistic than Nikolai Dobroliubov's reflections on the superfluous people of the 1860s, or even the analysis in *Signposts* that had so infuriated the Left. He claims to have observed in 1905 that Russians were beginning to develop a "Western" mentality (which he defines as an aptitude for disciplined effort and a faith in reason and science as the principal instruments of progress), but his few generalized references to this phenomenon make thin reading beside the exhaustive catalogue, illustrated with relentless repetitiveness in his critical essays over a decade, of the Eastern traits in the Russian national character. Russians were either mystics or nihilists (or both simultaneously). They were by turns servile, despotic, fanatical, fatalistic, dogmatic, and anarchic; but they were always lacking in the capacity to engage with a modern world that demanded the qualities of rationality and discipline.[51] In Gorky's view the folk hero Ivan the Fool, whose triumphs were due not to will or cunning but to inertia and luck, was an appropriate symbol for a people that, from its barbaric government down to its peasant sects, was characterized by one overwhelming urge: to withdraw from a world with which it could not cope. The intelligentsia (to whom even *Signposts* had conceded some virtues) was not spared in this damning analysis: in its mentality of part policeman, part slave, it is richly endowed with the qualities of the "broad Russian soul"—defined by Gorky as an incapacity for sustained effort in pursuit of its ideals and a propensity to turn all conflicts of principle into vulgar brawls.[52]

"We must remodel ourselves or . . . perish"[53] was a conclusion with which *Signposts* would have agreed, but Gorky was calling not forward but backward, to the model of the monolithic hero, with one significant change: what Mathewson called that model's "censorious potential" was realized in Gorky's prescriptions to contemporary writers, which do not seek to justify positive heroes on grounds of typicality.[54] Dobroliubov had genuinely believed that the negative types that writers should refrain from portraying were the fast-disappearing vestiges of the past; Gorky concedes the ubiquity of Fyodor Karamazovs and their masochistic victims in current Russian life but argues that those who portray them lack the requisite perspective on the present: "People have become imprisoned by the . . . truth of the day and are unable to see the great truth of the century."[55]

"Man is always worthy of idealization"[56]—so much so that Gorky and Lunacharsky had together concocted a collectivist "religion" whose deity was the infinite potential of human beings and whose aim was to revitalize the flagging will of the masses after 1905. By this stratagem they hoped that the energies generated in the past by what they called the "religious" urge to transcend the limitations of finite existence could be channeled into the fight for socialism, presented as the battle to attain immortality through the species. A Bolshevik offshoot of "Nietzschean Marxism," "godbuilding"—as it was called—was denounced by Lenin, which did not prevent its Menshevik critics from greeting it as the philosophical expression of Leninist political practice. In the words of Yuly Martov it was "the formula of a movement in which the leader and the led, the shepherd and the sheep, are sharply differentiated and opposed: in which there exist two truths—the esoteric and the exoteric, in which the ideologist utters *lies* because the masses are not capable of *assimilating the truth*."[57]

This quotation could serve equally well as a summary of Gorky's view of the relationship between the writer and his public, in which the emphasis was moved away from self-censorship (the voluntary fettering of the heart, intellect, and will in the service of common beliefs) to censorship in a more familiar form: the deliberate distortion of reality and recourse to myth as an instrument of social manipulation.

Gorky made no attempt to disguise his belief in the manipulative function of the writer. Referring to a poll conducted among Russian writers on the causes of a current epidemic of suicides, he expressed disgust with those who had used the opportunity to speculate on the objective reasons for pessimism among the youth: "The question is not about the truth or falsity of some or other view of life, but the social value of those views, their potential influence on the individual. The question is, which one of them is more likely to increase vital activity, which to reduce it?"[58]

On this defense of what Lenin called the *partiinost* ("partyness") of truth (the approach to concepts and ideals as weapons in the class war), Gorky based his recommendations to writers on what they should and should not portray. He accused the vast majority of contemporary writers, from *Signposts* to Savinkov, of a concern with "the so-called 'higher demands of the spirit,' " which distracted attention from pressing social tasks. The writer must not "seek the meaning of life" or "squawk about the irreconcilable enmity between the interests of the individual and the world"; all forms of individualism (a concept variously defined by Gorky as "social cynicism" or "alienation from the interests of the age") were in direct contradiction with the writer's duty to promote the development of "a new collective personality."[59]

Like Chernyshevsky, Gorky was forced to construct the necessary model himself. In his total, unhesitating political commitment, the wooden hero of his 1907 novel *The Mother* is a Bolshevik reincarnation of Rakhmetov, but if the type was familiar, Gorky's method of encouraging emulation required a distinct change of emphasis in the intelligentsia's demands on writers and critics in its own ranks. In a 1911 article he implicitly recognized that it was no longer enough to rely on the self-censorship of the progressive forces of society. He announced that the "enemies of freedom" had now succeeded in infiltrating the ranks of the intelligentsia, where they poisoned the minds of the younger generation by "deliberately emphasizing the contradictions of the present, but concealing their *creative significance.*" In these circumstances, whether total artistic freedom was desirable was, he suggested, "a very complex question."[60]

That he was personally in no doubt as to the answer became clear in September 1913 when he wrote to the editor of the paper *The Russian Word* protesting the staging of a dramatized version of *The Possessed* by the Moscow Art Theater and asking all "spiritually healthy citizens" to support his demand that the play be removed from the stage in the interests of "social education."[61]

Expanding on his view of Dostoevsky as an "evil genius" who took a perverse delight in portraying the deformities of the Russian character, Gorky argued that his works could further infect a society already weakened by the preaching of pessimism and suggested that the stage production might be a factor in the current epidemic of suicides among the young. In any case, it could only impede the "enormous task of . . . reorganization, not only sociopolitical but also psychological" that confronted the Russian people. In view of the urgency of this task, he demanded that his fellow citizens take it upon themselves to determine "the socially educative significance of the ideas which the Moscow Art Theater is to portray." In another letter, responding to the first reactions to his proposal, he justifies this extreme measure by an eminently Dostoevskian assessment of his countrymen's deficiencies: "I know the frailty of the Russian character, I know the pitiful instability of the Russian soul, the torments, exhaustion and despair that make it susceptible to all varieties of infection." The artist's duty is clear and straightforward: "One must not show [the public] Stavrogins. . . . One must preach cheerfulness . . . activity, not self-contemplation. One must return to the sources of energy: democracy, the people, social interests and science."[62]

Gorky's appeal was the last intellectual sensation in a society on the verge of extinction. Meetings of the intelligentsia were held to discuss it in Russia and abroad (one group of Left Bank Russians in Paris convened for three days).[63] The press carried detailed reports of the debates, and actors, directors, writers, and critics were canvased for their opinions; some expressed them at length in articles. The issue aroused intense passions: a correspondent of the paper *Moscow* describes the scene in a debate organized by the editors: "Dostoevsky's defenders foamed at the mouth and beat their breasts: the opposing side replied with protests, shouts, whistles, uproar. In the public gallery people jumped to their feet and waved their arms, their faces contorted with fury. On both sides unparliamentary expressions burst forth."[64] Once again, as in the *Signposts* debate, the self-image of the radical intelligentsia was at issue. Given that group's united hostility to the criticism leveled by *Signposts,* one might have expected substantial support for the proposal that a work that portrayed the Left in an unflattering light should be withdrawn from public performance. On the contrary, the response to Gorky's proposal was overwhelmingly negative, revealing the degree to which the traditional taboo on self-criticism had been eroded by the events of recent years.

There were, of course, exceptions. The Russians of the Paris Left Bank sent Gorky a telegram of congratulation after their marathon debate, and the Bolshevik paper *For Truth* expressed predictable and vociferous support for "the proletarian writer Gorky" in his battle with the bourgeois literary establishment. Collective letters to the paper by such bodies as "a group of students and workers" and a "Society for Education beyond the Moscow Gates" expressed solidarity with his campaign against writers who used art as a weapon in the service of capital.[65] The tradition of social criticism at its crudest was shown still to have staunch adherents, such as Yekaterina Kuskova, who declared in a letter to the paper *Russian News* that "theatrical productions, literature, etc., exist precisely in order that one may either sympathize with them or condemn them."[66] Most of the disputants who shared this belief, however, advanced it as an argument against censorship. A critic in the same paper argued that any work of genius, even if ideologically flawed, could serve truth by being made the object of "serious collective work" on the analysis and correction of its ideas.[67] In its official response to Gorky the Moscow Art Theater had defended itself against the charge of social irresponsibility, pointing out that its repertoire of recent years (which had included some of Gorky's own plays) was adequate proof of its social conscience, a view that received wide support.[68] There was widespread puzzlement over the logic of the argument in Gorky's letter of protest that by focusing attention on the maladies depicted by Dostoevsky, the theater would make "the dreaming conscience of society sleep more deeply."[69] If Dostoevsky had (as Gorky admitted) correctly diagnosed the negative traits of the Russian psyche, why, it was asked, not take advantage of the production to generate a debate on how they could be overcome?

In general, the intelligentsia overwhelmingly opposed supporting the concept of the social function of literature by what one critic called the methods of the police state.[70] At the end of 1905 new press rules had abolished preliminary censorship: the irony of Gorky's attempts to turn the clock back was not lost on most. Referring to the plea in Gorky's letter for "unity of thought and will" among the intelligentsia, the critic Dmitry Filosofov remarked that he seemed determined to divide it on the one point on which a consensus existed: namely, respect for freedom of speech.[71] Filosofov, Merezhkovsky, and Ivanov-Razumnik were among the most prominent of the left-wing critics who accused Gorky of confusing two very different things: convincing the opposition and silencing it.[72] Many others pointed out that Gorky's concept of social censorship, if consistently applied, would demand the suppression not only of dramatized versions of Dostoevsky's novels but also of the novels themselves and, ultimately, of all literature that lacked a happy ending or was otherwise detrimental to the nerves. He had embarked on a slippery path that led to the burning of books and the banishment of poets from a republic. As Filosofov inquired rhetorically, "Which is worse, The Possessed or censorship?"[73]

A substantial proportion of the writers and critics who took part in the debate found Gorky's view of the function of literature as repulsive as his methods. The force with which this point was made reflects the extent to which the theory of the freedom and self-sufficiency of art had made inroads on the traditional outlook of the radical intelligentsia. Contrary to the situation half a century before, it was now the doctrine of the social function of literature that was on the defensive, no longer identified with secular saints like Belinsky but with the programs of specific political parties. Gorky's own party adherence considerably weakened his debating position; he was accused of speaking not as a writer but as a Social Democrat—in the words of the novelist Mikhail Artsybashev, a man wearing the blinkers of a party whose program had solved all questions.[74] Slogans that in the previous century had demanded moral adherence from all who called themselves progressive had lost their credibility. There was no outraged reaction from the Left when the artist Aleksandr Benois accused Gorky of devaluing the past and present and, like a charlatan at a fair, enticing the public into "endless booths of the future" that held only deceit and disappointment.[75] A number of critics pronounced the measuring of great works of art by the "transient demands of social hygiene" as patently absurd.[76] Leonid Andreev's friendship with Gorky did not prevent him from publicly castigating him for believing that artists like Tolstoy or Dostoevsky could be assessed "within the narrow framework of the contemporary social movement."[77] Members of the Moscow Art Theater, while stressing their social conscience, were not afraid to proclaim to Gorky that the fundamental purpose of the theater and their duty as artists was to serve "those 'higher demands of the human spirit,' in which you see only idle rhetoric, distractions from the vital cause."[78]

A participant in the public debate organized by *Moscow* interpreted the noisy support for Gorky as a depressing sign that "we still . . . measure everything by the yardstick of politics," while the paper's own reporter, commenting on the manner in which the most complex questions were instantaneously disposed of, remarked that one could almost see Dostoevsky's devils wheeling over the disputants' heads. Another correspondent reported on a debate held on Gorky's motion by a group of teachers, who, though making no reference to the psychological analysis in Dostoevsky's novels, "crucified" him as a slanderer of the revolution: "And this after all the betrayals, all the Azevs. Truly, we are still possessed by demons."[79]

From a cooler historical perspective one might argue that, on the contrary, all the Azevs had helped to promote a degree of public self-criticism among the radical intelligentsia that would have seemed unthinkable at the time of the scandal over *Signposts*. Gorky's attack on Dostoevsky came nearly a decade too late. Familiar with Savinkov's novels and with critical works on Dostoevsky by Merezhkovsky and others, the intelligentsia saw the great writer not as a political enemy but (as Artsybashev put it in the debate) as the author of "an overwhelming portrayal of the disintegration of the human personality" that was of great relevance to contemporary experience. Members of the Moscow Art Theater pointed out that their dramatization of *The Possessed* concentrated not on its political content but on the spiritual drama of Stavrogin and declared themselves "distressed" to learn that Gorky saw no more than sadism, hysteria, epilepsy, and political libel in Dostoevsky's work.[80] By 1913 the Russian Left's most famous writer, with his simple model of the human consciousness, had become something of an embarrassment to it. Lenin, who greeted Gorky's novel *The Mother* with enthusiasm, was in a minority of one among influential critics: Plekhanov and others on the Left found it sentimental, schematic, and crudely didactic, an opinion that was not officially reversed until the promulgation of Socialist Realism in 1932.[81] In 1913, the limitations that the tradition of self-renunciation had imposed on the intellect, heart, and will were no longer generally acceptable to the Left. The belief that there were some areas of human experience outside the competence of political ideologies, and some conflicts that these could not resolve, was no longer seen as incompatible with radical politics or even, as in Veresaev's case, with membership of the Social Democratic Party. In the debate over Gorky's attempt at censorship, refusal to gloss over or suppress such conflicts was interpreted as a sign of political maturity.[82] Artsybashev accused Gorky of confusing psychology with pathology, and Filosofov declared that "for a conscious people harmful plays are preferable to a censor's muzzle."[83] Several contributors to the debate applied Dostoevsky's insights to Gorky himself. In his assumption of the moral guardianship of society he was compared to the Grand Inquisitor, determined to suppress all human strivings that did not advance the goal of healthy nerves and a full stomach.[84]

The two debates that I have discussed dispose of the myth that the Russian intelligentsia marched forward to 1917 with its model of heroism and its intolerance of criticism fundamentally unchanged since the 1860s. On the contrary, in the discussion of Savinkov's novels, very few individuals or groups on the Left, apart from the Bolsheviks, had not favored the abolition of self-censorship. When the question was put more crudely by Gorky, the dominant voices in the ensuing discussion were those of writers and critics, but again (with the exception of the Bolsheviks) the parties of the Left registered no coherent protest against the majority verdict.[85]

But if no spiritual descendant of Belinsky or Bazarov appeared to give Gorky's proposal the support of reasoned argument, it often carried the day in one arena of debate: the rowdy meetings reported in the press, where arguments were won by those with the loudest voices and the heaviest fists.[86] The Bolsheviks' ability to harness and organize those primitive forces proved in the end more historically significant than all the agonized debates among their rivals over the ethics of self-censorship.

Which Signposts?

CHAPTER NINE

Look harder! After all, we don't even know where "real life" is lived nowadays, or what it is, what name it goes by. . . . Soon we shall invent a means of being born from an idea.
—Fyodor Dostoevsky, *Notes from Underground*

Its appearance in Russian bookshops in March 1909 caused a sensation: it quickly ran into five editions. The intelligentsia to whom it was addressed repudiated it en masse; it was denounced in public meetings across the country, a bitter campaign was waged against it in the progressive press, and few who called themselves enlightened dared to write or speak in its defense. Yet less than a decade later many such people hailed it as a prophetic work. Its memory was kept alive by dissident Soviet intellectuals, and it was among the first of once-forbidden books to be republished under glasnost. This was directly followed by a succession of editions, all received, as one commentator observed, "with warm declarations of affection" from a post-Soviet readership.[1]

Such has been the remarkable career of *Signposts,* the volume of essays in which seven authors, including Pyotr Struve, an eminent economist, journalist, and liberal politician, and the philosophers Nikolai Berdiaev, Sergei Bulgakov, and Semyon Frank, subjected the Russian intelligentsia's political messianism to a devastating critique. The work began to attract notice in the West in the mid-1950s, after Leonard Schapiro cited it as a profound commentary on the Russian radical tradition and as proof that (contrary to the views of some Marxist historians) there existed in prerevolutionary Russia a genuine intellectual alternative to that tradition, one which professed the liberal values of tolerance, political pluralism, and respect for individual rights and the rule of law. More recently, commentators have stressed the relevance of *Signposts* to current debates in literary and cultural theory in Europe and the United States; Gary Saul Morson has pointed to the resemblance between its analysis of the utopian mentality and Mikhail Bakhtin's influential critique of "monological," dogmatic thought. Like Schapiro, he argues that despite disagreements among the authors, the volume reflects a coherent set of humanistic values clearly distinct from (and opposed to) the reductive vision of ethics, history, and culture that it attacks, and he interprets the current Russian interest in *Signposts* as an encouraging sign that Russia's new intelligentsia has not inherited the sectarian mentality of the old.[2]

But *Signposts* has also been praised by sections of the new Russian Right, and its appeal to some neo-romantic nationalists cannot be attributed solely to a misreading of its ideas. Some of its contributors were uneasy about the company they kept; Struve subsequently commented that the volume reflected traditional divisions between Slavophiles and Westernizers. Echoing this view, Frank observed that what separated Bulgakov and Berdiaev (the authors whom he regarded as the two principal Slavophiles) from the other contributors was the dogmatic nature of their religious beliefs.[3]

My intention is to show that the differences of principle between Struve and Frank, on the one hand, and Berdiaev and Bulgakov, on the other, are as significant a feature of *Signposts* as its collective opposition to the Left. They were the symposium's core contributors, all former leading ideologists of Russian Marxism. Their apostasy and the conflicting directions that it took can be seen as an early expression of a fundamental shift in European thought that began in the last century with the questioning of teleological thinking in all domains of intellectual activity. In its conflicts and confusions, as well as its insights, *Signposts* reflects the beginnings of a transition toward new representations of the self and the world that is still in progress.

This process is often described as the dismantling of the grand narratives of the Enlightenment, those universalizing theories that began to crumble in the late nineteenth century when developments in the natural sciences, psychology, and philosophy progressively revealed the radical contingency of our world and the fragmentary character of experience. These discoveries brought with them the sense of acute moral disorientation that has come to pervade our culture. As the philosopher Alasdair MacIntyre has put it, concepts of timeless rules and universal systems that have traditionally grounded notions of liberty, equality, justice, progress, and the good remain as "a present absence," a scheme of belief that may have been widely disowned but against which we continue to measure the fragmentation of our own enquiries.[4] We may have learned to distrust what Nietzsche described as the "craving for metaphysical comfort," but it shows no signs of diminishing. In the words of Isaiah Berlin:

> One of the deepest of human desires is to find a unitary pattern
> in which the whole of experience, past, present, and future, ac-

tual, possible, and unfulfilled, is symmetrically ordered. It is often expressed by saying that once upon a time there was a
harmonious unity—"the unmediated whole of feeling and
thought," "the unity of the knower and the known," of "the
outer and the inner," of subject and object, form and matter,
self and not-self; that this was somehow broken; and that the
whole of human experience has consisted in . . . an endless
quest to find an answer to the puzzle, return to the seamless
whole, to the paradise whence we were expelled, or to inherit
one which we have still not done enough to earn.[5]

Both in the former Communist countries and in the West this search is being expressed in new forms of religious and political messianism, which many
see as the only viable alternatives to the corrosive skepticism and Nietzschean
nihilism of so much postmodern thought. But a number of philosophers insist
that other options exist: that it is possible to contextualize and historicize our
moral concepts without collapsing into a Nietzschean relativism.

Russian intellectuals faced a very similar set of choices during the political
and cultural upheavals of the early twentieth century. Nietzsche's "revaluation
of all values" had a particular appeal to Russians who were disenchanted with
the empirical and logical shortcomings of the great secular eschatologies of the
century. Prominent among these were the four "core" authors of Signposts
who, abandoning their Marxist faith in a socialist utopia, embarked on a radical reformulation of the nature of the historical process and the individual's
relation to it. This would lead them to two opposing sets of views on the issue
of whether the human race should seek an answer to the great puzzle. By focusing principally on the symposium's prehistory I aim to show that the di-
verging paths of its authors anticipated a conflict that has become familiar in
our own time, between those who profess old eschatological faiths in new
forms and those who are moving toward a genuinely new understanding of the
meaning of history and human endeavor. We shall see that the divisions between the principal Signposts authors expose, in an extraordinarily illuminating way, some of the practical moral and political consequences of each of
these two major options.

In the darkest days of the despotism of Nicholas I, the critic Vissarion Belinsky
sought to convince his generation that rebellion against the status quo was not
only futile, but morally wrong. Faced with a monstrous reality that the individual seemed powerless to change, he found comfort and hope in devolving responsibility onto the historical process, deducing from Hegel's axiom "the
actual is rational" that the existing Russian state had its appointed place in the

harmony of the cosmic scheme, as one of the instruments by which history was destined to realize its transcendent goals.

This curious episode has a parallel in the enthusiasm with which many Russian intellectuals embraced Marxism in the early 1880s. Revolutionary populism had just suffered a crushing defeat following the assassination of Alexander II, and the country, embarked on the road to capitalism in Europe's wake, seemed in the grip of forces as inexorable and dehumanizing as the police state of Nicholas I. But a Marxist could argue that this process was not only inevitable but also desirable: the ultimate goal of socialism could be attained only through the prior formation of a proletariat. Georgy Plekhanov, the founder of Russian Marxism, stressed the "scientific" nature of the laws that allowed no exceptions to this iron rule: "We . . . know where we are going and board the train of history that takes us at full speed to our goal."[6] The actual is rational: as suggested by the incantatory emphasis on the theme of determinism in Russian Marxist writings of that time, this was a very consoling belief.

All recent university graduates, Struve (1870–1944), Bulgakov (1871–1944), and Berdiaev (1874–1948) were (together with the economist M. I. Tugan-Baranovsky) the most influential Marxists in Russia in the 1880s and 1890s. Frank (1877–1950) became prominent only at the turn of the century. They were known as "Legal Marxists" because, unlike those who operated in the revolutionary underground, their work was published legally in periodicals, where they sought to refute the populists' belief that history could be influenced by the wills and moral ideals of individuals. They insisted that freedom, as demonstrated by Marx and Engels, meant only the correct understanding of necessity. Ethical systems and ideals were entirely class-determined; in Struve's phrase, historico-economic materialism "simply disregards the individual personality as a sociologically negligible quantity." They prided themselves on the scientific detachment with which they viewed the intensification of the suffering of the peasantry, driven from the land into factories—a necessary precondition of socialism, they explained. In contrast to "weeping ideologists" (the populists) who lamented the sacrifice of the present generation to the future, Marxists were realists who never shed tears over the "painful paths" of economic development. Bulgakov pointed out the advantage of reconciling oneself to the inevitable: "Any rational person agrees that one acts more energetically when one *knows* that one's acts will be crowned with victory than when one acts only with guesses."[7]

But in Western Europe Marxism was already proving to be far from an exact science. Marx's revolutionary dialectic, according to which an intensification of the contradictions within the capitalist system led ineluctably to its revolutionary overthrow by a desperate proletariat, had not anticipated the effectiveness of organized labor in forcing social and economic reforms. This phenomenon, together with the revisionism of Edward Bernstein (who argued that it was not true that socialism could be attained only through revolution), made a strong impression on Struve, who attended conferences of the German Social Democrats in Germany and Switzerland in the 1890s. He concluded that there were two contradictory strands in Marxism—evolutionary and revolutionary, the former being closer to the observable reality of social processes. In 1899 (following the appearance that year of Bernstein's heretical *The Premises of Socialism and the Tasks of Social Democracy*) Struve published a major essay questioning the basic assumptions of historical dialectical materialism on the nature of the transition from capitalism to socialism. He pointed out that Marx's goal—a system that would embody and develop the highest cultural achievements of capitalism—was inconsistent with the means of revolutionary catastrophe. In its claim to explain processes in the real world by reference to a rigid conceptual schema of opposites originating in Hegel's dialectic, Marxism was a system of idealism "in the worst sense."[8]

As Struve remarked in 1899, the very phrase "scientific socialism" was "merely one big Utopia." If Marxism's claims to scientific prediction were unfounded, and the ethically desirable could not be shown to coincide with the objective laws of history, there was no philosophical justification for deriving values from the phenomenal world nor (as Bulgakov pointed out) for demanding the sacrifice of the interests of individuals in the present in the name of Marx's vision of future happiness. The same arguments had been leveled against Marxism by the leading ideologist of populism, Nikolai Mikhailovsky, but while the four erstwhile legal Marxists now echoed his condemnation of their former faith, they argued that his individualism was fatally undermined by his hostility to metaphysics. In Berdiaev's *Subjectivism and Individualism in Social Philosophy* (1901), to which Struve contributed a long preface, the two point out that as an ethical positivist Mikhailovsky had refused to recognize any a priori truths outside the world of experience; hence his defense of the free will of the individual and his right to self-development had been built on sand. His revolt against absolutes had led him to an extreme relativism which all too easily identified truth with the interests of a particular class. They note the inconsistency between his almost Nietzschean defense of the individual's right to a full and rich development of all his powers and his demand that the Russian educated minority should set aside its battle for civil and political rights in order to concentrate its efforts on social and economic reforms that would benefit the masses. Struve pronounces this disregard for natural rights a "moral impossibility" which could not be justified in the name of any concept of happiness. Berdiaev declares that it is time to reject "the sophism that finds the highest form of morality in the sacrifice of one's own soul for the welfare of others." Happiness without rights is "the greatest ignominy."[9] Only the recognition of a transcendental moral world order as the source and justification of values could safeguard the rights of individuals against the pressure to sacrifice them to the goals of specific groups or classes.

Subjectivism and Individualism outlined a general position at which Bulgakov and Frank had by then also arrived through a similar critique of the empirical and logical defects of deterministic materialism: a Kantian dualism that placed human goals and values in a transcendental realm, the source of the categorical imperative that humans must be regarded always as an end and never as a means. The four pointed out that the ideal of all ethical systems based on this principle was not (as in the eudaemonistic ethic of Marxism) collective happiness but individual moral perfection, achieved through the satisfaction of the metaphysical thirst of each human being for good, truth, and beauty. In their pursuit of material goals the Russian intelligentsia had neglected what should be the ultimate aim of the battle for progress: in Berdiaev's words, to create a new kind of individual, "spiritually reborn, the bearer of ideal values."[10]

This new individualism reflected a widespread mood among the Russian intelligentsia, who had come to find materialist and positivist doctrines inadequate as explanations of the world and guides to action and had started to explore the irrational and creative urges that their predecessors had sought to repress in the name of service to social tasks. Beginning in the early 1890s, this movement would lead to the explosion of creativity in the arts, philosophy, and religious thought that became known as Russia's Silver Age. It was shaped by two dominant influences: the revival of metaphysics by German neo-Kantian idealism and the philosophy of Nietzsche, whose exhortation to "smash the old table of values" evoked a passionate response among Russian intellectuals profoundly alienated from their society. Frank describes himself as having been "completely overwhelmed by the depth and intensity of Nietzsche's spiritual struggle . . . and his testing of the foundations of moral life. Under Nietzsche's influence I underwent a spiritual revolution."[11]

In his introduction to Berdiaev's book, Struve argues that Nietzsche's great achievement as a moralist lay in his aesthetic critique of eudaemonism, in which he had posed the most tormenting problem of the age: how to reconcile the individual's Faustian striving toward absolute good, truth, and beauty with the collective goals of social justice and equality. This view was echoed in the symposium of 1903, *Problems of Idealism,* in which the four ex-Marxists joined with eight other contributors—philosophers, historians, and legal theorists—to sketch out idealist positions in the fields of ethics, sociology, the philosophy of history, and law as the basis of a systematic defence of the proposition that the individual was not just a cog in society but the source of its values.

The editor, the philosopher and professor of jurisprudence Pavel Novgorodtsev, noted in his preface that the turn to idealism was part of a "general striving for moral renewal" among the intelligentsia, who were no longer satisfied with ideologies that gave political answers to moral problems. The symposium aroused fierce debate, but even hostile critics agreed that it was responding to a widespread and deeply felt need for a revaluation of values (Nietzsche's phrase had become part of the intellectual currency of the time) which would give due importance to aspects of creativity that the socially conscious intelligentsia had tended to ignore. One critic cited the essays as proof that the narrow personality of the traditional Russian radical, animated by an ethic of self-denial, was being supplanted by a "new man," a many-sided individual who was attracted to the fight for progress as a means of moral self-fulfillment.[12]

The new man required a new ethic. Struve, Berdiaev, and Frank were among several contributors who attempted to develop a theory of "moral creativity" by supplementing Kant's concept of moral autonomy with Nietzsche's aesthetic immoralism: this, they believed, was a necessary corrective to the narrow rationalism of Kant's concept of duty, which implied a personality divided against itself, the sensual side suppressed in the name of universal norms. Berdiaev protested against the "humiliating" view of morality as a "sort of external measure against the individual . . . something almost hostile to him." The life-denying asceticism of traditional morality, which celebrated altruism and defined self-love as a vice, was spiritually destructive and politically reactionary: "By formulating a whole succession of limitations . . . and denials of the self in the name of 'the other' one cannot obtain as a sum total the affirmation and development of all selves." The new idealism must embrace the "Dionysian" element in human existence, recognizing the intrinsic value of the individual's thirst for life and intensity of experience. Its slogan must be "live to the full" (*zhit vo vsiu*). Such an ethic would regard sanctity as "the total harmony between what is sensually desired and what is morally required." Frank contends that the fight for social justice should be motivated not by "the oppressive burden of moral obligation" but (paraphrasing Zarathustra) by "that wholesome, vital, sacred self-love, which in the name of its happiness banishes from its presence whatever is contemptible and all that is cowardly, and hates all forms of slavery." The good of society would be better served if morally conscious individuals "thought not only about the interests of the 'other,' but of what is sacred and inviolable in . . . their own selves," striving to attain the "many-sided integrality" of the Nietzschean ideal, a synthesis of artist, philosopher, and saint. Aesthetically integrated personalities of this type, Struve asserts, would not need the compulsive force of externally imposed norms to prompt them to act altruistically; their ethic would be one of "freely performed duty."[13]

Several contributors to *Problems of Idealism* coupled the ideal of an integral personality with another desideratum: an "integral worldview," despite the fact that the recent history of these two concepts in Russian thought could be read as a warning against any such linkage.

Although Nietzsche gave it new content, the ideal of individual integrality was no novelty for the intelligentsia. The romantic idealists of the 1830s had ascribed their spiritual suffering to a preponderance of their rational over their intuitive powers: they viewed the healing of their inner divisions as both an immediate goal and a foreshadowing of the idealist dream of ultimate wholeness, according to which the individual and the general, knowledge and faith, the Absolute and the created world, would form one indissoluble unity. For that generation, to be an integral personality one must have an "integral view of the world" (*tselnoe mirovozzrenie*): an understanding of the unitary pattern of existence as a movement toward the ideal goal and of one's own predetermined place in this universal schema. Only such certainty, they believed, could bring about the inner harmony that was a necessary condition of useful and creative action. This conviction had been the psychological impulse behind Belinsky's Hegelian determinism; but in 1840, in one of the greatest voltes-face in Russian intellectual history, he rejected all deterministic doctrines of progress as pretexts for preventing individuals in the present from fulfilling themselves in their own way and, in a celebrated challenge to his former idol, declared that if he were to reach the top rung of the Hegelian ladder of progress, he would demand an explanation of the sufferings of those past generations whose fate it had been to serve as a means to the final end. If no explanation was forthcoming, "I would throw myself down headlong from the highest rung." A similar humanistic revolt against historical determinism led Belinsky's contemporary Herzen to develop a proto-Nietzschean view that human beings could fulfill their creative potential only by overcoming the "fear of freedom" that attracted them to metaphysical systems. The "integral personality" that was Herzen's ideal would regard all such systems as unnecessary and pernicious fictions that prevented us from exploiting the creative potential of our contingent reality and our empirical selves. A future society composed of such individuals would regard their contingency as the source of their freedom, shaping their mutual relationships according to the aspirations and values of their time and place, unconstricted by the need to conform to any preset historical agenda.[14]

The certainties offered by such an agenda were, however, irresistible to the next generation of radicals, the men of the sixties, who held that socialism would be the inevitable outcome of a biologically determined process. But at the end of the decade their determinism provoked a strong reaction in the form of the personalism of Pyotr Lavrov and Mikhailovsky, whose subjectivist approach to society took account of human will, goals, and values as components of the historical process, defined by Mikhailovsky as the "struggle for individuality." Its only goal, he argued, was the development of many-sided and harmonious human beings, in whose name he rejected all deterministic systems that laid claim to an all-encompassing explanation of human existence and total predictive power.

For the neo-idealists of the early 1900s the defense of the integral personality meant affirming the unity of the physical and the spiritual in the human being against what they saw as the one-sidedness of traditional materialism and idealism which both demeaned the individual, presenting him or her either as an object in nature or as the pale reflection of a higher truth.[15] They sought to formulate what Frank (with reference to his own philosophy) would call an "ideal realism," one concerned with spiritual values in their concrete individual and historical embodiment. Such an approach implied a war on two fronts; a humanistic defense of the self-sufficient value of every individual against the depredations both of dogmatic metaphysics and of skeptical relativism. But for many in the new movement the second of these represented by far the greater danger, which could be countered only by the all-embracing certainty of an integral worldview; Berdiaev and Bulgakov were among those who found this in the apocalyptic vision of Vladimir Solovyov.

Although in tune with the times in insisting that spiritual advance was bound up with the battle for social and economic progress, Solovyov's philosophy was essentially a throwback to the religious romanticism of the Slavophiles. He believed like them that alienation and social conflict were the results of the divorce of reason from religious faith: the spiritual unity of the psyche would be restored only when philosophy, science, and theology were united in the pursuit of the supreme aim of knowledge—an understanding of the "pan-unity" of all existence through communion with its source, God (the Absolute), to which it must return. The goal of the historical process was the unification of all endeavors to this end: an "integral life" achieved by "integral creativity" in the pursuit of "integral knowledge" within an "integral society": a theocratic utopia uniting East and West, church and state, the temporal world and the divine. Solovyov believed, like the Slavophiles, that Russia had a universal religious mission: to be the first bearer of the new integral life among humankind.

Solovyov's messianic vision was in harmony with the apocalyptic mood that began to grip many Russian intellectuals at the turn of the century, as the country lurched toward revolution. A dominant influence on the cultural renaissance, his ideas are echoed by several contributors to *Problems of Idealism*. The philosopher S. A. Askoldov (the pseudonym of S. A. Kozlov) explains that previous philosophical systems, by privileging either the intellect or the will, had contributed to the inner divisions of the personality. The task of the new philosophy was to reintegrate reason and feeling. It was now "only a question of time before the demands of theory and practice, of philosophical thought, moral duty and aesthetic feeling will coincide." As another contributor put it, in order to become a personality in the full (integral) sense, each individual must construct a metaphysical system of integral knowledge: "Only then does he receive an answer to the question of why and for what purpose he exists."[16]

Solovyov believed that Nietzsche's anti-Christian ideal of human perfection ("Man-Godhood") was a perversion of the vision of "God-manhood," the synthesis of the divine with humanity and the world at the end of history; but in the religious and philosophical thought of the time the two influences often blended into a single apocalyptic vision of the Second Coming. A dissenting minority of thinkers, however, would insist that all eschatological thinking, whether religious or secular, devalued the historical present and was thereby incompatible with the notion of freedom preached by the new idealism: the search for individual integrality could not be prescribed or bounded by the dogmas of any system of beliefs claiming universal validity. Struve and Frank were to follow this path: Berdiaev and Bulgakov would pursue Solovyov's dream of pan-unity.

The split among the four former Marxists grew out of the differing motives that had led them first to Marxism and then to idealism.

Berdiaev and Bulgakov were both maximalists whose search for personal self-fulfillment was bound up with the need to find an answer to the cosmic puzzle. As Bulgakov put it in *Problems of Idealism,* disappointment in the millenarian promises of early Marxism had left a vacuum that must be filled: "We can and must create a new faith, find a new and more reliable source of moral enthusiasm." Berdiaev, too, believed that the priority for his generation was to construct an "organically whole, positive view of the world: at this historical moment . . . skepticism can play only a reactionary role." Both found what they were seeking in Solovyov's philosophy, which Bulgakov greets as the herald of a "higher synthesis" in which all conflicts between faith and reason would be resolved. It provided contemporary human beings with what they most desired: an integrating principle "which would unite the depths of being with everyday labor, giving meaning to individual life by placing it *sub specie aeternitatis.*" As Bulgakov explains, all individuals and nations have their particular historical mission, "foreordained in the moral world order." Historical progress is the unfolding of a divine plan, the march of the Absolute towards its goals; our role in this process can be discovered by consulting our conscience, the voice of the divine will within each individual. Unlike Berdiaev, Bulgakov shared Solovyov's disapproval of Nietzsche's Prometheanism, stressing that only a religious elite could claim true insight into the designs of Providence and provide an answer to the perennial Russian question: "What is to be done?"[17]

Berdiaev had initially rejected the dualism of fact and value that flowed logically from the adoption of Kant's critical philosophy, on the ground that this did not provide the proof of the inevitable victory of one's ideals, without which "life is meaningless." In his book of 1901 he had attempted to construct a synthesis of Kantian epistemology with Marx's sociopolitical determinism, arguing that an "immanent teleology in the lawful process of history" gave "an objectively logical, scientific sanction to the socialist ideal, that allows us to look bravely ahead."[18] Soon abandoned, this attempt at combining Kant with Marx is interesting only in showing the importance that Berdiaev, like Bulgakov, attached to the possession of unambiguous answers to ultimate questions.

Both thinkers have left revealing comments on the initial motivations of their intellectual quest. The son of a provincial priest and an ex-seminarian, Bulgakov lost his religious faith before becoming a Marxist, a process that he describes as moving from one eschatological faith to another, capable of inspiring the same "raptures" that he had known as a religious believer. Berdiaev (who came from an aristocratic background) asserts that early in his life he had regarded political upheavals with a certain disdain: his revolutionary impulse sprang from "a fundamental inability to acquiesce in the world-order, to submit to anything in this world." He had been initially drawn to Marxism because its goal of an emancipated humanity seemed to correspond to his yearning for "a spiritual revolution . . . against the slavery and meaninglessness of the world." His defection from Marxism came about through the awareness of what he describes in 1901 as "a terrible and tragic contradiction: we are ready to wear a martyr's crown for our ideal and to display greatness of soul. But the ideal itself has turned out to be so philistine . . . that there is no place in it for greatness of soul." He maintained that in Russia (as in the West) the working-class movement's concern with questions of economic organization and short-term material goals was the sign of a spiritual philistinism that must logically lead to the society of Dostoevsky's Grand Inquisitor, where freedom has been surrendered in the name of the material well-being of the herd. The task of intellectuals such as himself was to raise humanity above its petty everyday existence, in order to prevent the "home of the future" from being settled by "philistine contentment and bourgeois satisfaction." But such people could be only spiritual leaders, with no temporal power: the "battle for the aristocratization of the human soul" could be waged only on the level of the spirit. As a Marxist Berdiaev had expected history to realize his goal in full: as a no less uncompromising idealist, he would revolt against history in the name of a mystical aristocracy.[19]

In the motives that had drawn them to Marxist eschatology, Bulgakov and Berdiaev represent two distinct but related Russian radical types. Bulgakov had followed the path of the radical leaders of the 1860s, Nikolai Chernyshevsky and Nikolai Dobroliubov, both ex-seminarians, whose painful loss of religious faith was succeeded by a devotion to a new materialist gospel. (Bulgakov's conversions went full circle: in 1918 he became an Orthodox priest.) Berdiaev's disdain for compromise recalls that of the aristocratic rebel Mikhail Bakunin, whose legendary maximalism was inspired by the need to satisfy a craving for "absolute liberty."[20]

In contrast to the utopianism of these two, Struve, in retrospect, would emphasize the pragmatic motives that had drawn him to Marx's theories. His love of freedom had made him "by passion and by conviction" a constitutionalist and a liberal before he became, "*by conviction* only," a Social Democrat. Marx's theories attracted him because of the answers they gave to immediate, vital questions: "What economic processes, what social relations and forces will determine the downfall of absolutism (autocracy), the conquest of civil and political liberties, the establishment of a constitutional regime?" Even when he believed with Marx that capitalism was only a transitional system, Struve focused on the attainable goals of the immediate future rather than on a distant ideal. He devoted careful empirical analysis to the positive role of Western capitalism in furthering the political enfranchisement and cultural development of the individual citizen. He believed (as he wrote in 1894) that Russia's immediate task was clear: "from a poor capitalist country to become a wealthy capitalist country."[21] Frank, as we shall see, was to emulate Struve's pragmatic approach.

The contrast between Struve's pragmatism and Berdiaev's maximalism was already evident in their early enthusiasm for Nietzsche. Berdiaev was so wholehearted in his embrace of Nietzsche's exaltation of the individual who bows to nothing but his own ideal of authenticity that he upheld the romantic concept of demonic protest as symbolizing the refusal of the exceptional individual to bow to the limitations of historical existence. Struve, in contrast, while presenting the Nietzschean model of the aesthetically whole personality as an inspiring ideal, warns that as long as the propositions "I wish" and "I ought" varied in content, duty in the Kantian sense would continue to exist.[22] He would exemplify this belief in his dogged efforts to cooperate with a liberation movement whose goals and methods he often disapproved of. In 1900 he made the transition from Social Democracy to liberalism; two years later, from Stuttgart, he launched the first independent Russian liberal publication, *Liberation*, which sought to unite the nation across class and party barriers in the cause of the liquidation of autocracy and the establishment of constitutional rule. From his campaign there emerged the Union of Liberation, a coalition of liberals and radicals whose mobilization of public opinion in 1904–05 played a major role in the downfall of autocracy. He was elected to the central committee of the newly formed liberal Constitutional Democratic (Kadet) Party in 1905 and served in the Second Duma. He continued research and teaching in economics while maintaining a prolific journalistic output on current problems in Russia. From 1907 on, as editor of *Russian Thought,* one of Russia's leading monthly journals, he directed his main efforts to exposing the antilibertarian implications of the intelligentsia's maximalism. In this he was assisted by Frank, who had followed him into the Kadet Party and became his closest friend.

The two would frequently cross swords with Berdiaev and Bulgakov. Berdiaev followed Struve into the Union of Liberation but not into the Kadet Party, which he branded as philistine. Instead he became deeply involved in the apocalyptic seekings of the religious and philosophical circles of the period; with Bulgakov he founded *Questions of Life,* a journal concerned with the new religious ideas, and in 1907, under Bulgakov's influence, he began to move closer to Orthodoxy. During the 1905 revolution Bulgakov had begun to work for the creation of a Christian Socialist Party which (following Solovyov) would approach the struggle for social and political justice as part of the religious process of transfiguration of the world, through the recapturing of humanity's lost unity with nature and God. Although he was elected to the Second Duma, he aligned himself with no existing party. His priorities were those of Alesha Karamazov, whom he quotes in *Problems of Idealism:* "For real Russians the question of the existence of God, of immortality . . . are the first questions, above all others, and that is how it ought to be."[23] He played a leading role after 1905 in the Religious-Philosophical Societies founded in Moscow and Petersburg to discuss contemporary problems from a religious point of view. From this platform and in print he condemned the individualism of liberals such as Struve and Frank for perpetuating the divisions that stood in the way of the pan-unity prophesied by Solovyov and called for a monolithic party which would pursue transcendent goals on the basis of a shared system of belief in the divine aims of history and Russia's predestined role in their attainment. His hopes that the Orthodox Church would assume the leadership of such a movement were dashed by the latter's collusion with the government reaction after 1907. Bulgakov would continue to teach courses in political economy at Moscow University and other institutes, but his thinking became increasingly mystical: drawing on Solovyov and on Friedrich Schelling's philosophy of identity, he began to elaborate his own vision of the end of history as the uniting of subject and object.

We shall see that by the time the four former Marxists came to contribute to the critique of radical utopianism in *Signposts,* their views on the nature of freedom and history had diverged so far as to result in two contradictory mes-

sages to the intelligentsia. The content of these can be best defined by comparing the reactions of Berdiaev and Struve to the 1905 revolution and its
aftermath.

Berdiaev spent from 1904 through 1907 in St. Petersburg at the center of the literary, religious, and philosophical ferment that became known as the Russian
cultural renaissance. He attended the famous Wednesday sessions in Viacheslav Ivanov's "tower," where philosophers and symbolist writers discussed epistemology, aesthetics, and problems of social and political reform. He was also
one of the intimate circle of the novelist and critic Dmitry Merezhkovsky and
his wife, the poet Zinaida Hippius. Merezhkovsky was the founder and chief
proselytizer of an apocalyptic religion influenced by Nietzsche's critique of the
"slave morality" of traditional Christianity and based on the notion of a forthcoming new revelation, a "Third Testament" which would preach a morality
beyond conventional notions of good and evil, reconciling Christ and Antichrist, the flesh and the spirit, pagan self-affirmation and Christian brotherhood. This "New Religious Consciousness" was to herald the Second Coming
of Christ and the Kingdom of God on Earth.

Berdiaev (who later described himself as being "penetrated not only by the
breath of the Spirit but also by that of Dionysus" during those years) enthusiastically embraced this doctrine, whose vision of Promethean self-affirmation
as the path to theocratic harmony was particularly attractive to those who were
unwilling to choose between Nietzsche and Solovyov. In his writings of that
period he paints a radiant picture of the "new Church": unlike Orthodoxy,
which was tainted by its links with a despotic system, it would not see the deity
as a symbol of the individual's subjection to powers outside himself. It would
embrace "all the fullness of life," all that was valuable in the the world and human history: "the Renaissance . . . and the revolt of Reason, and the Declaration of Human Rights . . . and contemporary socialism and anarchism, and the
revolt of Ivan Karamazov and of Nietzsche . . . and the thirst for infinite freedom."[24]

Along with Merezhkovsky and his group, Berdiaev greeted the 1905 revolution
as the prelude to the Second Coming, a misjudgment that he would later ascribe to the infectious excitement of the time. With millenarian urgency he
proclaimed: "There is no return to paganism, as to a thesis, and to Christianity,
as to an antithesis. . . . The New Religious Consciousness thirsts for a synthesis,
must . . . unite two poles, two opposing abysses." He urged religious believers
to support the revolutionary Left, which, despite its professed positivism and

atheism, was characterized by an "unconscious religious sanctity." Berdiaev sketched out his own eschatological hopes in mid-1905 in a study of the thinker Konstantin Leontiev, often known as the "Russian Nietzsche," whose aestheticist contempt for bourgeois values he holds up for emulation: "One senses in him a Romantic's yearning . . . for the apostles, the martyrs, the poets and the knights. . . . We sense . . . a great truth in Leontiev's mad romanticism. We shall see whether it is possible for a romantic not to be a reactionary, for a mystic not to justify the *ancien régime*, but to challenge it in the name of freedom and the limitless rights of the individual spirit. Might it not be that the future belongs to mystical anarchism and to an aristocracy transcending history . . . ?"[25]

But the government's capitulation in October after a year of violent peasant disturbances and workers' strikes did not herald the transformation Berdiaev had prophesied. The October Manifesto, with its promise of a truncated constitution, was rejected as a sham by the parties of the Left. Continuing confrontations between the government and its opponents, which involved escalating violence on both sides, led to the end of Russia's constitutional experiment with the dissolution of the Second Duma in June 1907.

Bitterly disappointed at the failure of his hopes, Berdiaev turned on those who had helped to inspire them. In essays published between 1907 and 1909 he drew scathing parallels between the religious maximalism of Merezhkovsky and his group and the utopianism of the Left. Merezhkovsky's view of the revolution as "the last act in the tragedy of universal liberation" now seemed to him culpably naive. Their gaze fixed on the future goal, for which they saw the "flesh of history" as a mere means, Russian religious and revolutionary extremists perceived the world in terms of grand antitheses, vast collective forces from whose clash they expected that universal harmony would miraculously emerge. But this reliance on miracles had catastrophically distracted attention from real and intractable problems: "The agrarian question cannot be solved mystically, the position of the workers cannot be mystically improved, just as questions of physics and chemistry cannot be mystically solved." Nor would an intensification of these problems lead to some religious transformation of the world. "Bloody ravings and chaos" were not conducive to the genesis of a new religious reality.[26]

But this was no defense of compromise. On the contrary, Berdiaev believed that the mysticism of the Left was bogus, because its rejection of the existing order was not uncompromising enough. He later claimed that the violence of 1905 had convinced him that everything that was "objectivized" in the world was infected with evil: "I came at last to recognize that truth and spirit signify freedom and revolution, but that matter signifies necessity and reaction and that it imparts that character to revolutions themselves. Here we have . . . the theme of the Grand Inquisitor: for the sake of bread people agree to renounce their spiritual freedom." He saw himself as a precursor of the "mystical anarchism" preached by Viacheslav Ivanov and Georgy Chulkov in the wake of 1905, whose slogan was "nonacceptance of the world" (*nepriiatie mira*).[27]

In 1908 he moved to Moscow, where through Bulgakov he became close to religious thinkers who (like Bulgakov himself) had returned to the Orthodox Church. The two renewed their collaboration with a new journal and a publishing enterprise specializing in religion and philosophy. According to Berdiaev, it was then that he began to turn towards Orthodox Christianity: but the move was made strictly on his own terms. He had accused Merezhkovsky of betraying "a lack of faith in his own human depth" by appropriating the Orthodox concept of *sobornost* (religious togetherness) during 1905 in order to underline the resemblance of his forthcoming "Religious Revolution" to the socialist ideal of the Left; Berdiaev compares this notion to the "tribal thinking" of the radical intelligentsia. Traditional Christian teaching on the need to submit to God's will seemed to him a deplorable expression of humanity's tendency to seek support from forces outside itself; he censures his friend Bulgakov for an excessive emphasis on the virtue of humility, which showed him to be "the enemy of the heroic, the Promethean principle."[28]

The religious personalism that Berdiaev began to profess after 1907 differed from his earlier Nietzschean individualism principally in the fact that he no longer emphasized the dignity and value of earthly, physical existence. The self-affirming individual, striving to attain his or her goal of personal authenticity in a lonely spiritual revolt against the irredeemable philistinism of the norms and values of all earthly societies, was the "flesh" that he defended against the ideal abstractions of the Left.

"Should the whole world vanish into thin air or should I not drink my tea? I say, let the world vanish if I can always drink my tea": Berdiaev interpreted these words of Dostoevsky's Underground Man as a challenge to the "philosophers of the commonplace" who seek to place limits on the individual's self-fulfillment in the name of social tasks and norms. He was fascinated by the Dostoevskian type who professed a morality beyond conventional notions of good and evil, in particular the "proud aristocrat" Stavrogin, possessor of a hypnotic power over others. He maintained that the only true philosophers were "philosophers of tragedy" such as Nietzsche and Dostoevsky, who exposed the hollowness of theories of universal progress. In this category he put Ibsen, one of the formative influences on his early thought, whom he later described as an "aristocratic radical" whose individualism, like Nietzsche's, was of the kind that "makes 'enemies of society' " and whose work was devoted to the eternal tragic conflict between "the creative individual, with his vision of another, better life, and the social collective, which subjects every individual to its impersonal power." Ibsen "stands outside social trends, he represents no social collective, he fights equally against inert conservatism, against the pillars of contemporary society and against radical opinion, against the united majority, against democratic philistinism. He is for freedom of the spirit and against equality which destroys individuality. He is always for ascent, for the heroic personality. He is a spiritual revolutionary, but not at all a revolutionary in the external social and political sense."[29]

This could be a fair summary of Berdiaev's self-image after he embarked on the path from Marxism to idealism. Never distinguished by modesty, he would later note that he shared Nietzsche's "demand . . . for ecstasy, combined with [his] contemptuous attitude to empirical existence." He frequently and admiringly referred to Nietzsche's "loneliness," noting in retrospect that his own gifts always became weakened in political or social association with others but were at their strongest in situations of "conflict and isolation"; he stresses in his memoirs that his involvement in politics was from the first accompanied by a strong sense of alienation. He became "estranged" from Struve because the latter appeared more interested in politics than in matters of the spirit (this at a time when Berdiaev himself was still a member of the Social Democratic Party.) He followed Struve into the Union of Liberation because he wished "to take some part in the freedom movement" and even attended its congresses in Germany, maintaining his estrangement by taking more interest in the landscapes than the meetings. He was elected to the Union's central committee but records that he played no active role on it, sensing "a terrible estrangement" from Russian liberal circles. He experienced a similar sense with regard to the religious and philosophical milieu in which he subsequently moved. He continued to make periodical forays into the political and social arena, though, inevitably, "remaining estranged from it."[30]

Berdiaev's ambivalence has its comic side, but it springs from the classic dilemma of the utopian thinker. As he writes in his memoirs, his abhorrence of politics had led him "not to rejection of the world, but to a desire to overturn . . . it." He felt a compulsion "to realize my ideas in life. I did not want to be an abstract thinker." Characteristically, having lost faith in Merezhkovsky's solution to this problem, he at once hit on another, also based on the synthesis of opposing principles: an approach to Russian reality that would unite the "day" and "night" regions of Russian thought—the hitherto mutually hostile strands of secular Westernism and Slavophile religious messianism. He explains that thinkers such as the Slavophiles, Leontiev, Dostoevsky and Solovyov, whose insights were rooted in the transcendent consciousness of the Russian people, had revealed that the Russian state rested on a divine foundation: the truths embodied in the Orthodox faith. As the obedient instrument of Divine Providence, it was destined to point the way to the spiritual regeneration of the world by counterposing its dream of the Kingdom of God on Earth to the "human kingdom," the Westernizers' ideal of the bourgeois state. But Russia could not embark on its role as spiritual mediator between East and West until the obstacles of economic and cultural backwardness were overcome. The final goal was "absolute freedom and . . . the absence of authority," but this could be attained only through through the instrumentality of the state and its institutions: "One must affirm the state relatively in order to overcome it absolutely."[31]

In this transitional period, Berdiaev argues, the mystical strand of Russian thought had much to learn from the political pragmatism and tactical expertise of the liberal Westernizers; it was the intelligentsia's task to synthesize these two mutually hostile traditions by grafting the methods of the second onto the ideals of the first. "To transform the insight and the visions of the night into the powerful forces of the sunny day: this is our great . . . historical mission." Berdiaev's own attempts at synthesis result in a confusing alternation of messianic enthusiasm with appeals to gradualism and common sense. In prophetic mode he asserts that Russia's spiritual aspirations make it unlikely that it will ever be attracted by the "abstract constitutionalism" of the bourgeois West, while in polemics with the Left he pronounces liberal constitutionalism a civilizing force, asserts his preference for the "ordinary philistine who loves his country," over the narrow asceticism of the dedicated revolutionary, and defends Struve against the charge that he sought to make Russia bourgeois: it was essential to do so "if one understands by that . . . a transition to the highest forms of national economy."[32]

The logical weakness of this approach was pointed out by the historian and liberal deputy to the Second Duma, A. A. Kizevetter, who commented in response to one of Berdiaev's criticisms of Kadet tactics that it was hardly consistent for him to discuss the pros and cons of specific political policies when, as a professed religious anarchist, he deemed them all to be equally devoid of intrinsic value. "One cannot renew the world when one despises it."[33]

Berdiaev's forays into the arena of practical politics recall the political thinking of Dostoevsky, who prophesied the coming of a worldwide kingdom of brotherly love headed by Orthodox Russia while simultaneously pouring scorn on radical utopias which ignored the intractable obstacles presented by Russia's current poverty, ignorance, and backwardness. In Berdiaev's alternations between prophecy and pragmatism (as in Dostoevsky's) one sees the clash of two different perspectives, employed for two different purposes. To expose the abstract schematism of radical theory Berdiaev focuses on the conflicts of an irreducibly complex present; but such problems become vanishingly unimportant sub specie aeternitatis when he contemplates the religious meaning of history as the progression to a divine goal. But unlike Dostoevsky, who acknowledged that his readers had good grounds for finding his own dreams "fantastic" and "hysterical," Berdiaev seems curiously unaware that his criticism of others' utopias could be used with equal effect against his own.[34]

This was particularly the case with regard to Merezhkovsky, who came to epitomize for him a dominant radical type: "a politician among mystics and a mystic in politics" (surely an apt description of Berdiaev himself). By resorting to apocalyptic syntheses to resolve the contradictions between their religious vision and empirical reality, Merezhkovsky and his group were choosing the "easy way out." In intelligentsia circles at that time "it was not the word that became flesh, but flesh that was turned into words. Verbal constructions frequently took the place of real relationships."[35]

"Merezhkovsky's work," he would write later, "reveals, hidden beneath schemas and antitheses, . . . an incapacity to choose." Berdiaev's career as a member and critic of the intelligentsia between 1905 and 1917 shows a similar reluctance to face the fact that in concrete situations choices frequently have to be made between equally desirable but conflicting values: democracy and aristocracy, equality and excellence, the demands of the flesh and the spirit. Berdiaev's ideal of fullness of life embraced all these goods, and it was unnegotiable. Although conceding the tactical usefulness of liberal methods, he seems to have been blind to their moral foundation; he was ultimately no more prepared than his radical opponents to come to terms with the compromises and accommodations of day-to-day political and social life. In his memoirs he writes that long before 1917 he had come to believe that political change could do nothing to raise the spiritual level of human societies; it merely generated new forms of "philistinism."[36] Like that of the religious and radical extremists he attacked, his thought revolved around one central antithesis. They demonized the present and idealized the future; he demonized history and society and glorified the inner world of the exceptional individual. As his liberal critic Kizevetter put it, he attacked the radical intelligentsia for worshipping idols different from his own, without noticing that he had raised the question of whether idols should be worshiped at all.

It was this question precisely that Struve urged the intelligentsia to address in the aftermath of 1905. In an essay of 1908 (optimistically entitled *The Collapse of Tendentiousness*) he observes that the issue of dogma is "the most profound and . . . intractable philosophical problem in the spiritual existence of contemporary people in general, and Russians in particular." The decline of faith in the claims of metaphysical systems such as Marxism had not lessened the attraction of these systems for those who yearned for answers to all questions, and many Russians were now seeking to fill the void by attributing absolute significance to their chosen political, social, and moral objectives, in the belief that dogmatic certainty was the only safeguard against paralyzing skepticism, a notion that Struve categorically rejects. "I am strongly repelled by all kinds of dogmatism, and skeptical of all the pretensions of dogma to absolute validity. But this revulsion against dogma is, after all, a world view of a sort, imbued with the strongest convictions."[37]

His view that dogmatism was "the most subtle, the most spiritual form of despotism" brought him into direct collision with Berdiaev, whom he cites as one of those intellectuals who had recently made a "headlong transition" from positivist to religious dogmatism. At the meetings of the Religious-Philosophical Societies and in print he attacked Bulgakov's idea of a "Christian socialism." Although "all parties and political systems rest on certain religious ideas," it was wrong to believe that these ideas could be formulated in the precepts of a church to which all the members of a party had to assent. Bulgakov's "dogmatic" cast of mind made it impossible for him to accept that "subjective religiosity" was a more appropriate standpoint than dogmatic faith from which to approach life and politics.[38]

Criticism from Merezhkovsky, Berdiaev, and Bulgakov forced Struve to be explicit on the nature of his own "religiosity." He defines religion as "the acceptance and experience of values that transcend the boundaries of personal or social existence, that is, of life in the empirical sense of that word." But he emphasizes that contemporary religious thought could not ignore the revolt against dogmatic metaphysics headed by some of the most creative minds in Europe, from Goethe and Herzen to Nietzsche and Ibsen, and supported by the discoveries of empirical science about the limits of human knowledge and certainty. Struve points to the undogmatic religion (as opposed to the dogmatic morality) of Tolstoy as evidence of a transformation in the modern religious consciousness: "This does not mean that real religion has died. . . . But it has retreated inside the individual, it has become diffident, intimate, undemonstrable." Human beings were moving away from the chiliastic expectations of the materialization of the Kingdom of God that had characterized early Christianity.[39] Russians, however, lagged behind this general development. The theology of Vladimir Solovyov's disciples was a case in point: it was based on a cosmic fantasy just as bogus as the "economic fairy tale" concocted by the radical intelligentsia. Its "childlike" expectation of the miraculous transfiguration of human societies contradicted historical experience and degraded humanity. True mysticism

consists in touching on a mystery, not in uncovering it, not in
the material and complete possession of it. By materializing
God, one displays religion in materialized dogmas, while mysticism hides it in intimate experiences. The world is wrapped in
mystery, but no one can serve it to me on some apocalyptic
plate. Hence mysticism is . . . distinguished by a certain . . .
likeness to healthy intellectual skepticism, by diffidence and
moderation. It is imperative that this be emphasized in our
time, when the name of mysticism is used to cover shameless
. . . excess.[40]

Struve made no distinction between religious and revolutionary forms of
apocalyptic thought, insisting that the "all or nothing" mentality of the New
Religious Consciousness showed as little respect for individual freedom as the
messianism of the Left: both groups shared an ascetic contempt for values that
did not serve their chosen goals. In two essays written with Frank and published in 1905 Struve counters this cultural "nihilism" with a defense of humanism, "by which we mean idealism, a faith in absolute values which is
linked with faith in humanity and its creative tasks on earth." The concept of
culture set out in these essays would henceforth be the basis of Struve's critique
of utopian thought.

Culture in its metaphysical sense, Struve writes, is "humanization, the subordination of natural spontaneity and social spontaneity to the spirit of thinking humanity: it is the struggle of consciousness and will against 'primeval
chaos.'" To love culture was to be concerned with the process of history,
rather than its end; to respect ideals not merely as pure abstractions but in their
incarnation in living individuals and their artefacts:

We do not know and cannot conceive of another creator and
bearer of absolute values than the individual and his spiritual
life. The embodiment of the ideal in reality which is the essence
of cultural creation can be accomplished only by crossing the
point of existence where the world of the ideal intersects the
world of the real, and the creation of absolute values is combined with their realization in empirical life. This point is the
individual consciousness, the spiritual life of the thinking and
acting individual. All ideals, regardless of their content, are free
creations of the individual. It is he who creates science, art,
morality; even in religion, in which the individual often renounces himself, bowing to a higher principle, even here the
principle is the work of man.[41]

An understanding of culture as "the embodiment of the absolute values of the spirit in earthly life, using the means that life supplies" is for Struve the ultimate argument against all theories that reduce the historical past and present to the status of mere staging posts on the way to a state of perfection to be attained in a remote future. Culture is the tangible and visible proof that we should think of humanity's freedom and self-fulfillment not as a future goal but as a present process, acted out through the artifacts, institutions, and social structures which human beings create and sustain in their struggle to shape the contingent world. Only by cultivating a love of culture could Russian society learn to respect individual freedom: the concept of culture includes the battle of ideas but is intrinsically alien to sectarian intolerance:

> Culture holds equally dear the stern travail of solitary thought
> and the passionate song of triumphant flesh. Culture embraces
> the religious rapture of those who sense God in the beating of
> their hearts and see him in the skies. But it gives equal rights
> to the godlessness of rebellious, subversive, doubting human
> thought. Every idea, so long as it is profound and original, every
> work of art, so long as it is beautiful, every moral effort, so
> long as it is sincere and creative, every search for truth, beauty,
> and justice, creates culture.[42]

The link between culture and freedom is therefore such that "even at the most revolutionary moments, culture is never an unimportant trifle"—thus wrote Struve at the height of the 1905 revolution.[43] This sentiment might seem uncontentious, yet the practical conclusions that he drew from it were so novel and shocking to the vast majority of the Russian intelligentsia that they turned him into a political pariah.

Struve believed that the October Manifesto, for all its shortcomings, marked the end of autocratic rule in Russia and the opening up of new opportunities for economic and social construction, and he was dismayed by the Kadet leadership's strategy of confrontation with the government in broad alliance with the Left, which continued to incite the masses to further violence in the hope of destroying the monarchy. In articles and speeches on current events he sought to persuade the more moderate elements of the intelligentsia to use the powers provided by the Duma to school themselves and the masses in concepts of political responsibility, social construction, and the rule of law. With the dissolution of the Second Duma in June 1907 he withdrew from active participation in politics to devote himself to an analysis of the deeper causes of the failure of Russia's constitutional experiment.

Although Struve blamed the government and bureaucracy for their reluctance to honor the spirit and the letter of the 1905 constitution, he focused primarily on the radical intelligentsia's oppositional mentality, itself a product of autocracy. "The [intelligentsia's] lack of political and historical sense, the urge for destruction which borders on lunacy, is not a matter of tactics, it is a whole system of mind which was preceded by a whole ideological education." Its enforced alienation from the political and economic life of the state had led it to an obsession with ideals and absolutes unrelated to historical circumstances. This, allied with its conviction that all forms of compromise with the existing order were immoral, had generated two powerful anticultural movements: populism and Tolstoyism, which combined a wholesale rejection of the values and institutions of existing societies with an ascetic dedication to narrowly defined religious or political absolutes. "The typical Russian *intelligent,* whose conception of the world and whose spiritual mould determine the cultural and moral philosophy of contemporary society . . . is a mixture of the nihilist and the Tolstoyan."[44]

Struve points to the catastrophic effect of this anticultural ethos in the wake of 1905: the Left had pressed on with their attempt to destroy the political and economic structures of the state, not realizing that they were thereby also destroying the patrimony which the Russian people had begun to claim back for themselves. Their efforts had been supported by religious radicals, who had done nothing to help foster the qualities of self-discipline and self-control that were essential both to individual development and economic productivity. It was time that the latter clarified their thinking on the nature of religious self-perfecting and its relation to the perfecting of society: "We need more realism, more attention to the 'material' foundations of life, and at the same time more individualism, more personal creativity, personal effort. . . . We need, in fact, the qualities that created bourgeois society."[45]

The notion of bourgeois virtues was equally alien to religious and radical circles, whose attitude to the European middle class as an ethical and aesthetic phenomenon was expressed in the dual meaning of the word *meshchanstvo:* bourgeoisie and philistinism. Struve contended that Russian progressive thought had so far avoided confronting the central dilemma facing all reforming idealists: the relation between material and spiritual power and wealth. "How is good linked with strength? Negatively or positively?" We have seen that Berdiaev had no doubts on the matter; in his memoirs he recalls: "I never liked strength in this world, disliked the triumphant. And I was always conscious of the agonizing clash between fact and value—the greater strength of the lesser value, the lesser value of the greater strength." Struve believed the dogmatic otherworldliness of a Tolstoy or a Berdiaev to be an evasion of a problem whose dimensions constituted a "metaphysical abyss." True "moral creativity," he argued, consists not in the search for final answers but in an

"uninterrupted process" of effecting provisional balances between complementary or competing goods in response to particular circumstances.[46]

Struve applied this approach to what he considered the most urgently relevant aspect of the metaphysical problem of strength: the question of the relation between the power of the Russian state and the cultural creativity of its
citizens. He quotes Lezhnev in Turgenev's novel *Rudin:* "Russia can do without each of us, but none of us can do without her. . . . Cosmopolitanism . . . is
nonsense. . . . Without a national identity there is no art, no truth, no life;
there is nothing. Without a physiognomy there is not even an ideal face." The
Left's continuing determination to destroy the state after 1905 was based on a
misconception: "As the bearers of power have up to the present day confused
themselves with the state, so those who fight them have confused and continue
to confuse the state with the bearers of power." But "with reference to a state
one cannot speak merely of material . . . strength. All real strength acting
through a state is cultural and therefore spiritual strength. The state . . . depends on the nation, and the nation is a spiritual concept and a spiritual
force."[47] Instead of appealing to the masses' destructive instincts, the intelligentsia should seek to inculcate in them a sense of patriotism based on an identification with the state as an entity transcending the "government," the
guardian of national culture.

To defend the concept of patriotism in Russia at that time was sufficient to
be stigmatized as a reactionary, but Struve went further in two essays of 1908,
expressing views that caused a scandal in progressive circles. Contending that
every state is an organism that needs to assert itself among its peers in order to
maintain its health, he argued that Russia could help heal its internal wounds
by pursuing an expansionist foreign policy based on a vigorous nationalism.

Struve's exaggerated hopes that cultural unity would prove the instrument
of Russia's political and moral regeneration forced him into doctrinaire positions (notably his intolerance of Ukrainian claims to national distinctiveness)
which could not be reconciled with his political liberalism or his notion of
"moral creativity." His views on nationalism can be seen as a blind spot, the result of an overreaction against the cultural nihilism of Russian religious and
radical maximalists, though they did not lead him into any alliances with the
Right.[48] He advised one radical journalist to save himself the trouble of "the ge-
ographical definition of my political position as somewhere between the Kadets and the Octobrists. . . . With the help of party-political meridians he will
never find me on his globe." Struve's vision was his own, formed through the
trials and errors of reflection on the reality around him, not through the hallowed doctrine of any school of thought. On the ground that "true Liberalism
demands the all-round development of the personality, in all the breadth of its
individuality," he called himself a liberal. But he was never a party man, as-

cribing his political isolation to the fact that he adhered to no school of thought with pretensions to sole possession of the truth. His views were "foreign to the 'populists' and the 'Marxists,' the 'Mensheviks' and the 'Bolsheviks,' and even rather shocking to the 'Kadets.' "[49]

His principal offence was to have outraged the conservatism of all these groups: "The Russian intelligentsia as a whole is probably the most conservative breed of people in the world." They refused to adapt their dogmas to changing circumstances, in the belief that all compromise between the purity of their principles and life was "an immoral bargain with evil": "In fact, in its intellectual essence, compromise is the very opposite: it is the moral basis of social existence as such. The antithesis of accord or compromise in human societies is either coercion of others, aimed at subordinating them to my will, or estrangement from others . . . the severance of my will from theirs. The enemies of compromise are either despotism, force, or a hermitlike existence . . . [resulting in] impotence in the world."[50]

Struve emphasizes that his defense of compromise is based not on tactics but on a vision of history which he illustrates with a passage from Tolstoy's story "Lucerne":

> What a miserable, pitiful creature is man with his demand for
> positive solutions, thrown into the eternally moving, endless
> ocean of good and evil, of facts, calculations and contradictions!
> For centuries people have been battling and laboring in order to
> move good onto one side and evil to the other. Centuries pass
> and whatever the dispassionate intellect throws onto the scales
> of good and evil, in whatever place, the scales do not move: on
> each side there is as much evil as there is good. If only man
> could learn not to make harsh and absolute judgments, and not
> to give answers to questions that have been put to him only in
> order that they should eternally remain questions! If only he
> could understand that every idea is both false and true; false in
> its one-sidedness, because of the impossibility of grasping the
> truth in its entirety, and true because it expresses one aspect of
> human strivings. People have made subdivisions for themselves
> in this ceaselessly shifting, infinite, eternal, chaotic confusion
> of good and evil, have drawn lines on this sea, and expect the
> sea to divide accordingly. As if there were not millions of other
> subdivisions, made from a completely different point of view, on
> a different plane. True, these new subdivisions take centuries to
> formulate, but millions of centuries have passed and millions
> more will pass. Civilization is good, barbarism evil; freedom is

good, slavery evil. But who will define for me freedom, despotism, civilization, barbarism? And where are the boundaries of
one and the other? In whose soul is the yardstick of good and
evil so unshakeable that he can use it to measure the tangle of
fleeting facts? Whose mind is so great as to be able, even in the
immobile past, to encompass all facts and weigh them? And who
has seen a state in which good did not exist together with evil?
And why do I know that I do not see more of one than of the
other merely because I am not standing in the right place? And
who is able to detach his mind from life completely, even for an
instant, so as to look at it independently from above?[51]

That there is no "view from nowhere," that all our judgments about truth
and morality are historically and contextually embedded, was still a novel
proposition at the beginning of the twentieth century. Struve could cite few authorities other than Tolstoy in its support: he mentions Ibsen's artistic vision,
Goethe's realism, Herzen's and Nietzsche's attacks on teleological thinking.
The dogmatic moralist in Tolstoy, contradicting the insights of the artist, he
sees as demonstrating the tenacity of the pull in an opposing direction, toward
the security of a system of eternal rules and final goals, an integral worldview.
But this last term is habitually misused: "My integral worldview is myself as an
individual; I can't obtain one from somewhere outside me. At first sight this
seems a proclamation of extreme spiritual anarchism. But the recognition that
a 'view of the world' can be based only on a subjective and individual linking
of parts is only the recognition of the . . . freedom of each individual spirit."[52]

Struve was asking the intelligentsia to think of freedom not as self-
transcendence but as self-creation, to shift its focus from changeless ideals and
ultimate goals to the competing values and perspectives of the present, and to
view the individual as creative interpreter of his or her world. He emphasized
that what he was demanding was not a change in tactics but a process of self-
education starting with "a revaluation of one's feelings and ideas."[53] He commented wryly that he was at a polemical disadvantage with regard to his
opponents; he could offer no set of doctrines to compete with theirs. But he
frequently used a method more appropriate to the content of his message: an
embodied portrayal of his ideal of inner freedom—most strikingly, in the person of Aleksandr Herzen.

Although Herzen was recognized as an original and outstanding thinker,
the radical intelligentsia met his detachment from all parties and doctrines and
his protest against the dehumanizing effect of metaphysical systems with incomprehension and hostility. His views were also anathema to the messianic

strand of Russian religious idealism: in an essay of 1903 Bulgakov describes Herzen as a tragic figure, a "moral corpse," whose refusal to acknowledge a transcendent meaning in history had deprived him of the "integral worldview . . . that every individual needs."[54]

In two speeches, Struve presented an opposing assessment of Herzen as "one of our national heroes of the spirit," a true humanist, to whom nothing human was alien except the spirit of despotism. "Such people are capable of all passions, except the most cruel, the dogmatic. Such people sometimes die on the barricades, but they never call others to [them], and never drag them to the scaffold."[55] His example both as a thinker and a human type could help lead Russian society to a better awareness of the true nature of freedom. Struve illustrated his point by quoting from *To an Old Comrade*, in which Herzen takes issue with Bakunin's slogan "the urge to destroy is a creative urge," asserting that great revolutions are not made by the unleashing of destructive passions:

> Blown up by gunpowder, the bourgeois world, once the smoke settles and the ruins are cleared, will arise again . . . with just a few changes, because it still retains its hold on people's minds, and also because the new world in the process of construction . . . is not yet ready to take its place. . . . The people's consciousness . . . is the *raw* product of the succession of efforts, endeavors, events, successes and failures that make up human coexistence. One must accept it as a natural fact and grapple with it . . . by studying it, mastering its workings. . . . I don't believe in the seriousness of people who prefer demolition and brute force to development and bargaining. . . . We need apostles, not . . . sappers equipped for destruction, apostles who will preach not only to their own, but also to the enemy.[56]

Struve observes that such passages reveal a profound understanding of the evolutionary nature of true progress and of the moral meaning of compromise as an attempt to reconcile theories and principles with the real-life needs of human beings. This was why Herzen's writings offered "no ready-made solutions or firm recipes" but revealed a greater "religious respect" for the human personality than some of Russia's most revered religious seekers—Dostoevsky, for example, who sought "with a dogmatic passion to discover the final, ultimate solution, before which one must submit, which would free one from further seeking"; and Tolstoy, who believed that he had found the truth and aimed to smash everything that stood in its way.[57]

In the concluding lines of *To an Old Comrade* Herzen pleads for pity, not only for people but also for "things":

A savage, unrestrained upheaval . . . will spare nothing. . . . Together with the capital amassed by usurers, it will destroy another kind of capital, passed from generation to generation and
from nation to nation. A capital in which is sunk the character
and creativity of various periods, in which the annals of human
life have stratified and history has crystallized. . . . The raging
force of destruction will obliterate, along with all boundary
lines, those that mark the limits of human forces, toward which
individuals have striven in all directions . . . from the beginning
of civilization.

It is enough that Christianity and Islam shattered the ancient world, that the French Revolution exacted punishment on
statues, paintings, and monuments. It does not become *us* to
play at being iconoclasts.

I felt all that so acutely, standing in dull sadness and almost
in shame . . . in front of some custodian who was pointing to a
bare wall or a smashed sculpture, a tomb that had been dug up
repeating: "All that was destroyed during the revolution."[58]

This passage seems to encapsulate Struve's view of the embeddedness of absolute values and ideals in the contingent lives and goals of individuals and in
the continuity of culture. He himself cites a remarkably similar text in reviewing the letters of a more recent critic of the intelligentsia, the writer Aleksandr
Ertel, who had died in 1908. A performance of Chekhov's play *The Cherry Orchard* had caused Ertel to reflect on the violence and expropriations carried out
by some sections of the Left in 1905 in the name of revolutionary justice. He remarks that the indiscriminate destruction of family possessions handed down
over generations had a deep spiritual significance:

Here you have . . . the crude destruction of a kind of sacred
thing, a pogrom carried out on intimate objects, which link
whole generations in a common bond through material things,
memories, a way of life. . . . Let us admit that . . . according to
mathematical calculations the safekeeping of these "sacred
things" existed at the cost of others' work, hardship, discomfort,
humiliation, even downright slavery; but . . . all the same, in all
revolutionary destruction there is something deeply unjust. Oh,
if only it could destroy just decaying vestiges, laws, customs
and institutions that have outlived their time, but not organisms with blood circulating in their veins, with . . . living
hearts. But the "institution of private property" is just such an
organism, and in reality the great majority of so-called revolu-

tionaries are working, consciously or unconsciously, for the sake
of this very institution, but only in order to transfer its benefits
to other classes. When you watch *The Cherry Orchard,* you see
something that is merely sad, just as natural death is sad; but
when cherry orchards are destroyed by a frenzied crowd, according to the recipe of the SRs, that is as shocking as murder.[59]

The images in this passage convey more compellingly than any logical argument the sense of history that Struve regarded as essential to an understanding of the moral basis of political compromise. He held that the Russian
maximalists lacked this sense of the rootedness of all human creativity and ideals in particular historical contexts and in the humble paraphernalia of everyday existence. They believed that all compromise was morally wrong, whereas,
on the contrary, genuine compromise was inspired by "an honest attitude to
life," an acceptance that the endless variety of empirical existence could never
be reduced to one common denominator, whether that be Tolstoy or Christ.

Struve contrasts the "formalism" of Tolstoy, who sought to regulate moral
life by a set of fixed rules, with the moral "artistry" of Ertel, who cultivated an
openness to the variety of concrete existence that would prevent him from being "harnessed between any sectarian shafts." He describes Ertel's moral outlook as an "aesthetics of behavior." This could be a conscious echo of a famous
passage in a letter from Herzen to his son: "There are no general rules, but
there is improvisation . . . an aesthetics of behavior, which a developed person
strives to attain."[60]

In his biography of Struve, Frank records that he liked to quote a phrase of
Goethe: "Das Leben müss als Kunstwerk gestaltet werden" (One must shape
one's life so that it is a harmonious artistic creation). But Struve's aesthetic individualism was far removed from the Nietzschean (and Berdiaevian) view of
self-creation as the exceptional individual's romantic stance of defiance against
a historical reality that is unworthy of him. He constantly emphasizes that freedom can be achieved only within that reality, "using the means that it supplies," an approach that Frank suggests is best characterized by Goethe's term
"object-thinking" (*gegenständliches Denken*): thought that is riveted to reality.[61]

For Struve, as for the writers whom he holds up as models, personal moral
development involved the cultivation of a sense of relationships that allowed
one to reconcile competing demands in any given situation without being
bound by fixed rules or absolute principles. He believed that his contemporaries' predilection for the latter showed how far they had yet to go in that direction. Struve points to the way in which individuals' relations with themselves
govern their attitude to the external world: Tolstoy was as unsparing in his
moral demands on others as he was to himself, demanding the crippling of real

personalities in the name of an absolute ideal. Moral maximalism was fed by hatred, conciliation (when not a concession to evil) by a benevolent acceptance of the limitations and imperfections of contingent existence. Struve quotes Herzen: "I try to understand the size of the human step in the past and present, so as to judge how to keep pace with it, neither lagging behind nor advancing so far ahead that people won't keep up with me." There was, he believed, no one form of social existence that was the best for all times and places. One should instead look for structures that could be constantly and sensitively adjusted to maintain a balance between the individual and the social whole. But (as Struve and Frank warned the warring sides in 1905) "this balance will always be fluctuating and unstable, and it is precisely this instability that creates the conditions for creativity and cultural life."[62]

In his reminiscences of Struve, Frank argues that his "sobriety"—his opposition on religious and moral grounds to what he construed as "the dreamer's irresponsible attitude to reality"—distinguished him from the dominant type of Russian religious thinker.[63] This quality was undoubtedly the cause of his rift with Berdiaev and Bulgakov.

They both began to criticize Struve in 1906. Berdiaev claimed that he lacked the spiritual resources to furnish an antidote to the poison of revolution. His position was "very tragic": the "most outstanding man in the Kadet Party" and "perhaps the only creative political mind in Russia," he adhered to a moderate platform which (unlike the doctrines of the Left and Right) could never appeal to the people's religious enthusiasm:

> Russia has been handed over by the will of fate into the power
> of extremes: the red and black colors hold sway. What are
> needed here are not pale theories, moderate and devoid of en-
> thusiasm, but fresh, flaming ideas.
>
> Such ideas can only be religious and no less radical than
> those of the Social Democrats or the Black Hundreds. Until
> Struve will acknowledge this, all the potential in him will yield
> few results. He is, after all, a skeptic, and therefore he does not
> know the secret of how to rule hearts, the secret known to men
> of red and black.

As a skeptical rationalist, Berdiaev contends, Struve could comprehend neither the "mystery of history" nor the "mysteries of the Russian soul." Bulgakov criticizes Struve on the same grounds: he and Frank had sown immense confusion with a religious individualism that contradicted the mystical notion of sobornost, to which the Russian people were destined to give historical shape.[64]

Viewed from within the tradition of Russian religious messianism, Struve appeared to represent a rival orthodoxy: the rationalist optimism of the Enlightenment. Neither of his two critics perceived that his position was incompatible with all eschatological interpretations of the historical process, whether religious or secular. "The Apocalypse versus History . . . : two different perceptions of the historical process and of religion confront each other. There can be no intellectual reconciliation between them." This comment, from one of Struve's polemics with Merezhkovsky and his group, expresses a prescient awareness of the scale of the revolution in thought that had begun with the questioning of dogmatic metaphysical systems. Like Herzen, he believed that "in passing from the old world to the new, you can bring nothing with you."[65] Rejection of the belief in predestined progress, by shifting our attention from the goals of history to the process itself, must radically transform our perception of the present.

In his attempt to map out the consequences of this shift for our understanding of truth and morality, Struve was ahead of his time. His emphasis on the cultural context of beliefs and values anticipates.that distinctive line of late twentieth-century moral inquiry which seeks to jettison the problematic assumptions of moral absolutism without sinking into a Nietzschean relativism, holding onto the notion of progress through concepts of narrative and embodiment. A comparison with the approach of Alasdair MacIntyre, one of the most influential of such philosophers, will illustrate my point.

MacIntyre rejects the belief that moral ideals are timeless concepts, independent of historical context: all moral inquiry is embodied in individuals, whose lives have the unitary nature of a quest to discover and live out what is the good for themselves. This quest is intelligible only as part of a longer and larger narrative: the self acquires its moral identity only within a community, as a bearer of a tradition. Moral inquiry conducted within living traditions resembles participation in a craft whose practitioners share an ideal of perfection that they seek to reach by interpreting and reinterpreting their tradition, the better to comprehend at any given historical moment the future possibilities that the past has made available to the present. MacIntyre's analogy highlights the complementary role of theory and narrative in moral inquiry and the moral life: we do not know a theory until we can answer the question of what type of enacted narrative would be its embodiment. Such answers cannot be deduced from sets of rules; knowing what rules apply to what situations is a matter of judgment that depends on an adequate sense of the traditions to which one belongs or which one confronts. The same kind of judgment is required for the understanding of political processes of change, development, or revolution, which are also inescapably narratives of embodied moral inquiry, successful or unsuccessful. This position is quite distinct from a Nietzschean perspectivism: it acknowledges truth as a standard independent of the tradition that seeks to measure itself by truth, while at the same time pointing out that there is no thesis or doctrine to be so measured which is not presented as the thesis of a particular set of "tradition-informed and tradition-directed" individuals and groups. "It is only when theories are located in history, when we view the demand for justification in highly particular contexts of a historical kind, that we are freed from either dogmatism or capitulation to scepticism."[66]

Struve would have concurred with this: he once remarked that Russians "like to enthuse about the charms of an integral worldview. But . . . they forget . . . that every worldview is integrated in a living personality and is incomplete on pages of paper."[67] Like MacIntyre, he presents his concept of the historical situatedness of the self as a corrective to two distorted approaches to morality: that which identifies personal desires and motives with universal principles, and the solipsistic view of a self creating its own laws in opposition to society and history. He believed that neither was compatible with the sense of personal responsibility which was the source of true morality. The Nietzschean self-creator was accountable only to himself; the revolutionary or religious utopian believed himself the obedient tool of history or of Providence. As Struve showed, in the nightmarish atmosphere of revolutionary Russia they all shared a symbiotic existence, divided on goals and tactics but bound together by the fact that, devoid of a sense of history, they lived in eschatological time.

"Apocalyptic religion is based on faith in the materialization of God's Kingdom by supernatural means. . . . But there is another kind of religion which has taken from Christianity the basic defining idea of 'The Kingdom of God is within you.' These different conceptions of religion determine differing attitudes to the Russian revolution and to the 'intelligentsia.' "[68] Thus wrote Struve in February 1908. The truth of the last sentence would be demonstrated one year later in *Signposts*. Semyon Frank recalls that after its publication he remarked to the literary historian Mikhail Gershenzon, who had initiated the volume, that the two of them had really intended to attack each other, but "because the 'Russian intelligentsia' stood in the gap between us, we began to attack it together, although from different sides."[69] We shall see that the contributions of the four ex-Marxists stood in a somewhat similar relationship.

The symposium's purpose was outlined in Gershenzon's preface. In 1905–06 the values of the Left had been tried and found wanting. The nature of the revolution and of its failure had provided the contributors to the volume (all long-term critics of the intelligentsia) with new and compelling evidence for their position. Their desire to speak out was reinforced by the belief that their critique would meet a generally recognized need for a fundamental reexamination of the radical intelligentsia's traditional outlook.

Gershenzon had selected his authors carefully: the volume would owe much of its impact to the fact that it could not credibly be dismissed as yet another attack on the intelligentsia from the Right. All seven authors had been prominent opponents of autocracy, and some (including Frank, Berdiaev, and Struve) had been imprisoned or exiled for their views. Five (the former Marxists and the legal philosopher B. A. Kistiakovsky, a member of the Kadet Party) had contributed to *Problems of Idealism*. A. S. Izgoev was a journalist and Kadet Party activist. Gershenzon (whose personal philosophy was a compound of Slavophile romanticism and a Tolstoyan cult of simplicity) notes that the contributors differed greatly among themselves "both on basic questions of 'faith' and in their practical preferences" but that they agreed on a common platform: "the recognition of the theoretical and practical primacy of spiritual life over the external forms of community."

> They mean by this that the individual's inner life is the sole creative force in human existence, and that this inner life, and not the self-sufficient principles of the political realm, constitutes the only solid basis on which a society can be built. . . . [They] see the Russian intelligentsia's ideology, which rests entirely on the opposite principle—recognition of the unconditional primacy of social forms—as inherently erroneous and futile in practice. That is, it both contradicts the nature of the human spirit and is incapable of achieving the goal which the intelligentsia has set for itself, the emancipation of the people.[70]

Subsequent commentators have commonly argued that the differences alluded to by Gershenzon did not detract from the ideological coherence of the volume, a view shared by most of Russian society at the time, which saw *Signposts* as the product of a united anti-intelligentsia front.[71] But in discussions in the Religious-Philosophical Societies and in print, Struve accused his radical opponents of exaggerating the work's ideological unity: the traditional division in Russian thought between Slavophiles and Westernizers was "patently evident" in it. Gershenzon's and Bulgakov's contributions, he pointed out, were much closer to Merezhkovsky's apocalyptic brand of thinking than to those of Frank, Kistiakovsky, Izgoev, and himself.[72]

The Apocalypse versus History: this debate, which runs as a leading thread through the polemics of Russian Slavophiles and Westernizers, dogmatists and skeptics, is reflected in *Signposts* in contrasting diagnoses of the intelligentsia's spiritual disease, and the opposing remedies for it. Following the debate through the essays of the four thinkers whose development I have traced so far, it becomes evident that while one tendency makes a radical break with the intelligentsia's dominant traditions, the other is merely a form of sectarian dissension within its ranks. *Signposts* pointed in two directions: forward, to a new vision of the self and the world, and backward, to alternative versions of the old.

There is agreement among the *Signposts* authors on one point. The dominant characteristics of the intelligentsia's outlook are a thirst for justice and equality (expressed in the legendary selflessness of its leaders and its long martyrology as champion of the oppressed), combined with a denial of the existence of absolute, universally binding values. Ranging over the intelligentsia's attitudes toward law, philosophy, culture, the people, and the state, they come to broadly similar conclusions.

Frank's essay "The Ethic of Nihilism" addresses the question of why the revolutionary movement created and shaped by the intelligentsia's moral values had so rapidly degenerated into unprincipled violence and licentiousness. He finds the answer in the relationship between their nihilism and the moralism that had engendered it: the suspicion of all self-sufficient values, scientific, aesthetic, or religious, whose claims on the individual might distract him from the task of improving the lot of the majority. Denying all objective values, they had come to deify the subjective interests of the people:

> Nihilism and moralism; non-belief and fanatically stringent
> moral demands; lack of principle in the metaphysical sense—for
> nihilism is the denial of judgments made on principle and of
> the objective distinction between good and evil—and the fierc-
> est conscientiousness in observing empirical principles, which
> are in essence conditional, non-principled demands: this distinc-
> tive, rationally incomprehensible and yet vitally powerful fusion
> of antagonistic elements into a mighty psychological force is
> the mentality that we term nihilistic moralism.

It had found an appropriate outlet in the social philosophy of "revolutionism": the faith that social struggle and the violent destruction of existing social forms constitute the primary means for achieving one's moral and social ideals. Revolutionism was based on the optimistic theory that the factors preventing the establishment of earthly happiness lie not within human beings but outside, and that the harmonious organization of life is a natural condition that will set in of its own accord once the obstacles barring its path are swept away. In 1905 the contradiction between the universally binding, religiously absolute *character* and the nihilistically unprincipled *content* of the intelligentsia's faith had produced "real, poisonous fruits," providing a justification for the primacy of might over right in the name of partisan interests. As party ranks swelled during the revolution, class and party nihilism were frequently replaced by personal nihilism, as hoodlums and murderers took advantage of the fact that the intelligentsia's faith involuntarily allowed them to assume the mantle of ideological commitment and progressive thought.[73]

In his contribution, "Philosophical Verity and Intelligentsia Truth," Berdiaev accuses the intelligentsia of seeking in philosophy only a sanction for its social goals and ideals; hence its "almost insane tendency" to divide philosophical doctrines into "proletarian" and "bourgeois," "Left" and "Right," and its implacable hostility to idealism, which it suspected of being unfavorable to its cause. "It does not care if metaphysics is possible, or if metaphysical truths exist; its only concern is whether metaphysics harms the people's interests by distracting attention from the struggle with autocracy and from service to the proletariat." Its interest in truth had been almost destroyed by love for the people's welfare: but this was a false love, which did not respect their human dignity. It had succumbed to the temptation of the Grand Inquisitor, who demanded the renunciation of truth in the name of humanity's material well-being.[74]

In "Heroism and Asceticism," Bulgakov argues that the intelligentsia's yearning for justice has led it to an atheistic deification of the human race, based on a faith in the natural perfection of human beings and their potential for infinite progress. Above all, the intelligentsia worshiped itself, as the bearer of enlightenment in Russia and the future savior of the people. "Consciously or unconsciously, [it] lives in an atmosphere of expectation, awaiting the social miracle, the universal cataclysm—it lives in an eschatological frame of mind." Hence the maximalism that had been characteristic of all the parties of the Left in the revolution. Their programs were religious credos, ideological monoliths which could be accepted or rejected only in toto and were based on a simplistic view of the task of historical construction: in the eyes of the self-worshiping hero this required little more than "strong muscles and nerves." Maximalist ends were matched by a total lack of scruple with regard to means, a necessary consequence of the mentality of self-worship.[75]

Struve's essay "The Intelligentsia and Revolution" contends that the key to an understanding of the revolution lies in the radical intelligentsia's alienation from the state, reinforced by its socialist optimism, which held that the root of all oppression lay in imperfect institutions. Its propaganda in 1905, aimed at inflaming the people's destructive appetites, had been much more than a tactical lapse: "It was a moral error. It was based on the notion that society's 'progress' need not be the fruit of human improvement, but could be instead a jackpot to be won at the gambling table of history by appealing to popular unrest."[76]

The other three authors develop similar themes. In his essay "In Defense of

Law," Kistiakovsky argues that the intelligentsia's emphasis on force and destruction as the path to an ideal moral world order has led it to overlook the role of law as the safeguard of individual rights and social stability. Izgoev examines how the radical culture of the Russian student youth has schooled them in evaluating ideas and individuals by political standards, whereas Gershenzon, in an essay entitled "Creative Self-Consciousness," argues that the pressure of radical opinion, by impelling the intelligentsia to concentrate its energies on social and political problems, has distorted its members' personalities and arrested their spiritual development.

The *Signposts* authors were agreed on the recent and potential effects of the intelligentsia's belief in the primacy of social forms over the inner lives of individuals. But they were divided on a key question: whether the messianic faith that had been the driving force of both the radical movement's nihilism and its moralism should be abandoned or merely redirected into other channels. This issue was addressed most directly by the four with whom we are principally concerned; their conclusions, consistent with the views they had expressed for a decade on the nature of the religious perception of the world, present two contrary sets of proposals for Russia's spiritual regeneration.

The question at stake was the relation of the intelligentsia's maximalism to a religious understanding of the world. According to Bulgakov, "a certain otherworldliness, an eschatological dream of the City of God and the future reign of justice (under various socialist pseudonyms) and a striving for the salvation of mankind—if not from sin, then from suffering—are . . . the immutable and distinctive pecularities of the Russian intelligentsia." Berdiaev, too, discerned an "unconscious religiosity" in the intelligentsia's maximalism, "the promise of positive and valuable qualities: a thirst for an integral world-view that would fuse theory and life, and a thirst for faith." He points to the affinities of this trait with the eschatological tradition of Dostoevsky and Vladimir Solovyov, arguing that only "historically conditioned prejudices" had prevented the intelligentsia from finding the answers to its quest for freedom, brotherhood, and progress in the teachings of Russian religious philosophy rather than in those of Western atheistic socialism.[77]

Struve and Frank, on the contrary, categorically reject the notion that the intelligentsia's outlook was even unconsciously religious. Frank argues that this currently "fashionable" claim is true only if one equates religion with mere fanaticism. The intelligentsia's hostility to religious values was not due simply to a mistaken belief in the reactionary nature of all religions: "On the contrary, we see here the inherent and inevitable metaphysical repulsion of two modes of contemplating and perceiving the world; it is the primordial and irreconcilable struggle between the religious attitude that strives to draw human life closer to a superhuman, absolute principle and to discover an eternal and universal support for it, and the *nihilistic* attitude that strives to immortalize and absolutize what is only 'human, too human.' "[78]

Struve dismisses claims about the intelligentsia's "otherworldliness" as a myth propagated by Vladimir Solovyov. He points out that the Left's rejection of existing institutions and "bourgeois" values is inspired not by mystical intuition but by a set of rationalistic political dogmas: "It denies the world in the name of the world, and thereby serves neither the world nor God." The fundamental elements of Christianity are faith in God, combined with faith in the "redemptive power and decisive importance of personal creation." Hence the intelligentsia's maximalism should not be confused with forms of radicalism inspired by religious principles:

> No matter how decisively religious radicalism may pose political and social problems it cannot fail to see them as problems of a person's education. Even if this education is accomplished through direct communion with God, by superhuman means, so to speak, it remains human education and improvement: it is addressed to the individual person, his inner powers and his sense of responsibility. Conversely, all forms of atheistic maximalism brush aside the problem of education in politics and social reform, replacing it with the external organization of life.

Education in the religious sense "is completely alien to socialist optimism. It believes not in organization but only in creation, in a person's positive labor on himself, in his inner struggle for the sake of creative tasks." The intelligentsia's rejection of the opportunity to educate the masses in political responsibility in favor of continuing a struggle to the death against the state and the "bourgeois" social structure showed that it had no glimmer of a religious idea: "Credulity without faith, struggle without creation, fanaticism without enthusiasm, intolerance without reverence—in a word, here were all the external features of religiosity without its content."[79]

Gershenzon had stipulated that there be no prior discussion of the contents of *Signposts*, and most of the contributors did not see one another's articles before publication.[80] The polemical confrontation between the two pairs of authors was therefore unplanned, but it was also inevitable. No amount of editorial discussion could have bridged the gulf between them on the question of the merits of religious and political messianism. *Signposts* had the unintended effect of publicly exposing the fundamental disagreement among these critics of the intelligentsia on the very questions on which they were most eager to enlighten it: the nature of progress and Russia's relation to the culture of the West. The character of the division can be illustrated best by a comparison of

Bulgakov's and Frank's moral evaluations of the intelligentsia's hostility to what it termed "bourgeois culture."

Bulgakov observes that (as Dostoevsky, among others, had perceived) "the intelligentsia is psychologically alien . . . to the solid bourgeois tenor of life of Western Europe, with its everyday virtues and its economy based on hard work, but with its barrenness and limitations as well. . . . This constricted and spiritually earthbound way of life sickens the Russian *intelligent*." In this attitude to the West there was a element of "plain slovenliness," an aversion to disciplined habits of work, but there was also evidence of "an unconsciously religious aversion to spiritual philistinism, to 'the kingdom of this world,' with its placid self-satisfaction." Although Russians needed to emulate the "technology" of life in the West, its spiritual life was dominated by "bourgeois philistinism," the fruit of a combination of negative philosophical developments (skepticism, rationalism, positivism, materialism, and humanistic individualism) which derived from the "so-called Enlightenment." The face of Europe "is being steadily disfigured, its features stiffening in the chill of philistinism as the popular philosophy of the Enlightenment permeates the masses," edging out the positive aspects of European culture which sprang from its religious roots. Among these Bulgakov cites the English Reformation's proclamation of political freedom, freedom of conscience, and the rights of man, as well as the role of the Protestant ethic in the development of capitalism. But he looks elsewhere for a model of discipline to set before the intelligentsia—namely, to the ascetic tradition of the Orthodox Church, arguing that although the atheistic socialism of the Russian Left was a construct of the European Enlightenment, it owed its most positive qualities (the puritanism, asceticism, and readiness for self-sacrifice that characterized such leaders as Dobroliubov and Chernyshevsky) to the pervasive influence of the Church on Russian society. The atheistic hero took on himself the role of Providence in an act of spiritual usurpation; the Christian ascetic saw himself as Providence's tool, seeking to fulfill God's plan for him through a life of unremitting self-renunciation and self-control. The intelligentsia's spiritual affinity with this ideal gave grounds for hope that its current ideological crisis might be overcome by a process of "religious healing."[81]

In Frank's view, the intelligentsia's ascetic suspicion of the aspiration to earthly well-being was an indication of a spiritual deficiency: the inability to grasp the metaphysical concept of culture that was inherent in the consciousness of the educated European:

> The objective, intrinsically valuable development of the external
> and internal conditions of life; increased material and spiritual
> productivity; perfection of political, social and domestic forms

of intercourse; progress in morality, religion, science and art; in a word, the multifarious labor of raising collective existence to an objectively higher level—this is the vital concept of culture . . . that inspires the European. . . . From this point of view, culture exists not for some good or purpose, but only for itself; cultural creation signifies the improvement of human nature and the embodiment of ideal values in life, and as such it is in itself a superior and self-sufficient object of human activity.

In contrast to this concept, culture as we usually understand it here is stamped with utilitarianism throughout. When our people speak of culture they mean either railroads, sewage systems and highways, or the development of popular education, or the improvement of the political mechanism. They always offer us something useful, a *means* for achieving some other end— namely the satisfaction of life's subjective needs. But a wholly utilitarian concept is incompatible with the pure idea of culture, just as a wholly utilitarian concept of science or art destroys the very essence of what we call science or art.[82]

This notion of culture (echoing the essays that Frank had written with Struve in 1905) is the starting point for an analysis of the intelligentsia's "otherworldliness" which comes to very different conclusions from Bulgakov's.

Several *Signposts* authors had noted as a feature of the intelligentsia's mechanistic theory of progress its tendency to absolutize the principle of distribution and undervalue the processes of creation and production. Frank points out that this trait extends to material as well as spiritual production. To ignore the claims of either was "a philosophical error and a moral sin." It was time to understand that "our life is not simply unjust, but is primarily poor and squalid, and that the poverty stricken cannot become rich if they devote all their attention solely to the equal distribution of their few pennies." He observes that he is using the concept of wealth in a metaphysical sense, "which regards material well-being as only an accessory and a symbolic index of spiritual power and productivity . . . [and] coincides with the idea of culture as the aggregate of ideal values embodied in historical life." Clearly, national wealth did not in itself ensure popular welfare, but for Russia at that juncture it was "infinitely more important to keep in mind the simpler and more obvious truth that without national wealth popular welfare is quite inconceivable. . . . It is time we advanced from distribution and the struggle for it to cultural creation and the production of wealth."

But to produce wealth, one must value it, and the intelligentsia did not. Its moralism impelled it to renounce material gratification until life's blessings were available to all, and with many this led to an intense personal asceticism, a quality which Frank, unlike Bulgakov, believes to be devoid of spiritual value because of its link with cultural nihilism:

> The Russian *intelligent* feels a positive love for the simplifica-
> tion, impoverishment and constriction of life. A social reformer,
> he is also, and even more so, a monk who hates worldly vanity
> and diversions, all luxury, whether material or spiritual, all
> wealth and substance, all power and productivity. He loves the
> weak, the poor, the wretched in body and spirit, but not just as
> unfortunates whom he can help make strong and rich, thereby
> eliminating them as social or spiritual types; he loves them pre-
> cisely as ideal types of humanity. He wants to make the people
> wealthy but fears wealth itself as a burden and temptation, and
> believes that all the rich are evil while all the poor are good
> and kind. He strives for the "dictatorship of the proletariat" and
> dreams of giving power to the people, yet fears any contact
> with power; he considers it evil and all who wield it oppressors.
> He wants to give the people enlightenment, spiritual benefits
> and spiritual strength, but in the depth of his soul he feels that
> spiritual wealth, too, is a luxury and believes that purity of in-
> tention can compensate for and outweigh any knowledge or
> skill. The ideal of a simple, guileless, squalid but innocent life
> attracts him. The Russian national hero Ivanushka the Fool,
> "the blessed," whose simplicity of heart and holy naiveté con-
> quer all the strong, rich and clever ones, is the Russian intelli-
> gentsia's hero as well. . . .
>
> In summary, we can define the classic Russian *intelligent* as
> a *militant monk of the nihilistic religion of earthly well-being.*

Frank notes that the intelligentsia's asceticism should not be confused with other varieties (such as Tolstoy's) which had a religious foundation. Although their version seemed to contradict the nihilistic hedonism of their social philosophy (whose ultimate goal was the broadest possible satisfaction of human needs), "when it comes to appreciating spiritual wealth or the general idea of culture . . . [the Left's] ascetic self-restraint is reinforced by nihilistic unbelief and materialism; these two elements then join forces in endorsing a negative attitude toward culture, consolidating barbarism and giving it a principled justification."[83]

Frank and Struve feared that the intelligentsia's messianic drive would plunge the Russian people into barbarism: Berdiaev and Bulgakov hoped that, appropriately redirected, it would lead them to the City of God. These two prognoses were based on two mutually irreconcilable approaches to history, culture, and the individual personality, each of which is presented in *Signposts* as the key to the regeneration of Russian culture.

The two dogmatic idealists believed that the historical process derives its meaning from its future end, a spiritual transfiguration of human societies which would realize Russian philosophy's dream of an "organic fusion of truth and goodness, of knowledge and faith." Their belief that humanity's mission on earth was to strive for the ultimate triumph of spirit over matter dictated a narrowly utilitarian view of the intelligentsia's immediate tasks. Berdiaev is concerned in *Signposts* with only one feature of the Left's negative attitude to creativity: its hostility to philosophical idealism, specifically to the apocalyptic tradition of Dostoevsky and Solovyov. As a "Christian socialist" Bulgakov believed the attainment of economic and social justice to be an inseparable part of spiritual progress, but there is an unresolved tension in his essay between recognition of the need for the intelligentsia to contribute to Russia's economic recovery by developing disciplined habits of work and the fear that such habits might turn them into "solid bourgeois." His ambivalence toward the "everyday virtues" fostered in the West by the Protestant work ethic leads him to advocate a very different kind of discipline: the solitary self-renunciation of the Christian ascetic.[84]

Those who believe that human societies are moving toward the harmonizing of all purposes tend not to be enthusiastic defenders of the right of individuals in the present to pursue their own concept of the good in their own way. Bulgakov's hostility to liberal individualism finds expression in *Signposts* in an almost hysterical denunciation of the European Enlightenment for shattering the spiritual unity of humanity by proclaiming the autonomy of human reason and for spawning the positivism that had led to an excessive emphasis on the material conditions for progress: "Measured by religious standards European philistinism's deification of itself—in socialism and individualism alike—is nothing but repulsive complacency and spiritual rapine, a temporary dulling of consciousness." Obedience is the primary virtue of Bulgakov's Christian hero, whose mission is to be the tool of Providence, while Berdiaev's variety of anarchism seemingly does not embrace the notion of the individual's freedom to pursue a personal vision of freedom. He maintains that Russia's spiritual redemption depends on its people's attaining a "communality of philosophical consciousness." The intelligentsia must overcome its hostility to the tradition of Vladimir Solovyov, whom Berdiaev believed should be acknowledged as Russia's national philosopher.[85]

Dogmatic religious belief is not inherently incompatible with a liberal social philosophy that supports ideological diversity and political pluralism—the values with which critics have commonly identified *Signposts* as a whole. But the religious messianism of both thinkers is unambiguously opposed to these values, demanding, as a sine qua non of Russia's spiritual recovery, general adherence to a body of doctrine that makes no clear distinction between religious and political tasks.

Bulgakov asserts that the intelligentsia can regain contact with the people and play a positive national role only by adopting the national religion. It would thereby come to comprehend Russia's "world mission" of spiritual and cultural enlightenment, as expounded by the Slavophiles, Dostoevsky, and Solovyov. There was an urgent national need for a "church intelligentsia" able to elucidate Russia's historical tasks as one of that elite of nations destined to follow ancient Israel as bearer of the "religious-messianic idea."

A church army of propagandists bent on ensuring unanimity of faith would be unlikely heralds of the "joyous renaissance, the awakening of dormant spirits," to which Berdiaev looked forward when Russian thought was freed from the oppressive power of politics. But he too regards this event as the exchange of one form of doctrinal unity for another. The "national philosophical tradition" whose creation he sees as an urgent priority will provide the intelligentsia with "a synthesis of knowledge and faith . . . which will satisfy its valuable demand for an organic union of theory and practice, of 'just truth' and 'true justice.' "[86] In the theocratic idyll of these two thinkers, theory and political practice will form a seamless whole as Russia leads the world toward the materialization of God's Kingdom in earthly institutions.

"The Kingdom of God is within you": such, Struve asserts, is the "fundamental philosopheme of any religion predicated not on fear but on love and reverence." His and Frank's message is unambiguous: all forms of eschatological expectation devalue the historical present and threaten the right of individuals to pursue the truth in their own way, using the cultural resources of their particular time and place. As Frank puts it: "The abstract ideal of absolute happiness in the remote future destroys the concrete moral relationship of one individual to another and the vital sensation of love for one's neighbor, one's contemporaries and their current needs. The socialist . . . is striving for human happiness, but he does not love living people, only his *idea*, the idea of universal human happiness. Since he is sacrificing himself to this idea, he does not hesitate to sacrifice others as well." There was cruelty of a similar order in the eagerness of *Signposts'* religious maximalists to strip the human psyche of its baser, fleshly humanity in preparation for its blissful union with the divine. Their outlook was as alien as that of the Left to the concept of culture as Frank defines it: "The ideal force and creative activity of the human spirit that impels it to master and humanize the world and to enrich its life with the values of science, art, religion and ethics."[87]

Berdiaev and Bulgakov believed that Russia's spiritual and cultural regeneration depended on the intelligentsia's retaining its identity as an ideologically cohesive group. Struve and Frank maintain that the erosion of that monolithic unity was one of the few positive results of the failed revolution: "The Russian *intelligent* as we have tried to portray him, a complete and integral moral character type despite all his contradictions, is beginning to disappear before our eyes."

Struve notes that the intelligentsia's sectarian mentality is being broken down by the process of *embourgeoisement* which is assimilating it into existing social groupings, a process which will continue if Russia's economic and constitutional development is not halted by force. Frank points to an unprecedented ferment of ideas on the Left: the Bolshevik heresy of empiriocriticism, which sought to synthesize Marxism with the voluntarism of Nietzsche, Avenarius, and Mach; Gorky's and Lunacharsky's attempts to create a new religion of the proletariat; the interest of radicals in mystical experience and decadent literature. One should regret only that this new revaluation of values had not yet got down to first principles. Russian radical thought could learn from the boldness and originality of the thinkers of the English and French revolutions: "a striving for new values, intellectual initiative, and a thirst to organize one's life in accordance with one's own independently derived concepts and convictions"—on these qualities, as yet confined to isolated individuals among the intelligentsia, Frank places his hopes for Russia's future.

Both thinkers abstain from prescriptions on the direction of future development. Struve maintains that firm tactical directives are neither possible nor helpful: to ensure a positive outcome from the current transitional period "we need ideas and the creative struggle of ideas." Frank has only one positive directive to offer: "We must pass from unproductive, anti-cultural *nihilistic moralism* to creative, culturally constructive *religious humanism*."[88]

Two sets of signposts to the future—one pointing to cultural pluralism, the other to religious and national messianism: as Struve observed, the volume clearly reflects the old battle lines of the Slavophiles and Westernizers. Among the former is Gershenzon, who believed that the intelligentsia could recover from its crisis only by following the "radiant ideal" of the Slavophiles, rejecting the illusory constructions of analytical reasoning and merging with the "organic wholeness" of the people's traditional life.[89] Berdiaev's and Bulgakov's vision of the universal mission of Russian Orthodoxy was vague, but in the tradition to which they adhered religious messianism and militant nationalism were often two sides of the same coin. During the Polish uprising of 1863, Slavophile polemicists had demanded the severest measures against the Poles both as rebels against the Russian state and as renegades from the Orthodox faith. Dostoevsky had interpreted the tensions between Russia and the European powers in the 1870s as heralding a cataclysmic struggle between the Orthodox East and the faithless West, in the course of which Orthodoxy would reconquer its ancient capital, Constantinople, and preside over Europe's spiritual rebirth.

The Westernizers in *Signposts* (who include Kistiakovsky and Izgoev) viewed the historical apartness of Russia from the West as one of the side effects of its despotic tradition of government rather than as the mark of a messianic destiny. Struve pointed out that Russia's intellectual life was increasingly linked with that of more advanced European countries, a factor that made it more difficult to predict its future. But he and the other three were prepared to live with unpredictability as a consequence of openness to ideas (such as concepts of legal order and individual rights as preached and practiced in the West), which could extend the freedom of individuals in the present to determine their own destinies.

But *Signposts* was not just an episode in Russia's longest-lived (and ongoing) ideological debate. The question of Russia's relation to the West was only one of the issues on which its authors differed fundamentally. At the root of all their differences was the question of the desirability of an "integral worldview." On this issue the volume reflects a division which cuts across all the accepted categories of Russian thought. On one side are the dogmatic systematizers, religious and rational: Slavophiles, nineteenth-century Hegelian Westernizers such as Boris Chicherin, the radical materialists of the 1860s, the Marxists, Tolstoy (as moralist), Dostoevsky (as political thinker), and many of the luminaries of Russia's philosophical and religious renaissance. The other side includes Herzen, Tolstoy, and Dostoevsky (as novelists), together with a pleiad of other writers and thinkers from Pushkin's era into the Soviet period who rejected the claims of dogma to explain, regulate, and predict contingent existence. The demoralization of the Left after 1905 brought many new recruits to what has been called the "counter-tradition" of Russian thought.[90] Prominent among these were intellectuals of the SR Party, heirs to the humanistic populism of Herzen and Mikhailovsky. In essays, reviews, and fictional works (including a story by the terrorist Boris Savinkov which appeared two months before *Signposts*) they attacked the Left's traditional revolutionary mystique and affirmed the autonomy of the individual conscience against the tyranny of dogma.[91]

The antidogmatists of *Signposts* had hoped that their critique would contribute to the debate from which this new humanism was emerging, but in the polarized political atmosphere of the time, the volume's having been welcomed by the Right ensured it a hostile reception in progressive circles. Even the Kadet leadership, who sympathized with many of the criticisms expressed, was forced for tactical reasons (the need to maintain its alliance with the Left in the Duma) to condemn it in public. The so-called *"Signposts* controversy" was mainly a platform for party propaganda: the real debate between the two traditions of Russian thought was being waged elsewhere.[92] But the intelligentsia's united front against the symposium has had the effect of creating a myth: that in 1909 a tiny, farsighted group defended a liberal view of freedom against the precursors of Communist totalitarianism and were vindicated by subsequent events.

This view of *Signposts* contained a reassuring message about the universality of Western liberal values (it is perhaps significant that the volume was "discovered" in the West at the height of the Cold War). Now that the very existence of universal values is frequently brought into question, the issue that divided the *Signposts* authors seems of far greater interest than their few areas of agreement. As the Man from Underground declared, "We . . . find it a burden to be human beings with *real* flesh and blood *of our own; . . .* soon we shall invent a means of being born from an idea."[93] The *Signposts* messianists derived their human significance from their identification with impersonal cosmic forces, whereas the humanists insisted that only flesh and blood can create and sustain the values that give life meaning.

The Apocalypse versus History: this argument continued among some of the *Signposts* authors after 1917. Struve broke with Berdiaev in the 1920s over the latter's interpretation of the revolution as a great historical cataclysm which had revealed the bankruptcy of the West's rationalist and materialist culture. Berdiaev argued that the Russian people's special insight into the "tragedy of historical destiny" had equipped it for its sublime mission: to live through a terrible process of expiation and purification in order to prepare the world for a new era of the spiritual transfiguration of earthly life, guided (in some unspecified way) by "light from the East."[94] Struve protested the moral repulsiveness of thinking that glibly justifies the suffering and sacrifice of human beings in the name of some purpose visible only to an elite of initiates. He noted two vices in Berdiaev's writings: "On the one hand there is the detachment [*otreshennost*] from real life: on the other, a prideful mania to proceed directly from some general postulate of a philosophical or theological kind to . . . conclusions of a concrete quality."[95] But Struve also observed that for all their lack of content, Berdiaev's visions were deeply seductive. They earned him his fame as chief interpreter of the "Russian soul" to the West and his popularity among many Soviet dissidents and have helped to secure him a greater following than any other Russian philosopher in some circles of the post-Soviet intelligentsia, where his apocalyptic vision, appropriately updated, is the subject of keen interest.

If the interest in *Signposts* in the new Russia is focused primarily on its messianic strand, we all have cause for concern. But any careful reading of the volume provides an antidote to the moral poison secreted by what Struve (in his critique of Berdiaev) described as "a certain type of Russian philosophizing intellect." This type is prone to project its personal nightmares onto some imaginary historical perspective, which it then proceeds to foreshorten or to fill with mystical vapors: "This is why it happened that they wished to replace what, for all their difficulty and complexity, are clear and simple problems of concrete human politics with apocalyptic visions which are as superfluous as they are enticing: for no one is empowered to interpret the Apocalypse in concrete historical terms, let alone to 'apply it' in historical action."[96]

The Chaotic City

CHAPTER TEN

O n October 1, 1991, the city of Leningrad officially regained its original
name—Sankt-Peterburg. This marked the end of a tense debate that
began in the early years of glasnost. Supporters of the change were accused of monarchism and a lack of patriotism (it was pointed out that
the name St. Petersburg had been on the maps of Hitler's commanders, who
intended to rename the city immediately after they had taken it). Aleksandr
Solzhenitsyn had recommended a Russified rendering: Sviato-Petrograd.

As Solomon Volkov observes in *St. Petersburg,* the passions aroused by this
debate reveal the symbolic importance Russians attach to a name that evokes
one of the most controversial periods of their history.[1] To some Russian nationalists the name denotes the showpiece of a project of Europeanization that
cut the nation off from its traditional values, subjecting it to corrosive cosmopolitan influences. Other, more liberal political groups see the return to the old
name as a symbol of national regeneration, in which they hope the city will regain the cultural leadership bestowed on it by its foundation, nearly three centuries ago, as Russia's "window on the West." As the then-mayor Anatoly
Sobchak declared in a speech (alluding to the city's growing economic importance as a port after the Baltic republics broke off from the new Russian nation), Petersburg was once again "the only Russian door to Europe."[2]

These discussions have attracted attention in the West as indicators of the
new Russia's future political direction; but their cultural significance is no less
important. For the intellectuals and creative artists of prerevolutionary Russia,
Petersburg symbolized and reflected painful divisions in the national psyche.
Dostoevsky's exploration of those conflicts in *Notes from Underground* has
profoundly influenced the way in which our century has interpreted the predicament of human beings torn between opposing values and confronted at
every turn with the absurd. Under the Soviet regime, Petersburg's fate inspired
writing, art, and music of great artistic power (little of which could be published, exhibited, or performed). The city's renaming has given new promi-
nence to this body of work, which includes attempts to comprehend and
transcend the horror of Stalin's dictatorship. These, as well as the new work
they have inspired, may come to affect our understanding of the century as

much as the reflections of Dostoevsky's man from the (Petersburg) underground.

In one sense Petersburg is like all other great cities. As Burton Pike has pointed out, throughout the history of Western culture the image of the city stands as the "great reification of ambivalence."[3] It has served to crystallize anxieties about man's relation to his created world: Babylon, Babel, Rome, Sodom, the New Jerusalem, furnished the Christian imagination with images of power and perversion, heaven and hell. The destruction of cities has exercised a hypnotic power over the imagination, while, from the late nineteenth century on, the literary image of the modern city has been explored as a source of new ways of conveying and transcending states of dislocation and estrangement.

But Baudelaire's Paris, Kafka's Prague, Brecht's Berlin, and the "unreal city" of Eliot's *Waste Land* are all cities of the mind, visionary transfigurations of the ordinary. In contrast, the surreal quality of Petersburg has an immediate impact on any observer. In the words of one celebrated tourist, the Marquis de Custine,

> The effect on the spectator is something that can only imperfectly be expressed in words. . . . The lowlands of the city, with the buildings that crouch along the banks of the Neva, seem to hover between sea and sky, so that one expects to see them fade into the void. . . . Can this be the capital of a vast Empire, this scrap of earth that one sees shimmering against the water like froth carried on the flood; these little spots, black and uneven, hardly distinguishable between the whiteness of the sky and the whiteness of the river? Or is it a mere apparition, an optical illusion?[4]

The phantasmagoria that Custine observed on one of the white nights of the northern summer of 1839 seemed a visible manifestation of an "incomprehensible mystery": a mighty city whose existence defied the physical and moral order of things.[5] Like most visitors before and since, Custine was taken to the shrine at the heart of the mystery: the small cabin in which Peter the Great had planned the great city that would rise up on the swampy wasteland before him, the crowning achievement of his effort to transform his country into a modern Westernized state. In that hut at the mouth of the Gulf of Finland the will of one man set itself against natural forces, historical experience, and the aspirations of an entire nation.

The symbolic significance of a capital on Russia's most western border impelled Peter to choose the most unpromising of sites: marshy, often flooded lowlands vulnerable to invaders who could strike at the heart of the empire a few miles from its border. His city was built not for his people but against them. The ubiquitous onion spires of the old capital, Moscow, symbolized the religious and national traditions to which the Russian people remained fiercely attached: Petersburg would long figure in popular literature as the Antichrist. The tsar's impatience to complete his city (it was declared the new capital of Russia in 1717, fourteen years after the first house was built) took a heavy toll on the lives of his people: many thousands of conscripted workers died from hunger, disease, and exhaustion during the Egyptian labors required to hammer in the piles that would defend the city against the water on which it was built.

Designed entirely by Western architects (one of whom is reputed to have died after a beating administered by the tsar himself), the city was lavishly embellished in successive reigns, first in baroque style by the Italian architect Bartolomeo Rastrelli at the command of the empress Elizabeth. Later, Catherine the Great lined the city's vast squares, the banks of the Neva, and its network of canals with magnificent neoclassical buildings. The spectacle of "prodigious grandeur" that greeted Custine in 1839 was undoubtedly, he wrote, one of the wonders of the world. Yet one had only to travel to the end of the Nevsky Prospect, the great avenue extending from the center to the boundaries of the city, to reach the squalid habitations of another Russia. Beyond were the destinations toward which couriers flew through the city in their light carriages: Siberia, Kamchatka, the Salt Desert, the Glacial Sea.

Custine reflects that in this city without roots in history or the soil, perpetually under threat from natural disaster or human vengeance, normality is a state of siege. The military-style discipline imposed on the people was "a forced calm, an apparent order . . . more frightful than anarchy," a veil thrown over chaos, like the facades of villages erected by Catherine's favorite, Grigory Potemkin, to assure her as she traveled southward, that she presided over an empire of happy peasants. There was something deeply ominous in the theatricality of the capital's public rituals and royal festivals, enacted against the backcloth of Rastrelli's marvelous palaces and stupendous in their scale and magnificence: "You think . . . what I am seeing is too great to be real, it is the dream of a lovesick giant told by a mad poet." St. Petersburg was what it seemed on a first impression: a splendid decor "designed to serve as the theatre for a real and terrible drama."[6]

The city had already witnessed two such dramas. In 1824 it experienced a devastating flood. On 14 December of the following year a troop of revolutionary guardsmen was mown down by artillery fire on Senate Square, the site of the equestrian statue of Peter which Catherine had commissioned from the French sculptor Falconet. A typical Petersburg monstrosity, it stands on a hunk of granite weighing over fifteen hundred tons which took thousands of people three years to move from its location twelve miles from the city. The hind feet of the horse are rooted in the rock, its front feet rear high into the air; the out-stretched arm of its rider points toward the sky.

To Russia's would-be reformers that pointing arm symbolized the ascent of historical progress. The officers who led the revolt believed that by forcing the autocracy to share power they would be steering Peter's great project of West-ernization to its logical conclusion. To their sympathizers among the intellec-tual elite, the bodies lying in the snow under the hooves of Peter's rearing horse raised tormenting questions about the significance of his achievement. Their ambivalence was crystallized in Pushkin's great narrative poem of 1833: *The Bronze Horseman*. Beginning with a solemn encomium to the mighty tsar and his capital, it abruptly changes tone to recount the tragedy of a poor clerk, Yev-geny, who loses his beloved in the flood of 1824. In the poem's climax, mad-dened by grief, he shakes his fist at the statue of the tsar who built his city on water, and flees as the mounted "idol" seems to descend from its plinth to pur-sue him. All night long the chase continues, the terrible hooves echoing through the deserted streets.

The poem's imagery, evoking the barbarism of Russia's great civilizer and the fragility of his mighty city, has a cumulative hallucinatory effect which calls into question all reasoned explanations of history and human life. When Push-kin's hero wonders if he has not dreamed the horror of the flood, the poet in-terjects: "Is not all life an empty dream, a joke played by heaven at earth's expense?" The city that Custine saw as imbued with a sense of the imperma-nence of human affairs was invested by Pushkin's poem with the grandeur of tragic myth. In the same decade Gogol added to the myth with his unique brand of surrealism, exemplified in the famous passage from one of his *Peters-burg Tales*: "O, do not trust that Nevsky Prospect! . . . All is deceit, all is a dream, all is not what it seems! . . . It lies at all times, this Nevsky Prospect, but most of all when night settles on it in a thick mass . . . when the whole city turns into thunder and glitter, myriads of carriages come pouring over the bridges, the postilions shout and leap on their horses, and the devil himself lights the lamps expressly in order to show everything off in an unreal guise."[7]

Petersburg was a riddle which would fit none of the doctrines of universal and rational progress that dominated nineteenth-century historical thinking, and for this reason it fascinated two of the most iconoclastic minds of the age—Dostoevsky and Aleksandr Herzen. According to Herzen, there was no way of deciphering the mysterious existence of this city built on an element that must surely one day engulf it. His native Moscow, rooted in the past, was secure in its identity and its aspirations. Petersburg, child of a tsar "who rejected his country for its own good and oppressed it in the name of . . . civilization," was a tragic enigma. But this was its virtue: there was no place more conducive to somber thoughts on the predicament of modern human beings, torn by allegiances to incompatible ideals. For that reason Herzen had come to love Petersburg, "just as I ceased to love Moscow because it is incapable of inflicting torture."[8]

The rootless city—"the most abstract and intentional city in the whole round world," in the words of Dostoevsky's Man from Underground—was the breeding ground of the rootless intelligentsia whose significance Dostoevsky believed he was the first to have perceived. It is the background of many of his stories and novels whose characters, often subject to fevers and hallucinations induced by the unhealthy atmosphere of the surrounding swampland, seek desperately to formulate new rules for moral and social existence in a world where former certainties no longer apply. Tormented by the intensity of their mental existence, they hate the city whose grotesque contradictions mirror their own inner state. On misty Petersburg mornings the hero of *A Raw Youth* is haunted by a strange dream: "And what if this mist suddenly evaporates and goes upwards, won't all this rotten, slimy city go up with it, rise with the mist and vanish like smoke, and there will remain the former Finnish swamp, and in its midst, perhaps, for decoration, the bronze horseman on his hotly breathing, exhausted horse?"[9]

Such fantasies began to seem prophetic as Russia's revolutionary drama was played out on the Petersburg streets. In 1881 Tsar Alexander II was killed by a terrorist bomb as his carriage drove through the city. On January 22, 1905, with the country on the verge of revolution, vast columns of workers, singing hymns and holding icons aloft, approached the Winter Palace with a robed priest at their head to deliver a petition at the feet of Nicholas II. Soldiers fired into the unarmed crowd, killing or wounding hundreds. For many of the cultured elite the workers' bodies in Palace Square signified the completion of a process that had begun with the shootings under Peter's statue eighty years before: the Petersburg regime had now severed its ties with both the intelligentsia and the Russian people. The Symbolist movement that dominated Russian poetry between the revolutions of 1905 and 1917 was predominantly Slavophile and apocalyptic in tone. The Petersburg-born poet Aleksandr Blok looked forward to the destruction of his city and its foreign culture as a fiery purification, retribution exacted by the elemental forces of the people. In Andrei Bely's surrealist novel *Petersburg*, whose action is dominated by the ticking of a terrorist's bomb, the city is a "fourth dimension" which exists on no maps.[10]

Reality soon outstripped poetic imagination. A few months after Bely's novel appeared, Petersburg was renamed Petrograd to satisfy patriotic sentiment after the outbreak of the First World War. Two years later it ceased to be the capital of Russia. Its second renaming on Lenin's death, in 1924, was seen by many of its intelligentsia as an attempt to stamp out the memory of their traditional independence. Stalin sought to complete that task by making the city a prime target of his terror. Those who survived the mass shootings and deportations of the 1930s were subjected by Hitler's armies to the longest siege of a city in modern history. When it was lifted after nine hundred days, three-quarters of the city's population had perished. Leningrad's slow resurrection was hampered first by Stalin's continuing vengefulness and subsequently by a particularly reactionary local party apparatus. But by the 1960s the city was the scene of a flourishing (if largely underground) activity in literature and the arts, a dominant feature of which was a fascination with the culture of prerevolutionary Petersburg. This was not simply an exercise in nostalgia but part of a search for cultural roots after the discrediting of Stalinism. The search continues amid the current debates about the meaning of the city's past. By defining "true" Petersburg culture as distinct from values associated only with the former imperial power, many Petersburg intellectuals hope to rebuild a sense of historical continuity, national identity, and moral purpose.

To provide such a definition is one of the aims of Solomon Volkov's book. Its title is misleading: this is no scholarly study, but the result of a personal odyssey that began in 1965 when, as part of a string quartet of young musicians from the Leningrad Conservatory, the author was invited to play Dimitry Shostakovich's Ninth Quartet for the poet Anna Akhmatova at her dacha near the city. The fates of the composer and the poet had been closely tied to Petersburg, where in the decade before the Revolution Akhmatova had been part of an astonishing pleiad of writers, composers, painters, choreographers, and theater directors who seminally influenced the art of this century. What was it in the culture of Petersburg that in a short span of years nourished the genius of Igor Stravinsky, Kazimir Malevich, Vsevolod Meyerhold, Vladimir Nabokov, and Sergei Diaghilev? To ask this question in Leningrad in the 1960s was to invite the reply: "We have only one culture—the Soviet one!" Nor did Volkov find an answer in the West (to which he emigrated in 1972). Unlike Paris, Berlin, Vienna, or New York, Petersburg did not exist in the general consciousness as a great center of cultural revolution: "All these splendid accomplishments and famous names floated in some kind of space and time vacuum and remained strangely unconnected."[11]

Volkov came to define the common factor as the "Petersburg mythos"—his term for the complex of philosophical and moral ideas concerned with the special place of Petersburg on Russian soil and in Russian history. In his chronologically and thematically chaotic book, which ranges over the major movements in all the arts connected with the city in the twentieth century (and, much more sketchily, the two preceding ones), the author's impressively broad culture allows him to shape an absorbing narrative out of a mixture of anecdote, memoir, critical discussion, and historical fact.

He argues that at the beginning of this century the image of Petersburg, previously demonized by the radical intelligentsia and socially concerned writers, was transformed by Russian modernism. The *World of Art* movement (named after the journal founded by Benois and Diaghilev) sought to bring Russia abreast of the latest cultural developments in Western Europe and found the inspiration for new painting, music, and ballet in the city's neoclassical beauty and imperial pomp. Petersburg's theatricality also fascinated the avant-garde that emerged in the feverish decade before the Revolution. Its leaders saw the theater as a means for bringing about the transformation of human consciousness which they anticipated with millenarian fervor. The Futurists idealized the dynamism of Petersburg's urban culture and staged in the city their electrifying productions, such as Mayakovsky's *Vladimir Mayakovsky, A Tragedy,* that flouted all conventional canons and beliefs. They hailed the October Revolution as the merging of theater with life. The Bolshevik leaders, however, disliked both the avant-garde and the city that had bred these anarchic artists. Volkov contends that the regime's vindictiveness toward the former capital intensified the intelligentsia's attachment to it. Never had there been so extraordinary a transformation in the mythos of a city. Once repudiated by Russia's creative geniuses as a foreign implant on their soil, the former capital survived both the Great Terror and the attack of Hitler's armies, to emerge, buoyed up by the sympathy of the nation and the world, as a new national legend, a symbol of the suffering and resilience of the Russian people.

No wonder that Volkov sees something miraculous in this process. He set out to describe the evolution of one myth and seems to have ended by constructing another: an epic saga of repudiation, destruction, and rebirth far removed from the real complexities of history and human motivation. But his material resists the interpretation he places on it. The Petersburgers and Leningraders with whom his book is concerned regarded their city sometimes with love, sometimes with fear and revulsion, but always with ambivalence and irony. Volkov himself recognizes these qualities as central to what he describes as the "Petersburg spirit." He makes a convincing case for the existence of a specifically "Petersburg" style of musical composition (stretching from Glinka to Stravinsky, Prokofiev, and Shostakovich), characterized by "a solid grounding of craftsmanship, . . . restrained irony, and nostalgia without sentimentality"; and he observes that as modernists with Petersburg roots, Nabokov and Stravinsky "were related by the theatricality of their works, the paradoxicality of their creative thought . . . as well as an incorrigible tendency toward irony and the grotesque."[12] But he gives few insights into the complex attitude toward the city as idea and reality that shaped this ironic vision over the past two centuries. He argues that Dostoevsky rejected all that Petersburg stood for; yet Dostoevsky chose to spend his most creative years there, tied to the city by a strange attraction that Herzen defined in his own case as amounting to love: no other place provided so formidable a test of their responses both as artists and as human beings. The great radical critic Vissarion Belinsky made the same point as follows: "Saint-Petersburg is the touchstone of a man: he who living in it has not been carried away by the whirlpool of phantom life, who has managed to keep both heart and soul, but not at the expense of common sense, to retain his human dignity without falling into quixotism—to him you can extend your hand . . . as to a man."[13]

Belinsky's distinction is equally relevant to Russian intellectual life after 1917, when many took the rituals and facades of Bolshevism for reality and built utopias on them. Those writers and artists who did so tended to perish early, victims of a cruel power and of their own illusions. Much of the greatest art of the Soviet period was produced by another breed—former Petersburgers who managed to preserve both heart and soul by means of that subversive irony which Herzen once predicted would be the "hope and salvation" of the Russian nation.[14]

One of the latter—Anna Akhmatova—is the heroine of Volkov's book, and he writes revealingly about many others. But in keeping the theme of the former Petersburg intelligentsia's love of their victimized city in the foreground, he blurs a more important issue: the distinction between those who clearly understood the moral essence of the new regime and those who clung to their illusions. That some of the latter met tragic ends with great courage has tended in the past to inhibit criticism of their outlook. But the rare quality of Akhmatova's response to the Stalin epoch becomes plain only when one approaches that terrible age in an unsentimental, skeptical "Petersburg" spirit.

In 1918 Aleksandr Blok published his long poem "The Twelve," which tells of twelve Red Guardsmen, ignorant and violent and driven only by the desire for revenge on the bourgeois, who march through a Petrograd blizzard, killing and plundering on their way. But they are guided by an invisible force; in the last stanza of the poem a white-clad figure appears at the head of their column: Jesus Christ.

Blok's likening of the Bolshevik seizure of power to the spiritual revolution preached by Christ and his twelve apostles aroused bitter controversy; but he was typical of the avant-garde in reading a deeply symbolic meaning into the revolutionary drama being acted out on the streets and squares of the capital. The new regime encouraged the intelligentsia to see themselves as participants in an unprecedented experiment in the transformation of human existence. The Bolshevik revolution, like the Petrine one, sought to construct a mystique of power through show and ritual, and the public spaces of Petrograd served its purpose well. The Bolsheviks' "storming" of the Winter Palace during a session of the cabinet of the provisional government was hardly a heroic affair (only a few military cadets and a battalion of women attempted resistance), but it was instantly transformed into myth in paintings, posters, and film, along with the cruiser *Aurora*, which, moored on the Neva within range of the Palace, had fired the blank shells that helped frighten the provisional government into surrendering.

On May 1, 1918, Petrograd was the scene of a festival on the scale that had inspired Custine with fascinated horror. The city and the fleet were festooned with flags and banners; huge parades wound through the streets as airplanes circled overhead and artillery salutes resounded, concluding with the blaze of fireworks in the night sky. Such public rituals gave the avant-garde the chance to transpose their artistic experiments from the stage to the streets. A semiofficial newspaper in late 1918 contained these lines from a poem by the Futurist Mayakovsky, "Order to the Army of Art":

> Wipe the old from your heart.
> The streets are our brushes.
> The squares our palettes.[15]

To merge theater with life was the aim of the Theatre of Worker Youth (TRAM), formed in 1922 as an amateur studio at the House of Communist Upbringing in Petrograd. With the government's encouragement they dramatized revolutionary events in performances in which thousands took part, illuminated by projectors from battleships, with sound effects provided by real cannon. Appropriately, it was in Leningrad in the mid-1920s that Mikhail Bakhtin developed his theory of the influence of carnival on world culture. Bakhtin noted that carnival life "is life taken out of its usual ruts." As Volkov observes, Petrograd after the revolution "was the quintessential carnival city. All the hierarchical barriers that had formed over centuries were broken down there, traditional values were tossed out the window." No hope seemed too extravagant; the critic Nikolai Punin later wrote: "We imagined . . . perhaps even a dictatorship of art over the government."[16]

The chasm between the expectations of the avant-garde and the intentions of the Bolsheviks could not have been greater. For the artists the rituals in the public spaces of Petrograd were the acting out of a new freedom; for the Bolsheviks they were the means of consecrating a new order. The avant-garde's indiscipline severely limited their usefulness in this regard, and it became increasingly clear that art would not be exempt from the regimentation being imposed on all other social activities. Blok was one of the first to succumb to despair. He died in August 1921—from "spiritual asthma," as Andrei Bely put it.[17] In the same month the poet Nikolai Gumilyov was arrested on a charge (now known to have been fabricated) of anti-Soviet conspiracy: he was shot in Petrograd along with sixty others. During the first postrevolutionary decade, the city that had been the birthplace of Russian modernism witnessed its gradual suffocation. Mayakovsky, the avant-garde's most strident propagandist for the new regime, shot himself in 1930. The year before, Bakhtin had been arrested during an attempt by the police to liquidate underground philosophical and religious circles in Petrograd. Describing the dissolution of Bakhtin's circle, one of its members, the young writer Konstantin Vaginov, concluded: "But it is time to lower the curtain. The performance is over. It is confusing and quiet on the stage. Where is the promised love, the promised heroism? Where is the promised art?"[18]

Here was the voice of the Petersburg spirit. Vaginov was one of a number of Leningrad experimentalists in prose whose work began to appear in the early 1920s. Almost all these authors knew, and learned from, one another, and many lived in or frequented the "House of the Arts" founded by Maksim Gorky to provide support for writers in the first hungry years of the new regime. St. Petersburg–Leningrad was a dominant theme of their work, which both measured itself against and parodied the work of the Petersburg masters of the past. They included the Serapion Brothers, a group founded in 1921, whose most famous member was the satirist Mikhail Zoshchenko. With great daring, in a style that recalled Gogol and the early Dostoevsky, he depicted the "new Soviet man" not as the proletarian hero of official mythology but as a truculent, greedy philistine.

Volkov writes illuminatingly on this "new Petersburg prose," which has rarely been given its due in studies of the period; he notes that its ironic self-commentary was a daring challenge to official ideology. But it is also worth stressing that such irony struck an equally dissonant note in the chorus of the avant-garde, whose most prominent groups (such as the Futurists and the proletarian culture movement, Proletkult) equated revolutionary art with revolutionary politics and clamored for the suppression of rival artistic movements. The new prose writers did not allow rosy visions of the future to cloud their moral perceptions in the present. Yevgeny Zamiatin, one of the movement's mentors, set its tone in his article "I Am Afraid," published in a Petrograd journal in 1921. He declared that servile conformism was now the rule in Soviet literature, forcing some writers into silence: "Real literature can exist only where it is made not by industrious and dependable clerks, but by madmen, hermits, heretics, dreamers, rebels and skeptics."[19]

Zamiatin's protest was the more effective because of his radical credentials (he had once been a member of the Bolshevik Party). In the same year, he completed his antiutopian novel *We*, which was to influence Orwell's *1984*. It was passed around in manuscript, and after a version appeared in an émigré review, he was allowed to publish no more work in Russia. In 1931, he wrote to Stalin asking for permission to go abroad, "so that I may come home as soon as it is possible for literature to serve great ideas without crawling before small men." Miraculously, permission was granted.[20]

Heresy took a surrealist form in the writings of the Oberiu group (an acronym for the Association for Real Art), founded in 1928. Its central figure was Daniil Kharms, whose absurdist prose depicts a dark and cruel Leningrad, where, on Nevsky Prospect, people "come trampling from all sides, growling and shoving." Vaginov, who belonged to this group, portrays in his novel *The Goat Song* remnants of the old Petersburg intelligentsia carrying on their philosophical and moral discussions in the forlorn hope of escaping from the ugliness of Soviet reality and taking refuge "in a tall tower of humanism."[21]

"Fantastic realism"—a term often used to describe Dostoevsky's technique—is an apt description of the prose that emanated from Leningrad's House of the Arts, described by an inmate as a "crazy ship" that had appeared out of nowhere and was speeding to an unknown destination. The new writing, like Dostoevsky's, blended the tragic and the grotesque in its depiction of individuals attempting to assert their human dignity in an implacably hostile environment. Memoirs of the early 1920s portray a dark, hungry, and freezing city threatened by a vindictive power. The sense of menace hanging over the city was conveyed by many oblique means, from surrealist fiction to the historical prose of the critic Yury Tynianov, who depicted the clash of the individual with the Russian state in works which, according to one account, "agitated contemporaries more than stories by others about the present, because the Bronze Horseman was still galloping after the fleeing Yevgeny and with every year the ringing hoofbeats sounded louder along the stunned cobblestones."[22]

Peter's statue and the flooding of his city were a frequent source of ambivalent metaphors in the prose of the 1920s. There was much discussion of the symbolism of the flooding of Leningrad in 1924 (exactly a hundred years after the flood that had inspired Pushkin's poem), which coincided with the year of Lenin's death and the renaming of the city. Volkov remarks on the frequency with which the city is described as a ship in the literature of the time, recalling the ancient image of a "ship of the dead," wandering between death and rebirth.[23]

Herzen had observed that Petersburg induced a permanent state of physical and moral fever, an intensity of existence for which the price was an early death. Many Leningrad writers paid the price: several leading figures in Oberiu, including Kharms, died in prison. Emigration continued in a steady stream throughout the 1920s. Those who remained faced the choice between spiritual suffocation and physical extinction. But a number retained their artistic integrity and recorded the fantastic reality of Stalin's Terror. It is no co-incidence that the most prominent of these had their roots in the ironic culture of prerevolutionary Petersburg. Volkov gives two of them—Shostakovich and Akhmatova—the principal credit for turning the city into a symbol both of Russia's tragic fate and of its hopes for a rebirth.

Shostakovich, who entered the Petrograd Conservatory in 1919, at the age of thirteen, was one of the great alumni of the Petersburg school of composition. He was also deeply imbued with the city's literary culture. His first opera, *The Nose,* was based on Gogol's absurdist tale about the nose of an official which leaves its owner's face to assume an autonomous existence until finally captured by the police. The opera could be read as a satire on power and the fear of power. This, together with its avant-garde character, ensured that its premiere in Leningrad in 1930 received a hostile press. His opera *Lady Macbeth of the Mtsensk District* turned a melodramatic tale by the nineteenth-century Petersburg writer Nikolai Leskov into a complex psychological drama which succeeds in eliciting sympathy for the multiple murderess in the title role. In 1936 Stalin attended a performance and expressed displeasure—the signal for a ferocious campaign in the party press against all forms of deviation from "socialist realism" in the arts.

Leningrad was already the primary target of the Great Terror: following the assassination there in December 1934 of the Leningrad party chief Sergei Kirov (probably engineered by Stalin as a pretext for extinguishing all opposition in the city), mass arrests and executions became part of daily life. Shostakovich had to tread a very dangerous path to survive without compromising his integrity. Although in an interview with his critics he claimed that his Fifth Symphony (first performed in November 1937) was about "man with all his feelings," the Leningrad audience (who gave him a thirty-minute ovation) interpreted it as a work about the Terror.[24] His Seventh Symphony, dedicated to the blockaded city of Leningrad, was first performed there in August 1942, before an audience weak from starvation. Broadcast all over Russia, this performance was adroitly used by Stalin's propaganda machine as evidence of the patriotic spirit of Leningraders, but many of the latter were aware that, as Shostakovich told trusted friends, the Seventh Symphony was not only about fascism but about all forms of oppression. His music crystallized the new image of the city as victim; but, as Volkov observes, that image already had an underground currency in the poetry of Anna Akhmatova.

Unlike so many of the other victims in Volkov's narrative, Akhmatova had no difficulty in distinguishing between the theatrical charades of Petrograd in 1917 and the true moral nature of Bolshevism. In the decade before the revolution, she was (along with her then-husband Gumilyov and Osip Mandelstam) a leader of the acmeist movement which arose in Petersburg in reaction to symbolism. The acmeists' manifestos demanded clarity and concreteness of expression in contrast to the "fogginess" of the Symbolists. Akhmatova once observed that unlike the Symbolist poets, she felt herself "responsible for every word." In 1918 she refused to attend a literary evening where Blok's poem "The Twelve" was to be read. She saw Petersburg as the city of her Muse, "loved with bitter love."[25] She foresaw that the destruction of its culture would lead to barbarism, yet she did not contemplate emigrating after the Revolution—and had harsh words for those who did:

> I am not with those who abandoned their land
> To the lacerations of the enemy.
> I am deaf to their coarse flattery,
> I won't give them my songs.[26]

Yet (unlike Mayakovsky) neither did she give them to Russia's new rulers. In *Anno Domini MCMXXI*, a volume of poems written between 1917 and 1921, she subverts the reader's expectations with true Petersburg irony. Her epigraph is a phrase from the nineteenth-century poet Tiutchev, "In those legendary years . . . ." But the poems that follow are concerned not with epic events but with private emotions—dramas of love, jealousy, and betrayal—played out in a city where monstrous rumors roam the streets and death chalks the doors with crosses.[27]

The critical hostility that greeted *Anno Domini*'s lack of "socialist optimism" forced Akhmatova into silence for many years. The critics suggested that she had been born too late or had not died soon enough, but she sensed that her time was still to come. The first poem of the cycle, addressed "To my Fellow-Citizens," ends:

> A different time is drawing near,
> The wind of death already chills the heart,
> But the holy city of Peter
> Will be our unintended monument.[28]

A decade later she emerged from her silence to produce what is arguably the greatest artistic work about the Terror: the cycle *Requiem*. Its subject is the years when Leningrad dangled "like a useless appendage . . . from its prisons," outside whose walls a line of women stood every day hoping to deliver parcels or receive news of their relatives' fate. Akhmatova had stood there during the seventeen months that her son Lev Gumilyov was held before being deported to a labor camp. As the poet through whose "exhausted mouth . . . a hundred million people scream," she records the daily, exhausting terror of those years.[29]

It was too dangerous to write the poem down; over a period of five years verses scribbled on pieces of paper were memorized by trusted friends and then burned. The target of an ideological attack mounted on Stalin's initiative in 1946, Akhmatova was treated as a pariah until Stalin's death, but her poetry was widely circulated in samizdat. As Volkov notes, *Requiem* in particular became bred into the intelligentsia's bones. Yet his relentless insistence on the poem's importance in creating a "new mythos of the martyr city" tends to sentimentalize and diminish it.[30] Like all the greatest works of Petersburg culture, *Requiem* was the creation of an artist whose identification with her city was a compound of many ambivalent feelings. Volkov himself cites a conversation that he had in New York with Joseph Brodsky (who as a young poet in Leningrad in the 1960s was part of what Akhmatova called her "magic choir"), in which Brodsky observed that the literature created in Petersburg is marked by "the awareness that it is all being written from the edge of the earth. And if we can speak of some general concept, or tonality . . . of Petersburg culture, it would be alienation."[31]

This tonality can be traced to one major influence, that of Dostoevsky. As Donald Fanger has put it, Dostoevsky's myth of Petersburg is infused with a spirit of searching and anguish which gives it an extraordinarily modern tone: "He raised the chaotic city to the position of a symbol of the chaotic moral world of man, so that the contradictions of the second find their counterpart in the contrasts of the first. He showed . . . human consciousness striving in a world where there were few of the usual categories of normality, striving with a terrible and unsought freedom, isolated and rootless, together without community, [to discover] a new or an old morality—something to fill the void."[32]

In the classic Petersburg novel, *Crime and Punishment,* the city's fetid heat, its sudden deluges, stirring up images of a primeval flood, and the contrasts between its classic facades and the teeming slum life behind them reflect and intensify the characters' spiritual states, impressing on us the fragile nature of what we call normality and the ever-present threat of the irruption of monstrous evil into the everyday. Dostoevsky believed that his fantastic realism had a prophetic element—a view borne out by the fate of his city. One image from Volkov's book conveys all the bizarre horror of life in Leningrad in the 1930s: the festively dressed audience gathered for the premiere of Shostakovich's Fifth Symphony, all of them aware that later that night some of their number would be dragged off to prison or execution. As he puts it:

> Stalin had declared a genocidal war against his own people, and Leningrad was one of his most visible victims. And yet the terror wanted to remain anonymous, unnamed. "Enemies of the

people" were harangued daily on the radio, in newspapers, at
countless meetings, but it was forbidden to speak of where they
were being sent as they disappeared. The words "terror,"
"prison," "camp," and "arrest" were not spoken aloud and
seemed not to exist in the everyday vocabulary. The infamous
black vans that carried off the arrested had fake signs on their
side: "Meat" or "Milk." . . . The official slogan for the country,
by which everyone allegedly lived at that time, was Stalin's constantly quoted "Life has become better, life has become mer-
rier."[33]

Akhmatova's importance as a chronicler of this horror lies not merely in her
capacity to evoke pity for its victims, but in the Dostoevskian power with
which she uses her city's concrete reality to convey the grotesque banality of
the evil that some of her compatriots tried to justify in the name of great historical goals. She ignores the Bolsheviks' official downgrading of Peter's city: it
is the "savaged capital," where old crones howl like wounded beasts, where
fear "trembles in a dry laugh," where "only the dead smiled, happy to be at
peace." The extremes of Petersburg's climate and its impenetrable fogs are in-
terwoven into the experience of the poem: the lines of women standing beneath the prison's blind red wall "both in cruel cold and in July's heat," the
streets bordering the misty Neva, where people "more lifeless than the dead"
trudge at dawn on their way to queue at the prison gates.[34]

Akhmatova's fellow acmeist Osip Mandelstam (whom Volkov unjustly
neglects) conveyed the same monstrous reality in his poem of 1930, "Leningrad":

> I returned to my city, familiar to tears,
> to my childhood's tonsils and varicose veins.
>
> You have returned here—then swallow
> the Leningrad streetlamp's cod-liver oil.
>
> Recognise now the day of December fog
> when ominous street-tar is mixed with the yolk of egg.
>
> Petersburg, I do not want to die yet:
> You have my telephone numbers in your head.
>
> Petersburg, I still have addresses
> at which I will find the voice of the dead.

> I live on a black stair, and into my temple
> strikes the doorbell, torn out with flesh.
>
> And all night long I await the dear guests,
> and I jangle my fetters, the chains on the door.[35]

This was the world that Dostoevsky had dimly foreseen: the somber, sooty, slimy, foggy city and the dark, claustrophobia-inducing staircases and landings of its tenements are at the same time tangible realities and symbols of the savagery of a system in which all is permitted. Dostoevsky's characters had speculated on the grotesque consequences of such a doctrine: Akhmatova and Mandelstam illustrated them in their poetry when outspokenness was punishable by death.

> We live without feeling the country beneath us,
> our speech at ten paces inaudible.[36]

The poem about Stalin that began with those lines sealed Mandelstam's fate. He would die in a camp. Akhmatova's caustic irony rings as a counterrefrain throughout the Stalin years. Mandelshtam's wife, Nadezhda, recalls her fury whenever she heard someone speculating about why an individual had been arrested: "What do you mean, what for? It's time you understood that people are arrested for nothing at all."[37]

The work of these two poets is a powerful demonstration that sanity, moral integrity, and even hope can survive in an absurd world. Mandelstam expressed his faith that "the word"—poetry—would not perish:

> For that blessed senseless word
> I shall pray in the Soviet night.[38]

Requiem ends with the hope that if a monument is raised to the poet, it will be before the prison walls:

> where I stood for three hundred hours,
> And where they never unbolted the doors for me. . . .
> And may the melting snow stream like tears
> From my motionless lids of bronze,
>
> And a prison dove coo in the distance,
> And the ships of the Neva sail calmly on.[39]

One of the paradoxes of Petersburg is that the "deepest hell of senseless and abnormal life" (as one of Dostoevsky's characters describes the city) could produce such luminous personalities. But over the past three centuries it also produced multitudes of docile believers in its official myths. This is why I am uneasy about Solomon Volkov's emphasis on the city's "tragic mythological aura" as the basis for its hope to be once again recognized as the spiritual capital or, at least, the cultural arbiter of the new Russia.[40] The cults of imperial Petersburg and revolutionary Petrograd manipulated mythology for the ends of political power. It is not inconceivable that a cult of the martyred and resurrected city may be created for the same purpose.

In Petrograd in 1919 the artist Vladimir Tatlin was commissioned to design a monument to the Third International. Tatlin's tower was to be a colossal metal spiral structure, far exceeding the Eiffel Tower in height, which would straddle the Neva, dominating the city as both a symbol and a nerve center of the new communist world. It would consist of three levels: the first two, housing the legislative and executive committees of the International, would be topped by a communications center equipped with all the latest techniques for the dissemination of propaganda round the world. As the critic Nikolai Punin explained admiringly at the time, the monument's form was chosen to express humanity's ascent to freedom. But the spectator would not be left free to indulge in passive contemplation of this concept: "You will be carried upwards or downwards by mechanical methods, involuntarily swept along, while before you there will flash a propagandist's forceful, laconic phrase; then, further up, the latest news, resolution or decree, the latest invention—all delivered in bursts of simple, clear ideas."[41]

Designed to suck the citizens of Petrograd into the whirlpool of phantom life, the tower was never built. The city's dominant monument remains the Bronze Horseman, a symbol of the riddle of history that no ideology has yet managed to solve.

PART III

Delusions and Evasions

The Rational Reality of Boris Chicherin

C H A P T E R   E L E V E N

Few Russian thinkers have profited so much from historical hindsight as Boris Chicherin. Politically isolated and widely detested, he was described by Pyotr Struve as a "superfluous" figure in the Russia of his time;[1] the leader of the right wing of the Kadet Party, V. A. Maklakov (one of Chicherin's few contemporaries who sympathized with his ideas), subsequently expressed regret that Chicherin had had absolutely no influence on the Russian liberal movement.[2] But historians have presented him very differently: he is commonly described both as a leading theorist of Russian liberalism and one of the most outstanding thinkers of his period.[3]

There is still a marked lack of consensus as to the nature of Chicherin's liberalism (he has been described both as an ardent individualist and as a defender of the unlimited sovereignty of the state;[4] as a new kind of liberal and as an old-fashioned one;[5] as among the "more typical" Russian liberals and as a "solitary" figure to their right).[6] But historians in the West have tended to agree on the reason for his unpopularity in mid-nineteenth-century Russia: his belief that the principal threat to freedom came from the Left. In the Soviet period this made Chicherin a key figure for Western liberal historians who broadly interpreted the ideological and political conflicts that led to the Russian Revolution in terms of the classic dichotomy between proponents of liberal and totalitarian democracy.[7] They attributed the triumph of the latter in 1917 in great part to the attachment of a majority of educated society (including large numbers of liberals sympathetic to the Left) to various programs for the total transformation of society. But they dismissed the view that no middle way between revolution and reaction had been possible for Russia, that the liberal mentality was an alien phenomenon that could not have taken root there. On the contrary, the argument goes, in the century before the Revolution Russia possessed a tenuous but highly significant tradition of conservative liberalism whose principal theorist was Chicherin. In the ideologically charged field of Russian history, Chicherin came to symbolize liberal values that the Russian radical intelligentsia had fatally ignored in its deluded pursuit of a socialist utopia.

A more contextual approach to Russian history has brought into question

many of the assumptions on which this interpretation of the fundamental conflicts in Russian thought was based. Chicherin in particular has come to be
seen as a more ambivalent figure; hence the continuing uncertainty as to where
to place him on the liberal spectrum. But that he belongs there is generally accepted, on the ground that he devoted most of his life to opposing what Martin
Malia has defined as the distinguishing characteristic of the intelligentsia of
that period: their belief in the primacy of principles over the "intractability of
everyday life, or what the vulgar call reality."[8] Against this prevailing stream
Chicherin, it is argued, preached the defense of freedom through evolution,
gradualism, and compromise. His ideas would thus seem relevant to our own
pragmatic, postideological age.

I believe that they are relevant, but only as a warning of the ideological contraband that can be carried under the flag of realism. Beneath the language that
sounds so reassuringly familiar to Western liberals, there lurked an alien vision
of freedom, whose underlying affinities were with the totalitarian democrats
whom Chicherin loathed so deeply. My intention is to examine his thought at
the height of his political involvement in the mid-nineteenth century, focusing
on the notion of realism that was his battle cry against the Left, a notion that
was rooted in Hegelian categories. The influence of Hegel on his political philosophy is not disputed, but it has been argued that this did not prevent him
being a pragmatist. I maintain that it did: the reality to which he expected Russians to submit was the "rational reality" of Hegelian fantasy. On this he built
his own fantasies, which were generically akin to those that later plunged his
country into darkness.

Chicherin's political thought was shaped by the frustrations of Russia's Westernized intellectual elite under the stifling despotism of Nicholas I. He describes in his memoirs how men of independent minds, with no arena of
public activity open to them, channeled their energies into philosophical speculation in order to decipher the enigma of their lives and of their nation's destiny. Hegel's idealism provided many with the answers they needed. It was at
the height of its fashion in Russia when in 1844, at the age of sixteen, the intellectually precocious Boris Chicherin arrived in Moscow to prepare for en-
trance to the university. Like many of his contemporaries he believed that with
the discovery of Hegel he had emerged from the realm of subjective dreams
and fantasies onto the firm ground of reality—by which he meant nothing so
banal as the everyday world. Hegelian reality was a dialectical pattern of development purporting to be universal, rational, and necessary and to give sense
and coherence to the disparate phenomena of the external world. By the mid-

1840s, following the split of the German Hegelian school into Right and Left tendencies, the Russian Hegelians had divided similarly over the interpretation of Hegel's identification of Reason with reality;[9] and it was from conservative Hegelians such as the professor of law P. G. Redkin and the historian Timofei Granovsky that the student Chicherin took a view of the dialectic that emphasized the necessity of reconciling oneself with the predetermined pattern of historical progress. He subsequently recalled that he was "totally captivated by the new world view that revealed to me the marvelous harmony of the supreme principles of existence."[10]

News of the European upheavals of 1848 intruded on this beguiling vision. Like his mentors, Chicherin was shocked by the violence of the revolution in France which, he claims, brought his thoughts "down from the level of ideals to that of reality," leading him to dismiss socialist ideals as utopian dreams, "the delirium of overheated minds." "Realism" (defined as the "sober" view that only those ideals could be attained which were in harmony with the given stage in the advance of Reason through history) was henceforth to be Chicherin's slogan in his battle with the Left. His new realism, however, was in essence no different from the old. It was not empirical criteria that Chicherin used to distinguish between attainable and unattainable ideals but the determinism of the conservative Hegelian. The failure of the revolutionaries to control and direct the events of 1848 confirmed him in the belief that he later defined as the central theme of all his writings: that history was the development of the infinite spirit "in accordance with the eternal laws of Reason intrinsic to it." All the phenomena of experience could therefore be organically integrated into "a single living picture" which (it goes without saying) could be deciphered only by those initiated into the workings of the absolute.[11] This conclusion was the fruit of an intensive study of Hegel, as a result of which, Chicherin claimed, the meaning of the whole course of human history became clear to him: its fundamental law was "the movement of the spirit from unity to division and from division back to unity."[12] Together with the historian Konstantin Kavelin, he founded the etatist school of Russian historiography, based on Hegel's doctrine that the human being was the vehicle through which the rational necessity immanent in the cosmos came to comprehend its own laws; this was done through the advance of human societies toward the modern state, which in its perfected form would be a community grounded in reason.[13] The etatist historians believed that Russia and Europe were destined ultimately to converge on this goal, and when Alexander II came to the throne in 1855, Chicherin joined with other prominent Westernizers in urging the new tsar to proceed with the emancipation of the serfs, the granting of civil rights, and other administrative reforms that would propel Russia along the Western path of progress.

As one historian has put it, in the 1840s Hegel's thought served Russian academic jurists and historians as an "organizing paradigm" for interpretations of Russia's past and predictions about her future.[14] In the late 1850s Chicherin took the lead in transforming it into a weapon of political polemic, in the context of discussion about the impending reforms. Alarmed by the socialist propaganda emanating from Aleksandr Herzen's Free Russian Press in London, he and Kavelin wrote a joint letter to Herzen, contending that the latter's ideal of peasant socialism could be justified only if he could prove that it represented "the inevitable consequence of what has gone before, the ripened fruit of the rational development of human societies." In fact, the two asserted, the opposite was the case: communal association represented a primitive stage of historical development, long since superseded. All Herzen's errors flowed from one source—his failure to perceive that "history advances gradually from one imperfect stage to the next, with each stage moving closer to perfection."[15]

Although differences in ultimate goals did not prevent Kavelin from supporting Herzen's campaign for immediate reforms, Chicherin's opposition to Herzen became increasingly vehement. In particular he criticized Herzen's warnings that if the government did not initiate reform with all possible speed, it would be brought about by revolution from below.[16] Herzen replied in an article in his paper *The Bell*, describing his critic as a dogmatist more concerned with imposing his own views about the shape of the reforms than with defending reform itself against reaction. In reply, Chicherin accused Herzen of seeking to incite violence instead of using his influence to calm the people. The responsible conduct of public affairs, he reminded Herzen, demands patience, a sense of timing, moderation, and a respect for law.[17]

This polemic has been viewed as a paradigm of the conflict between two political archetypes, or "temperaments," as Chicherin calls them—the liberal pragmatist and the doctrinaire extremist.[18] As such it has been interpreted (in accordance with the schema that I have outlined) as marking the division of Russian thought into two mutually hostile strands. But Chicherin's contemporaries took a different view of the debate. In a foreword to Chicherin's letter, Herzen emphasized that it came from an entirely different camp than previous criticism of *The Bell*—the camp of official ("governmental") doctrinairism, and the most prominent Russian liberals took his side in the dispute.[19] In a letter to Chicherin, Kavelin pointed out that Herzen had never preached violent revolution as a desirable outcome; on the contrary, he had urged the government to forestall it by reform, a view with which no liberal could disagree. By representing Herzen as an insurrectionist, Chicherin was playing the game of the tsar's reactionary advisers, giving them carte blanche for any repressive action they cared to take. "In exalted circles, everyone is delighted by your letter.

. . . Their only reproach is that you did not present this fine and noble missive to the government for approval before you published it; [they] would have approved it without fail."[20]

In a letter he wrote but did not send to Chicherin at the time, and which was later published in his memoirs, Herzen draws attention to the philosophical basis of their dispute, originating in the intelligentsia's earlier polemics on the nature of Hegelian "reality." Although he does not refer directly to these, his letter recapitulates the central argument of his celebrated Hegelian article of 1843, "Buddhism in Science," inspired by a recent episode in which Vissarion Belinsky and Mikhail Bakunin, then conservative Hegelians, had used Hegel's axiom "What is real is rational" as the basis of a brief but notorious "reconciliation with reality," which was a justification of all aspects of life under the regime of Nicholas I as necessary and inevitable manifestations of the Absolute. Herzen accused the Hegelian Right of committing the cardinal sin of all doctrinaire idealists, religious and secular, that of condoning the sacrifice of living individuals to abstract principles unrelated to real situations.

Herzen depicts Chicherin as a doctrinaire of this type. Having adopted Hegel's theory of the Rechtsstaat as the goal of universal history, he was logically obliged to oppose all popular aspirations which might lead in a different direction. Present reality being an inevitable stage in the unfolding of a "program" of progress, Chicherin cannot rebel against it: "You know that if the past was *thus and thus,* the present must be *thus and thus,* and lead to *that particular* future." Chicherin is not disconcerted by those who find the given reality intolerable: "Aware of the inevitability of suffering, the doctrinaire stands, like Simon Stylites, on a pillar, sacrificing all the temporal to the eternal, the living and particular to universal ideas." The parallel with the Russian Right Hegelians of two decades earlier would have been clear to Herzen's readers.

Herzen argues that Chicherin is defending the modern bureaucratic state not on empirical grounds but as the central tenet of a new "civic religion": "You have replaced the heavenly hierarchy by state rank, . . . substituted centralisation for God and the policeman for the priest."[21] In an oblique reference to Chicherin's frequently expressed belief that Russia was not yet "ready" for constitutional freedoms,[22] Herzen asserts that for all his talk of liberty, Chicherin is in the tradition of those priestly castes who saw the mass of human beings as a submissive flock and themselves as the sole interpreters of eternal truth.

What was Chicherin, a "bureaucratic Saint-Just"[23] fanatically devoted to the state as the embodiment of Reason in the world (Herzen's image of him) or a pragmatic liberal seeking a middle way between revolution and reaction? A closer look at his ideas will show that Herzen's view was nearer to the truth.

✳

There has been much debate as to what constituted liberalism in the context of nineteenth-century Russia. Some historians have argued that etatist liberalism, which viewed the state as the chief guarantor of individual freedom and preferred enlightened absolutism to the specter of the despotism of the masses, was the only true Russian liberalism, or at least the variety most appropriate to the country's backwardness.[24] Others have quoted the views of Ivan Turgenev (who described himself as a liberal "in the English sense" and had little sympathy for etatist doctrines) as the touchstone of true liberalism,[25] although at least one history of the Russian liberal movement includes those who felt that to keep faith with their liberal ideals they had no alternative but to seek the violent overthrow of the existing order.[26]

But all these commentators seem to agree that in Russia, as elsewhere, liberalism entails adherence to "a theory holding that political authority must be restrained by law and representative institutions" in the name of the rights of individuals.[27] Despite the diversity of opinion as to what sort of liberal Chicherin was, it is commonly accepted that he was a liberal in this generic sense of the term (which includes the disparate traditions of Locke and Mill, Burke and the proponents of the Rechtsstaat). My view that he was not rests on the theory of "liberal conservatism" with which his name is identified, which he formulated in the crucial first decade of Alexander's reign and which became the criterion for his judgments of events, policies, and political figures in those years, as the new tsar began to move back from reform to retrenchment.[28]

At the time of Chicherin's polemic with Herzen, Russian liberalism was (as George Fischer describes it) little more than "a state of mind, a hazy cluster of political ideas and programmes."[29] Above all it was a mood of moral opposition to serfdom and of solidarity with the campaign for reform waged in Herzen's *Bell.* The importance of this common bond made Russian liberals content to treat their differences with Herzen in the prereform period as primarily a matter of emphasis. Even Chicherin is tentative when in 1858 he suggests that their respective positions "perhaps demonstrate the difference between liberalism and radicalism."[30]

It was in order to draw a clear line between these two tendencies that Chicherin, in a volume of essays on contemporary issues published in the early 1860s, set out to define "true" liberalism, as distinct from two other varieties. The first of these he calls "street liberalism"—the stance of those who equate liberal attitudes with the rejection of culture and tradition and the removal of all constraints (he is here aiming at the emerging *raznochintsy,* the young déclassés who despised gentry culture). But it is the category of "oppositional liberals," in which he includes Herzen and his liberal sympathizers, who are the main target of his attack. This type, he claimed, was more civilized than the street liberal, but no less opposed to the authority of the state and to tradition: "Abolish, dissolve, destroy—that is his whole system." His ideal of freedom took no account of reality: "The further a given principle is from the existing order, the more general and undefined, the more hidden in a mist of hazy concepts . . . the dearer it is to the oppositional liberal."[31] Such persons had a polarized vision of the world in which "the people," self-government, and public opinion were absolute goods, whereas centralization, bureaucracy, and the state were the embodiment of evil. Chicherin held the uncooperativeness of oppositional liberals to blame for the government and society remaining at loggerheads in the 1860s. In post-Emancipation Russia, he declares, "true liberalism is measured not by opposition, not by the glorification of liberty, not by advanced opinions, but by devotion to the Edict of 19 February."[32] True liberalism was therefore "liberal conservatism," whose slogan was "liberal measures and strong government."[33] It must respect law and the principle of power on the grounds that a strong central authority was the only safeguard against anarchy. Above all, liberalism must be pragmatic: it "must adapt to life, learn from history, act with an understanding of the nature of political power, . . . [without] making irrational demands . . . [while] encouraging and exercising restraint where necessary."[34] In short, what was needed was a thoroughgoing realism: "The whole task [of the political thinker] can be reduced . . . to a practical understanding of existing reality; one must discern those forces that possess an element of permanence, and on which at some given moment social structures can be built."[35]

This seems an admirably moderate and balanced approach to the problem of progress in Russia: it was later cited as such by Pyotr Struve, a genuinely pragmatic liberal whose writings have helped promote Chicherin's image as a realist heroically swimming against the utopian stream.[36] However, while Struve, seeking a tradition in which to set his own thought, took Chicherin's definition of liberalism at face value, Chicherin's contemporaries were more conscious of the ideological subtext of his frequent references to "realism" and the "laws of life." Nikolai Chernyshevsky spoke for his generation of radicals when he denounced Chicherin's manner of thinking as "scholasticism, proceeding from a false basis by means of twisted syllogisms, with utter contempt for . . . the facts."[37] But liberals too were conscious of the philosophical underpinnings of Chicherin's calls for moderation and restraint. Turgenev was repelled by his doctrinairism,[38] whereas Kavelin, who feared revolution no less than Chicherin, detected in the latter's "apotheosis" of state centralism a "terribly mistaken" ideology. As Kavelin wrote to M. N. Katkov (editor of the liberal journal *The Russian Messenger*), "Against the new Baal . . . to which he offers human sacrifices, we must take up arms with all our strength."[39]

To the Hegelian Kavelin, Chicherin's Baal and Hegel's ideal state were two distinct entities. Although it has often been argued that the emphasis on centralism in Hegel's theory of the state is not compatible with liberal doctrines, I shall assume for the purpose of this study that it is.[40] My argument is not that Chicherin was too Hegelian a liberal but rather that (as Kavelin perceived) he was not Hegelian enough: his peculiar adaptation of Hegel's theory of the state to Russian conditions cannot lay claim even to the questionable liberalism of the original.[41]

Like Hegel, Chicherin and other etatist theorists defined the ideal state as a constitutional monarchy with legal guarantees of rights, and Chicherin's writings on this theme constitute the liberal aspect of his doctrine.[42] He emphasizes that the realm of private law should not be absorbed in the state and defends the right to private property, freedom of conscience, and freedom of contracts. He goes further than most of his Russian contemporaries in advocating a laissez-faire economy, arguing that a large degree of individual economic initiative is an essential condition of national prosperity.[43] These views have been cited as proof of Chicherin's concern with protecting the individual against authoritarianism of the Right and the Left, but they are very heavily qualified.[44] While noting that "the free individual with his rights and interests" is the "basic and essential element" of the state, Chicherin stresses that individual liberty must never take such "extreme" forms as in contemporary England, where "overemphasis of the principle of individuality and suspicion of the government . . . have led to unwarranted limitations of the state's power."[45] His definition of civil rights has been described as narrow and idiosyncratic.[46] For instance, in *On Popular Representation* (1866), he recommended that the press and public speech should be subject to careful government supervision and argues that under a representative system the right of suffrage should be granted only to those citizens capable of rational participation in public life. "The individual is free to do as he wishes—so long as he does not transgress the laws of the Spirit": such dicta (abundant in Chicherin's work) remind the reader that what often seem to be crude contradictions in his attitude to liberal freedoms are the product of a mind at home in Hegel's dialectic.[47] It is this that binds the liberal with the conservative side of Chicherin's philosophy, the side to which he devotes by far the greater part of his writings. Here he diverges from other etatist historians on two crucial aspects of his interpretation of Hegel: his attitude to the concept of law and his prescriptions on the hierarchical nature of the state.

Chicherin's stress on law is commonly regarded as the distinctive characteristic of his liberalism; it has been argued that he was almost alone among Russian thinkers in pointing to the importance of legal guarantees of rights (the majority of the radical intelligentsia believing that freedom would follow as a logical consequence of the destruction of privilege).[48] But Chicherin's defense of law, based on Hegel's *Philosophy of Right,* is combined with a defense of hierarchy and tradition that is founded on a conservative interpretation of Hegel's *Philosophy of History.* The result is a crude logical contradiction, which opens the way to an absolute philosophical sanction for the despotic status quo.

Chicherin's conservatism flowed from a Right Hegelian interpretation of the dialectic whose emphasis was on continuity rather than change. He explains that history is a "succession of organic formations" which express a single spiritual essence.[49] Thus, the foundations of society must consist of principles "sanctioned by tradition." Every state needs a conservative party to preserve those "vital foundations" and restrain radical elements. It is on this Hegelian historicism, and not (as is often maintained) on empirical grounds, that Chicherin based his defense of contemporary Russian institutions against the general clamor for far-reaching reform. He is against such a reform of the bureaucracy, which "has been given to us by history and contemporary life." To the liberals who were calling for genuine local self-government he retorts that to demand a weakening of the central power is to go against a thousand years of history during which Russian society has been dominated by the "principle of power."[50] Such arguments, in particular the last, can scarcely have impressed those who did not share Chicherin's faith in the sanctity of tradition. Equally historicist was his response to those who pressed for a constitution: like Hegel, he asserts that representative government is based on a substructure of beliefs and habits which is the product of a specific stage of development. He warns that several generations will pass before the Russian people reach the level of consciousness necessary for the transition from absolutist to constitutional rule.[51]

Whatever its relation to the Russian realities of the mid-nineteenth century, Chicherin's use of Hegel's philosophy of history as a brake on demands for reform has at least a doctrinal consistency. This consistency is lost, however, when he attempts to defend the structure and legality of the existing Russian state with arguments of a different order—based on the concept of liberty outlined in Hegel's *Philosophy of Right.*

As Chicherin emphasized in his polemics with Russian liberals, his understanding of freedom was fundamentally different from theirs: to their "negative" view of liberty as the absence of constraints, he opposed a liberalism based on "positive" principles.[52] This corresponds to Hegel's distinction between "abstract" or "negative" liberty, on the one hand, and "concrete" liberty, on the other. Hegel identified the former with classical liberalism, which held individuals to be free only inasmuch as they were guaranteed an area of activity in which they could do as they liked without interference from others and had the freedom to consent to or dissent from particular forms of government. Hegel's concept of concrete or positive freedom, however, presupposed constraints. The individual could achieve liberty only through the state, which was the embodiment of his self-consciousness or reason, its institutions being perceived not as an external coercive force but the expression of human moral nature, the "actuality of the ethical Idea." In the identity of the personal and the universal will expressed in acts of obedience to law, Hegel held, "right and duty coalesce."[53]

Hegel's doctrine of positive liberty was the basis of his hierarchical concept of the state: being the incarnation of man's rational consciousness, its structure must embody his moral personality, ensuring the subordination of his subjective interests to the objective, universal will. Hegel's state is therefore a hierarchical structure reflecting three modes of consciousness. The agricultural class, composed of nobility at the top and peasants at the bottom, represents a consciousness circumscribed by quasi-familial relations; the middle class, for whom intelligence is essential, represents a higher, more "objective" level of consciousness; and a rational, modern bureaucracy, the "universal" class (motivated by the interests of society as a whole) plays the crucial role of mediator between subjective wills and the objective universal goals of the state. Finally, the monarch, standing above the clash of contending forces, expresses in his or her person the integration of the subjective principle with the universal will.

It has been pointed out that the doctrine of "positive liberty" can be used to justify tyranny of both the Left and the Right: once the state is identified with its citizens' higher rational nature, they are regarded as being free even when they are most coerced, their resistance to the force used against them being seen as the expression of their lower, irrational urges.[54] But Hegel did stress that positive liberty could exist only in a state whose institutions reflected the self-consciousness of the individuals who composed it, representing a true integration of subjective and objective wills. In the system of representation he saw primarily an instrument of mediation between the subjective interests of civil society and the objectivism of the state; systems whose balance was disturbed by excessive centralism he saw as despotic. Although no existing state could be more than an approximation to his ideal, none was further from it than Russia, which he cited as an illustration of his thesis that "a state without a middle class is still at a low stage of development."[55]

Chicherin revered the *Philosophy of Right* as the "crown of all the previous development of thought." In his view, no other thinker had defined so well the relations of the "two mutually contrary constituents of freedom—law and morality, which . . . are placed in opposition to each other and then brought to-gether in a higher unity in the organism of the social union . . . where man . . . as an individual and as a rational and moral being fulfills his supreme mis-sion."[56]

This enthusiastic appreciation of the subtle dialectic between the principles of freedom and constraint in Hegel's ideal state seems to leave no doubt as to the gulf between that state and the autocratic regime which (in the last years of the reign of Nicholas I) Chicherin himself had described as an Eastern despot-ism, and to whose continuation for the foreseeable future he had reconciled himself, with the help of Hegel's philosophy of history.[57] But to this legal phi-losopher, who always believed that the danger to the rule of law was far greater from the Left than from the Right, Hegel's arguments against negative liberty must have seemed an irresistible weapon to supplement the Hegelian philos-ophy of history against what he saw as the increasing threat of social instability and even anarchism after the Emancipation. His doctrine of liberal conserva-tism was clearly intended to embody the dialectical tensions of Hegel's concept of liberty, yet he seems to have been unaware of the logical contradiction in his use of that concept to support his conservative historicism. In the 1860s he ap-plies the principles of the *Philosophy of Right* with such dogmatic rigidity in support of the status quo that the real and the ideal, the autocracy of Alexander II and the Rechtsstaat of Hegel's imagination, seem to have coalesced in his thought. His attempts to force a recalcitrant Russian reality into Hegel's ideal scheme must surely rank as one of the most bizarre episodes in the history of Russian thought.

Chicherin's definition of liberty is closely modeled on Hegel's. As we have seen, he castigates those liberals for whom freedom is a "boundless concept," who feel oppressed by the most essential activities of the state, and he propounds the doctrine of positive liberty: the state is not an external form imposed me-chanically on an aggregate of people. It is the people itself, as a "moral person-ality." In obeying the law, the individual is obeying those "higher forces" which express the free spirit of the nation.[58]

But Chicherin's emphasis on the sanctity of law must be seen in context. At that time, the archaic Russian legal system, with a long tradition of arbitrary in-terpretation and abuse, was only in the preliminary stages of reform. Law in the Hegelian or constitutional sense did not begin to exist in Russia until after 1905. The legal reforms completed in 1864 proclaimed the establishment of an independent judicial system and equality of all before the law, but the incom-patibility between the rule of law and unlimited autocracy, and the tsar's de-termination to keep the latter intact, was to deprive of any effective force all aspects of the reform that encroached on the total obedience demanded of his subjects. Appeals against violations of the law by organs of the state were meaningless when, by virtue of his position, every order of the tsar and of the officials whose power derived from him alone had supralegal force. A few years later the shaky juridical guarantees of individual inviolability established in 1864 vanished when all crimes deemed political were removed from the jurisdiction of the courts to that of the political police.

To defend the rationality of Russian law at the beginning of the 1860s was, at the least, untimely. Nevertheless, in his inaugural lecture as professor of jurisprudence at Moscow University in 1861 Chicherin aroused a storm of protest from liberals and radicals alike by invoking his doctrine of obedience to law as the "primary condition of liberty" explicitly against the liberal movement, which was seeking to bring about the very rule of law he held so dear. The duty of obedience to law, he maintained, extends even to bad laws; for if people obeyed only those laws of which they approved, anarchy would prevail. He clinches his argument with this assertion: "For a jurist obedience to law is as basic an axiom as 'twice two is four' is for a mathematician."[59] His argument notably lacks the proviso which, for a jurist of the kind Chicherin professed to be, is at least as important as the axiom itself—namely, that this binding character does not extend to edicts emanating from an unconstitutional authority. Nor was the proviso omitted on the understanding that Chicherin was speaking of a hypothetical constitutional state. His speech was a political one, delivered from an important public platform and explicitly directed against opponents of the autocracy. As his audience perfectly understood, his trenchant defense of all laws, good or bad, and irrespective of their source, was a defense of the status quo against its critics.[60] He supports his argument with the dubious claim he had used in his polemic with Herzen—that in an autocracy which promises reform the obligation to exercise moderation and self-control rests primarily with the subjects of the autocrat: it is up to them to earn their right to freedom. Once again, he appears to be confusing the imperfect present with the ideal future; the inference from his arguments would seem to be the logically absurd proposition that as soon as a despot announces, however ambiguously, his intention to move toward legality, his arbitrary sanctions, enforced (as Chicherin admits) by corrupt courts, become in some way invested with the same morally binding character as those of the hypothetical future constitutional state.[61] Chicherin again makes no distinction between categories of laws when, in an article written in the same year, he informs the government's critics that it is only in the act of obedience to law that human beings realize their true nature as ends in themselves. "The absolute meaning of the law confers absolute meaning also on the . . . individual who submits to it."[62] The real is confused with the ideal, autocracy with the Rechtsstaat, and Hegel's *Philosophy of Right* is turned on its head as Chicherin assures his audience that submission to an autocrat's diktats will confirm them in their dignity as autonomous moral beings.

Having used Hegel's concept of liberty to defend the legality of the existing regime against the Left, Chicherin proceeded to apply it to another front under attack from liberals and socialists alike—the hierarchical structure of the Russian state, in particular the role of the nobility and the bureaucracy. Of Hegel's three modes of consciousness, Russia possessed only two: the nobility and peasants represented one mode, the bureaucracy a second. The future development of the third, a strong middle class, Chicherin saw as essential both for the cohesion of society and the strengthening of the central power. Meanwhile, he argued, its role as a "rational force" should fall to the nobility, which had shown through its awareness of its rights that it was the sole group in Russian society with the beginnings of political consciousness.[63] The bureaucracy, though in need of some reform, must remain as "one of the central supports of the state order." Like Hegel, Chicherin calls for the development of corporations, arguing that in the absence of a middle class these could provide a schooling in civil life by channeling subjective interests into a universal framework.[64]

Like its legal system, Russia's bureaucracy and nobility were far removed from Hegel's specifications. Even moderate liberals echoed Herzen in condemning their obstruction of the reform process. Chicherin himself, who clashed with the bureaucracy in the 1850s, described it in his memoirs as a servile and intellectually moribund milieu which drove to despair any gifted young man who entered its ranks.[65] He also shared the view of many liberals that the nobility would manipulate the reforms for its own self-aggrandizement; indeed, he uses this as an argument against the granting of a constitution which would extend their freedom.[66]

He is not disconcerted, however, by the poverty of the material at hand, nor by the gulf between reality and the Hegelian ideal. He recognizes that self-interest is the primary political motivation of the bureaucracy and nobility but believes that the government will be able to contain their ambition;[67] and at a time when many of the nobility were seeking to protect their privileges by blocking agrarian reform, he advances Hegel's argument that this group is particularly suited to political preeminence because its hereditary ownership of land makes it, unlike the other estates, independent of sectional interests. Because of the nobility's traditional position as the dependent of an autocratic power, presenting this class as a rationally conscious force in Hegel's sense was difficult, and Chicherin resorts to the curious argument that its moral qualification for political dominance lies in its sense of caste honor, its tradition of state service, and its long experience of exercising power over serfs.[68] In another bizarre twist of Hegel's schema, the mentality of the slave owner becomes that rational force on which the state, as the expression of humanity's moral essence, is to rest.

More curiously still, Chicherin contrives to present the autocracy of the 1860s as designed to meet Hegel's criteria for the head of state even more satisfactorily than Hegel's own model of a constitutional monarch. Such monarchies, he writes, are dominated by parties representing conflicting interests; in contrast, the absolute ruler represents the interests of the state as a whole. Moreover, he can call on the services of all his ablest subjects: in a constitutional system many of these would be in opposition. There, too, ministers were answerable first and foremost to their party, whereas an autocrat was responsible to all his subjects without distinction.[69] Chicherin would later point out that it was not possible in the 1860s to discuss openly all the defects of autocracy and all the advantages of a constitutional order (which, he declared subsequently, was always his ultimate ideal);[70] but if we are to accept his repeated insistence that the views he expressed were always his own, we must assume that in the 1860s at least, he saw autocracy as not incompatible with positive liberty.[71]

Chicherin's defense of the Russian status quo also draws on the *Philosophy of Right* to justify a restricted system of political rights. He argues that the call for universal suffrage is based on an "abstract" conception of equality which does not take into account the differing modes of consciousness (in the Hegelian sense) of each social group. He rejects the proposal being aired in the early 1860s for a consultative assembly composed of representatives of all social groups, on the grounds that the peasants' consciousness was circumscribed by the commune and that the emerging middle class was not yet competent to exercise power outside the field of its immediate interests. Although in the *Philosophy of Right* the divisions of civil society were reflected in a system of bicameral representation (consisting of an upper house made up of members of the nobility and a lower house of elected representatives of the other estates), Chicherin's system was much narrower. The right to representation and to participate in law making (in an advisory capacity only—he is still speaking of an autocracy) was to be confined to the nobility, because it alone possessed the requisite "universality" of outlook.[72]

The idea of such strict limits on rights was intrinsic to Chicherin's concept of state power. Hegel's system of representation by estates was intended to mediate between the particularism of civil society and the universalism of the state, which he saw as a pluralistic structure. He frequently condemned the centralized bureaucracy of France as a lifeless machine. Chicherin, on the contrary, admired it.[73] A strongly centralized state was his ideal, and he clearly intended limitation of rights and suffrage to contribute to that end. At a time when liberal opinion was united in calling for greater powers for the local zemstva assemblies to counterbalance the bureaucracy, Chicherin opposed such demands on the grounds that local interests would then take precedence over those of society as a whole, as represented by the central power.[74] In his lectures and writings on the state, his observance of the letter of the Hegelian law contrasts sharply with his neglect of its spirit. The concern with mediation and balance between particular and universal goals which permeates Hegel's system is almost entirely absent from Chicherin's version of it. We have seen that the slogan of his liberal conservatism was "liberal measures and strong government"; in his conception of the state the emphasis is almost exclusively on the latter. The bureaucracy must be retained primarily because it has proved its ability to "preserve order and . . . strengthen the state" in the past; the nobility's attachment to the existing order is an overwhelming reason for allowing it to keep its privileges.[75] The primary function of corporations should be as a support for the central power.[76]

Chicherin's slogan implies a balance between freedom and order, but in his ideal state the principle of order clearly takes precedence over freedom. Liberal themes are correspondingly given little place in his writings, the overwhelming majority of which are dedicated to a justification of state power. Andrzej Walicki has emphasized that Chicherin's idealism asserted the absolute value of the individual as the source of all social unions.[77] Nonetheless, we have seen that in his theory of the state, where the distinction between moral law and state authority is for practical purposes effaced (law being the "moral principle on which the state is founded"), it is the absolute value of the law, and obedience to it, that gives the individual human worth,[78] and reference to those rights which in liberal philosophies derive from the nature of persons as ends in themselves is notably missing from his journalism of the 1860s. In the preceding decade he had joined with liberals and radicals in calling for freedom of speech and the press and reform of the legal system as the essential premises of political liberty. In the mid-1860s, when none of those goals had been achieved and the government was clearly set on a course of repression, the constant refrain of his writings is that change must not be taken too far or too quickly. As we have seen, he is very sparing with political rights—the overwhelming mass of the population, the peasantry, is to be excluded from them; he even opposes any immediate extension of the rights of the nobility.[79]

What, then, does Chicherin mean by "liberal measures"? The answer is given in letters written in September and October of 1861 at the request of his brother, a councillor in the Ministry of Foreign Affairs, where he records for the benefit of the authorities (to whom the letters were intended to be passed on) his views on the student disturbances in Moscow and Petersburg that year.[80] Their immediate cause had been the introduction of new regulations aimed at eliminating freedom within the universities and representing a return to the policies of Nicholas I. Educated society in Petersburg and Moscow sympathized with the students' grievances and was incensed when the peaceful protests were met with a large force of soldiers and police, resulting in numerous injuries and arrests. Chicherin's former mentor, Kavelin, together with his colleagues in the Faculty of Law at St. Petersburg University, resigned in protest against the brutality of the authorities' actions.

Chicherin, however, was eloquent in his condemnation of the students. In his letters to his brother that year, although he criticizes the regulations which had caused the trouble as being petty and ineffectual, he accuses the government of not enforcing them resolutely enough: its most urgent task was to use the police to reassert its authority over the universities and society as a whole. Once this was done, it need not fear introducing "liberal measures," which Chicherin enumerates as removal of the more absurd aspects of the censorship and some curtailment of the activities of the secret police. This would be enough to satisfy the general demand for greater freedom and would strengthen the central authority in the long run, so long as these measures were combined with the continued exercise of strong government.

The authorities were quick to grasp the relation of Chicherin's liberalism to his conservatism. His brother wrote that the tsar would be pleased with his slogan, inasmuch as it did not impinge on the principle of absolutism. It was officially approved (the foreign minister, Prince Gorchakov, remarked that it had always been a motto of his own), and Chicherin was asked to write more on this theme. His assessment of the state of public opinion was pronounced particularly valuable:[81] he had emphasized that the government should not be deterred from the use of strong measures by the widespread indignation at the truncation of the reforms and at the rough treatment of the students. These protests were not to be taken seriously—they had been stirred up by "trash and nonentities, little twenty-one-year-old officers and first-year students." The sole reason for them was the "absence of strong government."

This insight into the causes of political opposition in Russia in the early 1860s was worthy of a policeman rather than a member of the intellectual elite, and it completed that break with the liberal camp which had begun with Chicherin's inaugural lecture at Moscow University. When his liberal conservatism is set in its historical context, it becomes clear that, contrary to a common view, his alienation from mainstream Russian liberalism was not due to the fact that his call for gradualism was too truly liberal to be attractive to people whose real sympathies were with the Left. In fact, as is well known, in the 1860s a polarization occurred between liberals and the Left; such figures as Kavelin and Turgenev were at least as emphatic as Chicherin in their calls for compromise and their opposition to revolution as a means of social change. But they had few illusions as to the compatibility of unlimited autocracy with liberal ideals, however moderate. Their support for the autocracy was a tactical maneuver in their effort to attain the goals of political rights and the rule of law, but they never expressed approval of its repressive measures and (as in Kavelin's case) were sometimes roused to public protest against them. This was the gulf that separated them from Chicherin. As we have seen, by 1861 he had come to confuse reality and the ideal so much as to use the *Philosophy of Right* to justify a regime based on brute force. It was his ideological support and active encouragement of the government, his acceptance of its absolute right to repress, and his consistent opposition to all extensions of individual rights which might encroach on its power that alienated liberals from him; they sensed, as Herzen had done, that he belonged to "another camp." In March 1862 *The Bell* published the text of a secret report by a university commission appointed by the government to investigate the causes of the student protests in Moscow. Among the signatories was Chicherin, who reveals in his memoirs that he had drafted the report. It echoed the sentiments expressed in the letter to his brother on the same subject and ends with the hope that the university can rely on a more prompt response from the police in the event of any future illegal actions by the students.

The publication of this document made Chicherin a pariah in liberal circles. Kavelin wrote to him that it was "too shameful . . . even to be discussed."[82] Turgenev informed Herzen that Chicherin was widely shunned in Moscow: "In Petersburg he would be unable to exist."[83] But his sense of righteousness was unshaken: as he had pointed out to his brother in one of the letters from which he quotes liberally in his memoirs, it was important to reassure the government that the current protests, whether in the universities, in literature, or in society as a whole, represented *"not only nothing dangerous, but not even anything remotely serious"*—nothing, in fact, that a show of force would not cure.[84]

Quite apart from its moral nastiness, this monumental miscalculation about the strength of purpose of the opposition to autocracy would seem to indicate that Chicherin was even less a realist than he was a liberal. His rehabilitation by historians came after the Russian liberal movement had been swept away by the 1917 Revolution. In the light of subsequent developments Chicherin's loathing of the Left has seemed to some commentators remarkably prescient. This point has been made most forcefully by Walicki, who contends that Chicherin was much ahead of his time in perceiving that liberalism and democracy were two quite different things. Given that classical liberalism revolves around the problem of the limitation of all political power, socialism (as a form of democracy which devolves powers to a bureaucratic apparatus independent of democratic control) must, Walicki argues, be "enemy number one of a liberalism so conceived."[85]

Walicki does not deny that Chicherin himself came very late (at the end of his life) to an acceptance of the necessity of limiting the power of the tsar and transforming Russian absolutism into a constitutional monarchy.[86] But his insights into the totalitarian implications of socialist democracy are seen to compensate for such deficiencies: Walicki is emphatic that although Chicherin was not a liberal democrat, he was nonetheless a liberal.

Undoubtedly, the concept of liberalism has been much enlarged by political theory and practice in this century. The "night watchman" theory of the state—the ideal of a classical liberalism concerned with defending the individual against the encroachments of state power—has given way to communitarian theories of liberalism which emphasize the social essence of human beings, and as a result the boundaries between positive and negative liberty have become progressively blurred. So have distinctions between liberalism and conservatism. As John Plamenatz has pointed out, "No liberal is only a liberal."[87] This tolerant church can accommodate even the conservatism of the *Philosophy of Right,* described by one critic as "a grand endeavor to insert modern 'civil society' . . . into the framework of a holist state accommodating the traditional hierarchies of the ancien regime."[88]

But if the concept of liberalism is to have any meaning at all, it must exclude theories that seek to justify arbitrary power. Chicherin did so, not as a passing aberration but for over forty years. He was not, however, just a conservative or (as some Soviet scholars portrayed him) a cynical spokesperson for the selfish interests of his caste. He was something much more interesting. His true historical significance is not as a critic of the totalitarian mentality but as a prime specimen of it.

Chicherin's relation to liberalism can perhaps best be described in terms of Isaiah Berlin's characterization of two opposing human types, the hedgehog and the fox. If the stereotypical liberal, with his belief in the value of diversity and many-sidedness in personal and social existence, is the fox of the Greek poet, who "knows many things," Chicherin is the hedgehog, who "knows one big thing." Chicherin once declared that the aim of all his intellectual activity was to demonstrate the fundamental unity underlying the diversity of phenomena, "to reduce the totality of human history, philosophy and law to a few universal, simple and clear principles, and to deduce from that basis a general law of the development of mankind."[89] He exemplifies that fanatical consistency which led many Russian intellectuals, in Herzen's words, to march "in a fearless phalanx . . . . to the very limit, and beyond, in step with the dialectic, but out of step with the truth."[90] There are striking parallels between Chicherin and one of the most notorious of these dialecticians, Belinsky in his Right Hegelian period. Like Belinsky, Chicherin had experienced a moment of revelation, when he perceived the "marvelous harmony of the supreme principles of existence" and the "entire historical path of human thought."[91] The immediate consequence for both was a "reconciliation" with existing political realities as a necessary stage in the unfolding of the rational pattern of existence.

As Herzen pointed out, all Chicherin's prescriptions on the future structure of the Russian state spring from his view of its place in the Hegelian scheme of things. He opposes all forms of federalism on the grounds that only nations in hierarchically centralized states "possess a higher consciousness . . . [and] are called to play a role in history." The rights of all the estates should depend on what they are "appointed" to do (in the Hegelian scheme of things); just as the purpose of the nobility is to stand at the head of society, so, "by the very nature of things," the lowest position in society is given to the peasants, whose purpose ("rational consciousness" being least developed in this group) is to stay within the bounds of their commune. Women are "naturally" incapable of taking part in political life. History proves that a state must have a developed bureaucratic structure; the less uniform a society the stronger must be the central power. It is Russia's fate eventually to have a bourgeoisie, "because this is the eternal law of development of human societies."[92]

In 1859 Chernyshevsky predicted that Chicherin's philosophy would soon lead him "to prove by means of philosophical constructions the historical inevitability of every . . . police edict," and that what was historically inevitable would soon become rational for him. Three years later, after the student disturbances, Chernyshevsky was to congratulate himself on his prescience: Chicherin had indeed come to "comprehend the duties of a policeman in a light more absolute than the police itself."[93] This was no exaggeration: Chicherin had criticized the governor of Moscow, P. A. Tuchkov, for showing insufficient energy in suppressing the student disturbances. He also (in one of his reports to his brother) expressed the fear that the government would appoint as minister of popular enlightenment an official who had permitted a polemic about his policies in the press. Such a person, Chicherin wrote, has no conception of what authority is.[94]

Chicherin believed that his distinguishing virtue was his refusal to allow personal attachments or emotions to blur his picture of the cosmic whole. He maintained that only by rising above the world of "everyday aspirations and passions" could one attain that "broad and free contemplation of life" which allowed one to speak with authority on day-to-day political questions.[95] In fact, his attempt to maintain an Olympian distance from the political and moral debates that engrossed his contemporaries led them to regard him as something of a curiosity. His treatise *On Popular Representation* (in which he warned against premature hopes of a Russian constitution), though an impressive feat of scholarship, was coolly received even by academic lawyers. As the jurist A. D. Gradovsky commented, in Chicherin's methodology "the form [of government] is the main thing—something exalted and unique that the people can achieve only after generations. The characteristics of this abstract form having been stated, there is nothing easier than to raise it to such a height that its attainment will always be impossible for a given nation."[96] Some conservatives, too, were struck by Chicherin's inability to realize that what might be true in the realm of abstract logic could be inapposite and even false in the context of the battle of historical forces. Thus, the government censor Aleksandr Nikitenko observed that although Chicherin had been justified in seeing Herzen's radicalism as harmful, his public attack on Herzen in 1858 had been more damaging still, as it had given support to reactionary elements in the government at a time when even conservatives recognized the need for reform.[97] A similar point was put pungently by Chernyshevsky. Referring to Chicherin's predilection for uttering abstract truths without regard to their bearing on existing social realities, he points out that in the Russia of the early 1860s to use the threat of anarchy as grounds for defending extreme bureaucratic centralism was like trying to frighten Hottentots with the dangers of too much intellectual activity. "Only a person in the grip of scholasticism can imagine that Russian society needs to defend the bureaucracy."[98]

Although Chicherin insisted that the Left adapt their principles to historical circumstances, he made no attempt to do so himself. When The Bell published the secret report of his commission, with the comment that history would not forget the names of the signatories, he was incensed: it was, he notes bitterly in his memoirs, "as if we had committed some heinous crime, instead of setting down quite objectively all the facts of the affair."[99] When even the conciliatory Kavelin broke off relations with him over his stance on the university protests he complained that he could not comprehend this snub from his former friend—he had not changed his views since the time when they both stood on common ground against Herzen; now, as then, he was opposed to despotism and intolerance whether from "above" or "below."[100] To Kavelin, it was little comfort that Chicherin's views on the potential despotism of the Left were theoretically correct when, by expressing them at that juncture in events, he had denied much-needed support to the liberal professors in their unequal battle with the actual despotism of the Right.[101]

Chicherin's thinking was equally foreign to those whose interests he was most interested in protecting: the conservative nobility were suspicious of the lofty philosophical significance with which he invested their material interests. As one of their representatives remarked, "Monsieur nous défend trop."[102] The only force wholeheartedly on his side in the early 1860s was the government, and its support became an increasing embarrassment to him. By its orders, all press criticism of his notorious inaugural lecture at Moscow University was banned. Chicherin protested, arguing that the influence he hoped to exercise on Russian society depended on his being seen as an independent thinker and not as the government's mouthpiece. This distinction was clearly not appreciated, for in the same year Chicherin was asked to contribute to its official propaganda organ, *The Northern Bee*, and, subsequently, after Kavelin's resignation from the chair of jurisprudence in Petersburg, to take his place in order to imbue the rebellious university with a more obedient spirit. He refused both requests on the same grounds as before.[103] The predicament into which his confusion of the real and the ideal had led him was satirized by Kavelin, in reply to a letter in which Chicherin had dissociated himself from the government's action in banning criticism of his inaugural Lecture. Kavelin urges him, on the contrary, to accept the government's canonization of him as the logical consequence of his consistent defense of its rationality and good intentions against those who "by their foolish chattering are destroying the triumphant accomplishment of the destiny of our fatherland"—the progressive intelligentsia. "Why are you so embarrassed that our wise government in its unremitting concern for the good of its loyal subjects, has closed the mouth of calumny and disloyalty and thereby secured the total triumph of the truths expressed in your writings?" But perhaps when declaring war on all the enemies of the government, Chicherin had had in mind not the government with which they all had to deal, with its reactionary ministers and corrupt bureaucrats, but a government of his imagination, and was therefore dissatisfied when the real government thanked him in its characteristic way. If so, noted Kavelin, that was his own fault—he should have made some reservations in his defense of the autocracy: "Otherwise from your words one would think that you are talking not about an imaginary ideal, but about reality, which is far from being the same thing."[104]

Chicherin's tragedy was that he had lost the capacity to make this distinction. It is true that reality begins to impinge on his thinking in the mid-1860s; if his account in his memoirs is correct, it was then that he first became aware of a characteristic of autocracy that had long been self-evident to his contemporaries. Hearing that the tsar was encouraging his advisers to intrigue against one another, he is led to reflect that an autocrat expects his ministers to be passive instruments of his will.[105] In 1868 Chicherin suffered personal humiliation when an intrigue among members of his faculty involving a government minister forced him to resign his chair; this incident provoked the bitter realization that the regime placed more value on court favorites than on independent conservatives like himself, whom it should have cherished "as the apple of its eye."[106] It was not until thirty years later, however, that he first publicly suggested that the time might be ripe for constitutional reform—and then he did so anonymously, in a pamphlet published abroad.[107]

This precaution, contrasting with his fearless public denunciations of the regime's opponents, testifies perhaps to some sensitivity as to the true "reality" of autocracy. If so, it was belated; in 1883, when he was dismissed from his post as head of the Moscow City Duma on suspicion of having hinted in a speech at the necessity for constitutional reform, he indignantly rejected the charge as "libelous."[108] His doubts about the personal qualities of the autocrat did not seriously undermine his view of the existing Russian state as an embodiment of Reason, with the result that up to the last years of his life he displayed a truly staggering blindness as to the strength and the nature of the oppositional forces—a blindness that can have had few parallels outside court circles. We have seen his assessment of the ferment of the early 1860s as the work of "little twenty-one-year-old officers" and "first-year students." Even more bizarre is the assertion attributed to him two decades later, that the revolutionary activity culminating in the assassination of Alexander II was all the work of one ill-intentioned individual: "It is all Chernyshevsky's fault; it is he who has injected revolutionary poison into our lives."[109]

Like Belinsky, when his idealization of the Russian autocracy, its brutal police, and self-serving bureaucracy earned him the contempt of those who had been his friends, and the favor of sycophants whom he despised, Chicherin bore his fate with self-righteous resignation, as a martyrdom imposed by his dedication to truth. But the parallel between Belinsky's and Chicherin's reconciliations with Russian reality should not be taken too far. Belinsky's was brief and tortured and was followed by a passionate humanism which would inspire future generations of the intelligentsia. Chicherin's was much more self-assured and was to last nearly all his life. There is no reason to doubt that as a Hegelian student he had drawn a sharp line between the regime of Nicholas I and Hegel's ideal state, but with the increasing threat from the Left, Hegel's Rechtsstaat became less a goal to be attained than the basis of a defense of the status quo. Inevitability had, as Chernyshevsky observed, become rationality for Chicherin. Those philosophical arguments that had led him to embrace Hegel's state as the crown of history were now applied to justify the regime of Alexander II, and one aspect missing from that regime—constitutional legality—came to seem little more than an extra flourish on an already completed structure. True, he never renounced his view that it was an ideal for the future, but he relegates it to such a distance that it fades into insignificance. It should also be noted that his first real doubts about the rationality of the tsar's rule were due not to indignation at injustice done to others (as in Belinsky's case) but to his own wounded vanity. Even at the height of his aberration, Belinsky would not have commented, as Chicherin did in a letter intended for the eyes of the tsar: "The Russian likes to be whipped from time to time."[110] Contrary to a common view, it was not his moderation or his gradualism that alienated Chicherin from Russian liberals; it was his aloof indifference to the fate of real individuals and the realities of their experience, his total lack of the humanism that distinguished liberals like Kavelin and Turgenev, enabling them to understand and sympathize with ideas and aspirations foreign to their own. The judgment of Chicherin's contemporaries was expressed by Kavelin when he wrote to him that although he was prepared to vouch for his sincerity, he could not attempt to defend the "clarity of your understanding of the reality around you, the subtlety of your sense of justice and injustice in that milieu in which we are fated to live."[111]

Had Chicherin been merely deficient in moral understanding, he would not have been so interesting. I believe that he is historically significant above all as an early proponent of a vision of right and wrong that was still rare in his time. He once expressed the belief that a rational human being could experience "no greater satisfaction" than to be the conscious instrument of historical Reason.[112] A similar motivation has since provided totalitarian states with some of their most devoted servants.

The following two extracts from letters unearthed in Chicherin's archives will help to support my case. Written in 1863 to his brother, they concern the Polish revolt of that year. The first addresses the fear in government circles that repression of the Poles might spark a war with the Great Powers. Chicherin suggests that a war may even be useful: "The Crimean War was necessary for the government; a new war is necessary for society, and afterward not a trace will remain of the insanity that has infected part of Russian youth. . . . I fear only that the government . . . will prove too weak." By mid-October, when Russian forces had crushed the revolt, Chicherin urged his brother to recommend to the authorities that no mercy be shown to the defeated Poles: "I hope that in the future we will also make no concessions . . . that for the next ten years the Poles shall live under terror so that they may be convinced that they are completely in our hands. . . . In my view, there can be only one solution [to the Polish question]: the complete impotence of Poland with respect to Russia. . . . For this to happen we must smash anyone who approaches us with any sort of demand. Russia cannot permit any other solution of the Polish question."[113] Chicherin was truly ahead of his time. The Russian government was not wholly indifferent to moral opinion at home or abroad. It used limited terror against the Poles, just as, despite Chicherin's urgings, it had shown some restraint against the students. Chicherin's absolute faith in the state as moral arbiter had much more in common with Leninism than with old-fashioned autocracy. Herzen described him at their first meeting: "There was a cold light in his eyes, a challenge in the timbre of his voice and a terrible and repellent self-assurance."[114] The twentieth century was to become well acquainted with such types who were able calmly and dispassionately to recommend the mass slaughter of human beings, secure in the belief that they were history's instruments and, if necessary, its executioners.

Bakunin and the Charm of the Millennium

CHAPTER TWELVE

Only when we can say "Ce que je veux, Dieu le veut" will our sufferings be at an end.
—Mikhail Bakunin, 1835

"One of the completest embodiments in history of the spirit of liberty," to quote E. H. Carr, Mikhail Bakunin has come to symbolize the rebellion of the human spirit against all the constraints imposed on it by authorities, systems, and institutions.[1] But there is another image of Bakunin, equally well documented: a scheming megalomaniac with aspirations to dictatorship. The first image was sedulously promoted by his followers, the second by his enemies. Historians have been almost as divided on the question of the true Bakunin, their differences depending often on whether they have chosen to focus primarily on his personality or on his texts.

Carr's biography—first published in 1937—is still by far the best example of the first type of approach. It finds the key to Bakunin's extraordinary career in a personality embodying with exceptional intensity the "pure instinct to rebel."[2] Born in 1814 into an aristocratic landowning family, he began his revolt when at the age of twenty he gave up the army career for which he had been destined to join the intellectual circles of Moscow, where romantic thought and idealist philosophy reigned supreme. In Germany, where he went in 1840 to escape the stifling atmosphere of autocratic Russia, he was converted to radical politics by the Left Hegelians. Thus began a turbulent career which was interrupted in 1849 when his activities as a revolutionary Pan-Slavist led to arrest in Germany, followed by deportation to Russia, prison, and exile in Siberia. In 1861 he escaped to Europe, to embark on a new revolutionary life as an anarchist. In the intervals of attempting to foment risings in Italy, France, and (through his contacts with radical emigres) Russia, he mounted a challenge to the domination of the Socialist International by the authoritarian communism of Marx. The ensuing contest between Marxists and Bakuninists ended with Bakunin's expulsion from the International after evidence was uncovered that he had set up within it a secret society under his autocratic control. He died in Switzerland in 1876.

Carr has drawn a superbly vivid portrait of this "intense, bizarre, destructive personality" whose complexity is reflected in the bewildering contradictions in his ideas and actions. He preached unrestrained liberty while
simultaneously drawing up statutes, programs, and codes for a series of half-
real, half-imaginary secret societies; organized to act in strict obedience to his
will, they were to direct the revolution and establish a dictatorship. But none of
these societies (including the secret Alliance, which caused the scandal within
the International) had any real existence. Bakunin's methods of recruitment
were haphazard, and his conspiracies tended to collapse in farce: his devious-
ness was continually frustrated by his gullibility, his megalomania defeated by
his tendency to blurt out his secrets to any sympathetic listener. He was an in-
veterate dreamer, an eternal optimist and, in his lifelong rebellion against all
authority, a perpetual adolescent. According to Carr, "The determination of
the object against which his rebellions were directed . . . was decided by more
or less transient conditions or motives; and the arguments provided by his reason to justify the revolt were more adventitious still."[3]

It is presumably this judgment that accounts for the absence in Carr's book
of any serious analysis of the nature and provenance of Bakunin's ideas. All the
emphasis is on his personality, his penchant for intrigue, and his childish
weaknesses. It is in terms of these that Carr explains the contradiction between
his anarchism and his dictatorial leanings: his urge to dominate was as strong
as his urge to rebel. It may be, as Carr maintains, that Bakunin's mind was "to
an almost unparalleled degree the servant . . . of his impulses," and it is true
that his theories were incoherent and derivative.[4] But to conclude that his influence cannot be explained in rational terms and derived solely from the hypnotic effect of his extraordinary eloquence is to beg too many questions.
Although he never had more than a small core of devoted disciples, he managed to orchestrate the opposition to Marxist communism within the socialist
movement by offering a radical alternative, the continuing relevance of which
has often been vehemently argued in the twentieth century. Even if some of Bakunin's defenders have been even more incoherent than he, reference to the ju-
venile urge to rebel will not take us very far in understanding the recurring
attraction of his anarchism.

The more common approach to Bakunin, while not ignoring his remarkable personality, concentrates on analysis of his texts. This difficult challenge
(Bakunin's oeuvre, much of it existing only in unfinished manuscripts, is as
chaotic as his life) has been met with much devoted scholarship, notably by Arthur Lehning, editor of the massive Bakunin archives, who has also succeeded
in squeezing a representative selection of Bakunin's output into one volume.[5]
Two early pieces—a letter to his sisters on the delights of the inner life and the
famous article of 1842, "The Reaction in Germany," which launched him on

his revolutionary career—are followed by a range of writings (programs for secret and open revolutionary organizations, extracts from his principal theoretical works, and his polemics with Herzen's populism and Marx's communism) which convey the essence of his anarchism.

But this material comes with a heavily biased editorial interpretation. Scholarly exegesis tends naturally to seek out an underlying coherence in the most contradictory of texts, a method that Lehning takes to an extreme, maintaining that Bakunin's writings constitute a coherent and consistent exposition of libertarian socialism. This entails presenting his battle with Marx (and his secret Alliance) as motivated solely by the defense of an anarchist ideal of liberty against an opponent whose principal concern was to maintain his own supremacy in the socialist movement. This is, of course, the official anarchist view of Bakunin's contest with Marx for control of the International, and Lehning accepts without question the denials of Bakunin's followers that Bakunin had established, or intended to establish, within the International a clandestine elite under his personal authority. But this is to ignore the wealth of evidence, not least in Bakunin's own correspondence, of his intrigues directed to just that end. That the group had no effective existence was due only to his spectacular incompetence as a conspirator.

Nor do the texts in this selection support the editor's claim that Bakunin's political philosophy was original and profound. On the contrary, they amply illustrate Isaiah Berlin's observation that his concept of liberty was "glib Hegelian claptrap," his positive doctrines "mere strings of ringing commonplaces, linked together by vague emotional relevance or rhetorical afflatus rather than a coherent structure of genuine ideas."[6] (A typical example: "Freedom can be created only by freedom.")

But for all its intellectual shoddiness, Bakunin's rhetoric cannot be lightly dismissed. Its power to motivate his followers in the battle with Marx proves that he was far more than just the colorful eccentric that Carr makes him out to be. Bakunin had the ability to dazzle the simple-minded with high-sounding phrases and to galvanize the perennial alienated intellectual by masterfully articulating his or her fantasies. Together, Bakunin's personality and rhetoric illuminated a phenomenon about which we need to know much more: the patterns of thinking and willing which generate extremist ideologies that are logically flawed but psychologically compelling.

In Bakunin's case these patterns were formed in Russia in the 1830s. Carr's treatment of these years is a highly entertaining account of Bakunin's friendships, entanglements, and quarrels in the course of his "philosophical philandering" as mentor to admiring women friends in German idealist philosophy and the romantic cult of elevated feelings.[7] But this was only one, and not the most important, aspect of the passionate absorption with idealism that was so strikingly characteristic of the first generation of the Russian intelligentsia, who applied themselves to the thought of Schelling, Fichte, and Hegel with an intensity unparalled in Germany itself.

This generation was a product of Russia's increasing contact with Western culture. The gulf between the ideas they assimilated in the universities and their backward environment led the cultured elite to look to the secular eschatology of German romantic idealism for reassurance about their own and their country's destiny. Idealism compensated them for their isolation and frustrations by assuring them that the knowing self and the external world were in the deepest sense one unitary whole, that it was only in human consciousness that the essence of all reality—the World Spirit, universal Reason, or absolute Mind—came to knowledge of itself. When this process was finally accomplished (whether through some mystical transcendence or, as Hegel taught, through the historical progress of human societies to ever more rational forms), all duality and conflict between the parts and the whole—all alienation—would end.

In the meantime, many of Bakunin's generation found idealism a source of compensating fantasies through which they could escape the grim reality around them and achieve a foretaste of the wholeness that they craved. It allowed them to sublimate two urges that were equally frustrated in the alienated: the drive for self-affirmation through subjection of external reality to the will, and the urge for self-surrender, for identity with some transcendent whole which would endow the isolated ego with universal meaning and purpose. Russian intellectuals of the 1830s could imagine themselves in communion with the Absolute through religious or aesthetic contemplation or through idealized platonic relationships with other members of their circle (the Schillerian cult of the Beautiful Soul); alternatively, they could identify with the limitless self-affirmation of Fichte's absolute Ego, engaged in a struggle to reappropriate the world that was its own creation. The colossal egocentrism of Fichte's idealism opened the way to visions of absolute liberty as an earthly ideal to be attained through a protean exercise of will. Both categories of fantasy could be satisfyingly combined in the notion of a "mission," the belief that chosen individuals such as themselves were destined to accomplish some great feat as instruments of the designs of Providence.

Fantasies of self-assertion and self-surrender alternate obsessively in the young Bakunin's letters to his adoring sisters and women friends and to the members of his Moscow circle, in which he had appointed himself the principal interpreter of idealist doctrines. At times, he yearns to "dissolve into the Absolute" by renouncing all personal hopes and desires; in other moods, he glorifies his "proud will," the sign, surely, of some sublime destiny: "I am a man and I shall become God."[8]

Bakunin's preoccupation with his future mission struck even his fellow idealists as excessive. Ivan Turgenev later depicted him as the eponymous hero of his novel *Rudin*, who expatiates to his circle on the mysterious harmony of all things and on their own exalted role as agents in the accomplishment of cosmic purposes: "There should be no greater joy for a person than to sense oneself the instrument of . . . higher forces."[9]

By the end of the decade these young people had come to view their obsession with an ideal future as an unhealthy sublimation of the need to find fulfillment in their own time and place. Whereas most began to adapt their aspirations to historical circumstances, Bakunin took the opposite course. Soon after his arrival in Europe in 1840, he wrote his brother Pavel: "When [our ideals] clash with everyday reality we call them . . . empty fantasies . . . . but it is reality that is the most terrible of . . . fantasies; we must break its bonds by force of faith and will!" He would remain true to this Fichtean program all his life.[10]

He believed fervently that he had been born anew as a man of action, but his contempt for "theorizers" and their abstractions was based on a theory of extreme abstraction: the romantic faith in the regenerative power of primitive spontaneity. He interpreted the unrest among the peoples of the Russian and Austro-Hungarian empires in the mid-1840s as the expression of the elemental force of "natural" life which would soon sweep away all the artificial systems and institutions that had hitherto sought to contain and oppress it. This instinct of revolt—the sole creative force in history—was, he believed, to be found in its purest form in the most primitive, and thereby the least corrupt, of the common people: the peasantry. The most promising of these were the Russians, who had behind them a tradition of savage rebellion against the state. Bakunin scoffs at his fellow democrats' fear of the "evil passions" unleashed by peasant revolution, and in his *Appeal to the Slavs* of 1846 he paints a visionary picture of the Russian peasantry as a "fiery ocean" which will engulf Moscow in blood and flame and bury all the slavery in Europe beneath its own ruins.[11]

This millenarian faith was based on Bakunin's version of the revolutionary dialectic of the Left Hegelians, as expressed in *The Reaction in Germany*, which gave him his entrée into radical circles in Europe. He proclaims that the total destruction of the "positive principle" (the existing order) by the forces of "negation" will lead to "a new heaven and a new earth . . . in which all the discords of our time will be resolved in harmonious unity." He concludes with the most famous sentence he ever wrote: "The urge to destroy is also a creative urge!"[12]

There is a passionate impatience in these predictions of universal destruction. Bakunin had discovered his mission: to act out his private drama of self-realization on an apocalyptic scale. On the eve of the 1848 revolutions he announced to his friend the German radical poet Georg Herwegh: "I await my

... fiancée, revolution. We will ... become our true selves only when the whole world is engulfed in fire."[13]

The anarchism which became his political creed in the 1860s was a logical consequence of his cult of spontaneity. He now declared all states (including the revolutionary state which was Marx's goal) to be oppressive by their nature as institutionalizations of the rule of system and theory over life. The infallible instincts of the masses were the only guide to freedom and the good. These instincts had created the peasant commune, which survived only in Russia; but this form of self-government would become universal if the masses were allowed to make their revolution without the interference of an intellectual elite, who could teach the people nothing and would merely perpetuate the tyranny of theory over life.

The worst offender in this respect was the "scientific socialism" of Marx. In his anarchist propaganda Bakunin argues that the Germans, creators both of philosophical idealism and of the most bureaucratic state in Europe, are the most "abstract" of peoples. Their determination to subordinate life to theory had inspired the Marxists' ideal of a centralized revolutionary state. Bakunin airs his anti-Semitism in declaring Marx himself to be "triply authoritarian" as a German, a Hegelian, and a Jew. He was fond of emphasizing how he himself had broken completely with his philosophical past. The insults he heaped on Marx can be seen as a form of exorcism of his own devils; he once asserted (apropos of the role of Germanophobia in uniting the Slavs): "I say as Voltaire said of God: 'If the Germans did not exist, we should have to invent them.' "[14] It is a measure of his success in promoting himself as the champion of "life" against "theory" that his self-image has tended to be taken at face value. The Bakunin of revolutionary mythology is passionate, unreflective, instinctively hostile to all attempts to categorize or constrain the rich variety of everyday life and individual character by general rules and norms.

This was not how his Russian contemporaries had seen him. Pavel Annenkov, the author of a brilliant memoir of Bakunin's generation, describes him in his philosophical heyday: "The whole of life presented itself to him through the prism of abstraction, and he spoke of it with striking enthusiasm only when it was translated into idea."[15] Bakunin himself, in a rare moment of self-understanding, admitted in 1840: "A striving toward the universal is the basic characteristic of my life. . . . Everything individual . . . has meaning and importance for me only to the degree to which it is illuminated by the rays of universal . . . Spirit." His transformation into a revolutionary changed nothing in this respect; he continued to see the world in terms of the same grand antitheses as when he had been the main exponent of the dialectic in his circle. "Reaction is theory . . . but revolution is instinct," he declared to Herwegh in the 1840s. More than two decades later, in his two longest writings (*The Knouto-*

Germanic Empire and the Social Revolution [1870–71] and *The State and Anarchy* [1873]), he refines this definition, equating reaction with the state and all its defenders, revolution with anarchy: all contemporary conflicts, he argues, can be traced to the opposition between these "two polarities." These works, which offer a historical outline of the development of the state in Europe, are composed of sweeping generalizations and hackneyed stereotypes: "all history shows" that aristocrats are "vain," the bourgeoisie is given to "corruption and debauchery," and so on.[16] Bakunin's writing reaches the heights of abstraction in the definition of the people that is the cornerstone of his anarchism. He defines their primary characteristic as the spirit of rebellion; this forces him to exclude from the category of the "true" people all those who showed a disappointing disinclination to rebel. His criterion was fully met only by a construct of romantic fantasy, based on legends about individuals who, in the great Russian peasant risings of the seventeenth and eighteenth centuries, had taken to the forests to live a life outside the law, murdering and plundering. In propaganda pamphlets addressed to the Russian revolutionary youth, Bakunin exalts these "primitive, brutal men" with "fresh, strong, untainted natures" as revolutionaries "without cant, without bookish rhetoric, tireless and invincible in action." Half romantic demon, half noble savage, Bakunin's version of the Russian bandit is presented as "the sole means . . . of the moral regeneration and salvation of the Russian people." The young Russian radical intelligentsia, who Bakunin hoped would make common cause with them, are depicted as a collective version of Karl von Moor, the rebel hero of Friedrich Schiller's drama *The Robbers*. In his secret correspondence he portrays the members of his Alliance as formed from the same mold: they are utterly ruthless but devoid of personal ambition or cupidity, the epitome of aristocratic honor. These noble individuals, the "unseen pilots of popular passions" would set up an "invisible dictatorship" which would ensure the unhindered expression of the people's will. "Absolute liberty"—a favorite phrase of Bakunin's—would automatically ensue: Bakunin's concept of freedom took no account of any limitations imposed by time, place, or circumstance. "It is quite untrue," he asserts in a draft of statutes for a secret "brotherhood," "that the freedom of the individual is bounded by that of every other individual."[17]

The Marxists who got wind of his secret projects viewed them with deadly seriousness, as a sinister plot to gain control of the socialist movement and subsequently the socialist state. But the doyen of the Russian émigré revolutionaries, Aleksandr Herzen (who had had a disastrous collaboration with Bakunin over propaganda for the Polish rising of 1863), dismissed his conspiracies as futile games of make-believe, proof that he still inhabited the "world of phantoms" that German idealism had conjured up to satisfy those who could find no adequate fulfillment in the real world.[18]

Herzen's observations were based on close personal knowledge of Bakunin and of the Russian philosophical circles of the 1830s; they are borne out by the tone of near-religious exaltation in which, both in his published writings and his secret correspondence, Bakunin describes the relationship of the revolutionary intellectual to the masses. As in his philosophical outpourings of the 1830s, the theme of self-assertion alternates with that of self-surrender. Addressing the Russian radical youth in the expectation of a peasant rising at the end of the 1860s, he urges them with incantatory insistence to unite body and soul with the peasantry, to "melt," "drown," "dissolve" in the purifying stream of popular revolt. At the same time he warns his co-conspirators that the masses may sometimes "cling to ideas that contradict their own instincts." It was up to his secret Alliance to articulate those instincts for them, and even, if necessary, to carry out the revolution so that the people may at last comprehend that their aspirations coincide with the "revolutionary idea."[19] In Bakunin's dialectical world there was no contradiction between self-abasement before the masses and manipulation of them. Just as the Absolute could come to know itself only through the consciousness of spiritually developed individuals engaged in its contemplation, so the people's idealized will could be interpreted only by its servant, the revolutionary elite.

The same dialectic operated in Bakunin's conception of relations within the secret Alliance. He describes as follows its mythical Russian section (of whose existence he had become convinced through misinformation from his associate Sergei Nechaev): this "invisible . . . omnipresent host . . . are caught in tens, they are resurrected in hundreds; individuals perish, but the host is immortal." The collective demands the "total dissolution of individual personalities" in its ranks, but such self-renunciation is merely the sacrifice of "appearance for reality, empty ambition for real power, words for action. I want not to be 'I,' I want to be 'We.' . . . Only on that condition can we triumph."

This, he writes, "is the organization of which I have dreamed."[20] Quite so. It was a pure projection of the ideal of personal wholeness that he had failed to achieve on the plane of the inner life. As in those early years of philosophical reflection, the external world was real to him only inasmuch as it mirrored his ideals and aspirations. In Dresden in 1849, hearing Wagner conduct Beethoven's Ninth Symphony, Bakunin is said to have assured him that this work, at least, would be spared in the future holocaust. Behind his constant invocations of the spirit of destruction lay the conviction that it would possess the aesthetic sensibility of a Russian aristocrat of the romantic age.

In his *Letters to an Old Comrade* of 1869, Herzen attempted to propel Bakunin into the real world. He pointed out that humanity had outgrown the age when a simple faith in the truth of one's beliefs was sufficient justification for forcibly imposing them on others. Historical experience, economic and social theory, all provided overwhelming evidence that the masses were not a sheet of blank paper on which revolutionaries could inscribe their vision of liberty. Ignorance, prejudices, and attachment to the past were as much an obstacle to the socialist ideal as the institutions of the old order. To convert the majority to a free acceptance of that ideal would involve a long and tortuous process of persuasion, a path despised by those who yearned to implement the messianic vision of the early socialists in its purity. But to do so they would have to meet popular resistance by force: yet one could not create a new world by the methods of the old, civilizing people with the whip, liberating them by means of the guillotine.[21]

As his secret writings show, Bakunin had more than an inkling that the masses might have to be persuaded to be free by those who understood their true needs and their historical destiny better than they did themselves. But the unreality of his conspiracies made it unlikely that he would be faced on a practical level with the kinds of moral choices involved in doing violence to individuals in the name of ideals. As he hurried around the centers of radical activity in Europe in the late 1860s, addressing workers' meetings and terrifying the bourgeoisie with his calls for the unleashing of "evil passions," he reminded Herzen of an old nanny, frightening children with stories of the bogeyman yet knowing full well that the bogeyman would not come.[22]

But the bogeyman did come—in the person of Sergei Nechaev. Bakunin's relationship with this terrifying young man, whose philosophy of violence was a deromanticized mirror image of his own, is a moral drama no less compelling than Dostoevsky's fictional rendering of the "Nechaev affair" in *The Possessed*.

The principal motivation of Nechaev's revolutionary activity seems to have been a seething hatred of all aspects of the existing order. His simple philosophy, embodied in his notorious Revolutionary Catechism, was that the sole aim of revolutionaries and the moral criterion of all their actions must be the triumph of their ideal. They must be prepared to kill without compunction all who threaten it and should seek to intensify the misery of the masses, so that despair would drive them to revolt. The use of blackmail and intimidation is recommended not only against the enemy but within the revolutionary organization itself, as a means of gaining recruits and strengthening the resolve of existing members. Nechaev acted out this last precept in November 1869 by forcing three members of his own revolutionary group, The People's Revenge, to participate in the murder of a fourth, a student named Ivanov: his aim appears to have been to cement his little group by complicity in crime. His methods caused consternation among the Russian Left when the text of his catechism was made public during the trial of his associates; Nechaev was arrested in 1872 and died ten years later in prison, uncompromising to the end.

Nechaevism, as it came to be called, has been seen as a landmark in the development of revolutionary socialism. Many Western historians and writers have followed Dostoevsky and Camus in interpreting it as the extreme logical consequence of the "religion of humanity" preached by messianic socialism.[23] The god of that religion was a wholly transformed and ideally free future humanity in whose name many socialists were prepared to sacrifice individuals, even whole classes, with the exception of those oppressed groups whose interests they sought to defend. But Nechaev took the further step of stating, as a corollary of the absolute nature of the future ideal, that all human beings in the present, without exception, should be seen as expendable material in the fight to attain it. The horror felt in all sections of Russian society at the details of Ivanov's murder reflected the sense that there was something quite unprecedented in that act; in retrospect one might see it as prefiguring the transition of utopian socialism from millenarian theory to totalitarian practice, with the appearance of a type who combined fanatical faith in a personal ideal with a cold calculation of the steps that must be taken in order to carry out a utopian experiment. As the Nechaevist Shigalev puts it in The Possessed: "My conclusion is in direct contradiction to the original idea from which I start. Starting from absolute freedom, I arrive at unlimited despotism. I will add, however, that there can be no solution of the social equation other than mine."[24]

In the spring of 1869 Nechaev left Russia to make contact with leading Russian émigré radicals in advance of a peasant rising which, it was rumored, might break out the following year. Herzen, who had formed his own conclusions about Nechaev, refused to have any dealings with him, but he was received ecstatically by Bakunin, who construed his virulent hatred as a noble passion and confided to his closest associates that this "charming" young fanatic was the embodiment of his ideal revolutionary. Nechaev soon took Bakunin's measure, dazzling him with invented stories about his escape from an impregnable fortress and about the size of the force he represented, and the two embarked on a close collaboration which lasted more than a year. Its chief fruit was a number of pamphlets for use in the hoped-for Russian rising. Bakunin vied with Nechaev in the bloodthirstiness of his style, advocating the use of terrorism, "poison, the knife, the noose, and so on! The revolution sanctifies all means."[25] The difference was that Nechaev practiced what he preached. During a brief return visit to Russia, he organized the murder of Ivanov. Rumors about the crime soon became known in Western revolutionary circles, where Nechaev's other methods had already made him detested, but even after Nechaev had ended their relationship by stealing letters from him for purposes of future blackmail, Bakunin sought to defend his "young barbarian," explaining to his astonished friends that the killing of Ivanov had been the act of a pure and saintly nature, inspired by a passionate love for the people. He explained that Nechaev had judged correctly that the creation of a secret organization was the essential first step to revolution in Russia. When methods of persuasion had failed to recruit sufficient numbers, it had become necessary to resort to force and deception. Because those enlisted by such methods would be eager to defect, they had had to be compromised by being forced to commit a crime that would cut them off irrevocably from their society. This "despairing step" had been taken with great repugnance, but the alternative—to abandon the revolutionary cause—would have been much worse.[26]

To Nechaev himself Bakunin wrote that he accepted that "real" revolutionaries had to dispense with all scruples about joining ranks with the "bandit world" but that he recognized his own "total inability" to adopt its methods. To do so one must be equipped with "solid nerves, a herculean strength, passionate convictions, and a will of iron. Such people may be found in your ranks. But people of our generation, formed by our education, are incapable of it."[27]

Nechaev's crime had punctured Bakunin's self-image. He had come to realize that his glorification of evil passions and the "grim poetry of destruction" was so much romantic hot air: when faced with the actual choice, he could not have killed Ivanov. Nonetheless, he saw this as a weakness, not as a virtue; it is significant that he was the only prominent revolutionary of his time who defended Ivanov's murder. The defense was made in full *connaissance de cause*. As his letter to Nechaev shows, he perfectly understood the latter's reasoning; it was only his motivation that he got wrong. This astonishing blindness as to moral character was not surprising: people and events were for Bakunin merely props on the stage on which he acted out his dramas of self-assertion and self-escape. As his contemporary Belinsky once noted, "This unhappy man, born to cause grief to himself and others" was incapable of distinguishing between service to the objective truth and the satisfaction of his subjective urges.[28] As such, he was the prime material of which totalitarian movements are made. He was not a Nechaev, but he was eager to become a Nechaevist; had he lived a century later, he could have put his eloquence at the service of real dictators, who would have found ways of exploiting his greatest talent: his ability to infect an audience with his own delusions.

Of all those who came under Bakunin's spell, it is Turgenev who best defined its secret. Here is the middle-aged Lezhnev in *Rudin*, describing how, with other idealistic youths in his circle, he had once listened avidly to Rudin expatiating on philosophy, science, and life: "Everything we knew came together in harmonious unity. . . . Nothing remained senseless or accidental. Everything expressed rational inevitability and beauty, everything acquired a meaning that was simultaneously clear and mysterious, every individual phenomenon of life resonated in harmony, and we ourselves, with a kind of sacred worshipful awe, with a sweet quivering of our hearts, felt as if we were living vessels of eternal Truth, called to accomplish something great."[29]

Here is the simple formula behind the charm of all millenarian ideologies: a compound of extreme clarity and profound mystery, replacing doubt with the security of a collective purpose, while simultaneously giving full play to vague but delicious fantasies of self-aggrandizement. To those interested in the social psychology of extremist politics, Bakunin's writings offer a rich mine of material, valuable above all for the light it sheds on the hold exercised on the will and the emotions by ideas that in logical argument are absurdly easy to refute.

A Bolshevik Philosophy?

CHAPTER   THIRTEEN

Russian Marxism produced two revisionist movements at the turn of the century: the neo-Kantian and the empiriocriticist. The first of these had an important influence on Russian philosophy, literature, and religious thought and on the theory of Russian liberalism. Consequently, it has received much more attention from historians than the much more narrowly circumscribed attempt by a group of Bolsheviks to synthesize Marxism with the philosophy of empiriocriticism. Intellectually and politically, their influence was slight and short-lived; their major claim to interest is commonly seen as the role they played in causing Lenin to write his only philosophical work. The brief existence of their movement has seemed less significant than its rapid demise, which is often cited as an instance of Lenin's ability to bring dissidents to heel.[1]

But the empiriocriticist movement takes on a very different significance when approached from the perspective of the sociology of knowledge. It represents a crisis point in the history of the Russian intelligentsia at which the fundamental conflicts and dilemmas of Russian radical thought emerge with particular clarity. The movement's goal can be defined as the formulation of an integral worldview centered on the ideal of an integral personality. These two concepts (*tselnoe mirovozzrenie* and *tselnaia lichnost*) reverberate through Russian thought from the 1830s, when an intelligentsia first emerged, deeply alienated from the existing order and obsessed with the millenarian goal of wholeness as expressed in the doctrines of the romantics, the German idealists, or the French utopian socialists. The political ideals of later generations had in common a vision of the personality of the future as a many-sided being whose powers, physical, intellectual, and moral, would be maximally developed and integrated in creative harmony. Each generation of the intelligentsia sought to situate this ideal within an integral worldview, a unitary and all-embracing schema of history and progress which could provide reassuring answers to the questions that tormented them about their own and Russia's place in the universal scheme of things. But such deterministic visions, whether Hegelian or Marxist, proved difficult to reconcile with their ultimate ideal of the personality. The more comprehensive the explanation of history and current reality, and the more clearly it defined each stage in the pattern of human progress, the less place it gave to the aesthetic and ethical individualism implicit in the notion of a many-sided and creatively fulfilled personality. It was this dilemma that gave rise to Russian neo-Kantian revisionism, which began as a revolt against the mechanistic determinism of Russian Marxist philosophy. With the help of Kantian criticism its proponents asserted the autonomy of the sphere of ethics and of subjective ideals. They soon found it impossible to synthesize their neo-Kantianism with any form of Marxism and moved to idealist positions in philosophy.[2]

The empiriocriticist movement addressed the same problem, seeking to succeed where the neo-Kantians had failed: to reconcile the demands of the integral personality with Marxism as an integral worldview. Seen in this light, the movement represents the last attempt by the Russian radical intelligentsia to construct an ideology which would resolve a fundamental conflict in its view of the self and the world. I discuss two aspects of the movement below: first, its significance and its achievements as an attempt to reconcile the two traditionally conflicting goals of the radical intelligentsia; and second, the debate among the members of the movement and its critics after the 1905 revolution on the intelligentsia's collective psychology, the relation of its subjective aspirations to objective social goals, and the social and political implications of this relationship.

The empiriocriticist movement in Russian Marxism, while more diffuse than that of the neo-Kantians, included, as they had done, a number of the most prominent Marxist intellectuals of the time. Its principal theorists were Aleksandr Bogdanov,[3] Vladimir Bazarov[4] (both of whom were concerned mainly with the construction of a Marxist ethic), and Anatoly Lunacharsky,[5] who with Maksim Gorky expounded a new socialist "religion." The only two prominent members of the movement who did not join the Bolshevik faction after the split of the Marxist-inspired Russian Social Democratic Workers' Party (the SDs) in 1903 were P. S. Yushkevich and Nikolai Valentinov.[6]

Memoirs by members of the group reveal a close similarity between their initial motivation and that of the neo-Kantian revisionists. They had been drawn to Marxism in the 1890s above all because it offered what every generation of the intelligentsia had sought: "not merely views, but one integral worldview" which could answer all questions. In Valentinov's words, the "economic factor" of which they made much play in their polemics was "a sort of magic carpet bearing us across the gloomy sea of inequality, of deprivation, of exploitation, onto the azure shore of the future system."[7] For Bogdanov, Marxism was not only a new faith but also the liberating negation of an old one that had intolerably constricted the personality—the crudely mechanistic materialism inherited from the 1860s that had been the philosophical basis of much radical theory.[8] Lunacharsky, who describes his adoption of Marxism as an "ecstatic conversion," emphasizes that for his generation Marxism was not merely an economic theory; it was "a synthesising philosophy that harmoniously united the ideal with practice, crowning in a realistic and revolutionary way the immense . . . aspirations of Marx's teachers, the great German idealists."[9] He compares the effect of Marxism on his contemporaries to the influence of Left Hegelian philosophy on the first generation of the intelligentsia at the beginning of the 1840s. The comparison is revealing: the Left Hegelians had believed that, as the dialectically inevitable outcome of the historical process, human beings would realize their potential as integral personalities by reappropriating (through the revolutionary negation of outworn institutions) the qualities they had projected onto fictitious entities. Lunacharsky and his group sought in Marxism a similar reassurance that while doing the work of history they were not merely the instruments of an inexorable collective process but were engaged in actively conquering their freedom as whole and harmonious human beings. They found a satisfying reflection of their aspirations in Lenin's pamphlet of 1902, *What Is to Be Done?* with its call for a disciplined elite to lead the revolution: "Give us an organization and we will overturn Russia!" Inspired by this "fiery voluntarism,"[10] they became increasingly critical of the official party philosophy as formulated by Georgy Plekhanov, the founder and chief ideologist of the SD Party. In his book *On the Development of the Monist View of History* and in numerous articles, Plekhanov interpreted the doctrine of the primacy of being over consciousness in the spirit of Engels's mechanistic materialism, according to which consciousness was historically and causally a product of matter, which Plekhanov defined as "that which, acting on our sense organs, gives rise to certain sensations in us." Matter is consequently "an aggregate of things-in-themselves, inasmuch as these things are the source of our sensations."[11] The materialists' thing-in-itself, he argued, differs from the Kantian noumenon in that it is not in principle unknowable—the forms and relations of phenomena are "symbols" which correspond precisely to the forms and relations of things-in-themselves; through this symbolic correspondence we may understand the action of matter on us and in turn act on it. Consciousness for Plekhanov is merely a mirror reflecting the objective world, whose laws and relations are independent of it, although these laws may be used to humans' advantage. Freedom was, therefore, to echo Engels's definition, the consciousness of necessity. "Human reason can triumph over blind inevitability only by apprehending its inner laws."[12]

In the view of the young voluntarists, Plekhanov's doctrine of the primacy of matter over consciousness totally failed to come to grips with the "great and subtle problems of philosophy."[13] In its complete denial of the role of subjective ideals as movers of history, it had made no advance on the mechanistic materialism of the eighteenth century. "For us," Valentinov writes, "socialism was expressed in the verbs 'sollen,' 'wünschen' [ought, wish]. For Plekhanov it was a . . . historical inevitability": its triumph would come about through economic laws immanent in society, independently of the will of socialists, whose role was reduced, in Valentinov's words, to that of the fifth spoke in a wheel. "In one's youth, when one is bursting with energy, the role of a fifth spoke is especially galling."[14]

Thus, the new voluntarist revolt against the orthodoxy represented by Plekhanov began (as the neo-Kantian movement had done) as a demand for the reassessment of the relation of objective historical laws to subjective goals and values. Its proponents were well aware of the resemblance: Lunacharsky describes an occasion in Kiev in 1898 when he read a paper on the role of subjective values as movers of progress. Nikolai Berdiaev (one of the leaders of the neo-Kantian group) was in the audience, and in the ensuing discussion it became clear that they were both asking the same question, which Lunacharsky puts in Berdiaev's formulation: "For Marx, socialism is a sociological inevitability: but does it follow from this that it is a good? . . . Can one prove that socialism is the highest possible ideal of our time without regard to the interests of particular classes and independently of the question of its inevitable arrival?"[15]

Both groups believed that in treating subjective goals and values as mere epiphenomena, reflections of material processes, orthodox Marxism was in contradiction with instinctive human convictions and that its claim to offer an all-embracing interpretation of the world could be justified only when its economic doctrines were supplemented by a satisfactory epistemology. But at this point the two groups radically diverged; while the neo-Kantians sought to replace an unsatisfactory monism by a consistent dualism, separating the realms of fact and value, their rivals saw this as a step back to "bourgeois" idealism: indeed their main criticism of Plekhanov's philosophy was that the concept of matter as thing-in-itself was dangerously close to the idealist concept of substance. A truly Marxist philosophy would have to be consistently monist, and in their view Marx himself, in his *Theses on Feuerbach,* had indicated the direction it should take, particularly in the first *Thesis,* where he wrote: "The chief defect of all hitherto existing materialism—that of Feuerbach included—is that the thing [*Gegenstand*], reality, sensuousness, is conceived only in the form of the *object [Objekt]* or of *contemplation [Anschauung],* but not as *human sensuous activity, practice,* not subjectively. Hence it happened that the *active* side, in contradistinction to materialism, was developed by idealism—but only abstractly, since, of course, idealism does not know real, sensuous activity as such."[16]

To the new revisionists, Marx's intentions were clear: Marxism as social practice must be allied to a new activist form of cognition which would transcend the one-sidedness of idealism and materialism alike. As Bogdanov put it, Marx had indicated in the *Theses* how collectivist practice would create new social forms; the task of a Marxist philosophy was, by using Marx's view of the sociality of cognition as its guiding principle, to sketch out the corresponding conceptual forms, the "collectivist philosophy of the proletariat."[17] But they would not have to break entirely new ground: the direction of the new epistemology, they believed, had already been outlined in the neopositivism developed independently in Prague and Vienna by the scientist Ernst Mach and in Zurich by the philosopher Richard Avenarius, who had given it the name empiriocriticism.

The new philosophy (which owed much to the empiricism of George Berkeley and David Hume) was at the height of its popularity in the 1890s, when Avenarius was professor of philosophy at the University of Zurich. Its aim was to construct a monistic view of the world. It rejected, as not given in experience, the distinction made by all dualistic systems between subject and object, the inner and the outer world, the thing and its impression. Experienced reality, Avenarius taught, was a homogeneous world, in which the self, conceived as the central nervous system, was coordinated with the environment as the "central part" to its counterpart, both being components of reality in an identical sense. Similarly, Mach held that the world of experience, including both physical processes (bodies) and psychical processes (thoughts and impressions) were combinations of one and the same primary material or "elements": the world (and the human ego) is neither mind nor matter but a complex of elements known to us only through our sense experience.

Both Avenarius and Mach (who was much influenced by Charles Darwin) interpreted the cognitive process in terms of a biological voluntarism, as a process of adaptation to the environment arising from the struggle for survival. The more "economically" thought systematizes and communicates the data of experience, the more perfect is our collective orientation in this struggle. The principle of economy of thought demanded the rejection of classical materialist concepts of laws and causality as metaphysical assumptions with no basis in experience. Matter was merely a mental symbol standing for "a relatively stable complex of sensational elements," and the categories of cause and purpose were replaced by the functional concept of the permanence of certain connections.[18] According to Mach, laws did not denote the underlying relations of realities but were methods of orientation in the flow of experience; their role being to select and order its components, they changed in accordance with the practical demands of the struggle for survival. Both thinkers propounded an ethical monism, rejecting the autonomy of the sphere of the ought-to-be in relation to what is (*sollen* versus *sein*), on the grounds that no such opposition is given in experience; ethical problems fall within the sphere of science and can be solved by its methods.

This attempt to return to a "natural" view of the world, stripped of scientific and philosophical prejudices, bears some resemblance to the biological voluntarism of Nietzsche but differs from it in its anti-individualism and its emphasis on the cumulative nature of experience. Survival is seen as attained through cooperation, aided by the communication of experiences which are stored in science. It is not individual consciousnesses but the universal contents of consciousness and their continuity that are important: in Mach's words, "The ego must be given up."[19]

The doctrines of Avenarius and Mach began to arouse interest among Russian Marxists in the mid-1880s; the University of Zurich, where Avenarius taught, had long been a center for Russians studying abroad, in particular young radicals in exile. The suspicion of metaphysics traditional among the intelligentsia predisposed these young people to the doctrines of Avenarius, and some of them became his most enthusiastic students.[20] Among these was Lunacharsky, who studied in Zurich in 1895. A number of commentaries on empiriocriticism and translations of individual works appeared in Russia at the turn of the century;[21] one of the most active popularizers of the new philosophy was Bogdanov, who wrote the introduction to the Russian edition of Mach's most influential work, *The Analysis of Sensations*. In the view of the group which began to form around Bogdanov and Lunacharsky, the monist and voluntarist approach of Avenarius and Mach was singularly well suited to serve as a support for the *Theses on Feuerbach* and a framework for the new philosophy of the proletariat.

First, empiriocriticism seemed to have demonstrated that a monist approach to knowledge was an essential precondition for the attainment of Marx's ultimate goal: the unification of human endeavors in the battle with nature. Mach taught that all dualism was a hidden form of fetishism, rooted in primitive animism; Bogdanov in particular gave much emphasis to Mach's demonstration of how the fetishes inherent in traditional philosophical conceptions of causality, matter, and force hindered human understanding of the world. Matter and ideas could be defined only in their relation to human activity in society; materialism and idealism, by making absolutes of one or the other, effected an artificial break in experience. Here "machism" (as empiriocriticism was sometimes called) echoed Marxism: Bogdanov pointed out that whereas in the *Theses* Marx had referred only obliquely to the fetishism inherent in the classic materialist concept of matter, in the first chapter of *Capital* he had shown fetishism to be characteristic of capitalist relations, where the objects of human activity become subjects and humans are degraded to the status of objects: the products of one's labor become one's master, just as in religion the products of the brain acquire authority over the individual. The revolutionary destruction of fetishism in practical life must therefore be accompanied by the destruction of its intellectual counterparts.[22]

Second, empiriocriticism's approach to knowledge as the organization of experience seemed to correspond closely to the dynamism of the approach to reality as social practice outlined in the *Theses*—namely, Marx's "collectivist method" (as Bogdanov called it) of ordering the data of experience from the viewpoint of the human race engaged in a battle with nature.[23] It seemed to provide an appropriate epistemological basis for the revolutionary voluntarism of the last *Thesis:* "The philosophers have only interpreted the world in various ways. Our task is to change it."[24]

Bogdanov was generally regarded as the group's leading philosopher;[25] with two exceptions—the empiriosymbolism of Yushkevich[26] and the godbuilding of Lunacharsky and Gorky, other empiriocriticists did not attempt to construct independent systems of their own.

The survey that follows is concerned with the dominant characteristics of the movement and not with individual contributions to it. Thus, I shall refer mainly to the writings of its three most representative and prominent members: Bogdanov, Lunacharsky and Bazarov.

In his work *Empiriomonism* and other books and articles, Bogdanov propounded a modified form of empiriocriticism (which he considered insufficiently monist to be the basis of a "proletarian philosophy"). He regarded the concept of a functional link between conditions and the conditioned as a watered-down version of fetishistic notions of causality and proposed instead a concept of causality based on the energeticism of Wilhelm Ostwald, who, like Mach, was a critic of mechanical interpretations of physical phenomena and who substituted the notion of energy for that of "ultimate" particles such as atoms or molecules. According to Bogdanov, cause and effect should be conceived as a sum of energies in successive phases. He pointed out that this monistic view of causality was appropriate for the proletariat, the principle of the conservation and transformation of energy being the "ideological essence" of machine technology. For what he saw as the empiriocriticists' "dualistic" distinction between two types of experience, the physical and the mental (each being regarded as irreducible to the other), he substituted another distinction (also more in line, in his view, with proletarian practice in production) between two phases or types of organization: individually organized experience (of practical validity only for the individual) and socially organized experience (in harmony with the accumulated experience of society at a given time).[27]

Finally, Bogdanov believed that the founders of empiriocriticism took too passive a view of the role of cognition in relation to reality, maintaining like the materialists that its task was to orientate itself in the world rather than to change it. He pointed out that Marx, as the *Theses* revealed, had perceived that the role of cognition must be active and organizing: in the dynamic process of the battle between the human race and nature, to understand the world was *eo ipso* to change it.

Armed with the theories of Avenarius and Mach and the *Theses on Feuerbach,* the Russian empiriocriticists launched an attack on Plekhanov's postulate of an objective suprahistorical truth, summarized in a phrase that they frequently quoted against him: "No fate will move us from the correct point of view which has finally been revealed."[28] They pointed out that this was the standpoint of "contemplative," unhistorical materialism described by Marx in the *Theses* as unable to rise to an understanding of the dynamics of social relations, because it saw the cognitive process as the description or reflection of a world forever given.[29] Marx had explicitly refuted it in the second *Thesis:* "The question whether objective [*gegenständliche*] truth can be attributed to human thinking is not a question of theory but is a *practical* question. . . . The dispute over the reality or non-reality of thinking which is isolated from practice is a purely *scholastic* question."[30]

One of the most telling attacks on Plekhanov and his followers was made by Bazarov in 1908, in a contribution to an empiriocriticist symposium on Marxist theory. By a judicious use of texts, including not only the *Theses* but also Marx's criticism of Bruno Bauer in the *Nachlass,* and his analysis (in *The Holy Family*) of the concept of substance as a metaphysical illusion, Bazarov foreshadowed many later critics in demonstrating that the "reflection" theory of cognition, with its opposition of subject and object, was an inverted form of idealist dualism: its proponents believed that "there is only one way whereby the materialist-metaphysician can humble the creative pretensions of this unsympathetic 'subjective' substance: by subordinating it to another, sympathetic, 'objective' substance—supraexperiential nature." Yet Marx in the *Theses,* with his monist conception of reality as human practice, "was infinitely far removed from this naive 'either-or.' "[31]

Bogdanov argued that Plekhanov's thing-in-itself was a fetish characteristic of "authoritarian social relations" and "bourgeois individualism," which distinguished between experience (perceived as necessarily individual and subjective) and the objective reality which caused it but was outside its bounds.[32] He pointed out that this naive dualism had led Plekhanov and his followers to misinterpret Marx's statement in his *Critique of Political Economy* that "social being determines the social consciousness of man." They took "being" to be external to consciousness, whereas, as the *Theses on Feuerbach* showed, Marx believed that economic factors were inseparable from consciousness: they were the labor relations of human beings, not the physical relations of bodies, and labor was a conscious activity: "Social being and social consciousness . . . are identical."[33]

This perception of Marx's fundamental activism was rare at a period when Marx was generally held to be an economist who offered a scientific demonstration of the inevitable breakdown of capitalism; with few of Marx's early writings available, Engels's later works were the source of the Russian Marxists' interpretation of materialism. It was nearly two decades before the early manuscripts, showing Marx's thinking to be far removed from the mechanistic determinism preached by Engels, began to be generally known. But the empiriocriticists' understanding of what Marx meant by "social practice" was severely distorted by the fact that they knew nothing of the conception of the dialectic that Marx had elaborated in his early writings on alienation. Like Plekhanov, they identified Marx's view of the dialectic with the mechanistic formulation given by Engels in the *AntiDühring* and the *Dialectics of Nature*. It is to these works that Bogdanov referred when he launched an attack on the dialectic, arguing that the triadic system of development through contradictions was a relic of idealist thought and had meaning only in the world of abstract logic;[34] he substituted a formulation of dialectical conflict based on the biological evolutionism of Avenarius and Mach as "an organizational process proceeding by means of contradictions, or (what is the same thing) by a conflict between various tendencies," some leading to a loss of energy, others to a gain, the resolution of conflict being marked by a return to equilibrium.[35] As such, dialectical conflict was only one of the forms taken by the battle for survival. The world, including human society, consisted of "endless rows of complexes . . . at different stages of organization."[36] The criterion of progress in human societies was thus the same as in the animal and organic world: "an increase in the organization of complexes."[37] In the human species this could be defined as an increase in the harmony and quality of experience. From this perspective Bogdanov interpreted the phenomena of capitalism and class war as representing a state of disorganization in which individually and socially organized experiences were at odds with one another. With the end of class war the boundaries between physical and mental experience would be effaced. Human beings were progressing toward a unified experience as the content of a unified cognition. The social and legal forms and moral norms which developed in this process were, like biological forms, adaptations in the battle for survival and subject to the law of selection, their fate being determined by the extent to which the net gain in vital energy in the production process (mea-

sured by the "growth in energy of the mental apparatus of the members of society") outweighed the loss incurred by the disturbance of the existing
equilibrium.[38] In the words of Lunacharsky (who saw Bogdanov as the foremost Marxist philosopher of his time), "science," in the form of empiriocriticism, had, by replacing the dialectic with a biological voluntarism, once and for
all refuted what (quoting Croce) he called the "subjective category of inevitability."[39] It had shown that there existed no immutable laws, only hypotheses
and probabilities: the proposition that progress is an immanent law of nature
was metaphysical, and therefore meaningless. The initial dependence of labor
on the environment "does not limit its liberty . . . but merely places external
impediments on it. The thirst for life—this is the free principle in the organism, and insofar as it can, it processes its environment in its own way."[40]

In believing that this biological voluntarism represented a Marxist philosophy
the empiriocriticists were much mistaken; their voluntarism came from a philosophical stable very different from that of Marx. Ironically, it was closer to the
vulgarized Darwinism of Engels (whose mechanistic determinism, by applying
dialectics to nature, divorced it from the mediation of human consciousness)
than to the voluntarism of Marx, which, as the early manuscripts show, was
rooted in Hegel's categories and in the Hegelian dialectic, with its view of the
world as self-estrangement of Spirit. For Engels, matter was the source of the
evolution of consciousness; in Marx's materialist version of Hegel's metaphysics, the human being was the conscious creator of his or her world. In
Marx's dialectic, although the human satisfies needs through contact with nature, the process whereby the gap between being and consciousness was to be
closed was a historical one, brought about not by mechanistic responses of the
organism to material stimuli but by the conscious shaping of historical conditions, in the course of which people, in the act of satisfying their needs, dialectically create both new needs and new possibilities of satisfying them.

Empiriocriticism was thus theoretically incompatible with Marxism—a
poor qualification for the role envisaged for it by the aspiring "philosophers of
the proletariat." But it was designed to fulfill a need that was emotional as
much as intellectual. Its proponents had an immediate practical goal: to sustain and increase the revolutionary intelligentsia's enthusiasm by allowing it to
justify and defend its voluntarist notion of the integral personality against encroachments by the integral worldview of orthodox Marxism. In this area, too,
the empiriocriticists' achievements were minimal; but their attempt, and the
reactions that it provoked among their opponents, shed much light on the psychology of the Marxist intelligentsia and the degree of its self-awareness in the
years immediately following the 1905 revolution.

✳

Initially, the empiriocriticists had concentrated their attacks on what they saw as the theoretical defects of the official philosophy of Russian Marxism. After the 1905 revolution, the emphasis in the movement changed: the new theories were advanced above all as a solution to a moral crisis among the Marxist intelligentsia. For many of these, the events of 1905 marked the end of a long honeymoon with Marxism. The outbreaks that began the revolution owed nothing to Marxist propaganda, and the party that Lenin had confidently predicted would turn Russia upside down had been as much overtaken by events as the other political groupings. The radical intelligentsia's sense of its impotence and of its lack of contact with the masses was sharpened during the subsequent reaction, when the revolutionary parties found it difficult to rally mass support. The result was the intensification of factional squabbles among the Social Democrats and an increase in self-questioning on such matters as the party's goals and the relation of intellectuals to the mass movement. In the view of the empiriocriticists this was the crisis whose seeds they had discerned several years previously. In 1910 Yushkevich characterized it as follows:

> Marxism . . . is sick: . . . in the hands of narrow-minded people
> it is being transformed from a broad and liberating idea and
> doctrine into the instrument of ideological enslavement. . . . Its
> spring of theoretical creativity has dried up, its internal differ-
> ences of opinion have taken on the character of intellectual
> slaughter. . . . As though possessed by the spirit of mutual de-
> struction . . . we are ready to tear out each other's throats on
> any pretext: for a paragraph of the regulations on organization,
> for a point in the agrarian program, for a philosophical dis-
> agreement, for a difference in the evaluation of some political
> group, or for a crime such as that of drinking tea with the
> "philistine Kadets." Around every contentious trifle there begins
> a rapid process of crystallization. Bolsheviks, Mensheviks, par-
> tyites, workers'-congressites, boycottists, antiboycottists, materi-
> alists, Machists, then otzovists, ultimatists, liquidators . . .
> Potresovites, and so on, endlessly. . . . In sum, an endless mark-
> ing of time, an atmosphere permeated with hatred and enmity.[41]

It was time, wrote Yushkevich, that the party theoreticians understood that these destructive polemics had ceased to interest the mass of the Marxist intelligentsia, who yearned for a socialism imbued with a constructive spirit, an enthusiasm and faith comparable to that which had inspired the great religions.

A similar diagnosis was made in a flurry of books and articles, including two symposiums in which the empiriocriticists offered their doctrines as a remedy for the prevailing malaise. The seven contributors to the symposium *Essays on the Philosophy of Marxism* stated that although their theoretical positions were far from identical, they were united in seeing socialism as concerned not merely with material reforms but also with the "higher demands of the human spirit";[42] although they had no intention of defecting to the idealist camp, they had ceased to find a response to these demands in orthodox Marxism. The symposium's central theme was that historical determinism, in the narrow interpretation of the party's theorists, had destroyed the revolutionary enthusiasm of socialism and turned its poetry into dull prose: allegiance to "one-sided" doctrines that ignored the moral and emotional demands of individuals had led to a painful sense of inner conflict among the more idealistic revolutionaries, while others had begun to use the movement for their own corrupt purposes.

Lunacharsky treats this problem at length in the symposium and in his book *Religion and Socialism*. He asserts that "if our materialists are confident and active . . . it is in spite of their materialism and not because of it."[43] To be consistent, a Marxist of Plekhanov's school had to discard such sentiments as love of humanity and hatred of oppression as "merely froth, merely unmaterial and unnecessary reflections of a materially inevitable process." The role of such a person was "simply, prosaically to do the work foreordained by history: may what the prophets have spoken come to pass."[44]

Lunacharsky contended that what had been regarded as the principal strength of Marxism, namely, its claim to be "scientific," was its main weakness. Deducing the goals of society from an objective analysis of the laws of social development, it dismissed subjective ideals and values as epiphenomena. But human beings were evaluating as well as cognizing creatures, and their actions flowed from these two attributes, allied in "the fullness of a *human* attitude to the world."[45] Marxism had precluded itself from offering answers to the questions which most tormented the human race: "How and in the name of what shall I live?"[46]

The empiriocriticists claimed that by devaluing vital instincts and feelings, Plekhanov's fetish of the thing-in-itself was no less destructive in its effect on the personality than the idols set up by religious and metaphysical systems. Lunacharsky characterized his orthodox opponents as the spiritual descendants of Bazarov, the "nihilist" hero of Turgenev's *Fathers and Children*, a narrow rationalist who sought to base his actions uniquely on scientific principles, uninfluenced by moral or aesthetic feelings or ideals. He pointed out that Marx himself had criticized eighteenth-century materialism for the one-sidedness of its mechanistic view of the movement of matter: this movement was also characterized by "striving, vital spirit, tension."[47] The individual's moral and emotional demands could be reconciled with "scientific socialism" only through an approach which, by postulating the equal reality of physical and mental phenomena, made Marxism both "a science and a practical philosophy, a synthesis of inevitability and the ideal."[48]

Within the framework of empiriocriticism the rebel philosophers developed an ideal of the "new man" of the future, an "integral personality" who would not suffer from the divisions of their own "epoch of contradictions."[49] Progress, they stressed, was an increase both in the quantity and the harmony of experience. Its goal must be "a personality harmonious in all its desires . . . a society composed of such people."[50] This "wholeness" would be the outcome of a triadic development. Bourgeois materialism had been the destructive antithesis of idealism: "The proletariat requires a harmonious synthesis . . . that will assimilate and destroy [them both]."[51]

In formulating their ideal of the integral human being the Russian empiriocriticists were (as the neo-Kantian revisionists had been) strongly influenced by Nietzsche.[52] Lunacharsky describes his ethical position as "aesthetic amoralism," based on a Nietzschean voluntarism and on contemporary aesthetic theories whose ideal was "fullness of life." He supports his aesthetic voluntarism with a physiological explanation of ethics derived from Avenarius: all organisms share the "thirst for life," expressed in a striving for the maximum intensity and quantity of experiences. All ethical demands may thus be subsumed under the principle of "the greatest possible flowering of the life of the species," which Lunacharsky proposes as the basis of "a universal science of evaluation."[53]

The empiriocriticists rejected traditional Kantian ethical systems based on the concepts of duty and self-denial as irreconcilable with the goal of harmony. Bogdanov describes all legal and ethical norms as fetishes,[54] and in an essay in the symposium *Studies in a Realistic World View* Bazarov points out that empiriocriticism has invalidated the normative ethics of the past by showing that cognition presents human beings not with obligatory laws but with heuristic norms elaborated according to the demands of the struggle for survival and the principle of the harmonization of life: "The psychology of a free person cannot be reconciled with any form of leadership. That person is not free who is afraid of his own self, who does not dare to acknowledge that all of his sensations are in principle of equal value, [and who does not] seek in . . . the testimony of direct feeling the norms of his life. The demand for an absolute non-empirical norm . . . is psychological slavery."[55]

Echoing Nietzsche, Bazarov denies that altruism and self-sacrifice, as traditionally conceived, are virtues; like Nietzsche's *Übermensch,* the new socialist human being will use others as instruments in his creative battle with nature and will expect others to use him in the same way. The Kantian ethic which presupposed a conflict between duty and pleasure corresponded to a psychology that was regrettably widespread in Russian society, epitomized by the phenomenon of the "repentant nobleman" who yearned to sacrifice his rights to happiness and self-fulfillment in repayment of his debt to the people and by the heroes of Dostoevsky's novels, for whom torment and suffering, duality and division, were the "pearl of creation." To the notion of obligation Bazarov opposes the heuristic principle of the "harmonization of life": the search for norms which would permit each individual to include all attainable pleasures in his or her life. As distinct from the Dionysian apotheosis of instinct, this goal would demand a conscious and critical evaluation of experience by one criterion—that of harmony, defined as "a general feeling of heightened sensation, of fullness of life, of spiritual uplift."[56]

Their enthusiasm for the type exemplified by the Übermensch earned the Russian empiriocriticists the title of "Nietzschean Marxists." However, they were unanimously opposed to the individualism which was central to Nietzsche's ideal. They all endorsed the collectivist emphasis of empiriocriticism: Bazarov affirmed that "the recognition of the individual personality as an absolute principle has always been and will always be alien to the proletariat,"[57] while Lunacharsky observed that individualism was characteristic of social decadence: "For a true socialist, reality is the species, humanity." Theirs was a collective Übermensch: the proletariat. They argued that the individual personality achieved "integrality" by harmonizing its experience with that of the most progressive class. In the words of Lunacharsky: "[The individual] is a part, and without the corresponding whole has no meaning."[58]

To sum up: by their revolt against official Marxist philosophy the empiriocriticists were seeking to resolve a tension endemic in the outlook of the Russian radical intelligentsia—namely, between a rebellious voluntarism and the search for reassuring absolutes. Their revolt followed a pattern very similar to that of the neo-Kantian revisionists: criticism of the one-sidedness of orthodox Marxist determinism, perceived as constricting and distorting the development of the individual, followed by the demand for a revaluation of ideals and values from the standpoint of the aspirations of the integral human being, whose harmony and self-fulfillment (conceived in terms strongly influenced by Nietzsche's aesthetic amoralism) were set up as the goal of progress. However, while the neo-Kantians held that the concept of individual wholeness was grounded in an ethical individualism incompatible with Marxism as a collectivist philosophy of progress, the empiriocriticists believed that their task was to synthesize the ideal of the whole and harmonious individual with the Marxist vision of humanity as collectively moving to a single, unitary view of reality.

For them the ideal of the integral personality was inseparable from an integral view of the world. The author of the introduction to the symposium *Studies in a Realistic Worldview* put it as follows: "The fullest and strongest life is life that is integral and harmonious: this means that the most perfect and powerful cognition must be unitary and harmonious; this means that truth is monist."

The same writer attacks the "subjective sociology" through which some Russian populists had sought to defend the interests of the "integral personality" against the encroachment of political and moral absolutes. He accuses them of eclecticism, which he calls the "professional illness of the intelligentsia": "Eclecticism is a sign of weakness, the expression of a pitiful, unharmonious life."[59]

Curiously, Bogdanov, who had been the most enthusiastic of the empiriocriticists in welcoming Marxism as the liberating "negation of all eternal truths," nonetheless frequently insists that the innate tendency of the human mind is to organize all knowledge into a "harmonious and integral system."[60] In the future philosophy of the proletariat all phenomena, "from the most primitive complex of cosmic elements to artistic creativity, the . . . highest and most mysterious form of organizing activity, will be . . . elucidated and harmoniously synthesized by the formalized, organized experience of humanity."[61] In this apparent inconsistency he is directly following Avenarius and Mach. Their demystification of knowledge and their attacks on fetishes were the means of achieving what they saw as the final goal of human reason: the construction of a unitary vision of the world as a basis for the unification of all human intellectual and practical endeavors. As Mach asserted, by reducing the material world to a complex of identical elements, "we may reasonably hope to build a unified monistic structure . . . and thus to rid ourselves of the distressing confusions of dualism."[62] The tool for this task was philosophy, which (as the only discipline concerned with all areas of human experience) could, they believed, integrate all the data of the sciences into a single harmonious system.

This desire to eliminate the distressing effects of the divisions of consciousness led both Avenarius and Mach into contradiction with their own empiricism. As their critics have pointed out, their assertion that the goal of reason is a unitary worldview was not a deduction from experience but an a priori assumption, a metaphysical hypothesis designed to satisfy the human's need to overcome the sense of an inner split.[63] Whatever its psychological justification, the view (stressed by Avenarius more than Mach) that knowledge is moving in a continuous progression toward a single all-embracing synthesis was in direct contradiction with the radical reaction against dogmas and absolutes which had led both to emphasize the relative, provisional, and exclusively methodological significance of scientific laws.

This combination of iconoclasm and faith proved irresistible to empiriocriticism's Russian adherents; but as a result they were caught in a vicious circle. Their revolt against Marxist determinism had been a defense of the individual personality, with its subjective goals and values against immutable historical laws; but these philosophers were not individualists. Like Mach they believed that "the ego must be given up." The integrality, creativity, and even the free will that they defend against abstract norms and sanctions are themselves lodged in an abstraction: the collective. It is true that Lunacharsky admits that in the contemporary world "it is not always possible to reconcile the ideals of fullness of life for myself and maximum benefit to the species,"[64] but he believes that this is due to the distorting effects of capitalist society, which has suppressed the generic instinct and led individuals to focus on their personal urge for wholeness as opposed to the interests of the collective. In the socialist society "the personal and the generic instinct [will] fuse; . . . the individual will value himself as a moment in the great life of the species."[65] Bogdanov sees the individual ego as a temporary "adaptation" designed to cope with the disharmony between individually and socially organized experience. When this conflict is resolved, the ego will disappear.[66]

Thus, the Promethean revolt of the Marxist *Übermensch* leads to a very tame conclusion: absolute obedience to a new set of universal moral norms. According to Lunacharsky, the individual personality increases its strength tenfold by denying itself in the name of the species. "Classes and nations are, as it were, modalities of pan-human society. . . . Individuals are modalities, living expressions of their classes, receiving their spiritual identity from them and determined in general . . . by their fate."[67]

The self-affirming new man turns out to be only another disembodied absolute. The empiriocriticists had gone full circle, to arrive back at that orthodoxy from which they had once retreated in indignant revolt. Real human beings were merely predicates of an abstraction as much beyond experience as Plekhanov's thing-in-itself: "The individual is merely a particular expression of the essence of humanity."[68] A new god had been proclaimed: all that remained was to found a new cult. This was done in the theory of godbuilding; an offshoot of empiriocriticism, it exposes at its most candid and naive the thirst for faith which inspired the Marxist rebels.

Godbuilding (*bogostroitelstvo*) was developed by Lunacharsky in conjunction with Maksim Gorky, who expounded it in literary form in his novel *Confession* (1908). Lunacharsky elaborated it in his book *Religion and Socialism* and in a number of articles. He attributes the skepticism and apathy prevailing among revolutionaries to the fact that the movement was not satisfying the human need to feel part of a great whole, to transcend the limits of one's individuality by fusing with an "infinite life force." This need was especially acute in conditions of disorientation and social pessimism such as those prevailing after 1905, and it could be satisfied only by religion—"a conception and sense of the world which resolves the contradiction between the ideal and reality" and which provided faith in the future by positing "a higher force kindred to the individual, close to him, on which he can place his hopes."[69] "[Religion] will unite the romantic, self-sacrificing, religiously supra-individual practice of Social Democracy with its philosophy, which has been prompted by a stern modesty to assume a dry and calculating facade, with great detriment to its cause."[70]

Lunacharsky's new proletarian religion is anthropocentric: "The species, the collective, is the center: the individual personality revolves round it but feels itself deeply at one with it."[71] Among the prophets of his faith he counts Fichte, whose voluntarism he defines as a "collectivist" philosophy in which the individual is the instrument for "the manifestation of the pure Ego in the aggregate of rational beings" (he traces the initial inspiration for his religion to his enthusiasm for the idealism of Fichte and Schelling, to which, ironically, he had been introduced by Plekhanov in 1895).[72] Another prophet is Nietzsche, whose concept of "love of the distant ones" in *The Joyous Science* is construed by Lunacharsky as a call to worship the "supra-individual beings" who express the essence of humankind. He names Feuerbach as "father" of the new religion, with his teaching that humans must reappropriate their alienated essence, which they had projected onto fictitious deities. This anthropotheism had been developed by Marx, "the last prophet to issue from the bowels of Israel," who taught that the way to redemption lay through the organized battle of the human race with nature.[73] Progress is the eschatology of the new religion: Lunacharsky expresses the confident expectation that the awareness of being a link in the development of history's drama will inspire Social Democrats with "religious" enthusiasm. Through the worship of their infinite potential individuals will transcend their own finiteness; by fusing their subjective desires with the objective progress of the proletariat they will gain immortality in the species.

"Si Dieu n'existait pas, il faudrait l'inventer" . . . Lunacharsky's exhortation—"Let us adore the potential of mankind, our own potential, and represent it in an aureole of glory, so that we may love it yet more passionately"[74]— has an embarrassingly hollow ring, as have the saccharine ecstasies of Gorky's novel, in which a cripple is cured through the collective will of the "people-god." Their preaching has all the manufactured enthusiasm and false cheerfulness of scoutmasters whipping up support for an unpopular but necessary chore: Lunacharsky frequently insists that after the setbacks of 1905 only the enthusiasm generated by his religion can provide the strength and motivation needed for the victory of socialism.

✳

In a campaign that began in 1904 and reached its climax in 1909, orthodox Russian Marxists attacked the empiriocriticist heresy on two grounds: its theoretical shortcomings and its social effects. The first category of criticism, which includes one of the sacred texts of Soviet Marxism, is both better known and much less interesting than the second and requires only a brief summary here.

The first published attack on empiriocriticism was an article by Liubov Akselrod, written in 1904, apparently at the request of Lenin.[75] A faithful pupil of Plekhanov, Akselrod maintained that the essence of materialism lies in the doctrine of the primacy of being over consciousness; the latter being causally dependent on the former, its task is to reflect and adapt to the objective reality which exists outside it and independently of it. By conceiving of the physical world as experience, empiriocriticism was asserting that nature had no existence outside consciousness: it was thus a form of subjective idealism verging on solipsism and was irreconcilable with a Marxist vision of the world.

The principal Marxist counterattacks on the new heresy were a lengthy refutation of Bogdanov by Plekhanov, published in 1908, and Lenin's work of 1909, *Materialism and Empiriocriticism.*[76] Both are no more than a restatement of the main theses of Plekhanov's work *On the Development of the Monist View of History,* accompanied by vicious personal attacks on their opponents' integrity. Lenin's famous work is remarkably unoriginal. Its central thesis, that "consciousness reflects being which is independent of it," is supported by copious quotations from Engels (in particular his *AntiDühring* and *Ludwig Feuerbach and the End of Classical German Philosophy*).[77] He does point to the incompatibility between Marx's view of history and the biological voluntarism of empiriocriticism, but his treatise is remarkable above all for what one critic has described as Lenin's "inability to understand the nature of philosophical worry."[78] Coarse and contemptuous in tone, it exudes the conviction that all philosophical problems can be solved by the application of a dose of common sense. His central argument is starkly simple: all doctrines that do not regard matter as primary and spirit as secondary belong to the category of "subjective idealism" and lead inescapably to "the purest solipsism."[79] This crude reductionism makes short work of philosophical subtlety: Avenarius's proposition that natural scientists cannot abstract themselves (i.e., their thinking consciousness) from their picture of the world is interpreted by Lenin as the denial of something "not doubted by anyone who is to any degree educated or healthy," namely, that "the world existed *when there could be no* life, no sensations . . . on it."[80]

Lenin concludes by defining the role of empiriocriticism in the class war. He reminds his readers of the "*partiinost*" of truth (that all concepts are weapons of contending parties in this war): behind the "gnosiological agnosticism" of empiriocriticism there lurks the ideology of a class hostile to the proletariat. Contemporary professors of philosophy are the "scientific henchmen" of theologians, and the "objective, class role [of empiriocriticism] can be entirely summed up as subservience to the fideists in their battle against materialism in general and historical materialism in particular."[81]

This definition raises an obvious question: Why did a philosophy so antagonistic to the class interests of the proletariat find its main defenders among the leading Bolshevik theorists? Lenin devotes no more than four lines in his long work to this embarrassing point. It is, he writes, the "misfortune" of the Russian "Machists" that they "put their trust in reactionary professors of philosophy."[82] Having done so, they slid down a slippery slope.

If Lenin found it politically expedient to attribute the popularity of empiriocriticism among his followers to an intellectual aberration that could be remedied by repentance and a return to the fold, Menshevik theorists had no reasons for refraining from a closer examination of what Liubov Akselrod described as the "conspicuous historical significance" of the heresy on their doorstep.[83] They were at one with the empiriocriticists themselves in seeing the movement as the expression of a crisis in relations between the Russian intelligentsia and the revolutionary movement; but their interpretation of that crisis was very different.

The Mensheviks' commentaries on the social significance of empiriocriticism in Russia are closely connected with their opposition to the Bolsheviks on the issue of the "liquidation" of the party. After 1905 Lenin envisaged the next phase of the revolution in terms of a proletarian and peasant rising, and he continued to preach the view (which had led to his break with the Mensheviks) that the revolution must have strong leadership in the form of a secret organization consisting of a small vanguard of disciplined, professional revolutionaries. The Mensheviks, however, believed that Russia was still in a "bourgeois democratic" phase of revolution that had not been completed in 1905 because the liberal parties had been insufficiently strong to seize power; and although most of them believed that in the conditions of repression illegal party committees had to continue to exist, they called for the Social Democrats to devote their energies to the creation of a mass proletarian party on the Western model, on the ground that the existing movement of underground conspirators was out of touch with the everyday interests and activities of the masses.

In 1908 Lenin bitterly attacked the leading proponents of this view as "liquidators" whose aim was to disband the existing party and to confine social democratic politics to legally permitted trade union activities. The "liquidators" saw in Lenin's attitude the same Jacobin mistrust of the spontaneous mass movement that had led to the split in the party in 1903. One of their leading figures, A. N. Potresov, repeatedly pointed out that as yet there existed in Russia only the embryo of a party in the Marxist sense. Its development was frustrated by the continued and unnatural hegemony of the intelligentsia over the mass movement, which it was using as "an instrument on which to play its heroic symphony." Instead of the party's supporting the proletarian movement, the latter was being used to support the party, as an apparatus in the hands of the intelligentsia.[84]

Potresov's conclusions were judged too extreme by many in his own faction; but his approach reflected a general interest among Menshevik theorists in the social and political significance of new movements of ideas. This led them to interpret empiriocriticism as symptomatic of a disturbing trend among the intelligentsia. In a two-part article published in 1909, entitled "On the So-Called Religious Seekings in Russia," Plekhanov pointed to similarities between Lunacharsky's "godbuilding" and the religious revival in intelligentsia circles at the turn of the century, which had been closely tied to the neo-Kantian revision of Russian Marxism.[85] He argued that Lunacharsky's ideology represented a phenomenon recurrent among the radical intelligentsia, but especially evident after 1905: the loss of faith in a collective ideal, a resurgence of individualism, expressed in anxious introspection about their personal fate in an alien world, and a turn to religion in a search for the "meaning of life." Lunacharsky was "a typical Russian *intelligent,* one of the most impressionable sort."[86] Although he claimed to speak for the proletariat, he had nothing in common with it; his new god had been created "for the improvement, edification and encouragement of languishing *intelligenty*."[87]

Plekhanov's analysis of the intelligentsia's malaise does not go very deep. But other Menshevik intellectuals, notably Potresov, believed that the time had come for the Marxist intelligentsia to take stock of itself, examine its subjective goals in relation to the mass movement, and decide whether to identify with the latter or to preserve its "intelligentsia" values by reneging from Marxism altogether. Such was the theme of a symposium by ten leading Menshevik theorists (including Potresov, Akselrod, F. I. Dan, and Yu. O. Martov) published in 1909 and entitled *On the Boundary*.[88]

The authors present a Marxist interpretation of the religious, literary, and philosophical movements that had arisen at the turn of the century, focusing on what they see as their common feature: a pessimistic sense of a rift between the individual and society. According to Dan, all these movements had represented the "impotent revolt" of bourgeois individualism against an environment that it could not control, a revolt that had spread to the radical intelligentsia when the revolution of 1905 failed to fulfill their rosy hopes. The

masses had not played the role expected of them; they had not leapt trium-
phantly over the historical obstacles to freedom. Instead, there had ensued a
protracted and inglorious phase of class war, in the course of which the specific
class characteristics and aspirations of the proletariat had emerged more
clearly, causing "a dissonance in the common 'radical' music."[89] Notes
sounded from the depths that elicited no intellectual or emotional response
from the intelligentsia. The poetry of lofty ideals had been replaced by the
prose of material class interests and by mundane antlike labors which required
neither heroes nor leaders but cooperation, patience, and technical skill. The
intelligentsia's characteristic individualism and voluntarism, previously channeled into a cult of the revolutionary hero, began to express itself in a sense of
affinity with other less radical sections of society. Many started to break their
ties with a cause that had become spiritually alien to them and to search for a
faith more specifically their own. As this could not be a proletarian faith, it
could only be a bourgeois one. The "bourgeois rebirth of the intelligentsia's
psyche," taking place in a period of reaction, found expression in social apathy
and religious mysticism or, alternatively, in the impotent pretense of vitality—
as exemplified in a Nietzschean cult of strength or the hedonistic ethic characteristic of much contemporary literature and philosophy. Dan suggested that
this development was not wholly negative: it was the sign of the "inevitable liquidation" of the intelligentsia's dominance over the social movement. Some
would join the ranks of the liberals; others would follow those who had already
made common cause with the proletariat and been "ideologically reborn in
their innermost depths."[90]

Dan's essay did not refer specifically to empiriocriticism as an illustration of
this process, but Martov and Akselrod did. Martov, after offering an interpretation similar to Dan's of the current crisis among the intelligentsia, concludes
with an analysis of godbuilding as an expression of the intelligentsia's traditional voluntarism. He quotes Lunacharsky's exhortation "By faith . . . alone
will you be saved; by faith alone will you rise above the 'everyday level' of the
contemporary class battle." This, Martov asserts, is the language of a dema-
gogue: "It is the formula of a movement in which the shepherd and the sheep,
the leader and the led, are sharply differentiated and opposed; in which there
exist two truths—the esoteric and the exoteric; in which the ideologist utters
lies because the masses are not capable of *assimilating the truth.*" According to
Martov, Lunacharsky's "religion of the social myth," like all utopian theories
emanating from the intelligentsia, was designed to justify the latter's hegemony
over the radical movement. But he confidently predicts the failure of this aim.
Jacobinism, sectarianism, and other manifestations of an intelligentsia aristocracy in the proletarian movement were "relics of the past."[91]

There is no such optimism in Akselrod's analysis. Her first attack on empiriocriticism had been written at Lenin's request. Now, however, she points out that it is no coincidence that the majority of Bolshevik theorists are empiriocriticists—Bolshevism is "permeated through and through with the methodology of empiriocriticist philosophy."[92] It shares the latter's two fundamental characteristics: a "boundless subjective arbitrariness," and a rigid dogmatism.[93] By allowing no clear boundary in principle between subjective and objective truth, empiriocriticism's theory of the identity of physical and mental phenomena offered no firm criteria for distinguishing between reality and utopian illusions; it encouraged the "Machist romantic" to ignore the objective limits on his or her will. It also encouraged a dogmatic rigidity in social and political theory: in a view of the world in which the principles of cause and effect were understood as functional relations coordinated by consciousness, there was no place for the concepts of historical process and development in time.[94]

She argued that Bolshevism embodied the same paradoxical combination of boundless voluntarism and dogmatic inflexibility. Its theoretical basis was the view of the relation of consciousness to spontaneity expressed by Lenin in his pamphlet *What Is to Be Done?*—that the role of the critically thinking Marxist intelligentsia was to lead the spontaneous working-class masses. However, the theory of the power of the will of politically conscious individuals used by the Bolsheviks to justify the dictatorship of Social Democrat intellectuals over the masses was based on illusion. The people followed "conscious" individuals only when there was intellectual contact between them—namely, when the people themselves had reached a high level of consciousness. Otherwise, in order to attract them, the intellectual was forced to adapt to their instincts, using demagogic methods to stir up their "immature revolutionary passions."[95] This was the path the Bolsheviks had chosen: their relationship with the masses was that of the hero and the crowd. But Akselrod pointed out that although their general approach to the political struggle was opportunistic, they were inflexible regarding their ultimate goal: the seizure of power. They had discarded the concept of process central to Marxist theory, according to which the revolutionary consciousness of the masses developed in historical stages which made it necessary for the revolutionary party to resort to tactical compromises and alliances. The Bolshevik method was to reject all such tactics and to seek instead to incite the masses to immediate action through simple slogans designed to arouse violent passions.

In sum, Akselrod concluded, the philosophy of empiriocriticism was ideally suited to those lacking a sense of historical process, whether they be "peaceful bourgeois" or romantic utopians. In its mixture of dogmatism and "vulgar empiricism" it was what its proponents claimed it to be—the theoretical counterpart to Bolshevik practice.[96]

Akselrod's analysis, although overburdened with the jargon of Marxist polemics, is the most interesting of the contributions to the debate on empiriocriticism's significance as an intelligentsia ideology. It was the fate of the empiriocriticists that their claim to be the theorists of Bolshevik practice was taken seriously only by the Mensheviks. But in the last analysis the strongest support for their claim (and for Akselrod's interpretation of it) may be seen to have come from Lenin himself. For what is most significant in his reaction to empiriocriticism is not what he wrote against it but when he chose to attack it and why.

Lenin's initial reaction to the attempt to marry empiriocriticism with Social Democracy was no less extreme than Plekhanov's. Valentinov, who took on the task of acquainting Lenin with the theories of Avenarius and Mach in 1904, relates that Lenin was driven to "frenzy" by his attempt to defend their ideas. Agreeing with Plekhanov that "Marx and Engels had said all that needs to be said," Lenin asserted that "to revisionism there is only one reply: thump it on the snout [v mordu]."[97] But for five years he refrained from making such comments in public, breaking his silence on the subject only in 1909. His reasons were very practical: the movement's main philosopher, Bogdanov, was essential to him in the battle to establish the dominance of his group in the SD Party. Bogdanov's decision to join the Bolshevik faction in 1904 was a windfall for Lenin—he had an impressive intellectual reputation and a wide network of literary and political contacts (including Gorky) in Moscow and Petersburg. He soon became editor of the Bolshevik organ Forward and Lenin's right hand in the task of building up the new faction, in particular, its finances. With Lenin and Leonid Krasin he formed a secret group controlling large sums of money obtained by questionable methods, especially what was euphemistically known as "expropriation": bank robberies. It was in the interests of this fruitful collaboration that, as Lenin explained to Gorky on 25 February 1908, "In the summer and autumn of 1904 we finally came to an understanding with Bogdanov and concluded as Bolsheviks a tacit alliance which tacitly excluded philosophy as being a neutral area. This alliance . . . gave us the possibility of carrying out jointly in the revolution [of 1905] that tactic of revolutionary Social Democracy (i.e., Bolshevism) which according to my deepest conviction was the sole correct one."[98]

According to V. Bonch-Bruevich, then a close associate of Lenin's, the latter called all the Bolsheviks together after Bogdanov had joined the party and told them that although they were not to agree with Bogdanov's views, they must refrain from all polemics with him on the subject, so that all their energies could be focused on immediate questions of strategy and tactics in the revolutionary battle.[99]

In a conversation with Bonch-Bruevich, Plekhanov described Lenin's cooption of Bogdanov as the sheer opportunism of a man who, like one of Gogol's characters, "picks up everything he finds on the road: you never know, it may come in handy."[100] Bonch-Bruevich's reply, apparently without intended irony, was a classic example of the same approach: he explained that the Bolsheviks were not prepared to attack Bogdanov in print but would welcome any public refutation of his views that the Mensheviks might care to make.

Plekhanov's taunts against the heretic in his camp eventually stung Lenin into a public reply at the party congress held in April 1905, known by the Bolsheviks as the Third (the Mensheviks repudiated its legality). Referring to attempts by Plekhanov to drag the names of Avenarius and Mach into polemics within the party, he blandly asserted: "I positively cannot understand what relation these writers, with whom I have not the slightest sympathy, have to the question of social revolution."[101]

By 1907, however, Lenin's alliance with Bogdanov had began to disintegrate. Bogdanov became (as did Lunacharsky) a leader of the ultra-left wing, the otzovist, or ultimatist group of the Bolsheviks, which opposed Lenin on the issue of SD participation in the Duma. In addition, the policy of expropriations which he directed together with Krasin (who was closely connected with some of the empiriocriticists) began to be an embarrassment to Lenin. It had come to attract undesirable publicity for the SDs, and in 1908 the party's central committee condemned it and ordered an investigation into the matter. Lenin managed to smother this, but in August 1908 the Bolshevik center replaced Bogdanov and Krasin by a new financial commission. By mid-1908 Lenin had ousted Bogdanov from the editorial board of *The Proletarian,* the Bolshevik mouthpiece that had succeeded *Forward,* and in a secret vote on 23 February 1909 the Bolshevik center censured Bogdanov and Krasin for misappropriating party funds and expelled them from the faction. The public break came in June 1909 at a meeting of the Bolshevik center which denounced otzovism and ultimatism, expelled Bogdanov and Lunacharsky, and in a special resolution condemned godbuilding as "a movement implying a breach with the very foundations of Marxism."[102]

In the first issue of *The Proletarian* in early 1908 Lenin had repeated the view that questions of philosophy were a matter of individual opinion, but the secret condemnation of Bogdanov in February 1909 was followed by a public attack on his philosophical views in *The Proletarian.* In March *Materialism and Empiriocriticism,* on which Lenin had been working for nearly a year, appeared.

In his correspondence with Gorky, Lenin presents his decision openly to attack the empiriocriticists as the result of a final loss of patience with their public utterances. In his letter to Gorky of 25 February 1908 he asserts that the publication by Bogdanov and others of *Essays in the Philosophy of Marxism* had "greatly exacerbated long-standing disagreements among the Bolsheviks on philosophical problems." The preaching of varieties of agnosticism, idealism, religious atheism, and so on was "going too far. Of course we rank and file Marxists are not well read in philosophy, but why should we suffer this indignity, why should we be offered this sort of stuff as Marxist philosophy!" Further, in a letter of 24 March 1908, announcing his intention to launch a public attack on empiriocriticism, he writes: "You must and will of course understand that, if a party man has come to the conviction that certain propaganda is deeply wrong and *harmful,* he is in duty bound to speak out against it. I would not have started the row were I not absolutely convinced . . . that [*Essays in the Philosophy of Marxism*] is ridiculous, harmful, philistine and obscurantist from beginning to end."[103]

Lenin's protest carries no conviction. It is true that the number of empiriocriticist publications increased in 1908, but their first symposium had appeared in 1904 and there had since been no significant change in their theories. What had changed was that not only had Bogdanov ceased to be useful to Lenin's political strategy but an attack on Bogdanov and his allies would be tactically advantageous in Lenin's battle with his Menshevik opponents. As he asserts in his letter to Gorky of 24 March, far from weakening the Bolsheviks, as Gorky feared, a break with Bogdanov would strengthen them, as the Mensheviks would no longer be able to attack them on theoretical grounds and would have to restrict their polemics to questions of practical politics, where they were no match for their opponents.

In its timing, Lenin's attack on empiriocriticism seems a particularly skillful application of what Akselrod had called "vulgar empiricism." To emphasize the partiinost of all philosophy four years after he had stressed the irrelevance of empiriocriticism to social revolution was a volte-face difficult to reconcile with the reigning orthodoxy expressed in Plekhanov's phrase "No fate will move us from the correct point of view which has finally been revealed." Lenin might well have countered this with Engels's dictum (which he used frequently) that Marxism was not a dogma but a guide to action. But this maxim, as expressed in his political practice, was not consistent with the reflective theory of cognition to which he paid lip service in *Materialism and Empiriocriticism.* It was far closer to the voluntarist view of truth propounded by the self-styled Bolshevik theorists and expressed in Bogdanov's thesis: "Truth is . . . not a petty and exact representation of [the facts]: it is an instrument for domination over them."[104] As we have seen, for the empiriocriticists laws and norms had an exclusively functional significance as methods of orientation, changing in accordance with the practical demands of the collective battle for survival. Lenin's primary objective was to secure a monopoly of power for that collective which he held to embody the principle of progress—the Bolsheviks, and in the pursuit of this aim he showed a similar functionalist approach to

Marxist dogma, maintaining the domination of his group by a skillful combination of extreme flexibility, even arbitrariness, in his interpretation of historical laws, with an extreme dogmatism and authoritarianism in enforcing a given interpretation, once the choice had been made. As Akselrod had pointed out, his position on ultimate ends was uncompromising, but this in no way restricted his choice of means. She might well have quoted the history of Lenin's relations with Bogdanov as an illustration of her thesis: ironically, it is the methods that Lenin used to defeat Bogdanov and his group which provide the most convincing support for their claim to be the philosophers of Bolshevism.

The question remains: Why, if Lenin's political practice had more affinity with the theories of empiriocriticism than with the determinism of Plekhanov, was he so strongly opposed to the former? Contemporary accounts leave no doubt of his genuine loathing of them, however much expediency may have impeded its expression. Two reasons may be advanced: first, in his outlook and psychology Lenin was very much in the tradition of the Russian intelligentsia's radical extreme, for whom the term *idealism* traditionally stood for all the forces that lent moral and practical support to Russian backwardness and despotism—the impotent dreams of superfluous people, liberal cant, and the social apathy of mystical and religious trends in literature. Lenin's hatred of these tendencies was fanatical, and the label of "subjective idealism" fixed on empiriocriticism by the SD theorists is sufficient to explain his extreme reaction against it. Second, on the evidence of his later philosophical notebooks, his defense in 1909 of a mechanistic materialism so much at odds with his own political practice may be attributed to philosophical laziness. In his concern with practical politics he was prepared to take his philosophy at second hand from those who had more time to devote to it. His famous "discovery" of Hegel, recorded in his philosophical notebooks of 1914–16, shows that his first serious study of the sources of Marxism had the same electrifying effect on him as the *Theses on Feuerbach* had had on the empiriocriticists. The influence of Hegel's dialectic on Marx was a revelation to him: "One may not fully understand Marx's *Capital*, especially his first chapter, without having studied and understood the *whole* of Hegel's Logic. Therefore no Marxist has understood Marx for half a century!" Plekhanov's dualistic materialism was incompatible with Lenin's new understanding of the dialectic. He quotes Hegel: "It is wrong to see subjectivity and objectivity as a kind of stable and abstract opposition. They are both fully dialectical"; he observes that "objective" idealism "in a zigzag fashion *went right up* to materialism and partly *turned into it.*" He is severe on Plekhanov's critique of empiriocriticism, arguing that it was made "more from a vulgar materialist than from a dialectical materialist point of view"; and he asserts that "intelligent idealism is closer to intelligent materialism than is stupid materialism."[105]

The advent of the Revolution prevented Lenin from pursuing his philosophical investigations, but it is clear from the philosophical notebooks that well before 1917 he had arrived at what had been the starting point of the first Bolshevik revision of Marx: repudiation of the dualism of the "reflective" theory of cognition.

If Lenin had read Hegel five years earlier, he would not have written *Materialism and Empiriocriticism,* but, given the role of tactical considerations in determining his attitude to theory, it is idle to speculate whether the fate of the empiriocriticists in 1909 would have been much different. Their expulsion from the party ended the group's political significance. They founded an opposition group called Forward, but this had little influence. In August 1909 they established a party school on the island of Capri, where Gorky was living; they invited collaboration from the Bolshevik center, but the latter did not respond and by the end of 1909 succeeded in engineering a split in the school. Lenin's philosophical development had no effect whatever on the ultimate fate of those empiriocriticists who remained in Russia after the Revolution: by then philosophical radicalism was too firmly associated with political indiscipline. Those who had fulsomely recanted, like Lunacharsky, were readmitted into the Bolshevik fold.[106] Bogdanov never renounced his views, but he took no part in public polemics. Empiriocriticism had no defenders left in Russia when in 1938 it was officially credited with a new and sinister significance as a secret weapon of Hitler's Germany: it was enigmatically alleged in *Pravda* that by combining Marxism with Machism the Austrian Marxists had betrayed the working class and prepared the ground for Hitler's annexation of Austria.[107]

The unqualified success of Lenin's defeat of empiriocriticism cannot be ascribed to mere pusillanimity on the part of its proponents. They were locked in a vicious circle in which defeat was forced on them by the demands of consistency with their own philosophical premises. Unlike their revisionist predecessors, whose Kantian dualism placed the ultimate criterion of truth in the individual consciousness, the empiriocriticists lodged it in the collective; when the latter, in the form of the Bolsheviks, condemned them as bourgeois revisionists, they were trapped in a catch-22 dilemma. The party demanded that they cease to be empiriocriticists; rejecting that demand would mean that they *had* ceased to be empiriocriticists. Valentinov, describing his own crisis of conscience in this respect, likens the plight of the group to that of the Old Bolsheviks condemned at the Moscow trials of 1936–38 for deviation from the party line. Their public self-incrimination, incomprehensible to observers in the West, was not due to torture alone: "There was also something else there, something very complex, which caused them to 'confess,' to regard as 'criminal' their deviation from the 'general line.' "[108]

The empiriocriticist heresy, the controversy that it aroused, and the manner of its defeat together shed considerable light on the psychology of a significant section of the Russian Left before 1917. The new philosophy had been presented as a final answer to the problem that had preoccupied successive generations of the intelligentsia: that of the conflict between its radical voluntarism and its need for absolutes. The empiriocriticists claimed to have performed the miracle of synthesizing Marxism as an "integral worldview" with a defense of the "integral personality." But this "synthesis" of voluntarism with determinism was not the answer to the intelligentsia's dreams of wholeness; its most obvious function, as some of its critics pointed out, was to provide a philosophical justification of the dictatorship of an elite. It was the neatest of historical ironies that the heresy of the Bolshevik theorists produced a ready-made defense of the authoritarianism that finally defeated them.

Brave New Worlds

In the introduction to their book *Utopia in Power,* the exiled Russian historians Aleksandr Nekrich and Mikhail Heller wrote that in the great wars of history, defeat for the losers has always meant more than extermination or slavery. It means that "the conquerors write the history of their wars; the victors take possession of the past, establish their control over the collective memory."[1] In the Soviet utopia, they argued, manipulation of the past in the service of power was carried to a level previously unknown in human history. Following the formulas of Marx, Lenin, and Stalin, history was rewritten in order to deprive citizens of the faculty of memory, a distinguishing characteristic of human beings, and to allow those who controlled the past to do what they wished.

Their book was written in 1982. The dramatic changes that have happened since then owe much to the efforts of Russian historians such as these two to keep the people's memory alive. In a tenacious guerrilla warfare against the official view of the past, they recorded testimonies, fought for the physical preservation of monuments, and sometimes even managed (as Nekrich did with his book on the German invasion of Russia, which appeared in the mid-1960s) to print accounts of the Soviet past which questioned the judgment of the top leaders.

These historians must have found ironic satisfaction in seeing the Soviet press, in its final phase, energetically engaged on the reconstruction of the national memory. Pravda publishing house embarked on an ambitious project to reprint the writings of previously banned Russian thinkers. Bukharin, who challenged Lenin's and Stalin's vision of socialism, was rehabilitated, his works published and discussed. The official version of history as the inevitable and triumphal march to the Soviet utopia was quietly abandoned; with encouragement from above, the Soviet intelligentsia began to discuss paths that had not been taken but might still be open. Some looked back to the unrealized, alternative utopias of almost-forgotten thinkers as beacons of hope in the surrounding confusion. Even skeptics were drawn into the search to find pointers to the future by resurrecting the past; there was a general sense that new ideas and movements had a better chance of succeeding if they were rooted in the national experience.

At the same time the changes in Russia were stimulating new debate among historians in the West on what might have been or might yet be. Stephen Cohen's book of 1985, *Rethinking the Soviet Experience: Politics and History since 1917*, was followed by a number of studies suggesting that the outcome of the Russian Revolution was by no means as predetermined as had been believed, that there were other strands in Russian radical thought, and in the Bolshevik Party itself, which might have led to a more humanist form of socialism. This revision of Soviet history aroused much interest among Russian intellectuals in the Gorbachev period (Cohen's book on Bukharin was published in Russian translation in Moscow in 1988). But Russians concerned with a balanced reconstruction of the Soviet past will be poorly served by some of the studies that have followed that work, which are less concerned with rehabilitation than with idealization. History presented from the losers' point of view is scarcely more reliable than the official versions, and a sentimental view of Russia's alternative utopias is a sign of yet another return to the rewriting of the Russian past as myth.

Both the seductiveness and the moral dubiousness of this path are well illustrated by two studies of alternative Russian utopias—Richard Stites's book on utopian visions and experiments in the Soviet state of the 1920s and Zenovia Sochor's work on Aleksandr Bogdanov.[2]

According to Stites the utopian vision—"a surging altruism accompanied by towering confidence and free-flowing social fantasy—was the best thing that nineteenth century Russian intellectual and cultural history bequeathed to the twentieth century, and not the disaster that some critics have called it." His book is an account of the social and cultural experiments that took place during the immediate postrevolutionary period, when, as one observer put it, "all aspects of existence . . . were opened to purposeful fashioning by human hands. . . . Everywhere the driving passion was to create something new, to effect a total difference with the 'old world' and its civilization. . . . The storm passed nobody by: neither those who hailed it as a blessing nor those who spurned it as a curse."[3]

Such was the extraordinary atmosphere of Russia between 1917 and 1928, when extravagant hopes flourished against a background of civil war, economic breakdown, rural backwardness, and social misery, and people in government or in sympathy with it attempted to fashion a human type previously unknown to history. The Bolshevik Revolution was the first in modern times to attempt a fundamental reordering of all aspects of social life. Stites argues that, until Stalinism, the utopian propensity of Russian society fused with the Bolshevik programs to modernize Soviet life and to bring about social justice, and that this fusion added emotional force to the efforts to build an earthly paradise. His book discusses specific experiments in "culture building": attempts to create a new aesthetic by revolutionary artists such as the Futurists; new values, as in the efforts to replace bourgeois and peasant morality with a more proletarian and egalitarian one; new rituals designed to supplant the Orthodox Church, like the cult of Lenin in the 1920s; and new patterns of personal and social behavior, inspired by a revolt against deference and the urge for social leveling. He presents a brief survey of visions of the ideal society expressed in architecture and in social theories and experiments in collective living by proponents of the "Urbanist" school, such as L. M. Sabsovich, who envisaged "industrial-agrarian cities" formed from complexes of communal buildings, and by the "Disurbanists," such as Mikhail Okhitovich, who advocated the dissolution of cities altogether. Stites also evokes the fictional fantasies of ideal communities of the future by novelists and popular science-fiction writers such as Yakov Okunev and V. D. Nikolsky, now mostly forgotten.

We are left in no doubt concerning the range and inventiveness of the millenarian fantasies circulating after the Bolsheviks came to power; but Stites tries also to convince the reader of the positive moral force of these fantasies. He argues that the utopian experiments of the 1920s gave the Revolution its "human dimension," a sense of justice and dignity that was swept away when Stalin declared his war on utopias. Although he admits that Stalinism was itself a utopia (in the sense that it was based on a myth of well-being and a cult of the benevolent ruler), he believes that its bureaucratic authoritarianism distinguished it from even the least libertarian of the social visions of the 1920s. This view, however, is not supported by the evidence in his book.

There seem to have been remarkably few libertarian visions of the ideal society in the Soviet Union during the decade after 1917. A number of anti-Bolshevik (mostly anarchist) attempts to establish communal societies were snuffed out soon after the Revolution. The most significant of these was the commune of sailors on the naval base of Kronstadt. Between 1917 and 1921 they formed a virtually independent community whose methods of decision making were inspired by the traditional Russian village assemblies. Their attacks on the Bolshevik "commissarocracy" and their demands for democratic control by the workers led to their bloody repression by the Red Army under Trotsky.

The story of the Kronstadt rebellion has been well documented, as have the adventures of the "mobile army" organized in the Ukraine by the anarchist leader Nestor Makhno. But it would be interesting to know more about other libertarian models, of which Stites notes only that some were eccentric and bizarre, others serious and practical. Pyotr Kropotkin is the only serious social theorist cited in his book who is also clearly a libertarian. In outlining his ideal of a stateless federation of communes, Kropotkin declined to provide specific details, on the grounds that the needs and aspirations of a future generation could not be predicted or prescribed. Yet he is allotted just two paragraphs. We are, however, given a satisfyingly detailed account of the "conductorless orchestra," known as Persimfans, which flourished throughout the 1920s and whose seventy musicians formed an anarchist utopia in miniature (although they claimed to be inspired by Marxist principles). Their spokesman attacked the "absolutism and dictatorship" of the modern conductor: an orchestra was a community of players, not a vehicle for the ego of one individual. Besides equality of pay, each player enjoyed an equal voice in the choice and interpretation of the repertoire (all performers learned the entire score). They were very popular in the factories and workers' clubs, where they performed tirelessly, and critical response was mainly favorable. Their instrumentalists were of exceptionally high quality; Prokofiev, who played with the orchestra many times, praised their interpretation of his music. Their experiment in collective labor had a number of imitators; by 1928 there were a dozen conductorless orchestras in Russia, and in the same year the movement spread to Europe and the United States. The Leipzig Symphony Orchestra gave a number of conductorless concerts, and a short-lived American Symphonic Ensemble was founded on the principles of Persimfans (which dissolved, under circumstances that are unclear, in 1932).[4]

With such exceptions, hostility to the spirit of anarchism and to the unruly, unregimented, and unpredictable elements of life seems the single most important factor uniting the diverse cultural experiments of the period. The visions of a new world that dominated Russia in the 1920s were for the most part founded on a cult of reason and of the virtues of urban life, technology, and the machine. They were variations of the view of the socialist future described by Lenin in *State and Revolution* (itself an adaptation of Marx's utopia to Russian conditions). In such a future a system of rational harmony would replace the conflict of egos; there would be communal sharing of resources in work and life, and technology would triumph over nature. The machine was perceived by writers, artists, and ideologists as the creator of modernity and happiness, the instrument of the victory of social justice over greed and hunger. Celebration of the magic of the machine reached its heights in the Soviet infatuation with "Taylorism," the time-and-motion theories of Frederick Winslow Taylor, one of the first prophets of "scientific management," who had gained fame in the United States in 1899 when he taught a Dutchman to shovel forty-seven instead of twelve and a half tons of pig iron a day.

Some of the small communes set up in the early 1920s to exemplify the communist ideal were Taylorist in inspiration, designed to regulate every aspect of life through strict timetables that permitted no private time or space. Stites points out that these experiments in living were intended to get rid of passivity, sloth, and indiscipline, which were the source of much of the traditional misery of Russian life. He takes an equally favorable view of the technological utopias of popular science fiction of the 1920s. But he mentions only obliquely that one prerevolutionary dystopia, by an obscure author, had already opposed this optimism with a nightmare vision of societies of conformity and repression founded on a cult of machine technology.

One of the most prominent of the cultist writers of the 1920s was Aleksei Gastev, who also ran an experimental laboratory of human robotry until 1938. Gastev usually is given no more than a footnote in any history of Soviet literature, but Stites believes that he represents a convergence, common in the 1920s, between the revolutionary pragmatism of the Bolsheviks and the utopianism of the Russian artistic avant-garde. The Futurist and Constructivist movements identified with the Bolshevik Revolution, seeing it as a continuation of their own revolution in literature and painting. Although much influenced by European Modernist currents, they were specifically Russian in their conceptions of social conscience, and even Leninist in the political discourse in which they framed their ideas; they saw art as ancillary to industry in the task of creating the new socialist society.

The fervor of the Constructivists and other allied artistic movements was initially welcomed by the state; for the first time in modern history artists and writers were invited to help fashion a new society in alliance with the reigning political power. New art schools were established, staffed by avant-garde artists, and theories and manifestos proliferated: the Left Front, formed by the Futurists, including Vladimir Mayakovsky and the artist Aleksandr Rodchenko, declared its intention to "re-examine the theory and practice of so-called 'Left' art, freeing it from individualist distortions, and developing its valuable Communist aspects." Constructivism, or "production art," which grew out of the experiments of the painter Vladimir Tatlin, declared war on "pure art" as a form of escapism for which there was no place in a socialist society, rejecting easel painting in favor of the technical mastery of the properties of "real materials in real space."[5]

Taking to the streets, the squares, and the countryside, artists and writers set out to satisfy the "social demand" (a term launched by the leftist intelligentsia and later used by the party to crush them). In a frenzy of activity they designed agitational posters, composed revolutionary poetry and slogans, and decorated cities for the festivals that celebrated the new order. Gifted artists such as Liubov Popova strove to reach the masses by constructing sets and scenery for the theater and applied their ideas in textiles, porcelain, and dress design as well.

Attempting to embody his own ideal of the "artist-engineer," Tatlin turned to the design of workers' clothes, a wood-fueled stove, and plans for the Tower of the Third International, an information and community center twice the height of the Empire State Building and capable of being rotated. Avant-garde literature, art, architecture, music, dance, theater, and film of the 1920s were all suffused with technological fantasy, exalting functionality, speed, and efficiency. The theater director Vsevolod Meyerhold developed a theory of organized movement, "Biomechanics," as a means of creating the new "high-velocity man."[6]

Unfortunately, though much exciting art and design emerged from those years, idealism was not sufficient to turn these artists into engineers. Like the glider on which he worked for many years, Tatlin's tower was no more than a potent symbol of his faith in a future in which human creativity and machine technology would form one harmonious whole.

Clearly, though, because of their visionary energy and self-appointed role as propagandists, Russian avant-garde artists helped to stimulate and guide the utopian imagination of the mass of Soviet society; but the images, ideas, and personalities of their leading representatives are mentioned only briefly in Stites's book. Although he remarks that the Russian avant-garde has been treated extensively by scholars in recent years, he fails to note that many of those studies have reached conclusions on the relationship between political power and the artistic avant-garde sharply at variance with the harmonious picture he presents of a "rich interaction between . . . life and art, one imitating the other and each reshaping both." He acknowledges that the early Bolsheviks were sometimes downright hostile to artistic experiment, which they saw as irrelevant to the urgent task of raising the level of literacy and social consciousness; but this, he argues, was understandable: "No one should blame revolutionary leaders for not succumbing to all the rosy appeals of utopia as they faced the gruelling and exacting tasks of state-building." In the resulting sunny picture of the 1920s, the Bolshevik leadership, while more "hesitant and tentative" than the intelligentsia in its attitude to utopian experimentation, was united with them in pursuit of the dream of human liberty.[7]

The view that the political culture of the 1920s was, in the degree of its openness and tolerance, qualitatively different from what followed is no longer widely supported by Western historians; and Stites would not have been able to state it so unequivocally had he been a little more specific about the careers and ultimate fates of some of the writers and artists he mentions in his book. Mayakovsky, leader of the Futurists, is called the "irrepressible bard of the Russian Revolution":[8] there is no reference to his suicide in 1930, which was the result of pressures that began over a decade before with the discovery that his vision of the renewal of humanity differed fundamentally from that of the Bolsheviks.

To most of the Russian avant-garde, 1917 was a part of a universal revolution of the spirit against the old world of fixed and hallowed forms, closed and prejudiced minds. The Russian word *byt* (variously translated as "convention," "daily grind," "established pattern of life") became, in Mayakovsky's poetry, the symbol for the bourgeois values that must be liquidated to make place for the new world. Through their innovation in language and visual imagery, the Russian Modernists sought to transform perception and thereby create a new type of human being and a new social environment. This process of destruction and creation had no predetermined path or final goal; these artists and writers saw the revolutions in art and politics as a voyage into the unknown and infinite sphere of human creative potential. For all their fascination with futurology, utopia for them was not a final destination but (to quote a utopian philosopher of our own age) "an endless process—an endless, proliferating realisation of Freedom."[9]

The Bolsheviks had a contrary view: for them social and economic transformation would be the cause, not the effect, of a revolution in consciousness. Lenin had little to say about the nature of the new Soviet person who would emerge, he believed, only in the distant future; but we can deduce from his writings that the dominant characteristic of such a person would be not dynamic creativity but conformity to a set and final pattern of social existence, historically predetermined and legitimized by science and reason. Stalin's bureaucratic centralism was not a betrayal of Leninist idealism but could be described instead as the set of practices that ultimately proved best suited to Lenin's theory.

The fate of experimental artists and writers under such a system began to be decided in 1920, when Lenin signed a resolution authorizing the establishment of the Soviet successor to the Moscow College of Painting, Sculpture and Architecture as an institution for "the training of artists for the benefit of the national economy." The members of the avant-garde who were eager to serve that goal did not enjoy the party's favor for very long. They were soon challenged by a number of organizations of writers and artists who, calling themselves "proletarian," exalted the new collectivist ideal of the personality in artistic forms that were modeled on the realism of the past and were thought to be easily accessible to the newly literate. Few of these writers and artists are known today in the West. They formed the powerful Russian Association of Proletarian Writers (RAPP) and, with the increasing support of the party, accused the avant-garde of bourgeois individualism and decadent modernism.

Mayakovsky, the most flamboyant and vociferous of the modernists, came increasingly to suspect that technological progress and spiritual revolution were two different, and not necessarily connected, things. His play *The Bedbug,* written in 1928, satirized a future Soviet society built on machine technology. But there was no way out for him, as is clear from his contempt for the irrational, unreconstructed human being of his own day who, in the play, survives into the twenty-first century in a frozen state.

Mayakovsky's fate provides a very different perspective on the faith in the fusion of man and machine, of the artist and the social collective, that is often seen as the main source of creative inspiration in the Russia of the 1920s. This faith led Mayakovsky to exalt a collectivist society in whose future perfection he had little belief, and whose conformist mediocrity in the present he despised. As Trotsky commented in a perceptive essay, the real hero of Mayakovsky's revolutionary epics is himself: even the "hundred and fifty million" (the title of one of his poems) assume the personality of the poet.[10] Increasingly hounded by RAPP for not fulfilling the "social demand"—his own definition of the primary function of a writer—he finally capitulated by joining it. Two months later he shot himself; his suicide note contained the line "Love's boat has smashed against byt."

As Trotsky put it, Mayakovsky's poetry flowed enthusiastically into the Revolution but did not merge with it. None of the other major artists and writers of the avant-garde achieved such a fusion; but many lived in hopes of it, repudiating their own gifts in theory if not always in practice. Without conscious irony Liubov Popova cites, as an inspirational example for the revolutionary artist, Tolstoy's "brilliant discrediting" of art after his religious conversion. If, as was held in radical circles, every living organism is governed by the principle of expediency, "then why the hell should the most . . . uncertain of all subjective judgments—the notorious *aesthetic* judgment—be able to serve as a *criterion?*"[11]

Of the three major avant-garde movements that flowed into the Revolution only one refused on principle to merge with it. That was Suprematism, which as both a Russian and a European movement was at least as important as Constructivism and Futurism, producing painters of the quality of Kazimir Malevich and El Lissitsky (whose works represent a combination of Suprematist and Constructivist ideas). Vassily Kandinsky was also closely associated with the movement before his emigration in 1922. Radical and visionary, it had a pervasive influence on the design and architecture of the 1920s. (Inexplicably, Stites does not mention this movement.)

Suprematism was founded by Malevich around 1913. The first systematic school of abstract painting in modern art, it attempted, through the geometric simplification of forms, to create self-referential harmonies devoid of associative meaning. Malevich's painting possesses a mystical element, which he described as a "sensation of infinity." Like other Modernists, he sought to create a new language that would enable humans to discover "things still outside of cognition," allowing art for the first time in history not merely to represent the existing world but to take part in the construction of a new one. His weightless primary forms float in a space that is not determined by the laws of gravity, expressing what he described as humanity's yearning "to break free from the globe of the earth."[12] In 1920 he published a pamphlet on the possibility of interplanetary flight and of mastery of the cosmos through satellites and space stations.

Malevich taught in the art schools founded in Vitebsk, Leningrad, and Moscow after the Revolution to work out a theoretical approach to art in a socialist society. There he began to investigate the possibilities for a Suprematist architecture in a series of idealized sketches, while his followers applied his ideas in the design of a variety of objects (including teapots). But unlike the Constructivists he emphasized the spiritual, as opposed to the utilitarian, function of art, insisting that if artists saw themselves merely as craftspeople fulfilling a social demand, they would cease to create the ideal forms from which new design would emerge.

This led to a break with Tatlin and his Constructivist followers in 1921 over the question of the social function of art. This event has been seen as having historic significance for Russian art. It was historic in another sense as well, however, as the first open confrontation in the new state between utopia as "an endless, proliferating realization of freedom" and the systems of control erected by utopia in power.

Malevich argued his case at length in an article published in 1928. There should be a place for both Constructivism and Suprematism in Soviet culture; but their goals should not be confused. Utilitarian functions were historically relative, whereas the value of artistic form was constant and invariable:

> The influence of economic, political, religious, utilitarian phe-
> nomena on art is the disease of art. . . . Our contemporaries
> must understand *that life will not be the content of art, but
> rather that art must become the content of life, since only thus
> can life be beautiful.*
>   . . . Not one engineer, military leader, economist or politician
> has ever managed to achieve in his own field a *constant, beauti-
> ful, forming element such as that achieved by the artist.*[13]

Malevich was notorious for the impenetrability of his theoretical writing, but this defense of the independence of art could not have been more clearly put. In the historical circumstances in which he wrote, its forthrightness represents an act of great courage. His polemic with Tatlin had earned him the wrath of the proletarian and realist artists and writers. In 1926 the institute he directed was accused of "counterrevolutionary propaganda" in the Soviet press and was closed shortly afterward. In 1929 he had his last public exhibition, the catalogue for which stressed the alienation of his art from current ideology. In much of his work in the late 1920s he returned to figurative art, but this was no concession to the "social demand" for inspirational icons to mobilize the masses. In his "peasant series," painted at the time of the death and deportation of millions of kulaks, figures with featureless faces stand with chilling monumentality against a landscape composed of stark strips of primary colors.

Malevich's vision had none of the otherworldliness of traditional aesthetic idealism. He believed that the proper understanding of art as an end in itself would lead not to philosophical or religious escapism but to a revolutionary transformation of human societies far beyond what politics alone was capable of doing. He insisted on the global significance of the change to nonobjectivity in art. It had reversed a process of thousands of years in which art had been tied to the representation of visible reality. In their rejection of representation, the new movements in art had freed the imagination from its historical clutter and opened the way for a renewal of life through artistic form. "In the art of Suprematism . . . each form is free and individual. Each form is a world." In 1915 he declared: "Objects have vanished like smoke."[14] A new artistic culture was emerging in which the principle of creation as an end in itself would lead to domination over nature.

The Modernist vision of the relation of art to society is summed up in a phrase from Malevich's manifesto of 1919, *On New Systems in Art:* "Art must grow together with the stem of the organism, . . . to lend it form, to take part in its purpose and function."[15] Malevich believed that by seeking to serve rather than to shape the aspirations of a historical class and state, the Russian avant-garde had turned its back on the most significant discovery in the history of art. His ideal of a dynamic world where art has transformed human perception, freeing it from subservience to authority and routine, is far more abstract and unattainable than the machine utopias that many other Modernists settled for. And yet, as he observed with satisfaction, both before and after 1917 the guardians of the status quo saw his dream as a serious threat. He ironically records the horror of the Russian artistic establishment when faced by his famous *Black Square:* "In my desperate attempt to free art from the ballast of the objective world, I fled to the form of the square. . . . The critics moaned and with them the public. 'Everything we have loved, we have lost; . . . before us stands a black square on a white ground.' " Malevich was parodying the outraged reaction of such critics as the artist Aleksandr Benois, who had led the attack on Suprematism: *"Black Square on a White Background* is not just a joke, not a simple challenge, not a small chance episode.... It is an act of self-affirmation—of the principle of vile desolation. Through its aloofness, arrogance, and desecration of all that is beloved and cherished, it flaunts its desire to lead everything to *destruction*."[16]

In the eyes of the Modernists on the eve of the Revolution, Benois was a man of the past. They were mistaken. In the 1920s, despite the protests of the "proletarian" writers and the avant-garde, the party gave encouragement to many "fellow travelers" (as Trotsky labeled them), artists and writers in the prerevolutionary realist tradition who sympathized in general with the aims of the communist leaders, who in turn saw their style as a model for an art and literature that could be harnessed to propaganda tasks. Benois was one of several such artists popular during that decade.

But Malevich's art was useless as an instrument of propaganda; worse still, its effect on the imagination could not be predicted, channeled, or contained. Malevich's painting, described by the critic Nikolai Punin as "a rocket sent by the human spirit into nonexistence," is an eternal protest against the entropy of utopia in power. To those artists who yearned to be workers in the idealized universal factory of the "machine utopia," he retorted: "Is not my brain the foundry from which the new transfigured world of iron flows, and from which lives, which we call *inventions*, take wing?"[17]

There were many other dissidents among the dreamers of the 1920s, people whose utopia of freedom could not be reconciled with utopia in power. One of these was the poet Osip Mandelstam. He greeted the Revolution as a cosmic event; but, unlike Mayakovsky's thundering oratory, his poetry of the 1920s expresses the silences of those whose voices (as he writes in his famous poem against Stalin) could not be heard more than ten paces away. It is rich in veiled allusions to the Revolution's brutality and corruption and to his fears for the survival of poetry's "sacred, senseless word in the Soviet night." He died in a transit concentration camp in 1938, but (as his widow notes in her memoirs) Soviet journals, with remarkable unanimity, refused to print his poetry as early as 1922. The poems in praise of Stalin that he wrote in exile in the mid-1930s have been seen as a last attempt to find an authentic voice for the poet as prophet of the national destiny. If so, it was a hopeless effort: his was the kind of vision which, as Joseph Brodsky put it, "casts doubt on more than a concrete political system: it questions the entire existential order."[18]

Although it was Stalin who declared all-out war on the dreamers after 1928, the ostracism and petty persecution of many of them started much earlier, as the zealots in the party and in the writers' and artists' unions began to identify those who would never conform. Sometimes such people became rebels against their will. The painter Pavel Filonov tried hard to turn himself into a so-called proletarian artist but could not suppress his powerful vision of human alienation in the claustrophobic chaos of the modern city. An exhibition of his paintings was not permitted to open in 1929, though he had begun to be persecuted as early as the mid-1920s, when his intricate and hypnotic canvases were denounced for their "bourgeois pessimism" by the dominant realist school.

Only one of the dissident voices who discerned the shape of things to come appears in Stites's book, in a reference to Yevgeny Zamiatin's famous futurological satire *We*. In it, a monstrous United State, whose citizens are known as Numbers, is represented as a satire on the general tendency of political power to misuse technology. But Zamiatin (who held views close to Malevich's on the power of artistic innovation to transform perception) devoted much of his writing during the 1920s to an analysis of what he saw as the disease of the Soviet system in particular: fear of the power of the heretical word. Arguing that a truly revolutionary writer should disturb rather than reassure, he deplored the eagerness of Soviet artists to take on the functions of journalists and propagandists, embracing such topics as the introduction of tractors into the countryside or the improvement of sanitation in the cities: "I find it hard to imagine a work of Tolstoy based on the question of sanitary improvements."[19] Zamiatin perceived that the intelligentsia of the 1920s was not collaborating with the state in building a dream but colluding with it in creating a myth of unanimity that could end in nightmare. Nadezhda Mandelstam, writing much later, had no doubt of that generation's moral responsibility for what followed:

> There are now many people who would like to bring back the twenties and recreate the self-imposed unity of those days. Survivors from those times do their best to persuade the younger generation that this was an age in which everything—science, literature, the theatre—flourished as never before, and that if everything had continued to develop on the lines then laid down, we should by now have attained the height of perfection. . . . In other words, they deny responsibility for what happened later. But how can they? It was, after all, these people of the twenties who demolished the old values and invented the formulas which even now come in so handy to justify the unprecedented experiment undertaken by our young State: you can't make an omelette without breaking eggs.
>
> Every new killing was excused on the ground that there would be no more violence, and that no sacrifice was too *great for it.*
>
> Nobody noticed that the end had begun to justify the means, and then, as always, gradually been lost sight of. It was

> the people of the twenties who first began to make a neat dis-
> tinction between the sheep and the goats, between "us" and
> "them," between upholders of the new and those still mindful of
> the basic rules that governed human relationships in the past.
> . . . In reality it was the twenties in which all the foundations
> were laid for our future: the casuistical dialectic, the dismissal
> of older values, the longing for unanimity and self-abasement.[20]

Nadezhda Mandelstam believed that the myth about the 1920s would be shattered once the facts were known. The appeal of myth, however, can be stronger than rational proof.

It is possible to contrast the spirit of the experimentation of the 1920s, carried on in an atmosphere of coexistence, with Stalinism, which abhorred experimentation and tolerated no rivals. But Stalin exploited the utopian enthusiasm of the time to launch his programs of industrialization and collectivization, and huge numbers of Russians willingly cooperated in creating the cult of the leader. The question of the collusion of utopia with power deserves to be explored in any future cultural history of the early Soviet period.

Many utopians of that time tolerated rivals only because they did not have the power to eliminate them. This was the case with Proletkult, a movement founded to create a new proletarian culture through the intensive training of working-class writers in literary "studios." Although it produced some of the most interesting cultural experiments of the age, its most militant members also fought to exclude the nonproletarian intelligentsia (whose experiments tended to be of a higher artistic quality) from cultural life. During the late 1920s the successors of Proletkult tried to enlist the party's authority in enforcing their demand for control over Soviet literature: a nasty case of the kind of collusion that Nadezhda Mandelstam had in mind.

Another example of utopian inventiveness that was less innocent than it seemed was "godbuilding." Formulated before the Revolution by Gorky and Lunacharsky as a means of inspiring a religious sense of community, it deified the collective force of the proletariat. Although condemned by Lenin as a form of philosophical idealism, godbuilding became (thanks to Lunacharsky's position as commissar of enlightenment) an ingredient in the rituals of communist festivals. Stites sees this movement as the expression of a strong subconscious bond between intelligentsia and working class—a common "utopian spirit of hope and humanism," but he notes that these festivals soon lost their spontaneity and became instruments of political manipulation. This is not surprising: there was nothing spontaneous about godbuilding, which was specifically concocted as a manipulative myth by Bolshevik intellectuals when the 1905 revolution failed to realize their expectations. Dismayed at mass desertions from the party, they hit on the idea of inspiring enthusiasm for the cause by inventing (in Lunacharsky's words) "an infinite higher force . . . on which [the individual] can place his hopes."[21]

It would be hard for a student of Russian culture of the 1920s not to see ironies of collusion and collision at every step. The science-fiction writer Gastev is a case in point. A genuine idealist, he found favor with Stalin for his ideas of social engineering, while personally endorsing the Stakhanovite movement, devised to encourage high output by individual shock-workers, as a logical outcome of his system. The dream came to an end in 1938, when he disappeared into a camp. He is now best remembered for having provided some of the inspiration for Zamiatin's *We*, one of the greatest of modern dystopias.

According to the mythological version of the 1920s, the system that destroyed such people was fundamentally hostile to their ideals. In reality, it derived both its claim to legitimacy and the justification for its violence from a belief that the revolutionary leaders of the 1920s, with the willing collaboration of large numbers of the intelligentsia, had unremittingly sought to inculcate in their society: namely, that the aim of progress was to establish a single, correct (because wholly rational) system of social existence and that total identification with the system's collective goals would give meaning and purpose to individual lives.

Nadezhda Mandelstam writes that the need to belong, not to be isolated from the main current of history, was the dominant psychological cause of the moral capitulation of writers and artists to the principle that might equals right. Conflicts between the creative imagination and the desire to serve narrowly defined political goals were central to the Russian art and literature of the 1920s, but only in discussing the gruesome inventions designed to replace the festive rituals of capitalist societies does Stites note that the elements of spontaneity and humor in Bolshevism were dampened by "its need to moralize, congratulate itself, teach, speechify, punish, and organize."[22]

The picture of the intelligentsia that he presents is an extraordinarily attractive one of creative dissonance. Every aspect of the new society became a subject of passionate debate, from architecture to morality and dress. Among the major responses to the last problem were "to dress down, to dress up, to dress equally, and not to dress at all" (the proponents of the last option believing that the only egalitarian apparel was the human skin itself—a point they made in street demonstrations in 1922).[23] But the other side of the picture is missing from the book: the unceasing pressure for conformism, the desire to establish once and for all the right way to build, think, behave, and dress. As the 1920s progressed, these debates were resolved by an implicit consensus among the police (who removed the nudists from the streets), Bolshevik moralists, and the radical intelligentsia, who favored the rejection of all forms of dress and behavior that smacked of "bourgeois individualism" or "hooliganism" in favor of neatness and discipline. The colorful feminism preached by Aleksandra Kollontai was a short-lived phenomenon: full sexual liberation turned out to be an impediment to the task of socialist construction. In the ending of experimentation that marks the prelude to Stalinism, it is difficult to separate the elements of pressure from above and voluntary conformism from below.

Stites claims that Russian utopians en masse believed that people were inhibited only by bad institutions from expressing their natural goodness in a state of brotherhood, whereas Stalin's system held that human beings are wicked, lazy, and stupid and must be controlled by coercion. However, a closer consideration of the record suggests that the difference between the two views corresponds to a difference between utopias in the mind and utopias in power. It may be true, as Stites contends, that the "utopian propensity" is the principal mechanism whereby mankind protects and preserves its most sacred values, but his argument would have been more balanced had he been less reluctant to acknowledge that utopian thinking has also been the source of some of the most horrible crimes of the human race. He finds it depressing that even many liberals in our "self-consciously brutal" age tend to scorn ideals of perfection, universal justice, harmony, and peace. But there is a good reason why liberals should be skeptical of the "warmhearted visions of a lovely land . . . graced by justice and prosperity" that Stites presents in his book.[24] The rationalist utopias of the types he describes embody a concept of freedom that is difficult to reconcile with liberal ideals.

The importance of this distinction between "two concepts of liberty" and their vastly differing political and social implications was stressed in Isaiah Berlin's famous essay of that name.[25] Berlin's argument helps to introduce some much-needed clarity into the discussion of whether any of the utopias conceived in the 1920s might have been a genuinely humanist alternative to the one that became "Utopia in Power."

Berlin outlined the tortuous path by which the Enlightenment's vision of freedom as rational self-direction—the historical root of liberal individualism—became the ideological justification of totalitarian despotism. In attempting to free people from subordination to divine powers, rationalist metaphysics in turn made reason, perceived as the true eternal core of human nature, quasi-divine. The authority of reason was identified with freedom, on the grounds that in conforming to rational necessity the individual was obeying the laws of his or her own nature. This had the effect (as in Kantian ethics) of dividing the personality into two parts. Freedom was seen as self-mastery, the bringing of the "lower" part of the psyche, the passions and desires, into line with the "higher," rational self. According to the socialized version of this ethic (the basis of all rationalist visions of the Golden Age), reason being universal, all valid human values and goals must be ultimately compatible, fitting into a single, harmonious pattern. If all people were sufficiently rational, social conflict would cease. From this premise it is only one step to the argument that in the present imperfect world it may be the duty of the more enlightened to force the less enlightened to be free, by coercing their lower, animal natures into patterns of action consistent with the demands of their higher, rational selves.

Berlin argues that the belief in a single solution to all social problems has no basis in empirical experience, which suggests that conflict is an inalienable feature of the human condition. But it seems that the desire for wholeness and unity is just as fundamental, and Berlin sees this metaphysical need as the source of the unacknowledged tension in much contemporary liberalism between a commitment to pluralism and diversity for its own sake (based on the view that people should be permitted to pursue as many ends as possible with minimal interference, except insofar as they frustrate the needs of others for self-fulfillment), and the belief that societies are moving toward one correct way of life, when all their members will acknowledge the primacy of reason over the passions and will freely choose conformity to widely shared norms in preference to chaotic individualism. But Berlin argues that those who recommend, for whatever reason, that individual liberty be sacrificed to some more desirable goal, such as fraternity or justice, should not deceive themselves into believing that they are thereby defending liberty in some much deeper sense. To say that in some all-reconciling synthesis, duty is self-interest, the authoritarian state enhances freedom, or benign despotism promotes humanism "is to throw a metaphysical blanket over either self-deceit or deliberate hypocrisy."[26]

Berlin contends that many liberals, with the best of intentions, have blinded themselves to irreconcilable differences between their own deeply held values of plurality and tolerance and the values of collectivist democracies whose sense of purpose they admire. In the reassessment of twentieth-century Russian history that has followed the collapse of the Soviet regime, a number of thinkers seem to have profited from such a metaphysical coverup. One of the most notable was Aleksandr Bogdanov.

Bogdanov, a philosopher and economist who was trained as a medical doctor and wrote two utopian novels about collectivist society on Mars, was Lenin's main intellectual rival in the Bolshevik Party. His philosophical ideas (which led to his expulsion from the party in 1910) became the theoretical inspiration of Proletkult. His activities in this organization after the Revolution and the linking of his name with dissident groups aroused Lenin's hostility, causing him to turn increasingly to medical research. He died in 1928, as the result of an experimental blood transfusion he performed on himself. Like Bukharin (another Bolshevik dissident), Bogdanov has been rescued from oblivion by the interest in the different and more desirable paths that Russia might have taken to socialism. Zenovia Sochor's study presents him as the proponent of such a path.

Bogdanov had an impressive record of independent thinking. He joined the Bolsheviks in 1904 because, unlike more orthodox Marxists, Lenin emphasized the role of human will in making history, though he opposed Lenin's view of the party as a vanguard interpreting Marxism for the masses. He was one of the first to predict that a "new class" would appear in the Soviet Union, arguing that the capitalist fetishes denounced by Marx would survive into socialist society and would produce new exploitative relationships unless the economic transformation of society was accompanied by a revolution in human consciousness. His philosophy, known as "empiriomonism," rejected all universal laws and eternal truths, together with all self-appointed interpreters of such truths. He believed that truth corresponded to the experience of the most progressive class (the proletariat) in its revolutionary struggle. He attempted to sketch out an ambitious "organizational science" that would draw on new developments in technology and would replace all hierarchical relationships in the productive process by cooperation, thereby eliminating the fragmentation of knowledge. In the new "proletarian culture," the insights of the sciences and the arts would be systematized into one coherent body of knowledge.

Sochor presents Bogdanov's ideas as a grassroots challenge to authoritarianism and the rule of dogma. But she admits that there is a curious disjunction between his protest against coercive norms and his theories about proletarian culture, according to which individual deviations from the "collective consciousness" would not be tolerated. Nonetheless, she argues that Bogdanov's ideal of cooperation represented a clear alternative to the despotic path chosen by Lenin and Stalin and that the difference would have been even clearer if he had managed to rid himself of the vestiges of authoritarianism that ran counter to most of his thinking.

I believe, on the contrary, that a study of Bogdanov's priorities makes it clear that only by renouncing his democratic leanings could he have been wholly true to his basic ideas. It is not surprising that the godbuilders Gorky and Lunacharsky were among his most enthusiastic fans; his philosophy was based on an extreme version of the rationalist idealization of the human being that is the soul of the Marxist utopia. What principally distinguished him from other Marxist ideologues of the time was the mystical fervor with which he expressed his longing for transcendence and for a new age when the "illusion of the independent ego" would give way to the reality of the omnipotent collective. Knowledge and being would then form a seamless whole, and humanity would achieve its goal: "all-understanding" and "all-mastery." He believed that with a little persuasion from him and other sympathetic intellectuals the proletariat was on the verge of fashioning the new, undivided consciousness which would reject coercive norms and worship no authorities yet wholly identify with the collective in "will, mind, and feelings."[27] He saw no reason why the originality and initiative that he demanded of proletarian art should conflict with this collectivism; when it did, he attributed this to remnants of bourgeois individualism persisting in the psyche. He defended the instincts of the proletariat against the party's attempts to control them, but it was he who defined what those instincts were.

It was Bogdanov, not Lenin, who demanded, some years before the Revolution, that the Bolshevik Party have a single line in philosophy—his own. During the period of the "New Economic Policy," a temporary return to the principle of the free market, Proletkult's millenarian impatience led it to accuse the party of not being authoritarian enough and to object to the tolerance of the so-called fellow travelers in cultural life, on the grounds that the arts were primary instruments in the ideological battle to create a collective psyche. As Proletkult proclaimed in 1920: "Art can organize the feelings in exactly the same way as propaganda organizes thought." The visual art of the new world "will be productional art, or there will be none at all."[28]

The enthusiastic support of Proletkult's successors for Stalin's class war would seem to indicate a natural symbiosis between its collectivism and the party's authoritarianism. What puzzles Sochor is how Bogdanov could reconcile his humanistic vision of social harmony with his "rather chilling" indictment of deviant groups.[29]

She is troubled, it seems clear, because she identifies Bogdanov's ideal of harmony roughly with the liberal principle of mutual tolerance. That she can do so is evidence of the ambiguity in contemporary liberalism noted by Berlin, who detected an unresolved contradiction between the defense of pluralism and the attraction of some liberals to a rationalist utopia in which all ends will coincide.

There seem few empirical grounds for Bogdanov's belief that the human psyche was undergoing a revolutionary transformation in the direction of collectivism in the early years of the twentieth century; the Bolsheviks, most historians now agree, owed their success in 1917 less to proletarian solidarity than to their skill in exploiting the selfish interests of separate groups. Yet Sochor does not question Bogdanov's claim that his collectivist philosophy was no more than a response to the autonomous development of a proletarian culture based on comradely cooperation. She claims there is a fundamental difference between the Stalinist conception of *partiinost* (the view that adherence to the party line established the validity of beliefs and actions) and Bogdanov's collectivism, which she interprets (with some reservations) as a consensus of free spirits, a willingness to explore and tolerate diversity.

She does, however, admit that the very notion of there being one best way to act contains an "authoritarian implication."[30] Unfortunately she does not keep this suggestion in mind when she stresses the differences between Stalin, who controlled culture for the purpose of consolidating power, and Proletkult, whose conception of self-transformation was designed to enhance human dignity rather than submissiveness. Such distinctions prove nothing, except that Bogdanov was less of a realist than Stalin and a nicer man. Some of his disciples, who were not nice men, took his ideas to their logical conclusion and joined the ranks of Stalin's executioners.

Sochor's defense of Bogdanov serves to illustrate Berlin's claim that contemporary liberals are insufficiently aware of the conflict between the urge for transcendence and the liberal values of pluralism and tolerance. She seems to interpret the mood that brought down the communist regimes of Eastern Europe—people's weariness with a controlled society, their desire for democratic discussion, for humanist values—as a demand for such pluralism. And yet, as an answer to those who still have hopes of "socialism with a human face," she proposes the ideas of Bogdanov, whose own face was resolutely turned away from the empirical world of diverse and conflicting purposes and toward the abstract entity that he saw as the only true reality—the omnipotent collective.

Isaiah Berlin reminds us: "Enough manipulation with the definition of man, and freedom can be made to mean whatever the manipulator wishes."[31] Bogdanov and the collectivist utopians of the 1920s were, intentionally or otherwise, engaged in such manipulation. The admiration of some contemporary liberal scholars for this group seems as morally undiscriminating as the wholesale condemnation of the Russian radical intelligentsia by leading liberal academics in the past. The new phenomenon can perhaps be explained by a pervasive yearning in the West for a new spirit of idealism to fill the vacuum left by the collapse of old ideological certainties—liberal as well as radical. Stites condemns the fear and selfish materialism that he sees as the main barrier to the spread of utopian visions in our own age, and cites as an inspiring counterexample Lev Kopelev, an early Communist and one of Stalin's victims, who, while expressing bitter disappointment in the ways the communist vision "degenerated in some men into the fervent desire to serve as executioners," has reaffirmed his faith in the ideals themselves.[32]

I doubt whether the reconstruction of the Russian national memory that began with the fall of communism will produce many new converts to that cause. It has already been argued by post-Soviet Russian scholars that the conflict between Stalin and the avant-garde was fundamentally (in the words of G. Tulchinsky) "a battle over authors' rights to the program for restructuring the world and the human being."[33] Now that the archives have begun to disgorge their evidence of the collaboration of some varieties of idealism with brute force, no historian is justified in rhapsodizing about the innocence of the revolutionary visions of the 1920s without attempting to assess their ultimate cost in ruined human lives. With the failure of the greatest utopian experiment in history, it is time to take a long, cool look at the concept of liberty that underpins the dream of universal harmony. As Nikolai Berdiaev (himself an unreconstructed utopian) remarked in the wake of 1917, utopias have proved much easier to realize than we anticipated; the problem we now face is how to stop their being realized in full.

PART IV

Another Shore

Irony and Utopia in Herzen and Dostoevsky

CHAPTER FIFTEEN

What is a social ideal? . . . Its essence lies in the attempt of human beings to discover a formula of social organization, as faultless as possible, and satisfying everybody. Is this not so? But humans know of no such formula. . . . The ant knows the formula of its anthill; the bee the formula of its beehive. . . . But humans do not know their formula.
—Fyodor Dostoevsky, *A Writer's Diary*

In *A Writer's Diary*, Dostoevsky records that on visiting Aleksandr Herzen in London in 1862, he praised *From the Other Shore*, Herzen's philosophical meditation on the revolutionary defeat of 1848–49, presented mainly as a series of dialogues with an imaginary opponent. What he liked most about the book, Dostoevsky told Herzen, was that "your opponent is also very clever" and that "many a time he has driven you into a corner."[1]

There has been much commentary on the echoes of Herzen's writings in Dostoevsky's work,[2] but only one critic has focused on the resemblance between the dialogical structures of *A Writer's Diary* and *From the Other Shore*. In his illuminating study of the *Diary*, whose structure he believes to have been primarily inspired by Herzen's work, Gary Saul Morson has observed that the two works represent similar dialogues of utopia and antiutopia, faith and doubt—typical of all such encounters in their lack of ultimate resolution.[3] Yet although the works restate a familiar dilemma, they do so in a way that breaks new ground. This becomes clear when we examine their central concern: the dissonances of modern societies.

The point of departure of Herzen's discussion is the disorientation and pessimism of European intellectuals after a revolution that discredited, but did not destroy, the relics of the old European order and at the same time exposed the hollow rhetoric in its opponents' programs. Dostoevsky's analysis of events in the Russia of the 1870s records the dislocation and confusion of a society in process of transition from traditional structures and values toward an unknown destination. Both writers focus on the phenomena of an unprecedented questioning of the beliefs that had previously formed the moral basis of society and of the search to replace them by new formulas for personal relations and social organization. I call these two phenomena "irony" and "utopia" and argue that the dialogues in both works, and their complex mutual relationship, spring from the authors' very different responses to one question: whether it is possible for modern man or woman to be at one and the same time an ironist and a utopian.

Although, as one writer on irony contends, "Every attempt to define irony unambiguously is in itself ironical," I shall still attempt to do so here.[4] As I use it, the term denotes "general" or romantic irony, which may be defined, in the words of René Wellek, as "recognition of the fact that the world in its essence is paradoxical and that an ambivalent attitude alone can grasp its contradictory totality."[5] Romantic irony challenged the metaphysical visions of the world that posit any single, unitary principle, whether Divine Providence or Universal Reason, as the key to the meaning and purpose of all existence, and the source of eternal laws that, once understood and obeyed, will lead humanity to a predestined state of harmony and happiness.

In contrast to such "closed" visions of the world, the open-ended philosophy of the German post-Kantian idealists formulated a new historicist approach to values, ideals, and goals as contingent to time and place in a dynamic universe that is in a constant state of becoming, where paradox and change are normal, and conflict is the moving principle of existence. Idealism and romanticism focused on the inescapable contradiction between free will and determinism, between the longing for the infinite, for absolute perfection, and the limitations of finite existence; the romantic artist explored the existential predicament of the self in an inescapably absurd world. Richard Rorty has pointed to the fundamental differences between the way ironist and metaphysical "vocabularies" describe the self, freedom, and history.[6] The metaphysician sees freedom as the recognition of necessity, the bringing of the individual self into line with universal and eternal laws. The ironist sees the attainment of freedom as the acceptance of contingency, a process not of self-transcendence, but of self-creation, whereby individuals come to terms with their contingency by creating their own values and meaning. Like the romantic artist, the ironist seeks not harmony, but the maximum fullness of experience, always aware of the impossibility of reaching the ideal but constantly generating new possibilities in the attempt.

Irony thus defined is incompatible with the traditional conception of utopia as the attainment of a perfect form of society; the natural affinity of irony would seem to be with the liberal pragmatism that is willing to live with plurality rather than demand harmony and seeks to maximize individual freedom through temporary accommodations rather than a final synthesis of conflicting goals and values. However, the consistent ironist is rarely encountered in reality. German idealism, in particular, was a mixture of ironic negation and utopian affirmation. *From the Other Shore* is a polemic against such incoherence: an attempt, of striking originality, to articulate a consistently ironist view of history, freedom, and the self and to point to the dangers of seeking to ally such a vision with the utopian dream.

In two cycles of essays on Hegel's philosophy that Herzen wrote between 1842 and 1846, he stressed the enormous significance of the revolution in thought represented by the dialectic as interpreted by the German Left Hegelians. Their interpretation of the historical process as perpetual struggle and change, together with Feuerbach's analysis of religious alienation, exposed the absurdity of the faith in absolute truths and transcendent goals which Herzen saw as the principal obstacle to rational self-determination. Although the philosophical premises of a new anthropocentric civilization were thereby established, Herzen warned that the struggle to emancipate consciousness from the metaphysical baggage of the past had merely begun. His first essay commenced by asserting: "We live on the boundary between two worlds. Our former vision of the world has been shaken in its entirety, but remains precious to us. Our new convictions promise to bear strong fruits, but those fruits have not as yet appeared, while the ideas themselves are still foreign to our hearts."[7]

The result was a painful disorientation, which many tried to overcome by seeking somehow to reconcile the new vision with the old. Foremost among them was Hegel himself, who, Herzen believed, had taken fright at the consequences of his own logic, promising the human race a final destiny that was inconsistent with the principles of dialectical negation.

The belief that humanity feared freedom inspired the title of Herzen's reflections on 1848. He claimed that the most radical thinkers of the age, having set sail from the shore of illusion, have recoiled before the vistas of freedom before them and returned to safer waters. They have erected new authorities and absolutes—progress, humanity, the republic—to replace those they had cast down, failing to understand that the time has come to put on trial not only religion and the monarchy but "all our notions about the citizen and his relations to other citizens and to the State."[8] In the essays and dialogues that comprise his book, Herzen set out to give the view from the "other shore"—to show how history, morality, and the human psyche look when stripped of the belief in transcendent authorities and final solutions.

Each dialogue is a confrontation between what one may call a metaphysician, and an ironist, who is the vehicle for Herzen's own views. The metaphysician ascribes the defeat of attempts at revolution to the failure of the masses to heed their "inner voice" and follow the path prescribed to them by reason. His opponent finds it curious that those who dismiss notions of Divine Providence should believe in the existence of a "universal, hereditary, transcendental reason" that has programmed humanity for future bliss: "Could you please explain to me why belief in God is ridiculous and belief in humanity is not; why belief in the kingdom of heaven is silly, but belief in utopias on earth is clever?" If one looked at history without moralistic preconceptions, one perceived progress, in the sense of the increasing sum and extent of ideas, improvement in some capacities of the brain at the expense of others, but no single rational line of development. History resembled nature more than was generally believed: it aborted and improvised; physiological contingency continually triumphed over rational intention. The masses, far from the noble savages of radical mythology, were moved by "dark instincts, incalculable passions," which defied prediction or rational explanation. Empirical evidence did not support the postulate of an a priori rational human nature. In all ages, only a tiny minority had craved independence, whereas the majority had yielded to the power of heredity and circumstance; ideals were therefore always realized in a form different from what their creators intended. One should not demand from people and history more than they could give but rather attempt to understand the limits of the possible.

The metaphysician protests that if our ideals are not to be realized even in the future, then it is scarcely worth the effort to fight for them in the present. Shakespeare puts it well: history is "a tale told by an idiot, signifying nothing." The ironist is accused by his (in this case) female opponent of Olympian detachment from the struggles of his time, which leaves him one option: "sterile criticism and idleness to the end of your days." She would rather believe that the masses had reneged on their destiny than concede to the ironist's defense of them.[9] Dostoevsky admired Herzen for mounting against himself this moral argument for utopian hope as the necessary stimulus to social altruism and struggle for progress. Many later commentators have been unimpressed by Herzen's counterargument: if there were a "libretto" to history, we would be deprived of moral freedom and turned into "wheels in a machine."[10] *From the Other Shore* has been seen as a manifesto of anarchic egoism based on a vision of a meaningless universe, its mood characterized as a "thorough pessimism," or an early expression of existentialist angst about spiritual loneliness. It has been argued that Herzen, tormented by the bleakness of his own skepticism, shows himself in this work to be torn between the positions of his two protagonists, identifying alternately with one or the other.[11]

The latter view is not borne out by the text, where the choice is set out between acceptance of the facts of history and human nature, a worldview with which Herzen (however painfully) identifies, and the dubious consolations of self-delusion. Moreover, the view that this is a pessimistic, even nihilistic work, is, I believe, based on a misreading of Herzen's main argument. He does not deny meaning and purpose in human existence but rather claims that people have habitually looked for them in the wrong place: in the future or the next world, and not in the present. Instead of seeking to escape from contingency, we should accept it as the source of our freedom and creativity. To do this we must change the way we speak. The moral and political vocabulary of modern Europeans is permeated with the religious and idealist dualism that conceives of abstract principles as authorities independent of and superior to real individuals. In our images, our metaphors, "idealism sides with one shadow against another, granting spirit the monopoly over matter, species the monopoly over the particular, sacrificing man to the state, the state to humanity." The categories in which we are taught to see the world are a chaotic mix, all too often at odds with experience: "The prejudices of the Roman world alongside the prejudices of the Middle Ages, the Gospel and political economy, Loyola and Voltaire, idealism in theory and materialism in practice, an abstract rhetorical morality and behavior directly opposed to it." The time has come to submit our moral vocabulary to rigorous scrutiny and to make even more "terrible sacrifices" than the revolutionaries were prepared to make—namely, to abandon the charms and security of dependence on powers outside ourselves.[12]

Richard Rorty has argued that the revolution in thought that began at the end of the eighteenth century was inspired by "a dim sense that human beings whose language changed so that they no longer spoke of themselves as responsible to nonhuman powers would thereby become a new kind of human beings."[13] This idea, no longer dim, forms the main argument of *From the Other Shore*, which is best understood not as a dialogue between belief and skepticism but, rather, as the opposition of two vocabularies, two incompatible ways of describing the self, morality, and history.

Herzen stresses the distance separating the new vocabulary from the old: its users "do not use the same logic; their brains are different." In his approach to history the idealist is "misled by categories not fitted to catch the flow of life." Reason looks for ends, but the final end of everything living is death. To the *memento mori* of the idealist, Nature opposes her *memento vivere*, pouring all of herself into the present with an "unbridled creative passion," the profligacy of her "poetic fantasy" unrestrained by the transience of all finite being. Such an aesthetic concern with the plenitude of being Herzen proposes as a model for historical thinking; he finds it "comforting" that one's ideals cannot be guaranteed to survive into the future—proof that "every historical phase has its complete reality, its own individuality," that "each is an aim achieved, not a means." Norms for personal and social morality change "with circumstances, like everything living. . . . What was admirable behavior yesterday may be abominable today." Unprogrammed by rationalist determinism, the individual is free to *"create"* his or her own morality. If one's ideals are out of step with one's time, this is no cause for despair—by striking some chord in a few, they may become an ingredient of the future. If not, no matter: "We do not live to entertain others, we live for ourselves."

If only people wanted to save themselves instead of saving the world, Herzen observes, "to liberate themselves instead of liberating humanity, how much they would do for the salvation of the world and the liberation of humanity!" By labeling altruism a virtue and egoism a vice, the radicals have set up an artificial opposition, whereas "the real point is not to fulminate against egoism and extol brotherhood . . . but to unite freely and harmoniously these two ineradicable elements of human life."[14]

Unlike the contemporary Left, Herzen viewed the creative individual and society as irreconcilably at odds while at the same time essential to each other's existence. As he put it in a subsequent essay: "These kinds of antinomies . . . are insoluble because in effect their resolution would be the indifference of death, whereas life exists only in *movement*."[15] In *From the Other Shore*, Herzen engages with the concept of utopia through the dialogue of irony. I believe that much of the confusion over the interpretation of this work is owed to the mistaken view that Herzen's irony is a feature of his style rather than the basis of his vision of the world. The confusion has been increased by attempts to explain his position with the help of parallels with Nietzsche and Kierkegaard, neither of whom was an ironist in the sense defined here.[16] Much more light can be shed on Herzen's view of the personality by comparison with Schiller, a thinker whose philosophical writings on freedom he ardently admired.[17]

Herzen referred on several occasions to Schiller's famous polemic with Kant, in which he argued that, by demanding the subordination of the individual's sensual drives to the universal imperatives of reason, Kant gave virtue the appearance of subjection to a transcendent authority. In his treatise *On the Aesthetic Education of Man*, Schiller proposed a model of moral freedom as achieved through a form of aesthetic "play," which, by reconciling the perceptions of sense with the insights of reason, releases the individual from the compulsions of both instinct and rigid principle, enabling him to respond to moral challenges as an integrated personality. Schiller feared that those who saw the task of morality as the subordination of affective drives to reason would incline to a vision of the state (perceived as the "ideal being") achieving order through the regimentation of empirical individuals. He was an early proponent of the classical liberal ideal of the minimum of state power necessary to guarantee the maximum development of the talents and aspirations of the citizens. His humanism prefigured the dialectic of the Left Hegelians but also showed a prescient awareness of the threat to individual freedom posed by all doctrines that hypostatized human reason.

Herzen greeted Schiller's treatise as "a great and prophetic work."[18] There seems little doubt that it alerted him to the despotic implications of the new "religion of reason," and his vision of freedom in *From the Other Shore* is remarkably close to Schiller's. For centuries, his ironist argues, human beings have been urged to fear what is natural and to yearn for "some unattainable bliss"; in contrast, he wanted to "reconcile people with themselves," to encourage them to seek the maximum of self-realization consistent with the limitations of their empirical natures and of the historical time at which they lived. For this to happen, Herzen believed that a change was necessary not only in the ideals but also in the mode of perception of modern human beings. As he had put it in one of his essays on Hegel's philosophy: "Thought must take on flesh, descend into the marketplace of life, unfold in all the splendor and beauty of transient existence."[19] In *From the Other Shore* the future-directed perception of the metaphysician is contrasted with a present-oriented perception focused on the dynamism of process, which, as in Schiller's ideal type, unites a sense of form with an aesthetic delight in the multiplicity of contingent existence and the richness of creative fantasy. The concept of aesthetic "play" appears at key places in the work to denote the fundamental opposition between the protagonists. The metaphysician protests that if our goals are not destined to be realized, "Why . . . do they come into our heads at all? It's a sort of irony." If history has no purpose, "The life of peoples becomes mere idle play." Herzen's alter ego mocks his indignation: "What you want is that the world should, out of gratitude for your devotion, dance to your tune, and, as soon as you realize that it has its own step and rhythm, you feel angry; you're cross, you despair. You haven't enough curiosity to watch it doing its own dance."

His opponent finds this "poetic curiosity" morally repugnant at a time of historical catastrophe; he is told that such reversals of human hopes are part of "the eternal play of life . . . the *perpetuum mobile* of the pendulum."

In the introduction to the work, Herzen advises the reader: "Do not look for solutions in this book—there are none." The contradictions that offend his imaginary interlocutors are a permanent feature of human existence; but by grasping their dialectical "play" one can seek to devise social forms that will accommodate humanity's competing needs and drives in a way best suited to one's particular time and place. Herzen's belief was that in his time such a balance could be best achieved through an anarchist federation of communes; but (aware that his hopes for Russia in this respect made him, too, vulnerable to the charge of utopianism), the mature Herzen would stress that no social ideal should be regarded as final, no progress as inevitable. Of socialism itself, he predicts in *From the Other Shore:* "[It] will develop in all its phases until it reaches its own extremes and absurdities. Then once again a cry of denial will break from the titanic chest of the revolutionary minority, and again a mortal struggle will begin, in which socialism will play the role of contemporary conservatism and will be overwhelmed in the subsequent revolution, as yet unknown to us."[20]

In its affirmation of an ideal whose transience and imperfection are simultaneously stressed, this passage perfectly expresses that "incessant and self-creating alternation of two contradictory thoughts," the "marvelous and eternal alternation of enthusiasm and irony," which Friedrich Schlegel saw as the characteristic of the true romantic ironist.[21]

D. C. Muecke has noted a tendency among literary critics and social commentators to equate irony as a social attitude with a subjectivism that validates and invalidates at pleasure, a disease of the spirit leading fatally to a pessimistic nihilism or cynical detachment. Yet, he argues, such attitudes fail to achieve the unresolvable tension, the detached involvement of true irony:

> Romantic irony is not negative; it does not, for example, negate subjectivity by objectivity, the imaginative by the critical, the emotional by the rational. Nor does it steer a middle course between them. . . . The Romantic Ironist will be consciously subjective, enthusiastically rational, and critically emotional. . . . Caught between his aspirations for an ideal he knows is beyond his reach, and his limitations of which he is equally aware, the only possibility for the ironist is a continual dialectic process of ironic affirmations and negations.[22]

This passage perfectly encapsulates the argument of *From the Other Shore.* Herzen was not a nihilist, an idealist, or a hesitant inhabitant of some middle ground. Among his contemporaries, only Dostoevsky seems to have seized on the essential characteristic of his thought: "Self-reflection—the ability to make an object of one's deepest feeling, to set it before oneself, to bow down to it, and perhaps immediately after, to ridicule it—was developed in [Herzen] to the highest degree."[23]

This comment from the first chapter of *A Writer's Diary* was not intended as a tribute: Dostoevsky here constructs an image of Herzen that recurs throughout the work as the symbol of a national moral sickness that can only be cured by faith in Russia's religious mission. The *Diary* has been seen as the conclusion of a dialogue with Herzen that began with *Winter Notes on Summer*

Impressions.[24] The product of Dostoevsky's European travels of the previous year (during which he visited Herzen in London), the *Winter Notes* were strongly influenced by Herzen's critique of Western bourgeois culture.[25] But as Dostoevsky's opposition to socialism increased, his attitude to Herzen became more negative. It has been argued that although Herzen is omnipresent in the *Diary*, he figures exclusively as a representative of ideas against which Dostoevsky wishes to warn his readers, that he imitates Herzen's style (in particular paradox and the dialogical form) in order to refute his ideas more forcefully.[26] But although irony was indeed used to this end in the *Diary*, at a deeper level his engagement with Herzen's vision reflects the struggle of the ironist with the utopian in Dostoevsky himself.

Notes from Underground echoes Herzen's arguments against the view that the human race is predestined by the laws of its rational nature ultimately to arrive at a final perfect social organization.[27] As the Underground Man remarks, any assertion about history, however fantastic, can be defended: "There's only one thing you can't say—that it is rational." He challenges the belief that it is in humanity's interest to become more rational, pointing to the irresolvable conflict between the irrational desire for freedom and all universalist and deterministic prescriptions for happiness and social harmony.

Two central themes of *From the Other Shore* appear in this work. First, the paradoxalist questions the notion of a final purpose in history. The empirical evidence suggests that human beings are not programmed to construct "one marvelous building, eternal and indestructible"—a human version of the ant heap. He muses: "[Man] likes only the process of creation, and not the end itself. And who knows . . . perhaps the whole goal on earth, toward which mankind is striving, consists only in that uninterrupted process of attainment, in other words, in life itself, and not in its aim which, naturally, must be none other than two times two is four, that is—a formula; but two times two is not life, gentlemen, but the principle of death."

Second, like Herzen's ironist, the Underground Man attributes the metaphysical yearnings of contemporary intellectuals to a cultural distortion of the psyche. "We have all become unused to life, . . . we sometimes feel a sort of revulsion against real 'living reality' . . . [and] secretly agree that it's better in books. . . . When we are left to our own devices, without our books, at once we get muddled and confused; we don't know what . . . to love and what to hate, what to respect and what to despise."[28]

Like Herzen's ironist, the Underground Man views liberty as a continual process of self-creation based on the acceptance of contingency, seeking to "invent" his life rather than discover its laws, to escape, through denial and paradox, the finality of definition.

But unlike Herzen, Dostoevsky had no faith in the ability of human beings to create their own morality without appeal to a power outside themselves; his misshapen hero believes that the answer to his urge for freedom lies not in the Underground but in "something else, quite different."[29]

In *A Writer's Diary*, Dostoevsky set out to formulate that transcendent ideal which he believed could alone resolve the dissonances of the modern personality. From Herzen's perspective, the kind of religious utopia that Dostoevsky would ultimately construct was a classic product of that fear of freedom which had led even the boldest of contemporary thinkers to seek new absolutes to replace those they had cast down. The Underground Man had predicted that modern human beings so longed to escape from the torments of their physical existence that they would one day devise a way to be born from an idea.[30] According to Dostoevsky's subsequent religious schema of history, humankind was already in this happy state. He argued that the nations of Europe embodied three "ideas"—the Catholic, the socialist, and the Orthodox. Only Russian Orthodoxy had preserved the divine image of Christ, the true foundation of morality and order; Western Christianity's alliance with material power had generated its antithesis, socialism, which preached a false and divisive freedom based on egoistic rationalism. Throughout the 1870s the *Diary* interpreted the growth of the socialist threat to the established order in Europe, the intensification of conflict between states, and the confrontation between Europe and Russia over the Balkan question as signs that the struggle of opposing principles was approaching a universal denouement. In this cataclysm the old European order would be shattered, while Russia as leader of the liberated Slavs would establish a reconquered Constantinople as the seat of Orthodoxy and bring about the preordained rebirth of Europe within a universal community in which, at last, all contradictions would be resolved.

Like Hegel's immanent Reason, Dostoevsky's Idea moves through conflict and contradiction to its predestined embodiment in a final state of social harmony. He claimed that, unlike the socialists', his utopia would answer the needs of humans' entire spiritual being, not merely their rational nature; but it clearly belongs in the category of ideals of freedom as the recognition of necessity that are the subject of Herzen's ironist critique.[31]

But as Morson has shown, throughout the *Diary* utopia alternates with its parody. Dostoevsky periodically concedes that his faith in the fraternal instincts of the Russian people may be too strong, that his readers may find his "dreams" exaggerated, fantastic, even hysterical.[32] He repeatedly draws attention to the current disorientation of Russian society, the disintegration of traditional structures, and the lack of moral leadership, and in the January 1877 issue of the *Diary* he even despairs of finding a "leading thread" in the prevailing chaos. These inconsistencies have been ascribed to Dostoevsky's hesitation between religious faith and doubt. I shall interpret them rather as a vacillation between two conflicting views of the nature of freedom and the self. Herzen had argued with great cogency that one cannot be both an ironist and a utopian: one must choose. *A Writer's Diary* can be seen as an evasion of that choice.

The polemicist of the *Diary* is commonly viewed as an "ex-humanitarian radical," dissecting his former ideology with a mixture of condescension and contempt.[33] But a closer look at the *Diary* reveals Dostoevsky's rejection of his past to have been less than total: a recurring concern is the attempt to reconcile some of the insights of radical humanism with traditional Christianity.

Dostoevsky's comments on the "new people" of his time show that he attached as much significance as Herzen to the humanist revolt against transcendent authorities; he believed it to have caused an irreversible disintegration of traditional notions of social and moral order, a perception which, as he repeatedly noted, was not shared by his fellow writers. In a well-known passage in the *Diary,* he describes Tolstoy as the "historian" of a structured and ordered world that no longer exists, while in his notebooks for *The Adolescent,* he comments on the condescension of writers who have labeled him "poet of the Underground": "Silly fools, it is my glory, for that is where the truth lies. . . . The reason for the Underground is the destruction of our belief in certain general rules. *'Nothing is sacred.'* "[34]

Much of the *Diary* is devoted to a study of the type of the "restless and unpacifiable personality," the "Russian majority" whose minds are in ceaseless ferment as they search for "new formulas of the ideal, a new word, essential for the progress of the human organism." In the chapter "Isolation" and elsewhere Dostoevsky notes the unprecedented confusion and pessimism produced in Russian society by a state of affairs in which no one is satisfied with the feelings and ideas that were formerly shared in common; "each seeks to invent something of his own, something new and unheard of."

Some have even reduced progressive ideas to the formula: "if nothing is sacred, this means that one can play any dirty trick"; but Dostoevsky refuses to dismiss all the new iconoclasts as villains or poseurs. Many are seekers after truth who "languish and suffer," indeed who "sever all their former ties, and are *compelled* to begin anew, because no-one is offering them any light."[35]

He identifies with their search for a new formula of social existence, offering his own religious ideal as "something . . . in no way resembling anything in the past." He proposes it as a response to the material as well as the spiritual needs of the human race, as expressed in the current struggle for social emancipation, whose history is charted in the *Diary* in terms similar to Herzen's political writings. He traces its beginnings back to the scientific advances of the eighteenth century and the French Revolution, which had expanded conceptions of the humanly possible and led to demands for autonomy that the Revolution itself, by merely effecting a transfer of power, had not realized. Then the utopian socialists uttered their "new word"—the vision of a society no longer founded on exploitative relationships. In a tribute published on the death of George Sand, Dostoevsky recalls the veneration he had felt for this champion of the new humanism, whose social idealism and defense of women's rights had inspired his generation. He observes that her socialism was based on "the moral feeling of humanity and its striving for perfection and purity, not on ant-necessity" (the biological determinism preached by the Russian radicals of the 1860s).[36] Declaring her to have been one of the most farseeing of contemporary social prophets, he remarks that his readers might be amused at this view.

Some are more likely to have been scandalized by the contrast between Dostoevsky's enthusiasm for this French humanist and his comments on the contemporary Russian church, portrayed in the *Diary* as tainted by power and materialism. He sees its clergy as a bureaucratic arm of the state, divorced from the needs of the people (which, he emphasizes, include universal access to education). Repeatedly, he defends the right of women to higher education and to equality with men before the law. In his notes for the *Diary* (though not in the published work), he accuses the official ideologists of Orthodoxy and autocracy of a callous indifference to injustice and the material deprivation of the mass of the population.[37] In 1881, in the penultimate chapter of the *Diary*, he affirms that the true church has "not yet wholly come into being." It is prefigured in the Russian people's thirst for "universal, brotherly union in Christ's name"—in "our Russian socialism." He comments that it may seem strange that, in order to clarify his ideal, he has recourse to a concept "diametrically opposed to what the Church stands for."

As he was well aware, "Russian socialism" was Herzen's term for a social organization modeled on the self-governing structure of the Russian peasant commune. Through a "paradoxalist" (a recurring figure in the *Diary*), for whose views Dostoevsky claims he is not responsible, he conveys his own "socialist" vision of a regenerated humanity, which has done away with the "horrible cities" loved by the bourgeoisie, whose land is distributed among communes and whose factories are built amid gardens.[38] Unlike Herzen's, Dostoevsky's fraternal socialism drew its inspiration from the peasants' Christian faith and was more akin to the Slavophile concept of sobornost (a fusion of the part with the whole in what Konstantin Aksakov described as a "moral choir")[39] than to Herzen's dynamic of shifting balances between incompatible interests. But Dostoevsky's Pushkin Speech, printed in the August 1880 edition of the *Diary*, reminds us that, unlike the Slavophiles, he acknowledged the positive role of Peter's Westernization in introducing into Russia the principles of rational autonomy and respect for science, in spite of the resulting dissonances in the Russian "choir." In 1861 he had attacked the Slavophile periodical *Day* for its hostility to the critical spirit of contemporary Russian literature, arguing that the Slavophiles' fear of "this passionate negation through laughter, this voluntary self-condemnation, unheard of in any other literature," showed how deficient was their sense of reality; theirs was the kind of idealism that "majestically distances itself from everything that lives and breathes in its vicinity."[40]

Like Herzen, Dostoevsky equated the absence of irony with the absence of life. Both writers use irony as a means of defending the disorderly plenitude of concrete existence against the tyranny of abstraction. In *From the Other Shore*, Herzen satirizes the liberals of 1848, who had constructed an abstract ideal of the proletariat, part Roman plebs, part Rousseauian natural man, and who, when confronted with the real proletariat, hastened to protect themselves with bayonets. In the *Diary*, Dostoevsky excoriates Russian "cosmopolitan" humanitarians who ignore the Russian peasant: "You see, to love universal humanity necessarily means to despise, and, at times, to hate, the real person standing by your side." The malaise of contemporary society is the consequence of its loss of contact with "the so-called 'living force,' the vital sense of being, without which no society can exist" and which had been crushed by the dead weight of ideas.[41]

While the *Diary* was being published, Dostoevsky was working on *The Brothers Karamazov*, one of whose central themes is the opposition between "life" and "theory," reason and nature. Schiller's hymn *To Joy*, with its celebration of the joy of life, has been identified as a basic element in the ideological conception of the novel.[42] Some commentators have noted Alesha Karamazov's resemblance to Schiller's aesthetic ideal of the personality, a point that the author seems to emphasize when he has Alesha expound Schiller's notion of aesthetic play in a discussion with Kolia Krasotkin. Dostoevsky, who saw religious faith, not beauty, as the means of reconciling the contending forces of the psyche, clearly intended to represent Alesha as the epitome of "religious man"; nevertheless, Schiller's aesthetic ideal is not refuted in the novel. V. V. Zenkovsky claims that the work represents a fusion of the aesthetic and religious ideals of the human personality, but the two conceptions—one resting on faith in the inherent nobility of human nature, the other stressing its weakness and dependence on the mediation of the divine—are not easily reconcilable.[43]

The *Diary*, like *The Brothers Karamazov*, is ambivalent because it operates with two sets of criteria for making sense of reality and human conflict that are never harmonized. Dostoevsky the utopian believes that history derives its meaning from the transcendent purpose it is destined to accomplish, whereas Dostoevsky the ironist sees human freedom threatened by attempts to impose a single coherent pattern on the chaotic multiplicity of contingent reality. In his utopian mode, in the *Diary*, Dostoevsky constantly addresses Herzen as his unnamed principal opponent, but when he frequently subverts his own utopia with arguments that echo *From the Other Shore*, Herzen is no less present.

In the *Diary* of December 1876, Dostoevsky attacks dogmatic belief in terms reminiscent of Herzen's playful deflation of the earnest idealist in *From the Other Shore*. He laments the disappearance of "many-sidedness" from both literature and life and the appearance of a new phenomenon: "linearity" (*priamolineinost*): "The instinct for adaptation, for metaphor, for allegory, is noticeably beginning to disappear. People have ceased . . . to understand jests and humor—and this, according to the observation of a certain German thinker, is one of the clearest symptoms of the intellectual and moral degeneration of an epoch. Instead, there have come into being gloomy blockheads with frowning brows and narrow minds moving in a straight line, in one direction, toward one fixed point." He identifies as culprits certain "strange, inflexible conservatives" who were "even more rigorous, more cruel and more stupid than . . . the 'new people' " (of the Left). He concedes, however, that "in denouncing linearity, I myself have digressed too far."

This was hardly possible in a work whose generic nature was digression: Dostoevsky's apology invites his readers to consider whether he had gone too far in challenging their shared convictions. As the 1870s progress, however, the *Diary* records the development in all areas of Russian society of that tendency to simplification that he had once equated with atheistic rationalism. For example, he was appalled at how easily the newly reformed Russian courts delivered their verdicts on intractable human problems. He made the experiment of formulating a judgment of his own on a reported criminal case, and his lack of success convinced him that reasoning which by some moral criteria is legitimate and just can, by other (equally valid) criteria, be "illegitimate and unjust to the highest degree." "In fact, why is everything so arranged that nothing can be brought into accord?"

It was very much *à contre-coeur* that Dostoevsky was obliged to recognize the existence of incompatible perspectives on reality that could not be synthesized by reference to some ultimate criterion, but when he writes in this vein, the resemblance between his thought and Herzen's is particularly striking. For example, he slyly puts this comment on Tolstoy into the mouth of "an old Moscow acquaintance":

> The author of *Anna Karenina* possesses one of those Russian intellects which see clearly only what stands directly before their eyes, and therefore, keep emphasizing that one point. Appar-

> ently, they lack the faculty of turning their head to the right or
> to the left in order to discern also that which is to one side: to
> do that, they need to turn the whole body. . . . Then, maybe,
> they might start saying something quite contrary, since, at all
> events, they are always strictly sincere.[44]

Compare the following lines from an essay by Herzen, remarking on the tendency to notice only those aspects of reality that correspond to one's preconceptions: "People like things to be decorative; even in truth they see only the side that looks the best. They don't care if round the back the grass is growing wild. But *real* truths are always cubic, and all three dimensions are essential to their existence."[45]

The "one-sidedness" of all dogmatic thinking and the demand that social theorizing should "take on flesh" and embrace the untidy reality of contingent existence were dominant themes in Herzen's political journalism. Since Dostoevsky was demonstrably well acquainted with Herzen's writing, it is not surprising that Herzen's influence is detectable in those passages in the *Diary* where the author or his "paradoxalist" slyly (and wittily) subverts the notional reader's established beliefs.[46]

The relationship to Herzen's outlook, however, is complex. The ironist in Dostoevsky constantly invokes the empirical data of "real life" to defeat the simplifications of idealists and romantics. But while Herzen uses such facts in his battle with all utopias, Dostoevsky seeks to employ them in utopia's defense. In December 1876 (when the *Diary* had been in existence for a year as an independent publication), he explains that its main aim has hitherto been to elucidate "the idea of our national spiritual independence . . . as far as possible, through the concrete facts as they present themselves." This is rather as if Ivan Karamazov were to undertake to construct a proof of ultimate harmony from his dossier of the gross disharmonies of empirical existence. This was not a mere polemical strategy: Dostoevsky generally made no attempt to massage the facts, conscientiously recording the evidence that contradicted his thesis and expressing his own bewilderment before it.

Dostoevsky seeks to prove by "the facts," first, that morality is rooted in the religious belief in the immortality of the soul, and second, that God has implanted this religious instinct in human beings as the means of achieving a final state of harmony on earth. Evil occurrences such as the "Nechaev affair" are cited to demonstrate that atheistic socialism leads logically to the murderous doctrine that "all is permitted."[47] The proposition that love of humanity is impossible without belief in immortality is, he concedes, "as yet unsubstantiated," but he quotes frequent newspaper reports of suicides among the unbelieving youth as evidence of their despair when faced with the aimlessness and absurdity of an existence to which they deny a transcendent meaning.

But, on the other side of the scales, the *Diary* cites the moral idealism of the young radicals who took part in the "movement to the people" of the mid-1870s as one of the few causes for hope in the current crisis (in a note for the *Diary*, Dostoevsky remarked that they put believers like himself to shame). Although he had claimed that George Sand's moral idealism sprang from her deism, he could not apply this argument to the radicals of the 1870s. Laconically, he observes: "This movement . . . still continues, and, it seems, is determined not to come to a stop. I have no intention of speaking here either for or against the movement."[48] Such ironic reticence seems intended to have dramatic effect on a readership that might have expected him to express himself unambiguously on this theme.

Dostoevsky's hopes for an earthly paradise rested principally on his observations of a Christian instinct in the peasants (recorded in the *Diary* in his autobiographical account "The Peasant Marei"). That this had survived in the brutish conditions of their life seemed to him proof of its strength. But the *Diary* also presents another picture of the peasants, culled from court reports and other sources, which reveals them to be habitual drunkards sunk in ignorance, morally disoriented, and corrupted by materialism. Two interpretations of the "concrete facts" are set out, with no attempt to mediate between them. We see the peasants now as the hope for the renewal of humanity, now as being in desperate need of the moral leadership of others.

Dostoevsky's vacillation between these two views is most evident in his treatment of the Russo-Turkish war, which threatened to spark a major conflict between Russia and Europe. Initially he confidently interprets events as evidence of that spiritual solidarity among the Orthodox Slavs which will qualify them to lead Europe to rebirth; but as the war progresses he notes that the other Slavs, much like the rest of Europe, suspect Russia of imperialist aspirations "and will still be suspecting her a century hence." He alternates between a view of the war as an event predestined to express Russia's spiritual unity and as a welcome contingency that might create the moral consensus that was so sadly lacking and arrest the nation's spiritual decay. This second interpretation is developed at the expense of the first when Dostoevsky uses his "paradoxalist" to argue in favor of the morally regenerative function of war.

"We nearly always perceive reality as we *wish* to perceive it . . . at times, I swear, we would rather believe in a miracle and an impossibility than in a reality *that we do not wish to see*": this statement (apropos of a discussion of miracles) reveals that affinity with Herzen's "self-reflection" which leads Dostoevsky on occasion to regard his own utopian hopes with the same disabused gaze that is turned on the idealist in *From the Other Shore*. Thus, in October 1876 he reflects that the old has been destroyed or has worn itself out and the new exists only in fantasy, whereas in actual life "there appears before our eyes something abominable which has reached unheard-of proportions." In 1881, in the penultimate chapter of the *Diary*, he declares that everything in Russia is "pregnant with questions . . . there is no calmness in our convictions, in our views, in our nerves, in our appetites." The masses, in particular, were in a state of such moral confusion that it was only the incompetence of the "nihilistic" propagandists that had prevented them from succeeding: "with the slightest skill they could have infiltrated the people."[49]

The possibility that there may exist no "leading thread" or, as Herzen put it, no libretto for human history is not directly addressed in the *Diary*, but one of the notebooks contains this reflection: "Christ himself preached his teaching only as an ideal, himself predicted that until the end of the world there would be struggle and development . . . for this is the law of nature. . . . And thus on earth the individual strives toward an ideal that is *contrary* to his nature."[50]

As the metaphysician of *From the Other Shore* indignantly remarked, if humans have been endowed with ideals that are not destined to be realized, this would indeed be "some sort of irony."

The evidence that exists on what Dostoevsky described as the "terrible torments" of his struggle with religious doubt suggests that he was torn between the faith of an Alesha Karamazov, which did not require the support of visible proof, and the temptation to judge Christian belief like Ivan, by its effectiveness in alleviating human suffering.[51] This functionalist approach to religion actually dominates the *Diary*. Whatever Dostoevsky's personal religious beliefs, his journalistic defense of religion is that of an ironist, who approaches values and concepts as tools for specific purposes rather than as approximations to some ultimate truth. The purpose Dostoevsky has in mind is the creation of that sense of moral cohesion that he believes constitutes "the greatest happiness in the life of a nation." The practical benefits of religious faith as a remedy for pessimism and a social cement are stressed throughout the *Diary*— an approach not inconsistent with traditional Christian belief; but Dostoevsky's reflections on the nature of belief itself are far from orthodox.

In the course of discussing spiritualism and a séance he had attended, Dostoevsky asserts that "he who *wishes* to have faith in spiritualism can't be prevented from doing so by anything . . . while the unbeliever, if only he fully *does not wish* to believe, will be swayed by nothing." Dostoevsky counts himself in the second category:

> I suddenly learned . . . not only that I don't believe in spiritualism, but in addition, that I *do not wish* to believe in it, so that

> no proofs will ever shake me. . . . I vaguely sense here some
> special law of human nature, some law common to everyone,
> specifically pertaining to faith and incredulity in general. . . .
> What force incredulity may find and develop in one, at a given
> moment, completely against one's will, although in accordance
> with one's secret desire. . . . The same is also probably true of
> faith.[52]

He remarks that he had intended to discuss his mental experiment in the current *Diary* but would postpone it to the next issue—a promise he does not fulfill. Again the diarist's tantalizing withdrawal emphasizes the subversive nature of the little he has chosen to say. Anticipating Freud's derivation of moral sense from the contingencies of our upbringing, Dostoevsky's experiment questions the belief, fundamental to religious and rationalist metaphysics, that the principles by which we rule our lives have their source in necessary, a priori truths, unconditioned by historical contingency and immanent in all human consciousnesses. The view that such principles are subject to the vicissitudes of time and chance is the basis of Herzen's ironist defense of freedom in *From the Other Shore*. Dostoevsky's *Diary* reveals that he shared the capacity of his own fictional heroes to bow down to a belief and, like Herzen, "immediately after, to ridicule it."

Why, then, in view of Dostoevsky's understanding of Herzen's thought and his affinities with it, does he present in the *Diary* an image of Herzen disfigured almost beyond recognition?

In a letter of 1870 to the critic Nikolai Strakhov, Dostoevsky asserts that the key to all Herzen's activity is that he was "always and everywhere, a *poet above all else.*"[53] However, as Nina Perlina has pointed out, this characteristic is given negative overtones in the *Diary*, where Herzen is referred to as a dreamer, a utopian cut off from his native soil. In the first chapter of the *Diary*, he is represented as a "gentilhomme russe et citoyen du monde," one of the *déraciné* liberals of the 1840s who aped Western fashions by preaching an atheistic and deterministic doctrine of progress that denied the moral responsibility, and thereby also the freedom, of the individual. Thus discredited, Herzen becomes a symbol of the contemporary ideological confusion.[54]

Yet Dostoevsky was undoubtedly both well acquainted with and (notably in the case of *Notes from Underground*) influenced by Herzen's writings, which consistently exposed the cognitive and moral deficiencies of a determinist outlook. It could be argued that in Dostoevsky's eyes the fact that Herzen was not a religious believer outweighed all his insights and placed him squarely in the category of those he condemned. From the published *Diary* this would seem to be the case. On two occasions he refers to the suicide of Herzen's youngest daughter (described only as the child of a "well-known emigrant"). He interprets her death as a protest against the vision of life devoid of transcendent meaning conveyed to her in her father's house: "Her soul proved instinctively unable to bear linearity, and instinctively demanded something more complex."[55]

The recurrence of the words "Herzen's daughter" in Dostoevsky's notebooks for the *Diary* of 1876–77 would seem to confirm Perlina's view that Dostoevsky was fascinated by this death as evidence that Herzen's unbelief was the source of a profound and infectious pessimism.[56] But a draft, in the same notebooks, of his reflections on the suicide reveals a quite different reason for his obsession with it. He remarks that even though she was brought up in a household where the question of God was never discussed, one would expect Herzen's daughter to have inherited some of her father's spiritual qualities. The problem that puzzles him is how a man of such talent, "a thinker and a poet, . . . could not have passed on to this suicide anything . . . of his passionate love of life, that life which he so treasured, valued so highly, and in which he so deeply believed. . . . Of course, she did not have her deceased father's convictions, his aspirations and his faith in them, otherwise she would not have destroyed herself. It is unthinkable even to imagine that so passionate a *believer* as Herzen could have killed himself."[57]

Here perhaps is the reason for Dostoevsky's unambiguously negative portrayal of Herzen in the *Diary*. Herzen's personality provided so strong a refutation of his thesis that love of life and faith in the human personality were impossible without religious belief that, for all his readiness to cite evidence that contradicted his theories, he could not bring himself to print this passage. The grossly distorted picture of Herzen that appears in the printed *Diary* speaks eloquently of Dostoevsky's sense of the threat that Herzen's irony posed to his utopia.

Herzen versus Schopenhauer

CHAPTER SIXTEEN

If I can't cheerfully describe myself as an optimist, I must insist that I'm an anti-pessimist of the utmost vehemence—ferociously anti-pessimist, in fact, for there's no other realistic form my anger can take.
—Robert Simpson, "The Ferociously Anti-Pessimist Composer"

A philosophy of *"despair, hopelessness and disbelief"*—this view of Aleksandr Herzen's thought in V. V. Zenkovsky's authoritative history of Russian philosophy has been echoed by other commentators, who have classed Herzen with Nietzsche as a precursor of modern pessimism.[1] This is not a labeling he would have welcomed. It is commonly maintained that to deny the existence of an a priori rational or providential order in the world is to be, by definition, a pessimist.[2] Herzen vigorously rejected the possibility of such an order but denied equally strongly that this rejection was equivalent to pessimism. He pressed his point home with arguments that are particularly relevant to our own time, when the philosophy of Nietzsche and his mentor, Schopenhauer, are often presented as the most consistent and courageous responses to a world without transcendence. Herzen did not live long enough to take issue with Nietzsche's ideas, but he was well acquainted with Schopenhauer's. Ivan Turgenev, Herzen's friend and intellectual sparring partner, was the first of many major artists to find Schopenhauer's vision compelling, a position that caused Herzen to reproach him for succumbing to the influence of the "philosopher of death."[3] But although the first known references to Schopenhauer in Herzen's writings occur in the course of his polemics with Turgenev in the 1860s, his most devastating attack on Schopenhauerian pessimism was made more than a decade before, in *From the Other Shore,* the volume of essays on the nature of history that was the fruit of his reflections on the debacle of 1848. In two of these essays (written in dialogical form) Herzen's imaginary companion bears more than a passing resemblance to Turgenev's philosophical mentor.

A recent commentator, emphasizing the depth and scope of Schopenhauer's influence on twentieth-century sensibility, through such figures as Tolstoy, Zola, Proust, Hardy, Conrad, and Mann, notes that the Schopenhauerian case for a tragic view of the human condition is "extremely formidable. One looks in vain for a comparably sustained case for optimism."[4] I contend that in the two dialogues discussed below Herzen erects, at the very least, an impressive scaffolding—not for optimism but for an "antipessimism" which, according to the composer Robert Simpson, understands that things are going seriously wrong but hopes there is a chance.[5] His position rests on the original and provocative view that Schopenhauerian pessimism (later to be greeted by Nietzsche as a philosophy of unparalleled daring) is a fainthearted evasion of the consequences of our dependence on contingency. We shall see that this forcefully argued case is the basis of Herzen's own heavily qualified hope.

"Sors de l'enfance, ami, et réveille-toi!" These words of Rousseau introduce what has been described as the first breakthrough of reality into philosophical thought: Schopenhauer's *The World as Will and Representation* (1819).[6] When Schopenhauer published this work, Hegel's fame and influence were at their height. Consequently, Schopenhauer failed miserably in his attempt to outshine and discredit the philosopher whom he described (in the preface to the second edition of his treatise) as an "intellectual Caliban." His reputation finally began to grow in the 1850s, when many intellectuals who sought to explain the defeat of their radical hopes in 1848 were drawn to his critique of the metaphysical systems that presented reality as the incarnation of an a priori rational or moral order. The philosophers of his century had, he maintained, cynically used such systems to prop up intellectual and political power, ignoring the fact that Kant had shown definitively that human cognition, limited to the phenomena of experience, had no access to a priori truths.

This did not mean that it was not legitimate to speculate about the ultimate nature of reality: the human being was an *"animal metaphysicum,"* unable to orient itself in the world without finding answers to the riddles of death, suffering, and evil. Schopenhauer maintained that this could be done without stepping beyond Kant's strict criteria of the limits of knowledge, by recourse to a method hitherto insufficiently used by philosophers: reflection on direct inner experience, unmediated by analytical categories. This intuitive approach brings one to the certainty that the kernel of one's being is will (Schopenhauer's name for the force or energy constitutive of everything in the cosmos from galaxies to subatomic particles.)[7] That force (Kant's thing-in-itself) of which all phenomena are representations is, he argues, no distant divinity but our own inner self, to which we have immediate access through self-awareness. Unprejudiced reflection on lived experience reveals that the self is not (as Descartes, Kant, and Hegel would have us believe) a free rational agent acting in conformity with beliefs arrived at through conscious mental processes: in reality, reason is the instrument of the will, whose desires, often unconscious and unarticulated, dictate our goals. The role of the intellect is to determine the optimal means to their attainment. Shifting the center of gravity from consciousness or reason (and its hypostasis in God, the soul, Spirit, or Idea) to the irrational and creative side of the self, Schopenhauer began that radical review of the categories of our experience usually associated with Sigmund Freud. Schopenhauer points to the role of primal impulses in motivating our conduct, the part played by the will in repressing awareness of desires which we are reluctant to admit, and the pervasive influence of the sexual drive, "the invisible central point of all action and conduct, [which] peeps up everywhere, in spite of all the veils thrown over it."[8]

The real, Schopenhauer contends, is demonstrably not the rational: all theories of progress based on belief in the perfectibility of human beings contradict experience. In its phenomenal manifestations, the will is a blind, insatiable struggle for existence which in Nature is directed to the maintenance of the species. Only in the human race is the individual set against the species: consciousness experiences the will to live as immediate reality only in the perceiving subject, approaching others as alien objects to be used as means in pursuit of its egocentric aims. The result is *bellum omnium contra omnes,* a struggle in which all victories are hollow; for the basis of all willing is need, lack, and pain, a restless striving that by its nature cannot be assuaged. Attainment quickly ceases to satisfy. "The goal was only apparent; possession takes away its charm. The wish, the need, appears again on the scene under a new form; if it does not, then dreariness, emptiness, and boredom follow. . . . For desire and satisfaction to follow each other at not too short and not too long intervals, reduces the suffering occasioned by both to the smallest amount, and constitutes the happiest life."[9]

This passage has been greeted as a prescient description of the anomie that haunts the twentieth century. Schopenhauer has been seen as equally farsighted in insisting that economic and political adjustments can never eliminate, but only contain, the aggression of the egoistic will which is the chief cause of human misery.[10] The historical process is a continuation of zoological strife:

> The world is the battle-ground of tormented and agonized beings who continue to exist only by each devouring the other. Therefore, every beast of prey in it is the living grave of thousands of others, and its self-maintenance is a chain of torturing deaths. Then in this world the capacity to feel pain increases with knowledge, and therefore reaches its highest

degree in man, a degree that is the higher, the more intelligent the man. To this world the attempt has been made to adapt the system of *optimism,* and to demonstrate that it is the best of all possible worlds. The absurdity is glaring."[11]

Historical theodicies such as Hegel's ("this assumed plan of the world according to which all is managed for the best") are dismissed with contempt: optimism, writes Schopenhauer, "seems to me to be not merely an absurd, but *also a really wicked, way of thinking*":

> If we were to conduct the most hardened and callous optimist through hospitals, infirmaries, operating theatres, through prisons, torture chambers and slave-hovels, over battle-fields and to places of execution; if we were to open to him all the dark abodes of misery, where it shuns the gaze of cold curiosity, and finally were to allow him to gaze into the dungeon of Ugolino where prisoners starved to death, he would certainly see in the end what kind of world is this *meilleur des mondes possibles.* For whence did Dante get the material for his hell, if not from this actual world of ours?[12]

One may well argue that ours is "the *worst* of all possible worlds ... if it were a little worse, it would be no longer capable of continuing to exist." Powerful as are the weapons of reason and understanding, they have not saved nine-tenths of humanity from a miserable existence of conflict and want in which, prey to disease, natural disasters, and their own violent instincts, they balance themselves "with difficulty and effort on the brink of destruction." To see some form of progress in this sorry process is absurd: "The chapters of the history of nations are at bottom different only through the names and dates; the really essential content is everywhere the same."[13]

The first sustained philosophical assault on nineteenth-century historical optimism, Schopenhauer's treatise demands that we jettison the fantasy of progress in favor of the only goal that we have the power to attain: self-knowledge. This we achieve through reflection on the "immediate, intuitive conviction" that we do not end with our deaths.[14] Schopenhauer maintains that this sense (innate in most humans) has been clouded by doctrines that equate our existence with our consciousness and promise the continued survival of the latter after death. But observation of the continuities and patterns of recurrence common to historical, evolutionary, and natural processes leads us to a different conception of immortality: "Because the strong arm that three thousand years ago bent the bow of Ulysses no longer exists, no reflective and well-regulated understanding will look upon the force that acted so energetically in it as entirely annihilated. Therefore, on further reflection, it will not be assumed that the force that bends the bow today, first began to exist with that arm. Much nearer to us is the idea that the force that formerly actuated a life now vanished is the same force that is active in the life now flourishing: indeed this thought is almost inevitable."[15]

Those doctrines that have led human beings to claim a status superior to animals "under the boastful name of immortality" have obscured the nature of our true inner being, which is not tied to our individuality and will survive it, as the species (the most enduring objectification of Nature's will to live) survives the plants or animals that compose it. The first modern Western philosopher to become immersed in the teachings of Oriental religions, Schopenhauer held that the doctrines of metempsychosis common to these express a true intuition about the forms of recurrence which are "Nature's great doctrine of immortality." But he is at pains to stress that his own system confines itself to consideration of the only problem with which philosophy should be concerned—the world of experience: "With this alone it has to do, and it leaves the gods in peace."[16]

Although it is beyond the competence of philosophy to speculate on why the world-as-will could have gone so far astray as to produce the egoistic human will, observation of the natural world reveals how the error is ultimately corrected: Nature delivers its own "great reprimand," returning us to our true being as timeless will by destroying the aberration of individual consciousness. Death is "the great disillusionment. At bottom, we are something that ought not to be; therefore we cease to be."[17]

Understanding death in this way, we will embrace it as "the great opportunity no longer to be I."[18] Such a perception can be reached through two forms of awareness: aesthetic and ethical. Aesthetic contemplation releases us from the prison of our individual wills: detached from the needs and interests that condition our everyday modes of knowledge and understanding, we penetrate to the universal forms and structures of the world (its archetypal Ideas in the Platonic sense), which are the immediate objectifications of the unitary Will. A similar understanding is expressed in the altruism of those who identify with the sufferings of others. What we call virtue, Schopenhauer contends, emanates not (as Kant believed) from an abstract conception of duty but from an intuitive sense of the unitary nature shared by all beings. The dedicated altruist, however, soon becomes aware of the futility of efforts to relieve human misery. Ethical and aesthetic awareness alike help prepare the psyche for the highest mode of understanding, expressed in a turning of the will from the world: an ascetic renunciation of the vanity of phenomenal existence and a yearning for "that nothingness, which as the final goal hovers behind all virtue and holiness."[19]

Schopenhauer contended that the features of his philosophy that his contemporaries found least attractive were those that coincided most evidently with the accumulated experience of humanity. Rousseau's shallow doctrine of the "original goodness and unlimited perfectibility" of the human race was an instance of the failure of optimistic philosophies to give due weight to insights into the wretchedness of human existence. One could find such insights in the great religions of the East, in the writings of Christian ascetics and quietists, and in the pessimism common to poets and great minds through the ages, from Socrates and Homer to Shakespeare, Pascal, Byron, and Giacomo Leopardi.[20]

In according imaginative insights equal status with the data of empirical observation and analytical thought as sources of truth about the world, Schopenhauer was consciously staking out new ground for philosophy. He believed the great merit of his system to be that it had "wide-spreading roots in . . . the reality of perception from which all the nourishment of abstract truths springs."[21] This quality may account for the wave of interest in his philosophy in the latter part of the twentieth century. As has been said of Nietzsche (whom he foreshadows in many respects), he seems to express "a modern kind of truthfulness" in his rejection of hierarchies and compartmentalizations between varieties of knowledge and in his insistence (over half a century before the publication of Darwin's *The Descent of Man*) that human history presented no privileged exception to other natural and physical processes governed by time and chance.[22] (It has been argued that twentieth-century science, by revealing the constitution of all matter to be nothing but a concatenation of forces, supports his insights into the reality behind phenomenal appearance.)[23] He has been credited with unequalled boldness in facing the consequences for human freedom of a godless world. Nietzsche greeted him as a thinker who had triumphed over the greatest difficulties, boldly confronting the suffering and the monsters that other philosophers had only pretended to fight.[24] That he "does so little to clothe the negative in a semblance of meaning" has been seen to make him the most appropriate of teachers for our own disillusioned age.[25] Schopenhauer himself laid much stress on the pioneering integrity of his empirical approach, characterized by its fearless exposure of the myths, evasions, and self-deceit of previous philosophies, proclaiming himself the first to have revealed the "ancient, universal and radical error" of placing the kernel of human nature in consciousness.[26] His claim was exaggerated: other modern thinkers (notably Schiller in his treatise *On the Aesthetic Education of Man*) had already pointed to the importance of irrational drives as motivations of human behavior. However, from the perspective of our own age, a Schopenhauer, a Nietzsche, or a Freud seem to many to be more fearless in facing the truth about the human being than a Schiller, a Herzen, or a John Stuart Mill, whose

critiques of rationalist assumptions were balanced with a defense of the civilizing power of reason in human affairs. To seek to preserve such a balance is now
often seen as engaging in what Max Horkheimer has described as a "subtle res-
cue of Utopia"—an attempt, against losing odds, to preserve the ideal of human perfectibility.[27] As Bernard Williams notes, to defend in the late twentieth
century the idea that "philosophy and science can share a conception of truthfulness that is not merely an application of the will to power" is to invite the
charge of perpetuating old illusions.[28]

Herzen's polemics with his pessimistic friend in *From the Other Shore* present a counterblast to such arguments that has lost none of its relevance with
the passing of time: it is a powerful attack on the intellectual and moral confusions of pessimism as a response to the crumbling of old universalist faiths.

Schopenhauer's name does not appear in that work or its surviving drafts
(Herzen mentions him only in connection with his later debate with Turgenev); his opponent in the two dialogues in question appears to have been based
on a former member of his Moscow circle, who resurfaced in Paris just before
the 1848 revolution.[29] But (given the interest in German philosophy that had
made Herzen the leading interpreter of Hegel in Russia in the mid-1840s) it is
unlikely that by 1849 he did not know of Schopenhauer's ideas. Moreover, his
opponent's vocabulary and metaphors are often strikingly close to those of *The
World as Will*. We shall see that Herzen's criticism of the unquestioned assumptions of philosophical pessimism is supported by the inconsistencies in
Schopenhauer's main theses, which lend weight to Herzen's view that the underlying motivation of such doctrines is the fear of freedom. Whether he had
Schopenhauer in particular in his sights at that time is a matter for conjecture,
and irrelevant to this discussion: he was attacking not an individual or a theory
but a perception of the world in which he sensed the beginnings of a new orthodoxy, resembling the systems it condemned in its tendency to confer absolute and all-explanatory status on certain relative and conditional truths.

These truths—"Schopenhauerian" theses about the nature of history at
which Herzen had arrived independently through historical study, philosophical reflection, and observation of the European scene—form the shared premises from which he and his imaginary opponent draw their differing
conclusions.[30] When the first dialogue begins (the first is set before the catastrophe of 1848; the second takes place in its aftermath), Herzen has all but succeeded in converting his companion, a disillusioned idealist, to his view that in
history as in Nature chance, "dark forces" and primal drives defeat attempts to
impose a rational direction on events. But the former idealist refuses to accept

the possibility of any form of freedom or creative maneuvering within such a reality. He accuses Herzen of destroying his last hopes by convincing him that history has no goal: once faith in progress is lost, the only consistent attitude is despair, a withdrawal from the conflict of existence into passive resignation. There is no way of imposing form and stability on the chaotic turbulence of the world, no escape from "moral impotence, from opinions pitifully divorced from practice, from the chaos in which we ultimately cease to distinguish friend from foe." The hopes of theorists are derided by the demonic pattern of history, where civilizations strain upward for centuries, to disappear, leaving only a dim memory. "With melancholy anxiety, [man] contemplates the infinite road ahead of him and sees that he is just as far from his end after all efforts as he was a thousand, two thousand years ago!" We are conscious of life "through dull pain, through regrets which gnaw the heart, through the monotonous ticking of clocks. . . . It is hard to enjoy life to the full, to get drunk, knowing that the whole world is crumbling around you." He angrily protests against the intolerable consequences of admitting that history has neither transcendent meaning nor final goals; if the struggles of each generation lead to no cumulative improvement in the human condition, "then our whole civilization is a lie. . . . Our labours are absurd, our efforts ludicrous."[31] The pessimist laments that history "piles grain on grain, pebble on pebble, until once again everything comes tumbling down to earth and men begin to crawl out from under the ruins, to clear a space and build huts for themselves out of moss, boards and fallen capitals, only to achieve, after centuries of long effort, destruction once more. It was not for nothing that Shakespeare said that history was a tale told by an idiot, signifying nothing."[32]

Like Schopenhauer, Herzen's interlocutor perceives an iron law in human existence: "The higher the degree of development the greater the suffering." The present slips through our fingers, all enjoyment vitiated by the speed of its passing; loss of faith in the future will remove the last reason for attachment to life: "All that is left is to wait with folded hands for the waters to flood over us."[33]

"Is the game worth the candle?" Herzen's opponent demands bitterly. This phrase recurs as a distinctive refrain in Schopenhauer's treatise, where the same angry rhetoric relentlessly batters the reader into accepting the worthlessness of an existence in which "the present is always inadequate, . . . the future is uncertain, and the past irrecoverable."[34]

It is possible, Schopenhauer admits, to deduce from the transitoriness of existence that "the greatest *wisdom* consists in enjoying the present and making this enjoyment the goal of life, because the present is all that is real and everything else merely imaginary. But you could just as well call this mode of life the greatest *folly;* for that which in a moment ceases to exist, which vanishes as completely as a dream, cannot be worth any serious effort."[35]

"To look at the end and not at the action itself is the greatest of errors" is Herzen's response to the "gloomy *memento mori*" of his opponent.[36] Schopenhauer, however, is intent on proving the contrary. He sees contingency ("the scornful mastery of chance") as playing a purely destructive role in the "tragicomedy of world-history." It is Nature's way of declaring that "the individual is nothing and less than nothing. I destroy millions of individuals every day for sport and pastime; I abandon their fate to chance, to the most capricious and wanton of my children, who harasses them at his pleasure."[37] The prodigality with which, as Herzen put it, Nature "pours the whole of herself into the present moment"[38] and the infinite variety and resourcefulness of the evolutionary adaptations of animals are for Schopenhauer the most compelling of proofs of the futility of all sentient existence:

> We cannot help asking what comes of all this, and what is attained by animal existence that demands such immense preparations. And there is nothing to show but the satisfaction of hunger and sexual passion, and in any case a little momentary gratification, such as falls to the lot of every individual animal, now and then, between its endless needs and exertions. If we put the two together, the inexpressible ingenuity of the preparations, the untold abundance of the means, and the inadequacy of what is thus aimed at and attained, we are driven to the view that life is a business whose returns are far from covering the cost.[39]

It might be argued that no real debate is possible between the two discontinuous visions of the human condition set out by Schopenhauer: which one seems to us to be "wisdom" and which "folly" depends on our individual perspective, dictated by temperament and circumstances. But Herzen believed that only one was consistent with the rejection of all a priori assumptions about the nature of the self and the world. Thus, he challenges his intransigent friend: "Tell me frankly: how did you convince yourself that your demands were real?"

The pessimist retorts in Schopenhauerian style: "I did not invent them; they were born naturally within me; the more I thought about them afterwards, the more clearly I perceived their wisdom, their justice—these are my proofs. This is neither perversion nor aberration. Thousands of others, our whole generation, suffer in almost the same way, to a greater or less extent, according to circumstances and their degree of development—the higher the degree of development the greater the suffering."[40]

Herzen suggests that his friend has misinterpreted his data: there are no empirical grounds for assuming that the demands whose frustration causes us such suffering are written into the human condition. On the contrary, the evidence is that they have been fostered by the dualism that has dominated all teaching, preaching, writing, and action for a millennium and a half, causing "sadness and morbid longings" by inculcating a yearning for "some unattainable bliss." "Is it so strange that after this we are unable to organize either the inner or the outer life, that we demand too much, sacrifice too much, scorn the possible, are indignant because what is impossible scorns us?"[41]

His friend is less of an iconoclast than he believes: "You imagine that you despair because you are a revolutionary, and you are mistaken. You despair because you are a conservative." Accepting that his demands are unrealizable, he continues to believe them legitimate. His indignation betrays a colossal egotism: "You believe that there is no salvation for the world except along the paths you have found." Idealists are "beside themselves with anger because life does not obey their haughty commands, their private whims. You, for instance, expected from life something quite different from what it gave you; instead of appreciating what it has given, you are angry with it." You are irritated, Herzen tells him, "because the nations don't fulfill the conception that is dear and clear to you, because they are unable to save themselves with the weapons you offer them and to cease suffering." These are the "tantrums of a sulky lover"; "why do you think that the nation is obliged to fulfil your conception and not its own, and precisely at this time, and not another?" This "didactic, pontifical attitude" had had its justification in ages of universal faith, "but now it has become ridiculous and casts us for the stock role of the disillusioned."[42]

Herzen points out that there is nothing new in such disenchantment: "The idea of retreating into oneself, severing the umbilical cord which binds us to our country, to the present . . . appeals to people after every failure, after every loss of faith; mystics and freemasons, philosophers and *illuminati* have turned to it for refuge." Nor is there anything very admirable in the attitude of the noble sufferer. To assume such a stance with regard to the world is "not merely vanity—it is immense cowardice. Do not be offended by these words; fear of discovering the truth makes many prefer suffering to analysis. Pain distracts, absorbs, comforts . . . yes, yes, it comforts, and above all, like every occupation, it prevents men from looking into themselves, into life."[43]

We clutter up our lives with invented preoccupations, unreal misfortunes, artificial complexities, to conceal our "fear of all enquiry, fear lest the absurdity of the subject of enquiry be glimpsed." Within us all there slumbers an "ominous truth": that it makes no sense to introduce our human demands for meaning and purpose into the economy of a universe in which we make so marginal and fleeting an appearance.[44]

In a passage in his memoirs written some years later, Herzen presents the pessimism of his time as a confused and transitional stage in the process of shedding foundationalist notions of ultimate purpose. It had a quality peculiar to the age: the result of the death of that faith in humanity and civilization which was the "final religion." "It grieves us to realize that the idea is impotent, that truth has no binding power over the real world. A new kind of Manichaeism takes hold of us, and we are ready, *par dépit,* to believe in rational (that is, purposive) evil, as we believed in rational good—that is the last tribute we pay to idealism."[45]

In his treatise, Schopenhauer muses on the fact that in Nature "it is precisely the most perfect beings, namely living things with their infinitely complicated and inconceivably ingenious organizations," which are the most fragile and transient, whereas the lowest, the inorganic, continue to exist unassailed. "This is something so obviously absurd that it can never be the true order of things, but rather a mere veil concealing such an order."[46] Like Herzen's conservative friend, he never entertains the hypothesis that the absurdity of natural processes when judged by rational criteria may cast doubt on the appropriateness of the latter. Schopenhauer's allegiance to humanity's household rules is a priori and unconditional. In his view, the error of the "optimists" is to have discerned only one purpose in the cosmic process, whereas there are "two fundamental purposes, diametrically opposed": that of the individual will, directed to chimerical happiness, and that of fate and the "course of things," which by tragically frustrating that urge teaches us to seek the oblivion of death.[47] There is a certain inconsistency in attributing purpose to blind, unconscious will, but Schopenhauer's *dépit* is stronger than his logic: at times he seems, as one commentator puts it, "possessed by the idea that there is something inherently evil, monstrous, wicked about the ultimate force that constitutes the world."[48]

The same critic stresses, in Schopenhauer's defense, that his speculations about the noumenal world should be seen as marginal to his system, on the grounds that it denied them cognitive validity.[49] It seems all the more curious, then, that propositions of such doubtful status should be the source of a set of ethical prescriptions more rigid, dogmatic, and extreme than the doctrine of self-mastery that Kant deduced from his a priori categories. There are no gray areas in Schopenhauer's ethic. Virtue and the egoistic urge for self-affirmation are fundamentally opposed: acting "in open contradiction" to that urge, the virtuous person "denies the will, and gives the lie to the body; he desires no sexual satisfaction on any condition."[50] In its schematic reductiveness Schopenhauer's system is a mirror image of the rationalist theodicies he rejects, substituting will for reason as the basic explanatory principle of history and being. Herzen discerned a prior agenda behind his opponent's "stubborn . . . desire to remain at odds with the world."[51] Schopenhauer is driven by similar unnegotiable demands. He maintains that if one compared the sum of the pleasures that are possible in the course of a human life with the sum of the sufferings that may be encountered, it could be safely presumed that the second category would outweigh the first; but his rejection of the world is not, in the last analysis, based on any such empirical calculation of profit and loss:

> In the long run . . . it is quite superfluous to dispute whether there is more good or evil in the world; for the mere existence of evil decides the matter, since evil can never be wiped off, and consequently can never be balanced, by the good that exists along with or after it. . . . That thousands had lived in happiness and joy would never do away with the anguish and death-agony of one individual; and just as little does my present well-being undo my previous sufferings. Therefore, were the evil in the world even a hundred times less than it is, its mere existence would still be sufficient to establish . . . that [the world] is something which at bottom ought not to be.[52]

What Schopenhauer rejects are the limitations of finite being *tout court:* "The vanity of existence is revealed in the whole form existence assumes: in the infiniteness of time and space contrasted with the finiteness of the individual in both; in the fleeting present as the sole form in which actuality exists; in the contingency and relativity of all things; in continual becoming without being; in continual desire without satisfaction; in the continual frustration of striving of which life consists. . . . Time is that by virtue of which everything becomes nothingness in our hands and loses all real value."[53]

In a prescient reflection on the new anthropotheism of Feuerbach and his followers, Proudhon (the only European radical whom Herzen acknowledged as a mentor) observed that humans' perennial yearning for the qualities traditionally assigned to their divinities had now led to the philosophically confused belief that they had only to abolish those gods in order to appropriate their perfections. This enterprise, he predicted, would end in despair, followed by a retreat into the service of some vast impersonal entity: "Les dieux sont partis: L'homme n'a plus qu'à s'ennuyer et mourir dans son égoïsme. Quelle effrayante solitude s'étend autour de moi et se creuse au fond de mon âme! Mon exaltation ressemble à l'anéantissement, et depuis que je me suis fait Dieu, je ne me vois plus que comme une ombre" (The gods have departed. There is nothing left to man but to grow weary and die in his egoism. What a terrifying solitude extends around me and burrows into the depths of my soul! My exaltation resembles annihilation, and since I made myself god, I no longer see myself as anything but a phantom).[54]

There are traces of the same psychological progression in Schopenhauer's thought. He had claimed to be the first philosopher to grant morality "its complete and entire rights; for only if the true nature of man is his own *will*, consequently only if he is, in the strictest sense, his own work, are his deeds actually entirely his and attributable to him."[55] But freedom resides only in that noumenal will which, although it is the core of our (and all) being, is "wholly inaccessible" to the intellect. As phenomenal beings we are therefore determined, our characters shaped by some act of will that takes place outside space and time. Schopenhauer's treatise contains the following revealing reflection on its own project of self-knowledge: "As soon as we . . . wish for once to know ourselves fully by directing our knowledge inwards, we lose ourselves in a bottomless void; we find ourselves like a hollow glass globe, from the emptiness of which a voice speaks. But the cause of this voice is not to be found in the globe, and since we want to comprehend ourselves, we grasp with a shudder nothing but a wavering and unstable phantom."[56]

Schopenhauer argues that our intuitions about the mystery of the self are consonant with those Eastern teachings which interpret each life as a reward or punishment for behavior in an earlier incarnation. He is particularly attracted by the notion that each successive form assumed by the will represents a progression toward that state of self-understanding that will prompt it to "abolish" the phenomenal world entirely.[57] He sees such doctrines as the "natural" result of unprejudiced observation and reflection, supported by the moral and aesthetic insights of humanity throughout its history. In the way he formulates them, they also present an obvious parallel with Hegel's notion of the human consciousness as the vehicle whereby Absolute Spirit reaches self-awareness. The metaphysical rhetoric, representing the individual ego as "bearer" of the universal will, is the same. Schopenhauer would not have welcomed the comparison, although he is happy to compare his insights into noumenal reality with those of Christianity, interpreted as "the doctrine of the deep guilt of the human race by reason of its very existence, and of the heart's intense longing for salvation therefrom."[58]

There are still critics who echo Schopenhauer's claim that his philosophy's great merit lies in the fact that "all its truths have been found independently of one another, through a consideration of the real world."[59] But others have noted that he much exaggerates the degree of unanimity among the mystical movements that he quotes in his support: they are far from being sightings of one and the same thing.[60] Nor does the empirical evidence favor the view that the content of consciousness is "often in fact entirely . . . nothing but a stream of paltry, earthly, poor ideas, and endless worries and anxieties," that reason is invariably the servant of the will, happiness merely the negative sensation of the absence of pain, and history a monotonous repetition devoid of development.[61]

> "Warum willst du dich von uns Allen
> Und unsrer Meinung entfernen?"—
> Ich schreibe nicht euch zu gefallen,
> Ihr sollt was lernen.

> Ist's denn so grosses Geheimnis was Gott und der Mensch und
> die Welt sei?—
> Nein, doch niemand hoert's gerne, da bleibt es geheim.

The first of these two quotations from Goethe serves as an opening epigraph to the second book of *The World as Will;* the second introduces *From the Other Shore.* It is not greatly surprising that two thinkers who were equally aware of a profound and general resistance to their ideas should each independently introduce their most polemical works in this way. But it is also not too fanciful to surmise that among the targets of Herzen's attack was the philosopher who had anticipated him in the same enterprise but had failed to observe its cardinal rule: "In passing from the old world to the new, you can take nothing with you."[62] Both men perceived that the erosion of religious belief demanded a review of all our notions about the nature of the self, but Herzen was the more consistent in carrying it through. Behind the obsessive question that his disillusioned idealist addresses to history—"What is the purpose of all this?"—he sees a conservatism compounded of arrogance and fear: "Idealists are chary of surrendering themselves; they are just as stubbornly egotistical as monks who can stand any privations, but never forget themselves, their personality, the reward." The last illusion to which we cling is the faith that we are central to the scheme of things; Herzen suggests that it is less painful to believe that we are uniquely punished in that scheme, frozen in a tragic pose of opposition to the universe, than that we are peripheral to its operations, dependent for our survival, like all other living things, on a successful interaction with our natural and historical environment.[63] But this "humility" in the face of the prosaic reality of our status as physical beings is the sign of a mature understanding, and it can also be a source of hope. Our brain "has been formed under the influence of past conditions. There is much that it cannot grasp, or sees from the wrong angle." It has grown "onesidedly" because of idealism; people have begun to notice this and are now moving in another direction. "We used to be great and strong, even happy in our detachment, in the bliss of our theories, but now we have gone beyond this state and it has become intolerable to us." People will be cured of idealism "as they have been of other historical diseases—chivalry, Catholicism, Protestantism." This movement will be long, confused, and difficult, full of false starts and unfulfilled potential, like all processes in history and Nature. One example of such a confused beginning, the indignation of the disenchanted idealist, "is perhaps a good thing—a sharp ferment that spurs man to action and movement, but, after all, that is merely the initial impulse; one cannot remain merely indignant and spend one's life lamenting one's failures, in a constant state of struggle and resentment!" Pessimism is indeed manifest on all sides; the more reason to seek a way of escape. "Suffering, pain—is a challenge to battle; it is the warning cry of life, calling attention to danger."[64]

Herzen's belief in the adaptive potential of the human psyche was founded on personal experience. The young Herzen had been apt to complain, like Schopenhauer, that happiness "lies always in the future, or else in the past, and the present may be compared to a small dark cloud driven by the wind over the sunny plain; in front of and behind the cloud everything is bright, only it itself always casts a shadow." Herzen's diaries and letters of the early 1840s (when the frustrations of political exile in the Russian provinces were followed by a series of domestic tragedies) are variations on the Schopenhauerian theme of the senselessness of life, "with its deluded hopes and accidents bringing all calculations to nought";[65] but he succeeded in overcoming inertia and despair by resolving to exploit to the fullest the freedom offered by the indeterminateness of human existence. As he pointed out in his remarkable essay of 1860, *Robert Owen*, that Nature is not *for us* does not mean that she is *against us:* "Both nature and history *are going nowhere,* and therefore they are ready to go *anywhere* to which they are directed, *if this is possible,* that is, if nothing obstructs them. . . . In history and nature a multitude of possibilities, episodes, discoveries, lies slumbering at every step." The role of chance in history does not make it a random process: laws exist, probabilities can be calculated. The accumulated experience of humanity, stored in its collective memory, makes it possible to progress. It is not a tragedy that human progress does not lead in a linear fashion to a single goal. If there were an overall plan, whether divine or rational, we would be merely needles and threads in the hands of fate as it sews the tapestry of history: our value and our moral dignity reside in the fact that in the improvisation that is history, each of us can be "an irreplaceable reality," able to influence our own time and place in ways that no one else can replicate.[66]

The "eternal play of life"[67] (in which Schopenhauer saw only monotonous repetition) was for Herzen comforting proof that "every historical phase has its complete reality, its own individuality, that each is an aim achieved, not a means." He would make no messianic claims for the theory of "Russian socialism" that he based on the potential of the peasant commune, defending it principally as an empirical solution to a contemporary problem, which exploited a chance set of circumstances, namely, that Russia's traditional system of communal land tenure was still intact at a time when the more advanced countries of Western Europe were facing the severe social consequences of the creation of a landless proletariat. He was fond of comparing the poetic fantasies of conservative Slavophiles and utopian socialists to his own "prosaic" approach to the possibilities of the fleeting historical moment.[68] As he wrote in *From the Other Shore,* "I am neither a pessimist nor an optimist; I watch, I examine, without any preconceived notion, without any prepared idealism, and I am in no hurry to reach a verdict."[69]

We have seen that Herzen hoped that philosophical pessimism would be no more than a short-lived transitional stage in the movement away from teleological explanations of the visible world. In this he was mistaken. Schopenhauer's atheism, irrationalism, and mockery of "optimistic" theories of progress were a potent mixture that continues to exercise a pervasive (some have suggested all-pervasive) influence on ethics, aesthetics, and cultural theory, not least by way of the man who claimed him as his educator—Nietzsche.[70] Although Schopenhauer's ascetic denial of the will may appear the antithesis of the Nietzschean *Übermensch*'s "yes" to life, it has often been argued that the latter is the affirmation of a despair that refuses to recognize itself as such. The Übermensch asserts his will to be the meaning of the earth, in defiance of a historical process dominated by the desire of the resentful for revenge and destined (according to Nietzsche's fatalistic theory of eternal recurrence) to repeat its absurdities, the future being a replica of the past. In a fundamentally irrational world his feat can have no aim other than itself; his own authenticity and the value of his actions derive from his readiness to undertake the most difficult moral and existential tasks, irrespective of their accepted moral worth. In this strange ethic, moral strenuousness is an end in itself: in Nietzsche's purposeless world there is "no better purpose . . . than to be destroyed by that which is great and impossible." This "penitential theory of a God-less universe" (as J. P. Stern describes it) can be seen as an activist variation on the Schopenhauerian theme of the self-renunciation of a will irrevocably at odds with a meaningless reality.[71] Schopenhauer's model of virtue, it will be recalled, "gives the lie to the body": in his 1886 preface to *Human, All-Too-Human,* Nietzsche tells us: "I took sides *against* myself, and *for* everything that hurt me and was hard for me; thus I found the way . . . to that courageous pessimism that is the antithesis of all romantic fraud."[72]

It is still debated whether, in its nazified form, the doctrine that all is permitted to the self-sacrificing hero was a terrible abuse or a logical application of Nietzsche's ethic. But undoubtedly, for many self-designated Nietzscheans, as for the master himself, the compelling attraction of his doctrine consists in its claim to dare and bear a truth from which all but the strongest flinch.[73] In the last quarter of the twentieth century, the same claim has been made ever more insistently on Schopenhauer's behalf; we are told that, in the face of the crumbling of the last of our traditional structures, faiths, and ideologies, pessimistic quietism is not (as it might seem) a form of moral cowardice but rather the only consistent response to the final proofs of the death of God.

Herzen dismissed this kind of argument: the pessimists, and the optimists whom they despised, were brothers under the skin, equally motivated by a secret fear of confronting the fact that we are not central to the cosmic scheme of things and equally cavalier in their disregard for evidence that did not suit their purposes. In an essay published in 1869, a year before his death, Herzen reflects that although the utopian optimism of the contemporary Russian Left conjures up something out of nothing, the "destructive creativeness" of pessimistic nihilism achieves "the turning of facts and thoughts into nothing, into barren scepticism, into haughty folding of the arms, into the despair which leads to inaction." Two of the greatest of such contemporary nihilists, he observes, are the novelist Ivan Turgenev and "his favorite philosopher, Schopenhauer."[74]

Herzen's readers would have recognized the allusion to Turgenev's bleak story "Enough," whose narrator recommends (as an appropriate reaction to a world order that seems implacably opposed to human aspirations) that one calmly turn one's back on it all, fold one's "useless arms," and say "Enough!"[75] It was in his polemics with Turgenev in the early 1860s that Herzen first referred explicitly to Schopenhauer's doctrines, which had helped to shape Turgenev's vision of a tragic discontinuity between the highest aspirations of human beings and the conditions of their finite existence. Turgenev argued that although Herzen had grasped the irrationality of the historical process, he had recoiled from the implications of his discovery. A more attentive reading of Schopenhauer, he suggests, might cure his friend of his illusions on the question of Russia's potential for progress.[76]

In his response, "Ends and Beginnings," Herzen rejects Turgenev's belief that Russia is condemned to repeat the historical course of Europe, with all its tragedies and disillusionments. In life and Nature, Herzen asserts, "there are no monopolies, no measures for preventing and suppressing new zoological species, new historical destinies and political systems—they are limited only by practical possibility. The future is an improvisation on a theme from the past."[77] At any instant a cosmic catastrophe might put an end to such experiments, but until then the lack of a historical script offered an infinity of challenges to human creativity. In his appraisal of the chances of individual self-fulfillment, Herzen could not be accused of optimism in Schopenhauer's sense. As he tells the pessimist in *From the Other Shore,* "I prize every fleeting pleasure, every minute of joy, for there are fewer and fewer of them. . . . I should not say that my present point of view is a particularly consoling one, but I have grown calmer; I have stopped being angry with life because it does not give what it cannot give—that is all I have managed to achieve."[78] The human individual exists "between two voids—the void before his birth and the void after his death": on this Herzen and Turgenev could agree.[79] Nor would Herzen dispute that this brief existence is dominated by suffering: Turgenev, meeting him at the end of a decade of personal and political tragedies, notes that he is only beginning to emerge from the "gnawing sadness" of those years.[80] His favorite poet, for whom he professed a "boundless love," was Giacomo Leopardi, whom he describes as an "apologist of death . . . who represents the world as a league of the wicked, waging savage war against a few virtuous madmen." He recalls defending him in a conversation with Giuseppe Mazzini, one of those fanatical believers who were incapable of comprehending "these poisonous reflections, these shattering doubts. They see in them only fruitless complaint, only weak despair."[81]

Schopenhauer, too, greatly admired Leopardi as a poet whose understanding of life's "tragic farce" was unsurpassed in his century.[82] But while Schopenhauer sees Leopardi's despair as expressing the eternal truth about humanity's predicament, Herzen points to the historical context of his "gloomy, satanic laughter": the reaction after 1848, which blighted the prospects for Italian independence. In Herzen's view it was no coincidence that Mikhail Lermontov— the only other modern poet "who made the somber chords of the human soul vibrate with such force"—died before the first stirrings of political liberation in his country.[83] Where Schopenhauer saw terminal despair, Herzen saw the "warning cry of life" spurring others on to action.

The hope of the fighter is our compensation for surrendering the secret aspirations that fuel the pessimist's despair, along with the arrogant belief that we have been somehow cheated of the destiny we deserve. Only when we renounce our unreal expectations and cease to judge the hazardous processes of life and history by inappropriate criteria can we exploit our contingency and make it work for us. For Herzen, this was a matter of logical consistency: "Events move rapidly but the brain develops slowly"; "Quantitatively, reason will always have to give way." But human reason is nonetheless a component of the historical process, which can, therefore, never be totally irrational and uncontrollable. In Smoke, Turgenev's most Schopenhauerian novel, he declares that Nature has its own logic, which we come to recognize only after it has crushed us. Herzen, too, notes that Nature's ways do not conform to rational categories but points out to Turgenev that recognition of the inevitable is a source of strength. Of course, sub specie aeternitatis our tiny area of creative maneuverability vanishes into nothingness, a point that Herzen makes with a nicely calculated irony in "Ends and Beginnings," comparing their debate on the nature of history to a dialogue between two friends, one of whom recalls

> a certain German book, in which the laborious existence of the mole is described—it is very funny. The little beast, with big paws and little slits instead of eyes, digs in the dark, underground, in the damp, digs day and night, without weariness, without diversion, with passionate persistence. It barely stops to snatch a bite—some little grains and worms, and sets to work again; but in return for all this a burrow is ready for the children, and the mole dies in peace; and the children begin digging holes in all directions for their own children. What is the price paid for a lifetime of toil underground? What is the relation between effort and attainment? Ha, ha, ha![84]

The German book in question is *The World as Will and Representation*, in which the life of the mole is selected as an outstanding example of the "evident want of proportion between the effort and the reward" of all phenomenal existence.[85] Herzen concludes this essay with a reminder to Turgenev: "Within two days we shall have the New Year, and I wish you a happy one; we must summon up fresh strength for the molelike labors ahead; my paws are itching to begin."[86]

Turgenev saw Herzen as a secret idealist who sought to poeticize the prosaic nature of the everyday. But Herzen did not hold reality to be other than prosaic: where he differed from Schopenhauer and his followers was on the creative possibilities of humble daily prose.

The Divine Inventor, Chance

CHAPTER SEVENTEEN

In 1852 the French historian Jules Michelet published a tirade against the Russian government and people. The vast majority of the population of that country, he pointed out, were barbarous serfs, and the gentry who owned them were themselves the cringing servants of a tyranny that threatened the freedom of the whole of Europe. The Russians, he suggested, were devoid of moral sense.[1] This attack drew an angry response from an obscure Russian political refugee who argued that the Russian people might indeed be politically enslaved but that, unlike their European critics, they were not morally shackled by the formidable legacy of a theological and philosophical culture which routinely sacrificed the aspirations of real individuals to idealized abstractions such as Spirit, the state, or universal progress. His people were fortunate, he wrote, in that their miserable past had left them with no such heritage. The most daring among them had, in fact, begun to dream of a revolution which would sweep away not only the tsar, but all those metaphysical fictions that devalued the real world in which they had to live.

The refugee was Aleksandr Herzen, one of the first to predict the erosion of that faith in a purposeful universe in which the basic assumptions of all the great optimistic systems of the nineteenth century—Christian theism, utopian socialism, Marxism and Comtian positivism—were grounded. From our postmodern perspective we can appreciate the size of that shift in representations of the world which Nietzsche would characterize with the lurid metaphor of the death of God. Darwin's discovery of the primary role of chance in evolutionary processes, Nietzsche's unmasking of the devices language uses to impose an illusory stability on the flux of life, Freud's revelations about the power of the unconscious, and the failure of political utopias have all helped to shape a sense of the world as inherently fragmentary, at the mercy of time and chance. This sense has already filtered through from intellectual debate to everyday social practices. As Jean-François Lyotard put it, "The temporary contract is . . . supplanting permanent institutions in the professional, emotional, sexual, cultural, family and international domains, as well as in political affairs."[2] Some philosophers claim that we are in the midst of a revolution which will ultimately erase the picture of the self that has been common to

Greek metaphysics, Christian philosophy, and Enlightenment rationalism: a self rooted in some timeless reality which serves as the source of universal norms. If this is so, it seems a remarkably joyless revolution, rarely accompanied by any sense of liberation. For many, the end of ideology is just the beginning of a nihilistic pessimism.

Philosophical pessimism in its modern form dates back to Schopenhauer, who interpreted human history as an anarchic and absurd struggle for existence among beings doomed to death. The vanity of existence, he declared, "is revealed in the whole form existence assumes . . . in the contingency and relativity of all things." Schopenhauer's thought was an inspiration for Nietzsche's "pessimism of *strength*," built on a heroic acceptance of humanity's tragic dependence on chance.[3] Nietzsche's vision of an intrinsically meaningless world has profoundly, and sometimes catastrophically, influenced social and moral philosophy and practice in our century, and pessimism is now widely perceived as the only intellectually honest reaction to a world without an a priori moral or rational order. But the most effective challenge to these ideas was raised while they were still being shaped, by the Russian exile who maintained that even the most radical European thinkers of his time were conservatives, clinging sentimentally to outworn interpretations of the world. Herzen would argue that pessimism was a confused, half-way stage in the process of coming to terms with the contingent nature of human existence. In answer to those who fear that our progress in this direction has already led us to a new dark age, his views can be a source of hope and inspiration.

In 1849, just one year after the Communist Manifesto had proclaimed the coming of a revolution which would end "exploitation, oppression, and enmity among nations," Herzen wrote that nobody should expect that the victory of socialism would provide a conclusive solution to the problems of society. Socialism would generate its own inner contradictions and absurdities, until "a mortal struggle will begin, in which socialism will play the role of contemporary conservatism, and be overwhelmed in the subsequent revolution, as yet unknown to us."[4]

This prediction was all the more remarkable in that it was made by the founder of Russian socialism. Herzen is best known outside Russia for his memoirs as an exile and an observer of the European social and political scene in the mid-nineteenth century. These, together with his outstandingly original essays on the nature of history, rank among the masterpieces of Russian writing. His principal activity, however, was political journalism. He emigrated in 1847 at the age of thirty-five in order to devote his life to the struggle against the Russian autocracy. In the 1850s he performed the feat of single-handedly creating and shaping a public opinion in his country by means of the Free Russian

Press that he set up in London, whose smuggled publications, aimed at inform-
ing and awakening the consciences of Russia's educated elite, helped prepare
the ground for the emancipation of the serfs in 1861. He preached a form of
anarchism inspired by the cooperative structure of the Russian agrarian commune but did not present his ideal as a universal answer to social problems. In
an age of visionary utopias, he took the unpopular view that there were no empirical grounds for believing that history was an ascent toward any final goal,
whether preprogrammed by a benevolent Creator or inherent in the rational
structure of the universe. History, like Nature, gave no guarantees, continually
suppressing developments that were full of promise or rerouting them into
new and unexpected channels. Chance and unexplained forces intervened at
every step to defeat rational intention. No model of society could claim to be
more than a provisional experiment whose life expectancy depended on contingent circumstances. Why was the modern mind so resistant to this idea?
Herzen saw the answer in the dualism characteristic of Western interpretations
of the world since Plato and Aristotle, in which appearance and essence, the
real and ideal worlds, were polarized. Anticipating Nietzsche's critique of "nihilistic" otherworldly values which degrade the world of experience, Herzen
notes that all the great moral systems have been built on the assumption that
process, chance, and change are less real than timelessness and stasis, singular
events less significant than universal norms and laws. We prefer symmetry and
finality to paradox and open-endedness. Our concepts and images are all
rooted in the idea that the world of phenomena can be made intelligible and
given legitimacy only by reference to notions of ultimate design: the revolutionary atheist who denies God deifies a perfected future humanity. This urge
to escape from the precariousness and conflicts of contingent existence into a
changeless idyll, Herzen argued, is understandable but misconceived. We hate
and fear chance as a malign and brutal force, "but it is only by depriving history of any predestined path that man and history become something serious,
effective, filled with profound interest. If events are stacked in advance, if the
whole of history is the unfolding of some prehistorical plot that is confined to
. . . a single mise en scene, then at least let us too take up wooden swords and
tin shields. . . . With a prearranged plan history is reduced to the insertion of
numbers in an algebraical formula; the future is mortgaged before our birth."[5]

Herzen's assessment of his compatriots' mentality in his letter to Michelet
was overoptimistic: the Russian revolutionary parties preferred to fight the autocracy with the messianic certainties of imported socialism rather than with
his brand of iconoclastic humanism. But many intellectuals in the populist
movement that he founded emulated his revolt against the despotism of systems over human beings. The same antidogmatic humanism can be seen in the
works of Russia's great writers as well—for example, in Chekhov's plays and

stories and in the novels of Dostoevsky and Tolstoy, whose heroes have the habit of making eccentric but deeply disturbing objections to propositions deemed self-evident by more sophisticated Western minds. The ironic outsider of Dostoevsky's *Notes from Underground* suggests that the human race's well-known passion for creating disorder may arise from its instinctive dread of constructing the perfect social edifice and then having to cease its building operations, from its sense that the aim of life is in the living of it, in the process of attainment rather in its goal, which has to be some simple formula such as two times two equals four. "But two times two is four is no longer life, gentlemen, but the beginning of death!"[6] In Tolstoy's *Anna Karenina,* Levin's search for a grand meaning in existence leads him to a state of suicidal despair, from which he is saved by a renewed sense of the richness and intrinsic value of everyday life. "I looked for miracles," he declares, "grieved because I did not see a miracle that would convince me. And here is a miracle, the only miracle possible, continually existing, surrounding me on all sides, and I never noticed it!"[7]

This distinctive strand in Russian thought was cited to me by an eminent Russian scientist on a visit to Cambridge from Siberia in the summer of 1993, when the revolution that Herzen had predicted was well under way. With the demise of the communist dream, Russians were facing for the first time that comprehensive loss of faith in universal systems which intellectuals in the West had begun to experience over a century earlier. News reports began to hint at what we now know to be true: that many were reacting with the kinds of cynicism and despair that are depressingly familiar to Europeans and Americans, while a significant number were seeking to revive precommunist traditions of messianic nationalism to fill the intolerable void. But the scientist placed his hopes for the future of his country on the reaffirmation of a more tenuous Russian tradition, of which Herzen can claim to be one of the fathers and which locates the miraculous in the daily flux of life, with its limitless opportunities for discovery, invention, and creation. As well as appealing to the scientific mind, my visitor pointed out, Herzen's ideas coincided with the intuitions of Russia's greatest writers. He quoted from memory some lines by Russia's national poet, Aleksandr Pushkin:

> O, how many and marvelous are the discoveries
> prepared for us by the spirit of enlightenment,
> by Experiment, the child of painful error,
> by Genius, the friend of paradox,
> and by the divine inventor, Chance."[8]

Herzen sometimes referred to his perception of the world as "true nihilism," a clear alternative both to comforting illusions and to the despair of those who can see no meaning in transitory existence. His option offers an escape from the dilemma of those who hold that honesty rules out optimism but cannot come to terms with the denial of freedom that pessimism seems to entail. In *From the Other Shore*, Herzen addresses this predicament in dialogues in which he and an imaginary companion attempt to map out the unfamiliar and terrifying landscape of a world without a governing purpose. Herzen's friend asserts that if no such purpose exists, we should cease to struggle for our ideals and wait with resignation for the waters to close over our heads. The game of life is not worth the candle.

This protest is a faithful echo of Schopenhauer's attack on nineteenth-century historical optimism, much praised by Nietzsche for its pioneering courage in confronting a purposeless universe. But Herzen suggests that the real motives of such cosmic pessimism are human vanity and fear. Rather than judge the world by its capacity to fulfill our "private whims," he recommends that we learn to adapt our categories to the ex tempore nature of history, which "uses every chance, every coincidence . . . knocks simultaneously at a thousand gates." The unprogrammable and unpredictable nature of finite existence can empower as well as thwart the individual. As Herzen put it in a later essay, anyone is at liberty to insert his verse into the tattered improvisation of history, and "if it is resonant, it will remain *his* verse until the poem breaks off, as long as the past ferments in its blood and memory.[9]

Herzen frequently used aesthetic images to describe an attitude to life that has clear affinities with Nietzsche's *amor fati:* the demand that we face up to the "beautiful chaos" of existence, joyfully accept the historicity of the human condition with its attendant suffering, finitude, and mortality, and embrace "dear chance" by shaping arbitrary, random events into the aesthetic unity of a unique self. But had Herzen lived long enough to respond to Nietzsche's ideas, he would certainly not have assented to Nietzsche's view that there is no reality independent of our shifting perspectives on it; that "nothing is true, all is permitted"; that our concepts—moral, social, even scientific—are no more than convenient fictions used to justify the pragmatic strategies of the single moving force of all living things: the will to power.[10] Herzen, on the contrary, used the empirical methods of the natural sciences to demonstrate that the view of the world as a chaotic battleground of irrational forces is an overreaction to the failure of unrealistic expectations, a muddled transitional stage on the way to understanding reality without metaphysical preconceptions. Observation and experience reveal that chance operates within a framework of laws which allow us to calculate probabilities, to control events within certain boundaries, and even to progress, though not to utopia. Herzen's world, unlike Nietzsche's, contains no boltholes for supermen—that lonely elite who obey no laws except those they make for themselves, in triumphant independence of all social norms and institutions, which they identify with the life-denying values of the herd. Nietzsche's fantasy has been interpreted as an exciting anticipation of what human societies can become in a postmetaphysical age: that is, communities of "self-creating" individuals experimenting with different moral and philosophical vocabularies in a spirit of ironic play. Herzen would have seen this vision as a romantic retreat from history. When the anarchist Mikhail Bakunin glorified the "will to destroy" as the sole creative force in history, Herzen accused him of a naive disregard for the "physiology" of historical and social change, the painful slowness of processes of growth in real time.[11] In his dialogues with the pessimist he suggests that it is ridiculous to shake one's fist at an unsympathetic universe, cowardly to hope to escape from the prosaic constraints of the everyday. We like to assume that Nature and history are two wholly different processes, but the truth is that "the development of nature passes imperceptibly into the development of mankind, that these are two chapters of one novel, two phases of one process, very far apart at the extremities, very close together in the centre." We shall grow in freedom and dignity only by first humbling ourselves, accepting that it is futile to apply "our own petty household rules," our human demands for intentionality and purpose, to the economy of a world in which we make so brief and peripheral an appearance.[12]

Ten years after Herzen wrote these lines, the human species was humbled by a scientific demonstration that its arrival on earth was not the culmination of a goal-directed process but a by-product of adaptive responses to changes in local environments. Herzen's dialogues with his imaginary friend uncannily anticipate Darwin's exchanges with anxious or irate correspondents who believed that his revolution had set them adrift in an unfeeling universe. Replying to the Christian evolutionist Asa Gray, who feared that the theory of natural selection could be held to imply that the universe was shaped entirely by blind chance, Darwin acknowledges the existence of laws which direct the broad channels of life but insists that the details, whether good or bad, are "left to the working out of what we may call chance."[13] The general laws may or may not have been expressly designed: to those who demanded his opinion on the ultimate origin and purpose of life, Darwin responded that science could throw no light on such matters. Herzen professed a similar agnosticism. Nietzsche would declare the concept of God to be "far too extreme a hypothesis"; Herzen would have said the same of Nietzsche's dogmatic atheism.[14] Pressed for his views on the existence of an intelligent first cause, Darwin famously replied: "The safest conclusion seems to me that the whole subject is beyond the scope of man's intellect, but man can do his duty."[15] Herzen defends the notion of free will against the crude scientific materialism of his age as, at the very least, a "psychological or, if you wish, an anthropological reality," without which we could not function as social beings.[16] He was among the first to grasp the importance of the challenge that the *Origin of Species* posed to teleological thought in all branches of intellectual activity; he recommends the work to his Russian readers as an antidote to the profound conservatism of most current European thought. He believed, like Darwin, that to accept the chanciness of phenomenal existence was in no way to demean it. Asked to admit to some consoling sign of an overarching providential scheme in evolution, Darwin responded that, on the available evidence, natural selection "is not perfect in its action, but tends only to render each species as successful as possible in the battle for life with other species, in wonderfully changing and complex circumstances." In one of his notebooks he wrote: "What a chance it is . . . that has made a man!"—an exclamation that denotes wonder, not despair.[17] Herzen shared this attitude of wonder before the miraculousness of the accidents that had created human reason, so marginal and fragile a development in the history of the universe. The reassurance we seek regarding our freedom and moral responsibility was, he believed, to be found not in some inaccessible transcendent sphere but all around us, in the wonderfully changing circumstances of the everyday world, which ensured that no two moral choices, no two creative acts, could ever be identical. If this is so, he asks, *"how then can one sit back and fold one's arms!"*[18]

This was no shallow optimism. The young Herzen had cursed the "outrageous power of chance" and the "precariousness of all that is best and most sacred in life."[19] A series of personal tragedies (the drowning at sea of his mother and younger son, followed a few months later by the death of his wife and newborn child) exposed him to chance in its most destructive forms, and his memoirs contain a moving account of his struggle to resist the attractions of some compensating vision of rational progress. Dostoevsky interpreted Herzen's faith in the self-sufficing value of contingent existence as a form of religious belief. From the perspective of our time he can be seen as anticipating hermeneutic philosophers who argue that the historicity of the self does not render moral generalizations meaningless and who detect in history the unifying thread of a spiritual quest: the search to articulate our intuitive sense of the good.

Herzen himself was clear about the tradition in which he stood. One of his heroes was Francis Bacon, the founder of modern science, whose inductive method was based on a close observation of the physical world and who exhorted his fellow scholars not to exclude "things that are mean and low" from the field of their investigations: "The sun enters the sewer no less than the palace, yet takes not pollution."[20] Bacon's belief that progress in knowledge was made by purging the human mind of "idols" (false representations of the external world enshrined in systems and sanctified by authority and tradition) made a deep impression on Herzen when he was a student in the Faculty of Physics and Mathematics at Moscow University in the early 1830s. At the same time the evolutionist theories of Erasmus Darwin and Geoffroy Saint-Hilaire (which were beginning to challenge the doctrine of the immutability of species) had helped to shape his view of history. He retained a lifelong interest in the natural sciences, and it was as a scientist that he opposed the doctrinaire intolerance that he encountered among Russian radicals. A true understanding of science, he maintained, would persuade them not to treat the ideas of others with contempt: "Science even more than the Gospel teaches us humility. She cannot look down on anything, she does not know what condescension means, she despises nothing, never lies for the sake of a pose, and conceals nothing out of coquetry. She stops before the facts as an investigator, sometimes as a physician, never as an executioner, and still less with hostility and irony. . . . Science is *love,* as Spinoza said of thought and understanding."

Defiantly, he asserts that he is not obliged to keep those last words "hidden in the silence of the spirit."[21] He was aware that his view of science was far removed from the popular stereotype, according to which scientific method was unemotional, analytic, aimed at the discovery of some single explanatory formula under which all the complexity of empirical reality could be subsumed. But in our own age (despite the continuing stereotype) the natural sciences have come increasingly to focus on the unrepeatable phenomena in which Herzen saw the engrossing interest of history and Nature. The evolutionary biologist Stephen Jay Gould has argued that in exploring the theme of contingency, science can learn from the way writers like Tolstoy describe the cascading effects of individual human actions and choices on the lives around them.[22] The sense of freedom and moral responsibility with which Gould contemplates an unprogrammed (but not random) world is symptomatic of the revolution in thought that Herzen hoped would counter utopian expectations and nihilistic despair. It has yet to fulfill that promise, but it *is* beginning to lay to rest some of the more sterile debates between science and religion by transferring our attention from ultimate ends and origins to the miracles wrought daily by "the divine inventor, Chance."

Notes

Introduction

1. *Hegel's Lectures on the Philosophy of History*, trans. E. S. Haldane and F. H. Simson, 3 vols. (London, 1963), 3:217; A. I. Herzen, *Sobranie sochinenii*, 30 vols. (Moscow, 1954–66), 3:242.

2. For the history of the term *intelligentsia* in Western Europe and Russia, see O. W. Müller, *Intelligenciia: Untersuchungen zur Geschichte eines politischen Schlagwortes* (Frankfurt, 1971). It became popular in Russia in the mid-nineteenth century when, as Isaiah Berlin has observed, its members "thought of themselves as united by something more than mere interest in ideas; they conceived themselves as being a dedicated order, almost a secular priesthood, devoted to the spreading of a specific attitude to life, something like a gospel" (Berlin, *Russian Thinkers* [London, 1978], 117).

   No simple and uncontroversial definition of this ideologically charged term is possible. With the notable exception of Berlin, Western liberal historians have tended to regard the Russian intelligentsia en masse as an unattractive and extreme species of doctrinaire. See Martin Malia's definition of the "classical" intelligentsia of the 1840s and 1860s as "men of ruthlessly logical ideology" (Malia, "What Is the Intelligentsia?" in *The Russian Intelligentsia*, ed. R. Pipes [New York, 1961], 12). The term will be generally used in this book in a broad sense, denoting politically conscious and committed men and women who shared a deep concern with social justice and a moral opposition to the status quo. By the early twentieth century this group included many liberals who were sympathetic to the ideals of the Left: hence I use the adjective *radical* when I want to emphasize the revolutionary subset of the intelligentsia. See also "Which Signposts?" n. 69.

3. M. Malia, *Alexander Herzen and the Birth of Russian Socialism, 1812–1855* (Cambridge, Mass., 1961), 419.

4. Edward Acton, *Rethinking the Russian Revolution* (London, 1990), 39. In a lucid and balanced survey of the interpretations that have shaped conventional wisdom about the revolution, Acton points out that until the 1960s the approach of scholars to the Russian radical intelligentsia was usually determined by their adherence to one of three traditional schools of thought on the origins and nature of the revolution: the Soviet, the liberal, and what he calls the "libertarian" (Western historians on the far left of the political spectrum who saw the intelligentsia as representatives of a new technocratic, managerial class spawned by Western capitalism, who sought to take power into their own hands, and who found a congenial expression for that aspiration in Marx's "scientific socialism" and Bolshevik political centralism). As the tensions between East and West eased in the late 1950s, a revisionist school gained ground among Western historians, influenced by the approaches and techniques of historians such as the French

Annales school. While drawing on the insights of each of the three traditional schools, revisionists have attempted to demythologize the intelligentsia, arguing that as a group it was neither as isolated from social realities, as ideologically monolithic, as utopian, or as important in the Russian revolutionary movement as it had been traditionally presented, and that the roots of the fall of tsarism and of the failure of liberals and moderate socialists are deeper and more complex than had been believed by most Western or Soviet commentators (28–48, 83–106).

5. Berlin, *Russian Thinkers,* 148.
6. K. S. Vincent, *Pierre-Joseph Proudhon and the Rise of French Republican Socialism* (Oxford, 1984), 125.
7. Ibid., 11.
8. See G. S. Morson and C. Emerson, *Mikhail Bakhtin: Creation of a Prosaics* (Stanford, Calif., 1990); and Morson, "Prosaic Bakhtin: Landmarks, Anti-Intelligentsialism, and the Russian Counter-Tradition," *Common Knowledge* 2, no. 1 (1993): 35–74.
9. See R. Rorty, *Contingency, Irony and Solidarity* (Cambridge, Eng., 1989). For a critique of Rorty's view, see B. Williams, "Auto-da-Fé: Consequences of Pragmatism," in *Reading Rorty: Critical Responses to* Philosophy and the Mirror of Nature *(and Beyond),* ed. A. R. Malachowski (Oxford, Eng., 1990), 26–36.
10. C. Norris, *What's Wrong with Postmodernism: Critical Theory and the Ends of Philosophy* (London, 1990), 3–4.
11. F. M. Dostoievsky, *The Diary of a Writer,* trans. B. Brasol (Salt Lake City, 1985), 760.
12. F. Nietzsche, "Ecce Homo," in *Werke in Drei Bänden,* ed. K. Schlechta (Munich, 1954–56), 2:1066.
13. See my essays in the *New York Review of Books:* "Revealing Bakhtin," 24 September 1992; and "Chekhov the Subversive," 6 November 1997. (These essays, together with my studies of Herzen's thought mentioned in this volume, are collected in my forthcoming book *Views from Another Shore: Essays on Herzen, Chekhov and Bakhtin.*)
14. P. Waugh, ed., *Postmodernism: A Reader* (London, 1992), 9.

CHAPTER ONE
A Complex Vision

1. *The Autobiography of Bertrand Russell* (London, 1978), 354.
2. J. Gray, *Berlin* (London, 1995), 2.
3. I. Berlin, *Four Essays on Liberty* (London, 1969), 116.
4. Ibid., 198, 112, xxvii.
5. Berlin, *Russian Thinkers,* 1–21.
6. Ibid., 83.
7. Ibid., 197–98.
8. Ibid., 51.
9. Ibid., 262.
10. L. Kolakowski, *Marxism and Beyond: On Historical Understanding and Individual Responsibility,* trans. Jane Zielonko Peel (London, 1971), 162.

11. Berlin, *Russian Thinkers,* 197.

12. Berlin, *Four Essays on Liberty,* 172.

CHAPTER TWO
Leonard Schapiro's Russia

1. L. Schapiro, *Rationalism and Nationalism in Russian Nineteenth-Century Political Thought* (New Haven, 1967).

2. L. Schapiro, *Russian Studies,* ed. E. Dahrendorf, introd. H. Willetts (New York, 1987).

3. Ibid., 18.

4. S. F. Cohen, *Rethinking the Soviet Experience: Politics and History since 1917* (Oxford, 1985).

5. See, e.g., Aleksandr Zinoviev's proclamation to the emigration, warning them not to fall for Soviet propaganda and support the authorities' "hypocritical pretense of liberalization" *(Kontinent* 51 [1987]: 240–41). Sakharov's belief that Gorbachev should be "encouraged" in his reforms (see his interview with Nicholas Bethell in *Kontinent* 52, 425–45) was bitterly attacked by exiled dissidents; but see Vladimir Voinovich's conclusion that "we are in a moment of hope. . . . I am definitely for this process of reform" ("Vladimir Voinovich, Satirist in Exile," *International Herald Tribune,* June 9, 1987).

6. As examples of the two approaches see, S. Cohen, "An Anti-Stalinist Tide Is Flowing Again," and A. M. Rosenthal, "How to Make This Glasnost More Interesting Than Ever," *International Herald Tribune,* February 3, 1987.

7. Schapiro, *Russian Studies,* 45.

8. Ibid., 24.

9. Ibid., 64.

10. Ibid., 47.

11. See M. Raeff, *Understanding Imperial Russia* (New York, 1984), and T. von Laue, "The Chances for Liberal Constitutionalism," *Slavic Review* 24, no. 1 (1965): 34–46.

12. Schapiro, *Russian Studies,* 90.

13. See D. Field, "Kavelin and Russian Liberalism," *Slavic Review* 32, no. 1 (1973): 59–78.

14. On this curious example of continuity in Russian and Soviet historiography, see chaps. 8 and 9 of A. Yanov, *The Origins of Autocracy: Ivan the Terrible in Russian History,* trans. S. Dunn (Berkeley: University of California Press), 1981.

15. Berlin, *Russian Thinkers,* 302.

16. Schapiro, *Russian Studies,* 351.

17. Ibid., 125, 326.

18. L. Schapiro, *Turgenev: His Life and Times* (Oxford, 1978), 287.

19. Cohen, *Rethinking the Soviet Experience,* 165.

20. Schapiro, *Russian Studies,* 291.

21. Ibid., 297.

22. Cohen, *Rethinking the Soviet Experience,* 4–5. For a particularly illuminating summing-up of past conflicts among historians of communism, see D. Joravsky,

"Communism in Historical Perspective," *American Historical Review* 99, no. 3 (1994): 837–57.

23. Schapiro, *Russian Studies,* 301.

CHAPTER THREE
Carnival of the Intellectuals

1. N. Shelgunov, quoted in A. Walicki, *A History of Russian Thought from the Enlightenment to Marxism* (Stanford, Calif., 1979), 186.
2. N. V. Shelgunov, *Vospominaniia,* ed. A. A. Shilov (Moscow, 1923), 67.
3. See the chapter "Bakhtin, Marxism, and the Carnivalesque," in D. La Capra, *Rethinking Intellectual History: Texts, Contexts, Language* (Ithaca, N.Y., 1983), 291–324. For Bakhtin's theory of carnival, see M. M. Bakhtin, *Problemy poetiki Dostoevskogo* (Moscow, 1979), chap. 4; and *L'oeuvre de François Rabelais et la culture populaire au Moyen Age et sous la Renaissance,* trans. A. Robel (Paris, 1970; hereafter cited as *Rabelais*), chaps. 1 and 7.
4. Bakhtin, *Rabelais,* 101.
5. "Epos i roman. (O metodologii issledovaniia romana)," M. Bakhtin, *Voprosy literatury i estetiki: Issledovaniia raznikh let* (Moscow, 1975), 466.
6. H. Granjard, *Ivan Tourguénev et les courants politiques et sociaux de son temps* (Paris, 1966), 258.
7. A. V. Nikitenko, *Dnevnik v trekh tomakh* (Leningrad, 1955), 1:403; to A. Saffi, 6 March 1855, Herzen, *Sobranie sochinenii,* 25:244.
8. L. N. Tolstoi, *Polnoe sobranie sochinenii,* ed. V. G. Chertkov, 90 vols. (Moscow, 1928–58), 47:37.
9. Nikitenko, *Dnevnik,* 1:405, 410–11, 414.
10. To Tolstoy, 15 October 1855, I. S. Turgenev, *Polnoe sobranie sochinenii i pisem,* 28 vols. (Moscow, 1960–68), *Pis'ma,* 2:316.
11. To T. A. Ergolskaia, 4 September 1855, *Polnoe sobranie,* 59:334.
12. To S. T. Aksakov, 17 September 1855, *Pis'ma,* 2:311–12.
13. Shelgunov, *Vospominaniia,* 167.
14. F. Venturi, *Roots of Revolution: A History of the Populist and Socialist Movements in Nineteenth-Century Russia,* trans. F. Haskell (Chicago, 1960), 236–37.
15. Ibid., 255.
16. Nikitenko, *Dnevnik,* 1:418, 419.
17. Shelgunov, *Vospominaniia,* 83.
18. F. M. Dostoevskii, *Polnoe sobranie sochinenii,* 30 vols. (Leningrad, 1972–88), 26:129, 22:80.
19. To M. N. and V. P. Tolstoy, 20 December 1855, *Pis'ma,* 2:326.
20. A. A. Fet, *Moi vospominaniia,* Slavische Propylaen, vol. 105 (Munich, 1971), 106; P. A. Annenkov, *Literaturnye vospominaniia* (Moscow, 1960), 399.
21. Tolstoi, *Polnoe sobranie sochinenii,* 47:41, 38, 61, 37.
22. See I. Berlin, introduction to A. Herzen, *My Past and Thoughts,* trans. C. Garnett, rev. H. Higgens, 4 vols. (London, 1968), 1:xiv.
23. Herzen, *Sobranie sochinenii,* 24:184, 6:7.
24. Ibid., 12:250.
25. Herzen, "Le peuple russe et le socialisme: Lettre à M. J. Michelet," ibid., 7:299.

26. To his parents, 16 May 1855, N. G. Chernyshevskii, *Polnoe sobranie sochinenii*, 15 vols. (Moscow, 1939–50), 14: 299–300.

27. Shelgunov, *Vospominaniia*, 166.

28. To A. V. Druzhinin and D. V. Grigorovich, 22 July 1855, *Pis'ma*, 2:293; to I. I. Panaev, 22 July 1855, 2:297.

29. To V. P. Botkin, 29 June 1855, *Pis'ma*, 2:282.

30. To S. T. Aksakov, 28 October 1855, *Pis'ma*, 2:317–18.

31. Turgenev, "Gamlet Shchigrovskogo uezda," *Zapiski okhotnika*, *Sochineniia*, 4:281–82.

32. See Bakhtin, *Rabelais*, chap. 7.

33. To Druzhinin, 1 September 1855, *Pis'ma*, 2:309.

34. Cited in Granjard, *Tourguénev*, 241

35. Bahktin, "Slovo v romane," *Voprosy literatury i estetiki*, 147, 200ff.

36. Turgenev, *Rudin*, *Sochineniia*, 6:269.

37. Ibid., 348.

38. See Annenkov's comment in *Literaturnye vospominaniia*, 400–01.

39. See Turgenev's lecture of 1860, "Gamlet i Don Kikhot," *Sochineniia*, 8:169–92.

40. Bahktin, "Slovo v romane," *Voprosy literatury i estetiki*, 144.

41. Turgenev, "Predislovie k romanam," *Sochineniia*, 12:303.

42. To P. V. Annenkov, 21 December 1855, *Pis'ma*, 2:329. On Nekrasov's comments, see the editors' notes to *Rudin*, *Sochineniia*, 6:572.

43. To M. N. and V. P. Tolstoy, 20 December 1855, *Pis'ma*, 2:326.

44. To P. Annenkov, 21 February 1855, *Pis'ma*, 2:328.

45. Ibid.

46. "Dva slova o Granovskom," *Sochineniia*, 6:371–74; to S. T. Aksakov, 28 October 1855, *Pis'ma*, 2:318.

47. To N. A. Nekrasov, 22 July 1855, *Pis'ma*, 2:296–97.

48. Turgenev, *Rudin*, 366–67.

49. To V. P. Botkin and N. A. Nekrasov, 6 August 1855, *Pis'ma*, 2:300–01.

50. Bakhtin, *Rabelais*, 122ff.

51. Herzen, "Eshchë raz Bazarov," *Sobranie sochinenii*, 20:335–50; Herzen, *My Past and Thoughts*, 2:1348–50.

52. Turgenev, "Gamlet Shchigrovskogo uezda," *Sochineniia*, 4:282.

53. Herzen, *Sobranie sochinenii*, 12:106–07.

54. Venturi, *Roots of Revolution*, 206.

CHAPTER FOUR
Dostoevsky and the Divided Conscience

1. See my "Attitudes to the Individual in Russian Thought and Literature, with Special Reference to the Vekhi Controversy" (Ph.D. diss., Oxford University, 1970), chap. 8.

2. See, e.g., P. Pomper, *Sergei Nechaev* (New Brunswick, N.J., 1979), 217ff.

3. C. Pike, "Formalist and Structuralist Approaches to Dostoevsky," in *New Essays on Dostoevsky*, ed. M. Jones and G. Terry (London, 1983), 200.

4. R. Wellek, ed., *Dostoevsky: A Collection of Critical Essays* (Englewood Cliffs, N.J., 1962), 5. Wellek's dismissal of Bakhtin is based on a misunderstanding—that

Bakhtin's view that the authorial "voice" participates in unresolved dialogue makes Dostoevsky out to be a relativist; "Bakhtin's View of Dostoevskii: 'Polyphony' and 'Carnivalesque,' " *Dostoevsky Studies* (Klagenfurt) 1 (1980): 35. Bakhtin's real position is equally far removed from Wellek's view that Dostoevsky is "objective" only "in the sense that he knows how to expound ideas of which he disapproves"—an observation that "does not refute the fact that Dostoevskii makes a clear judgment about the values of the points of view presented by the speakers [in the novels]" ("Bakhtin's View of Dostoevsky," 33).

5. E. Dalton, *Unconscious Structure in* The Idiot: *A Study in Literature and Psychoanalysis* (Princeton, 1979), 159.

6. E. Sandoz, *Political Apocalypse: A Study of Dostoevsky's Grand Inquisitor* (Baton Rouge, La., 1971), 170; S. Linnér, *Starets Zosima in "The Brothers Karamazov": A Study in the Mimesis of Virtue,* Stockholm Studies in Russian Literature, no. 4 (Stockholm, 1975), 189, 237; B. K. Ward, "Dostoevsky and the Problem of Meaning in History," *Dostoevsky and the Twentieth Century: The Ljubljana Papers,* ed. M. C. Jones (Nottingham, 1993), 50. While acknowledging that Dostoevsky "hesitated before the notion of [the] inevitability" of a future universal Christian society, Ward argues that the entire corpus of his work offers "powerful support" for a religious interpretation of history (61, 51). See also the article by the philosopher A. Guliga, " 'Filosofiia est' tozhe poesiia' (Dostoevskii-myslitel')," *Nash sovremennik* 11 (1996): 181–88. In this article (with which the journal marks the 175th anniversary of Dostoevsky's birth, Guliga argues that the "strongest aspect" of Dostoevsky's work was its underlying Orthodox Christian philosophy, embodied in the "Russian idea" (his belief that Orthodox Russia was destined to resolve the spiritual contradictions of Europe) and that the argument in all his novels ends with "the triumph of the good" against the evils of positivist, materialistic, and socialist doctrines. He contends that Bakhtin's theory of polyphony in the novels was forced on him by the Soviet censorship, which would not have permitted him to write positively about the Christian outlook; he was therefore constrained to assert falsely that Dostoevsky gave it no more than "equal rights" with the arguments for atheism (83, 186, 187).

7. M. Jones, *Dostoevsky: The Novel of Discord* (London, 1976), 37–38.

8. R. Jackson, "The Testament of F. M. Dostoevskij," *Russian Literature* 4 (1973): 87, 99. Jackson asserts that Dostoevsky's "belief in a viable human existence was based on the clearest acknowledgment of . . . evil, yet on the necessity of permanently negating it through constant striving"—a formulation of the problem that "implies the need for a 'leap' in faith and action"—surely an orthodox Christian position? See the same inconsistency in his essay "Dimitrij Karamazov and the 'Legend,' " *Slavic and East European Journal* 11, no. 3 (1965): 257–67, where, after emphasizing the polyphony of Dostoevsky's last novel and warning the reader not to subsume "all of Dostoevskii under one or another truth: to hear, for example, Alesha and not Ivan," he concludes, monologically: "It is the truth (and therefore the reality) of the ideal [of Christ] and of man's constant yearning for it that renders *incomplete* the Grand Inquisitor's view of man—that, in the end, makes viable man's tragic actuality" (258, 266).

9. Jones, *Dostoevsky,* 192.

10. J. Drouilly, *La pensée politique et religieuse de Dostoievski* (Paris, 1971), 455.

11. G. S. Morson, *The Boundaries of Genre: Dostoevsky's* Diary of a Writer *and the Traditions of Literary Utopia* (Austin, Tex., 1981).

12. J. Meijer, "The Author of Brat'ya Karamazovy," *The Brothers Karamazov by F. M. Dostoevskij: Essays by Jan van der Eng and Jan M. Meijer,* Dutch Studies in Russian Literature, vol. 2 (The Hague, 1971), 44.

13. R. F. Fernandez, "Dostoevsky, Traditional Domination and Cognitive Dissonance," *Social Forces* 49 (December 1970): 299–303, 302; R. Jackson, *The Art of Dostoevsky: Deliriums and Nocturnes* (Princeton, 1981), xi.

14. Jones, *Dostoevsky,* 191.

15. J. Frank, *Dostoevsky: The Years of Ordeal, 1850–1859* (Princeton, 1983), 117.

16. In his monumental study of Dostoevsky's epilepsy, James Rice demonstrates that, although Dostoevsky's records of his seizures do not refer to this aura (whose content, according to Rice, had both sexual and religious overtones), there is no reason to question the evidence of contemporaries to whom he confided this experience or to doubt that it was the source for his depiction of Myshkin's seizures. J. L. Rice, *Dostoevsky and the Healing Art: An Essay in Literary and Medical History* (Ann Arbor, 1985), 83–86.

17. M. M. Dostoevskii, *Idiot,* in *Polnoe sobranie sochinenii,* 8:188.

18. See the records of Dostoevsky's seizures in Rice, *Dostoevsky and the Healing Art,* 287–98.

19. To N. D. Fonvizina, February 1854, in Dostoevskii, *Pis'ma,* ed. A. S. Dolinin (Moscow, 1928–59), 1:142.

20. Frank, *Years of Ordeal,* 161.

21. Dostoevskii, *Polnoe sobranie sochinenii,* 8:433.

22. Ibid., 8:192.

23. See J. Frank, *Dostoevsky: The Seeds of Revolt, 1821–1849* (London, 1977), 182ff.

24. See Dostoevsky's notebook for 1863–64 in *Neizdannyi Dostoevskii: Zapisnye knigi i tetradi, 1860–1881,* vol. 83 of *Literaturnoe nasledstvo* (Moscow, 1971), 176 (hereafter cited as *L.N.*); Dostoevskii, "Dnevnik pisatelia" (1876), *Polnoe sobranie sochinenii,* 22:83.

25. Dostoevskii, *Polnoe sobranie sochinenii,* 4:154.

26. Dostoevskii, notebook, 1861–62, *L.N.,* 83:149; Dostoevskii, *Polnoe sobranie sochinenii,* 23:58.

27. N. Berdiaev, *Dostoievsky,* trans. D. Attwater, 5th ed. (New York, 1960), 25. Comparisons of Dostoevsky with Gogol are not always admiring. See Linnér's comment: "Was Dostoevskii aware of how close he came to Gogol in his reasoning? The distrust of institutional change harboured by both is combined with a colossal faith in the effect of attitudinal change within the individual. Although they excel in drawing man as his own caricature, they have a boundless faith in his ability to improve himself" (*Starets Zosima,* 226, n. 6).

28. Draft of a letter to M. Katkov, September 1865, *Pis'ma,* 1:419.

29. To S. A. Ivanova, 13 January 1868, *Pis'ma,* 2:71.

30. R. F. Miller, *Dostoevsky and the Idiot: Author, Narrator, and Reader* (Cambridge, Mass., 1981).

31. To S. A. Ivanova, 6 February 1869, *Pis'ma,* 2:160.

32. Dostoevskii, *Polnoe sobranie sochinenii,* 8:142.

33. To Maikov, 6 April 1870, 23 December 1868, *Pis'ma,* 2:263, 264, 150.

34. To Maikov, 28 August 1867, *Pis'ma*, 2:31; also 21 October 1870, 2:291. See also letter to Maikov, 23 December 1868, 2:149; and letters to Strakhov, 5, 30 May 1871, 2: 357, 364.

35. On Dostoevsky's relations with the major political groupings in Russia in the 1870s, see L. M. Rosenblium, "Tvorcheskaia laboratoriia Dostoevskogo-romanista," in *F. M. Dostoevskii v rabote nad romanom "Podrostok": Tvorcheskie rukopisi, L.N., 77*:7–55; and Rosenblium, "Tvorcheskie dnevniki Dostoevskogo," ibid., 83:9–91.

36. E.g., see entries in Dostoevsky's notebooks in *L.N.*, vol. 83: (1875–76) 439; (1876–77) 557; (1880–81) 613, 670, 680, 686. See also "Dnevnik pisatelia" (1877), *Polnoe sobranie sochinenii*, 25:137–38.

37. See notebooks in *L.N.*, vol. 83: (1875–76) 367, 409; (1876–77) 574; and "Dnevnik pisatelia" (1876) and "Dnevnik pisatelia" (1877), *Polnoe sobranie sochinenii*, 22:30, 25:178ff.

38. Dostoevskii, notebook, 1875–76, *L.N.*, 83:404, 367.

39. "Dnevnik pisatelia" (1876), 23:75; and notebooks in *L.N.*, vol. 83: (1872–75) 316, (1880–81) 682, (1875–76) 424ff.; "Dnevnik pisatelia" (1876) 22:50ff.; notebooks in *L.N.*, vol. 83: (1872–75) 316, (1875–76) 441, 448–49, (1876–77) 517, 550, 555, 574–75.

40. Dostoevskii, notebooks, *L.N.*, vol. 83, (1875–76) 404, (1876–77) 623.

41. Quoted in Rosenblium, "Tvorcheskaia laboratoriia Dostoevskogo-romanista," 75.

42. "Dnevnik pisatelia" (1876), 22:31.

43. Ibid.; also see notebooks in *L.N.*, vol. 83, (1875–76) 408, 416, (1876–77) 522.

44. Both quotations are from letters to Botkin, 8 September, 1 March 1841, *Polnoe sobranie sochinenii*, 12:69, 23.

45. A few months after its publication it was quoted in the journal *Notes of the Fatherland* by the radical critic Nikolai Mikhailovsky with whom Dostoevsky was engaged in friendly polemics at the time (see Rosenblium, "Tvorcheskie dnevniki Dostoevskogo," 64–65). Some critics, however, maintain that Ivan's challenge is an allusion to the third stanza of Schiller's poem *Resignation*: see E. Kostka, *Schiller in Russian Literature* (Philadelphia, 1965), 243.

46. Dostoevskii, "Starye liudi," "Dnevnik pisatelia" (1873), *Polnoe sobranie sochinenii*, 21:10; notebooks in *L.N.*, vol. 83, (1876–77) 530, 526, (1875–76) 466.

47. "Odna iz sovremennykh fal'shei," "Dnevnik pisatelia" (1873), 21:125–36.

48. Notebook, 1872–75, *L.N.*, 83:311.

49. Ibid., 1875–76, 83:458; letter to students, 18 April 1878, *Pis'ma*, 4:17.

50. See the preface in A. S. Dolinin, ed., *F. M. Dostoevskii: Materialy i issledovaniia* (Leningrad, 1935); and Rosenblium, "Tvorcheskaia laboratoriia Dostoevkogo-romanista" and "Tvorcheskie dnevniki Dostoevskogo."

51. Some examples include Drouilly's substantial study of Dostoevsky's religious and political thought, Kabat's study of *A Writer's Diary*, and Morson's work on genre. Drouilly's book devotes less than two pages to a summary dismissal of the significance of the changes in Dostoevsky's attitude to socialism in the 1870s (*La pensée*, 430–32) and focuses on the contradictions between Dostoevsky's nationalism and his religious belief. G. C. Kabat's *Diary of a Writer, Ideology and Imagination: The Image of Society in Dostoevsky* (New York, 1978) focuses on the contrast between Dostoevsky's concern with concrete social issues and his resolution of them in terms of his messianic ideology. Morson (in *Boundaries of Genre*) approaches the same work as an exercise in literary genre.

52. Jackson expresses a typical view in defining the content of Dostoevsky's social philosophy after his exile as "a passionate appeal for a Christian change in consciousness . . . coupled with a rejection of the path of action of the socialist and revolutionary forces of his day" (*Art of Dostoevsky*, 13). Jones comments that Dostoevsky was "not altogether immune to the attractions of atheistic socialism" but does not expand on this statement (*Dostoevsky*, 195).

53. K. Mochulsky, *Dostoevsky: His Life and Work*, trans. M. Minihan (Princeton, 1967), 502.

54. Dostoevskii, notebook, 1875–76, *L.N.*, 83:438, 446.

55. Ibid., 367.

56. Dostoevskii, "Otvet 'Russkomu vestniku' " (1861), *Polnoe sobranie sochinenii*, 19: 131–32.

57. Dostoevskii, notebooks in *L.N.*, vol. 83: (1875–76) 375, 379–80, 447, 449; (1872–75) 294–95; (1876–77) 546; (1875–76) 446, 375, 403. "Dnevnik pisatelia" (1873), 21:131.

58. Dostoevskii, notebooks in *L.N.*, vol. 83: (1875–76) 386, 420; (1872–75) 289; and "Dnevnik pisatelia" (1876), *Polnoe sobranie sochinenii*, 22:41. See Turgenev, *Sochineniia*, 14:28–29.

59. See Dostoevskii, notebook, 1875–76, *L.N.*, 83:450.

60. Ibid., 1876–77, 83:546. See also "Dnevnik pisatelia" (1876), *Polnoe sobranie sochinenii*, 23:37.

61. Dostoevskii, "Dnevnik pisatelia" (1876), 23:73.

62. Dostoevskii, *Podrostok: Rukopisnye redaktsii*, *Polnoe sobranie sochinenii*, 16:329.

63. Dostoevskii, "Dnevnik pisatelia" (1876), 22:43; notebook, 1875–76, *L.N.*, 83:463.

64. Dostoevskii, "Dnevnik pisatelia" (1876), 2:29-30; notebook, 1876–77, *L.N.*, 83:574–75.

65. Dostoevskii, notebooks in *L.N.*, 1875–76, 83:441; 1876–77, 83:611.

66. To M. Katkov, 20 October 1870, *Pis'ma*, 2:289.

67. To N. Strakhov, 21 October 1870, *Pis'ma*, 2:294; to Katkov, 20 October 1870, 2: 289. Dostoevskii, *Polnoe sobranie sochinenii*, 10:202.

68. Dostoevskii, *Polnoe sobranie sochinenii*, 10:198.

69. Ibid., 94, 469.

70. Ibid., 165.

71. Dostoevskii, *Podrostok, Polnoe sobranie sochinenii*, 16:17, 51.

72. Ibid., 13:171.

73. A. S. Suvorin, *Dnevnik A. S. Suvorina* (Moscow, 1923), 15–16.

74. Dostoevskii, *Polnoe sobranie sochinenii*, 14:290, 214.

75. Berdiaev, *Dostoevsky*, 188.

76. E. Wasiolek, *Dostoevsky: The Major Fiction* (Cambridge, Mass., 1964), 164ff.

77. To N. Liubimov, 10 May 1879, *Pis'ma*, 4:53.

78. Dostoevskii, *Polnoe sobranie sochinenii*, 14:221.

79. Ibid., 14:201.

80. Suvorin, *Dnevnik*, 16.

81. See Dostoevskii, notebook, 1875–76, *L.N.*, 83:449.

82. A. F. Koni, *Vospominaniia o dele Very Zasulicha* (Moscow, 1933), 139.

83. Dostoevskii, notebook, 1880–81, *L.N.*, 83:676.

84. To N. Strakhov, 5 December 1883, in L. N. Tolstoi, *Sobranie sochinenii*, 20 vols. (Moscow, 1960–65), 17:550.

CHAPTER FIVE
Tolstoy in Doubt

1. *Tolstoy's Letters*, selected, ed., and trans. R. F. Christian, 2 vols. (New York, 1978), 399, 396.
2. Ibid., 218.
3. Berlin, *Russian Thinkers*, 22–81.
4. *Tolstoy's Letters*, viii; see also *Tolstoy's Diaries*, ed. and trans. R. F. Christian, 2 vols. (London, 1985).
5. *Tolstoy's Letters*, 126.
6. Ibid., 126, 121, 122.
7. Ibid., 96.
8. "Iz zapisok kniazia D. Nekhliudova. Liutsern," L. N. Tolstoi, *Sobranie sochinenii* (Moscow, 1961), 3:31.
9. *Tolstoy's Letters*, 127.
10. Tolstoi, *Sobranie sochinenii*, 9:414.
11. *Tolstoy's Letters*, 122.
12. Tolstoi, *Sobranie sochinenii*, 19:163.
13. *Tolstoy's Letters*, 98, 106.
14. Ibid., 113, 110.
15. Ibid., 134, 142.
16. Ibid., 70, 82.
17. Ibid., 127, 182.
18. Tolstoi, *Sobranie sochinenii*, 19: 259–60.
19. *Tolstoi's Letters*, 197.
20. Tolstoi, *Sobranie sochinenii*, 19:260.
21. Ibid., 3:271.
22. *Tolstoy's Letters*, 261, 321, 314.
23. Ibid., 492.
24. Ibid., 415, 600.
25. Ibid., 661, 533, 503, 451.
26. Ibid., 303.
27. Ibid., 495.
28. Ibid., 478.
29. Ibid., 398, 377.
30. Ibid., 572.
31. Tolstoi, *Sobranie Sochinenii*, 19:310.
32. *Tolstoy's Letters*, 364.
33. Ibid., 363.

CHAPTER SIX
The Nihilism of Ivan Turgenev

1. Berlin, *Russian Thinkers*, 262.
2. Nietzsche, *Werke*, 2:1152.
3. To Turgenev, 17–18 November 1862, *Sobranie sochinenii*, 27:266.
4. See below, "Herzen versus Schopenhauer," this vol.

5. A. Walicki, "Turgenev and Schopenhauer," *Oxford Slavonic Papers*, vol. 10 (Oxford, 1962), 2.

6. See his review of M. Vronchenko's translation of Goethe's *Faust*: Turgenev, *Pis'ma*, 1:274; *Sochineniia*, 1:214–56. In a coded reference to the "philosophy of action" he argues that the "reconciliation" that Faust yearned for was false because it was sought "outside the sphere of human reality . . . although of other forms of reconciliation we can as yet but dream" (238).

7. To Pauline Viardot, 8, 19 December 1847, *Pis'ma*, 1:274, 279.

8. To Vestnik Evropy, 2 January 1880, *Sochineniia*, 15:185.

9. To P. Viardot, 19–21 July 1849, *Pis'ma*, 1:343.

10. Subsequent commentators (see n. 14, below) echo A. Walicki's assertion that Schopenhauer's philosophy became "an inestimably valuable framework for the integration of [Turgenev's] views" and that the specific Schopenhauerian ideas that he adopted became "a truly organic component of his own philosophical image of man" ("Turgenev and Schopenhauer," 17, 8).

11. To P. Viardot, 10 June 1849, *Pis'ma*, 1:324.

12. To E. E. Lambert, 9 November 1862, *Pis'ma*, 5:70.

13. "Poezdka v Poles'e," *Sochineniia*, 7:51–52.

14. S. McLaughlin, *Schopenhauer in Russland: Zur literärischen Rezeption bei Turgenev*, Opera Slavica, n.s., vol. 3 (Wiesbaden, 1984), 67 (this is the most exhaustive work on the subject; for a survey of earlier studies, see pp. 47–55).

15. A. Schopenhauer, *The World as Will and Representation*, 2 vols., trans. E. F. J. Payne (New York, 1966), 2:534 (hereafter cited as *WWR*).

16. Turgenev, "Faust," *Sochineniia*, 7:49.

17. See *Nakanune*, *Sochineniia*, 8:156–57, 165; *Dvorianskoe gnezdo*, *Sochineniia*, 7:293. Schopenhauer is fond of quoting Calderón's lines "For man's greatest offence / Is that he has been born" (see *WWR*, 1:355; and his description of man as "a being whose existence is a punishment and an atonement," 2:580).

18. To E. E. Lambert, 3 October 1860; to N. Nekrasov, 8 April 1858, *Pis'ma*, 4:133; 3: 209. See McLaughlin's enlightening discussion of the paradoxes in Turgenev's fatalistic ethic of duty, *Schopenhauer in Russland*, 74–75.

19. See *Rudin*, *Sochineniia*, 6:367; *Nov'*, *Sochineniia*, 12:139.

20. Turgenev, "Dovol'no," *Sochineniia*, 10:118–19.

21. Ibid., 122.

22. Ibid., 19, 120, 117. Compare the conclusion to the fantastic tale "Prizraki" (begun in 1855 and completed in 1863).

23. To V. Delessert, 28 July 1864. *Pis'ma*, 5:276.

24. See the chapters "On History" and "On the Vanity and Suffering of Life," in Schopenhauer, *WWR*, vol. 2.

25. To Turgenev, 14 September 1856, *Sobranie sochinenii*, 26:32. For a comparison of Turgenev's and Schopenhauer's "scientific mysticism," see McLaughlin, *Schopenhauer in Russland*, 132–43.

26. To M. V. Avdeev, 25 January 1870, *Pis'ma*, 8:172.

27. Turgenev, "Gamlet i Don Kikhot," *Sochineniia*, 8:178.

28. Ibid., 184.

29. See (as well as his novels and novellas) the short stories "Diary of a Superfluous Man," "Iakov Pasynkov," "Two Friends," "A Correspondence," "Faust," and "Asia," all in *Sochineniia*.

30. "Gamlet shchigrovskogo uezda," *Sochineniia*, 4:282.

31. Turgenev, *Sochineniia*, 6:298.

32. Ibid., 357; see Turgenev's characterization of the Hamlets: "They cannot lead [the masses] anywhere, because they themselves are going nowhere. In any case, how can one lead others, when one does not know whether there is any ground beneath one's feet?" (*Sochineniia*, 8:179).

33. *Pis'ma*, 4:366.

34. To Herzen, 26 September 1862, *Pis'ma*, 5:51.

35. *Pis'ma*, 2:107, 108.

36. To P. Annenkov, 4 June 1867, *Pis'ma*, 6:258.

37. To Ya. Polonsky, 23 November 1876, *Pis'ma*, 11:351.

38. The Arbat was a street lined with the houses of the old Moscow nobility; Antonina Bludova, daughter of a Slavophile family, was prominent in official patriotic circles.

39. To Yu. Vrevskaia, 22 March 1876, *Pis'ma*, 11:230.

40. See his letter to Annenkov, 4 June 1867, and to Herzen, 22 May 67, *Pis'ma*, 6: 258, 252.

41. Turgenev, *Sochineniia*, 9:173.

42. Ibid., 315.

43. Ibid., 399.

44. Ibid., 287–88.

45. To M. A. Miliutina, 6 March 1875, *Pis'ma*, 11:31.

46. Review of Goethe's *Faust, Sochineniia*, 1:244.

47. Herzen, "Eshchë variatsii na staruiu temu," *Sobranie sochinenii*, 22:43.

48. To V. F. Luginin, 8 October 1862. *Pis'ma*, 5:49.

49. Herzen, "Ends and Beginnings: Letters to I. S. Turgenev (1862–1863)," in *My Past and Thoughts*, 4:1686.

50. To Herzen, 8 October 1862, *Pis'ma*, 5:51–53.

51. To Herzen, 8 November 1862, *Pis'ma*, 5:67.

52. To Herzen, 4 November 1862, *Pis'ma*, 5:65.

53. Herzen, "Ends and Beginnings," 1747, 1748.

54. Ibid., 1747.

55. To Turgenev, 22, 29–30 November 1862, *Sobranie sochinenii*, 27:264–66.

56. Herzen, "Eshchë raz Bazarov," *Sobranie sochinenii*, 20:349.

57. To M. M. Stasiulevich, 20 May 1878, *Pis'ma*, vol. 12, pt. 1:322.

58. Although the novel was not published until 1868, Turgenev began working on it in 1862, shortly after discussions in London with Herzen, Ogarev, and Bakunin. The leader of the émigré circle in the book seems initially to have been partly modeled on Ogarev. One commentator has argued that the novel's entire ideological content was dictated by Turgenev's opposition to the propaganda of *The Bell.* See the editors' notes to Turgenev, *Sochineniia*, 9:507–8.

59. *Pis'ma*, vol. 12, pt. 1:322.

60. To Herzen, 25 November 1862, *Pis'ma*, 5:73.

61. See L. Schapiro, "Turgenev and Herzen: Two Modes of Russian Political Thought," *Russian Studies*, 321–37.

62. To Herzen, 25 December 1867, *Pis'ma*, 7:14.

63. Schopenhauer, *WWR*, 2:443.

64. To Herzen, 3 December 1862, *Pis'ma*, 5:74.

65. A. Herzen, *"From the Other Shore" and "The Russian People and Socialism,"* trans. M. Budberg and R. Wollheim (Oxford, 1979), 28, 32 (hereafter cited as *OS*).

66. Turgenev, "Dovol'no," *Sochineniia*, 9:117–18.

67. Herzen, *OS*, 107. For a discussion of these dialogues, see "Herzen versus Schopenhauer," this vol.

68. Schopenhauer, *WWR*, 1:311.

69. Turgenev, *Sochineniia*, 8:166.

70. Schopenhauer, *WWR*, 2:574.

71. To E. E. Lambert, 26 October 1859, *Pis'ma*, 3:354. Cf. Schopenhauer, *WWR*, 1:322: "The life of every individual, viewed as a whole . . . is really a tragedy."

72. To Herzen, 2 March 1869, *Pis'ma*, 7:310.

73. Schopenhauer, *WWR*, 1:312.

74. To E. E. Lambert, 24 December 1859, 14 March 1862, *Pis'ma*, 3:385, 4:349–50.

75. To O. D.Khilkova, 31 January 1861, *Pis'ma*, 4:190.

76. To P. B. Annenkov, 9 November 1881, *Pis'ma*, vol. 13, pt. 1:141.

77. To E. E. Lambert, 31 May 1861, *Pis'ma*, 4:236–37. Cf. Schopenhauer, *WWR*, 2:573: "Happiness lies always in the future, or else in the past, and the present may be compared to a small dark cloud, driven by the wind over the sunny plain; in front of and behind the cloud everything is bright, only it itself casts a shadow."

78. To L. N. Tolstoi, 18 April 1858, *Pis'ma*, 3:211; to E. E. Lambert, 20 January 1861, 4:184.

79. To E. E. Lambert, 31 July 1861, *Pis'ma*, 4:274. See his letter to Lambert, 4 August 1859: "Life is nothing other than an illness which sometimes intensifies, sometimes loosens its hold; one must learn to put up with its attacks" (3:331).

80. To A. F. Pisemsky, 7 November 1876, *Pis'ma*, 11:340.

81. As S. McLaughlin points out, they summarize in particular sec. 57 of vol. 1 of Schopenhauer, *WWR* (*Schopenhauer in Russland*, 130).

82. "Monakh" (Senilia), *Sochineniia*, 13:196. See A. Walicki's commentary on these works, which he describes as "the most important document of Turgenev's 'schopenhauerianism' " and sees as concerned with a set of ideas closely connected with Schopenhauer's ethic ("Turgenev and Schopenhauer," 10–15).

83. To G. Flaubert, 1 September 1877, *Pis'ma*, 12:199.

84. To E. E. Lambert, 24 June 1859, *Pis'ma*, 3:306.

85. See *The Possessed*, pt. 1, chap. 1, sec. 2; pt. 2, chap. 6, sec. 5; pt. 3, chap. 1, sec. 3. On this question, see A. S. Dolinin, "Turgenev i 'Besy'," in *Dostoevskii: Stat'i i materialy*, ed. A. S. Dolinin (Leningrad, 1925), 119–26.

86. To M. M. Stasiulevich, 3 January 1877, *Pis'ma*, 12:44.

87. Reminiscences of P. Lavrov, in *Turgenev v russkoi kritike: Sbornik statei*, ed. K. I. Bonetskii (Moscow, 1953), 414.

88. To P. B. Annenkov, 24 April 1879, *Pis'ma*, 12:64.

89. "Mne zhal' " (Senilia), *Sochineniia*, 13:200–01. Cf. Schopenhauer, *WWR*, 1:354: "Tormentor and tormented are one. The former is mistaken in thinking he does not share the torment, the latter in thinking he does not share the guilt."

90. To A. V. Toporov, 19 December 1882, *Pis'ma*, vol. 13, pt. 2:123.

91. Turgenev, "Po povodu 'Ottsov i Detei,' " *Literaturnye i zhiteiskie vospominaniia, Sochineniia*, 14:103.

92. Herzen, *OS*, 141.

93. Herzen, *Sobranie sochinenii*, 2:298.

94. See my "Herzen, Schiller and the Aesthetic Education of Man," in *Forschungen zur Osteuropäischen Geschichte* 44 (Berlin, 1990), 101, 114.

95. Williams, "Auto-da-Fé," in *Reading Rorty*, 28.

96. Schopenhauer, *WWR*, 1:196.

97. F. Schiller, *On the Aesthetic Education of Man* (Oxford, 1957), 189.

98. Schopenhauer, *WWR*, 2:433–34.

99. Ibid., 1:232–33; 2:443.

100. A. Schopenhauer, *On the Freedom of the Will*, trans. K. Kolenda (Oxford, 1985), 51.

101. Schopenhauer, *WWR*, 1:245; 2:442, 610, 441; 1:322.

102. Turgenev, *Sochineniia*, 12:303.

103. Schiller, *Aesthetic Education*, 47.

104. Herzen, *OS*, 120, 135.

105. A. Walicki, "Turgenev and Schopenhauer," 15–16.

106. To Herzen, 18 March 1869, *Pis'ma*, 7:334; "Monakh," *Sochineniia*, 13:196.

107. To E. E. Lambert, 27 November 1861, *Pis'ma*, 4:306.

108. Turgenev, "Monakh," *Sochineniia*, 13:196.

109. To I. P. Borisov, 4 January 1870, *Pis'ma*, 8:152.

110. Turgenev, "Po povodu 'Ottsov i Detei,' " *Sochineniia*, 14:100.

111. M. O. Gershenzon, *Mechta i mysl' I. S. Turgeneva*, Brown University Slavic Reprint Series (Providence, R.I., 1970), 94.

112. *Sochineniia*, 6:337. To S. T. Aksakov, 10 March 1856, *Pis'ma*, 2:340.

113. Herzen, *Sobranie sochinenii*, 11:359.

114. Turgenev, *Sochineniia*, 8:178.

115. Herzen, *Sobranie sochinenii*, 20:438.

116. Ibid., 10:67, 74, 75.

117. To P. Viardot, 5, 6 July 1868, *Pis'ma*, 7:172. On the self-contradictions in Schopenhauer's ethic, see B. Magee, *The Philosophy of Schopenhauer* (Oxford, 1983), 236–37. Magee points out that on Schopenhauer's assumptions there can be no morality.

118. See A. Kelly, *Mikhail Bakunin: A Study in the Psychology and Politics of Utopianism* (Oxford, 1982), chaps. 2, 3, 5, 6.

CHAPTER SEVEN
Liberal Dilemmas and Populist Solutions

1. Acton, *Rethinking the Russian Revolution*, 89. An early example of the genre is R. Payne, *The Terrorists: The Story of the Forerunners of Stalin* (New York, 1957).

2. A. Ulam, *In the Name of the People: Prophets and Conspirators in Prerevolutionary Russia* (New York, 1977), 144–45.

3. Ibid., 10.

4. A. Nikitenko, *Diary of a Russian Censor*, abr., ed., and trans. H. S. Jacobson (Amherst, Mass., 1975).

5. Ibid., 259, 308, 298, 320.

6. Ibid., 360.

7. Ibid., 305.

8. Ibid., 336.

9. Ibid., 239, 324, 352, 335.

10. Ibid., 338.

11. Ibid., 345.

12. Ibid., 350, 366.

13. Turgenev, *Sochineniia*, 4:282; *Pis'ma*, 7:14.

14. *Sochineniia N. K. Mikhailovskogo*, 6 vols. (St. Petersburg, 1896–97), 3:230, 4:451.

15. Cited in J. H. Billington, *Mikhailovsky and Russian Populism* (Oxford, 1958), 109.

16. R. Rocker, *The London Years*, trans. J. Leftwich (London, 1956), 162.

17. Cited in G. Woodcock and I. Avakumovic, *The Anarchist Prince: A Biographical Study of Peter Kropotkin* (London, 1950), 427.

18. Ibid., 249.

19. See, e.g., R. Pipes, *The Russian Revolution, 1899–1919* (London, 1990), esp. chap. 4, "The Intelligentsia"; and H. Carrère d'Encausse, *The Russian Syndrome: One Thousand Years of Political Murder,* trans. C. Higgitt, with a foreword by A. Ulam (New York, 1992).

20. Ulam, *In the Name of the People*, 296.

21. V. Figner, *Memoirs of a Revolutionist,* authorized translation from the Russian (De Kalb, Ill., 1991), 106.

22. Ulam, *In the Name of the People*, 248, 84, 251–52.

23. Herzen, *Sobranie sochinenii*, 20:588

24. Ibid., 16:196

25. J. S. Mill, *On Liberty: with, The Subjection of Women, and, Chapters on Socialism,* ed. S. Collini (Cambridge, 1989), 72.

CHAPTER EIGHT
The Intelligentsia and Self-Censorship

1. A. I. Herzen, *Pis'ma iz Frantsii i Italii, Sobranie sochinenii,* 30 vols. (Moscow, 1954–66), 5:202.

2. Quoted in G. L. Kline, "Darwinism and the Russian Orthodox Church," in *Continuity and Change in Russian and Soviet Thought,* ed. E. J. Simmons, (Cambridge, Mass., 1955), 308.

3. C. A. Moser, *Antinihilism in the Russian Novel of the 1860s* (The Hague, 1964), 185.

4. On the definitions of the intelligentsia as a group (a vast subject beyond the scope of this book), see my Introduction, n. 2, and "Which Signposts?" n. 69.

5. P. L. Lavrov, *Istoricheskie pis'ma* (St. Petersburg, 1906), 358.

6. Quoted in Venturi, *Roots of Revolution*, 365.

7. See N. Valentinov, "Chernyshevskii i Lenin," *Novyi zhurnal* 27 (1951): 193–94.

8. N. G. Chernyshevskii, *Polnoe sobranie sochinenii,* 15 vols. (Moscow, 1939–50), 14: 320.

9. Ibid., 5:166.

10. R. W. Mathewson, Jr., *The Positive Hero in Russian Literature,* 2d ed. (Stanford, Calif., 1975), 80.

11. Ibid., 49.

12. S. Kravchinskii [S. Stepniak], *Andrei Kozhukhov* (Geneva, 1898).

13. P. B. Struve, *Kriticheskie zametki k voprosu ob ekonomicheskom razvitii Rossii* (St. Petersburg, 1894), 30.

14. For an analysis of both movements, see my "Attitudes to the Individual," chap. 3; and "A Bolshevik Philosophy?" this vol.

15. See Struve's preface to N. Berdiaev, *Sub'ektivizm i individualizm v obshchestvennoi filosofii: Kriticheskii etiud o N. K. Mikhailovskom. S predisloviem P. B. Struve* (St. Petersburg, 1901), lxiff.

16. N. Berdiaev, "Eticheskaia problema v svete filosofskogo idealizma," in *Problemy idealizma: Sbornik statei,* ed. P. I. Novgorodtsev (Moscow, 1903), 130–31. A. Lunacharskii, *Religiia i sotsializm* (St. Petersburg, 1908), 291; "Osnovy pozitivnoi estetiki," *Ocherki realisticheskogo mirovozzreniia* (St. Petersburg, 1904), 122ff.

17. M. O. Gershenzon, "Tvorcheskoe samosoznanie," *Vekhi: Sbornik statei o russkoi intelligentsii,* 5th ed. (Moscow, 1910), 71.

18. Ibid., 80, 70.

19. Ibid., ii.

20. R. Pipes, *Struve: Liberal on the Right, 1905–1944* (Cambridge, Mass., 1980), 114. See the discussion in my Introduction, p. 1. See also G. S. Morson's article of 1993 on *Signposts* and the intelligentsia (cited in chap. 9, n. 2).

21. On Azev's career, see B. Nikolaievsky, *Aseff: The Russian Judas,* trans. G. Reavey (London, 1934).

22. V. Rozanov, "Mezhdu Azevom i 'Vekhami,' " *Novoe vremia,* 20 August 1909. See also the article by A. Belyi, "Pravda o russkoi intelligentsii: Po povodu sbornika 'Vekhi,' " *Vesy* 5 (1909): 68.

23. V. Chernov, *Pered burei: Vospominaniia* (New York, 1953), 285.

24. "Etika i politika: Ocherki," *Zavety,* no. 2, pt. 2 (May 1912): 56–86; no. 3, pt. 2 (June 1912): 90–120; no. 7, pt. 2 (October 1912): 77–97; quotations, pt. 1:74, pt. 3:92, 96.

25. For a detailed study of Savinkov's novels and the discussion of ethics in the SR Party, see my "Attitudes to the Individual," chap. 8.

26. See N. Ropshin [B. Savinkov], "Kon' blednyi," *Russkaia mysl',* no. 1, pt. 1 (1909): 1–77. See also Ropshin, "To, chego ne bylo (Tri brata)," *Zavety* (1912), 1:64–82; 2:33–55; 3:31–46; 4:5–43; 5:5–20; 6:5–41; 7:5–47; 8:5–40; (1913), 1:83–112, 2:12–33; 4: 11–48.

27. Ropshin, "To, chego ne bylo" (1912), 1:78, 7:18.

28. See M. Gor'kii, letters to M. Kotsiubinsky, 23 May 1912, and to V. Miroliubov, 26 May 1912, *Sobranie sochinenii,* 30 vols. (Moscow, 1949–56), 29:240, 241; and speech of 1934, 27:313.

29. F. Volkhovskii et al., "V redaktsiiu 'Zavetov,' " *Zavety* 8, pt. 2 (1912): 144.

30. *Redaktsiia,* ibid., 144–45; V. I. Lenin, letter to Gorky, 22 or 23 December 1912, *Sochineniia,* 5th ed. (Moscow, 1958–69), 48:137. See also Lenin's letter to Gorky of 1 August 1912, in which he claims that Savinkov's works indicate the SRs' "sympathy" with the thought of the Kadets and *Signposts* (*Sochineniia,* 25).

31. See the portraits of Ivan Kaliaev and Mar'ia Benevskaia in V. V. Zenzinov, *Perezhitoe* (New York, 1953); and of Kaliaev, Benevskaia, Yegor Sazonov, Dora Brill'iant, and Rashel' Lur'ie in B. Savinkov, *Vospominaniia terrorista* (Kharkov, 1926). See also Chernov's assertion (*Pered burei,* 294) that the dialogues of *The Pale Horse* reflected, "although in a weak and confused way," some of the most profound experiences of Kaliaev, Sazonov, and other terrorists. Compare this with Savinkov's public assertion, in a response to one of the *Signposts* authors, that the characters of *The Pale Horse* were entirely imaginary and that the SR

leadership could not be said to bear any responsibility for the events depicted there. V. Ropshin, "Pis'mo v redaktsiiu," *Zavety* 1, pt. 2 (1912): 222.

32. Zenzinov, *Perezhitoe*, 107–8.

33. This incident is quoted in Chernov, *Pered burei*, 294.

34. G. B. Plekhanov, "O tom, chto est' v romane 'To, chego ne bylo,' " *Sovremennyi mir* 2 (1913) 2:91.

35. See ibid., and the articles by V. Kranikhfel'd, "Literaturnye otkliki: Stavka na sil'nykh," "Literaturnye otkliki," and "Otvet G. V. Plekhanovu," *Sovremennyi mir* 5 (1909): 78–84; 10 (1912): 323–25; and 2 (1913): 99–104.

36. See, e.g., S. Adrianov, "Kriticheskie nabroski," *Vestnik Evropy* (March 1909): 343–54; E. Koltonovskaia, "Samotsennost' zhizni (evoliutsiia v intelligentskoi psikhologii)," *Obrazovanie* 2 (May 1909): 91; and "Byt' ili ne byt'? O romane Ropshina 'To, chego ne bylo,' " *Russiaia mysl'*, no. 6, pt. 2 (1913): 29–40.

37. D. S. Merezhkovskii, "Kon' blednyi," *Bol'naia Rossiia. Sbornik statei* (St. Petersburg, 1910), 15–38.

38. See K. Kachorovskii, "Narodnichestvo kak sotsiologicheskoe napravlenie," *Zavety* 3, pt. 2 (1913): 71–72; 4, pt. 2:72–89; 5, pt. 2:1–44.

39. Adrianov, "Kriticheskie nabroski," 354.

40. Gor'kii, letter to Andreev, 17 February–1 March 1908, *Gor'kii i Leonid Andreev: Neizdannaia perepiska*. Literaturnoe nasledstvo (Moscow, 1965), 72:305; V. L'vov -Rogachevskii, *Leonid Andreev: Kriticheskii ocherk s prilozheniem khronologicheskoi kanvy i bibliograficheskogo ukazatelia* (Moscow, 1923); R. V. Ivanov-Razumnik, *O smysle zhizni: F. Sologub, L. Andreev, L. Shestov*, 2d ed. (Moscow, 1910), 159–60.

41. See especially Andreev's stories: "Rasskaz o semi poveshennykh," "Iuda Iskariot," and "T'ma."

42. L. Andreev, *Sashka Zhegulëv, Literaturno-khudozhestvennye al'manakhi izdatel'stva 'Shipovnik,'* bk. 16 (St. Petersburg, 1911), 11–201.

43. See Lvov-Rogachevsky's description of him as "a man deeply involved in the thought and moods of his time, who recorded and diagnosed the successive stages of the progressive social movement with a rare conscientiousness and objectivity" (V. L'vov-Rogachevskii, "V. V. Veresaev," in *Russkaia literatura dvadtsatogo veka, 1890–1910*, ed. S. A. Vengerov [Moscow, 1914–16], 1:145–72). See also E. Koltonovskaia, "V. V. Veresaev," in *Novyi entsiklopedicheskii slovar'*, ed. F. Brokgauz and I. Efron, 29 vols. (St. Petersburg, 1911–16), 10:210. And see the Marxist critic Kranikhfeld's description of his third novel, *K zhizni*, as "a true and thoughtful . . . chronicle of the moods of the intelligentsia of our day" (Kranikhfel'd, "Literaturnye otkliki: Stavka na sil'nykh," 84).

44. See V. V. Veresaev [V. V. Smidovich], *Bez dorogi* (1895); *Na povorote* (1901); *K zhizni* (1908).

45. See Veresaev's personal vision expounded in his study of Dostoevsky and Tolstoy, *Zhivaia zhizn'*, vol. 1: *O Dostoevskom i L've Tolstom* (Moscow, 1911).

46. See, e.g., the novels by R. Grigor'ev, *Na ushcherbe* (1913); A. Derental', *V temnuiu noch'*, in *Russkoe bogatstvo* (1907), nos. 9, 10, 11; O. Mirtov [O. Kotyleva], *Mertvaia zyb'*, in *Russkaia mysl'*, nos. 8–12 (1909). See also the short stories of N. F. Oliger (1882–1919); I. Sugurchev, *Sosedka*, in *Vestnik Evropy*, January 1909; and M. Artsybashev, *Rabochii Shevyrev, Zemlia, Sbornik vtoroi* (Moscow, 1909), 249–360.

47. E. Koltonovskaia, "Pisatel'-intelligent (V. Veresaev, *Sochineniia*, tt. I–V)," *Russkaia mysl'*, no. 6, pt. 2 (1910): 62.

48. Gor'kii, "Zametki o meshchanstve," *Stat'i, 1905–16*, 2d ed. (St. Petersburg, 1918), 5. See also "Dve dushi" and "Izdaleka," 98–149, 174–87.
49. Gor'kii, "Izdaleka," 130, 114.
50. Gor'kii, "O sovremennosti," 93.
51. See esp. the essays "O sovremennosti" and "O durakakh i prochem," 76–97, 196–207.
52. Gor'kii, "O sovremennosti," 85.
53. Gor'kii, "O durakakh i prochem," 207.
54. Mathewson, *Positive Hero*, 45.
55. Gor'kii, "Izdaleka," 137.
56. Ibid.
57. Iu. Martov, "Religiia i marksizm," *Na rubezhe. (K kharakteristike sovremennykh iskanii). Kriticheskii sbornik* (St. Petersburg, 1909), 35.
58. Gor'kii, "Izdaleka," 142.
59. Gor'kii, "O karamazovshchine," 152; "Izdaleka," 132; "O tsinizme," 61–75; "Izdaleka," 114; "Dve dushi," 187.
60. Gor'kii, "Izdaleka," 134, 113.
61. Gor'kii, "O karamazovshchine" (letter to *Russkoe slovo* of 22 September 1913), 150–54.
62. Gor'kii, "Eshchë o karamazovshchine," 155–59.
63. See Belorussov, "O formakh obshchestvennoi bor'by," *Russkie vedomosti*, 19 November 1913.
64. M. Krinitskii, "Besy o 'Besakh,'" *Utro Rossii*, 10 November 1913.
65. See Belorussov, "O formakh"; A. Vitimskii, "Pokhod protiv M. Gor'kogo," *Za pravdu*, 4 October 1913; L. P., "K pokhodu protiv Gor'kogo," *Za pravdu*, 30 October 1913; and *Za pravdu*, 30 October and 13 November 1913.
66. E. Kuskova, *Russkie vedomosti*, 3 November 1913. See also D. Talnikov's article in the Marxist *Sovremennyi mir*, no. 11 (1913): 202–14, which expresses unqualified approval of Gorky's protest and the principle of social censorship.
67. I. Ignatov, "'Besy' i g. Gor'kii," *Russkie vedomosti*, 27 September 1913.
68. Moskovskii khudozhestvennyi teatr, "Otkrytoe pis'mo M. Gor'komu," *Utro Rossii*, 26 September 1913; see also "Chuzhoi," "Maksim Gor'kii i khudozhestvennyi teatr," *Rech'*, 27 September 1913.
69. See the typical comments by A. Koiranskii, "Doloi Dostoevskogo," *Utro Rossii*, 25 September 1913.
70. Belorussov, "O formakh."
71. D. Filosofov, "Pis'mo v redaktsiiu," *Russkoe slovo*, 29 September 1913.
72. D. Filosofov, D. Merezhkovskii, and R. Ivanov-Razumnik, "'O vypadke g. Gor'kogo protiv Dostoevskogo.' Mneniia," *Birzhevye vedomosti*, 8 October 1913; see also F. Sologub, in *Den'*, 1 October 1913.
73. In a response to this criticism, Gorky denied that he wanted Dostoevsky's novels to be suppressed. A stage production, by acting on the "dark area of the emotions," stunted the spectator's critical faculties; the attentive reader, however, "can correct the thoughts of [Dostoevsky's] heroes, whereby they gain significantly in beauty, depth and humanity" ("Eshchë o karamazovshchine," 158). See A. Aduev, "Gor'kii protiv Dostoevskogo," *Rul'*, 30 September 1913; A. Koiranskii, "Doloi Dostoevskogo"; M. Artsybashev, I. Potapenko, and F. Batiushkov, *Birzhevye vedomosti*, 8 October, 25 September 1913; and D. Filosofov, *Pis'mo*.

74. See A. I. Kuprin and I. I. Iasinskii in *Birzhevye vedomosti,* 8 October 1913; M. Artsybashev, *Vechernie izvestiia,* 24, 25 September 1913.

75. A. Benua, "Dnevnik khudozhnika," *Rech',* 30 September 1913.

76. A. Koiranskii, "Doloi"; see also A. G. Gornfel'd in *Den',* 1 October 1913, and F. Sologub in *Birzhevye vedomosti,* 8 October 1913.

77. "Leonid Andreev contra M. Gor'kogo," *Utro,* 26 September 1913.

78. Moskovskii khudozhestvennyi teatr, "Otkrytoe pis'mo."

79. Ia. Abramovich and M. Krinitskii, *Utro Rossii,* 10 November 1913. The teachers' debate was reported by S. Glagol, "Disputy o 'Besakh,'" *Stolichnaia molva,* 11 November 1913.

80. Artsybashev, *Vechernie izvestiia,* 25 September 1913. The Moscow Art Theater defended itself in "Khudozhestvennyi teatr i Gor'kii," *Rul',* 23 September 1913, and "Otkrytoe pis'mo."

81. See Mathewson, *Positive Hero,* 174.

82. See "L. Andreev contra Gor'kogo."

83. Artsybashev, *Vechernie izvestiia,* 24 September 1913; Filosofov, "Pis'mo v redaktsiiu."

84. Filosofov made this comparison, as did Artsybashev (*Vechernie izvestiia,* 24, 25 September 1913).

85. See D. Talnikov's survey of the debate, "Estetika i obshchestvennost': O sovremennoi literature," *Sovremennyi mir,* no. 2 (1914): 112–38. Admitting that "most of those who wrote about Gorky and *The Possessed* were not on Gorky's side," he is particularly disturbed by the opposition to Gorky of such radical intellectuals as Ivanov-Razumnik and concludes that such responses show that the intelligentsia "has not yet recovered from the period of reaction."

86. A fact noted with satisfaction by Gorky's supporters. See ibid., 136: "In all public lectures and debates the majority were for Gorky and against Dostoevsky."

CHAPTER NINE
Which Signposts?

1. A. A. Iakovlev, introduction to *Vekhi: Iz glubiny* (Moscow, 1991), 3.

2. See L. Schapiro, "The *Vekhi* Group and the Mystique of Revolution," *Slavonic and East European Review* 44 (December 1955): 6–76; G. S. Morson, "Prosaic Bakhtin: 'Landmarks,' Anti-Intelligentsialism, and the Russian Counter-Tradition," *Common Knowledge* 2, no. 1 (1993): 35–74. The hostile definitions of the intelligentsia in *Signposts* were bitterly contested, and the question of whether the *Signposts* authors were themselves *intelligenty* was much debated. See n. 69, below, and n. 2 of my Introduction.

3. See P. Struve, "O 'Vekhakh,'" in *Patriotica: Politika, kul'tura, religiia; Sbornik statei za 5 let. 1905–1910* (St. Petersburg, 1911), 231; S. L. Frank, "Kul'tura i religiia," *Russkaia mysl',* no. 7 (1909): 148.

4. A. MacIntyre, *Three Rival Versions of Moral Enquiry: Encyclopaedia, Genealogy, and Tradition* (London, 1990), 217.

5. Berlin, "Historical Inevitability," in *Four Essays on Liberty,* 106–07.

6. G. Plekhanov, "Our Disagreements," in *Selected Philosophical Works,* 5 vols. (Moscow, 1974), 1:338.

7. Struve, *Kriticheskie zametki,* 30; Nemo (S. Bulgakov), "Manifest narodnoi partii,"

Novoe slovo, August 1897, 24–25; P. Struve, "Nashi utopisti," ibid., March 1897, 19; S. Bulgakov, "O zakonomernosti sotsial'nikh iavlenii," *Voprosy filosofii i psikhologii*, November–December 1896. For a detailed analysis of the movement from Marxism to idealism, see A. P. Mendel, *Dilemmas of Progress in Tsarist Russia: Legal Marxism and Legal Populism* (Cambridge, Mass., 1961); and R. Kindersley, *The First Russian Revisionists: A Study of Legal Marxism in Russia* (Oxford, 1962).

8. P. B. Struve, "Die Marx'sche Theorie der Sozialen Entwicklung: Ein kritischer Versuch," *Archiv für Soziale Gesetzgebung und Statistik* 14 (1899): 688.

9. Ibid., 690; Struve, introduction to Berdiaev, *Sub'ektivizm*, lxxxiii; N. Berdiaev, "Bor'ba za idealizm," *Mir bozhii*, no. 1, pt. 1 (1906): 23–24.

10. Berdiaev, "Bor'ba za idealizm," 16.

11. S. L. Frank, *Biografiia P. B. Struve* (New York: Izdatel'stvo imeni Chekhova, 1956), 28–29.

12. "Predislovie," in Novgorodtsev, *Problemy idealizma*, ix; "A. B.," "Kriticheskie zametki: 'Problemy idealizma,' sbornik statei," *Mir bozhii*, no. 2, pt. 2 (1903): 2. See also the following reviews of the symposium: V. Rozhkov, "Znachenie i sud'by noveishego idealizma v Rossii (Po povodu knigi 'Problemy idealizma,' " *Voprosy filosofii i psikhologii* 2 (1903): 314–32; Iu. Aikhenval'd, "Obzor knig: 'Problemy idealizma,' " ibid., 333–56. Aikhenval'd asserts that "it is not what this book says, but 'the things it thinks about' that is its main attraction for many" (333).

13. Berdiaev, "Eticheskaia problema v svete filosofskogo idealizma," in *Problemy idealizma*, 107, 109, 131; *Sub'ektivizm*, 75, n. 1; Frank, "Fr. Nitsshe i etika 'liubvi k dal'nemu,' " in *Problemy idealizma*, 182, 183, 183–84; Struve, preface to *Sub'ektivizm*, lxxii. On the same theme, see also the essays by D. E. Zhukovskii, "K voprosu o moral'nom tvorchestve," in *Problemy idealizma*, 504–21; and S. A. Askol'dov, "Filosofiia i zhizn'," ibid., 196–215.

14. V. G. Belinskii, *Polnoe sobranie sochinenii*, 12 vols. (Moscow, 1953–56), 12:23; see my "Herzen and Proudhon: Two Radical Ironists," *Common Knowledge* 1, no. 2 (1992): 36–62.

15. See Frank's formulation of the distinctiveness of the new idealism: "Contemporary philosophical thought, guided by Kant's . . . synthesis of sober intellectual realism with daring idealistic flights of the moral spirit, draws a sharp distinction between critical positivism in the field of scientific cognition, and ethical idealism in the field of the integral moral consciousness. It must protest equally against doctrinaire tendencies to limit the richness of the inner experience of the human consciousness, and against rash attempts to hypostasize moral experiences and . . . to give them the shape of a logical system of objective knowledge. It thereby reconciles these two opposing tendencies of the human spirit, pointing out to each its boundaries" ("Fr. Nittshe," 194).

16. S. A. Askol'dov, "Filosofiia i zhizn'," 205; D. E. Zhukovskii, "K voprosu," 520.

17. Bulgakov, "Osnovnye problemy teorii progressa," in *Problemy idealizma*, 46; Berdiaev, *Sub'ektivizm*, 24; Bulgakov, "Chto daet sovremennomy soznaniiu filosofiia Vladimira Solov'ëva?" in Bulgakov, *Ot marksizma k idealizmu: Sbornik statei, 1896–1903* (St. Petersburg, 1903), 208, 195–96; "Dushevnaia drama Gertsena," ibid., 188; "Osnovnye problemy," 42.

18. Berdiaev, *Sub'ektivizm*, 92, 63.

19. Bulgakov, *Avtobiograficheskie zametki* (Paris, 1946), 32; Berdiaev, *Samopoznanie*

(Opyt filosofskoi avtobiografii) (Paris, 1949), 116–17; "Bor'ba za idealizm," 17, 23; "Eticheskaia problema," 127.

20. See my discussion of Bakunin's pursuit of "absolute liberty" in *Mikhail Bakunin*, 209–26.

21. Struve, "My Contacts and Conflicts with Lenin," pt. 1, *Slavonic Review* 12, no. 36 (April 1934): 577; *Kriticheskie zametki*, 250.

22. Struve, preface to Berdiaev, *Sub'ektivizm*, lxix–lxx.

23. Bulgakov, "Ivan Karamazov kak filosofskii tip," in *Ot marksizma*, 83.

24. Berdiaev, *Samopoznanie*, 134; introduction to *Dukhovnyi krizis intelligentsii: stat'i po obshchestvennoi i religioznoi psikhologii, 1907-1909* (St. Petersburg, 1910), 10; "K. Leont'ev: Filosof reaktsionnoi romantiki," *Voprosy zhizni*, no. 7 (1905): 180.
On Merezhkovsky's religious philosophy, see C. H. Bedford, "Dmitri Merezhkovsky, the third Testament and the third Humanity," *Slavonic and East European Review* 42, no. 98 (1963): 144–60.

25. Berdiaev, "O novom religioznom soznanii," *Voprosy zhizni*, no. 9 (1905): 151–52; "K. Leont'ev," 190.

26. Berdiaev, "Merezhkovskii o revoliutsii," in *Dukhovnyi krizis*, 106, 109, 112, 115.

27. Berdiaev, *Samopoznanie*, 145, 164. (The slogan refers to the words of Ivan Kara-mazov: "I accept God, but I do not accept his world.") Berdiaev emphatically distances himself from the "fashionable" mystical anarchism of the time (165).

28. Berdiaev, "Tipy religioznoi mysli v Rossii: Novoe khristianstvo," 65; "Idei i zhizn': Ob otnoshenii russkikh k ideiam," *Russkaia mysl'*, no. 1, pt. 2 (1917): 68; "Opyt filosofskogo opravdaniia khristianstva," *Dukhovnyi krizis*, 280–81; "Tipy religioz-noi mysli v Rossii: Vozrozhdenie pravoslaviia," *Russkaia mysl'*, no. 6, pt. 2 (1916): 21–22.

29. Berdiaev, "Tragediia i obydennost'" (L. Shestov: 'Dostoevskii i Nitsshe,' 'Apofeoz bezpochvennosti,'" *Voprosy zhizni*, no. 3 (1905): 268–69; "Stavrogin," *Russkaia mysl'*, no. 5, pt. 2 (1914): 80–89; "Tragediia i obydennost'," 255; "Tri iubileia (L. Tolstoi, Gen. Ibsen, N. Fëdorov)," *Put'*, no. 11 (1928): 84, 83.

30. Berdiaev, "Bunt i pokornost' v psikhologii mass," *Dukhovnyi krizis*, 77; *Samo-poznanie*, 134, 143, 141, 142, 145.

31. Berdiaev, *Samopoznanie*, 117, 126; "Russkie bogoiskateli," *Dukhovnyi krizis*, 35; "Rossiia i zapad: Razmyshlenie, vyzvannoe stat'ei P. B. Struve 'Velikaia Rossiia,'" *Dukhovnyi krizis*, 127; preface to *Dukhovnyi krizis*, 7.

32. Berdiaev, "Russkie bogoiskateli," 35; "Rossiia i zapad," 127; "Merezhkovskii o revoliutsii," 109; "K voprosu ob intelligentsii i natsii," *Dukhovnyi krizis*, 130.

33. A. Kizevetter, "Postscriptum k stat'e gospodina Berdiaeva," *Russkaia mysl'*, no. 7, pt. 2 (1908): 144.

34. Dostoevskii, *Polnoe sobranie sochinenii*, 26:148.

35. Berdiaev, "Tipy religioznoi mysli v Rossii. Novoe khristianstvo," 55; "K voprosu ob intelligentsii i natsii," 134; *Samopoznanie*, 165.

36. Berdiaev, *Samopoznanie*, 156.

37. P. Struve, "Krushenie napravlenstva," *Russkaia mysl'*, no. 2, pt. 2 (1908): 175.

38. Struve, "Gertsen," in *Patriotica*, 526; "Krushenie napravlenstva," 175; "Neskol'ko slov po povodu stat'i S. N. Bulgakova," *Poliarnaia zvezda*, 12 March 1906, 128–30.

39. Struve, "Religiia i sotsializm," *Russkaia mysl'*, no. 8 (1909): 148; "Krushenie na-pravlenstva," 179. Commenting on Struve's critique of Bulgakov, G. F. Putnam

has described Struve's "subjective religiosity" as "dubious religion" (*Russian Alternatives to Marxism: Christian Socialism and Idealistic Liberalism in Twentieth-Century Russia* [Knoxville, Tenn., 1977], 104), but the religious status of Struve's thought is outside the boundaries of this discussion.

40. Struve, "Spor s D.S. Merezhkovskim.II. Kto iz nas 'maksimalist'?" in *Patriotica*, 124.

41. Struve and Frank, "Ocherki filosofii kul'tury," pt. 1, "Chto takoe kul'tura?" *Poliarnaia zvezda*, no. 2 (1905): 115; pt. 2, "Kul'tura i lichnost'," ibid., no. 3, 174–75, 171. R. Pipes argues that the definition of culture in these articles seems to have been drawn directly from Kant (*Struve: Liberal on the Right*, 85–87).

42. Struve and Frank, "Chto takoe kul'tura?" 113–14, 116.

43. Ibid., 116; Struve, "Skoree za delo," *Patriotica*, 3.

44. Struve, "Taktika ili idei? Iz razmyshlenii o russkoi revoliutsii," *Russkaia mysl'*, no. 8, pt. 2 (1907): 233; "Chto takoe kul'tura?" 109.

45. "Intelligentsiia i narodnoe khoziaistvo," *Patriotica*, 367.

46. Struve, "Lev Tolstoi," *Russkaia mysl'*, no. 8, pt. 2 (1908): 222; Berdiaev, *Samopoznanie*, 122; Struve, "Lev Tolstoi," 222, 223.

47. Struve, "Gertsen," *Russkaia mysl'*, no. 4, pt. 2 (1912): 134; "Velikaia Rossiia i sviataia Rus,'" ibid., no. 12, pt. 2 (1914): 147–48, 178. See also "Velikaia Rossiia: Iz razmyshlenii o probleme russkogo mogushchestva," *Russkaia mysl'*, no. 1, pt. 2 (1908): 143–57; "Otryvki o gosudarstve i natsii," ibid., no. 5, pt. 2, 187–93.

48. Pipes suggests that Struve's intemperateness on the issue of nationalism was due to a combination of anxiety about his country's future and "an acute intellectual disorientation caused by his being isolated and under fire from so many quarters" (*Struve: Liberal on the Right*, 74).

49. Struve "Na raznye temy: Otvet g. Peshekhonovu," in *Patriotica*, 427; cited in D. Shub, "Liberalizm v Rossii," *Mosty*, no. 2 (1959): 381; "Pochemu zastoialas' nasha dukhovnaia zhizn'?" *Russkaia mysl'*, no. 3, pt. 2 (1914): 104.

50. Struve, "Konservatizm intelligentskoi mysli," *Russkaia mysl'*, no. 7 (1907): 174; "Iz razmyshlenii o russkoi revoliutsii," ibid., no. 1, pt. 2, 130.

51. Struve, "Lev Tolstoi," 219.

52. Struve, "Pochemu zastoialas' nasha dukhovnaia zhizn'?" 105.

53. Struve, "Taktika ili idei?" 233.

54. Struve, "Dushevnaia drama Gertsena," 114, 179.

55. Struve, "Gertsen" (speech given to the St. Petersburg Herzen Circle in January 1908), *Patriotica*, 530, 527.

56. Herzen, *Sochineniia*, 20:577, 579, 593.

57. Struve, "Gertsen" (1908), 530; "Gertsen" (speech to the Herzen circle in March 1912), *Russkaia mysl'*, no. 4, pt. 2 (1912): 138; "Gertsen" (1908), 527, 528.

58. Herzen, *Sochineniia*, 20:593.

59. Struve, "Na raznye temy: 'Vekhi' i pis'ma Ertel'ia; Po povodu stat'i kn. D. I. Shakhovskogo," *Russkaia mysl'*, no. 5, pt. 2 (1909): 121 n1.

60. Ibid., 119, 122, 121. See Herzen, *Sochineniia*, 29:148.

61. Frank, *Biografiia P. B. Struve*, 40, 230.

62. Herzen, *Sochineniia*, 20:586; "Kul'tura i lichnost'," 179.

63. Frank, *Biografiia P. B. Struve*, 79. He acknowledges himself as Struve's pupil in this respect.

64. Berdiaev, "Russkaia zhironda," in *Sub Specie Aeternitatis: Opyty filosofskie, sot-*

sial'nye i literaturnye (1900–1906g) (St. Petersburg, 1907), 392, 395, 396; "Rossiia i zapad," *Slovo*, 11 July 1908, 2–3; Bulgakov, "Individualizm ili sobornost'," *Narod*, no. 6 (1906): 3–4.

65. Struve, "Spor s D. S. Merezhkovskim," pt. 2, 124; Herzen, *OS*, 50.

66. MacIntyre, *Three Rival Versions*, 202; "Epistemological crises, dramatic narrative, and the philosophy of science," *Monist* 60 (1977): 471. Bakhtin's attack on "monologism" and his emphasis on the "prosaic" (which Morson's essay, cited above, illuminatingly compares with themes in *Signposts*) has much in common with MacIntyre's approach to morality.

67. Struve, "Pochemu zastoialas' nasha dukhovnaia zhizn'?" 105.

68. Struve, "Spor s Merezhkovskim.II," 123.

69. Frank, *Biografiia P. B. Struve*, 82. The use of quotation marks by both Frank and Struve points to the problems involved in using the term *intelligentsia* to denote the collective object of *Signposts'* critique. As we shall see, both authors acknowledge in *Signposts* that the "classical" alienated Russian intelligentsia was fast disappearing as a result of the processes of modernization. The "intelligentsia" outlook as defined in *Signposts*—a radical political messianism based on atheistic and rationalist principles—was dominant on the Left no later than the 1860s, after which it could be found in its pure form most commonly among Marxists. As I have indicated in earlier chapters, other strands of the radical movement (partly in reaction to the narrowness of the "men of the sixties") showed an increasing interest in cultural currents outside the movement and in the problem of reconciling personal development with social progress which was central to the agenda of *Signposts*. As used in the symposium, the word *intelligentsia* can be said to denote a composite mentality, aspects of which (such as dogmatism and messianism) were to be found equally among radicals, adherents of the new religious revival, and critics of the old atheistic intelligentsia, such as the Slavophiles and Lev Tolstoy—as well as some *Signposts* authors. On the use of the term in general, see my Introduction, n. 2.

70. *Signposts: A Collection of Articles on the Russian Intelligentsia*, trans. and ed. M. S. Shatz and J. E. Zimmerman (Irvine, Calif., 1986), xxvii.

71. Some representative examples: L. Schapiro describes the *Signposts* authors as "a group of thinkers whose views were . . . close to those of Struve" and whose ideas represented "a return to a . . . truly liberal Russian tradition" ("Vekhi Group," 59, 76). C. Read approaches the symposium as a thematic unity (*Revolution and the Russian Intelligentsia, 1900–1912* [London, 1979], 106–20); as do M. Shatz and J. Zimmerman, who cite among its (liberal) themes those of individualism, political Westernism, and the call for a productive culture (introduction to *Signposts*, xiii–xv, xxv). G. S. Morson argues that religious differences among the *Signposts* authors do not make it any less of a coherent statement, on the ground that the work's religious aspect is "highly attenuated" ("Prosaic Bakhtin," 51 n19). I advance a contrary view here.

72. Struve, "O 'Vekhakh,' " *Patriotica*, 231.

73. *Signposts*, 138, 143, 152.

74. Ibid., 5, 4–5.

75. Ibid., 30, 31.

76. Ibid., 125.

77. Ibid., 21, 5, 13, 14.

78. Ibid., 135.
79. Ibid., 119, 124, 127, 124.
80. Frank, *Biografiia P. B. Struve*, 82.
81. *Signposts*, 20, 20–21, 20, 24–25, 49.
82. Ibid., 138–39.
83. Ibid., 147, 147–48, 148, 150.
84. Ibid., 13, 20.
85. Ibid., 26, 15, 12.
86. Ibid., 44, 47, 44, 15, 13, 15.
87. Ibid., 120, 143, 148.
88. Ibid., 153, 154–55, 29, 155.
89. Ibid., 63.
90. See Morson, "Prosaic Bakhtin."
91. See "The Intelligentsia and Self-Censorship," this vol.
92. For a thorough survey of the "official" *Signposts* debate, see G. Oberländer, "Die Vechi-Diskussion 1909–1912" (Ph.D. diss., University of Cologne, 1965). On post-revolutionary sequels to *Signposts* (including the symposium *Out of the Depths*, in which five *Signposts* authors, with six others, approached the events of 1917–18 as a vindication of their warnings), see J. Burbank, *Intelligentsia and Revolution: Russian Views of Bolshevism, 1917–1922* (Oxford, 1986), chap. 5.
93. Dostoevskii, *Polnoe sobranie sochinenii*, 5:179.
94. *The Meaning of History* (New York, 1936), 223 (based on lectures delivered in Moscow in 1919–20); "Predsmertnye mysli Fausta," in N. A. Berdiaev et al., *Osval'd Shpengler i zakat Evropy* (Moscow, 1922), 66. See also Berdiaev, *Novoe srednevekov'e* (Berlin, 1924).
95. "Dnevnik politika: O gordyne, velemudrii i pustote," *Rossiia i slavianstvo*, no. 12 (1929): 1, cited in Pipes, *Struve: Liberal on the Right*, 365.
96. Pipes, *Struve: Liberal on the Right*, 366.

CHAPTER TEN
The Chaotic City

1. S. Volkov, *St. Petersburg: A Cultural History*, trans. A. W. Bouis (New York, 1995).
2. Ibid., 545.
3. B. Pike, *The Image of the City in Modern Literature* (Princeton, 1981), 8.
4. Marquis de Custine, *Letters from Russia*, trans. and ed. R. Buss (London, 1991), 151–52.
5. Ibid., 53.
6. Ibid., 53, 91, 110, 95.
7. A. S. Pushkin, "Mednyi vsadnik," *Sobranie sochinenii*, 10 vols. (Moscow, 1974–77), 3:262; N. V. Gogol', "Nevskii prospekt," *Sobranie sochinenii*, 8 vols. (Moscow, 1952–53), 3:42–43.
8. Herzen, *Sobranie sochinenii*, 2:39, 41.
9. Dostoevskii, *Podrostok, Polnoe sobranie sochinenii*, 13:113.
10. A. Bely, *Petersburg*, trans. and intro. R. Maguire and J. Malmstead (London, 1983), 207.
11. Volkov, *St. Petersburg*, xix.
12. Ibid., 324.

13. V. G. Belinskii, *Polnoe sobranie sochinenii*, 12 vols. (Moscow, 1953–56), 8:410.

14. Herzen, *Sobranie sochinenii*, 7:117.

15. Volkov, *St. Petersburg*, 212.

16. Ibid., 281.

17. Ibid., 232.

18. Ibid., 407.

19. E. Zamiatin, "Ia boius'," *Sochineniia*, 4 vols. (Munich, 1988), 4:255.

20. Zamiatin, "Pis'mo Stalinu," ibid., 313.

21. Volkov, *St. Petersburg*, 406.

22. Ibid., 388.

23. Volkov, *St. Petersburg*, 381.

24. Ibid., 423.

25. Ibid., 179, 221.

26. *The Complete Poems of Anna Akhmatova/* Anna Akhmatova, *Polnoe sobranie stikhotvorenii*, trans. J. Hemschemeyer, ed. and intro. R. Reeder, 2 vols. (Somerville, Mass., 1990), 1:547.

27. Ibid., 537.

28. Ibid., 539.

29. Ibid., 2:99, 113.

30. Volkov, *St. Petersburg*, 421.

31. Ibid., 516.

32. D. Fanger, *Dostoevsky and Romantic Realism: A Study of Dostoevsky in Relation to Balzac, Dickens, and Gogol* (Cambridge, Mass., 1965), 211.

33. Volkov, *St. Petersburg*, 418–19.

34. *The Complete Poems of Anna Akhmatova*, 2:97, 111.

35. O. Mandelstam, *Selected Poems*, trans. D. McDuff (London, 1983), 111.

36. O. Mandel'shtam, *Sobranie sochinenii*, ed. G. Struve and B. Filipoff, 3 vols. (Munich, 1967–69), 1:202.

37. N. Mandel'shtam, *Vospominaniia* (New York, 1970), 15.

38. Mandel'shtam, *Sobranie sochinenii*, 1:86.

39. *Complete Poems of Anna Akhmatova*, 2:113, 115.

40. Volkov, *St. Petersburg*, 547.

41. N. Punin, *O Tatline: Arkhiv russkogo avangarda* (Moscow, 1994), 16–17.

CHAPTER ELEVEN

The Rational Reality of Boris Chicherin

1. Novus (pseud. of P. Struve), "Na raznye temy: G. Chicherin i ego obrashchenie k proshlomu," *Novoe slovo* 7 (1897): 40.

2. V. Maklakov, "Iz proshlogo," *Sovremennye zapiski* [Paris] 40 (1929): 308–10. Another admirer, Prince E. Trubetskoy, describes Chicherin's life as "the story of a man who was ill-suited to Russia and was thrown overboard by life because he was too crystal-clear, too granite-firm, too whole-hearted"; quoted by D. Chizhevskii, *Gegel' v Rossii* (Paris, 1930), 289.

3. V. Leontovitsch describes him as "the greatest theoretician of Russian liberalism" (*Geschichte des Liberalismus in Russland* [Frankfurt, 1957], 129). See also Venturi, *Roots of Revolution*, 157, where Chicherin is described as "one of the strictest theorizers of the Liberalism of the time." D. Hammer, "Two Russian Liberals:

The Political Thought of B. N. Chicherin and D. K. Kavelin" (Ph.D. diss., Columbia University, 1962), describes Chicherin as "the theoretical forerunner, if not the main prophet," of the Kadet Party (9). He admits elsewhere, however, that "there is some difficulty in identifying Chicherin's place in the history of Russian liberalism" (373). See also G. Gurvich, "B. N. Chicherin," in *Encyclopaedia of the Social Sciences*, vol. 3 (London, 1930), 372: "Politically he . . . paved the way for the Russian Constitutional-Democratic Party." A. Walicki asserts that Chicherin's importance in Russian intellectual history is "very great" (*Legal Philosophies of Russian Liberalism* [Oxford, 1987], 109). G. M. Hamburg asserts that after 1855 Chicherin was regarded as the leading theoretician of Russian liberalism (*Boris Chicherin and Early Russian Liberalism, 1828–1866* [Stanford, Calif., 1992], 2).

Soviet scholars, too, were almost unanimous in seeing Chicherin as a leading liberal. Typical is the description by V. E. Illeritskii ("O gosudarstvennoi shkole v russkoi istoriografii," *Voprosy istorii* 5 [1959]: 143), where Chicherin and K. D. Kavelin are described as the "leaders of landowning-bourgeois liberalism, and its most eminent ideologists in the middle of the last century." See also L. Ginzburg, "Pis'mo k B. N. Chicherinu," in *Literaturnoe nasledstvo*, no. 61 (Moscow, 1953), 248: Chicherin was "a moderate liberal, an advocate of certain bourgeois reforms, as implemented by the monarchy, with the help of the privileged classes." The sole departure from this standard Soviet interpretation is that of S. Bakhrushin, who sees Chicherin as the ideologist of a form of enlightened absolutism already anachronistic in his time: introduction to B. N. Chicherin, *Vospominaniia: Moskva sorokovykh godov* (Moscow, 1929), x.

4. S. Utechin, *Russian Political Thought* (London, 1963), 107; Walicki, *Legal Philosophies*, 160.

5. Hammer, "Two Russian Liberals," 335 (he asserts that Chicherin's thought "does not fall short of, it goes beyond liberalism," in revealing the latter's "shortcomings"); Gurvich, "Chicherin."

6. Venturi, *Roots of Revolution*, 99. On Chicherin's isolation, see Schapiro, *Rationalism and Nationalism*, 90; and G. Fischer's curious description: "Typical of [a middle group of liberals] was a solitary figure—Chicherin" (*Russian Liberalism: From Gentry to Intelligentsia* [Cambridge, Mass., 1958], 19).

7. See the formulation of this distinction by J. L. Talmon, *The Origins of Totalitarian Democracy* (London, 1952), introduction. The most interesting and sustained attempt to view the course of Russian intellectual history in terms of such a schema has been made by L. Schapiro (*Rationalism and Nationalism*). In his article "The *Vekhi* Group," Schapiro emphasizes Chicherin's influence on the *Vekhi* (*Signposts*) writers who, he claims, belonged to the "same tenuous truly liberal Russian tradition" (56–76). See also Schapiro's essay entitled "The Prerevolutionary Intelligentsia and the Legal Order," in Pipes, *The Russian Intelligentsia*, 26, where he contends that it was their "emotion and passion" which made the intelligentsia reject liberalism: "If reason alone determined political convictions, Chicherin's influence . . . might have been greater." In the chapter "What Is the Intelligentsia?" in the same volume, M. Malia cites *Signposts* as one of the few attempts by the intelligentsia to "adapt to the real world." See also L. Haimson, "The Parties and the State: The Evolution of Political Attitudes," in *The Transformation of Russian Society: Aspects of Social Change Since 1861*, ed. C. E. Black (Cambridge,

Mass., 1960), 110–45; Haimson contrasts the Kadet Party's "old intelligentsia prejudices" with the *Signposts* authors' platform of political responsibility, realism, and moderation.

8. M. Malia, "What Is the Intelligentsia?" 12. See S. Benson's monograph, which presents Chicherin as a moderate reformist, one of the "few true 'liberals' " in a society polarized between conservatives and an intelligentsia whose "moderates" and radicals were united in their opposition to gradualism, liberal constitutionalism, and the entire existing order ("The Conservative Liberalism of Boris Chicherin," *Forschungen zur Osteuropäischen Geschichte* 21 [1975]: 17–111).

9. John Toews has pointed out that the terms *Left* (or Young) and *Right* (or Old) *Hegelians* that emerged in Germany in the 1830s oversimplified the nature of the split within the Hegelian school over the meaning (and ultimately the validity) of Hegelian theory and the relationship between theory and practice. On the focus of division—the question of Hegel's identification of Reason with reality (was it completed, an ongoing process, or a future goal?)—there was a wide spectrum of views between revolutionary tendencies at one extreme and political and religious accommodationists at the other (Toews, *Hegelianism: The Path toward Dialectical Humanism, 1805–1841* [Cambridge, Eng., 1980], chap. 7). The same was true in Russian in the early 1840s: between the revolutionary Hegelianism of Herzen (which led him ultimately to repudiate Hegel's philosophy altogether) and the conservatism of Chicherin, there were many "reformist" positions, such as that of T. N. Granovsky.

10. Chicherin, *Vospominaniia: Moskva sorokovykh godov*, 74.

11. Ibid., 75, 77, 89.

12. Ibid., 88–89.

13. On the etatist school, see P. Miliukov, "Iuridicheskaia shkola v russkoi istoriografii," *Russkaia mysl'*, no. 6 (1886): 80–92; and Illeritskii, "O gosudarstvennoi shkole."

14. See Hamburg, *Boris Chicherin*, 57ff.

15. The letter is reproduced in V. Baturinskii, "Gertsen, ego druz'ia i znakomye," *Vsemirnyi vestnik* 5 (1905): 20–33.

16. See the letters printed by M. Dragomanov, in *Vol'noe slovo* (Geneva, 1883), 61, 62.

17. "Nas uprekaiut," *Kolokol*, 1 November 1858; *Kolokol*, 1 December 1858.

18. See his letter to Herzen of 11 November 1858: "We are separated . . . by one thing, which is perhaps more important than all the rest: political temperament" (Dragomanov, *Vol'noe slovo*).

19. Only two of Herzen's former liberal friends, N. Ketcher and A. Korsh, took Chicherin's side in the dispute. A collective letter of protest, signed by Turgenev, Annenkov, I. Babst, N. Tiutchev, and A. Galakhov, was sent to Chicherin, who forwarded it to Herzen with an accompanying letter (letter to Herzen, 25 February 1859, in Dragomanov, *Vol'noe slovo*).

20. Baturinskii, "Gertsen," viii; *Vsemirnyi vestnik* 3 (1904): 23–29.

21. Herzen, *Sobranie sochinenii*, 9:250–53. On his reason for not sending the letter, Herzen writes that it had been intended "to initiate a friendly polemic, which was forestalled by his prosecutor's indictment" (11:250).

22. His arguments are laid out in *On Popular Representation*.

23. Herzen, *Sobranie sochinenii*, 11:300.

24. See V. Leontovitsch, *Geschichte des Liberalismus*, 18; D. Offord, *Portraits of Early Russian Liberals* (Cambridge, 1985), 74; P. R. Roosevelt, *Apostle of Russian Liberalism: Timofei Granovsky* (Newtonville, Mass., 1986).

25. See Berlin's essay "Fathers and Children," in *Russian Thinkers*, 261–305.

26. Fischer, *Russian Liberalism*, viii.

27. R. Pipes, *Struve: Liberal on the Left, 1870–1905* (Cambridge, Mass., 1970), 283.

28. I do not discuss developments in his later thought, when (after resigning from Moscow University in 1866) he moved to his family estate in Tambov. In my view these still did not make him a liberal.

29. Fischer, *Russian Liberalism*, 119.

30. To Herzen, 30 November 1858 (Dragomanov, *Vol'noe slovo*).

31. B. Chicherin, "Razlichnye vidy liberalizma," in *Neskol'ko sovremennikh voprosov* (hereafter cited as *Nsv*) (Moscow, 1862), 19, 193, 194.

32. Chicherin, "Chto takoe okhranitel'nye nachala?" *Nsv*, 181.

33. Chicherin, "Razlichnye vidy liberalizma," 200. According to Struve, the term "liberal conservative" was first used in Russia by Pushkin's friend Prince P. Viazemsky (preface to S. Frank, *Pushkin kak politicheskii myslitel'* [Belgrade, 1937], 9).

34. Chicherin, "Razlichnye vidy liberalizma," 197.

35. Chicherin, "Chto takoe," 156.

36. See in particular "B. N. Chicherin i ego mesto v istorii russkoi obrazovannosti i obshchestvennosti," in P. Struve, *Sotsial'naia i ekonomicheskaia istoriia Rossii* (Paris, 1952), 323–31.

37. Chernyshevskii, *Polnoe sobranie sochinenii*, 5:656.

38. I. Turgenev, letter to P. Annenkov, 6 April 1862, *Pis'ma*.

39. K. D. Kavelin, from an unpublished letter of 1857, quoted by Hammer, "Two Russian Liberals," 114.

40. In spite of Hegel's influence on subsequent liberal thought (which also emphasized the social essence of man and laid less stress on "negative freedom" than classical liberalism had, J. Plamenatz was able to assert in 1965 that the claim that Hegel and his most orthodox followers were liberals was "not often" made (*Readings from Liberal Writers* [Oxford, 1965], 25). One notable exception was G. Ruggiero (see *The History of European Liberalism*, trans. R. Collingwood [Boston, 1959], 229–40). The consensus has been that Hegel's idealization of the state, with its authoritarian and nationalist implications, "ran counter to the gradual acceptance of liberal doctrines throughout the nineteenth century" (G. Lichtheim, "Hegel," *International Encyclopaedia of the Social Sciences*, vol. 6 [1968]: 342). But this has begun to change. For example, C. Taylor has attributed the view that Hegel's glorification of the state is incompatible with liberalism to the "atomistic prejudices" of Anglo-Saxon liberals who are repelled by the concept of "positive liberty" based on the recognition of man's social nature (Taylor, *Hegel and Modern Society* [Cambridge, 1979], 87).

41. Despite my emphasis on this point, when this essay was first published A. Walicki attributed my criticism of Chicherin to a "liberal-democratic" standpoint opposed to Hegel's glorification of the modern centralized state. As a Hegelian in this sense, he argues, Chicherin was nonetheless a liberal (*Legal Philosophies*, 156–57). I hope the following argument will demonstrate that he was neither.

42. Chicherin describes nations that have attained the state form of organization as

the "crown of mankind" ("Vstupitel'naia lektsiia po gosudarstvennomu pravu," *Nsv*, 33). He distinguishes three stages in Russian history, corresponding to Hegel's three moments of the will (immediacy, in family relations; subjectivity, in the conflicts of individual purposes in civil society; and objective universality, the submission of individual wills to the higher social will of the state). The first stage was a primitive patriarchal society, the second a civil society which, though institutionally an advance on its predecessor, had lost its primitive unity, and the third the state. The other representatives of the etatist school present variants of this pattern.

43. Chicherin, *O narodnom predstavitel'stve* (Moscow, 1866).

44. See L. Schapiro, *Rationalism and Nationalism*, 92–94; Utechin, *Russian Political Thought*, 107; K. von Beyme, *Politische Soziologie im zaristischen Russland* (Wiesbaden, 1965), 34.

45. B. Chicherin, *Istoriia politicheskikh uchenii* (Moscow, 1869), 1:7; *O narodnom predstavitel'stve*, 569–73.

46. Hamburg, *Boris Chicherin*, 285.

47. B. Chicherin, *Istoriia politicheskikh uchenii* (Moscow, 1877), 4:602.

48. See, e.g., Hammer, "Two Russian Liberals," 336; and Schapiro, "Pre-revolutionary Intelligentsia," 22ff.

49. Chicherin, "Chto takoe okhranitel'nye nachala?" 149. In the introduction to the first volume of his *History of Political Thought*, Chicherin emphasizes his conservative interpretation of Hegel, asserting that he had learned to see past events as "not transitory moments of development, but expressions of eternal truths, inherent in human reason" (*Istoriia politicheskikh uchenii*, 1:ix). Elsewhere he writes: "I came to understand that those stages which Hegel calls moments of development are eternal elements of the human spirit, possessing the right to independent existence and being preserved in subsequent movement" (*Vospominaniia: Moskva sorokovykh godov*, 90).

50. Chicherin, "Chto takoe okhranitel'nye nachala?" 154; "Russkoe dvorianstvo," 150; "Chto takoe," 169, 166–67.

51. This is one of the central arguments of *O narodnom predstavitel'stve*. Although the censorship did not allow him to refer directly to Russia, he hoped that the Russian reader would read between the lines and understand that Russia was not ready for a constitution (*Vospominaniia: Moskovskii universitet* [Moscow, 1929], 164). In an unpublished article written in 1862 at the request of the tsar's minister N. Miliutin on the situation of the peasants in Poland, Chicherin took the opportunity of asserting that neither Russian public opinion nor the new institutions introduced after 1861 were yet stable enough to support a constitutional order. If introduced before the people were "educated" to its level, it would lead to "fruitless discontent . . . and dictatorship" (ibid., 113–14).

52. "Razlichnye vidy liberalizma," 193, 197.

53. Hegel, *Philosophy of Right*, § 257, 155.

54. See Berlin, "Two Concepts of Liberty," in *Four Essays on Liberty*, 118–72.

55. Hegel, *Philosophy of Right*, addition to § 297.

56. Chicherin, *Istoriia politicheskikh uchenii*, vol. 4:595, 596.

57. Chicherin, *Vospominaniia: Moskva sorokovykh godov*, 158.

58. Chicherin, "Mera i granitsy," *Nsv*, 78; "Vstupitel'naia lektsiia," 32–33; "Razlichnye vidy liberalizma," 199.

59. Chicherin, "Vstupitel'naia lektsiia," 34.

60. The lecture, though condemned by the progressive press, was welcomed in official circles: the tsar read it and wrote approving comments in the margin (Chicherin, *Vospominaniia: Moskovskii universitet,* 44).

61. He notes in his memoirs: "We do not yet possess the most essential conditions for a just court system" (ibid., 24).

62. "Razlichnye vidy liberalizma," 197. Here he is referring primarily to moral law, but he proceeds to assert that "[state] power and freedom are as inseparable as are . . . freedom and the moral law." It is true that he makes a highly ambiguous caveat: any citizen "without submitting unconditionally before the [state] power, of whatever kind it may be, is obliged, in the name of his own liberty, to respect the essence of the power itself." Whatever the meaning of the curious distinction between submission to some kinds of power, and respect for all power, he had, as his inaugural lecture showed, no sympathy for these who chose not to submit unconditionally to the kind of power represented by the Russian autocracy.

63. "Russkoe dvorianstvo," 93.

64. Chicherin, "Chto takoe," 170, 173–74.

65. In 1853 Chicherin's dissertation, "Oblastnye uchrezhdeniia Rossii v XVII veke," was rejected by Moscow University on the grounds that it contained "libel and abuse of ancient Russia." See *Vospominaniia: Moskva sorokovykh godov,* 122ff., 209–10.

66. Chicherin, *Vospominaniia: Moskovskii universitet,* 163.

67. Chicherin, *Nsv,* 91, 169.

68. "Russkoe dvorianstvo," 103–4.

69. Chicherin, "Sovet ministrov," *Nsv,* 205–35. He makes an unconvincing distinction between despotism and an "unlimited monarchy" (the latter being his term for the Russian autocracy) on the grounds that the autocracy, like a monarchy, acts through a subordinate body, the nobility ("Chto takoe," 176).

70. Chicherin, *Vospominaniia: Moskovskii universitet,* 164.

71. See, e.g., ibid., 50.

72. "Russkoe dvorianstvo," 123–31.

73. Chicherin, *Ocherki Anglii i Frantsii* (Moscow, 1859).

74. "O zemskikh uchrezhdeniiakh," *Nsv,* 258–59.

75. "Chto takoe," 170; "Russkoe dvorianstvo," 106. Chicherin advocates a property qualification for the privilege of belonging to the nobility, which would ensure both the supremacy of the upper classes and their attachment to the status quo, without making them a closed estate.

76. "Chto takoe," 173. He does, however, use the curious argument that in an "unlimited government" the corporations can protect the "independence of society"(!) from the "boundless dominion of the bureaucracy" (175).

77. Walicki, *Legal Philosophies,* 130ff.

78. Chicherin, *Istoriia politicheskikh uchenii,* 1:7. It is notable that the only assessment of Chicherin by a contemporary which emphasizes his defense of individual liberty was in an obituary published by a government journal, where he is praised for opposing those theories which exaggerated the "social principle" to the detriment of the moral freedom of the individual (V. Speranskii, "B. N. Chicherin, Nekrolog," *Zhurnal ministerstva narodnogo prosveshcheniia* 4 [1904]: 186–96). Because Chicherin saw the personality as achieving its moral freedom through obe-

dience to the state, this official blessing on his "individualism" is not as odd as it might seem.

79. "Vstupitel'naia lektsiia," 25. See also his argument against setting up an assembly of estates to advise the tsar, which would present "too much difficulty for the state." The government should not be distracted from its work on the Emancipation by any reproaches or demands on the part of Russian society ("Russkoe dvorianstvo," 131).

80. Chicherin, *Vospominaniia: Moskovskii universitet*, 23–25, 28–34, 37–41.

81. Ibid., 35, 26.

82. Ibid., 61. On Kavelin's attitude to the student disturbances, see Baturinskii, "Gertsen," 72ff.

83. Turgenev, letter to Herzen, 26 September 1862, *Pis'ma*, 4:335.

84. Chicherin, *Vospominaniia: Moskovskii universitet*, 25.

85. Walicki, *Legal Philosophies*, 159. Walicki bases his argument on F. A. Hayek's definition of classical liberalism (see Hayek, "Liberalism," in his *New Studies in Philosophy, Politics, Economics and the History of Ideas* [London, 1978], 119–51). G. M. Hamburg also considers Chicherin a leading Russian liberal, while observing that his failure to "carefully distinguish between the existing Russian state and an ideal Rechtsstaat" was a grave error (*Boris Chicherin*, 337).

86. Walicki, *Legal Philosophies*, 116. See n. 107, below.

87. Plamenatz, *Readings from Liberal Writers*, 37.

88. J. G. Merquior, *Liberalism Old and New* (Boston, 1991), 49.

89. Chicherin, *Istoriia politicheskikh uchenii*, pt. 1:ix. See Berlin, "The Hedghog and the Fox," *Russian Thinkers*, 22.

90. Herzen, *Sobranie sochinenii*, 10:320.

91. Chicherin, *Vospominaniia: Moskva sorokovykh godov*, 74.

92. "Vstupitel'naia lektsiia," 33; "Russkoe dvorianstvo," 121–23, 122, 137, 122; "Chto takoe," 169, 165; "Russkoe dvorianstvo," 93.

93. Review of Chicherin's *Ocherki Anglii i Frantsii*, *Sovremennik* 5 (1859): 58; Chernyshevskii, *Polnoe sobranie sochinenii*, 10:62.

94. Chicherin, *Vospominaniia: Moskovskii universitet*, 40.

95. "Vstupitel'naia lektsiia," 41.

96. A. D. Gradovskii, "Russkaia uchenaia literatura," *Russkii vestnik* 70 (1867): 730; quoted in Hamburg, *Boris Chicherin*, 297.

97. Quoted by V. Baturinskii in *Vsemirnyi vestnik* 3 (1904): 21. Kavelin makes the same point in his letter to Chicherin: by giving the bureaucracy a pretext to justify its reactionary measures, he is "selling [his] birthright for a mess of pottage" (ibid., 29).

98. Chernyshevskii, *Polnoe sobranie sochinenii*, 5:648–51.

99. Chicherin, *Vospominaniia: Moskovskii universitet*, 42. See *Kolokol*, 22 March, 1 April 1862.

100. Chicherin, *Vospominaniia: Moskovskii universitet*, 64–65.

101. Chicherin asserts that this is the reason Kavelin gave for refusing to shake hands with him when they met six years later (ibid., 66).

102. The remark was made by Count P. Shuvalov, the marshal of nobility of St. Petersburg, when Chicherin was introduced to him as "one of the rare defenders of the nobility" (ibid., 71).

103. For Chicherin's account of these events, see ibid., 47–52.

104. Kavelin, letter to Chicherin, n.d.; this letter is quoted in ibid., 61–63.
105. Ibid., 112–13.
106. Ibid., 221–22. On the details of this affair, see Hamburg, *Boris Chicherin.*
107. See "Rossiia nakanune dvadtsatogo stoletiia" (Berlin, 1900). (The pamphlet was signed "Russkii patriot.")
108. B. Chicherin, *Vospominaniia: Zemstvo i moskovskaia duma* (Moscow, 1934), 237.
109. He is reported to have made this assertion to I. M. Sechenov, professor of medicine at St. Petersburg University. See L. F. Panteleev, *Vospominaniia* (Moscow, 1958), 530.
110. From Chicherin's letter to his brother on the student disturbances. He expresses the hope that there will be found in the government "at least one brave man, who will take a stick into his hands, and then everything will return to the old order" (*Vospominaniia: Moskovskii universitet,* 25).
111. Quoted in ibid., 63.
112. Chicherin, *Istoriia politicheskikh uchenii,* 4:603.
113. Quoted in Hamburg, *Boris Chicherin,* 261.
114. Herzen, *Sobranie sochinenii,* 9:248.

CHAPTER TWELVE
Bakunin and the Charm of the Millennium

1. E. H. Carr, *Michael Bakunin* (New York, 1975), 440.
2. Ibid., 107.
3. Ibid., 24, 107.
4. Ibid., 107.
5. M. Bakunin, *Selected Writings,* ed. A. Lehning, trans. S. Cox and O. Stephens (New York, 1973).
6. Berlin, *Russian Thinkers,* 107, 106.
7. Carr, *Bakunin,* 73.
8. Bakunin to his sister Varvara, 10 January 1837, M. A. Bakunin, *Sobranie sochinenii i pisem, 1828–76,* ed. Iu. M. Steklov, 4 vols. (Moscow, 1934–35), 1:386; Bakunin to Aleksandra Beier, April 1836, *Sobranie sochinenii,* 1:262.
9. Turgenev, *Rudin, Sochineniia,* 6:270.
10. Bakunin, *Sobranie sochinenii,* 3:45. The determining influence of Bakunin's early idealist fantasies on his subsequent life and thought is the subject of my book *Mikhail Bakunin.*
11. Bakunin, *Sobranie sochinenii,* 3:360.
12. Ibid., 126–47.
13. Bakunin to G. and E. Herwegh, 6 September 1847, ibid., 265.
14. Bakunin, *Gosudarstvennost' i anarkhiia, Archives Bakounine,* ed. A. Lehning (Leiden, 1961–), 3:119; *Sobranie sochinenii,* 2:8.
15. P. V. Annenkov, *Vospominaniia i kriticheskie ocherki* (St. Petersburg, 1881), 272.
16. Bakunin, *Sobranie sochinenii,* 2:302; to G. Herwegh, August 1848, ibid., 317; Bakunin, *Archives,* 3:17; *Selected Writings,* 80, 81.
17. Bakunin to Nechaev, 2 June 1870, *Archives,* 4:114; M. A. Bakunin, *Rechi i vozzvaniia* (Moscow, 1906), 240; Bakunin to Herzen, 19 July 1866, *Pis'ma M. A. Bakunina k A. I. Gertsenu i N. P. Ogarevu,* ed. M. P. Dragomanov (Geneva, 1896), 177; *Selected Writings,* 181, 64–65.

18. Herzen to Bakunin, 1 September 1863, *Sobranie sochinenii*, 27:371.

19. See Bakunin, "Neskol'ko slov k molodym brat'iam v Rossii" and "Postanovka revoliutsionnogo voprosa," *Rechi i vozzvaniia*, 227–45; *Materialy dlia biografii M. Bakunina*, ed. V. Polonskii, 3 vols. (Moscow, 1923), 3:354: *Rechi i vozzvaniia*, 200.

20. Bakunin to A. Richard, 7 February 1870, *Materialy*, 3:25, 258, 259–60, 258.

21. Herzen, "K staromu tovarishchu," *Sobranie sochinenii*, 20: 585.

22. Herzen to Ogarev (?), 11 May 1869, *Sobranie sochinenii*, 30:109.

23. See M. Confino, *Violence dans la violence: Le débat bakounine-necaev* (Paris, 1973), 36.

24. F. Dostoevskii, *Besy, Polnoe sobranie sochinenii*, 10:311.

25. Bakunin to J. Guillaume, 13 April 1869, *Sobranie sochinenii*, 3:435; *Pis'ma M. A. Bakunina*, 482.

26. Bakunin, *Materialy*, 3:258; Bakunin to N. Ogarev, N. Herzen, V. Ozerov, and S. Serebrennikov, 20 June 1870, *Archives*, 4:144.

27. Bakunin to Nechaev, 2 June 1870, ibid., 115.

28. Quoted by Iu. Steklov, *Mikhail Aleksandrovich Bakunin: Ego zhizn' i deiatel'nost', 1814–1876*, 4 vols. (Moscow, 1926–27), 2:273–74; Belinskii to V. Botkin, 18–20 February 1840, *Polnoe sobranie sochinenii*, 11:499.

29. Turgenev, *Rudin, Sochineniia*, 6: 298.

CHAPTER THIRTEEN
A Bolshevik Philosophy

1. There has been little analysis of the empiriocriticist movement as a whole. See L. Kolakowski, *Main Currents of Marxism II: The Golden Age* (Oxford, 1978), chap. 17. The political issues are emphasized in R. Williams, *The Other Bolsheviks: Lenin and His Critics, 1904–1914* (Bloomington, Ind., 1986). On Nietzsche's influence on the movement, see *Nietzsche in Russia*, ed. B. Glatzer Rosenthal (Princeton, 1986), chaps. 11–13. References to the movement in works on Russian philosophy are brief. See, e.g., G. A. Wetter, *Dialectical Materialism: A Historical and Systematic Survey of Philosophy in the Soviet Union*, trans. P. Heath (London, 1958), 92–99. Bogdanov, the movement's main philosopher, has received more attention, but his thought has generally been treated in isolation from the movement as a whole. See references in note 25, below.

2. The conflict between these two conceptions of "integrality" in Russian radical thought is treated in my doctoral dissertation, "Attitudes to the Individual"; an interpretation of neo-Kantian revisionism in this light is given at 180–276.

3. Pseudonym of A. A. Malinovsky. Bogdanov's main works in the period under review were *Iz psikhologii obshchestva* (St. Petersburg, 1904); *Empiriomonizm: Stat'i po filosofii*, 3 vols. (Moscow, 1904–06); and *Filosofiia zhivogo opyta* (St. Petersburg, 1912). He also contributed to the three main symposiums of the movement: *Ocherki realisticheskogo mirovozzreniia* (St. Petersburg, 1904; hereafter cited as *ORM*); *Ocherki po filosofii marksizma* (St. Petersburg, 1908; hereafter *OFM*); and *Ocherki filosofii kollektivizma* (St. Petersburg, 1909; hereafter *OFK*). After the movement disintegrated, he continued to develop his philosophy in other works.

4. Pseudonym of V. A. Rudnev. Bazarov's main writings appeared in the empiriocriticist symposia.

5. See A. Lunacharskii, *Etiudy kriticheskie i polemicheskie* (Moscow, 1905); *Otkliki zhizni* (St. Petersburg, 1906); *Religiia i sotsializm* (St. Petersburg, 1908); and articles in the movement's main symposia.

6. Pseudonym of N. V. Vol'skii. See N. Valentinov, *Filosofskie postroeniia marksizma* (Moscow, 1908), and *E. Makh i marksizm* (Moscow, 1908).

7. N. Valentinov, *Vstrechi s Leninym* (New York, 1953), 240, 243.

8. Bogdanov, *Empiriomonizm*, 2d ed., 3 vols. (Moscow, 1905–06), 3:iii–v.

9. Lunacharskii, *Religiia i sotsializm*, 8.

10. Valentinov, *Vstrechi*, 242.

11. G. Plekhanov, "Kritika nashikh kritikov," in *Sochineniia*, vol. 2 (Moscow, 1925–27), 137.

12. G. Plekhanov, *K voprosu o razvitii monisticheskogo vzgliada na istoriiu*, in *Sochineniia*, 7, 246.

13. Valentinov, *Vstrechi*, 240.

14. Ibid., 242, 243–44.

15. Lunacharskii, *Religiia i sotsializm*, 3–14.

16. K. Marx and F. Engels, *Selected Works in One Volume* (London, 1968), 28. For commentaries on the *Theses* by members of the movement, see V. Bazarov, "Mistitsizm i realizm nashego vremeni," in *OFM*, 69–71; Bogdanov, *Filosofiia zhivogo opyta*, 25–127; Lunacharskii, *Religiia i sotsializm*, 326–27.

17. Bogdanov, "Filosofiia sovremennogo estestvoznaniia," in *OFK*, 127.

18. E. Mach, *The Analysis of Sensations and the Relation of the Physical to the Psychical*, trans. C. M. Williams, rev. S. Waterlow (London, 1914), 311.

19. Ibid., 24.

20. See V. Bonch-Bruevich, *Izbrannye sochineniia*, 3 vols. (Moscow, 1959–63), 2:349ff.; and A. Lunacharskii, *Vospominaniia i vpechatleniia* (Moscow, 1968), 19–20.

21. The first Russian popularizer of empiriocriticism was V. Lesevich, *Chto takoe nauchnaia filosofiia* (St. Petersburg, 1891). In 1905 Lunacharsky published a popular version of Avenarius's most important work, *Kritik der Reiner Entfahrung*: R. Avenarius, *Kritika chistogo opyta v populiarnom izlozhenii A. Lunacharskogo* (Moscow, 1905). By 1904, there was a considerable literature in Russian on empiriocriticism and widespread interest in it, particularly in socialist circles, which held lectures and discussions on the subject. See V. Bonch-Bruevich, *Izbrannye sochineniia*, 353.

22. Bogdanov, *Filosofiia zhivogo opyta*, 70–85; "Strana idolov i filosofiia marksizma," in *OFM*, 215–42; "Filosofiia . . . estestvoznaniia," 78–81. He points to the similarities between the voluntarism of the empiriocriticists and the thought of the socialist philosopher Joseph Dietzgen.

23. Bogdanov, "Filosofiia . . . estestvoznaniia," 138.

24. Marx and Engels, *Selected Works*, 30.

25. For a detailed study of Bogdanov's philosophy, see the monograph by D. Grille, *Lenins Rivale: Bogdanov und seine Philosophie* (Cologne, 1966); see also K. Jensen, *Beyond Marx and Mach: Aleksandr Bogdanov's Philosophy of Living Experience* (Dordrecht, 1982); and Z. Sochor, *Revolution and Culture: The Bogdanov-Lenin Controversy* (Ithaca, N.Y., 1988).

26. Yushkevich started out from a view of the world as a complex of sensations but argued that, because the latter differed from individual to individual, reality was to be found only in their "common multiple." This constitutes the subject matter

of science, which endows it with simplifying symbols, namely, laws and concepts. Reality lies in these "empirical symbols." See P. Iushkevich, *O materialisticheskom ponimanii istorii* (St. Petersburg, 1907); *Materializm i kriticheskii realizm* (St. Petersburg, 1908); and *Novye veiania* (St. Petersburg, 1910).

27. Bogdanov, "Filosofiia . . . estestvoznaniia," 3–87; *Filosofiia zhivogo opyta*, 267–74.

28. Plekhanov, *K voprosu*, 22; quoted, among others, by Lunacharskii, *Religiia i sotsializm*, 343.

29. See the eighth and ninth *Theses:* "The highest point attained by *contemplative* materialism, that is, materialism which does not understand sensuousness as practical activity, is the contemplation of single individuals in 'civil society' "; and "The philosophers have only *interpreted* the world, in various ways; the point however, is to *change* it" (Marx and Engels, *Selected Works*, 30).

30. Ibid., 28. Lunacharsky pointed out that Plekhanov's rendering of this *Thesis* (in notes to his translation of Engels's *Ludwig Feuerbach and the End of Classical German Philosophy*) conveyed the exact opposite of the meaning of the original, making it seem that Marx recognized the existence of the thing-in-itself. Plekhanov had written "man must show . . . that his thought does not stop on this side of phenomena" (*Religiia i sotsializm*, 343). Bazarov makes the same point in his essay "K voprosu o filosofskikh osnovakh marksizma," in *Pamiati Marksa* (Moscow, 1908), 70–71.

31. Bazarov, "K voprosu o filosofskikh osnovakh marksizma," 65, 73. See Lunacharsky's similar use of Marx's texts against the "thing-in-itself" (*Religiia i sotsializm*, 285–357).

32. Bogdanov, "Filosofiia . . . estestvoznaniia," 52–60.

33. Bogdanov, *Iz psikhologii obshchestva*, 57–58.

34. Bogdanov, *Filosofiia zhivogo opyta*, 216–66.

35. Ibid., 217.

36. Bogdanov, *Empiriomonizm*, 3:157.

37. Ibid., 1:181.

38. Ibid., 3:61, 1:47, 3:58–65; *Iz psikhologii obshchestva*, 52–59; *Filosofiia zhivogo opyta*, 317.

39. Lunacharskii, *Religiia i sotsializm*, 47. Like Bogdanov, he turns Marx into a Machist, asserting that Marx conceives of the material and the ideal as merely "different stages of organization of the same element" (ibid., 334).

40. Ibid., 331. In his article "Ateizm," in *OFM*, Lunacharsky expresses himself more circumspectly, though also more obscurely: he describes the world as "a battle of freedoms from which inevitability naturally arises as the result of the mutual restrictions imposed by phenomena": the future socialist society will accomplish "the destruction of the gulf between inevitability and freedom, through progress, through the perfecting of the species, at one and the same time material and deeply determined, and deeply spiritual and free" (135–36, 148).

41. Iushkevich, *Stolpy filosofskoi ortodoksii* (St. Petersburg, 1910), 5–6.

42. See preface, *OFM*, i.

43. Lunacharskii, "Ateizm," 160.

44. Ibid., 125.

45. Lunacharskii, *Religiia i sotsializm*, 10.

46. Lunacharskii, "Ateizm," 146.

47. Lunacharskii, *Religiia i sotsializm*, 291.

48. Lunacharskii, "Ateizm," 147.

49. Bogdanov, *Empiriomonizm*, 1:61.

50. Lunacharskii, "Osnovy pozitivnoi estetiki," in *ORM*, 139.

51. Lunacharskii, "Ateizm," 160.

52. On this aspect of their thought, see *Nietzsche in Russia*.

53. R. Avenarius, *Kritika chistogo opyta v populiarnom izlozhenii A. Lunacharskogo*, 206; Lunacharskii, "Osnovy . . . ," 122ff.; *Religiia i sotsializm*, 10–11.

54. Bogdanov, "Strana idolov . . . ," 215.

55. Bazarov, "Avtoritarnaia metafizika i avtonomnaia lichnost'," in *ORM*, 267.

56. Ibid., 36, 246–47. See also the essay by S. Suvorov, "Osnovy filosofii zhizni," in *ORM*, 1–113; and Lunacharsky's attack on Kantian ethics in *Otkliki zhizni*, 1–92.

57. Bazarov, *Na dva fronta* (St. Petersburg, 1910), 141.

58. Lunacharskii, *Religiia i sotsializm*, 45, 105.

59. *ORM*, v, vi.

60. Bogdanov, *Empiriomonizm*, 3:iv–v.

61. Bogdanov, *Filosofiia zhivogo opyta*, 324.

62. Mach, *Analysis of Sensations*, 312.

63. See L. Kolakowski's assessment in his *Positivist Philosophy from Hume to the Vienna Circle*, 4th ed. (London, 1972), 125–57.

64. Lunacharskii, "Osnovy pozitivnoi estetiki," 137.

65. Ibid.

66. Bogdanov, *Empiriomonizm*, 1:60–61.

67. Lunacharskii, *Religiia i sotsializm*, 146.

68. Ibid., 45.

69. Ibid., 43.

70. Lunacharskii, "Ateizm," 159.

71. Lunacharskii, *Religiia i sotsializm*, 395.

72. Ibid., 255; Lunacharskii, *Vospominaniia i vpechatleniia*, 21.

73. Lunacharskii, *Religiia i sotsializm*, 131, 189.

74. Lunacharskii, "Ateizm," 159.

75. L. Aksel'rod, "Novaia raznovidnost' revizionizma," in Aksel'rod (pseud. Ortodoks), *Filosofskie ocherki: Otvet filosofskim kritikam istoricheskogo materializma* (St. Petersburg, 1906), 171–85. She asserts that a year and a half earlier Lenin had asked her to write an attack on Bogdanov's philosophy (ibid., 171).

76. G. Plekhanov, "Materialismus militans (Otvet g. Bogdanovu)," in *Sochineniia*, 17: 1–99. This was a reply to Bogdanov's "Otkrytoe pis'mo g. Plekhanovu," *Voprosy zhizni* 7 (1907).

77. V. Lenin, *Materializm i empiriokrititsizm*, in Lenin, *Polnoe sobranie sochinenii*, 5th ed., 55 vols. (Moscow, 1958–69), 18:343. The only point on which Lenin differs with Plekhanov concerns the latter's view that an individual's representations of things and processes are not copies but symbols of things-in-themselves. Lenin sees this as introducing "an unnecessary element of agnosticism" into materialism (see ibid., 244–51). For an analysis of Lenin's philosophical views in general and *Materialism and Empiriocriticism* in particular, see A. Pannekoek, *Lenin as Philosopher: A Critical Examination of the Philosophical Bases of Leninism* (London, 1975); and R. S. Cohen, "Dialectical Materialism and Carnap's Logical Empiricism," in *The Philosophy of Rudolph Carnap*, ed. P. A. Schilpp (London, 1963),

99–158; G. Katkov, "Lenin as philosopher," in *Lenin: The Man, the Theorist, the Leader*, ed. L. Schapiro and P. Reddaway (London, 1967), 71–86.

78. G. Katkov, "Lenin as philosopher," 71.
79. Lenin, *Materializm i empiriokrititsizm*, 35–36.
80. Ibid., 74.
81. Ibid., 364, 380.
82. Ibid., 363.
83. L. Aksel'rod (Ortodoks), "Dva techeniia," in *Na rubezhe (K kharakteristike sovremennykh iskanii). Kriticheskii sbornik* (St. Petersburg, 1909), 255.
84. A. Potresov, "Nashi zlokliucheniia," in Potresov, *Posmertnyi sbornik proizvedenii* (Paris, 1937), 160. See also the article "Neotlozhnaia zadacha," in ibid., 173–78.
85. Plekhanov, "O tak nazyvaemykh religioznykh iskaniiakh v Rossii," *Sovremennyi mir* 9 (1909): 182–216; 10 (1909): 164–200.
86. Ibid., 10:185.
87. Ibid., 195.
88. See n. 83, above. The other contributors to the volume were A. Deborin, P. Maslov, V. Lvov, D. Koltsov, A. Martynov, and M. Nevedomsky.
89. F. Dan, "Geroi likvidatsii," in *Na rubezhe*, 83, 113.
90. Ibid., 114.
91. Iu. Martov, "Religiia i marksizm," in *Na rubezhe*, 35, 7.
92. L. Aksel'rod, "Dva techeniia," 266.
93. Ibid., 255.
94. Ibid., 256.
95. Ibid., 264.
96. Ibid., 265–66.
97. Valentinov, *Vstrechi*, 254.
98. Lenin, *Polnoe sobranie sochinenii*, 47:142.
99. Bonch-Bruevich, *Izbrannye sochineniia*, 355.
100. Ibid., 353.
101. Lenin, *Polnoe sobranie sochinenii*, 10:134.
102. *Bol'shaia sovetskaia entsiklopediia* (Moscow, 1927), vol. 6, col. 595.
103. Lenin, *Polnoe sobranie sochinenii*, 47:114, 151.
104. Bogdanov, *Filosofiia zhivogo opyta*, 192. See also Lunacharsky's definition: "The truth is what in any given conditions yields the most results per unit of effort expended" (*Religiia i sotsializm*, 344).
105. Lenin, *Polnoe sobranie sochinenii*, 29:162, 166, 250, 161, 248.
106. See Lunacharsky's expressions of contrition at having been "enticed" by the "crafty and confused" philosophy of Avenarius and Mach (Lunacharskii, *Lenin i literaturovedenie* [Moscow, 1934], 21–22).
107. Article of 24 December 1938, quoted by Valentinov, *Vstrechi*, 352–53.
108. Ibid., 258ff.

CHAPTER FOURTEEN
Brave New Worlds

1. M. Heller and A. Nekrich, *Utopia in Power: The History of the Soviet Union from 1917 to the Present* (New York, 1988), 9.

2. R. Stites, *Revolutionary Dreams: Utopian Visions and Experimental Life in the Russian Revolution* (Oxford, 1989). Sochor, *Revolution and Culture*.

3. Stites, *Revolutionary Dreams*, 9, 39.

4. See ibid., 135–40.

5. Cited in E. J. Brown, *Mayakovsky: A Poet in the Revolution* (Princeton, 1973), 212; C. Gray, *The Russian Experiment in Art, 1863–1922* (London, 1962), 180.

6. Stites, *Revolutionary Dreams*, 161.

7. Ibid., 7, 9–10, 7.

8. Ibid., 38.

9. R. Rorty, *Contingency, Irony and Solidarity*, xvi.

10. L. Trotsky, *Literature and Revolution* (Ann Arbor, Mich., 1960), 152.

11. L. Popova, "On Exact Criteria, Ballet Numbers, Deck Equipment on Battleships, Picasso's Latest Portraits, and the Observation Tower at the School of Military Camouflage in Kuntsevo," in *The Avant-Garde in Russia, 1910–1930: New Perspectives*, ed. S. Barron and M. Tuchman (Cambridge, Mass., 1980), 222.

12. D. Sarabianov, "Kazimir Malevich and His Art, 1900–1930," in *Kazimir Malevich, 1878–1935: Exhibitions: Leningrad, Moscow, Amsterdam* (Amsterdam, 1988), 70.

13. K. S. Malevich, *Essays on Art, 1915–33*, trans. X. Glowacki-Prus and A. McMillin, 4 vols. (London, 1968), 2:17–18.

14. Ibid., 1:38, 36.

15. Ibid., 87.

16. K. Malevich, "Die Gegenstandslose Welt," cited in C. Gray, introduction to *Kasimir Malevich, 1878–1935: An Exhibition of Paintings, Drawings and Studies* (London, 1959), 7. E. Kovtun, "Kazimir Malevich: His Creative Path," *Kazimir Malevich . . . Exhibitions*, 158.

17. C. Gray, introduction to *Kasimir Malevich*, 7; Malevich, *Essays on Art*, 1:86–87.

18. O. Mandel'shtam, *Sobranie sochinenii*, 1:86; J. Brodsky, introduction to O. Mandelstam, *Fifty Poems*, trans. B. Meares (New York, 1977), 15.

19. E. Zamiatin, "Tsel'," *Sochineniia*, 4:250.

20. N. Mandelstam, *Hope Against Hope: A Memoir*, trans. M. Hayward (London, 1976), 138.

21. Stites, *Revolutionary Dreams*, 231; Lunacharskii, *Religiia i sotsializm*, 43.

22. Stites, *Revolutionary Dreams*, 98.

23. Ibid., 118.

24. Ibid., 252–53.

25. Berlin, "Two Concepts of Liberty," *Four Essays on Liberty*, 118–72.

26. Ibid., 171.

27. A. Bogdanov, *Empiriomonizm*, 61; "Ten Laws of the New Conscience," cited in Sochor, *Revolution and Culture*, 199, 200.

28. Proletkult manifesto, in *Pravda*, 1 December 1920.

29. Sochor, *Revolution and Culture*, 198.

30. Ibid.

31. Berlin, "Two Concepts of Liberty," 134.

32. Stites, *Revolutionary Dreams*, 252.

33. G. L. Tul'chinskii, "Rossiiskii potential svobody," *Voprosy filosofii* 3 (1997): 23. This is a summary of the view argued at length in B. E. Grois, *Utopiia i obman. Stil' Stalina. O novom. Stat'i* (Moscow, 1993).

CHAPTER FIFTEEN
Irony and Utopia in Herzen and Dostoevsky

1. Dostoevskii, *Polnoe sobranie sochinenii*, 21:8.
2. See, e.g., A. S. Dolinin, "Dostoevskii i Gertsen," in *F. M. Dostoevskii: Stat'i i materialy*, ed. A. S. Dolinin (St. Petersburg, 1922), 275–324; N. Perlina, "Vozdeistvie gertsenovskogo zhurnalizma na arkhitektoniku i polifonicheskoe stroenie *Dnevnika pisatelia* Dostoevskogo," *Dostoevskii Studies*, vol. 5 (Klagenfurt, 1984), 141–56; Perlina, *Varieties of Poetic Utterance: Quotation in "The Brothers Karamazov"* (Lanham, N.Y., 1985), 118–35; and L. N. Dryzhakova, "Dostoevskii i Gertsen (u istokov romana 'Besy')," *Dostoevskii: Stat'i i materialy*, vol. 1 (Leningrad, 1974), 219–38.
3. G. S. Morson, *The Boundaries of Genre: Dostoevsky's "Diary of a Writer" and the Traditions of Literary Utopia* (Austin, Tex., 1981), 183.
4. E. Heller, *Thomas Mann: The Ironic German* (Cambridge, Eng., 1981), 235.
5. A summary of the position of the principal theorist of Romantic irony, Friedrich Schlegel. See R. Wellek, *A History of Modern Criticism*, vol. 2, *The Romantic Age* (London, 1955), 14.
6. Rorty, *Contingency, Irony and Solidarity*.
7. Herzen, *Sobranie sochinenii*, 3:7.
8. Herzen, *OS*, 52.
9. Ibid., 109, 120, 92, 28, 32, 121.
10. Ibid., 39, 35–36.
11. See M. Malia, *Alexander Herzen and the Birth of Russian Socialism, 1812–1855* (Cambridge, Mass., 1961), 379–80; J. E. Zimmerman, *Midpassage: Alexander Herzen and European Revolution, 1847–1852* (Pittsburgh, 1989), 161; and W. C. Wiedemaier, "Herzen and the Existential World View: A New Approach to an Old Debate," *Slavic Review* 40 (Winter 1981): 557–69. For the view that *From the Other Shore* represents an unresolved debate within Herzen himself, see Morson, *Boundaries of Genre*, 161; E. Acton, *Alexander Herzen and the Role of the Intellectual Revolutionary* (Cambridge, Eng., 1979), 54; and Zimmerman, *Midpassage*, 89. In contrast to these assessments, see Berlin's view in his introduction to *From the Other Shore*, vii–xxv.
12. Herzen, *OS*, 136, 153, 58. I discuss the "sacrifices" involved in Herzen's own resistance to the utopian urge in "Two Radical Ironists: Herzen and Proudhon."
13. Rorty, *Contingency, Irony and Solidarity*, 7.
14. Herzen, *OS*, 66, 35, 33, 67, 140–41, 142, 128, 140.
15. Herzen, *Sobranie sochinenii*, 19:184.
16. See W. C. Wiedemaier, "Herzen and Nietzsche: A Link in the Rise of Modern Pessimism," *Russian Review* 36 (October 1977): 477–88; and R. M. Davison, "Herzen and Kierkegaard," *Slavic Review* 25 (June 1966): 191–209. As D. C. Muecke points out, Kierkegaard's commitment as a Christian to a closed-world ideology made it impossible for him to take an ironical view of the totality of human existence (Muecke, *The Compass of Irony* [London, 1969], 240). Herzen's criticism of Bakunin's voluntarism indicates that he would have regarded the Nietzschean exaltation of the will over reason as an inverted form of rationalist "idealism."
17. For a discussion of Herzen's interest in Schiller in the 1840s, and the parallels

between their respective ideals of freedom, see my article "Schiller, Herzen and the Aesthetic Ideal of Man."

18. Herzen, diary of July 1843, *Sobranie sochinenii*, 2:298.
19. Herzen, *OS*, 23, 142; *Sobranie sochinenii*, 3:75–76.
20. Herzen, *OS*, 90, 32, 74, 147 (see also 69), 3, 147.
21. Quoted in Muecke, *Compass of Irony*, 201.
22. Ibid., 200–01.
23. Dostoevskii, *Polnoe sobranie sochinenii*, 21:9.
24. See Perlina, "Vozdeistvie."
25. See Dolinin's exposition of the textual parallels between the two works, "Dostoevskii i Gertsen," 312–17.
26. Perlina, "Vozdeistvie."
27. As several critics have noted, *Notes from Underground* was probably influenced, and certainly anticipated, by *From the Other Shore*.
28. Dostoevskii, *Polnoe sobranie sochinenii*, 5:116, 118–19, 178–79. Cf. the passage in *OS*, 38.
29. Dostoevskii, *Polnoe sobranie sochinenii*, 5:121.
30. Ibid., 179.
31. For a discussion of Dostoevsky's religious utopia, see B. K. Ward, *Dostoyevsky's Critique of the West: The Quest for an Earthly Paradise* (Waterloo, Ont., 1986).
32. Dostoevskii, *Polnoe sobranie sochinenii*, 23:42, 47, 25:63, 100, 129, 26:85, 148.
33. J. Frank, introduction to F. M. Dostoevsky, *The Diary of a Writer*, 2d ed., trans. B. Brasol (Salt Lake City, Utah, 1985), xiv.
34. Dostoevskii, *Polnoe sobranie sochinenii*, 25:34; F. Dostoevsky, *The Notebooks for "A Raw Youth,"* ed. E. Wasiolek, trans. V. Terras (Chicago, 1969), 426.
35. Dostoevskii, *Polnoe sobranie sochinenii*, 26:129, 25:152, 22:80, 25:179, 22:81.
36. Ibid., 26:132, 25:152, 23:37.
37. See "Dostoevsky and the Divided Conscience," this vol.
38. Dostoevskii, *Polnoe sobranie sochinenii*, 27:19, 23:96.
39. Quoted in Ward, *Dostoyevsky's Critique of the West*, 178.
40. Dostoevskii, "Poslednie literaturnye iavleniia: Gazeta 'Den,' " *Polnoe sobranie sochinenii*, 19:60, 62.
41. Dostoevskii, *Polnoe sobranie sochinenii*, 21:33, 23:24.
42. E. J. Simmons, *Dostoevskii: The Making of a Novelist* (New York, 1940), 348.
43. Zenkovsky, quoted in A. H. Lyngstad, *Dostoevskij and Schiller* (The Hague, 1975), 71–72. On the critical debate over the relationship between the two ideals, see ibid., 69–72; on Schillerian themes in *The Brothers Karamazov*, see 49–109.
44. Dostoevskii, *Polnoe sobranie sochinenii*, 24:45, 23:143, 23:23, 25:175.
45. Herzen, *Sobranie sochinenii*, 2:101.
46. See Dolinin, *Dostoevskii*; and Perlina, "Vozdeistvie."
47. On the Nechaev affair, see "Bakunin and the Charm of the Millennium," this vol.
48. Dostoevskii, *Polnoe sobranie sochinenii*, 24:61, 49, 46, 23:34.
49. Ibid., 26:80, 25:125, 23:160, 27:10, 11, 17.
50. *Neizdannyi Dostoevskii: Zapisnye knigi i tetradi, 1860–1881*, vol. 83 of *Literaturnoe nasledstvo* (Moscow, 1971), 174–75.
51. On this subject, see "Dostoevsky and the Divided Conscience," this vol.
52. Dostoevskii, *Polnoe sobranie sochinenii*, 23:121, 22:127–28.

53. Dostoevskii to Strakhov, 5 April 1870, *Pis'ma*, 2:259.
54. Perlina, "Vozdeistvie," 148.
55. Dostoevskii, *Polnoe sobranie sochinenii*, 24:52–54, 23:146.
56. *Neizdannyi Dostoevskii*, 556, 569, 573, 578, 580.
57. Ibid., 86.

CHAPTER SIXTEEN
Herzen versus Schopenhauer

1. V. V. Zenkovsky, *A History of Russian Philosophy*, trans. G. Kline (London, 1953), 296. See also Wiedemaier, "Herzen and Nietzsche," 477–88.
2. See, e.g., F. Copleston, "Schopenhauer and Nietzsche," in *Schopenhauer: His Philosophical Achievement*, ed. M. Fox (Brighton, 1980), 223. Copleston argues that Nietzsche's doctrine of eternal recurrence "logically involves pessimism, for it excludes the notion that there is any given end for life—all teleology is banished."
3. Herzen to Turgenev, 29–30 November 1862, *Sobranie sochinenii*, 3:7.
4. J. Young, *Willing and Unwilling: A Study in the Philosophy of Arthur Schopenhauer* (Dordrecht, 1987), 145–46.
5. R. Simpson, "Against Lipsius," *Tonic* 5 (Summer 1993): 12.
6. A. Hübscher, "Hegel and Schopenhauer: Aftermath and Present," in *Schopenhauer: His Philosophical Achievement*, 198.
7. B. Magee points out that Schopenhauer's use of the word *will* to denote phenomena (in two distinct senses) and the noumenon has caused widespread misunderstanding of his philosophy (*Philosophy of Schopenhauer*, 141ff). Magee notes that Schopenhauer's treatment of the noumenal will is self-contradictory; when discussing its nature directly, he insists on its blind aimlessness, but in other contexts (such as his discussion of evolutionary processes) he attributes conscious purpose to it. He never addresses the question of how a blind urge can manifest itself in, for example, Newton's laws (237–38). On the same question, see Young, *Willing and Unwilling*, 74ff.
8. Schopenhauer, *WWR*, 2:513.
9. Schopenhauer, *WWR*, 1:314.
10. See Magee, *Philosophy of Schopenhauer*, 220; Young, *Willing and Unwilling*, 143.
11. Schopenhauer, *WWR*, 2:581.
12. Ibid., 1:325.
13. Schopenhauer, *WWR*, 2:583, 584, 442.
14. Ibid., 475.
15. Ibid., 471.
16. Ibid., 482, 477, 187.
17. Ibid., 507.
18. Ibid.
19. Ibid., 1:411.
20. Ibid., 2:585.
21. Ibid., 2:185.
22. J. P. Stern, *A Study of Nietzsche* (Cambridge, Eng., 1979), 50. In his book, Magee notes unmistakable signs of a "serious revival of interest" in Schopenhauer over the preceding few years owing to, among other things, an increasing disenchantment with positivism and the empiricist tradition in general (*Philosophy of Scho-*

penhauer, 263). (He observes that Schopenhauer's influence was at its height from the 1880s until the First World War, when he sank into obscurity.)

23. See Magee, *Philosophy of Schopenhauer*, 145. Magee notes that the founder of quantum mechanics, Erwin Schrödinger, was an enthusiastic Schopenhauerian (146).

24. See M. Fox, preface to *Schopenhauer: His Philosophical Achievement*, xv; Nietzsche, "Schopenhauer als Erzieher," *Werke* (Munich, 1956), 1:287–365.

25. M. Horkheimer, "Schopenhauer Today," in *Schopenhauer: His Philosophical Achievement*, 20–33.

26. Schopenhauer, *WWR*, 2:409.

27. Williams, "Auto-da-Fé," in *Reading Rorty*, 36.

28. Horkheimer, "Schopenhauer Today," 25.

29. The model for the opponent is thought to be I. P. Galakhov. For Herzen's recollections of him, see *Sobranie sochinenii*, 9:115–20.

30. See "Irony and Utopia in Herzen and Dostoevsky," this vol.

31. Herzen, *OS*, 25, 35, 41, 28

32. Ibid., 32.

33. Ibid., 22, 28. See Schopenhauer, *WWR*, 1:310: "In proportion as knowledge attains to distinctness . . . pain also increases, and consequently reaches its highest degree in man; and all the more, the more distinctly he knows, and the more intelligent he is."

34. Schopenhauer, *WWR*, 2:573; see also 358, 572, and the discussion on 353ff.

35. A. Schopenhauer, *Essays and Aphorisms*, trans. R. J. Hollingdale (London, 1970), 52.

36. Herzen, *OS*, 33.

37. Schopenhauer, *WWR*, 1:253; 2:358, 600.

38. Herzen, *OS*, 35.

39. Schopenhauer, *WWR*, 2:353.

40. Herzen, *OS*, 22.

41. Ibid., 23, 24.

42. Ibid., 79, 74, 21, 77, 78, 77.

43. Ibid., 30, 20.

44. Ibid., 21.

45. *Sobranie sochinenii*, 10:120.

46. Schopenhauer, *WWR*, 2:474–5.

47. Ibid., 638.

48. Magee, *Philosophy of Schopenhauer*, 146. Self-contradiction is characteristic of Schopenhauer's philosophical style; see above, n. 7.

49. Magee, *Philosophy of Schopenhauer*, 218.

50. Schopenhauer, *WWR*, 2:492.

51. Herzen, *OS*, 20.

52. Schopenhauer, *WWR*, 2:576.

53. Schopenhauer, *Essays and Aphorisms*, 51.

54. "Système des contradictions économiques, ou philosophie de la misère," *Oeuvres complètes de P.-J. Proudhon*, 15 vols. (Paris, 1923–59), 1:41. On Proudhon's influence on Herzen, see my "Herzen and Proudhon: Two Radical Ironists."

55. Schopenhauer, *WWR*, 2:589.

56. Ibid., 1:278.

57. Ibid., 2:502.
58. Ibid., 505, 500, 625. Schopenhauer argues that his doctrine, which "candidly confesses the reprehensible nature of the world and points to the denial of the will as the road to redemption from it" could be called the "true Christian philosophy" (*Essays and Aphorisms*, 63).
59. Schopenhauer, *WWR*, 2:185.
60. See Young, *Willing and Unwilling*, 132–3.
61. Schopenhauer, *WWR*, 2:492. P. Gardiner suggests that "it must be possible to speak of the reality of effective conscious choice or purpose in at least some instances, if the notion of 'secret' or 'unconscious' operations of the will is to preserve an intelligible sense" (*Schopenhauer* [London, 1967], 167). Magee notes that Schopenhauer implicitly acknowledges a developmental aspect to history when he affirms his own philosophy's debt to Kant (*Philosophy of Schopenhauer*, 231).
62. Herzen, *OS*, 50.
63. Herzen's reflections in *From the Other Shore* on the chanciness of evolutionary processes appeared in print a decade in advance of *On the Origin of Species*. On the parallels between Herzen's and Darwin's views on the role of chance in evolution, see "The Divine Inventor, Chance," this vol.
64. Herzen, *OS*, 34, 79, 26, 38, 22.
65. Schopenhauer, *WWR*, 2:573–74.
66. Herzen, *Sobranie sochinenii*, 11:246, 253.
67. Herzen, *OS*, 147, 66.
68. See, e.g., Herzen, *Sobranie sochinenii*, 14:10–11.
69. Herzen, *OS*, 103.
70. See Hübscher, "Hegel and Schopenhauer," 204.
71. Stern, *A Study of Nietzsche*, 141.
72. Nietzsche, *Werke*, 1:740.
73. See Nietzsche's preface to *Ecce Homo*: "Philosophy, as I have hitherto understood and lived it, is a voluntary living in ice and on high mountains. . . . How much truth can a spirit *bear*, how much truth can a spirit *dare*? That became more and more for me the measure of real value" (*Werke*, 2:1066).
74. Herzen, *Sobranie sochinenii*, 20:349.
75. Turgenev, *Sochineniia*, 9:117. This work reads like a paraphrase of the chapters "On History" and "On the Vanity and Suffering of Life," in Schopenhauer, *WWR*, vol. 2.
76. See Turgenev's letters to Herzen of 4 and 8 November 1862, *Pis'ma*, 5:65, 67–68. On the polemic between the two, see "The Nihilism of Ivan Turgenev," this vol.
77. Herzen, *Sobranie sochinenii*, 16:198.
78. Herzen, *OS*, 20.
79. Herzen, *Sobranie sochinenii*, 20:442.
80. Turgenev, *Pis'ma*, 3:303.
81. Herzen, *Sobranie sochinenii*, 10:31, 7:296, 10:79.
82. Schopenhauer, *WWR*, 2:588.
83. Herzen, *Sobranie sochinenii*, 5:104, 7:296.
84. Ibid., 16:131, 11:218, 16:191–92.
85. Schopenhauer, *WWR*, 2:357. Herzen's source is the following: "Consider that indefatigable worker the mole; to dig strenuously with its enormous shovel-paws

is the business of its whole life; permanent night surrounds it; it has its embryo eyes merely to avoid the light. . . . What does it attain by this course of life that is full of trouble and devoid of pleasure? Nourishment and procreation, that is, only the means of continuing and beginning again in the new individual the same melancholy course. In such examples it becomes clear that the cares and troubles of life are out of all proportion to the yield or profit from it" (353–54).

86. Herzen, *Sobranie sochinenii*, 16:192.

CHAPTER SEVENTEEN
The Divine Inventor, Chance

1. On the content of Michelet's work (*Pologne et Russie: Légende de Kosciuszko* [Paris, 1852]), and on Herzen's reaction to it, see the editors' commentary in Herzen, *Sobranie sochinenii*, 7:437–39. His response, "Le peuple russe et le socialisme: Lettre à M. J. Michelet, professeur au Collège de France," was first published in a radically shortened version in the Paris paper *L'Avènement du Peuple* on 19 November 1851. For the full text, see Herzen, *OS*, 165–208.

2. J.-F. Lyotard, *The Postmodern Condition: A Report on Knowledge*, trans. G. Bennington and B. Massumi (Manchester, 1991), 66.

3. Schopenhauer, *Essays and Aphorisms*, 51; Nietzsche, "Versuch einer Selbstkritik," *Werke*, 1:9.

4. Herzen, *OS*, 147.

5. Herzen, "Robert Owen," *Sobranie sochinenii*, 11:247. For a fuller discussion of Herzen's view of history, see Chaps. 6, 15, and 16, this vol.

6. Dostoevskii, *Polnoe sobranie sochinenii*, 5:118–19.

7. Tolstoi, *Sobranie sochinenii*, 9:420.

8. A. S. Pushkin, *Polnoe sobranie sochinenii* (Moscow, 1937–49), 3:464. The scientist was the distinguished chemist Kirill Zamaraev, director from 1984 to 1994 of the largest institute of catalysis in the world, in Novosibirsk, Siberia. His visit to Cambridge (and his love of Pushkin) are also recorded in his obituary by Sir John Meurig Thomas: "Kirill I. Zamaraev (1939–96)," *Chemistry: A European Journal* 3 (1997).

9. Herzen, *OS*, 21, 34; "Robert Owen," 246.

10. Nietzsche, "Die fröliche Wissenschaft," *Werke*, 2:161, 162; "Zur Genealogie der Moral," ibid., 889.

11. Herzen, "K staromu tovarishchu," *Sobranie sochinenii*, 20:379.

12. Herzen, *OS*, 76, 69.

13. C. Darwin, letter to A. Gray, 22 May 1860, *Life and Letters of Charles Darwin*, ed. F. Darwin, 3 vols. (London, 1887), 2:311–12. Herzen's and Darwin's views on the role of chance in nature and history are compared in my forthcoming book *Views from Another Shore: Essays on Herzen, Chekhov and Bakhtin*.

14. Notes from Nietzsche's notebooks, cited in M. Warren, *Nietzsche and Political Thought* (Cambridge, Mass., 1988), 35.

15. Darwin, *Life*, 1:307.

16. Herzen, "Lettre sur le libre arbitre," *Sobranie sochinenii*, 20:438.

17. C. Darwin, *Notebooks on the Transmutation of Species: Bulletin of the British Museum (Natural History)*, Historical Series, vol. 2, no. 4 (London, 1960), 136.

18. Herzen, *Sobranie sochinenii*, 11:253.

19. Ibid., 2:390.

20. *The Works of Francis Bacon,* ed. J. Spedding, R. Ellis, D. Heath, 14 vols. (London, 1857–74), 4:106. On Bacon's influence on Herzen, see my article "Alexander Herzen and Francis Bacon," *Journal of the History of Ideas* (October 1908): 635–62.

21. Herzen, "Eshchë raz Bazarov," *Sobranie sochinenii,* 20:345.

22. S. J. Gould, *Wonderful Life: The Burgess Shale and the Nature of History* (London, 1990), 285.

Permissions

Grateful acknowledgment is made to the following editors and publishers for permission to make use of earlier versions of essays in this volume:

"A Complex Vision" first appeared as the Introduction to I. Berlin, *Russian Thinkers* (London: Hogarth Press, 1978) and is reprinted with permission from Chatto and Windus.

"Herzen versus Schopenhauer" is reprinted from the *Journal of European Studies* (March 1996) with the permission of the editor.

"The Rational Reality of Boris Chicherin" and "A Bolshevik Philosophy?" first appeared in *Cahiers du monde russe et soviétique*, vol. 18 (1977) and vol. 22 (1981); reprinted with the permission of *Cahiers du monde russe*, Editions EHESS.

"The Intelligentsia and Self-Censorship" and "Dostoevsky and the Divided Conscience" first appeared in the *Slavic Review*, vol. 46 (1977) and vol. 47 (1988); reprinted with permission of the American Association for the Advancement of Slavic Studies.

"Irony and Utopia in Herzen and Dostoevsky" is reprinted with permission from the *Russian Review*. Copyright 1991 by the Ohio State University Press. All rights reserved.

"Bakunin and the Charm of the Millennium," "Liberal Dilemmas and Populist Solutions," "Tolstoy in Doubt," "Leonard Schapiro's Russia," "Brave New Worlds," and "The Chaotic City" are reprinted with permission of the *New York Review of Books*. Copyright © 1976–97. NYREV, Inc.

I am indebted to Librairie Arthème Fayard for allowing me to publish "Carnival of the Intellectuals," which will appear in *Histoire de la littérature russe, Le XIXᵉ siècle: Le temps du roman* (forthcoming).

I am grateful to Dover Publications Inc. for permission to quote from Arthur Schopenhauer, *The World as Will and Representation*, 2 vols., translated from the German by E. F. J. Payne (Dover Publications, 1958).

I wish to acknowledge the permission of Orion Press to quote from Alexander Herzen, *From the Other Shore* and *The Russian People and Socialism*, translated by Moura Budberg and Richard Wollheim (first published in 1956 by Weidenfeld and Nicolson).

I thank David McDuff for permission to quote his translation of Osip Mandelstam's poem "Leningrad."

Quotations from *Tolstoy's Letters*, vols. 1 and 2, translated and edited by R. F.